A
TREASURY OF
IRISH MYTH,
LEGEND,
AND FOLKLORE

FAIRY MILLERS.

A TREASURY OF IRISH MYTH, LEGEND, AND FOLKLORE

FAIRY AND FOLK TALES
OF THE IRISH PEASANTRY

Edited and Selected by William Butler Yeats

and

CUCHULAIN OF MUIRTHEMNE
THE STORY OF
THE MEN OF THE RED BRANCH OF ULSTER

Arranged and Put into English by Lady Isabella Augusta Gregory

Compiled and Edited by Claire Booss

ILLUSTRATED

GRAMERCY BOOKS
New York

This 1986 edition was originally published by
Avenel Books and has been reprinted by
Gramercy Books, distributed by Outlet Book
Company, Inc., a Random House Company, 225
Park Avenue South, New York, New York
10003.

Printed and Bound in the United States of
America

**Library of Congress
Cataloging-in-Publication Data**

Main entry under title:

A Treasury of Irish myth, legend, and folklore.

   Contents: Fairy and folk tales of the Irish
peasantry / edited and selected by William
Butler Yeats—Cuchulain of Muirthemne /
arranged and put into English by Lady Isabella
Augusta Gregory.
   1. Tales—Ireland.   2. Fairy tales—Ireland.
3. Folklore—Ireland.   4. Ireland—Social life
and customs.   I. Booss, Claire.   II. Fairy and
folk tales of the Irish peasantry. 1986.
III. Cuchulain. English. 1986.
GR153.5.T734   1986   398.2'.1'09415
85-228569

ISBN 0-517-48904-X

12 11 10 9 8 7 6

CONTENTS

CUCHULAIN CARRIED FERDIAD ACROSS THE RIVER.

FOREWORD

THIS volume unites for the first time two classic works of Irish folklore and mythology which could well have been published together long ago, since they were both first printed near the turn of the century.

The opening book is *Fairy and Folk Tales of the Irish Peasantry*, selected and edited by Ireland's master poet, the Nobel Prize laureate, William Butler Yeats. First published in 1888, the beautiful, comic, and moving renditions of the tales in this collection have made it one of the most popular gatherings of folk material in our century.

Though not overly long, the anthology is indeed comprehensive, covering in fine detail the gamut of Irish folklore from the trooping or dancing fairies, the *Sidhe*, through the witches and sorcerers, shoemaking leprechauns, devils, ghosts, giants, robbers, kings and queens, to the fairy doctors and changelings— those children stolen by the fairies who leave one of their own in the child's place. In this collection, we witness weddings and burials, amble across meadows and through forests, and visit fairy drinking halls on the great feast of Samhain Eve (the Irish Halloween) and the land of the never-dying, ever-young Tir-na-n-Og. These stories were written by some of the best Irish writers of their time: the illustrious Irish scholar, Douglas Hyde, Samuel Ferguson, William Allingham, and William Carleton, among others. There are also offerings by Yeats himself. One, "The Stolen Child," has this haunting refrain:

> *Come away! O, human child!*
> *To the woods and waters wild,*
> *With a fairy hand in hand,*
> *For the world's more full of weeping than*
> *you can understand.*

Lady Isabella Augusta Gregory's *chef d'oevre*, *Cuchulain of Muirthemne*, constitutes the second half of this volume. Lady Gregory retold, by means of translation, adaptation, and rearrangement, the ancient stories from the Ulster cycle of Irish myths of the heroes of the House of the Red Branch, a group of warriors similar to the Knights of the Round Table. Chief among these warriors was Cuchulain, one of Ireland's foremost mythic heroes. Because Cuchulain was an important figure, Lady Gregory centered her rendition of the legends around his life, from birth to death. Even when young, Cuchulain never took the easy path, but rather the road which would bring him glory. While still a youth, he killed the menacing dog that guarded the warrior Culain, and then volunteered to guard Culain himself. Thus, the name Cuchulain, which literally means "Hound of Culain."

Cathbad the Druid had warned Cuchulain: "If any young man should take arms today, his name will be greater than any other name in Ireland. But his time of life will be short." Nevertheless, from his marriage to the beautiful Emer, first among the women of Ireland, through his participation in the war for the Bull of Cuailgne, until his final battle, Cuchulain always chose glory. Scholars have compared him to the sun god in classic Greek and Roman legend, yet he seems, to this writer, closer to the deity of the shooting star: brilliant and short-lived.

To the tales of Cuchulain, Lady Gregory added mythic stories from the Ulster cycle wherein Cuchulain is only a peripheral figure: the story of Angus Og who transformed himself into a swan so as to be with his bewitched beloved, and the renowned story of the beautiful, but sorrowing, Dierdre. In that tale, which closely parallels the ill-fated triangle of Iseult, Mark, and Tristan, Dierdre rejects the older King Conchubar for the young and handsome Naoise, runs off with him from Ireland to Scotland (or Alba), and lives happily with him until he is tricked by Conchubar into returning and is treacherously slain.

These heroes and heroines were the ancient Irish equivalents of the Greek and Roman demigods; with the coming of Christianity, they were changed into the fairies of Ireland, the *Sidhe*. As Yeats writes in his collection, *Fairy and Folk Tales of the Irish Peasantry:*

Who are they? "Fallen angels who were not good enough to be saved, nor bad enough to be lost," say the peasantry. "The gods of the earth," says the Book of Armagh. "The gods of pagan Ireland," say the Irish antiquarians, "the *Tuatha De Dañan*, who, when no longer worshipped and fed with offerings, dwindled away in the popular imagination, and now are only a few spans high."

In other versions before and after Lady Gregory's, the heroes of Ulster remain but "a few spans high," flat and lifeless. In her version, however, these gods are lifelike, vital presences, human, and somewhat more than human. She would later translate the Finn MacCool and Oisin cycles, but she would never again achieve either the continuity of the 1902 *Cuchulain* or its simple and intensely beautiful language, which is her version of the Kiltartan dialect, the English spoken by the peasants on the west coast of Ireland. Yeats, in his preface to *Cuchulain of Muirthemne*, compares this dialect to the English of William Morris and Robert Burns. Its very plainness becomes a lyric simplicity that hearkens back to Tudor and Elizabethan prose, a prose not too far removed from poetry. As Yeats writes:

> If we do not set Dierdre's lamentations among the greatest lyric poems of the world, I think that the wine-press of the poets has been trodden for us in vain.

Since Lady Gregory's intention was to set forth "in plain simple words" the history of the knights or warriors of the Red Branch, the demigods of the Ulster cycle, and especially "to give a fair account of Cuchulain's life and death," the language should present no difficulty to the modern reader. If any difficulty should arise—here, or in Yeats' collection of fairy tales—then one should simply read the passage aloud, as fine prose is meant to be read, and this should prove an excellent solution.

During the last part of the nineteenth century, an independent Ireland seemed a lost cause. Revolution, parliamentary maneuvering, agitation for agrarian reform, and the attempt to revive the native Irish language were all apparently unsuccessful in creating a modern state independent of British rule. At that time, the young William Butler Yeats (1865–1939) was casting about for a mythological basis for his poetry, as the Greek and Roman myths had become sterile from overuse and lacked freshness, and the Indian myths which Yeats had attempted to use were too alien. But the Irish myths were untapped territory. When Yeats and his colleagues—John Millington Synge, AE (George Russell), George Moore, and chiefly, Lady Isabella Augusta Gregory (1852–1932)—turned to the Irish material as the basis for their writings, they aroused the consciousness necessary to create a nation.

One part of this Irish Renaissance was the collecting of fairy tales and folklore, that is, the lore of the common people. Yeats, citing Plato, maintained in his introduction to *Fairy and Folk Tales of the Irish Peasantry* that, "The common opinion is enough for me." This Irish literature, then, was to be one where the ordinary Irish person played an important part. Further, as Yeats noted in that introduction, the collectors of "Irish folk-lore. . . . have made their work literature rather than science. . . . they have caught the very voice of the people, the very pulse of life."

As life includes both men and women, a surprising number of the writers and collectors included in this edition are women: Letitia MacLintock; Ellen O'Leary; and Lady Wilde, Oscar Wilde's mother, among others. Pleasant it is to see that they are the better writers in this collection, and Lady Wilde stands out as first among equals.

But more remained to be done to give Ireland a classical literary tradition that would stand up to all the literatures of all nations. As Yeats expressed it in 1904, Ireland had to "re-create the ancient arts, the arts as they were understood in Judaea, in India, in Scandinavia, in Greece and Rome, in every ancient land." This part of the program was the translation of the Irish epics, and, by default, it fell to Lady Gregory. After Yeats, a poor scholar in languages, turned down a commission to translate the Irish epics, Lady Gregory started her *Cuchulain of Muirthemne*. Yeats was initially skeptical, as, until that time, he had viewed Lady Gregory only as a patron and fund raiser for the Irish Literary Theatre but later, he was overwhelmed by her work. In his preface, reprinted here, he wrote:

I think this book is the best that has come out of Ireland in my time. Perhaps I should say that it is the best book that has ever come out of Ireland; for the stories which it tells are a chief part of Ireland's gift to the imagination of the world—and it tells them perfectly for the first time.

Some scholars have faulted Yeat's praise as extreme, but rather his admiration seems appropriate, for these stories of the brave and noble deeds of the Irish heroes and heroines *are* perfectly told for the first time. Next to Lady Gregory's version of the Cuchulain myths, all others seem to pale, and give only an inkling of the passions of these warriors. In addition to to their pure literary value, the stories of Cuchulain and Emer, of Conchubar and Fergus, of Dierdre and the sons of Usnach, of all these warriors and bards, were to be the basis for works by James Stephens, AE, Synge, Yeats, and Lady Gregory herself. Furthermore, for the first time, these legends passed into the consciousness of a worldwide literary public.

This was the foundation Yeats was looking for; here were the old pre-Christian gods of Ireland come alive again, not just "a few spans high," but full-blown and even larger than life. In the Ireland of his time—and even today—these gods had not passed entirely out of the mind of the people. Why not, then, asked Yeats, use these vital presences for an Irish theatre that would join king and commoner, peasant and aristocrat in common bond?

Moreover, as Yeats wrote in *The Rose,* his 1893 collection of poems:

> *Know that I would accounted be*
> *True brother of a company*
> *That sang, to sweeten Ireland's wrong,*
> *Ballad and story, rann and song. . . .*

Becoming this "true brother," Yeats created more than a literature. Later in life, he queried whether his writing—specifically *Cathleen ni Hoolihan,* a patriotic play he had written in collaboration with Lady Gregory in 1902—was responsible for the death of "certain men the English shot," the leaders of the 1916 Easter Rebellion in Dublin.

Even then, in the dark days following the execution of the six-teen revolutionary leaders, it was apparent to all that an independent Ireland was only a matter of a few short years. Ireland had captured the imagination of the world. On the west coast of Ireland, Yeats and Lady Gregory and John Synge and AE had gone looking for the ancient gods of their native land. Perhaps these gods of myth would speak once more to them, for myth is only myth to the nonbeliever. What these poets sought, they found, and the old gods of Ireland spoke again.

ARI SALANT

New York City
1986

FAIRY AND FOLK TALES
OF THE IRISH PEASANTRY

Edited and Selected by
William Butler Yeats

INSCRIBED

TO MY MYSTICAL FRIEND,

G. R.

CONTENTS.

INTRODUCTION.

——◆——

D R. CORBETT, Bishop of Oxford and Norwich, lamented long ago the departure of the English fairies. "In Queen Mary's time" he wrote—

> "When Tom came home from labour,
>   Or Cis to milking rose,
> Then merrily, merrily went their tabor,
>   And merrily went their toes."

But now, in the times of James, they had all gone, for "they were of the old profession," and "their songs were Ave Maries." In Ireland they are still extant, giving gifts to the kindly, and plaguing the surly. "Have you ever seen a fairy or such like?" I asked an old man in County Sligo. "Amn't I annoyed with them," was the answer. "Do the fishermen along here know anything of the mermaids?" I asked a woman of a village in County Dublin. "Indeed, they don't like to see them at all," she answered, "for they always bring bad weather." "Here is a man who believes in ghosts," said a foreign sea-captain, pointing to a pilot of my acquaintance. "In every house over there," said the pilot, pointing to his native village of Rosses, "there are several." Certainly that now old and much respected dogmatist, the Spirit of the Age, has in no manner made his voice heard down there. In a little while, for he has gotten a consumptive appearance of late, he will be covered over decently in his grave, and another will grow, old and much respected, in his place, and never be heard of down there, and after him another and another and another. Indeed, it is a question whether any of these personages will ever be heard of outside the newspaper offices and lecture-rooms and drawing-rooms and eel-pie houses of the cities, or if the Spirit of the Age is at any time more than a froth. At any rate, whole troops of their like will not change the Celt much. Giraldus Cambrensis found the people of the western islands a trifle paganish. "How many gods are there?" asked a priest, a little while ago, of a man from the Island of Innistor. "There is one on Innistor; but this seems a big place," said the man, and the priest held up his hands in horror, as Giraldus had, just seven centuries before. Remember, I am not blaming the man; it is very much better to believe in a number of gods than in none at all, or to think there is only one, but that he is a little sentimental and impracticable, and not constructed for the nineteenth century. The Celt, and his cromlechs, and his pillar-stones, these will not change much— indeed, it is doubtful if anybody at all changes at any time. In spite of hosts of deniers, and asserters, and wise-men, and professors, the majority still are averse to sitting down to dine thirteen at table, or being helped to salt, or walking under a ladder, or seeing a single magpie flirting his chequered tail. There are, of course, children of light who have set their faces against all this, though even a newspaper man, if you entice him into a cemetery at midnight, will believe in phantoms, for every one is a visionary, if you scratch him deep enough. But the Celt is a visionary without scratching.

Yet, be it noticed, if you are a stranger, you will not readily get ghost and fairy legends, even in a western village. You must go adroitly to work, and make friends with the children, and the old men, with those who have not felt the pressure of mere daylight existence, and those with whom it is growing less, and will have altogether taken itself off one of these days. The old women are most learned, but will not so readily be got to talk, for the fairies are very secretive, and much resent being talked of; and are there not many stories of old women who were nearly pinched into their graves or numbed with fairy blasts?

At sea, when the nets are out and the pipes are lit, then will some ancient hoarder of tales become loquacious, telling his histories to the tune of the creaking of the boats. Holy-eve night, too, is a great time, and in old days many tales were to be heard at wakes. But the priests have set faces against wakes.

In the Parochial Survey of Ireland it is recorded how the story-tellers used to gather together of an evening, and if any had a different version from the others, they would all recite theirs and vote, and the man who had varied would have to abide by their verdict. In this way stories have been handed down with such accuracy, that the long tale of Dierdre was, in the earlier decades of this century, told almost word for word, as in the very ancient MSS. in the Royal Dublin Society. In one case only it varied, and then the MS. was obviously wrong—a passage had been forgotten by the copyist. But this accuracy is rather in the folk and bardic tales than in the fairy legends, for these vary widely, being usually adapted to some neighbouring village or local fairy-seeing celebrity. Each county has usually some family, or personage, supposed to have been favoured or plagued, especially by the phantoms, as the Hackets of Castle Hacket, Galway, who had for their ancestor a fairy, or John-o'-Daly of Lisadell, Sligo, who wrote "Eilleen Aroon," the song the Scotch have stolen and called "Robin Adair," and which Handel would sooner have written than all his oratorios,* and the "O'Donahue of Kerry." Round these men stories tended to group themselves, sometimes deserting more ancient heroes for the purpose. Round poets have they gathered especially, for poetry in Ireland has always been mysteriously connected with magic.

These folk-tales are full of simplicity and musical occurrences, for they are the literature of a class for whom every incident in the old rut of birth, love, pain, and death has cropped up unchanged for centuries : who have steeped everything in the heart: to whom everything is a symbol. They have the spade over which man has leant from the beginning. The people of the cities have the machine, which is prose and a *parvenu*. They have few events. They can turn over the incidents of a long life as they sit by the fire. With us nothing has time to gather meaning, and too many things are occurring for even a big heart to hold. It is said the most eloquent people in the world are the Arabs, who have only the bare earth of the desert and a sky swept bare by the sun. "Wisdom has alighted upon three things," goes their proverb ; "the hand of the Chinese, the brain of the Frank, and the tongue of the Arab." This, I take it, is the meaning of that simplicity sought for so much in these days by all the poets, and not to be had at any price.

The most notable and typical story-teller of my acquaintance is one Paddy Flynn, a little, bright-eyed, old man, living in a leaky one-roomed cottage of the village of B——, "The most gentle—*i.e.*, fairy—place in the whole

* He lived some time in Dublin, and heard it then.

of the County Sligo," he says, though others claim that honour for Drumahair or for Drumcliff. A very pious old man, too! You may have some time to inspect his strange figure and ragged hair, if he happen to be in a devout humour, before he comes to the doings of the gentry. A strange devotion! Old tales of Columkill, and what he said to his mother. "How are you to-day, mother?" "Worse!" "May you be worse to-morrow;" and on the next day, "How are you to-day, mother?" "Worse!" "May you be worse to-morrow;" and on the next, "How are you to-day, mother?" "Better, thank God." "May you be better to-morrow." In which undutiful manner he will tell you Columkill inculcated cheerfulness. Then most likely he will wander off into his favourite theme—how the Judge smiles alike in rewarding the good and condemning the lost to unceasing flames. Very consoling does it appear to Paddy Flynn, this melancholy and apocalyptic cheerfulness of the Judge. Nor seems his own cheerfulness quite earthly—though a very palpable cheerfulness. The first time I saw him he was cooking mushrooms for himself; the next time he was asleep under a hedge, smiling in his sleep. Assuredly some joy not quite of this steadfast earth lightens in those eyes—swift as the eyes of a rabbit—among so many wrinkles, for Paddy Flynn is very old. A melancholy there is in the midst of their cheerfulness—a melancholy that is almost a portion of their joy, the visionary melancholy of purely instinctive natures and of all animals. In the triple solitude of age and eccentricity and partial deafness he goes about much pestered by children.

As to the reality of his fairy and spirit-seeing powers, not all are agreed. One day we were talking of the Banshee. "I have seen it," he said, "down there by the water 'batting' the river with its hands." He it was who said the fairies annoyed him.

Not that the Sceptic is entirely afar even from these western villages. I found him one morning as he bound his corn in a merest pocket-handkerchief of a field. Very different from Paddy Flynn—Scepticism in every wrinkle of his face, and a travelled man, too!—a foot-long Mohawk Indian tatooed on one of his arms to evidence the matter. "They who travel," says a neighbouring priest, shaking his head over him, and quoting Thomas Á'Kempis, "seldom come home holy." I had mentioned ghosts to this Sceptic. "Ghosts," said he; "there are no such things at all, at all, but the gentry, they stand to reason; for the devil, when he fell out of heaven, took the weak-minded ones with him, and they were put into the waste places. And that's what the gentry are. But they are getting scarce now, because their time's over, ye see, and they're going back. But ghosts, no! And I'll tell ye something more I don't believe in—the fire of hell;" then, in a low voice, "that's only invented to give the priests and the parsons something to do." Thereupon this man, so full of enlightenment, returned to his corn-binding.

The various collectors of Irish folk-lore have, from our point of view, one great merit, and from the point of view of others, one great fault. They have made their work literature rather than science, and told us of the Irish peasantry rather than of the primitive religion of mankind, or whatever else the folk-lorists are on the gad after. To be considered scientists they should have tabulated all their tales in forms like grocers' bills—item the fairy king, item the queen. Instead of this they have caught the very voice of the people, the very pulse of life, each giving what was most noticed in his day.

Croker and Lover, full of the ideas of harum-scarum Irish gentility, saw everything humorised. The impulse of the Irish literature of their time came from a class that did not —mainly for political reasons—take the populace seriously, and imagined the country as a humorist's Arcadia ; its passion, its gloom, its tragedy, they knew nothing of. What they did was not wholly false ; they merely magnified an irresponsible type, found oftenest among boatmen, carmen, and gentlemen's servants, into the type of a whole nation, and created the stage Irishman. The writers of 'Forty-eight, and the famine combined, burst their bubble. Their work had the dash as well as the shallowness of an ascendant and idle class, and in Croker is touched everywhere with beauty—a gentle Arcadian beauty. Carleton, a peasant born, has in many of his stories—I have been only able to give a few of the slightest—more especially in his ghost stories, a much more serious way with him, for all his humour. Kennedy, an old bookseller in Dublin, who seems to have had a something of genuine belief in the fairies, came next in time. He has far less literary faculty, but is wonderfully accurate, giving often the very words the stories were told in. But the best book since Croker is Lady Wilde's *Ancient Legends.* The humour has all given way to pathos and tenderness. We have here the innermost heart of the Celt in the moments he has grown to love through years of persecution, when, cushioning himself about with dreams, and hearing fairy-songs in the twilight, he ponders on the soul and on the dead. Here is the Celt, only it is the Celt dreaming.

Besides these are two writers of importance, who have published, so far, nothing in book shape—Miss Letitia Maclintock and Mr. Douglas Hyde. Miss Maclintock writes accurately and beautifully the half Scotch dialect of

Ulster; and Mr. Douglas Hyde is now preparing a volume of folk tales in Gaelic, having taken them down, for the most part, word for word among the Gaelic speakers of Roscommon and Galway. He is, perhaps, most to be trusted of all. He knows the people thoroughly. Others see a phase of Irish life; he understands all its elements. His work is neither humorous nor mournful; it is simply life. I hope he may put some of his gatherings into ballads, for he is the last of our ballad-writers of the school of Walsh and Callanan—men whose work seems fragrant with turf smoke. And this brings to mind the chap-books. They are to be found brown with turf smoke on cottage shelves, and are, or were, sold on every hand by the pedlars, but cannot be found in any library of this city of the Sassanach. "The Royal Fairy Tales," "The Hibernian Tales," and "The Legends of the Fairies" are the fairy literature of the people.

Several specimens of our fairy poetry are given. It is more like the fairy poetry of Scotland than of England. The personages of English fairy literature are merely, in most cases, mortals beautifully masquerading. Nobody ever believed in such fairies. They are romantic bubbles from Provence. Nobody ever laid new milk on their doorstep for them.

As to my own part in this book, I have tried to make it representative, as far as so few pages would allow, of every kind of Irish folk-faith. The reader will perhaps wonder that in all my notes I have not rationalised a single hobgoblin. I seek for shelter to the words of Socrates.*

"*Phædrus.* I should like to know, Socrates, whether the

---

* *Phædrus.* Jowett's translation. (Clarendon Press.)

place is not somewhere here at which Boreas is said to have carried off Orithyia from the banks of the Ilissus?

"*Socrates.* That is the tradition.

"*Phædrus.* And is this the exact spot? The little stream is delightfully clear and bright; I can fancy that there might be maidens playing near.

"*Socrates.* I believe the spot is not exactly here, but about a quarter-of-a-mile lower down, where you cross to the temple of Artemis, and I think that there is some sort of an altar of Boreas at the place.

"*Phædrus.* I do not recollect; but I beseech you to tell me, Socrates, do you believe this tale?

"*Socrates.* The wise are doubtful, and I should not be singular if, like them, I also doubted. I might have a rational explanation that Orithyia was playing with Pharmacia, when a northern gust carried her over the neighbouring rocks; and this being the manner of her death, she was said to have been carried away by Boreas. There is a discrepancy, however, about the locality. According to another version of the story, she was taken from the Areopagus, and not from this place. Now I quite acknowledge that these allegories are very nice, but he is not to be envied who has to invent them; much labour and ingenuity will be required of him; and when he has once begun, he must go on and rehabilitate centaurs and chimeras dire. Gorgons and winged steeds flow in apace, and numberless other inconceivable and portentous monsters. And if he is sceptical about them, and would fain reduce them one after another to the rules of probability, this sort of crude philosophy will take up all his time. Now, I have certainly not time for such inquiries. Shall I tell you why? I must first know myself, as the Delphian inscription says; to be curious about that which is not my business, while I am still in ignorance of my own self, would be ridiculous. And, therefore, I say farewell to all this; the common opinion is enough for me. For, as I was saying, I want to know not about this, but about myself. Am I, indeed, a wonder more complicated and swollen with passion than the serpent Typho, or a creature of gentler and simpler sort, to whom nature has given a diviner and lowlier destiny?"

I have to thank Messrs Macmillan, and the editors of *Belgravia, All the Year Round*, and *Monthly Packet*, for leave to quote from Patrick Kennedy's *Legendary Fictions of the Irish Celts*, and Miss Maclintock's articles respectively; Lady Wilde, for leave to give what I would from her *Ancient Legends of Ireland* (Ward & Downey); and Mr. Douglas Hyde, for his three unpublished stories, and for valuable and valued assistance in several ways; and also Mr. Allingham, and other copyright holders, for their poems. Mr. Allingham's poems are from *Irish Songs and Poems* (Reeves and Turner); Fergusson's, from Sealey, Bryers, & Walker's shilling reprint; my own and Miss O'Leary's from *Ballads and Poems of Young Ireland*, 1888, a little anthology published by Gill & Sons, Dublin.

W. B. YEATS.

FAIRY AND FOLK TALES.

◆

THE TROOPING FAIRIES.

THE Irish word for fairy is *sheehogue* [*sidheóg*], a diminutive of "shee" in *banshee*. Fairies are *deenee shee* [*daoine sidhe*] (fairy people).

Who are they? "Fallen angels who were not good enough to be saved, nor bad enough to be lost," say the peasantry. "The gods of the earth," says the Book of Armagh. "The gods of pagan Ireland," say the Irish antiquarians, "the *Tuatha De Danān*, who, when no longer worshipped and fed with offerings, dwindled away in the popular imagination, and now are only a few spans high."

And they will tell you, in proof, that the names of fairy chiefs are the names of old *Danān* heroes, and the places where they especially gather together, *Danān* burying-places, and that the *Tuath De Danān* used also to be called the *slooa-shee* [*sheagh sidhe*] (the fairy host), or *Marcra shee* (the fairy cavalcade).

On the other hand, there is much evidence to prove them fallen angels. Witness the nature of the creatures, their caprice, their way of being good to the good and evil to the evil, having every charm but conscience—consistency. Beings so quickly offended that you must not speak much about them at all, and never call them anything but the "gentry," or else *daoine maithe*, which in English means good people, yet so easily pleased, they will do their best to keep misfortune away from you, if you leave a

1

little milk for them on the window-sill over night. On the whole, the popular belief tells us most about them, telling us how they fell, and yet were not lost, because their evil was wholly without malice.

Are they "the gods of the earth?" Perhaps! Many poets, and all mystic and occult writers, in all ages and countries, have declared that behind the visible are chains on chains of conscious beings, who are not of heaven but of the earth, who have no inherent form but change according to their whim, or the mind that sees them. You cannot lift your hand without influencing and being influenced by hoards. The visible world is merely their skin. In dreams we go amongst them, and play with them, and combat with them. They are, perhaps, human souls in the crucible—these creatures of whim.

Do not think the fairies are always little. Everything is capricious about them, even their size. They seem to take what size or shape pleases them. Their chief occupations are feasting, fighting, and making love, and playing the most beautiful music. They have only one industrious person amongst them, the *lepra-caun*—the shoemaker. Perhaps they wear their shoes out with dancing. Near the village of Ballisodare is a little woman who lived amongst them seven years. When she came home she had no toes—she had danced them off.

They have three great festivals in the year—May Eve, Midsummer Eve, November Eve. On May Eve, every seventh year, they fight all round, but mostly on the "Plain-a-Bawn" (wherever that is), for the harvest, for the best ears of grain belong to them. An old man told me he saw them fight once; they tore the thatch off a house in the midst of it all. Had anyone else been near they would merely have seen a great wind whirling everything into the air as it passed. When the wind makes the straws and leaves whirl as it passes, that is the fairies, and the peasantry take off their hats and say, "God bless them."

On Midsummer Eve, when the bonfires are lighted on every hill in honour of St. John, the fairies are at their gayest, and sometime steal away beautiful mortals to be their brides.

TROOPING FAIRIES.

FLEEING A TROOP OF FAIRIES.

On November Eve they are at their gloomiest, for, according to the old Gaelic reckoning, this is the first night of winter. This night they dance with the ghosts, and the *pooka* is abroad, and witches make their spells, and girls set a table with food in the name of the devil, that the fetch of their future lover may come through the window and eat of the food. After November Eve the blackberries are no longer wholesome, for the *pooka* has spoiled them.

When they are angry they paralyse men and cattle with their fairy darts.

When they are gay they sing. Many a poor girl has heard them, and pined away and died, for love of that singing. Plenty of the old beautiful tunes of Ireland are only their music, caught up by eavesdroppers. No wise peasant would hum "The Pretty Girl milking the Cow" near a fairy rath, for they are jealous, and do not like to hear their songs on clumsy mortal lips. Carolan, the last of the Irish bards, slept on a rath, and ever after the fairy tunes ran in his head, and made him the great man he was.

Do they die? Blake saw a fairy's funeral; but in Ireland we say they are immortal.

THE FAIRIES.

WILLIAM ALLINGHAM.

Up the airy mountain,
   Down the rushy glen,
We daren't go a-hunting
   For fear of little men;
Wee folk, good folk,
   Trooping all together;
Green jacket, red cap,
   And white owl's feather!

Down along the rocky shore
    Some make their home,
They live on crispy pancakes
    Of yellow tide-foam;
Some in the reeds
    Of the black mountain lake,
With frogs for their watch-dogs,
    All night awake.

High on the hill-top
    The old King sits;
He is now so old and gray
    He's nigh lost his wits.
With a bridge of white mist
    Columbkill he crosses,
On his stately journeys
    From Slieveleague to Rosses;
Or going up with music
    On cold starry nights,
To sup with the Queen
    Of the gay Northern Lights.

They stole little Bridget
    For seven years long;
When she came down again
    Her friends were all gone.
They took her lightly back,
    Between the night and morrow,
They thought that she was fast asleep,
    But she was dead with sorrow.
They have kept her ever since
    Deep within the lake,
On a bed of flag-leaves,
    Watching till she wake.

By the craggy hill-side,
    Through the mosses bare,
They have planted thorn-trees
    For pleasure here and there.

Is any man so daring
   As dig them up in spite,
He shall find their sharpest thorns
   In his bed at night.

Up the airy mountain,
   Down the rushy glen,
We daren't go a-hunting
   For fear of little men ;
Wee folk, good folk,
   Trooping all together ;
Green jacket, red cap,
   And white owl's feather !

FRANK MARTIN AND THE FAIRIES.

WILLIAM CARLETON.

MARTIN was a thin pale man, when I saw him, of a sickly look, and a constitution naturally feeble. His hair was a light auburn, his beard mostly unshaven, and his hands of a singular delicacy and whiteness, owing, I dare say, as much to the soft and easy nature of his employment as to his infirm health. In everything else he was as sensible, sober, and rational as any other man ; but on the topic of fairies, the man's mania was peculiarly strong and immovable. Indeed, I remember that the expression of his eyes was singularly wild and hollow, and his long narrow temples sallow and emaciated.

Now, this man did not lead an unhappy life, nor did the malady he laboured under seem to be productive of either pain or terror to him, although one might be apt to imagine otherwise. On the contrary, he and the fairies maintained the most friendly intimacy, and their dialogues—which I fear were wofully one-sided ones—must have been a source of great pleasure to him, for they were conducted with much mirth and laughter, on his part at least.

" Well, Frank, when did you see the fairies ? "

"Whist ! there's two dozen of them in the shop (the weaving shop) this minute. There's a little ould fellow sittin' on the top of the sleys, an' all to be rocked while I'm weavin'. The sorrow's in them, but they're the greatest little skamers alive, so they are. See, there's another of them at my dressin' noggin.* Go out o' that, you *shingawn ;* or, bad cess to me, if you don't, but I'll lave you a mark. Ha ! cut, you thief you ! "

" Frank, arn't you afeard o' them ? "

" Is it me ! Arra, what ud' I be afeard o' them for ? Sure they have no power over me."

" And why haven't they, Frank ? "

" Because I was baptized against them."

" What do you mean by that ? "

" Why, the priest that christened me was tould by my father, to put in the proper prayer against the fairies—an' a priest can't refuse it when he's asked—an' he did so. Begorra, it's well for me that he did—(let the tallow alone, you little glutton—see, there's a weeny thief o' them aitin' my tallow)—becaise, you see, it was their intention to make me king o' the fairies."

" Is it possible ? "

" Devil a lie in it. Sure you may ax them, an' they'll tell you."

" What size are they, Frank ? "

" Oh, little wee fellows, with green coats, an' the purtiest little shoes ever you seen. There's two of them—both ould acquaintances o' mine—runnin' along the yarn-beam. That ould fellow with the bob-wig is called Jim Jam, an' the other chap, with the three-cocked hat, is called Nickey Nick. Nickey plays the pipes. Nickey, give us a tune, or I'll

---

* The dressings are a species of sizy flummery, which is brushed into the yarn to keep the thread round and even, and to prevent it from being frayed by the friction of the reed.

malivogue you—come now, 'Lough Erne Shore.' Whist, now—listen!"

The poor fellow, though weaving as fast as he could all the time, yet bestowed every possible mark of attention to the music, and seemed to enjoy it as much as if it had been real.

But who can tell whether that which we look upon as a privation may not after all be a fountain of increased happiness, greater, perhaps, than any which we ourselves enjoy? I forget who the poet is who says—

> "Mysterious are thy laws;
> The vision's finer than the view;
> Her landscape Nature never drew
> So fair as Fancy draws."

Many a time, when a mere child, not more than six or seven years of age, have I gone as far as Frank's weaving-shop, in order, with a heart divided between curiosity and fear, to listen to his conversation with the good people. From morning till night his tongue was going almost as incessantly as his shuttle; and it was well known that at night, whenever he awoke out of his sleep, the first thing he did was to put out his hand, and push them, as it were, off his bed.

"Go out o' this, you thieves, you—go out o' this now, an' let me alone. Nickey, is this any time to be playing the pipes, and me wants to sleep? Go off, now—troth if yez do, you'll see what I'll give yez to-morrow. Sure I'll be makin' new dressin's; and if yez behave decently, maybe I'll lave yez the scrapin' o' the pot. There now. Och! poor things, they're dacent crathurs. Sure they're all gone, barrin' poor Red-cap, that doesn't like to lave me." And then the harmless monomaniac would fall back into what we trust was an innocent slumber.

About this time there was said to have occurred a very remarkable circumstance, which gave poor Frank a vast deal of importance among the neighbours. A man named Frank Thomas, the same in whose house Mickey M'Rorey held the first dance at which I ever saw him, as detailed in a former sketch; this man, I say, had a child sick, but of what complaint I cannot now remember, nor is it of any importance. One of the gables of Thomas's house was built against, or rather into, a Forth or Rath, called Towny, or properly Tonagh Forth. It was said to be haunted by the fairies, and what gave it a character peculiarly wild in my eyes was, that there were on the southern side of it two or three little green mounds, which were said to be the graves of unchristened children, over which it was considered dangerous and unlucky to pass. At all events, the season was mid-summer; and one evening about dusk, during the illness of the child, the noise of a hand-saw was heard upon the Forth. This was considered rather strange, and, after a little time, a few of those who were assembled at Frank Thomas's went to see who it could be that was sawing in such a place, or what they could be sawing at so late an hour, for every one knew that nobody in the whole country about them would dare to cut down the few white-thorns that grew upon the Forth. On going to examine, however, judge of their surprise, when, after surrounding and searching the whole place, they could discover no trace of either saw or sawyer. In fact, with the exception of themselves, there was no one, either natural or supernatural, visible. They then returned to the house, and had scarcely sat down, when it was heard again within ten yards of them. Another examination of the premises took place, but with equal success. Now, however, while standing on the Forth, they heard the sawing in a little hollow, about a hundred and fifty yards below them, which was completely exposed to their view, but they could see nobody. A party of them immediately went down to ascertain, if possible, what this singular noise and invisible labour could mean; but on arriving at the spot, they heard the sawing, to which were now added hammering, and the driving of nails upon the Forth above, whilst those who stood on the Forth continued to hear it in the hollow. On comparing notes, they resolved to send down to Billy Nelson's for Frank Martin, a distance of only about eighty or ninety yards. He was soon on the spot, and without a moment's hesitation solved the enigma.

"'Tis the fairies," said he. "I see them, and busy crathurs they are."

"But what are they sawing, Frank?"

"They are makin' a child's coffin," he replied; "they have the body already made, an' they're now nailin' the lid together."

That night the child died, and the story goes that on the second evening afterwards, the carpenter who was called upon to make the coffin brought a table out from Thomas's house to the Forth, as a temporary bench; and, it is said, that the sawing and hammering necessary for the completion of his task were precisely the same which had been heard the evening but one before—neither more nor less. I remember the death of the child myself, and the making of its coffin, but I think the story of the supernatural carpenter was not heard in the village for some months after its interment.

Frank had every appearance of a hypochondriac about him. At the time I saw him, he might be about thirty-four years of age, but I do not think, from the debility of his frame and infirm health, that he has been alive for several years. He was an object of considerable interest and curiosity, and often have I been present when he was pointed out to strangers as "the man that could see the good people."

THE PRIEST'S SUPPER.

T. CROFTON CROKER.

It is said by those who ought to understand such things, that the good people, or the fairies, are some of the angels who were turned out of heaven, and who landed on their feet in this world, while the rest of their companions, who had more sin to sink them, went down farther to a worse place. Be this as it may, there was a merry troop of the fairies, dancing and playing all manner of wild pranks, on a bright moonlight evening towards the end of September. The scene of their merriment was not far distant from Inchegeela, in the west of the county Cork—a poor village, although it had a barrack for soldiers; but great mountains and barren rocks, like those round about it, are enough to strike poverty into any place: however, as the fairies can have everything they want for wishing, poverty does not trouble them much, and all their care is to seek out unfrequented nooks and places where it is not likely any one will come to spoil their sport.

On a nice green sod by the river's side were the little fellows dancing in a ring as gaily as may be, with their red caps wagging about at every bound in the moonshine, and so light were these bounds that the lobs of dew, although they trembled under their feet, were not disturbed by their capering. Thus did they carry on their gambols, spinning round and round, and twirling and bobbing and diving, and going through all manner of figures, until one of them chirped out,

> "Cease, cease, with your drumming,
> Here's an end to our mumming;
> By my smell
> I can tell
> A priest this way is coming!"

And away every one of the fairies scampered off as hard as they could, concealing themselves under the green leaves of the lusmore, where, if their little red caps should happen to peep out, they would only look like its crimson bells; and more hid themselves at the shady side of stones and brambles, and others under the bank of the river, and in holes and crannies of one kind or another.

The fairy speaker was not mistaken; for along the road, which was within view of the river, came Father Horrigan on his pony, thinking to himself that as it was so late he would make an end of his journey at the first cabin he came to. According to this determination, he stopped at the dwelling of Dermod Leary, lifted the latch, and entered with "My blessing on all here."

I need not say that Father Horrigan was a welcome guest wherever he went, for no man was more pious or better beloved in the country. Now it was a great trouble to Dermod that he had nothing to offer his reverence for supper as a relish to the potatoes, which "the old woman," for so Dermod called his wife, though she was not much past twenty, had down boiling in a pot over the fire; he thought of the net which he had set in the river, but as it had been there only a short time, the chances were against his finding a fish in it. "No matter," thought Dermod, "there can be no harm in stepping down to try; and maybe, as I want the fish for the priest's supper, that one will be there before me."

Down to the river-side went Dermod, and he found in the net as fine a salmon as ever jumped in the bright waters of "the spreading Lee;" but as he was going to take it out, the net was pulled from him, he could not tell how or by whom, and away got the salmon, and went swimming along with the current as gaily as if nothing had happened.

Dermod looked sorrowfully at the wake which the fish had left upon the water, shining like a line of silver in the moonlight, and then, with an angry motion of his right hand, and a stamp of his foot, gave vent to his feelings by muttering, "May bitter bad luck attend you night and day for a blackguard schemer of a salmon, wherever you go! You ought to be ashamed of yourself, if there's any shame in you, to give me the slip after this fashion! And I'm clear in my own mind you'll come to no good, for some kind of evil thing or other helped you—did I not feel it pull the net against me as strong as the devil himself?"

"That's not true for you," said one of the little fairies who had scampered off at the approach of the priest, coming up to Dermod Leary with a whole throng of companions at his heels; "there was only a dozen and a half of us pulling against you."

Dermod gazed on the tiny speaker with wonder, who continued, " Make yourself noways uneasy about the priest's supper ; for if you will go back and ask him one question from us, there will be as fine a supper as ever was put on a table spread out before him in less than no time."

" I'll have nothing at all to do with you," replied Dermod in a tone of determination ; and after a pause he added, " I'm much obliged to you for your offer, sir, but I know better than to sell myself to you, or the like of you, for a supper ; and more than that, I know Father Horrigan has more regard for my soul than to wish me to pledge it for ever, out of regard to anything you could put before him— so there's an end of the matter."

The little speaker, with a pertinacity not to be repulsed by Dermod's manner, continued, " Will you ask the priest one civil question for us ? "

Dermod considered for some time, and he was right in doing so, but he thought that no one could come to harm out of asking a civil question. " I see no objection to do that same, gentlemen," said Dermod ; " but I will have nothing in life to do with your supper—mind that."

" Then," said the little speaking fairy, whilst the rest came crowding after him from all parts, " go and ask Father Horrigan to tell us whether our souls will be saved at the last day, like the souls of good Christians ; and if you wish us well, bring back word what he says without delay."

Away went Dermod to his cabin, where he found the potatoes thrown out on the table, and his good woman handing the biggest of them all, a beautiful laughing red apple, smoking like a hard-ridden horse on a frosty night, over to Father Horrigan.

" Please your reverence," said Dermod, after some hesitation, " may I make bold to ask your honour one question ? "

" What may that be ? " said Father Horrigan.

" Why, then, begging your reverence's pardon for my freedom, it is, If the souls of the good people are to be saved at the last day ? "

"Who bid you ask me that question, Leary?" said the priest, fixing his eyes upon him very sternly, which Dermod could not stand before at all.

"I'll tell no lies about the matter, and nothing in life but the truth," said Dermod. "It was the good people themselves who sent me to ask the question, and there they are in thousands down on the bank of the river, waiting for me to go back with the answer."

"Go back by all means," said the priest, "and tell them, if they want to know, to come here to me themselves, and I'll answer that or any other question they are pleased to ask with the greatest pleasure in life."

Dermod accordingly returned to the fairies, who came swarming round about him to hear what the priest had said in reply; and Dermod spoke out among them like a bold man as he was: but when they heard that they must go to the priest, away they fled, some here and more there, and some this way and more that, whisking by poor Dermod so fast and in such numbers that he was quite bewildered.

When he came to himself, which was not for a long time, back he went to his cabin, and ate his dry potatoes along with Father Horrigan, who made quite light of the thing; but Dermod could not help thinking it a mighty hard case that his reverence, whose words had the power to banish the fairies at such a rate, should have no sort of relish to his supper, and that the fine salmon he had in the net should have been got away from him in such a manner.

THE FAIRY WELL OF LAGNANAY.

BY SAMUEL FERGUSON.

Mournfully, sing mournfully—
"O listen, Ellen, sister dear:
Is there no help at all for me,
  But only ceaseless sigh and tear?
Why did not he who left me here,

With stolen hope steal memory?
    O listen, Ellen, sister dear,
(Mournfully, sing mournfully)—
    I'll go away to Sleamish hill,
I'll pluck the fairy hawthorn-tree,
    And let the spirits work their will;
    I care not if for good or ill,
So they but lay the memory
    Which all my heart is haunting still!
(Mournfully, sing mournfully)—
    The Fairies are a silent race,
And pale as lily flowers to see;
    I care not for a blanched face,
    For wandering in a dreaming place,
So I but banish memory :—
    I wish I were with Anna Grace!"
Mournfully, sing mournfully!

Hearken to my tale of woe—
    'Twas thus to weeping Ellen Con,
Her sister said in accents low,
    Her only sister, Una bawn :
    'Twas in their bed before the dawn,
And Ellen answered sad and slow,—
    " Oh Una, Una, be not drawn
(Hearken to my tale of woe)—
    To this unholy grief I pray,
Which makes me sick at heart to know,
    And I will help you if I may:
    —The Fairy Well of Lagnanay—
Lie nearer me, I tremble so,—
    Una, I've heard wise women say
(Hearken to my tale of woe)—
    That if before the dews arise,
True maiden in its icy flow
    With pure hand bathe her bosom thrice,
    Three lady-brackens pluck likewise,

And three times round the fountain go,
   She straight forgets her tears and sighs."
Hearken to my tale of woe !

All, alas ! and well-away !
   " Oh, sister Ellen, sister sweet,
Come with me to the hill I pray,
   And I will prove that blessed freet ! "
They rose with soft and silent feet,
They left their mother where she lay,
   Their mother and her care discreet,
(All, alas ! and well-away !)
   And soon they reached the Fairy Well,
The mountain's eye, clear, cold, and grey,
   Wide open in the dreary fell :
How long they stood 'twere vain to tell,
At last upon the point of day,
   Bawn Una bares her bosom's swell,
(All, alas ! and well-away !)
   Thrice o'er her shrinking breasts she laves
The gliding glance that will not stay
   Of subtly-streaming fairy waves :—
   And now the charm three brackens craves,
She plucks them in their fring'd array :—
   Now round the well her fate she braves,
All, alas ! and well-away !

Save us all from Fairy thrall !
   Ellen sees her face the rim
Twice and thrice, and that is all—
   Fount and hill and maiden swim
   All together melting dim !
" Una ! Una ! " thou may'st call,
   Sister sad ! but lith or limb
(Save us all from Fairy thrall !)
   Never again of Una bawn,

Where now she walks in dreamy hall,
    Shall eye of mortal look upon!
    Oh! can it be the guard was gone,
The better guard than shield or wall?
    Who knows on earth save Jurlagh Daune?
(Save us all from Fairy thrall!)
    Behold the banks are green and bare,
No pit is here wherein to fall:
    Aye—at the fount you well may stare,
    But nought save pebbles smooth is there,
And small straws twirling one and all.
    Hie thee home, and be thy pray'r,
Save us all from Fairy thrall.

TEIG O'KANE (TADHG O CÁTHÁN) AND THE CORPSE.*

LITERALLY TRANSLATED FROM THE IRISH BY DOUGLAS HYDE.

[I FOUND it hard to place Mr. Douglas Hyde's magnificent story. Among the ghosts or the fairies? It is among the fairies on the grounds that all these ghosts and bodies were in no manner ghosts and bodies, but *pishogues*—fairy spells. One often hears of these visions in Ireland. I have met a man who had lived a wild life like the man in the story, till a vision came to him in County —— one dark night—in no way so terrible a vision as this, but sufficient to change his whole character. He will not go out at night. If you speak to him suddenly he trembles. He has grown timid and strange. He went to the bishop and was sprinkled with holy water. "It may have come as a warning," said the bishop; "yet great theologians are of opinion that no man ever saw an apparition, for no man would survive it."—ED.]

* None of Mr. Hyde's stories here given have been published before. They will be printed in the original Irish in his forthcoming *Leabhar Sgeulaigheachta* (Gill, Dublin).

THERE was once a grown-up lad in the County Leitrim, and he was strong and lively, and the son of a rich farmer. His father had plenty of money, and he did not spare it on the son. Accordingly, when the boy grew up he liked sport better than work, and, as his father had no other children, he loved this one so much that he allowed him to do in everything just as it pleased himself. He was very extravagant, and he used to scatter the gold money as another person would scatter the white. He was seldom to be found at home, but if there was a fair, or a race, or a gathering within ten miles of him, you were dead certain to find him there. And he seldom spent a night in his father's house, but he used to be always out rambling, and, like Shawn Bwee long ago, there was

"grádh gach cailin i mbrollach a léine,"

"the love of every girl in the breast of his shirt," and it's many's the kiss he got and he gave, for he was very handsome, and there wasn't a girl in the country but would fall in love with him, only for him to fasten his two eyes on her, and it was for that someone made this *rann* on him—

" Feuch an rógaire 'g iarraidh póige,
    Ni h-iongantas mór é a bheith mar atá
    Ag leanamhaint a gcómhnuidhe d'árnán na gráineóige
    Anuas 's anios 's nna chodladh 'sa' lá."

i.e.— " Look at the rogue, its for kisses he's rambling,
    It isn't much wonder, for that was his way ;
    He's like an old hedgehog, at night he'll be scrambling
    From this place to that, but he'll sleep in the day."

At last he became very wild and unruly. He wasn't to be seen day nor night in his father's house, but always rambling or going on his *kailee* (night-visit) from place to place and from house to house, so that the old people used to shake their heads and say to one another, "it's easy seen what will happen to the land when the old man dies; his son will run through it in a year, and it won't stand him that long itself."

He used to be always gambling and card-playing and drinking, but his father never minded his bad habits, and never punished him.   But it happened one day that the old man was told that the son had ruined the character of a girl in the neighbourhood, and he was greatly angry, and he called the son to him, and said to him, quietly and sensibly— "Avic," says he, "you know I loved you greatly up to this, and I never stopped you from doing your choice thing whatever it was, and I kept plenty of money with you, and I always hoped to leave you the house and land, and all I had after myself would be gone; but I heard a story of you to-day that has disgusted me with you.   I cannot tell you the grief that I felt when I heard such a thing of you, and I tell you now plainly that unless you marry that girl I'll leave house and land and everything to my brother's son.   I never could leave it to anyone who would make so bad a use of it as you do yourself, deceiving women and coaxing girls.   Settle with yourself now whether you'll marry that girl and get my land as a fortune with her, or refuse to marry her and give up all that was coming to you ; and tell me in the morning which of the two things you have chosen."

"Och! *Domnoo Sheery!* father, you wouldn't say that to me, and I such a good son as I am.   Who told you I wouldn't marry the girl?" says he.

But his father was gone, and the lad knew well enough that he would keep his word too ; and he was greatly troubled in his mind, for as quiet and as kind as the father was, he never went back of a word that he had once said, and there wasn't another man in the country who was harder to bend than he was.

The boy did not know rightly what to do.   He was in love with the girl indeed, and he hoped to marry her some-time or other, but he would much sooner have remained another while as he was, and follow on at his old tricks— drinking, sporting, and playing cards ; and, along with that, he was angry that his father should order him to marry, and should threaten him if he did not do it.

"Isn't my father a great fool," says he to himself.   "I

was ready enough, and only too anxious, to marry Mary; and now since he threatened me, faith I've a great mind to let it go another while."

His mind was so much excited that he remained between two notions as to what he should do. He walked out into the night at last to cool his heated blood, and went on to the road. He lit a pipe, and as the night was fine he walked and walked on, until the quick pace made him begin to forget his trouble. The night was bright, and the moon half full. There was not a breath of wind blowing, and the air was calm and mild. He walked on for nearly three hours, when he suddenly remembered that it was late in the night, and time for him to turn. "Musha! I think I forgot myself," says he; "it must be near twelve o'clock now."

The word was hardly out of his mouth, when he heard the sound of many voices, and the trampling of feet on the road before him. "I don't know who can be out so late at night as this, and on such a lonely road," said he to himself.

He stood listening, and he heard the voices of many people talking through other, but he could not understand what they were saying. "Oh, wirra!" says he, "I'm afraid. It's not Irish or English they have; it can't be they're Frenchmen!" He went on a couple of yards further, and he saw well enough by the light of the moon a band of little people coming towards him, and they were carrying something big and heavy with them. "Oh, murder!" says he to himself, "sure it can't be that they're the good people that's in it!" Every *rib* of hair that was on his head stood up, and there fell a shaking on his bones, for he saw that they were coming to him fast.

He looked at them again, and perceived that there were about twenty little men in it, and there was not a man at all of them higher than about three feet or three feet and a half, and some of them were grey, and seemed very old. He looked again, but he could not make out what was the heavy thing they were carrying until they came up to him, and then they all stood round about him. They threw the heavy thing down on the road, and he saw on the spot that it was a dead body.

He became as cold as the Death, and there was not a drop of blood running in his veins when an old little grey *maneen* came up to him and said, " Isn't it lucky we met you, Teig O'Kane ? "

Poor Teig could not bring out a word at all, nor open his lips, if he were to get the world for it, and so he gave no answer.

" Teig O'Kane," said the little grey man again, "isn't it timely you met us ? "

Teig could not answer him.

" Teig O'Kane," says he, " the third time, isn't it lucky and timely that we met you ? "

But Teig remained silent, for he was afraid to return an answer, and his tongue was as if it was tied to the roof of his mouth.

The little grey man turned to his companions, and there was joy in his bright little eye.   " And now," says he, " Teig O'Kane hasn't a word, we can do with him what we please. Teig, Teig," says he, " you're living a bad life, and we can make a slave of you now, and you cannot withstand us, for there's no use in trying to go against us.   Lift that corpse."

Teig was so frightened that he was only able to utter the two words, " I won't ; " for as frightened as he was, he was obstinate and stiff, the same as ever.

" Teig O'Kane won't lift the corpse," said the little *maneen*, with a wicked little laugh, for all the world like the breaking of a *lock* of dry *kippeens*, and with a little harsh voice like the striking of a cracked bell.   " Teig O'Kane won't lift the corpse—make him lift it ; " and before the word was out of his mouth they had all gathered round poor Teig, and they all talking and laughing through other.

Teig tried to run from them, but they followed him, and a man of them stretched out his foot before him as he ran, so that Teig was thrown in a heap on the road.   Then before he could rise up the fairies caught him, some by the hands and some by the feet, and they held him tight, in a way that he could not stir, with his face against the ground. Six or seven of them raised the body then, and pulled it over to him, and left it down on his back. The breast of the corpse was squeezed against Teig's back and shoulders, and the arms of the corpse were thrown around Teig's neck. Then they stood back from him a couple of yards, and let him get up. He rose, foaming at the mouth and cursing, and he shook himself, thinking to throw the corpse off his back. But his fear and his wonder were great when he found that the two arms had a tight hold round his own neck, and that the two legs were squeezing his hips firmly, and that, however strongly he tried, he could not throw it off, any more than a horse can throw off its saddle. He was terribly frightened then, and he thought he was lost. "Ochone! for ever," said he to himself, "it's the bad life I'm leading that has given the good people this power over me. I promise to God and Mary, Peter and Paul, Patrick and Bridget, that I'll mend my ways for as long as I have to live, if I come clear out of this danger—and I'll marry the girl."

The little grey man came up to him again, and said he to him, "Now, Teig*een*," says he, "you didn't lift the body when I told you to lift it, and see how you were made to lift it; perhaps when I tell you to bury it you won't bury it until you're made to bury it!"

"Anything at all that I can do for your honour," said Teig, "I'll do it," for he was getting sense already, and if it had not been for the great fear that was on him, he never would have let that civil word slip out of his mouth.

The little man laughed a sort of laugh again. "You're getting quiet now, Teig," says he. "I'll go bail but you'll be quiet enough before I'm done with you. Listen to me now, Teig O'Kane, and if you don't obey me in all I'm telling you to do, you'll repent it. You must carry with you this corpse that is on your back to Teampoll-Démus, and you must bring it into the church with you, and make a grave for it in the very middle of the church, and you must raise up the flags and put them down again the very same way, and you must carry the clay out of the church and leave the place as it was when you came, so that no one could know that there had been anything changed.   But that's not all. Maybe that the body won't be allowed to be buried in that church ; perhaps some other man has the bed, and, if so, it's likely he won't share it with this one.   If you don't get leave to bury it in Teampoll-Démus, you must carry it to Carrick-fhad-vic-Orus, and bury it in the churchyard there ; and if you don't get it into that place, take it with you to Teampoll-Ronan ; and if that churchyard is closed on you, take it to Imlogue-Fada; and if you're not able to bury it there, you've no more to do than to take it to Kill-Breedya, and you can bury it there without hindrance.   I cannot tell you what one of those churches is the one where you will have leave to bury that corpse under the clay, but I know that it will be allowed you to bury him at some church or other of them.   If you do this work rightly, we will be thankful to you, and you will have no cause to grieve; but if you are slow or lazy, believe me we shall take satisfaction of you."

When the grey little man had done speaking, his comrades laughed and clapped their hands together.   " Glic ! Glic ! Hwee ! Hwee ! " they all cried ; " go on, go on, you have eight hours before you till daybreak, and if you haven't this man buried before the sun rises, you're lost."   They struck a fist and a foot behind on him, and drove him on in the road.   He was obliged to walk, and to walk fast, for they gave him no rest.

He thought himself that there was not a wet path, or a dirty *boreen*, or a crooked contrary road in the whole county, that he had not walked that night.   The night was at times very dark, and whenever there would come a cloud across the moon he could see nothing, and then he used often to fall.   Sometimes he was hurt, and sometimes he escaped, but he was obliged always to rise on the moment and to hurry on.   Sometimes the moon would break out clearly, and then he would look behind him and see the little people following at his back.   And he heard them speaking amongst themselves, talking and crying out, and screaming like a flock of sea-gulls; and if he was to save his soul he never understood as much as one word of what they were saying.

He did not know how far he had walkéd, when at last one of them cried out to him, "Stop here!" He stood, and they all gathered round him.

"Do you see those withered trees over there?" says the old boy to him again. "Teampoll Démus is among those trees, and you must go in there by yourself, for we cannot follow you or go with you. We must remain here. Go on boldly."

Teig looked from him, and he saw a high wall that was in places half broken down, and an old grey church on the inside of the wall, and about a dozen withered old trees scattered here and there round it. There was neither leaf nor twig on any of them, but their bare crooked branches were stretched out like the arms of an angry man when he threatens. He had no help for it, but was obliged to go forward. He was a couple of hundred yards from the church, but he walked on, and never looked behind him until he came to the gate of the churchyard. The old gate was thrown down, and he had no difficulty in entering. He turned then to see if any of the little people were following him, but there came a cloud over the moon, and the night became so dark that he could see nothing. He went into the churchyard, and he walked up the old grassy pathway leading to the church. When he reached the door, he found it locked. The door was large and strong, and he did not know what to do. At last he drew out his knife with difficulty, and stuck it in the wood to try if it were not rotten, but it was not.

"Now," said he to himself, "I have no more to do; the door is shut, and I can't open it."

Before the words were rightly shaped in his own mind, a voice in his ear said to him, "Search for the key on the top of the door, or on the wall."

He started. "Who is that speaking to me?" he cried, turning round; but he saw no one. The voice said in his ear again, "Search for the key on the top of the door, or on the wall."

"What's that ?" said he, and the sweat running from his forehead ; "who spoke to me ?"

"It's I, the corpse, that spoke to you!" said the voice.

"Can you talk ?" said Teig.

"Now and again," said the corpse.

Teig searched for the key, and he found it on the top of the wall. He was too much frightened to say any more, but he opened the door wide, and as quickly as he could, and he went in, with the corpse on his back. It was as dark as pitch inside, and poor Teig began to shake and tremble.

"Light the candle," said the corpse.

Teig put his hand in his pocket, as well as he was able, and drew out a flint and steel. He struck a spark out of it, and lit a burnt rag he had in his pocket. He blew it until it made a flame, and he looked round him. The church was very ancient, and part of the wall was broken down. The windows were blown in or cracked, and the timber of the seats was rotten. There were six or seven old iron candlesticks left there still, and in one of these candlesticks Teig found the stump of an old candle, and he lit it. He was still looking round him on the strange and horrid place in which he found himself, when the cold corpse whispered in his ear, "Bury me now, bury me now; there is a spade and turn the ground." Teig looked from him, and he saw a spade lying beside the altar. He took it up, and he placed the blade under a flag that was in the middle of the aisle, and leaning all his weight on the handle of the spade, he raised it. When the first flag was raised it was not hard to raise the others near it, and he moved three or four of them out of their places. The clay that was under them was soft and easy to dig, but he had not thrown up more than three or four shovelfuls, when he felt the iron touch something soft like flesh. He threw up three or four more shovelfuls from around it, and then he saw that it was another body that was buried in the same place.

"I am afraid I'll never be allowed to bury the two bodies in the same hole," said Teig, in his own mind. "You corpse, there on my back," says he, "will you be satisfied if I bury you down here?" But the corpse never answered him a word.

"That's a good sign," said Teig to himself. "Maybe he's getting quiet," and he thrust the spade down in the earth again. Perhaps he hurt the flesh of the other body, for the dead man that was buried there stood up in the grave, and shouted an awful shout. "Hoo! hoo!! hoo!!! Go! go!! go!!! or you're a dead, dead, dead man!" And then he fell back in the grave again. Teig said afterwards, that of all the wonderful things he saw that night, that was the most awful to him. His hair stood upright on his head like the bristles of a pig, the cold sweat ran off his face, and then came a tremour over all his bones, until he thought that he must fall.

But after a while he became bolder, when he saw that the second corpse remained lying quietly there, and he threw in the clay on it again, and he smoothed it overhead, and he laid down the flags carefully as they had been before. "It can't be that he'll rise up any more," said he.

He went down the aisle a little further, and drew near to the door, and began raising the flags again, looking for another bed for the corpse on his back. He took up three or four flags and put them aside, and then he dug the clay. He was not long digging until he laid bare an old woman without a thread upon her but her shirt. She was more lively than the first corpse, for he had scarcely taken any of the clay away from about her, when she sat up and began to cry, "Ho, you *bodach* (clown)! Ha, you *bodach*! Where has he been that he got no bed?"

Poor Teig drew back, and when she found that she was getting no answer, she closed her eyes gently, lost her vigour, and fell back quietly and slowly under the clay. Teig did to her as he had done to the man—he threw the clay back on her, and left the flags down overhead.

He began digging again near the door, but before he had

thrown up more than a couple of shovelfuls, he noticed a man's hand laid bare by the spade. " By my soul, I'll go no further, then," said he to himself; " what use is it for me?" And he threw the clay in again on it, and settled the flags as they had been before.

He left the church then, and his heart was heavy enough, but he shut the door and locked it, and left the key where he found it. He sat down on a tombstone that was near the door, and began thinking. He was in great doubt what he should do. He laid his face between his two hands, and cried for grief and fatigue, since he was dead certain at this time that he never would come home alive. He made another attempt to loosen the hands of the corpse that were squeezed round his neck, but they were as tight as if they were clamped ; and the more he tried to loosen them, the tighter they squeezed him. He was going to sit down once more, when the cold, horrid lips of the dead man said to him, " Carrick-fhad-vic-Orus," and he remembered the command of the good people to bring the corpse with him to that place if he should be unable to bury it where he had been.

He rose up, and looked about him. " I don't know the way," he said.

As soon as he had uttered the word, the corpse stretched out suddenly its left hand that had been tightened round his neck, and kept it pointing out, showing him the road he ought to follow. Teig went in the direction that the fingers were stretched, and passed out of the churchyard. He found himself on an old rutty, stony road, and he stood still again, not knowing where to turn. The corpse stretched out its bony hand a second time, and pointed out to him another road—not the road by which he had come when approaching the old church. Teig followed that road, and whenever he came to a path or road meeting it, the corpse always stretched out its hand and pointed with its fingers, showing him the way he was to take.

Many was the cross-road he turned down, and many was the crooked *boreen* he walked, until he saw from him an old burying-ground at last, beside the road, but there was neither church nor chapel nor any other building in it. The corpse squeezed him tightly, and he stood. " Bury me, bury me in the burying-ground," said the voice.

Teig drew over towards the old burying-place, and he was not more than about twenty yards from it, when, raising his eyes, he saw hundreds and hundreds of ghosts— men, women, and children—sitting on the top of the wall round about, or standing on the inside of it, or running backwards and forwards, and pointing at him, while he could see their mouths opening and shutting as if they were speaking, though he heard no word, nor any sound amongst them at all.

He was afraid to go forward, so he stood where he was, and the moment he stood, all the ghosts became quiet, and ceased moving. Then Teig understood that it was trying to keep him from going in, that they were. He walked a couple of yards forwards, and immediately the whole crowd rushed together towards the spot to which he was moving, and they stood so thickly together that it seemed to him that he never could break through them, even though he had a mind to try. But he had no mind to try it. He went back broken and dispirited, and when he had gone a couple of hundred yards from the burying-ground, he stood again, for he did not know what way he was to go. He heard the voice of the corpse in his ear, saying "Teampoll-Ronan," and the skinny hand was stretched out again, pointing him out the road.

As tired as he was, he had to walk, and the road was neither short nor even. The night was darker than ever, and it was difficult to make his way. Many was the toss he got, and many a bruise they left on his body. At last he saw Teampoll-Ronan from him in the distance, standing in the middle of the burying-ground. He moved over towards it, and thought he was all right and safe, when he saw no ghosts nor anything else on the wall, and he thought he would never be hindered now from leaving his load off him at last. He moved over to the gate, but as he was passing in, he tripped on the threshold. Before he could recover himself, something that he could not see seized him by the neck, by the hands, and by the feet, and bruised him, and shook him, and choked him, until he was nearly dead ; and at last he was lifted up, and carried more than a hundred yards from that place, and then thrown down in an old dyke, with the corpse still clinging to him.

He rose up, bruised and sore, but feared to go near the place again, for he had seen nothing the time he was thrown down and carried away.

"You corpse, up on my back," said he, "shall I go over again to the churchyard ?"—but the corpse never answered him. "That's a sign you don't wish me to try it again," said Teig.

He was now in great doubt as to what he ought to do, when the corpse spoke in his ear, and said "Imlogue-Fada."

"Oh, murder !" said Teig, "must I bring you there? If you keep me long walking like this, I tell you I'll fall under you."

He went on, however, in the direction the corpse pointed out to him. He could not have told, himself, how long he had been going, when the dead man behind suddenly squeezed him, and said, "There !"

Teig looked from him, and he saw a little low wall, that was so broken down in places that it was no wall at all. It was in a great wide field, in from the road ; and only for three or four great stones at the corners, that were more like rocks than stones, there was nothing to show that there was either graveyard or burying-ground there.

"Is this Imlogue-Fada ? Shall I bury you here ?" said Teig.

"Yes," said the voice.

"But I see no grave or gravestone, only this pile of stones," said Teig.

The corpse did not answer, but stretched out its long fleshless hand, to show Teig the direction in which he was

to go.   Teig went on accordingly, but he was greatly terrified, for he remembered what had happened to him at the
last place.   He went on, "with his heart in his mouth," as
he said himself afterwards ; but when he came to within
fifteen or twenty yards of the little low square wall, there
broke out a flash of lightning, bright yellow and red, with
blue streaks in it, and went round about the wall in one
course, and it swept by as fast as the swallow in the clouds,
and the longer Teig remained looking at it the faster it
went, till at last it became like a bright ring of flame round
the old graveyard, which no one could pass without being
burnt by it.   Teig never saw, from the time he was born,
and never saw afterwards, so wonderful or so splendid a
sight as that was.   Round went the flame, white and yellow
and blue sparks leaping out from it as it went, and although
at first it had been no more than a thin, narrow line, it
increased slowly until it was at last a great broad band, and
it was continually getting broader and higher, and throwing
out more brilliant sparks, till there was never a colour on
the ridge of the earth that was not to be seen in that fire ;
and lightning never shone and flame never flamed that was
so shining and so bright as that.

Teig was amazed ; he was half dead with fatigue, and he
had no courage left to approach the wall.   There fell a
mist over his eyes, and there came a *soorawn* in his head,
and he was obliged to sit down upon a great stone to
recover himself.   He could see nothing but the light, and
he could hear nothing but the whirr of it as it shot round
the paddock faster than a flash of lightning.

As he sat there on the stone, the voice whispered once
more in his ear, " Kill-Breedya ; " and the dead man
squeezed him so tightly that he cried out.   He rose again,
sick, tired, and trembling, and went forwards as he was
directed.   The wind was cold, and the road was bad, and
the load upon his back was heavy, and the night was dark,
and he himself was nearly worn out, and if he had had
very much farther to go he must have fallen dead under his
burden.

At last the corpse stretched out its hand, and said to him,
" Bury me there."

"This is the last burying-place," said Teig in his own
mind ; "and the little grey man said I'd be allowed to bury
him in some of them, so it must be this ; it can't be but
they'll let him in here."

The first faint streak of the *ring of day* was appearing in
the east, and the clouds were beginning to catch fire, but it
was darker than ever, for the moon was set, and there were
no stars.

" Make haste, make haste ! " said the corpse ; and Teig
hurried forward as well as he could to the graveyard, which
was a little place on a bare hill, with only a few graves in it.
He walked boldly in through the open gate, and nothing
touched him, nor did he either hear or see anything. He
came to the middle of the ground, and then stood up and
looked round him for a spade or shovel to make a grave.
As he was turning round and searching, he suddenly perceived what startled him greatly—a newly-dug grave right
before him. He moved over to it, and looked down, and
there at the bottom he saw a black coffin. He clambered
down into the hole and lifted the lid, and found that (as he
thought it would be) the coffin was empty. He had hardly
mounted up out of the hole, and was standing on the
brink, when the corpse, which had clung to him for more
than eight hours, suddenly relaxed its hold of his neck, and
loosened its shins from round his hips, and sank down with
a *plop* into the open coffin.

Teig fell down on his two knees at the brink of the
grave, and gave thanks to God. He made no delay then,
but pressed down the coffin lid in its place, and threw in
the clay over it with his two hands ; and when the grave
was filled up, he stamped and leaped on it with his feet,
until it was firm and hard, and then he left the place.

The sun was fast rising as he finished his work, and the
first thing he did was to return to the road, and look out
for a house to rest himself in. He found an inn at last,
and lay down upon a bed there, and slept till night. Then

he rose up and ate a little, and fell asleep again till morning. When he awoke in the morning he hired a horse and rode home. He was more than twenty-six miles from home where he was, and he had come all that way with the dead body on his back in one night.

All the people at his own home thought that he must have left the country, and they rejoiced greatly when they saw him come back. Everyone began asking him where he had been, but he would not tell anyone except his father.

He was a changed man from that day. He never drank too much; he never lost his money over cards; and especially he would not take the world and be out late by himself of a dark night.

He was not a fortnight at home until he married Mary, the girl he had been in love with; and it's at their wedding the sport was, and it's he was the happy man from that day forward, and it's all I wish that we may be as happy as he was.

GLOSSARY.—*Rann*, a stanza; *kailee* (*céilidhe*), a visit in the evening; *wirra* (*a mhuire*), "Oh, Mary!" an exclamation like the French *dame*; *rib*, a single hair (in Irish, *ribe*); *a lock* (*glac*), a bundle or wisp, or a little share of anything; *kippeen* (*cipín*), a rod or twig; *boreen* (*bóithrín*), a lane; *bodach*, a clown; *soorawn* (*suarán*), vertigo. *Avic* (*a Mhic*) = my son, or rather, Oh, son. Mic is the vocative of Mac.

PADDY CORCORAN'S WIFE.

WILLIAM CARLETON.

PADDY CORCORAN'S wife was for several years afflicted with a kind of complaint which nobody could properly understand. She was sick, and she was not sick; she was well, and she was not well; she was as ladies wish to be who love their lords, and she was not as such ladies wish to be. In fact nobody could tell what the matter with her was. She had a gnawing at the heart which came heavily upon her husband; for, with the help of God, a keener appetite than the same gnawing amounted to could not be met with of a summer's day. The poor woman was delicate beyond belief, and had no appetite at all, so she hadn't, barring a little relish for a mutton-chop, or a "staik," or a bit o' mait, anyway; for sure, God help her! she hadn't the laist inclination for the dhry pratie, or the dhrop o' sour buttermilk along wid it, especially as she was so poorly; and, indeed, for a woman in her condition—for, sick as she was, poor Paddy always was made to believe her in *that* condition—but God's will be done! she didn't care. A pratie an' a grain o' salt was a welcome to her—glory be to his name!—as the best roast an' boiled that ever was dressed; and why not? There was one comfort: she wouldn't be long wid him—long troublin' him; it matthered little what she got; but sure she knew herself, that from the gnawin' at her heart, she could never do good widout the little bit o' mait now and then; an', sure, if her own husband begridged it to her, who else had she a better right to expect it from?

Well, as we have said, she lay a bedridden invalid for long enough, trying doctors and quacks of all sorts, sexes, and sizes, and all without a farthing's benefit, until, at the long run, poor Paddy was nearly brought to the last pass, in striving to keep her in "the bit o' mait." The seventh year was now on the point of closing, when, one harvest day, as she lay bemoaning her hard condition, on her bed beyond the kitchen fire, a little weeshy woman, dressed in a neat red cloak, comes in, and, sitting down by the hearth, says :—

"Well, Kitty Corcoran, you've had a long lair of it there on the broad o' yer back for seven years, an' you're jist as far from bein' cured as ever."

"Mavrone, ay," said the other; "in throth that's what I was this minnit thinkin' ov, and a sorrowful thought it's to me."

"It's yer own fau't, thin," says the little woman; "an', indeed, for that matter, it's yer fau't that ever you wor there at all."

"Arra, how is that?" asked Kitty; "sure I wouldn't be

here if I could help it? Do you think it's a comfort or a pleasure to me to be sick and bedridden?"

"No," said the other, "I do not; but I'll tell you the truth : for the last seven years you have been annoying us. I am one o' the good people; an' as I have a regard for you, I'm come to let you know the raison why you've been sick so long as you are. For all the time you've been ill, if you'll take the thrubble to remimber, your childhre threwn out yer dirty wather afther dusk an' before sunrise, at the very time we're passin' yer door, which we pass twice a-day. Now, if you avoid this, if you throw it out in a different place, an' at a different time, the complaint you have will lave you : so will the gnawin' at the heart; an' you'll be as well as ever you wor. If you don't follow this advice, why, remain as you are, an' all the art o' man can't cure you." She then bade her good-bye, and disappeared.

Kitty, who was glad to be cured on such easy terms, immediately complied with the injunction of the fairy; and the consequence was, that the next day she found herself in as good health as ever she enjoyed during her life.

CUSHEEN LOO.

TRANSLATED FROM THE IRISH BY J. J. CALLANAN.

[THIS song is supposed to have been sung by a young bride, who was forcibly detained in one of those forts which are so common in Ireland, and to which the good people are very fond of resorting. Under pretence of hushing her child to rest, she retired to the outside margin of the fort, and addressed the burthen of her song to a young woman whom she saw at a short distance, and whom she requested to inform her husband of her condition, and to desire him to bring the steel knife to dissolve the enchantment.]

SLEEP, my child! for the rustling trees,
Stirr'd by the breath of summer breeze,
And fairy songs of sweetest note,
Around us gently float.

Sleep! for the weeping flowers have shed
Their fragrant tears upon thy head,
The voice of love hath sooth'd thy rest,
And thy pillow is a mother's breast.
                              Sleep, my child!

Weary hath pass'd the time forlorn,
Since to your mansion I was borne,
Tho' bright the feast of its airy halls,
And the voice of mirth resounds from its walls.
                              Sleep, my child!

Full many a maid and blooming bride
Within that splendid dome abide,—
And many a hoar and shrivell'd sage,
And many a matron bow'd with age.
                              Sleep, my child!

Oh! thou who hearest this song of fear,
To the mourner's home these tidings bear.
Bid him bring the knife of the magic blade,
At whose lightning-flash the charm will fade.
                              Sleep, my child!

Haste! for to-morrow's sun will see
The hateful spell renewed for me ;
Nor can I from that home depart,
Till life shall leave my withering heart.
                              Sleep, my child!

Sleep, my child! for the rustling trees,
Stirr'd by the breath of summer breeze,
And fairy songs of sweetest note,
Around us gently float,

THE WHITE TROUT; A LEGEND OF CONG.

BY S. LOVER.

THERE was wanst upon a time, long ago, a beautiful lady that lived in a castle upon the lake beyant, and they say she was promised to a king's son, and they wor to be married, when all of a sudden he was murthered, the crathur (Lord help us), and threwn into the lake above, and so, of course, he couldn't keep his promise to the fair lady,—and more's the pity.

Well, the story goes that she went out iv her mind, bekase av loosin' the king's son—for she was tendher-hearted, God help her, like the rest iv us !—and pined away after him, until at last, no one about seen her, good or bad ; and the story wint that the fairies took her away.

Well, sir, in coorse o' time, the White Throut, God bless it, was seen in the sthrame beyant, and sure the people didn't know what to think av the crathur, secin' as how a *white* throut was never heard av afor, nor since ; and years upon years the throut was there, just where you seen it this blessed minit, longer nor I can tell—aye throth, and beyant the memory o' th' ouldest in the village.

At last the people began to think it must be a fairy ; for what else could it be ?—and no hurt nor harm was iver put an the white throut, until some wicked sinners of sojers kem to these parts, and laughed at all the people, and gibed and jeered them for thinkin' o' the likes ; and one o' them in partic'lar (bad luck to him ; God forgi' me for saying it !) swore he'd catch the throut and ate it for his dinner—the blackguard !

Well, what would you think o' the villainy of the sojer ? Sure enough he cotch the throut, and away wid him home, and puts an the fryin'-pan, and into it he pitches the purty little thing. The throut squeeled all as one as a christian crathur, and, my dear, you'd think the sojer id split his sides laughin'—for he was a harden'd villain; and when he thought one side was done, he turns it over to fry the other; and, what would you think, but the divil a taste of a burn was an it at all at all; and sure the sojer thought it was a *quare* throut that could not be briled. "But," says he, "I'll give it another turn by-and-by," little thinkin' what was in store for him, the haythen.

Well, when he thought that side was done he turns it agin, and lo and behould you, the divil a taste more done that side was nor the other. "Bad luck to me," says the sojer, "but that bates the world," says he; "but I'll thry you agin, my darlint," says he, "as cunnin' as you think yourself;" and so with that he turns it over and over, but not a sign of the fire was on the purty throut. "Well," says the desperate villain—(for sure, sir, only he was a desperate villain *entirely*, he might know he was doing a wrong thing, seein' that all his endeavours was no good)—"Well," says he, "my jolly little throut, maybe you're fried enough, though you don't seem over well dress'd; but you may be better than you look, like a singed cat, and a tit-bit afther all," says he; and with that he ups with his knife and fork to taste a piece o' the throut; but, my jew'l, the minit he puts his knife into the fish, there was a murtherin' screech, that you'd think the life id lave you if you hurd it, and away jumps the throut out av the fryin'-pan into the middle o' the flure; and an the spot where it fell, up riz a lovely lady—the beautifullest crathur that eyes ever seen, dressed in white, and a band o' goold in her hair, and a sthrame o' blood runnin' down her arm.

"Look where you cut me, you villain," says she, and she held out her arm to him—and, my dear, he thought the sight id lave his eyes.

"Couldn't you lave me cool and comfortable in the river where you snared me, and not disturb me in my duty?" says she.

Well, he thrimbled like a dog in a wet sack, and at last he stammered out somethin', and begged for his life, and ax'd her ladyship's pardin, and said he didn't know she was on duty, or he was too good a sojer not to know betther nor to meddle wid her.

"I *was* on duty, then," says the lady; "I was watchin' for my true love that is comin' by wather to me," says she, "an' if he comes while I'm away, an' that I miss iv him, I'll turn you into a pinkeen, and I'll hunt you up and down for ever-more, while grass grows or wather runs."

Well the sojer thought the life id lave him, at the thoughts iv his bein' turned into a pinkeen, and begged for mercy; and with that says the lady—

"Renounce your evil coorses," says she, "you villain, or you'll repint it too late; be a good man for the futhur, and go to your duty* reg'lar, and now," says she, "take me back and put me into the river again, where you found me."

"Oh, my lady," says the sojer, "how could I have the heart to drownd a beautiful lady like you?"

But before he could say another word, the lady was vanished, and there he saw the little throut an the ground. Well he put it in a clean plate, and away he runs for the bare life, for fear her lover would come while she was away; and he run, and he run, even till he came to the cave agin, and threw the throut into the river. The minit he did, the wather was as red as blood for a little while, by rayson av the cut, I suppose, until the sthrame washed the stain away; and to this day there's a little red mark an the throut's side, where it was cut.†

Well, sir, from that day out the sojer was an altered man, and reformed his ways, and went to his duty reg'lar, and fasted three times a-week—though it was never fish he tuk an fastin' days, for afther the fright he got, fish id never rest an his stomach—savin' your presence.

But anyhow, he was an altered man, as I said before, and in coorse o' time he left the army, and turned hermit at last; and they say he *used to pray evermore for the soul of the White Throut.*

* The Irish peasant calls his attendance at the confessional "going to his duty."

† The fish has really a red spot on its side.

[These trout stories are common all over Ireland. Many holy wells are haunted by such blessed trout. There is a trout in a well on the border of Lough Gill, Sligo, that some paganish person put once on the gridiron. It carries the marks to this day. Long ago, the saint who sanctified the well put that trout there. Nowadays it is only visible to the pious, who have done due penance.]

THE FAIRY THORN.

An Ulster Ballad.

SIR SAMUEL FERGUSON.

"Get up, our Anna dear, from the weary spinning-wheel;
  For your father's on the hill, and your mother is asleep;
Come up above the crags, and we'll dance a highland-reel
  Around the fairy thorn on the steep."

At Anna Grace's door 'twas thus the maidens cried,
  Three merry maidens fair in kirtles of the green;
And Anna laid the rock and the weary wheel aside,
  The fairest of the four, I ween.

They're glancing through the glimmer of the quiet eve,
  Away in milky wavings of neck and ankle bare;
The heavy-sliding stream in its sleepy song they leave,
  And the crags in the ghostly air:

And linking hand in hand, and singing as they go,
  The maids along the hill-side have ta'en their fearless way,
Till they come to where the rowan trees in lonely beauty
    grow
  Beside the Fairy Hawthorn grey.

The Hawthorn stands between the ashes tall and slim,
  Like matron with her twin grand-daughters at her knee;
The rowan berries cluster o'er her low head grey and dim
  In ruddy kisses sweet to see.

The merry maidens four have ranged them in a row,
  Between each lovely couple a stately rowan stem,
And away in mazes wavy, like skimming birds they go,
  Oh, never caroll'd bird like them!

But solemn is the silence of the silvery haze
  That drinks away their voices in echoless repose,
And dreamily the evening has still'd the haunted braes,
  And dreamier the gloaming grows.

And sinking one by one, like lark-notes from the sky
  When the falcon's shadow saileth across the open shaw,
Are hush'd the maiden's voices, as cowering down they lie
  In the flutter of their sudden awe.

For, from the air above, and the grassy ground beneath,
  And from the mountain-ashes and the old Whitethorn
    between,
A Power of faint enchantment doth through their beings
    breathe,
  And they sink down together on the green.

They sink together silent, and stealing side by side,
  They fling their lovely arms o'er their drooping necks so
    fair,
Then vainly strive again their naked arms to hide,
  For their shrinking necks again are bare.

Thus clasp'd and prostrate all, with their heads together
    bow'd,
  Soft o'er their bosom's beating—the only human sound—
They hear the silky footsteps of the silent fairy crowd,
  Like a river in the air, gliding round.

No scream can any raise, no prayer can any say,
　　But wild, wild, the terror of the speechless three—
For they feel fair Anna Grace drawn silently away,
　　By whom they dare not look to see.

They feel their tresses twine with her parting locks of gold,
　　And the curls elastic falling as her head withdraws;
They feel her sliding arms from their tranced arms unfold,
　　But they may not look to see the cause:

For heavy on their senses the faint enchantment lies
　　Through all that night of anguish and perilous amaze;
And neither fear nor wonder can ope their quivering eyes,
　　Or their limbs from the cold ground raise,

Till out of night the earth has roll'd her dewy side,
　　With every haunted mountain and streamy vale below;
When, as the mist dissolves in the yellow morning tide,
　　The maidens' trance dissolveth so.

Then fly the ghastly three as swiftly as they may,
　　And tell their tale of sorrow to anxious friends in vain—
They pined away and died within the year and day,
　　And ne'er was Anna Grace seen again.

THE LEGEND OF KNOCKGRAFTON.

T. CROFTON CROKER.

THERE was once a poor man who lived in the fertile glen of
Aherlow, at the foot of the gloomy Galtee mountains, and
he had a great hump on his back: he looked just as if his
body had been rolled up and placed upon his shoulders;
and his head was pressed down with the weight so much
that his chin, when he was sitting, used to rest upon his
knees for support. The country people were rather shy of

meeting him in any lonesome place, for though, poor creature, he was as harmless and as inoffensive as a new-born infant, yet his deformity was so great that he scarcely appeared to be a human creature, and some ill-minded persons had set strange stories about him afloat. He was said to have a great knowledge of herbs and charms; but certain it was that he had a mighty skilful hand in plaiting straws and rushes into hats and baskets, which was the way he made his livelihood.

Lusmore, for that was the nickname put upon him by reason of his always wearing a sprig of the fairy cap, or lusmore (the foxglove), in his little straw hat, would ever get a higher penny for his plaited work than any one else, and perhaps that was the reason why some one, out of envy, had circulated the strange stories about him. Be that as it may, it happened that he was returning one evening from the pretty town of Cahir towards Cappagh, and as little Lusmore walked very slowly, on account of the great hump upon his back, it was quite dark when he came to the old moat of Knockgrafton, which stood on the right-hand side of his road. Tired and weary was he, and noways comfortable in his own mind at thinking how much farther he had to travel, and that he should be walking all the night; so he sat down under the moat to rest himself, and began looking mournfully enough upon the moon, which—

> " Rising in clouded majesty, at length
> Apparent Queen, unveil'd her peerless light,
> And o'er the dark her silver mantle threw."

Presently there rose a wild strain of unearthly melody upon the ear of little Lusmore; he listened, and he thought that he had never heard such ravishing music before. It was like the sound of many voices, each mingling and blending with the other so strangely that they seemed to be one, though all singing different strains, and the words of the song were these—

Da Luan, Da Mort, Da Luan, Da Mort, Da Luan, Da Mort;

when there would be a moment's pause, and then the round of melody went on again.

Lusmore listened attentively, scarcely drawing his breath lest he might lose the slightest note. He now plainly perceived that the singing was within the moat; and though at first it had charmed him so much, he began to get tired of hearing the same round sung over and over so often without any change; so availing himself of the pause when *Da Luan, Da Mort,* had been sung three times, he took up the tune, and raised it with the words *augus Da Dardeen,* and then went on singing with the voices inside of the moat, *Da Luan, Da Mort,* finishing the melody, when the pause again came, with *augus Da Dardeen.*

The fairies within Knockgrafton, for the song was a fairy melody, when they heard this addition to the tune, were so much delighted that, with instant resolve, it was determined to bring the mortal among them, whose musical skill so far exceeded theirs, and little Lusmore was conveyed into their company with the eddying speed of a whirlwind.

Glorious to behold was the sight that burst upon him as he came down through the moat, twirling round and round, with the lightness of a straw, to the sweetest music that kept time to his motion. The greatest honour was then paid him, for he was put above all the musicians, and he had servants tending upon him, and everything to his heart's content, and a hearty welcome to all; and, in short, he was made as much of as if he had been the first man in the land.

Presently Lusmore saw a great consultation going forward among the fairies, and, notwithstanding all their civility, he felt very much frightened, until one stepping out from the rest came up to him and said—

> " Lusmore ! Lusmore !
> Doubt not, nor deplore,
> For the hump which you bore
> On your back is no more ;
> Look down on the floor,
> And view it, Lusmore ! "

When these words were said, poor little Lusmore felt himself so light, and so happy, that he thought he could have bounded at one jump over the moon, like the cow in the history of the cat and the fiddle; and he saw, with inexpressible pleasure, his hump tumble down upon the ground from his shoulders. He then tried to lift up his head, and he did so with becoming caution, fearing that he might knock it against the ceiling of the grand hall, where he was; he looked round and round again with the greatest wonder and delight upon everything, which appeared more and more beautiful; and, overpowered at beholding such a resplendent scene, his head grew dizzy, and his eyesight became dim. At last he fell into a sound sleep, and when he awoke he found that it was broad daylight, the sun shining brightly, and the birds singing sweetly; and that he was lying just at the foot of the moat of Knockgrafton, with the cows and sheep grazing peaceably round about him. The first thing Lusmore did, after saying his prayers, was to put his hand behind to feel for his hump, but no sign of one was there on his back, and he looked at himself with great pride, for he had now become a well-shaped dapper little fellow, and more than that, found himself in a full suit of new clothes, which he concluded the fairies had made for him.

Towards Cappagh he went, stepping out as lightly, and springing up at every step as if he had been all his life a dancing-master. Not a creature who met Lusmore knew him without his hump, and he had a great work to persuade every one that he was the same man—in truth he was not, so far as the outward appearance went.

Of course it was not long before the story of Lusmore's hump got about, and a great wonder was made of it. Through the country, for miles round, it was the talk of every one, high and low.

One morning, as Lusmore was sitting contented enough at his cabin door, up came an old woman to him, and asked him if he could direct her to Cappagh.

"I need give you no directions, my good woman," said

Lusmore, "for this is Cappagh ; and whom may you want here ? "

" I have come," said the woman, "out of Decie's country, in the county of Waterford, looking after one Lusmore, who, I have heard tell, had his hump taken off by the fairies ; for there is a son of a gossip of mine who has got a hump on him that will be his death ; and maybe, if he could use the same charm as Lusmore, the hump may be taken off him. And now I have told you the reason of my coming so far : 'tis to find out about this charm, if I can."

Lusmore, who was ever a good-natured little fellow, told the woman all the particulars, how he had raised the tune for the fairies at Knockgrafton, how his hump had been removed from his shoulders, and how he had got a new suit of clothes into the bargain.

The woman thanked him very much, and then went away quite happy and easy in her own mind. When she came back to her gossip's house, in the county of Waterford, she told her everything that Lusmore had said, and they put the little hump-backed man, who was a peevish and cunning creature from his birth, upon a car, and took him all the way across the country. It was a long journey, but they did not care for that, so the hump was taken from off him ; and they brought him, just at nightfall, and left him under the old moat of Knockgrafton.

Jack Madden, for that was the humpy man's name, had not been sitting there long when he heard the tune going on within the moat much sweeter than before ; for the fairies were singing it the way Lusmore had settled their music for them, and the song was going on : *Da Luan, Da Mort, Da Luan, Da Mort, Da Luan, Da Mort, augus Da Dardeen*, without ever stopping. Jack Madden, who was in a great hurry to get quit of his hump, never thought of waiting until the fairies had done, or watching for a fit opportunity to raise the tune higher again than Lusmore had ; so having heard them sing it over seven times without stopping, out he bawls, never minding the time or the humour of the tune, or how he could bring his words in properly, *augus Da Dardeen*, *augus Da Hena*, thinking that if one day was good, two were better ; and that if Lusmore had one new suit of clothes given him, he should have two.

No sooner had the words passed his lips than he was taken up and whisked into the moat with prodigious force ; and the fairies came crowding round about him with great anger, screeching and screaming, and roaring out, "Who spoiled our tune ? who spoiled our tune ?" and one stepped up to him above all the rest, and said—

> "Jack Madden ! Jack Madden !
> Your words came so bad in
> The tune we felt glad in ;—
> This castle you're had in,
> That your life we may sadden ;
> Here's two humps for Jack Madden !"

And twenty of the strongest fairies brought Lusmore's hump, and put it down upon poor Jack's back, over his own, where it became fixed as firmly as if it was nailed on with twelve-penny nails, by the best carpenter that ever drove one.   Out of their castle they then kicked him ; and in the morning, when Jack Madden's mother and her gossip came to look after their little man, they found him half dead, lying at the foot of the moat, with the other hump upon his back.   Well to be sure, how they did look at each other ! but they were afraid to say anything, lest a hump might be put upon their own shoulders.   Home they brought the unlucky Jack Madden with them, as downcast in their hearts and their looks as ever two gossips were ; and what through the weight of his other hump, and the long journey, he died soon after, leaving, they say, his heavy curse to any one who would go to listen to fairy tunes again.

A DONEGAL FAIRY.

LETITIA MACLINTOCK.

Ay, it's a bad thing to displeasure the gentry, sure enough—they can be unfriendly if they're angered, an' they can be the very best o' gude neighbours if they're treated kindly.

My mother's sister was her lone in the house one day, wi' a' big pot o' water boiling on the fire, and ane o' the wee folk fell down the chimney, and slipped wi' his leg in the hot water.

He let a terrible squeal out o' him, an' in a minute the house was full o' wee crathurs pulling him out o' the pot, an' carrying him across the floor.

"Did she scald you?" my aunt heard them saying to him.

"Na, na, it was mysel' scalded my ainsel'," quoth the wee fellow.

"A weel, a weel," says they. "If it was your ainsel scalded yoursel', we'll say nothing, but if she had scalded you, we'd ha' made her pay."

THE TROOPING FAIRIES.

CHANGELINGS.

SOMETIMES the fairies fancy mortals, and carry them away into their own country, leaving instead some sickly fairy child, or a log of wood so bewitched that it seems to be a mortal pining away, and dying, and being buried. Most commonly they steal children. If you "over look a child," that is look on it with envy, the fairies have it in their power. Many things can be done to find out in a child a changeling, but there is one infallible thing—lay it on the fire with this formula, "Burn, burn, burn—if of the devil, burn ; but if of God and the saints, be safe from harm" (given by Lady Wilde). Then if it be a changeling it will rush up the chimney with a cry, for, according to Giraldus Cambrensis, "fire is the greatest of enemies to every sort of phantom, in so much that those who have seen apparitions fall into a swoon as soon as they are sensible of the brightness of fire."

Sometimes the creature is got rid of in a more gentle way. It is on record that once when a mother was leaning over a wizened changeling the latch lifted and a fairy came in, carrying home again the wholesome stolen baby. "It was the others," she said, "who stole it." As for her, she wanted her own child.

Those who are carried away are happy, according to some accounts, having plenty of good living and music and mirth. Others say, however, that they are continually longing for their earthly friends. Lady Wilde gives a gloomy tradition that there are two kinds of fairies—one kind merry and gentle, the other evil, and sacrificing every year a life to Satan, for which purpose they steal mortals. No other Irish writer gives this tradition—if such fairies there be, they must be among the solitary spirits—Pookas, Fir Darrigs, and the like.

THE BREWERY OF EGG-SHELLS.

T. CROFTON CROKER.

MRS. SULLIVAN fancied that her youngest child had been exchanged by "fairies theft," and certainly appearances warranted such a conclusion ; for in one night her healthy, blue-eyed boy had become shrivelled up into almost nothing, and never ceased squalling and crying. This naturally made poor Mrs. Sullivan very unhappy ; and all the neighbours, by way of comforting her, said that her own child was, beyond any kind of doubt, with the good people, and that one of themselves was put in his place.

Mrs. Sullivan of course could not disbelieve what every one told her, but she did not wish to hurt the thing ; for although its face was so withered, and its body wasted away to a mere skeleton, it had still a strong resemblance to her own boy. She, therefore, could not find it in her heart to roast it alive on the griddle, or to burn its nose off with the red-hot tongs, or to throw it out in the snow on the road-side, notwithstanding these, and several like proceedings, were strongly recommended to her for the recovery of her child.

One day who should Mrs. Sullivan meet but a cunning woman, well known about the country by the name of Ellen Leah (or Grey Ellen). She had the gift, however she got it, of telling where the dead were, and what was good for the rest of their souls ; and could charm away warts and wens, and do a great many wonderful things of the same nature.

"You're in grief this morning, Mrs. Sullivan," were the first words of Ellen Leah to her.

"You may say that, Ellen," said Mrs. Sullivan, "and good cause I have to be in grief, for there was my own fine child whipped of from me out of his cradle, without as much as 'by your leave' or 'ask your pardon,' and an ugly dony bit of a shrivelled-up fairy put in his place ; no wonder, then, that you see me in grief, Ellen."

CHANGELING TWINS.

A CHANGELING EMERGING FROM AN EGG-SHELL.

"Small blame to you, Mrs. Sullivan," said Ellen Leah, "but are you sure 'tis a fairy?"

"Sure!" echoed Mrs. Sullivan, "sure enough I am to my sorrow, and can I doubt my own two eyes? Every mother's soul must feel for me!"

"Will you take an old woman's advice?" said Ellen Leah, fixing her wild and mysterious gaze upon the unhappy mother; and, after a pause, she added, "but maybe you'll call it foolish?"

"Can you get me back my child, my own child, Ellen?" said Mrs. Sullivan with great energy.

"If you do as I bid you," returned Ellen Leah, "you'll know." Mrs. Sullivan was silent in expectation, and Ellen continued, "Put down the big pot, full of water, on the fire, and make it boil like mad; then get a dozen new-laid eggs, break them, and keep the shells, but throw away the rest; when that is done, put the shells in the pot of boiling water, and you will soon know whether it is your own boy or a fairy. If you find that it is a fairy in the cradle, take the red-hot poker and cram it down his ugly throat, and you will not have much trouble with him after that, I promise you."

Home went Mrs. Sullivan, and did as Ellen Leah desired. She put the pot on the fire, and plenty of turf under it, and set the water boiling at such a rate, that if ever water was red-hot, it surely was.

The child was lying, for a wonder, quite easy and quiet in the cradle, every now and then cocking his eye, that would twinkle as keen as a star in a frosty night, over at the great fire, and the big pot upon it; and he looked on with great attention at Mrs. Sullivan breaking the eggs and putting down the egg-shells to boil. At last he asked, with the voice of a very old man, "What are you doing, mammy?"

Mrs. Sullivan's heart, as she said herself, was up in her mouth ready to choke her, at hearing the child speak. But she contrived to put the poker in the fire, and to answer, without making any wonder at the words, "I'm brewing, *a vick*" (my son).

"And what are you brewing, mammy?" said the little imp, whose supernatural gift of speech now proved beyond question that he was a fairy substitute.

"I wish the poker was red," thought Mrs. Sullivan; but it was a large one, and took a long time heating; so she determined to keep him in talk until the poker was in a proper state to thrust down his throat, and therefore repeated the question.

"Is it what I'm brewing, *a vick*," said she, "you want to know?"

"Yes, mammy: what are you brewing?" returned the fairy.

"Egg-shells, *a vick*," said Mrs. Sullivan.

"Oh!" shrieked the imp, starting up in the cradle, and clapping his hands together, "I'm fifteen hundred years in the world, and I never saw a brewery of egg-shells before!" The poker was by this time quite red, and Mrs. Sullivan, seizing it, ran furiously towards the cradle; but somehow or other her foot slipped, and she fell flat on the floor, and the poker flew out of her hand to the other end of the house. However, she got up without much loss of time and went to the cradle, intending to pitch the wicked thing that was in it into the pot of boiling water, when there she saw her own child in a sweet sleep, one of his soft round arms rested upon the pillow—his features were as placid as if their repose had never been disturbed, save the rosy mouth, which moved with a gentle and regular breathing.

THE FAIRY NURSE.

BY EDWARD WALSH.

SWEET babe! a golden cradle holds thee,
And soft the snow-white fleece enfolds thee;
In airy bower I'll watch thy sleeping,
Where branchy trees to the breeze are sweeping.
        Shuheen, sho, lulo lo!

When mothers languish broken-hearted,
When young wives are from husbands parted,
Ah! little think the keeners lonely,
They weep some time-worn fairy only.
        Shuheen sho, lulo lo!

Within our magic halls of brightness,
Trips many a foot of snowy whiteness;
Stolen maidens, queens of fairy—
And kings and chiefs a sluagh-shee airy.
        Shuheen sho, lulo lo!

Rest thee, babe! I love thee dearly,
And as thy mortal mother nearly;
Ours is the swiftest steed and proudest,
That moves where the tramp of the host is loudest.
        Shuheen sho, lulo lo!

Rest thee, babe! for soon thy slumbers
Shall flee at the magic koelshie's* numbers;
In airy bower I'll watch thy sleeping,
Where branchy trees to the breeze are sweeping.
        Shuheen sho, lulo, lo!

* *Ceól-sidhe—i.e.,* fairy music.

JAMIE FREEL AND THE YOUNG LADY.
A Donegal Tale.

MISS LETITIA MACLINTOCK.

DOWN in Fannet, in times gone by, lived Jamie Freel and his mother. Jamie was the widow's sole support; his strong arm worked for her untiringly, and as each Saturday night came round, he poured his wages into her lap, thanking her dutifully for the halfpence which she returned him for tobacco.

He was extolled by his neighbours as the best son ever known or heard of. But he had neighbours, of whose opinion he was ignorant—neighbours who lived pretty close to him, whom he had never seen, who are, indeed, rarely seen by mortals, except on May eves and Halloweens.

An old ruined castle, about a quarter of a mile from his cabin, was said to be the abode of the "wee folk." Every Halloween were the ancient windows lighted up, and passers-by saw little figures flitting to and fro inside the building, while they heard the music of pipes and flutes.

It was well known that fairy revels took place; but nobody had the courage to intrude on them.

Jamie had often watched the little figures from a distance, and listened to the charming music, wondering what the inside of the castle was like; but one Halloween he got up and took his cap, saying to his mother, "I'm awa' to the castle to seek my fortune."

"What!" cried she, "would you venture there? you that's the poor widow's one son! Dinna be sae venturesome an' foolitch, Jamie! They'll kill you, an' then what'll come o' me?"

"Never fear, mother; nae harm 'ill happen me, but I maun gae."

He set out, and as he crossed the potato-field, came in sight of the castle, whose windows were ablaze with light, that seemed to turn the russet leaves, still clinging to the crabtree branches, into gold.

Halting in the grove at one side of the ruin, he listened to the elfin revelry, and the laughter and singing made him all the more determined to proceed.

Numbers of little people, the largest about the size of a child of five years old, were dancing to the music of flutes and fiddles, while others drank and feasted.

"Welcome, Jamie Freel! welcome, welcome, Jamie!" cried the company, perceiving their visitor. The word "Welcome" was caught up and repeated by every voice in the castle.

Time flew, and Jamie was enjoying himself very much, when his hosts said, "We're going to ride to Dublin to-night to steal a young lady. Will you come too, Jamie Freel?"

"Ay, that will I!" cried the rash youth, thirsting for adventure.

A troop of horses stood at the door. Jamie mounted, and his steed rose with him into the air. He was presently flying over his mother's cottage, surrounded by the elfin troop, and on and on they went, over bold mountains, over little hills, over the deep Lough Swilley, over towns and cottages, when people were burning nuts, and eating apples, and keeping merry Halloween. It seemed to Jamie that they flew all round Ireland before they got to Dublin.

"This is Derry," said the fairies, flying over the cathedral spire; and what was said by one voice was repeated by all the rest, till fifty little voices were crying out, "Derry! Derry! Derry!"

In like manner was Jamie informed as they passed over each town on the rout, and at length he heard the silvery voices cry, "Dublin! Dublin!"

It was no mean dwelling that was to be honoured by the fairy visit, but one of the finest houses in Stephen's Green.

The troop dismounted near a window, and Jamie saw a beautiful face, on a pillow in a splendid bed. He saw the young lady lifted and carried away, while the stick which was dropped in her place on the bed took her exact form.

The lady was placed before one rider and carried a short way, then given another, and the names of the towns were cried out as before.

They were approaching home. Jamie heard "Rathmullan," "Milford," "Tamney," and then he knew they were near his own house.

"You've all had your turn at carrying the young lady," said he. "Why wouldn't I get her for a wee piece?"

"Ay, Jamie," replied they, pleasantly, "you may take your turn at carrying her, to be sure."

Holding his prize very tightly, he dropped down near his mother's door.

"Jamie Freel, Jamie Freel! is that the way you treat us?" cried they, and they too dropped down near the door.

Jamie held fast, though he knew not what he was holding, for the little folk turned the lady into all sorts of strange shapes. At one moment she was a black dog, barking and trying to bite; at another, a glowing bar of iron, which yet had no heat; then, again, a sack of wool.

But still Jamie held her, and the baffled elves were turning away, when a tiny woman, the smallest of the party, exclaimed, "Jamie Freel has her awa' frae us, but he sall hae nae gude o' her, for I'll mak' her deaf and dumb," and she threw something over the young girl.

While they rode off disappointed, Jamie lifted the latch and went in.

"Jamie, man!" cried his mother, "you've been awa' all night; what have they done on you?"

"Naething bad, mother; I ha' the very best of gude luck. Here's a beautiful young lady I ha' brought you for company.

"Bless us an' save us!" exclaimed the mother, and for some minutes she was so astonished that she could not think of anything else to say.

Jamie told his story of the night's adventure, ending by saying, "Surely you wouldna have allowed me to let her gang with them to be lost forever?"

"But a *lady*, Jamie! How can a lady eat we'er poor diet, and live in we'er poor way? I ax you that, you foolitch fellow?"

"Weel, mother, sure it's better for her to be here nor over yonder," and he pointed in the direction of the castle.

Meanwhile, the deaf and dumb girl shivered in her light clothing, stepping close to the humble turf fire.

"Poor crathur, she's quare and handsome! Nae wonder they set their hearts on her," said the old woman, gazing at her guest with pity and admiration. "We maun dress her first; but what, in the name o' fortune, hae I fit for the likes o' her to wear?"

She went to her press in "the room," and took out her Sunday gown of brown drugget; she then opened a drawer, and drew forth a pair of white stockings, a long snowy garment of fine linen, and a cap, her "dead dress," as she called it.

These articles of attire had long been ready for a certain triste ceremony, in which she would some day fill the chief part, and only saw the light occasionally, when they were hung out to air; but she was willing to give even these to the fair trembling visitor, who was turning in dumb sorrow and wonder from her to Jamie, and from Jamie back to her.

The poor girl suffered herself to be dressed, and then sat down on a "creepie" in the chimney corner, and buried her face in her hands.

"What'll we do to keep up a lady like thou?" cried the old woman.

"I'll work for you both, mother," replied the son.

"An' how could a lady live on we'er poor diet?" she repeated.

"I'll work for her," was all Jamie's answer.

He kept his word. The young lady was very sad for a long time, and tears stole down her cheeks many an evening while the old woman spun by the fire, and Jamie made salmon nets, an accomplishment lately acquired by him, in hopes of adding to the comfort of his guest.

But she was always gentle, and tried to smile when she perceived them looking at her; and by degrees she adapted herself to their ways and mode of life. It was not very long before she began to feed the pig, mash potatoes and meal for the fowls, and knit blue worsted socks.

So a year passed, and Halloween came round again. "Mother," said Jamie, taking down his cap, "I'm off to the ould castle to seek my fortune."

"Are you mad, Jamie?" cried his mother, in terror; "sure they'll kill you this time for what you done on them last year."

Jamie made light of her fears and went his way.

As he reached the crab-tree grove, he saw bright lights in the castle windows as before, and heard loud talking. Creeping under the window, he heard the wee folk say, "That was a poor trick Jamie Freel played us this night last year, when he stole the nice young lady from us."

"Ay," said the tiny woman, "an' I punished him for it, for there she sits, a dumb image by his hearth; but he does na' know that three drops out o' this glass I hold in my hand wad gie her her hearing and her speeches back again."

Jamie's heart beat fast as he entered the hall. Again he was greeted by a chorus of welcomes from the company— "Here comes Jamie Freel! welcome, welcome, Jamie!"

As soon as the tumult subsided, the little woman said, "You be to drink our health, Jamie, out o' this glass in my hand."

Jamie snatched the glass from her and darted to the door. He never knew how he reached his cabin, but he arrived there breathless, and sank on a stove by the fire.

"You're kilt surely this time, my poor boy," said his mother.

"No, indeed, better luck than ever this time!" and he gave the lady three drops of the liquid that still remained at the bottom of the glass, notwithstanding his mad race over the potato-field.

The lady began to speak, and her first words were words of thanks to Jamie.

The three inmates of the cabin had so much to say to one another, that long after cock-crow, when the fairy music had quite ceased, they were talking round the fire.

"Jamie," said the lady, "be pleased to get me paper and pen and ink, that I may write to my father, and tell him what has become of me."

She wrote, but weeks passed, and she received no answer. Again and again she wrote, and still no answer.

At length she said, "You must come with me to Dublin, Jamie, to find my father."

"I ha' no money to hire a car for you," he replied, "an' how can you travel to Dublin on your foot?"

But she implored him so much that he consented to set out with her, and walk all the way from Fannet to Dublin. It was not as easy as the fairy journey; but at last they rang the bell at the door of the house in Stephen's Green.

"Tell my father that his daughter is here," said she to the servant who opened the door.

"The gentleman that lives here has no daughter, my girl. He had one, but she died better nor a year ago."

"Do you not know me, Sullivan?"

"No, poor girl, I do not."

"Let me see the gentleman. I only ask to see him."

"Well, that's not much to ax; we'll see what can be done."

In a few moments the lady's father came to the door.

"Dear father," said she, "don't you know me?"

"How dare you call me your father?" cried the old gentleman, angrily. "You are an impostor. I have no daughter."

"Look in my face, father, and surely you'll remember me."

"My daughter is dead and buried. She died a long, long time ago." The old gentleman's voice changed from anger to sorrow. "You can go," he concluded.

"Stop, dear father, till you look at this ring on my finger. Look at your name and mine engraved on it."

"It certainly is my daughter's ring; but I do not know how you came by it. I fear in no honest way."

"Call my mother, *she* will be sure to know me," said the poor girl, who, by this time, was crying bitterly.

"My poor wife is beginning to forget her sorrow. She seldom speaks of her daughter now. Why should I renew her grief by reminding her of her loss?"

But the young lady persevered, till at last the mother was sent for.

"Mother," she began, when the old lady came to the door, "don't *you* know your daughter?"

"I have no daughter; my daughter died and was buried a long, long time ago."

"Only look in my face, and surely you'll know me."

The old lady shook her head.

"You have all forgotten me; but look at this mole on my neck. Surely, mother, you know me now?"

"Yes, yes," said the mother, "my Gracie had a mole on her neck like that; but then I saw her in her coffin, and saw the lid shut down upon her."

It became Jamie's turn to speak, and he gave the history of the fairy journey, of the theft of the young lady, of the figure he had seen laid in its place, of her life with his mother in Fannet, of last Halloween, and of the three drops that had released her from her enchantment.

She took up the story when he paused, and told how kind the mother and son had been to her.

The parents could not make enough of Jamie. They treated him with every distinction, and when he expressed his wish to return to Fannet, said they did not know what to do to show their gratitude.

But an awkward complication arose. The daughter would not let him go without her. "If Jamie goes, I'll go too," she said. "He saved me from the fairies, and has worked for me ever since. If it had not been for him, dear father and mother, you would never have seen me again. If he goes, I'll go too."

This being her resolution, the old gentleman said that Jamie should become his son-in-law. The mother was brought from Fannet in a coach and four, and there was a splendid wedding.

They all lived together in the grand Dublin house, and Jamie was heir to untold wealth at his father-in-law's death.

THE STOLEN CHILD.

W. B. YEATS.

WHERE dips the rocky highland
   Of Sleuth Wood in the lake,
There lies a leafy island
   Where flapping herons wake
The drowsy water-rats.
There we've hid our fairy vats
Full of berries,
And of reddest stolen cherries.
Come away, O, human child !
To the woods and waters wild,
With a fairy hand in hand,
For the world's more full of weeping than
       you can understand.

Where the wave of moonlight glosses
   The dim grey sands with light,
Far off by furthest Rosses
   We foot it all the night,
Weaving olden dances,
Mingling hands, and mingling glances,
   Till the moon has taken flight ;

To and fro we leap,
   And chase the frothy bubbles,
   While the world is full of troubles.
And is anxious in its sleep.
Come away ! O, human child !
To the woods and waters wild,
With a fairy hand in hand,
For the world's more full of weeping than
      you can understand.

Where the wandering water gushes
   From the hills above Glen-Car,
In pools among the rushes,
   That scarce could bathe a star,
We seek for slumbering trout,
   And whispering in their ears ;
   We give them evil dreams,
Leaning softly out
   From ferns that drop their tears
   Of dew on the young streams.
Come ! O, human child !
To the woods and waters wild,
With a fairy hand in hand,
For the world's more full of weeping than
      you can understand.

Away with us, he's going,
   The solemn-eyed ;
He'll hear no more the lowing
   Of the calves on the warm hill-side.
Or the kettle on the hob
   Sing peace into his breast ;
Or see the brown mice bob
   Round and round the oatmeal chest.
For he comes, the human child,
To the woods and waters wild,
With a fairy hand in hand,
For the world's more full of weeping than
      he can understand.

THE TROOPING FAIRIES.

THE MERROW.

The *Merrow*, or if you write it in the Irish, *Moruadh* or *Murrúghach*, from *muir*, sea, and *oigh*, a maid, is not uncommon, they say, on the wilder coasts. The fishermen do not like to see them, for it always means coming gales. The male *Merrows* (if you can use such a phrase—I have never heard the masculine of *Merrow*) have green teeth, green hair, pig's eyes, and red noses ; but their women are beautiful, for all their fish tails and the little duck-like scale between their fingers. Sometimes they prefer, small blame to them, good-looking fishermen to their sea lovers. Near Bantry, in the last century, there is said to have been a woman covered all over with scales like a fish, who was descended from such a marriage. Sometimes they come out of the sea, and wander about the shore in the shape of little hornless cows. They have, when in their own shape, a red cap, called a *cohullen druith*, usually covered with feathers. If this is stolen, they cannot again go down under the waves.

Red is the colour of magic in every country, and has been so from the very earliest times. The caps of fairies and magicians are well-nigh always red.

THE SOUL CAGES.

T. CROFTON CROKER.

JACK DOGHERTY lived on the coast of the county Clare. Jack was a fisherman, as his father and grandfather before him had been. Like them, too, he lived all alone (but for the wife), and just in the same spot. People used to wonder why the Dogherty family were so fond of that wild situation, so far away from all human kind, and in the midst of huge shattered rocks, with nothing but the wide ocean to look upon. But they had their own good reasons for it.

The place was just the only spot on that part of the coast where anybody could well live. There was a neat little creek, where a boat might lie as snug as a puffin in her nest, and out from this creek a ledge of sunken rocks ran into the sea. Now when the Atlantic, according to custom, was raging with a storm, and a good westerly wind was blowing strong on the coast, many a richly-laden ship went to pieces on these rocks ; and then the fine bales of cotton and tobacco, and such like things, and the pipes of wine, and the puncheons of rum, and the casks of brandy, and the kegs of Hollands that used to come ashore ! Dunbeg Bay was just like a little estate to the Dohertys.

Not but they were kind and humane to a distressed sailor, if ever one had the good luck to get to land ; and many a time indeed did Jack put out in his little *corragh* (which, though not quite equal to honest Andrew Hennessy's canvas life-boat, would breast the billows like any gannet), to lend a hand towards bringing off the crew from a wreck. But when the ship had gone to pieces, and the crew were all lost, who would blame Jack for picking up all he could find ?

"And who is the worse of it ?" said he. "For as to the king, God bless him ! everybody knows he's rich enough already without getting what's floating in the sea."

Jack, though such a hermit, was a good-natured, jolly fellow. No other, sure, could ever have coaxed Biddy Mahony to quit her father's snug and warm house in the middle of the town of Ennis, and to go so many miles off to live among the rocks, with the seals and sea-gulls for next-door neighbours. But Biddy knew that Jack was the man for a woman who wished to be comfortable and happy ; for, to say nothing of the fish, Jack had the supplying of half the gentlemen's houses of the country with the *Godsends* that came into the bay. And she was right in her choice; for no woman ate, drank, or slept better, or made a prouder appearance at chapel on Sundays, than Mrs. Dogherty.

Many a strange sight, it may well be supposed, did Jack see, and many a strange sound did he hear, but nothing daunted him. So far was he from being afraid of Merrows, or such beings, that the very first wish of his heart was to fairly meet with one. Jack had heard that they were mighty like Christians, and that luck had always come out of an acquaintance with them. Never, therefore, did he dimly discern the Merrows moving along the face of the waters in their robes of mist, but he made direct for them; and many a scolding did Biddy, in her own quiet way, bestow upon Jack for spending his whole day out at sea, and bringing home no fish. Little did poor Biddy know the fish Jack was after!

It was rather annoying to Jack that, though living in a place where the Merrows were as plenty as lobsters, he never could get a right view of one. What vexed him more was that both his father and grandfather had often and often seen them; and he even remembered hearing, when a child, how his grandfather, who was the first of the family that had settled down at the creek, had been so intimate with a Merrow that, only for fear of vexing the priest, he would have had him stand for one of his children. This, however, Jack did not well know how to believe.

Fortune at length began to think that it was only right that Jack should know as much as his father and grandfather did. Accordingly, one day when he had strolled a little farther than usual along the coast to the northward, just as he turned a point, he saw something, like to nothing he had ever seen before, perched upon a rock at a little distance out to sea. It looked green in the body, as well as he could discern at that distance, and he would have sworn, only the thing was impossible, that it had a cocked hat in its hand. Jack stood for a good half-hour straining his eyes, and wondering at it, and all the time the thing did not stir hand or foot. At last Jack's patience was quite worn out, and he gave a loud whistle and a hail, when the Merrow (for such it was) started up, put the cocked hat on its head, and dived down, head foremost, from the rock.

Jack's curiosity was now excited, and he constantly directed his steps towards the point; still he could never get a glimpse of the sea-gentleman with the cocked hat; and with thinking and thinking about the matter, he began at last to fancy he had been only dreaming. One very rough day, however, when the sea was running mountains high, Jack Dogherty determined to give a look at the Merrow's rock (for he had always chosen a fine day before), and then he saw the strange thing cutting capers upon the top of the rock, and then diving down, and then coming up, and then diving down again.

Jack had now only to choose his time (that is, a good blowing day), and he might see the man of the sea as often as he pleased. All this, however, did not satisfy him— "much will have more;" he wished now to get acquainted with the Merrow, and even in this he succeeded. One tremendous blustering day, before he got to the point whence he had a view of the Merrow's rock, the storm came on so furiously that Jack was obliged to take shelter in one of the caves which are so numerous along the coast; and there, to his astonishment, he saw sitting before him a thing with green hair, long green teeth, a red nose, and pig's eyes. It had a fish's tail, legs with scales on them, and short arms like fins. It wore no clothes, but had the cocked hat under its arm, and seemed engaged thinking very seriously about something.

Jack, with all his courage, was a little daunted; but now or never, thought he; so up he went boldly to the cogitating fishman, took off his hat, and made his best bow.

"Your servant, sir," said Jack.

"Your servant, kindly, Jack Dogherty," answered the Merrow.

"To be sure, then, how well your honour knows my name!" said Jack.

"Is it I not know your name, Jack Dogherty? Why, man, I knew your grandfather long before he was married to Judy Regan, your grandmother! Ah, Jack, Jack, I was fond of that grandfather of yours; he was a mighty worthy man in his time: I never met his match above or below, before or since, for sucking in a shellful of brandy. I hope, my boy," said the old fellow, with a merry twinkle in his eyes, "I hope you're his own grandson!"

"Never fear me for that," said Jack; "if my mother had only reared me on brandy, 'tis myself that would be a sucking infant to this hour!"

"Well, I like to hear you talk so manly; you and I must be better acquainted, if it were only for your grandfather's sake. But, Jack, that father of yours was not the thing! he had no head at all."

"I'm sure," said Jack, "since your honour lives down under the water, you must be obliged to drink a power to keep any heat in you in such a cruel, damp, *could* place. Well, I've often heard of Christians drinking like fishes; and might I be so bold as ask where you get the spirits?"

"Where do you get them yourself, Jack?" said the Merrow, twitching his red nose between his forefinger and thumb.

"Hubbubboo," cries Jack, "now I see how it is; but I suppose, sir, your honour has got a fine dry cellar below to keep them in."

"Let me alone for the cellar," said the Merrow, with a knowing wink of his left eye.

"I'm sure," continued Jack, "it must be mighty well worth the looking at."

"You may say that, Jack," said the Merrow; "and if you meet me here next Monday, just at this time of the day, we will have a little more talk with one another about the matter."

Jack and the Merrow parted the best friends in the world.

On Monday they met, and Jack was not a little surprised to see that the Merrow had two cocked hats with him, one under each arm.

"Might I take the liberty to ask, sir," said Jack, "why your honour has brought the two hats with you to day? You would not, sure, be going to give me one of them, to keep for the *curiosity* of the thing?"

"No, no, Jack," said he, "I don't get my hats so easily, to part with them that way; but I want you to come down and dine with me, and I brought you the hat to dine with."

"Lord bless and preserve us!" cried Jack, in amazement, "would you want me to go down to the bottom of the salt sea ocean? Sure, I'd be smothered and choked up with the water, to say nothing o' being drowned! And what would poor Biddy do for me, and what would she say?"

"And what matter what she says, you *pinkeen?* Who cares for Biddy's squalling? It's long before your grandfather would have talked in that way. Many's the time he stuck that same hat on his head, and dived down boldly after me; and many's the snug bit of dinner and good shellful of brandy he and I have had together below, under the water."

"Is it really, sir, and no joke?" said Jack; "why, then, sorrow from me for ever and a day after, if I'll be a bit worse man nor my grandfather was! Here goes—but play me fair now. Here's neck or nothing!" cried Jack.

"That's your grandfather all over," said the old fellow; "so come along, then, and do as I do."

They both left the cave, walked into the sea, and then swam a piece until they got to the rock. The Merrow climbed to the top of it, and Jack followed him. On the far side it was as straight as the wall of a house, and the sea beneath looked so deep that Jack was almost cowed.

"Now, do you see, Jack," said the Merrow: "just put this hat on your head, and mind to keep your eyes wide open. Take hold of my tail, and follow after me, and you'll see what you'll see."

In he dashed, and in dashed Jack after him boldly.

They went and they went, and Jack thought they'd never stop going. Many a time did he wish himself sitting at home by the fireside with Biddy. Yet where was the use of wishing now, when he was so many miles, as he thought, below the waves of the Atlantic? Still he held hard by the Merrow's tail, slippery as it was; and, at last, to Jack's great surprise, they got out of the water, and he actually found himself on dry land at the bottom of the sea. They landed just in front of a nice house that was slated very neatly with oyster shells! and the Merrow, turning about to Jack, welcomed him down.

Jack could hardly speak, what with wonder, and what with being out of breath with travelling so fast through the water. He looked about him and could see no living things, barring crabs and lobsters, of which there were plenty walking leisurely about on the sand. Overhead was the sea like a sky, and the fishes like birds swimming about in it.

"Why don't you speak, man?" said the Merrow: "I dare say you had no notion that I had such a snug little concern here as this? Are you smothered, or choked, or drowned, or are you fretting after Biddy, eh?"

"Oh! not myself, indeed," said Jack, showing his teeth with a good-humoured grin; "but who in the world would ever have thought of seeing such a thing?"

"Well, come along, and let's see what they've got for us to eat?"

Jack really was hungry, and it gave him no small pleasure to perceive a fine column of smoke rising from the chimney, announcing what was going on within. Into the house he followed the Merrow, and there he saw a good kitchen, right well provided with everything. There was a noble dresser, and plenty of pots and pans, with two young Merrows cooking. His host then led him into the room, which was furnished shabbily enough. Not a table or a chair was there in it; nothing but planks and logs of wood to sit on, and eat off. There was, however, a good fire blazing upon the hearth—a comfortable sight to Jack.

"Come now, and I'll show you where I keep—you know what," said the Merrow, with a sly look; and opening a little door, he led Jack into a fine cellar, well filled with pipes, and kegs, and hogsheads, and barrels.

"What do you say to that, Jack Dogherty? Eh! may be a body can't live snug under the water?"

"Never the doubt of that," said Jack, with a convincing smack of his under lip, that he really thought what he said.

They went back to the room, and found dinner laid. There was no tablecloth, to be sure—but what matter? It was not always Jack had one at home. The dinner would have been no discredit to the first house of the country on a fast day. The choicest of fish, and no wonder, was there. Turbots, and sturgeons, and soles, and lobsters, and oysters, and twenty other kinds, were on the planks at once, and plenty of the best of foreign spirits. The wines, the old fellow said, were too cold for his stomach.

Jack ate and drank till he could eat no more: then, taking up a shell of brandy, " Here's to your honour's good health, sir," said he; "though, begging you pardon, it's mighty odd that as long as we've been acquainted I don't know your name yet."

"That's true, Jack," replied he; "I never thought of it before, but better late than never. My name's Coomara."

"And a mighty decent name it is," cried Jack, taking another shellfull: "here's to your good health, Coomara, and may ye live these fifty years to come!"

"Fifty years!" repeated Coomara; "I'm obliged to you, indeed! If you had said five hundred, it would have been something worth the wishing."

"By the laws, sir," cries Jack, "*youz* live to a powerful age here under the water! You knew my grandfather, and he's dead and gone better than these sixty years. I'm sure it must be a healthy place to live in."

"No doubt of it; but come, Jack, keep the liquor stirring."

Shell after shell did they empty, and to Jack's exceeding

surprise, he found the drink never got into his head, owing, I suppose, to the sea being over them, which kept their noddles cool.

Old Coomara got exceedingly comfortable, and sung several songs; but Jack, if his life had depended on it, never could remember more than

> " *Rum fum boodle boo,*
> *Ripple dipple nitty dob ;*
> *Dumdoo doodle coo,*
> *Raffle taffle chittiboo !* "

It was the chorus to one of them; and, to say the truth, nobody that I know has ever been able to pick any particular meaning out of it; but that, to be sure, is the case with many a song nowadays.

At length said he to Jack, "Now, my dear boy, if you follow me, I'll show you my *curiosities !*" He opened a little door, and led Jack into a large room, where Jack saw a great many odds and ends that Coomara had picked up at one time or another. What chiefly took his attention, however, were things like lobster-pots ranged on the ground along the wall.

"Well, Jack, how do you like my *curiosities ?*" said old Coo.

"Upon my *sowkins,** sir," said Jack, "they're mighty well worth the looking at; but might I make so bold as to ask what these things like lobster-pots are?"

"Oh! the Soul Cages, is it?"

"The what? sir!"

"These things here that I keep the souls in."

"*Arrah!* what souls, sir?" said Jack, in amazement; "sure the fish have no souls in them?"

"Oh! no," replied Coo, quite coolly, "that they have not; but these are the souls of drowned sailors."

"The Lord preserve us from all harm!" muttered Jack, "how in the world did you get them?"

"Easily enough: I've only, when I see a good storm

---

* *Sowkins,* diminutive of soul.

coming on, to set a couple of dozen of these, and then, when the sailors are drowned and the souls get out of them under the water, the poor things are almost perished to death, not being used to the cold; so they make into my pots for shelter, and then I have them snug, and fetch them home, and keep them here dry and warm; and is it not well for them, poor souls, to get into such good quarters?"

Jack was so thunderstruck he did not know what to say, so he said nothing. They went back into the dining-room, and had a little more brandy, which was excellent, and then, as Jack knew that it must be getting late, and as Biddy might be uneasy, he stood up, and said he thought it was time for him to be on the road.

"Just as you like, Jack," said Coo, "but take a *duc an durrus** before you go; you've a cold journey before you."

Jack knew better manners than to refuse the parting glass. "I wonder," said he, "will I be able to make out my way home?"

"What should ail you," said Coo, "when I'll show you the way?"

Out they went before the house, and Coomara took one of the cocked hats, and put it upon Jack's head the wrong way, and then lifted him up on his shoulder that he might launch him up into the water.

"Now," says he, giving him a heave, "you'll come up just in the same spot you came down in; and, Jack, mind and throw me back the hat."

He canted Jack off his shoulder, and up he shot like a bubble—whirr, whirr, whiz—away he went up through the water, till he came to the very rock he had jumped off, where he found a landing-place, and then in he threw the hat, which sunk like a stone.

The sun was just going down in the beautiful sky of a calm summer's evening. *Feascor* was seen dimly twinkling in the cloudless heaven, a solitary star, and the waves of the Atlantic flashed in a golden flood of light. So Jack,

* *Recte,* deoch *án dorrus*—door-drink or stirrup-cup.

perceiving it was late, set off home; but when he got there, not a word did he say to Biddy of where he had spent his day.

The state of the poor souls cooped up in the lobster-pots gave Jack a great deal of trouble, and how to release them cost him a great deal of thought. He at first had a mind to speak to the priest about the matter. But what could the priest do, and what did Coo care for the priest? Besides, Coo was a good sort of an old fellow, and did not think he was doing any harm. Jack had a regard for him, too, and it also might not be much to his own credit if it were known that he used to go dine with Merrows. On the whole, he thought his best plan would be to ask Coo to dinner, and to make him drunk, if he was able, and then to take the hat and go down and turn up the pots. It was, first of all, necessary, however, to get Biddy out of the way; for Jack was prudent enough, as she was a woman, to wish to keep the thing secret from her.

Accordingly, Jack grew mighty pious all of a sudden, and said to Biddy that he thought it would be for the good of both their souls if she was to go and take her rounds at Saint John's Well, near Ennis. Biddy thought so too, and accordingly off she set one fine morning at day-dawn, giving Jack a strict charge to have an eye to the place. The coast being clear, away went Jack to the rock to give the appointed signal to Coomara, which was throwing a big stone into the water. Jack threw, and up sprang Coo!

"Good morning, Jack," said he; "what do you want with me?"

"Just nothing at all to speak about, sir," returned Jack, "only to come and take a bit of dinner with me, if I might make so free as to ask you, and sure I'm now after doing so."

"It's quite agreeable, Jack, I assure you; what's your hour?"

"Any time that's most convenient to you, sir—say one o'clock, that you may go home, if you wish, with the daylight."

"I'll be with you," said Coo, "never fear me,"

Jack went home, and dressed a noble fish dinner, and got out plenty of his best foreign spirits, enough, for that matter, to make twenty men drunk. Just to the minute came Coo, with his cocked hat under his arm. Dinner was ready, they sat down, and ate and drank away manfully. Jack, thinking of the poor souls below in the pots, plied old Coo well with brandy, and encouraged him to sing, hoping to put him under the table, but poor Jack forgot that he had not the sea over his own head to keep it cool. The brandy got into it, and did his business for him, and Coo reeled off home, leaving his entertainer as dumb as a haddock on a Good Friday.

Jack never woke till the next morning, and then he was in a sad way. "'Tis to no use for me thinking to make that old Rapparee drunk," said Jack, "and how in this world can I help the poor souls out of the lobster-pots?" After ruminating nearly the whole day, a thought struck him. "I have it," says he, slapping his knee; "I'll be sworn that Coo never saw a drop of *poteen*, as old as he is, and that's the *thing* to settle him! Oh! then, is not it well that Biddy will not be home these two days yet; I can have another twist at him."

Jack asked Coo again, and Coo laughed at him for having no better head, telling him he'd never come up to his grandfather.

"Well, but try me again," said Jack, "and I'll be bail to drink you drunk and sober, and drunk again."

"Anything in my power," said Coo, "to oblige you."

At this dinner Jack took care to have his own liquor well watered, and to give the strongest brandy he had to Coo. At last says he, "Pray, sir, did you ever drink any poteen? —any real mountain dew?"

"No," says Coo; "what's that, and where does it come from?"

"Oh, that's a secret," said Jack, "but it's the right stuff —never believe me again, if 'tis not fifty times as good as brandy or rum either. Biddy's brother just sent me a present of a little drop, in exchange for some brandy, and as you're an old friend of the family, I kept it to treat you with."

"Well, let's see what sort of thing it is," said Coomara.

The *poteen* was the right sort. It was first-rate, and had the real smack upon it. Coo was delighted: he drank and he sung *Rum bum boodle boo* over and over again; and he laughed and he danced, till he fell on the floor fast asleep. Then Jack, who had taken good care to keep himself sober, snapt up the cocked hat—ran off to the rock—leaped in, and soon arrived at Coo's habitation.

All was as still as a churchyard at midnight—not a Merrow, old or young, was there. In he went and turned up the pots, but nothing did he see, only he heard a sort of a little whistle or chirp as he raised each of them. At this he was surprised, till he recollected what the priests had often said, that nobody living could see the soul, no more than they could see the wind or the air. Having now done all that he could do for them, he set the pots as they were before, and sent a blessing after the poor souls to speed them on their journey wherever they were going. Jack now began to think of returning; he put the hat on, as was right, the wrong way; but when he got out he found the water so high over his head that he had no hopes of ever getting up into it, now that he had not old Coomara to give him a lift. He walked about looking for a ladder, but not one could he find, and not a rock was there in sight. At last he saw a spot where the sea hung rather lower than anywhere else, so he resolved to try there. Just as he came to it, a big cod happened to put down his tail. Jack made a jump and caught hold of it, and the cod, all in amazement, gave a bounce and pulled Jack up The minute the hat touched the water away Jack was whisked, and up he shot like a cork, dragging the poor cod, that he forgot to let go, up with him tail foremost. He got to the rock in no time, and without a moment's delay hurried home, rejoicing in the good deed he had done.

But, meanwhile, there was fine work at home; for our

friend Jack had hardly left the house on his soul-freeing expedition, when back came Biddy from her soul-saving one to the well.   When she entered the house and saw the things lying *thrie-na-helah** on the table before her—" Here's a pretty job !" said she ; "that blackguard of mine—what ill-luck I had ever to marry him !   He has picked up some vagabond or other, while I was praying for the good of his soul, and they've been drinking all the *poteen* that my own brother gave him, and all the spirits, to be sure, that he was to have sold to his honour."   Then hearing an outlandish kind of a grunt, she looked down, and saw Coomara lying under the table.   " The blessed Virgin help me," shouted she, "if he has not made a real beast of himself !   Well, well, I've often heard of a man making a beast of himself with drink !   Oh hone, oh hone !—Jack, honey, what will I do with you, or what will I do without you?   How can any decent woman ever think of living with a beast ?"

With such like lamentations Biddy rushed out of the house, and was going she knew not where, when she heard the well-known voice of Jack singing a merry tune.   Glad enough was Biddy to find him safe and sound, and not turned into a thing that was like neither fish nor flesh. Jack was obliged to tell her all, and Biddy, though she had half a mind to be angry with him for not telling her before, owned that he had done a great service to the poor souls. Back they both went most lovingly to the house, and Jack wakened up Coomara ; and, perceiving the old fellow to be rather dull, he bid him not to be cast down, for 'twas many a good man's case ; said it all came of his not being used to the *poteen*, and recommended him, by way of cure, to swallow a hair of the dog that bit him.   Coo, however, seemed to think he had had quite enough.   He got up, quite out of sorts, and without having the manners to say one word in the way of civility, he sneaked off to cool himself by a jaunt through the salt water.

Coomara never missed the souls.   He and Jack con-

---

* *Tri-na-cheile, literally through other*—*i.e.*, higgledy-piggledy.

tinued the best friends in the world, and no one, perhaps, ever equalled Jack for freeing souls from purgatory; for he contrived fifty excuses for getting into the house below the sea, unknown to the old fellow, and then turning up the pots and letting out the souls. It vexed him, to be sure, that he could never see them; but as he knew the thing to be impossible, he was obliged to be satisfied.

Their intercourse continued for several years. However, one morning, on Jack's throwing in a stone as usual, he got no answer. He flung another, and another, still there was no reply. He went away, and returned the following morning, but it was to no purpose. As he was without the hat, he could not go down to see what had become of old Coo, but his belief was, that the old man, or the old fish, or whatever he was, had either died, or had removed from that part of the country.

FLORY CANTILLON'S FUNERAL.

T. CROFTON CROKER.

THE ancient burial-place of the Cantillon family was on an island in Ballyheigh Bay. This island was situated at no great distance from the shore, and at a remote period was overflowed in one of the encroachments which the Atlantic has made on that part of the coast of Kerry. The fishermen declare they have often seen the ruined walls of an old chapel beneath them in the water, as they sailed over the clear green sea of a sunny afternoon. However this may be, it is well-known that the Cantillons were, like most other Irish families, strongly attached to their ancient burial-place; and this attachment led to the custom, when any of the family died, of carrying the corpse to the seaside, where the coffin was left on the shore within reach of the tide. In the morning it had disappeared, being, as was traditionally believed, conveyed away by the ancestors of the deceased to their family tomb.

Connor Crowe, a county Clare man, was related to the Cantillons by marriage. "Connor Mac in Cruagh, of the seven quarters of Breintragh," as he was commonly called, and a proud man he was of the name. Connor, be it known, would drink a quart of salt water, for its medicinal virtues, before breakfast; and for the same reason, I suppose, double that quantity of raw whiskey between breakfast and night, which last he did with as little inconvenience to himself as any man in the barony of Moyferta; and were I to add Clanderalaw and Ibrickan, I don't think I should say wrong.

On the death of Florence Cantillon, Connor Crowe was determined to satisfy himself about the truth of this story of the old church under the sea: so when he heard the news of the old fellow's death, away with him to Ardfert, where Flory was laid out in high style, and a beautiful corpse he made.

Flory had been as jolly and as rollicking a boy in his day as ever was stretched, and his wake was in every respect worthy of him. There was all kind of entertainment, and all sort of diversion at it, and no less than three girls got husbands there—more luck to them. Everything was as it should be; all that side of the country, from Dingle to Tarbert, was at the funeral. The Keen was sung long and bitterly; and, according to the family custom, the coffin was carried to Ballyheigh strand, where it was laid upon the shore, with a prayer for the repose of the dead.

The mourners departed, one group after another, and at last Connor Crowe was left alone. He then pulled out his whiskey bottle, his drop of comfort, as he called it, which he required, being in grief; and down he sat upon a big stone that was sheltered by a projecting rock, and partly concealed from view, to await with patience the appearance of the ghostly undertakers.

The evening came on mild and beautiful. He whistled an old air which he had heard in his childhood, hoping to keep idle fears out of his head; but the wild strain of that melody brought a thousand recollections with it, which only made the twilight appear more pensive.

"If 'twas near the gloomy tower of Dunmore, in my own sweet country, I was," said Connor Crowe, with a sigh, "one might well believe that the prisoners, who were murdered long ago there in the vaults under the castle, would be the hands to carry off the coffin out of envy, for never a one of them was buried decently, nor had as much as a coffin amongst them all. 'Tis often, sure enough, I have heard lamentations and great mourning coming from the vaults of Dunmore Castle; but," continued he, after fondly pressing his lips to the mouth of his companion and silent comforter, the whiskey bottle, "didn't I know all the time well enough, 'twas the dismal sounding waves working through the cliffs and hollows of the rocks, and fretting themselves to foam. Oh, then, Dunmore Castle, it is you that are the gloomy-looking tower on a gloomy day, with the gloomy hills behind you; when one has gloomy thoughts on their heart, and sees you like a ghost rising out of the smoke made by the kelp burners on the strand, there is, the Lord save us! as fearful a look about you as about the Blue Man's Lake at midnight. Well, then, anyhow," said Connor, after a pause, "is it not a blessed night, though surely the moon looks mighty pale in the face? St. Senan himself between us and all kinds of harm."

It was, in truth, a lovely moonlight night; nothing was to be seen around but the dark rocks, and the white pebbly beach, upon which the sea broke with a hoarse and melancholy murmur. Connor, notwithstanding his frequent draughts, felt rather queerish, and almost began to repent his curiosity. It was certainly a solemn sight to behold the black coffin resting upon the white strand. His imagination gradually converted the deep moaning of old ocean into a mournful wail for the dead, and from the shadowy recesses of the rocks he imaged forth strange and visionary forms.

As the night advanced, Connor became weary with watching. He caught himself more than once in the act of nodding, when suddenly giving his head a shake, he would look towards the black coffin. But the narrow house of death remained unmoved before him.

It was long past midnight, and the moon was sinking into the sea, when he heard the sound of many voices, which gradually became stronger, above the heavy and monotonous roll of the sea. He listened, and presently could distinguish a Keen of exquisite sweetness, the notes of which rose and fell with the heaving of the waves, whose deep murmur mingled with and supported the strain !

The Keen grew louder and louder, and seemed to approach the beach, and then fell into a low, plaintive wail. As it ended Connor beheld a number of strange and, in the dim light, mysterious-looking figures emerge from the sea, and surround the coffin, which they prepared to launch into the water.

"This comes of marrying with the creatures of earth," said one of the figures, in a clear, yet hollow tone.

"True," replied another, with a voice still more fearful, "our king would never have commanded his gnawing white-toothed waves to devour the rocky roots of the island cemetery, had not his daughter, Durfulla, been buried there by her mortal husband !"

"But the time will come," said a third, bending over the coffin,

> " When mortal eye—our work shall spy,
> And mortal ear—our dirge shall hear."

"Then," said a fourth, "our burial of the Cantillons is at an end for ever !"

As this was spoken the coffin was borne from the beach by a retiring wave, and the company of sea people prepared to follow it ; but at the moment one chanced to discover Connor Crowe, as fixed with wonder and as motionless with fear as the stone on which he sat.

"The time is come," cried the unearthly being, "the time is come ; a human eye looks on the forms of ocean, a human ear has heard their voices. Farewell to the

Cantillons; the sons of the sea are no longer doomed to bury the dust of the earth!"

One after the other turned slowly round, and regarded Connor Crowe, who still remained as if bound by a spell. Again arose their funeral song; and on the next wave they followed the coffin. The sound of the lamentation died away, and at length nothing was heard but the rush of waters. The coffin and the train of sea people sank over the old churchyard, and never since the funeral of old Flory Cantillon have any of the family been carried to the strand of Ballyheigh, for conveyance to their rightful burial-place, beneath the waves of the Atlantic.

THE SOLITARY FAIRIES.

LEPRACAUN. CLURICAUN. FAR DARRIG.

"THE name *Lepracaun*," Mr. Douglas Hyde writes to me, "is from the Irish *leith brog*—*i.e.*, the One-shoemaker, since he is generally seen working at a single shoe. It is spelt in Irish *leith bhrogan*, or *leith phrogan*, and is in some places pronounced Luchryman, as O'Kearney writes it in that very rare book, the *Feis Tigh Chonain*."

The *Lepracaun, Cluricaun*, and *Far Darrig.* Are these one spirit in different moods and shapes? Hardly two Irish writers are agreed. In many things these three fairies, if three, resemble each other. They are withered, old, and solitary, in every way unlike the sociable spirits of the first sections. They dress with all unfairy homeliness, and are, indeed, most sluttish, slouching, jeering, mischievous phantoms. They are the great practical jokers among the good people.

The *Lepracaun* makes shoes continually, and has grown very rich. • Many treasure-crocks, buried of old in war-time, has he now for his own. In the early part of this century, according to Croker, in a newspaper office in Tipperary, they used to show a little shoe forgotten by a Lepracaun.

The *Cluricaun*, (*Clobhair-ceann*, in O'Kearney) makes himself drunk in gentlemen's cellars. Some suppose he is merely the Lepracaun on a spree. He is almost unknown in Connaught and the north.

The *Far Darrig* (*fear dearg*), which means the Red Man, for he wears a red cap and coat, busies himself with practical joking, especially with gruesome joking. This he does, and nothing else.

THE LEPRACAUN, WHO CONTINUALLY MAKES SHOES.

THE CLURICAUN, WHO MAKES HIMSELF DRUNK IN GENTLEMEN'S
WINE CELLARS.

The *Fear-Gorta* (Man of Hunger) is an emaciated phantom that goes through the land in famine time, begging an alms and bringing good luck to the giver.

There are other solitary fairies, such as the House-spirit and the *Water-sheerie*, own brother to the English Jack-o'-Lantern ; the *Pooka* and the *Banshee*—concerning these presently ; the *Dallahan*, or headless phantom—one used to stand in a Sligo street on dark nights till lately ; the Black Dog, a form, perhaps, of the *Pooka*. The ships at the Sligo quays are haunted sometimes by this spirit, who announces his presence by a sound like the flinging of all "the tin porringers in the world" down into the hold. He even follows them to sea.

The Leanhaun Shee (fairy mistress), seeks the love of mortals. If they refuse, she must be their slave ; if they consent, they are hers, and can only escape by finding another to take their place. The fairy lives on their life, and they waste away. Death is no escape from her. She is the Gaelic muse, for she gives inspiration to those she persecutes. The Gaelic poets die young, for she is restless, and will not let them remain long on earth—this malignant phantom.

Besides these are divers monsters—the *Augh-iska*, the Water-horse, the Payshtha (*plast—bestia*), the Lake-dragon, and such like ; but whether these be animals, fairies, or spirits, I know not.

THE LEPRACAUN ; OR, FAIRY SHOEMAKER.

WILLIAM ALLINGHAM.

I.

LITTLE Cowboy, what have you heard,
   Up on the lonely rath's green mound ?
Only the plaintive yellow bird
   Sighing in sultry fields around,
Chary, chary, chary, chee-ee !—
Only the grasshopper and the bee ?—

" Yellow bird," the yellow-bunting, or *yorlin*.

" Tip tap, rip-rap,
   Tick-a-tack-too !
Scarlet leather, sewn together,
   This will make a shoe.
Left, right, pull it tight ;
   Summer days are warm ;
Underground in winter,
   Laughing at the storm ! "
Lay your ear close to the hill.
Do you not catch the tiny clamour,
Busy click of an elfin hammer,
Voice of the Lepracaun singing shrill
   As he merrily plies his trade ?
     He's a span
     And a quarter in height.
Get him in sight, hold him tight,
     And you're a made
      Man !

II.

You watch your cattle the summer day,
Sup on potatoes, sleep in the hay ;
   How would you like to roll in your carriage,
   Look for a duchess's daughter in marriage ?
Seize the Shoemaker—then you may !
   " Big boots a-hunting,
    Sandals in the hall,
White for a wedding-feast,
   Pink for a ball.
This way, that way,
   So we make a shoe ;
Getting rich every stitch,
   Tick-tack-too ! "
Nine-and-ninety treasure-crocks
This keen miser-fairy hath,
Hid in mountains, woods, and rocks,
Ruin and round-tow'r, cave and rath,
   And where the cormorants build ;

> From times of old
> Guarded by him;
> Each of them fill'd
> Full to the brim
> With gold!

III.

> I caught him at work one day, myself,
> In the castle-ditch, where foxglove grows,—
> A wrinkled, wizen'd, and bearded Elf,
> Spectacles stuck on his pointed nose,
> Silver buckles to his hose,
> Leather apron—shoe in his lap—
> "Rip-rap, tip-tap,
> Tick-tack-too!
> (A grasshopper on my cap!
> Away the moth flew!)
> Buskins for a fairy prince,
> Brogues for his son,—
> Pay me well, pay me well,
> When the job is done!"
> The rogue was mine, beyond a doubt.
> I stared at him; he stared at me;
> "Servant, Sir!" "Humph!" says he,
> And pull'd a snuff-box out.
> He took a long pinch, look'd better pleased,
> The queer little Lepracaun;
> Offer'd the box with a whimsical grace,—
> Pouf! he flung the dust in my face,
> And, while I sneezed,
> Was gone!

MASTER AND MAN.

T. CROFTON CROKER.

BILLY MAC DANIEL was once as likely a young man as ever shook his brogue at a patron,* emptied a quart, or handled a shillelagh; fearing for nothing but the want of drink; caring for nothing but who should pay for it; and thinking of nothing but how to make fun over it; drunk or sober, a word and a blow was ever the way with Billy Mac Daniel; and a mighty easy way it is of either getting into or of ending a dispute. More is the pity that, through the means of his thinking, and fearing, and caring for nothing, this same Billy Mac Daniel fell into bad company; for surely the good people are the worst of all company any one could come across.

It so happened that Billy was going home one clear frosty night not long after Christmas; the moon was round and bright; but although it was as fine a night as heart could wish for, he felt pinched with cold. "By my word," chattered Billy, "a drop of good liquor would be no bad thing to keep a man's soul from freezing in him; and I wish I had a full measure of the best."

"Never wish it twice, Billy," said a little man in a three-cornered hat, bound all about with gold lace, and with great silver buckles in his shoes, so big that it was a wonder how he could carry them, and he held out a glass as big as himself, filled with as good liquor as ever eye looked on or lip tasted.

"Success, my little fellow," said Billy Mac Daniel, nothing daunted, though well he knew the little man to belong to the *good people;* "here's your health, any way, and thank you kindly; no matter who pays for the drink;" and he took the glass and drained it to the very bottom without ever taking a second breath to it.

* A festival held in honour of some patron saint.

"Success," said the little man ; "and you're heartily welcome, Billy ; but don't think to cheat me as you have done others,—out with your purse and pay me like a gentleman."

"Is it I pay you ?" said Billy ; "could I not just take you up and put you in my pocket as easily as a blackberry ?"

"Billy Mac Daniel," said the little man, getting very angry, "you shall be my servant for seven years and a day, and that is the way I will be paid ; so make ready to follow me."

When Billy heard this he began to be very sorry for having used such bold words towards the little man ; and he felt himself, yet could not tell how, obliged to follow the little man the live-long night about the country, up and down, and over hedge and ditch, and through bog and brake, without any rest.

When morning began to dawn the little man turned round to him and said, "You may now go home, Billy, but on your peril don't fail to meet me in the Fort-field to-night ; or if you do it may be the worse for you in the long run. If I find you a good servant, you will find me an indulgent master."

Home went Billy Mac Daniel ; and though he was tired and weary enough, never a wink of sleep could he get for thinking of the little man ; but he was afraid not to do his bidding, so up he got in the evening, and away he went to the Fort-field. He was not long there before the little man came towards him and said, "Billy, I want to go a long journey to-night ; so saddle one of my horses, and you may saddle another for yourself, as you are to go along with me, and may be tired after your walk last night."

Billy thought this very considerate of his master, and thanked him accordingly : "But," said he, "if I may be so bold, sir, I would ask which is the way to your stable, for never a thing do I see but the fort here, and the old thorn tree in the corner of the field, and the stream running at the bottom of the hill, with the bit of bog over against us."

"Ask no questions, Billy," said the little man, "but go

over to that bit of bog, and bring me two of the strongest rushes you can find."

Billy did accordingly, wondering what the little man would be at; and he picked two of the stoutest rushes he could find, with a little bunch of brown blossom stuck at the side of each, and brought them back to his master.

"Get up, Billy," said the little man, taking one of the rushes from him and striding across it.

"Where shall I get up, please your honour?" said Billy.

"Why, upon horseback, like me, to be sure," said the little man.

"Is it after making a fool of me you'd be," said Billy, "bidding me get a horseback upon that bit of a rush? May be you want to persuade me that the rush I pulled but a while ago out of the bog over there is a horse?"

"Up! up! and no words," said the little man, looking very angry; "the best horse you ever rode was but a fool to it." So Billy, thinking all this was in joke, and fearing to vex his master, straddled across the rush. "Borram! Borram! Borram!" cried the little man three times (which, in English, means to become great), and Billy did the same after him; presently the rushes swelled up into fine horses, and away they went full speed; but Billy, who had put the rush between his legs, without much minding how he did it, found himself sitting on horseback the wrong way, which was rather awkward, with his face to the horse's tail; and so quickly had his steed started off with him that he had no power to turn round, and there was therefore nothing for it but to hold on by the tail.

At last they came to their journey's end, and stopped at the gate of a fine house. "Now, Billy," said the little man, "do as you see me do, and follow me close; but as you did not know your horse's head from his tail, mind that your own head does not spin round until you can't tell whether you are standing on it or on your heels: for remember that old liquor, though able to make a cat speak, can make a man dumb."

The little man then said some queer kind of words, out of which Billy could make no meaning; but he contrived to say them after him for all that; and in they both went through the key-hole of the door, and through one key-hole after another, until they got into the wine-cellar, which was well stored with all kinds of wine.

The little man fell to drinking as hard as he could, and Billy, noway disliking the example, did the same. "The best of masters are you, surely," said Billy to him; "no matter who is the next; and well pleased will I be with your service if you continue to give me plenty to drink."

"I have made no bargain with you," said the little man, "and will make none; but up and follow me." Away they went, through key-hole after key-hole; and each mounting upon the rush which he left at the hall door, scampered off, kicking the clouds before them like snow-balls, as soon as the words, "Borram, Borram, Borram," had passed their lips.

When they came back to the Fort-field the little man dismissed Billy, bidding him to be there the next night at the same hour. Thus did they go on, night after night, shaping their course one night here, and another night there; sometimes north, and sometimes east, and sometimes south, until there was not a gentleman's wine-cellar in all Ireland they had not visited, and could tell the flavour of every wine in it as well, ay, better than the butler himself.

One night when Billy Mac Daniel met the little man as usual in the Fort-field, and was going to the bog to fetch the horses for their journey, his master said to him, "Billy, I shall want another horse to-night, for may be we may bring back more company than we take." So Billy, who now knew better than to question any order given to him by his master, brought a third rush, much wondering who it might be that would travel back in their company, and whether he was about to have a fellow-servant. "If I have," thought Billy, "he shall go and fetch the horses from the bog every night; for I don't see why I am not, every inch of me, as good a gentleman as my master."

Well, away they went, Billy leading the third horse, and never stopped until they came to a snug farmer's house, in the county Limerick, close under the old castle of Carrigogunniel, that was built, they say, by the great Brian Boru. Within the house there was great carousing going forward, and the little man stopped outside for some time to listen; then turning round all of a sudden, said, " Billy, I will be a thousand years old to-morrow !"

" God bless us, sir," said Billy; " will you ? "

" Don't say these words again, Billy," said the little old man, " or you will be my ruin for ever. Now Billy, as I will be a thousand years in the world to-morrow, I think it is full time for me to get married."

" I think so too, without any kind of doubt at all," said Billy, " if ever you mean to marry."

" And to that purpose," said the little man, " have I come all the way to Carrigogunniel; for in this house, this very night, is young Darby Riley going to be married to Bridget Rooney; and as she is a tall and comely girl, and has come of decent people, I think of marrying her myself, and taking her off with me."

" And what will Darby Riley say to that ? " said Billy.

" Silence ! " said the little man, putting on a mighty severe look; " I did not bring you here with me to ask questions; " and without holding further argument, he began saying the queer words which had the power of passing him through the key-hole as free as air, and which Billy thought himself mighty clever to be able to say after him.

In they both went; and for the better viewing the company, the little man perched himself up as nimbly as a cocksparrow upon one of the big beams which went across the house over all their heads, and Billy did the same upon another facing him; but not being much accustomed to roosting in such a place, his legs hung down as untidy as may be, and it was quite clear he had not taken pattern after the way in which the little man had bundled himself up together. If the little man had been a tailor all his life he could not have sat more contentedly upon his haunches.

There they were, both master and man, looking down upon the fun that was going forward ; and under them were the priest and piper, and the father of Darby Riley, with Darby's two brothers and his uncle's son ; and there were both the father and the mother of Bridget Rooney, and proud enough the old couple were that night of their daughter, as good right they had ; and her four sisters, with bran new ribbons in their caps, and her three brothers all looking as clean and as clever as any three boys in Munster, and there were uncles and aunts, and gossips and cousins enough besides to make a full house of it ; and plenty was there to eat and drink on the table for every one of them, if they had been double the number.

Now it happened, just as Mrs. Rooney had helped his reverence to the first cut of the pig's head which was placed before her, beautifully bolstered up with white savoys, that the bride gave a sneeze, which made every one at table start, but not a soul said "God bless us." All thinking that the priest would have done so, as he ought if he had done his duty, no one wished to take the word out of his mouth, which, unfortunately, was preoccupied with pig's head and greens. And after a moment's pause the fun and merriment of the bridal feast went on without the pious benediction.

Of this circumstance both Billy and his master were no inattentive spectators from their exalted stations. "Ha !" exclaimed the little man, throwing one leg from under him with a joyous flourish, and his eye twinkled with a strange light, whilst his eyebrows became elevated into the curvature of Gothic arches ; "Ha !" said he, leering down at the bride, and then up at Billy, "I have half of her now, surely. Let her sneeze but twice more, and she is mine, in spite of priest, mass-book, and Darby Riley."

Again the fair Bridget sneezed ; but it was so gently, and she blushed so much, that few except the little man took, or seemed to take, any notice ; and no one thought of saying "God bless us."

Billy all this time regarded the poor girl with a most rueful expression of countenance; for he could not help thinking what a terrible thing it was for a nice young girl of nineteen, with large blue eyes, transparent skin, and dimpled cheeks, suffused with health and joy, to be obliged to marry an ugly little bit of a man, who was a thousand years old, barring a day.

At this critical moment the bride gave a third sneeze, and Billy roared out with all his might, "God save us!" Whether this exclamation resulted from his soliloquy, or from the mere force of habit, he never could tell exactly himself; but no sooner was it uttered than the little man, his face glowing with rage and disappointment, sprung from the beam on which he had perched himself, and shrieking out in the shrill voice of a cracked bagpipe, "I discharge you from my service, Billy Mac Daniel—take *that* for your wages," gave poor Billy a most furious kick in the back, which sent his unfortunate servant sprawling upon his face and hands right in the middle of the supper-table.

If Billy was astonished, how much more so was every one of the company into which he was thrown with so little ceremony. But when they heard his story, Father Cooney laid down his knife and fork, and married the young couple out of hand with all speed; and Billy Mac Daniel danced the Rinka at their wedding, and plenty he did drink at it too, which was what he thought more of than dancing.

FAR DARRIG IN DONEGAL.

MISS LETITIA MACLINTOCK.

PAT DIVER, the tinker, was a man well-accustomed to a wandering life, and to strange shelters; he had shared the beggar's blanket in smoky cabins; he had crouched beside the still in many a nook and corner where poteen was made on the wild Innishowen mountains; he had even slept on the bare heather, or on the ditch, with no roof over him but the vault of heaven; yet were all his nights of adventure tame and commonplace when compared with one especial night.

During the day preceding that night, he had mended all the kettles and saucepans in Moville and Greencastle, and was on his way to Culdaff, when night overtook him on a lonely mountain road.

He knocked at one door after another asking for a night's lodging, while he jingled the halfpence in his pocket, but was everywhere refused.

Where was the boasted hospitality of Innishowen, which he had never before known to fail? It was of no use to be able to pay when the people seemed so churlish. Thus thinking, he made his way towards a light a little further on, and knocked at another cabin door.

An old man and woman were seated one at each side of the fire.

"Will you be pleased to give me a night's lodging, sir?" asked Pat respectfully.

"Can you tell a story?" returned the old man.

"No, then, sir, I canna say I'm good at story-telling," replied the puzzled tinker.

"Then you maun just gang further, for none but them that can tell a story will get in here."

This reply was made in so decided a tone that Pat did not attempt to repeat his appeal, but turned away reluctantly to resume his weary journey.

"A story, indeed," muttered he. "Auld wives fables to please the weans!"

As he took up his bundle of tinkering implements, he observed a barn standing rather behind the dwelling-house, and, aided by the rising moon, he made his way towards it.

It was a clean, roomy barn, with a piled-up heap of straw in one corner. Here was a shelter not to be despised; so Pat crept under the straw, and was soon asleep.

He could not have slept very long when he was awakened

by the tramp of feet, and, peeping cautiously through a crevice in his straw covering, he saw four immensely tall men enter the barn, dragging a body, which they threw roughly upon the floor.

They next lighted a fire in the middle of the barn, and fastened the corpse by the feet with a great rope to a beam in the roof. One of them then began to turn it slowly before the fire. "Come on," said he, addressing a gigantic fellow, the tallest of the four—"I'm tired; you be to tak' your turn."

"Faix an' troth, I'll no turn him," replied the big man. "There's Pat Diver in under the straw, why wouldn't he tak' his turn?"

With hideous clamour the four men called the wretched Pat, who, seeing there was no escape, thought it was his wisest plan to come forth as he was bidden.

"Now, Pat," said they, "you'll turn the corpse, but if you let him burn you'll be tied up there and roasted in his place."

Pat's hair stood on end, and the cold perspiration poured from his forehead, but there was nothing for it but to perform his dreadful task.

Seeing him fairly embarked in it, the tall men went away.

Soon, however, the flames rose so high as to singe the rope, and the corpse fell with a great thud upon the fire, scattering the ashes and embers, and extracting a howl of anguish from the miserable cook, who rushed to the door, and ran for his life.

He ran on until he was ready to drop with fatigue, when, seeing a drain overgrown with tall, rank grass, he thought he would creep in there and lie hidden till morning.

But he was not many minutes in the drain before he heard the heavy tramping again, and the four men came up with their burthen, which they laid down on the edge of the drain.

"I'm tired," said one, to the giant; "it's your turn to carry him a piece now."

"Faix and troth, I'll no carry him," replied he, "but

there's Pat Diver in the drain, why wouldn't he come out and tak' his turn?"

"Come out, Pat, come out," roared all the men, and Pat, almost dead with fright, crept out.

He staggered on under the weight of the corpse until he reached Kiltown Abbey, a ruin festooned with ivy, where the brown owl hooted all night long, and the forgotten dead slept around the walls under dense, matted tangles of brambles and ben-weed.

No one ever buried there now, but Pat's tall companions turned into the wild graveyard, and began digging a grave.

Pat, seeing them thus engaged, thought he might once more try to escape, and climbed up into a hawthorn tree in the fence, hoping to be hidden in the boughs.

"I'm tired," said the man who was digging the grave; "here, take the spade," addressing the big man, "it's your turn."

"Faix an' troth, it's no my turn," replied he, as before. "There's Pat Diver in the tree, why wouldn't he come down and tak' his turn?"

Pat came down to take the spade, but just then the cocks in the little farmyards and cabins round the abbey began to crow, and the men looked at one another.

"We must go," said they, "and well is it for you, Pat Diver, that the cocks crowed, for if they had not, you'd just ha' been bundled into that grave with the corpse."

Two months passed, and Pat had wandered far and wide over the county Donegal, when he chanced to arrive at Raphoe during a fair.

Among the crowd that filled the Diamond he came suddenly on the big man.

"How are you, Pat Diver?" said he, bending down to look into the tinker's face.

"You've the advantage of me, sir, for I havna' the pleasure of knowing you," faltered Pat.

"Do you not know me, Pat?" Whisper—"When you go back to Innishowen, you'll have a story to tell!"

THE SOLITARY FAIRIES.

THE POOKA.

THE Pooka, *rectè* Púca, seems essentially an animal spirit. Some derive his name from *poc*, a he-goat ; and speculative persons consider him the forefather of Shakespere's "Puck." On solitary mountains and among old ruins he lives, "grown monstrous with much solitude," and is of the race of the nightmare. "In the MS. story, called 'Mac-na-Michomhairle,' of uncertain authorship," writes me Mr. Douglas Hyde, "we read that 'out of a certain hill in Leinster, there used to emerge as far as his middle, a plump, sleek, terrible steed, and speak in human voice to each person about November-day, and he was accustomed to give intelligent and proper answers to such as consulted him concerning all that would befall them until the November of next year. And the people used to leave gifts and presents at the hill until the coming of Patrick and the holy clergy.' This tradition appears to be a cognate one with that of the Púca." Yes ! unless it were merely an *augh-ishka* [*each-uisgé*], or Water-horse. For these, we are told, were common once, and used to come out of the water to gallop on the sands and in the fields, and people would often go between them and the marge and bridle them, and they would make the finest of horses if only you could keep them away from sight of the water ; but if once they saw a glimpse of the water, they would plunge in with their rider, and tear him to pieces at the bottom. It being a November spirit, however, tells in favour of the Pooka, for November-day is sacred to the Pooka. It is hard to realise that wild, staring phantom grown sleek and civil.

He has many shapes—is now a horse, now an ass, now a bull, now a goat, now an eagle. Like all spirits, he is only half in the world of form.

THE PIPER AND THE PUCA.

DOUGLAS HYDE.

Translated literally from the Irish of the *Leabhar Sgeulaigheachta.*

In the old times, there was a half fool living in Dunmore, in the county Galway, and although he was excessively fond of music, he was unable to learn more than one tune, and that was the "Black Rogue." He used to get a good deal of money from the gentlemen, for they used to get sport out of him. One night the piper was coming home from a house where there had been a dance, and he half drunk. When he came to a little bridge that was up by his mother's house, he squeezed the pipes on, and began playing the "Black Rogue" (an rógaire dubh). The Púca came behind him, and flung him up on his own back. There were long horns on the Púca, and the piper got a good grip of them, and then he said—

"Destruction on you, you nasty beast, let me home. I have a ten-penny piece in my pocket for my mother, and she wants snuff."

"Never mind your mother," said the Púca, "but keep your hold. If you fall, you will break your neck and your pipes." Then the Púca said to him, "Play up for me the 'Shan Van Vocht' (an t-seann-bhean bhocht)."

"I don't know it," said the piper.

"Never mind whether you do or you don't," said the Púca. "Play up, and I'll make you know."

The piper put wind in his bag, and he played such music as made himself wonder.

"Upon my word, you're a fine music-master," says the piper then; "but tell me where you're for bringing me."

"There's a great feast in the house of the Banshee, on the top of Croagh Patric to-night," says the Púca, "and I'm for bringing you there to play music, and, take my word, you'll get the price of your trouble."

"By my word, you'll save me a journey, then," says the

piper, "for Father William put a journey to Croagh Patric on me, because I stole the white gander from him last Martinmas."

The Púca rushed him across hills and bogs and rough places, till' he brought him to the top of Croagh Patric. Then the Púca struck three blows with his foot, and a great door opened, and they passed in together, into a fine room.

The piper saw a golden table in the middle of the room, and hundreds of old women (cailleacha) sitting round about it. The old women rose up, and said, "A hundred thousand welcomes to you, you Púca of November (na Samhna). Who is this you have with you?"

"The best piper in Ireland," says the Púca.

One of the old women struck a blow on the ground, and a door opened in the side of the wall, and what should the piper see coming out but the white gander which he had stolen from Father William.

"By my conscience, then," says the piper, "myself and my mother ate every taste of that gander, only one wing, and I gave that to Moy-rua (Red Mary), and it's she told the priest I stole his gander."

The gander cleaned the table, and carried it away, and the Púca said, "Play up music for these ladies."

The piper played up, and the old women began dancing, and they were dancing till they were tired. Then the Púca said to pay the piper, and every old woman drew out a gold piece, and gave it to him.

"By the tooth of Patric," said he, "I'm as rich as the son of a lord."

"Come with me," says the Púca, "and I'll bring you home."

They went out then, and just as he was going to ride on the Púca, the gander came up to him, and gave him a new set of pipes. The Púca was not long until he brought him to Dunmore, and he threw the piper off at the little bridge, and then he told him to go home, and says to him, "You have two things now that you never had before—you have sense and music (ciall agus ceól).

The piper went home, and he knocked at his mother's door, saying, "Let me in, I'm as rich as a lord, and I'm the best piper in Ireland."

"You're drunk," said the mother.

"No, indeed," says the piper, "I haven't drunk a drop."

The mother let him in, and he gave her the gold pieces, and, "Wait now," says he, "till you hear the music I'll play."

He buckled on the pipes, but instead of music, there came a sound as if all the geese and ganders in Ireland were screeching together. He wakened the neighbours, and they were all mocking him, until he put on the old pipes, and then he played melodious music for them ; and after that he told them all he had gone through that night.

The next morning, when his mother went to look at the gold pieces, there was nothing there but the leaves of a plant.

The piper went to the priest, and told him his story, but the priest would not believe a word from him, until he put the pipes on him, and then the screeching of the ganders and geese began.

"Leave my sight, you thief," says the priest.

But nothing would do the piper till he would put the old pipes on him to show the priest that his story was true.

He buckled on the old pipes, and he played melodious music, and from that day till the day of his death, there was never a piper in the county Galway was as good as he was.

DANIEL O'ROURKE.

T. CROFTON CROKER.

PEOPLE may have heard of the renowned adventures of Daniel O'Rourke, but how few are there who know that the cause of all his perils, above and below, was neither more nor less than his having slept under the walls of the Pooka's tower.　I knew the man well.　He lived at the bottom of Hungry Hill, just at the right-hand side of the road as you go towards Bantry.　An old man was he, at the time he told me the story, with grey hair and a red nose; and it was on the 25th of June 1813 that I heard it from his own lips, as he sat smoking his pipe under the old poplar tree, on as fine an evening as ever shone from the sky.　I was going to visit the caves in Dursey Island, having spent the morning at Glengariff.

" I am often *axed* to tell it, sir," said he, "so that this is not the first time.　The master's son, you see, had come from beyond foreign parts in France and Spain, as young gentlemen used to go before Buonaparte or any such was heard of; and sure enough there was a dinner given to all the people on the ground, gentle and simple, high and low, rich and poor.　The *ould* gentlemen were the gentlemen after all, saving your honour's presence.　They'd swear at a body a little, to be sure, and, may be, give one a cut of a whip now and then, but we were no losers by it in the end; and they were so easy and civil, and kept such rattling houses, and thousands of welcomes; and there was no grinding for rent, and there was hardly a tenant on the estate that did not taste of his landlord's bounty often and often in a year; but now it's another thing.　No matter for that, sir, for I'd better be telling you my story.

"Well, we had everything of the best, and plenty of it; and we ate, and we drank, and we danced, and the young master by the same token danced with Peggy Barry, from the Bohereen—a lovely young couple they were, though they are both low enough now.　To make a long story short, I got, as a body may say, the same thing as tipsy almost, for I can't remember ever at all, no ways, how it was I left the place; only I did leave it, that's certain.　Well, I thought, for all that, in myself, I'd just step to Molly Cronohan's, the fairy woman, to speak a word about the bracket heifer that was bewitched; and so as I was crossing the stepping-stones of the ford of Ballyashenogh, and was looking up at the stars and blessing myself—for why? it was

Lady-day—I missed my foot, and souse I fell into the water. 'Death alive!' thought I, 'I'll be drowned now!' However, I began swimming, swimming, swimming away for the dear life, till at last I got ashore, somehow or other, but never the one of me can tell how, upon a *dissolute* island.

"I wandered and wandered about there, without knowing where I wandered, until at last I got into a big bog. The moon was shining as bright as day, or your fair lady's eyes, sir (with your pardon for mentioning her), and I looked east and west, and north and south, and every way, and nothing did I see but bog, bog, bog—I could never find out how I got into it; and my heart grew cold with fear, for sure and certain I was that it would be my *berrin* place. So I sat down upon a stone which, as good luck would have it, was close by me, and I began to scratch my head, and sing the *Ullagone*—when all of a sudden the moon grew black, and I looked up, and saw something for all the world as if it was moving down between me and it, and I could not tell what it was. Down it came with a pounce, and looked at me full in the face; and what was it but an eagle? as fine a one as ever flew from the kingdom of Kerry. So he looked at me in the face, and says he to me, 'Daniel O'Rourke,' says he, 'how do you do?' 'Very well, I thank you, sir,' says I; 'I hope you're well;' wondering out of my senses all the time how an eagle came to speak like a Christian. 'What brings you here, Dan,' says he. 'Nothing at all, sir,' says I; 'only I wish I was safe home again.' 'Is it out of the island you want to go, Dan?' says he. ''Tis, sir,' says I: so I up and told him how I had taken a drop too much, and fell into the water; how I swam to the island; and how I got into the bog and did not know my way out of it. 'Dan,' says he, after a minute's thought, 'though it is very improper for you to get drunk on Lady-day, yet as you are a decent sober man, who 'tends mass well, and never fling stones at me or mine, nor cries out after us in the fields— my life for yours,' says he; 'so get up on my back, and grip me well for fear you'd fall off, and I'll fly you out of the bog.' 'I am afraid,' says I, 'your honour's making game of me ; for who ever heard of riding a horseback on an eagle before?' ''Pon the honour of a gentleman,' says he, putting his right foot on his breast, 'I am quite in earnest: and so now either take my offer or starve in the bog—besides, I see that your weight is sinking the stone.'

"It was true enough as he said, for I found the stone every minute going from under me. I had no choice; so thinks I to myself, faint heart never won fair lady, and this is fair persuadance. 'I thank your honour,' says I, 'for the loan of your civility ; and I'll take your kind offer.' I therefore mounted upon the back of the eagle, and held him tight enough by the throat, and up he flew in the air like a lark. Little I knew the trick he was going to serve me. Up—up—up, God knows how far up he flew. 'Why then,' said I to him—thinking he did not know the right road home—very civilly, because why? I was in his power entirely ; 'sir,' says I, 'please your honour's glory, and with humble submission to your better judgment, if you'd fly down a bit, you're now just over my cabin, and I could be put down there, and many thanks to your worship.'

"'*Arrah*, Dan,' said he, 'do you think me a fool? Look down in the next field, and don't you see two men and a gun ? By my word it would be no joke to be shot this way, to oblige a drunken blackguard that I picked up off of a *could* stone in a bog.' 'Bother you,' said I to myself, but I did not speak out, for where was the use? Well, sir, up he kept, flying, flying, and I asking him every minute to fly down, and all to no use. 'Where in the world are you going, sir?' says I to him. 'Hold your tongue, Dan,' says he : 'mind your own business, and don't be interfering with the business of other people.' 'Faith, this is my business, I think,' says I. 'Be quiet, Dan,' says he : so I said no more.

"At last where should we come to, but to the moon itself. Now you can't see it from this, but there is, or there was in my time, a reaping-hook sticking out of the side of the moon, this way (drawing the figure thus σ on the ground with the end of his stick).

"'Dan,' said the eagle, 'I'm tired with this long fly; I

had no notion 'twas so far.' 'And my lord, sir,' said I, 'who in the world *axed* you to fly so far—was it I? did not I beg and pray and beseech you to stop half an hour ago?' 'There's no use talking, Dan,' said he; 'I'm tired bad enough, so you must get off, and sit down on the moon until I rest myself.' 'Is it sit down on the moon?' said I; 'is it upon that little round thing, then? why, then, sure I'd fall off in a minute, and be *kilt* and spilt, and smashed all to bits; you are a vile deceiver—so you are.' 'Not at all, Dan,' said he; 'you can catch fast hold of the reaping-hook that's sticking out of the side of the moon, and 'twill keep you up.' 'I won't then,' said I. 'May be not,' said he, quite quiet. 'If you don't, my man, I shall just give you a shake, and one slap of my wing, and send you down to the ground, where every bone in your body will be smashed as small as a drop of dew on a cabbage-leaf in the morning.' 'Why, then, I'm in a fine way,' said I to myself, 'ever to have come along with the likes of you;' and so giving him a hearty curse in Irish, for fear he'd know what I said, I got off his back with a heavy heart, took hold of the reaping-hook, and sat down upon the moon, and a mighty cold seat it was, I can tell you that.

"When he had me there fairly landed, he turned about on me, and said, 'Good morning to you, Daniel O'Rourke,' said he; 'I think I've nicked you fairly now. You robbed my nest last year' ('twas true enough for him, but how he found it out is hard to say), 'and in return you are freely welcome to cool your heels dangling upon the moon like a cockthrow.'

" 'Is that all, and is this the way you leave me, you brute, you,' says I. 'You ugly unnatural *baste*, and is this the way you serve me at last? Bad luck to yourself, with your hook'd nose, and to all your breed, you blackguard.' 'Twas all to no manner of use; he spread out his great big wings, burst out a laughing, and flew away like lightning. I bawled after him to stop; but I might have called and bawled for ever, without his minding me. Away he went, and I never saw him from that day to this—sorrow fly away with him! You may be sure I was in a disconsolate condition, and kept roaring out for the bare grief, when all at once a door opened right in the middle of the moon, creaking on its hinges as if it had not been opened for a month before, I suppose they never thought of greasing 'em, and out there walks—who do you think, but the man in the moon himself? I knew him by his bush.

"'Good morrow to you, Daniel O'Rourke,' said he ; 'how do you do ?' 'Very well, thank your honour,' said I. 'I hope your honour's well.' 'What brought you here, Dan ?' said he. So I told him how I was a little overtaken in liquor at the master's, and how I was cast on a *dissolute* island, and how I lost my way in the bog, and how the thief of an eagle promised to fly me out of it, and how, instead of that, he had fled me up to the moon.

"'Dan,' said the man in the moon, taking a pinch of snuff when I was done, 'you must not stay here.' 'Indeed, sir,' says I, ''tis much against my will I'm here at all ; but how am I to go back ?' 'That's your business,' said he ; 'Dan, mine is to tell you that here you must not stay ; so be off in less than no time.' 'I'm doing no harm,' says I, 'only holding on hard by the reaping-hook, lest I fall off.' 'That's what you must not do, Dan,' says he. 'Pray, sir,' says I, 'may I ask how many you are in family, that you would not give a poor traveller lodging : I'm sure 'tis not so often you're troubled with strangers coming to see you, for 'tis a long way.' 'I'm by myself, Dan,' says he ; 'but you'd better let go the reaping-hook.' 'Faith, and with your leave,' says I, 'I'll not let go the grip, and the more you bids me, the more I won't let go ;—so I will.' 'You had better, Dan,' says he again. 'Why, then, my little fellow,' says I, taking the whole weight of him with my eye from head to foot, 'there are two words to that bargain ; and I'll not budge, but you may if you like.' 'We'll see how that is to be,' says he ; and back he went, giving the door such a great bang after him (for it was plain he was huffed) that I thought the moon and all would fall down with it.

"Well, I was preparing myself to try strength with him,

when back again he comes, with the kitchen cleaver in his hand, and, without saying a word, he gives two bangs to the handle of the reaping-hook that was keeping me up, and *whap!* it came in two.   'Good morning to you, Dan,' says the spiteful little old blackguard, when he saw me cleanly falling down with a bit of the handle in my hand; 'I thank you for your visit, and fair weather after you, Daniel.'   I had not time to make any answer to him, for I was tumbling over and over, and rolling and rolling, at the rate of a fox-hunt. 'God help me!' says I, 'but this is a pretty pickle for a decent man to be seen in at this time of night: I am now sold fairly.'   The word was not out of my mouth when, whiz! what should fly by close to my ear but a flock of wild geese, all the way from my own bog of Ballyasheenogh, else how should they know *me?*   The *ould* gander, who was their general, turning about his head, cried out to me, 'Is that you, Dan?'   'The same,' said I, not a bit daunted now at what he said, for I was by this time used to all kinds of *bedevilment,* and, besides, I knew him of *ould.*   'Good morrow to you,' says he, 'Daniel O'Rourke; how are you in health this morning?'   'Very well, sir,' says I, 'I thank you kindly,' drawing my breath, for I was mightily in want of some.   'I hope your honour's the same.'   'I think 'tis falling you are, Daniel,' says he.   'You may say that, sir,' says I.   'And where are you going all the way so fast?' said the gander.   So I told him how I had taken the drop, and how I came on the island, and how I lost my way in the bog, and how the thief of an eagle flew me up to the moon, and how the man in the moon turned me out.   'Dan,' said he, 'I'll save you: put out your hand and catch me by the leg, and I'll fly you home.'   'Sweet is your hand in a pitcher of honey, my jewel,' says I, though all the time I thought within myself that I don't much trust you; but there was no help, so I caught the gander by the leg, and away I and the other geese flew after him as fast as hops.

   "We flew, and we flew, and we flew, until we came right over the wide ocean.   I knew it well, for I saw Cape Clear to my right hand, sticking up out of the water.   'Ah, my lord,' said I to the goose, for I thought it best to keep a civil tongue in my head any way, 'fly to land if you please.'   'It is impossible, you see, Dan,' said he, 'for a while, because you see we are going to Arabia.'   'To Arabia!' said I; 'that's surely some place in foreign parts, far away.   Oh! Mr. Goose: why then, to be sure, I'm a man to be pitied among you.'   'Whist, whist, you fool,' said he, 'hold your tongue; I tell you Arabia is a very decent sort of place, as like West Carbery as one egg is like another, only there is a little more sand there.'

"Just as we were talking, a ship hove in sight, scudding so beautiful before the wind.   'Ah! then, sir, said I, 'will you drop me on the ship, if you please?'   'We are not fair over it,' said he; 'if I dropped you now you would go splash into the sea.'   'I would not,' says I; 'I know better than that, for it is just clean under us, so let me drop now at once.'

"'If you must, you must,' said he; 'there, take your own way;' and he opened his claw, and faith he was right—sure enough I came down plump into the very bottom of the salt sea!   Down to the very bottom I went, and I gave myself up then for ever, when a whale walked up to me, scratching himself after his night's sleep, and looked me full in the face, and never the word did he say, but lifting up his tail, he splashed me all over again with the cold salt water till there wasn't a dry stitch upon my whole carcass! and I heard somebody saying—'twas a voice I knew, too— 'Get up, you drunken brute, off o' that;' and with that I woke up, and there was Judy with a tub full of water, which she was splashing all over me—for, rest her soul! though she was a good wife, she never could bear to see me in drink, and had a bitter hand of her own.

"'Get up,' said she again: 'and of all places in the parish would no place *sarve* your turn to lie down upon but under the *ould* walls of Carrigapooka? an uneasy resting I am sure you had of it.'   And sure enough I had: for I was fairly bothered out of my senses with eagles, and men of the moons, and flying ganders, and whales, driving me through bogs, and up to the moon, and down to the bottom of the green ocean. If I was in drink ten times over, long would it be before I'd lie down in the same spot again, I know that."

THE KILDARE POOKA.*

PATRICK KENNEDY.

Mr. H—— R——, when he was alive, used to live a good deal in Dublin, and he was once a great while out of the country on account of the " ninety-eight " business. But the servants kept on in the big house at Rath—— all the same as if the family was at home. Well, they used to be frightened out of their lives after going to their beds with the banging of the kitchen-door, and the clattering of fire-irons, and the pots and plates and dishes. One evening they sat up ever so long, keeping one another in heart with telling stories about ghosts and fetches, and that when—what would you have of it?—the little scullery boy that used to be sleeping over the horses, and could not get room at the fire, crept into the hot hearth, and when he got tired listening to the stories, sorra fear him, but he fell dead asleep.

Well and good, after they were all gone and the kitchen fire raked up, he was woke with the noise of the kitchen door opening, and the trampling of an ass on the kitchen floor. He peeped out, and what should he see but a big ass, sure enough, sitting on his curabingo and yawning before the fire. After a little he looked about him, and began scratching his ears as if he was quite tired, and says he, " I may as well begin first as last." The poor boy's teeth began to chatter in his head, for says he, " Now he's goin' to ate me ; " but the fellow with the long ears and tail on him had something else to do. He stirred the fire, and then he brought in a pail of water from the pump, and filled

* *Legendary Fictions of the Irish Celts.*—Macmillan.

a big pot that he put on the fire before he went out. He then put in his hand—foot, I mean—into the hot hearth, and pulled out the little boy. He let a roar out of him with the fright, but the pooka only looked at him, and thrust out his lower lip to show how little he valued him, and then he pitched him into his pew again.

Well, he then lay down before the fire till he heard the boil coming on the water, and maybe there wasn't a plate, or a dish, or a spoon on the dresser that he didn't fetch and put into the pot, and wash and dry the whole bilin' of 'em as well as e'er a kitchen-maid from that to Dublin town. He then put all of them up on their places on the shelves; and if he didn't give a good sweepin' to the kitchen, leave it till again. Then he comes and sits fornent the boy, let down one of his ears, and cocked up the other, and gave a grin. The poor fellow strove to roar out, but not a dheeg 'ud come out of his throat. The last thing the pooka done was to rake up the fire, and walk out, giving such a slap o' the door, that the boy thought the house couldn't help tumbling down.

Well, to be sure if there wasn't a hullabullo next morning when the poor fellow told his story! They could talk of nothing else the whole day. One said one thing, another said another, but a fat, lazy scullery girl said the wittiest thing of all. "Musha!" says she, "if the pooka does be cleaning up everything that way when we are asleep, what should we be slaving ourselves for doing his work?" "*Shu gu dheine*,"* says another; "them's the wisest words you ever said, Kauth; it's meeself won't contradict you."

So said, so done. Not a bit of a plate or dish saw a drop of water that evening, and not a besom was laid on the floor, and every one went to bed soon after sundown. Next morning everything was as fine as fine in the kitchen, and the lord mayor might eat his dinner off the flags. It was great ease to the lazy servants, you may depend, and everything went on well till a foolhardy gag of a boy said he would stay up one night and have a chat with the pooka.

* Meant for *seadh go deimhin—i.e.*, yes, indeed.

He was a little daunted when the door was thrown open and the ass marched up to the fire.

"An then, sir," says he, at last, picking up courage, "if it isn't taking a liberty, might I ax who you are, and why you are so kind as to do half of the day's work for the girls every night?" "No liberty at all," says the pooka, says he: "I'll tell you, and welcome. I was a servant in the time of Squire R.'s father, and was the laziest rogue that ever was clothed and fed, and done nothing for it. When my time came for the other world, this is the punishment was laid on me—to come here and do all this labour every night, and then go out in the cold. It isn't so bad in the fine weather; but if you only knew what it is to stand with your head between your legs, facing the storm, from midnight to sunrise, on a bleak winter night." "And could we do anything for your comfort, my poor fellow?" says the boy. "Musha, I don't know," says the pooka; "but I think a good quilted frieze coat would help to keep the life in me them long nights." "Why then, in troth, we'd be the ungratefullest of people if we didn't feel for you."

To make a long story short, the next night but two the boy was there again; and if he didn't delight the poor pooka, holding up a fine warm coat before him, it's no mather! Betune the pooka and the man, his legs was got into the four arms of it, and it was buttoned down the breast and the belly, and he was so pleazed he walked up to the glass to see how he looked. "Well," says he, "it's a long lane that has no turning. I am much obliged to you and your fellow-servants. You have made me happy at last. Good-night to you."

So he was walking out, but the other cried, "Och! sure your going too soon. What about the washing and sweeping?" "Ah, you may tell the girls that they must now get their turn. My punishment was to last till I was thought worthy of a reward for the way I done my duty. You'll see me no more." And no more they did, and right sorry they were for having been in such a hurry to reward the ungrateful pooka.

THE SOLITARY FAIRIES.

THE BANSHEE.

[THE *banshee* (from *ban* [*bean*], a woman, and *shee* [*sidhe*], a fairy) is an attendant fairy that follows the old families, and none but them, and wails before a death. Many have seen her as she goes wailing and clapping her hands. The keen [*caoine*], the funeral cry of the peasantry, is said to be an imitation of her cry. When more than one banshee is present, and they wail and sing in chorus, it is for the death of some holy or great one. An omen that sometimes accompanies the banshee is the *coach-a-bower* [*cóiste-bodhar*]—an immense black coach, mounted by a coffin, and drawn by headless horses driven by a *Dullahan*. It will go rumbling to your door, and if you open it, according to Croker, a basin of blood will be thrown in your face. These headless phantoms are found elsewhere than in Ireland. In 1807 two of the sentries stationed outside St. James's Park died of fright. A headless woman, the upper part of her body naked, used to pass at midnight and scale the railings. After a time the sentries were stationed no longer at the haunted spot. In Norway the heads of corpses were cut off to make their ghosts feeble. Thus came into existence the *Dullahans*, perhaps; unless, indeed, they are descended from that Irish giant who swam across the Channel with his head in his teeth.—ED.]

HOW THOMAS CONNOLLY MET THE BANSHEE.

J. TODHUNTER.

Aw, the banshee, sir? Well, sir, as I was striving to tell ye, I was going home from work one day, from Mr. Cassidy's that I tould ye of, in the dusk o' the evening. I had more nor a mile—aye, it was nearer two mile—to thrack to, where I was lodgin' with a dacent widdy woman I knew, Biddy Maguire be name, so as to be near me work.

It was the first week in November, an' a lonesome road I had to travel, an' dark enough, wid threes above it; an' about half-ways there was a bit of a brudge I had to cross, over one o' them little sthrames that runs into the Doddher. I walked on in the middle iv the road, for there was no toe-path at that time, Misther Harry, nor for many a long day afther that; but, as I was sayin', I walked along till I come nigh upon the brudge, where the road was a bit open, an' there, right enough, I seen the hog's back o' the ould-fashioned brudge that used to be there till it was pulled down, an' a white mist steamin' up out o' the wather all around it.

Well, now, Misther Harry, often as I'd passed by the place before, that night it seemed sthrange to me, an' like a place ye might see in a dhrame; an' as I come up to it I began to feel a could wind blowin' through the hollow o' me heart. "Musha Thomas," sez I to meself, "is it yerself that's in it?" sez I; "or, if it is, what's the matter wid ye at all, at all?" sez I; so I put a bould face on it, an' I made a sthruggle to set one leg afore the other, ontil I came to the rise o' the brudge. And there, God be good to us! in a cantle o' the wall I seen an ould woman, as I thought, sittin' on her hunkers, all crouched together, an' her head bowed down, seemin'ly in the greatest affliction.

Well, sir, I pitied the ould craythur, an' thought I wasn't worth a thraneen, for the mortial fright I was in, I up an' sez to her, "That's a cowld lodgin' for ye, ma'am." Well, the sorra ha'porth she sez to that, nor tuk no more notice o' me than if I hadn't let a word out o' me, but kep' rockin' herself to an' fro, as if her heart was breakin'; so I sez to her again, "Eh, ma'am, is there anythin' the matther wid ye?" An' I made for to touch her on the shouldher, on'y somethin' stopt me, for as I looked closer at her I saw she was no more an ould woman nor she was an ould cat. The first thing I tuk notice to, Misther Harry, was her hair, that

was sthreelin' down over his showldhers, an' a good yard on
the ground on aich side of her. O, be the hoky farmer, but
that was the hair! The likes of it I never seen on mortial
woman, young or ould, before nor sense. It grew as
sthrong out of her as out of e'er a young slip of a girl ye
could see; but the colour of it was a misthery to describe.
The first squint I got of it I thought it was silvery grey, like
an ould crone's; but when I got up beside her I saw, be
the glance o' the sky, it was a soart iv an Iscariot colour, an'
a shine out of it like floss silk. It ran over her showldhers
and the two shapely arms she was lanin' her head on, for
all the world like Mary Magdalen's in a picther; and then
I persaved that the grey cloak and the green gownd undhernaith it was made of no earthly matarial I ever laid eyes on.
Now, I needn't tell ye, sir, that I seen all this in the twinkle
of a bed-post—long as I take to make the narration of it.
So I made a step back from her, an' "The Lord be betune
us an' harm!" sez I, out loud, an' wid that I blessed
meself. Well, Misther Harry, the word wasn't out o' me
mouth afore she turned her face on me. Aw, Misther
Harry, but 'twas that was the awfullest apparation ever I
seen, the face of her as she looked up at me! God forgive
me for sayin' it, but 'twas more like the face of the "Axy
Homo" bezand in Marlboro' Sthreet Chapel nor like
any face I could mintion—as pale as a corpse, an' a most o'
freckles on it, like the freckles on a turkey's egg; an' the
two eyes sewn in wid red thread, from the terrible power o'
crying the' had to do; an' such a pair iv eyes as the' wor,
Misther Harry, as blue as two forget-me-nots, an' as cowld
as the moon in a bog-hole of a frosty night, an' a dead-an'-
live look in them that sent a cowld shiver through the
marra o' me bones. Be the mortial! ye could ha' rung a
tay cupful o' cowld paspiration out o' the hair o' me head
that minute, so ye could. Well, I thought the life 'ud lave
me intirely when she riz up from her hunkers, till, bedad!
she looked mostly as tall as Nelson's Pillar; an' wid the two
eyes gazin' back at me, an' her two arms stretched out
before hor, an' a keine out of her that riz the hair o' me

scalp till it was as stiff as the hog's bristles in a new hearth broom, away she glides—glides round the angle o' the brudge, an' down with her into the sthrame that ran undhernaith it. 'Twas then I began to suspect what she was. "Wisha, Thomas!" says I to meself, sez I; an' I made a great struggle to get me two legs into a throt, in spite o' the spavin o' fright the pair o' them wor in ; an' how I brought meself home that same night the Lord in heaven only knows, for I never could tell; but I must ha' tumbled agin the door, and shot in head foremost into the middle o' the flure, where I lay in a dead swoon for mostly an hour ; and the first I knew was Mrs. Maguire stannin' over me with a jorum o' punch she was pourin' down me throath (throat), to bring back the life into me, an' me head in a pool of cowld wather she dashed over me in her first fright. "Arrah, Mister Connolly," shashee, "what ails ye?" shashee, "to put the scare on a lone woman like that?" shashee. "Am I in this world or the next?" sez I. "Musha! where else would ye be on'y here in my kitchen?" shashee. "O, glory be to God!" sez I, "but I thought I was in Purgathory at the laste, not to mintion an uglier place," sez I, "only it's too cowld I find meself, an' not too hot," sez I. "Faix, an' maybe ye wor more nor half-ways there, on'y for me," shashee; "but what's come to you at all, at all? Is it your fetch ye seen, Mister Connolly?" "Aw, naboclish!"* sez I. "Never mind what I seen," sez I. So be degrees I began to come to a little; an' that's the way I met the banshee, Misther Harry!

"But how did you know it really was the banshee after all, Thomas?"

"Begor, sir, I knew the apparation of her well enough; but 'twas confirmed by a sarcumstance that occurred the same time. There was a Misther O'Nales was come on a visit, ye must know, to a place in the neighbourhood—one o' the ould O'Nales iv the county Tyrone, a rale ould Irish family—an' the banshee was heard keening round the house that same night, be more then one that was in it :

* *Na bac leis*—*i.e.*, don't mind it.

an' sure enough, Misther Harry, he was found dead in his bed the next mornin'. So if it wasn't the banshee I seen that time, I'd like to know what else it could a' been."

A LAMENTATION

For the Death of Sir Maurice Fitzgerald, Knight, of Kerry, who was killed in Flanders, 1642.

FROM THE IRISH, BY CLARENCE MANGAN.

THERE was lifted up one voice of woe,
　　One lament of more than mortal grief,
Through the wide South to and fro,
　　For a fallen Chief.
In the dead of night that cry thrilled through me,
　　I looked out upon the midnight air?
My own soul was all as gloomy,
　　As I knelt in prayer.

O'er Loch Gur, that night, once—twice—yea, thrice—
　　Passed a wail of anguish for the Brave
That half curled into ice
　　Its moon-mirroring wave.
Then uprose a many-toned wild hymn in
　　Choral swell from Ogra's dark ravine,
And Mogeely's Phantom Women
　　Mourned the Geraldine!

Far on Carah Mona's emerald plains
　　Shrieks and sighs were blended many hours,
And Fermoy in fitful strains
　　Answered from her towers.
Youghal, Keenalmeaky, Eemokilly,
　　Mourned in concert, and their piercing *keen*
Woke to wondering life the stilly
　　Glens of Inchiqueen.

From Loughmoe to yellow Dunanore
 There was fear; the traders of Tralee
Gathered up their golden store,
 And prepared to flee;
For, in ship and hall from night till morning,
 Showed the first faint beamings of the sun,
All the foreigners heard the warning
 Of the Dreaded One!

" This," they spake, " portendeth death to us,
 If we fly not swiftly from our fate!"
Self-conceited idiots! thus
 Ravingly to prate!
Not for base-born higgling Saxon trucksters
 Ring laments like those by shore and sea!
Not for churls with souls like hucksters
 Waileth our Banshee!

For the high Milesian race alone
 Ever flows the music of her woe!
For slain heir to bygone throne,
 And for Chief laid low!
Hark! . . . Again, methinks, I hear her weeping
 Yonder! Is she near me now, as then?
Or was but the night-wind sweeping
 Down the hollow glen?

THE BANSHEE OF THE MAC CARTHYS.

T. CROFTON CROKER.

CHARLES MAC CARTHY was, in the year 1749, the only
surviving son of a very numerous family. His father died
when he was little more than twenty, leaving him the Mac

Carthy estate, not much encumbered, considering that it was
an Irish one.   Charles was gay, handsome, unfettered either
by poverty, a father, or guardians, and therefore was not, at
the age of one-and-twenty, a pattern of regularity and virtue.
In plain terms, he was an exceedingly dissipated—I fear I
may say debauched, young man.   His companions were, as
may be supposed, of the higher classes of the youth in his
neighbourhood, and, in general, of those whose fortunes
were larger than his own, whose dispositions to pleasure
were, therefore, under still less restrictions, and in whose
example he found at once an incentive and an apology for
his irregularities.   Besides, Ireland, a place to this day not
very remarkable for the coolness and steadiness of its youth,
was then one of the cheapest countries in the world in most
of those articles which money supplies for the indulgence of
the passions.   The odious exciseman,—with his portentous
book in one hand, his unrelenting pen held in the other, or
stuck beneath his hat-band, and the ink-bottle ('black
emblem of the informer') dangling from his waistcoat-
button—went not then from ale-house to ale-house,
denouncing all those patriotic dealers in spirits, who
preferred selling whiskey, which had nothing to do with
English laws (but to elude them), to retailing that poisonous
liquor, which derived its name from the British " Parliament "
that compelled its circulation among a reluctant people.
Or if the gauger—recording angel of the law—wrote down
the peccadillo of a publican, he dropped a tear upon the
word, and blotted it out for ever !   For, welcome to the
tables of their hospitable neighbours, the guardians of the
excise, where they existed at all, scrupled to abridge those
luxuries which they freely shared ; and thus the competition
in the market between the smuggler, who incurred little
hazard, and the personage ycleped fair trader, who enjoyed
little protection, made Ireland a land flowing, not merely
with milk and honey, but with whiskey and wine.   In the
enjoyments supplied by these, and in the many kindred
pleasures to which frail youth is but too prone, Charles Mac
Carthy indulged to such a degree, that just about the time

when he had completed his four-and-twentieth year, after a week of great excesses, he was seized with a violent fever, which, from its malignity, and the weakness of his frame, left scarcely a hope of his recovery. His mother, who had at first made many efforts to check his vices, and at last had been obliged to look on at his rapid progress to ruin in silent despair, watched day and night at his pillow. The anguish of parental feeling was blended with that still deeper misery which those only know who have striven hard to rear in virtue and piety a beloved and favourite child ; have found him grow up all that their hearts could desire, until he reached manhood ; and then, when their pride was highest, and their hopes almost ended in the fulfilment of their fondest expectations, have seen this idol of their affections plunge headlong into a course of reckless profligacy, and, after a rapid career of vice, hang upon the verge of eternity, without the leisure or the power of repentance. Fervently she prayed that, if his life could not be spared, at least the delirium, which continued with increasing violence from the first few hours of his disorder, might vanish before death, and leave enough of light and of calm for making his peace with offended Heaven. After several days, however, nature seemed quite exhausted, and he sunk into a state too like death to be mistaken for the repose of sleep. His face had that pale, glossy, marble look, which is in general so sure a symptom that life has left its tenement of clay. His eyes were closed and sunk ; the lids having that compressed and stiffened appearance which seemed to indicate that some friendly hand had done its last office. The lips, half closed and perfectly ashy, discovered just so much of the teeth as to give to the features of death their most ghastly, but most impressive look. He lay upon his back, with his hands stretched beside him, quite motionless ; and his distracted mother, after repeated trials, could discover not the least symptom of animation. The medical man who attended, having tried the usual modes for ascertaining the presence of life, declared at last his opinion that it was flown, and prepared to depart from the house of mourning. His horse was seen to come to the door. A crowd of people who were collected before the windows, or scattered in groups on the lawn in front, gathered around when the door opened. These were tenants, fosterers, and poor relations of the family, with others attracted by affection, or by that interest which partakes of curiosity, but is something more, and which collects the lower ranks round a house where a human being is in his passage to another world. They saw the professional man come out from the hall door and approach his horse; and while slowly, and with a melancholy air, he prepared to mount, they clustered round him with inquiring and wistful looks. Not a word was spoken, but their meaning could not be misunderstood; and the physician, when he had got into his saddle, and while the servant was still holding the bridle as if to delay him, and was looking anxiously at his face, as if expecting that he would relieve the general suspense, shook his head, and said in a low voice, "It's all over, James;" and moved slowly away. The moment he had spoken, the women present, who were very numerous, uttered a shrill cry, which, having been sustained for about half a minute, fell suddenly into a full, loud, continued, and discordant but plaintive wailing, above which occasionally were heard the deep sounds of a man's voice, sometimes in deep sobs, sometimes in more distinct exclamations of sorrow. This was Charles's foster-brother, who moved about the crowd, now clapping his hands, now rubbing them together in an agony of grief. The poor fellow had been Charles's playmate and companion when a boy, and afterwards his servant; had always been distinguished by his peculiar regard, and loved his young master as much, at least, as he did his own life.

When Mrs. Mac Carthy became convinced that the blow was indeed struck, and that her beloved son was sent to his last account, even in the blossoms of his sin, she remained for some time gazing with fixedness upon his cold features; then, as if something had suddenly touched the string of her tenderest affections, tear after tear trickled down her cheeks, pale with anxiety and watching. Still she continued looking at her son, apparently unconscious that she was weeping, without once lifting her handkerchief to her eyes, until reminded of the sad duties which the custom of the country imposed upon her, by the crowd of females belonging to the better class of the peasantry, who now, crying audibly, nearly filled the apartment. She then withdrew, to give directions for the ceremony of waking, and for supplying the numerous visitors of all ranks with the refreshments usual on these melancholy occasions. Though her voice was scarcely heard, and though no one saw her but the servants and one or two old followers of the family, who assisted her in the necessary arrangements, everything was conducted with the greatest regularity; and though she made no effort to check her sorrows they never once suspended her attention, now more than ever required to preserve order in her household, which, in this season of calamity, but for her would have been all confusion.

The night was pretty far advanced; the boisterous lamentations which had prevailed during part of the day in and about the house had given place to a solemn and mournful stillness; and Mrs. Mac Carthy, whose heart, notwithstanding her long fatigue and watching, was yet too sore for sleep, was kneeling in fervent prayer in a chamber adjoining that of her son. Suddenly her devotions were disturbed by an unusual noise, proceeding from the persons who were watching round the body. First there was a low murmur, then all was silent, as if the movements of those in the chamber were checked by a sudden panic, and then a loud cry of terror burst from all within. The door of the chamber was thrown open, and all who were not overturned in the press rushed wildly into the passage which led to the stairs, and into which Mrs. Mac Carthy's room opened. Mrs. Mac Carthy made her way through the crowd into her son's chamber, where she found him sitting up in the bed, and looking vacantly around, like one risen from the grave. The glare thrown upon his sunk features and thin lathy frame gave an unearthly horror to his whole aspect. Mrs.

Mac Carthy was a woman of some firmness; but she was a woman, and not quite free from the superstitions of her country. She dropped on her knees, and, clasping her hands, began to pray aloud. The form before her moved only its lips, and barely uttered "Mother"; but though the pale lips moved, as if there was a design to finish the sentence, the tongue refused its office. Mrs. Mac Carthy sprung forward, and catching the arm of her son, exclaimed, "Speak! in the name of God and His saints, speak! are you alive?"

He turned to her slowly, and said, speaking still with apparent difficulty, "Yes, my mother, alive, and—but sit down and collect yourself; I have that to tell which will astonish you still more than what you have seen." He leaned back upon his pillow, and while his mother remained kneeling by the bedside, holding one of his hands clasped in hers, and gazing on him with the look of one who distrusted all her senses, he proceeded: "Do not interrupt me until I have done. I wish to speak while the excitement of returning life is upon me, as I know I shall soon need much repose. Of the commencement of my illness I have only a confused recollection; but within the last twelve hours I have been before the judgment-seat of God. Do not stare incredulously on me—'tis as true as have been my crimes, and as, I trust, shall be repentance. I saw the awful Judge arrayed in all the terrors which invest him when mercy gives place to justice. The dreadful pomp of offended omnipotence, I saw—I remember. It is fixed here; printed on my brain in characters indelible; but it passeth human language. What I *can* describe I *will*—I may speak it briefly. It is enough to say, I was weighed in the balance, and found wanting. The irrevocable sentence was upon the point of being pronounced; the eye of my Almighty Judge, which had already glanced upon me, half spoke my doom; when I observed the guardian saint, to whom you so often directed my prayers when I was a child, looking at me with an expression of benevolence and compassion. I stretched forth my hands to him, and besought his intercession. I implored that one year, one month, might be given to me on earth to do penance and atonement for my transgressions. He threw himself at the feet of my Judge, and supplicated for mercy. Oh! never—not if I should pass through ten thousand successive states of being—never, for eternity, shall I forget the horrors of that moment, when my fate hung suspended— when an instant was to decide whether torments unutterable were to be my portion for endless ages! But Justice suspended its decree, and Mercy spoke in accents of firmness, but mildness, 'Return to that world in which thou hast lived but to outrage the laws of Him who made that world and thee. Three years are given thee for repentance; when these are ended, thou shalt again stand here, to be saved or lost for ever.' I heard no more; I saw no more, until I awoke to life, the moment before you entered."

Charles's strength continued just long enough to finish these last words, and on uttering them he closed his eyes, and lay quite exhausted. His mother, though, as was before said, somewhat disposed to give credit to supernatural visitations, yet hesitated whether or not she should believe that, although awakened from a swoon which might have been the crisis of his disease, he was still under the influence of delirium. Repose, however, was at all events necessary, and she took immediate measures that he should enjoy it undisturbed. After some hours' sleep, he awoke refreshed, and thenceforward gradually but steadily recovered.

Still he persisted in his account of the vision, as he had at first related it; and his persuasion of its reality had an obvious and decided influence on his habits and conduct. He did not altogether abandon the society of his former associates, for his temper was not soured by his reformation; but he never joined in their excesses, and often endeavoured to reclaim them. How his pious exertions succeeded, I have never learnt; but of himself it is recorded that he was religious without ostentation, and temperate without austerity; giving a practical proof that vice may be exchanged for virtue, without the loss of respectability, popularity, or happiness.

Time rolled on, and long before the three years were ended the story of his vision was forgotten, or, when spoken of, was usually mentioned as an instance proving the folly of believing in such things. Charles's health, from the temperance and regularity of his habits, became more robust than ever. His friends, indeed, had often occasion to rally him upon a seriousness and abstractedness of demeanour, which grew upon him as he approached the completion of his seven-and-twentieth year, but for the most part his manner exhibited the same animation and cheerfulness for which he had always been remarkable. In company he evaded every endeavour to draw from him a distinct opinion on the subject of the supposed prediction ; but among his own family it was well known that he still firmly believed it. However, when the day had nearly arrived on which the prophecy was, if at all, to be fulfilled, his whole appearance gave such promise of a long and healthy life, that he was persuaded by his friends to ask a large party to an entertainment at Spring House, to celebrate his birthday. But the occasion of this party, and the circumstances which attended it, will be best learned from a perusal of the following letters, which have been carefully preserved by some relations of his family. The first is from Mrs. Mac Carthy to a lady, a very near connection and valued friend of her's, who lived in the county of Cork, at about fifty miles' distance from Spring House.

"TO MRS. BARRY, CASTLE BARRY.

"*Spring House, Tuesday morning,*
October 15*th,* 1752.

"My dearest Mary,

"I am afraid I am going to put your affection for your old friend and kinswoman to a severe trial. A two days' journey at this season, over bad roads and through a troubled country, it will indeed require friendship such as yours to persuade a sober woman to encounter. But the truth is, I have, or fancy I have, more than usual cause for wishing you near me. You know my son's story. I can't tell you how it is, but as next Sunday approaches, when the prediction of his dream, or vision, will be proved false or true, I feel a sickening of the heart, which I cannot suppress, but which your presence, my dear Mary, will soften, as it has done so many of my sorrows. My nephew, James Ryan, is to be married to Jane Osborne (who, you know, is my son's ward), and the bridal entertainment will take place here on Sunday next, though Charles pleaded hard to have it postponed for a day or two longer. Would to God—but no more of this till we meet. Do prevail upon yourself to leave your good man for *one* week, if his farming concerns will not admit of his accompanying you; and come to us, with the girls, as soon before Sunday as you can.

" Ever my dear Mary's attached cousin and friend,

"ANN MAC CARTHY."

Although this letter reached Castle Barry early on Wednesday, the messenger having travelled on foot over bog and moor, by paths impassable to horse or carriage, Mrs. Barry, who at once determined on going, had so many arrangements to make for the regulation of her domestic affairs (which, in Ireland, among the middle orders of the gentry, fall soon into confusion when the mistress of the family is away), that she and her two young daughters were unable to leave until late on the morning of Friday. The eldest daughter remained to keep her father company, and superintend the concerns of the household. As the travellers were to journey in an open one-horse vehicle, called a jaunting-car (still used in Ireland), and as the roads, bad at all times, were rendered still worse by the heavy rains, it was their design to make two easy stages—to stop about midway the first night, and reach Spring House early on Saturday evening. This arrangement was now altered, as they found that from the lateness of their departure they could proceed, at the utmost, no farther than twenty miles on the first day ; and they, therefore, purposed sleeping at the house of a Mr. Bourke, a friend of theirs, who lived at somewhat less than that distance from Castle Barry.   They reached Mr. Bourke's in safety after a rather disagreeable ride.   What befell them on their journey the next day to Spring House, and after their arrival there, is fully recounted in a letter from the second Miss Barry to her eldest sister.

"*Spring House, Sunday evening,*
20th October 1752.

"Dear Ellen,

"As my mother's letter, which encloses this, will announce to you briefly the sad intelligence which I shall here relate more fully, I think it better to go regularly through the recital of the extraordinary events of the last two days.

"The Bourkes kept us up so late on Friday night that yesterday was pretty far advanced before we could begin our journey, and the day closed when we were nearly fifteen miles distant from this place.   The roads were excessively deep, from the heavy rains of the last week, and we proceeded so slowly that, at last, my mother resolved on passing the night at the house of Mr. Bourke's brother (who lives about a quarter-of-a-mile off the road), and coming here to breakfast in the morning.   The day had been windy and showery, and the sky looked fitful, gloomy, and uncertain.   The moon was full, and at times shone clear and bright ; at others it was wholly concealed behind the thick, black, and rugged masses of clouds that rolled rapidly along, and were every moment becoming larger, and collecting together as if gathering strength for a coming storm. The wind, which blew in our faces, whistled bleakly along the low hedges of the narrow road, on which we proceeded with difficulty from the number of deep sloughs, and which afforded not the least shelter, no plantation being within some miles of us.   My mother, therefore, asked Leary, who drove the jaunting-car, how far we were from Mr.

Bourke's? ' 'Tis about ten spades from this to the cross, and we have then only to turn to the left into the avenue, ma'am.' ' Very well, Leary; turn up to Mr. Bourke's as soon as you reach the cross roads.' My mother had scarcely spoken these words, when a shriek, that made us thrill as if our very hearts were pierced by it, burst from the hedge to the right of our way. If it resembled anything earthly it seemed the cry of a female, struck by a sudden and mortal blow, and giving out her life in one long deep pang of expiring agony. ' Heaven defend us !' exclaimed my mother. ' Go you over the hedge, Leary, and save that woman, if she is not yet dead, while we run back to the hut we have just passed, and alarm the village near it.' ' Woman !' said Leary, beating the horse violently, while his voice trembled, ' that's no woman ; the sooner we get on, ma'am, the better ;' and he continued his efforts to quicken the horse's pace. We saw nothing. The moon was hid. It was quite dark, and we had been for some time expecting a heavy fall of rain. But just as Leary had spoken, and had succeeded in making the horse trot briskly forward, we distinctly heard a loud clapping of hands, followed by a succession of screams, that seemed to denote the last excess of despair and anguish, and to issue from a person running forward inside the hedge, to keep pace with our progress. Still we saw nothing ; until, when we were within about ten yards of the place where an avenue branched off to Mr. Bourke's to the left, and the road turned to Spring House on the right, the moon started suddenly from behind a cloud, and enabled us to see, as plainly as I now see this paper, the figure of a tall, thin woman, with uncovered head, and long hair that floated round her shoulders, attired in something which seemed either a loose white cloak or a sheet thrown hastily about her. She stood on the corner hedge, where the road on which we were met that which leads to Spring House, with her face towards us, her left hand pointing to this place, and her right arm waving rapidly and violently as if to draw us on in that direction. The horse had stopped, apparently

frightened at the sudden presence of the figure, which stood
in the manner I have described, still uttering the same
piercing cries, for about half a minute. It then leaped upon
the road, disappeared from our view for one instant, and the
next was seen standing upon a high wall a little way up the
avenue on which we purposed going, still pointing towards
the road to Spring House, but in an attitude of defiance
and command, as if prepared to oppose our passage up the
avenue. The figure was now quite silent, and its garments,
which had before flown loosely in the wind, were closely
wrapped around it. 'Go on, Leary, to Spring House, in
God's name!' said my mother; 'whatever world it belongs
to, we will provoke it no longer.' ''Tis the Banshee,
ma'am,' said Leary; 'and I would not, for what my life is
worth, go anywhere this blessed night but to Spring House.
But I'm afraid there's something bad going forward, or *she*
would not send us there.' So saying, he drove forward;
and as we turned on the road to the right, the moon
suddenly withdrew its light, and we saw the apparition no
more; but we heard plainly a prolonged clapping of hands,
gradually dying away, as if it issued from a person rapidly
retreating. We proceeded as quickly as the badness of the
roads and the·fatigue of the poor animal that drew us would
allow, and arrived here about eleven o'clock last night.
The scene which awaited us you have learned from my
mother's letter. To explain it fully, I must recount to you
some of the transactions which took place here during the
last week.

"You are aware that Jane Osborne was to have been
married this day to James Ryan, and that they and their
friends have been here for the last week. On Tuesday
last, the very day on the morning of which cousin Mac
Carthy despatched the letter inviting us here, the whole of
the company were walking about the grounds a little before
dinner. It seems that an unfortunate creature, who had
been seduced by James Ryan, was seen prowling in the
neighbourhood in a moody, melancholy state for some days
previous. He had separated from her for several months,

and, they say, had provided for her rather handsomely ; but she had been seduced by the promise of his marrying her ; and the shame of her unhappy condition, uniting with disappointment and jealousy, had disordered her intellects. During the whole forenoon of this Tuesday she had been walking in the plantations near Spring House, with her cloak folded tight round her, the hood nearly covering her face ; and she had avoided conversing with or even meeting any of the family.

" Charles Mac Carthy, at the time I mentioned, was walking between James Ryan and another, at a little distance from the rest, on a gravel path, skirting a shrubbery. The whole party was thrown into the utmost consternation by the report of a pistol, fired from a thickly-planted part of the shrubbery which Charles and his companions had just passed. He fell instantly, and it was found that he had been wounded in the leg. One of the party was a medical man. His assistance was immediately given, and, on examining, he declared that the injury was very slight, that no bone was broken, it was merely a flesh wound, and that it would certainly be well in a few days. 'We shall know more by Sunday,' said Charles, as he was carried to his chamber. His wound was immediately dressed, and so slight was the inconvenience which it gave that several of his friends spent a portion of the evening in his apartment.

" On inquiry, it was found that the unlucky shot was fired by the poor girl I just mentioned. It was also manifest that she had aimed, not at Charles, but at the destroyer of her innocence and happiness, who was walking beside him. After a fruitless search for her through the grounds, she walked into the house of her own accord, laughing and dancing, and singing wildly, and every moment exclaiming that she had at last killed Mr. Ryan. When she heard that it was Charles, and not Mr. Ryan, who was shot, she fell into a violent fit, out of which, after working convulsively for some time, she sprung to the door, escaped from the crowd that pursued her, and could never be taken until last night, when she was brought here, perfectly frantic, a little before our arrival.

"Charles's wound was thought of such little consequence that the preparations went forward, as usual, for the wedding entertainment on Sunday. But on Friday night he grew restless and feverish, and on Saturday (yesterday) morning felt so ill that it was deemed necessary to obtain additional medical advice. Two physicians and a surgeon met in consultation about twelve o'clock in the day, and the dreadful intelligence was announced, that unless a change, hardly hoped for, took place before night, death must happen within twenty-four hours after. The wound, it seems, had been too tightly bandaged, and otherwise injudiciously treated. The physicians were right in their anticipations. No favourable symptom appeared, and long before we reached Spring House every ray of hope had vanished. The scene we witnessed on our arrival would have wrung the heart of a demon. We heard briefly at the gate that Mr. Charles was upon his death-bed. When we reached the house, the information was confirmed by the servant who opened the door. But just as we entered we were horrified by the most appalling screams issuing from the staircase. My mother thought she heard the voice of poor Mrs. Mac Carthy, and sprung forward. We followed, and on ascending a few steps of the stairs, we found a young woman, in a state of frantic passion, struggling furiously with two men-servants, whose united strength was hardly sufficient to prevent her rushing upstairs over the body of Mrs. Mac Carthy, who was lying in strong hysterics upon the steps. This, I afterwards discovered, was the unhappy girl I before described, who was attempting to gain access to Charles's room, to 'get his forgiveness,' as she said, 'before he went away to accuse her for having killed him.' This wild idea was mingled with another, which seemed to dispute with the former possession of her mind. In one sentence she called on Charles to forgive her, in the next she would denounce James Ryan as the murderer, both of Charles and her. At length she was torn away ; and the last words I heard her scream were, ' James Ryan, 'twas you killed him, and not I—'twas you killed him, and not I.'

"Mrs. Mac Carthy, on recovering, fell into the arms of my mother, whose presence seemed a great relief to her. She wept—the first tears, I was told, that she had shed since the fatal accident. She conducted us to Charles's room, who, she said, had desired to see us the moment of our arrival, as he found his end approaching, and wished to devote the last hours of his existence to uninterrupted prayer and meditation. We found him perfectly calm, resigned, and even cheerful. He spoke of the awful event which was at hand with courage and confidence, and treated it as a doom for which he had been preparing ever since his former remarkable illness, and which he never once doubted was truly foretold to him. He bade us farewell with the air of one who was about to travel a short and easy journey; and we left him with impressions which, notwithstanding all their anguish, will, I trust, never entirely forsake us.

" Poor Mrs. Mac Carthy——but I am just called away. There seems a slight stir in the family ; perhaps——"

The above letter was never finished. The enclosure to which it more than once alludes told the sequel briefly, and it is all that I have further learned of the family of Mac Carthy. Before the sun had gone down upon Charles's seven-and-twentieth birthday, his soul had gone to render its last account to its Creator.

GHOSTS.

GHOSTS, or as they are called in Irish, *Thevshi* or *Tash*
(*taidhbhse*, *tais*), live in a state intermediary between this
life and the next. They are held there by some earthly
longing or affection, or some duty unfulfilled, or anger
against the living. "I will haunt you," is a common
threat; and one hears such phrases as, "She will haunt
him, if she has any good in her." If one is sorrowing greatly
after a dead friend, a neighbour will say, "Be quiet now,
you are keeping him from his rest;" or, in the Western Isles,
according to Lady Wilde, they will tell you, "You are waking
the dog that watches to devour the souls of the dead." Those
who die suddenly, more commonly than others, are believed to
become haunting Ghosts. They go about moving the furniture,
and in every way trying to attract attention.

When the soul has left the body, it is drawn away, sometimes,
by the fairies. I have a story of a peasant who once saw,
sitting in a fairy rath, all who had died for years in his village.
Such souls are considered lost. If a soul eludes the fairies, it
may be snapped up by the evil spirits. The weak souls of
young children are in especial danger. When a very young
child dies, the western peasantry sprinkle the threshold with
the blood of a chicken, that the spirits may be drawn away to
the blood. A Ghost is compelled to obey the commands of the
living. "The stable-boy up at Mrs. G——'s there," said an old
countryman, "met the master going round the yards after he
had been two days dead, and told him to be away with him to
the lighthouse, and haunt that; and there he is far out to sea
still, sir. Mrs. G—— was quite wild about it, and dismissed

A GHOST, ONE OF THE DEAD ARISEN.

GHOST OF A LADY IN WHITE.

the boy." A very desolate lighthouse poor devil of a Ghost! Lady Wilde considers it is only the spirits who are too bad for heaven, and too good for hell, who are thus plagued. They are compelled to obey some one they have wronged.

The souls of the dead sometimes take the shapes of animals. There is a garden at Sligo where the gardener sees a previous owner in the shape of a rabbit. They will sometimes take the forms of insects, especially of butterflies. If you see one fluttering near a corpse, that is the soul, and is a sign of its having entered upon immortal happiness. The author of the *Parochial Survey of Ireland*, 1814, heard a woman say to a child who was chasing a butterfly, "How do you know it is not the soul of your grandfather." On November eve the dead are abroad, and dance with the fairies.

As in Scotland, the fetch is commonly believed in. If you see the double, or fetch, of a friend in the morning, no ill follows; if at night, he is about to die.

A DREAM.

WILLIAM ALLINGHAM.

I HEARD the dogs howl in the moonlight night;
I went to the window to see the sight;
All the Dead that ever I knew
Going one by one and two by two.

On they pass'd, and on they pass'd;
Townsfellows all, from first to last;
Born in the moonlight of the lane,
Quench'd in the heavy shadow again.

Schoolmates, marching as when we play'd
At soldiers once—but now more staid;
Those were the strangest sight to me
Who were drown'd, I knew, in the awful sea.

Straight and handsome folk ; bent and weak, too ;
Some that I loved, and gasp'd to speak to ;
Some but a day in their churchyard bed ;
Some that I had not known were dead.

A long, long crowd—where each seem'd lonely,
Yet of them all there was one, one only,
Raised a head or look'd my way.
She linger'd a moment,—she might not stay.

How long since I saw that fair pale face !
Ah ! Mother dear ! might I only place
My head on thy breast, a moment to rest,
While thy hand on my tearful cheek were prest !

On, on, a moving bridge they made
Across the moon-stream, from shade to shade,
Young and old, women and men ;
Many long-forgot, but remember'd then.

And first there came a bitter laughter ;
A sound of tears the moment after ;
And then a music so lofty and gay,
That every morning, day by day,
I strive to recall it if I may.

GRACE CONNOR.

MISS LETITIA MACLINTOCK.

THADY and Grace Connor lived on the borders of a large
turf bog, in the parish of Clondevaddock, where they could
hear the Atlantic surges thunder in upon the shore, and see
the wild storms of winter sweep over the Muckish mountain,

and his rugged neighbours. Even in summer the cabin by the bog was dull and dreary enough.

Thady Connor worked in the fields, and Grace made a livelihood as a pedlar, carrying a basket of remnants of cloth, calico, drugget, and frieze about the country. The people rarely visited any large town, and found it convenient to buy from Grace, who was welcomed in many a lonely house, where a table was hastily cleared, that she might display her wares. Being considered a very honest woman, she was frequently entrusted with commissions to the shops in Letterkenny and Ramelton. As she set out towards home, her basket was generally laden with little gifts for her children.

"Grace, dear," would one of the kind housewives say, "here's a farrel* of oaten cake, wi' a taste o' butter on it; tak' it wi' you for the weans;" or, "Here's half-a-dozen of eggs; you've a big family to support."

Small Connors of all ages crowded round the weary mother, to rifle her basket of these gifts. But her thrifty, hard life came suddenly to an end. She died after an illness of a few hours, and was waked and buried as handsomely as Thady could afford.

Thady was in bed the night after the funeral, and the fire still burned brightly, when he saw his departed wife cross the room and bend over the cradle. Terrified, he muttered rapid prayers, covered his face with the blanket; and on looking up again the appearance was gone.

Next night he lifted the infant out of the cradle, and laid it behind him in the bed, hoping thus to escape his ghostly visitor; but Grace was presently in the room, and stretching over him to wrap up her child. Shrinking and shuddering, the poor man exclaimed, "Grace, woman, what is it brings you back? What is it you want wi' me?"

"I want naething fae you, Thady, but to put thon wean back in her cradle," replied the spectre, in a tone of scorn. "You're too feared for me, but my sister Rose willna be

---

* When a large, round, flat griddle cake is divided into triangular cuts, each of these cuts is called a farrel, farli, or parli.

feared for me—tell her to meet me to-morrow evening, in the old wallsteads."

Rose lived with her mother, about a mile off, but she obeyed her sister's summons without the least fear, and kept the strange tryste in due time.

"Rose, dear," she said, as she appeared before her sister in the old wallsteads, "my mind's oneasy about them twa' red shawls that's in the basket. Matty Hunter and Jane Taggart paid me for them, an' I bought them wi' their money, Friday was eight days. Gie them the shawls the morrow. An' old Mosey McCorkell gied me the price o' a wiley coat; it's in under the other things in the basket. An' now farewell; I can get to my rest."

"Grace, Grace, bide a wee minute," cried the faithful sister, as the dear voice grew fainter, and the dear face began to fade—"Grace, darling! Thady? The children? One word mair!" but neither cries nor tears could further detain the spirit hastening to its rest!

A LEGEND OF TYRONE.

ELLEN O'LEARY.

CROUCHED round a bare hearth in hard, frosty weather,
Three lonely helpless weans cling close together;
Tangled those gold locks, once bonnie and bright—
There's no one to fondle the baby to-night.

"My mammie I want; oh! my mammie I want!"
The big tears stream down with the low wailing chant.
Sweet Eily's slight arms enfold the gold head:
"Poor weeny Willie, sure mammie is dead—

And daddie is crazy from drinking all day—
Come down, holy angels, and take us away!"
Eily and Eddie keep kissing and crying—
Outside, the weird winds are sobbing and sighing.

All in a moment the children are still,
Only a quick coo of gladness from Will.
The sheeling no longer seems empty or bare,
For, clothed in soft raiment, the mother stands there.

They gather around her, they cling to her dress;
She rains down soft kisses for each shy caress.
Her light, loving touches smooth out tangled locks,
And, pressed to her bosom, the baby she rocks.

He lies in his cot, there's a fire on the hearth;
To Eily and Eddy 'tis heaven on earth,
For mother's deft fingers have been everywhere;
She lulls them to rest in the low *suggaun** chair.

They gaze open-eyed, then the eyes gently close,
As petals fold into the heart of a rose,
But ope soon again in awe, love, but no fear,
And fondly they murmur, " Our mammie is here."

She lays them down softly, she wraps them around;
They lie in sweet slumbers, she starts at a sound,
The cock loudly crows, and the spirit's away—
The drunkard steals in at the dawning of day.

Again and again, 'tween the dark and the dawn,
Glides in the dead mother to nurse Willie Bawn:
Or is it an angel who sits by the hearth?
An angel in heaven, a mother on earth.

* Chair made of twisted straw ropes.

THE BLACK LAMB.*

LADY WILDE.

IT is a custom amongst the people, when throwing away water at night, to cry out in a loud voice, "Take care of the water;" or literally, from the Irish, "Away with yourself from the water"—for they say that the spirits of the dead last buried are then wandering about, and it would be dangerous if the water fell on them.

One dark night a woman suddenly threw out a pail of boiling water without thinking of the warning words. Instantly a cry was heard, as of a person in pain, but no one was seen. However, the next night a black lamb entered the house, having the back all fresh scalded, and it lay down moaning by the hearth and died. Then they all knew that this was the spirit that had been scalded by the woman, and they carried the dead lamb out reverently, and buried it deep in the earth. Yet every night at the same hour it walked again into the house, and lay down, moaned, and died; and after this had happened many times, the priest was sent for, and finally, by the strength of his exorcism, the spirit of the dead was laid to rest; the black lamb appeared no more. Neither was the body of the dead lamb found in the grave when they searched for it, though it had been laid by their own hands deep in the earth, and covered with clay.

SONG OF THE GHOST.

ALFRED PERCIVAL GRAVES.

WHEN all were dreaming
    But Pastheen Power,
A light came streaming
    Beneath her bower:

* *Ancient Legends of Ireland.*

A heavy foot
   At her door delayed,
A heavy hand
   On the latch was laid.

"Now who dare venture,
   At this dark hour,
Unbid to enter
   My maiden bower?"
"Dear Pastheen, open
   The door to me,
And your true lover
   You'll surely see."

"My own true lover,
   So tall and brave,
Lives exiled over
   The angry wave."
"Your true love's body
   Lies on the bier,
His faithful spirit
   Is with you here."

"His look was cheerful,
   His voice was gay;
You speech is fearful,
   Your face is grey;
And sad and sunken
   Your eye of blue,
But Patrick, Patrick,
   Alas! 'tis you!"

Ere dawn was breaking
   She heard below
The two cocks shaking
   Their wings to crow.

"Oh, hush you, hush you,
    Both red and grey,
Or you will hurry
    My love away.

"Oh, hush your crowing,
    Both grey and red,
Or he'll be going
    To join the dead ;
Or, cease from calling
    His ghost to the mould,
And I'll come crowning
    Your combs with gold."

When all were dreaming
    But Pastheen Power,
A light went streaming
    From out her bower ;
And on the morrow,
    When they awoke,
They knew that sorrow
    Her heart had broke.

THE RADIANT BOY.

MRS. CROW.

CAPTAIN STEWART, afterwards Lord Castlereagh, when he
was a young man, happened to be quartered in Ireland. He
was fond of sport, and one day the pursuit of game carried
him so far that he lost his way. The weather, too, had
become very rough, and in this strait he presented himself
at the door of a gentleman's house, and sending in his card,
requested shelter for the night. The hospitality of the Irish
country gentry is proverbial ; the master of the house
received him warmly ; said he feared he could not make

him so comfortable as he could have wished, his house being full of visitors already, added to which, some strangers, driven by the inclemency of the night, had sought shelter before him, but such accommodation as he could give he was heartily welcome to; whereupon he called his butler, and committing the guest to his good offices, told him he must put him up somewhere, and do the best he could for him. There was no lady, the gentleman being a widower.

Captain Stewart found the house crammed, and a very jolly party it was. His host invited him to stay, and promised him good shooting if he would prolong his visit a few days: and, in fine, he thought himself extremely fortunate to have fallen into such pleasant quarters.

At length, after an agreeable evening, they all retired to bed, and the butler conducted him to a large room, almost divested of furniture, but with a blazing turf fire in the grate, and a shake-down on the floor, composed of cloaks and other heterogeneous materials.

Nevertheless, to the tired limbs of Captain Stewart, who had had a hard day's shooting, it looked very inviting; but before he lay down, he thought it advisable to take off some of the fire, which was blazing up the chimney in what he thought an alarming manner. Having done this, he stretched himself on his couch and soon fell asleep.

He believed he had slept about a couple of hours when he awoke suddenly, and was startled by such a vivid light in the room that he thought it on fire, but on turning to look at the grate he saw the fire was out, though it was from the chimney the light proceeded. He sat up in bed, trying to discover what it was, when he perceived the form of a beautiful naked boy, surrounded by a dazzling radiance. The boy looked at him earnestly, and then the vision faded, and all was dark. Captain Stewart, so far from supposing what he had seen to be of a spiritual nature, had no doubt that the host, or the visitors, had been trying to frighten him. Accordingly, he felt indignant at the liberty, and on the following morning, when he appeared at breakfast, he took care to evince his displeasure by the reserve of his demeanour, and by announcing his intention to depart immediately. The host expostulated, reminding him of his promise to stay and shoot. Captain Stewart coldly excused himself, and, at length, the gentleman seeing something was wrong, took him aside, and pressed for an explanation; whereupon Captain Stewart, without entering into particulars, said he had been made the victim of a sort of practical joking that he thought quite unwarrantable with a stranger.

The gentleman considered this not impossible amongst a parcel of thoughtless young men, and appealed to them to make an apology; but one and all, on honour, denied the impeachment. Suddenly a thought seemed to strike him; he clapt his hand to his forehead, uttered an exclamation, and rang the bell.

"Hamilton," said he to the butler; "where did Captain Stewart sleep last night?"

"Well, sir," replied the man; "you know every place was full—the gentlemen were lying on the floor, three or four in a room—so I gave him the *Boy's Room;* but I lit a blazing fire to keep him from coming out."

"You were very wrong," said the host; "you know I have positively forbidden you to put anyone there, and have taken the furniture out of the room to ensure its not being occupied." Then, retiring with Captain Stewart, he informed him, very gravely, of the nature of the phenomena he had seen; and at length, being pressed for further information, he confessed that there *existed* a tradition in the family, that whoever the "Radiant boy" appeared to will rise to the summit of power; and when he has reached the climax, will die a violent death, and I must say, he added, that the records that have been kept of his appearance go to confirm this persuasion.

THE FATE OF FRANK M'KENNA.

WILLIAM CARLETON.

THERE lived a man named M'Kenna at the hip of one of the mountainous hills which divide the county of Tyrone from that of Monaghan.   This M'Kenna had two sons, one of whom was in the habit of tracing hares of a Sunday, whenever there happened to be a fall of snow.   His father, it seems, had frequently remonstrated with him upon what he considered to be a violation of the Lord's day, as well as for his general neglect of mass.   The young man, however, though otherwise harmless and inoffensive, was in this matter quite insensible to paternal reproof, and continued to trace whenever the avocations of labour would allow him. It so happened that upon a Christmas morning, I think in the year 1814, there was a deep fall of snow, and young M'Kenna, instead of going to mass, got down his cockstick—which is a staff much thicker and heavier at one end than at the other—and prepared to set out on his favourite amusement.   His father, seeing this, reproved him seriously, and insisted that he should attend prayers.   His enthusiasm for the sport, however, was stronger than his love of religion, and he refused to be guided by his father's advice. The old man during the altercation got warm ; and on finding that the son obstinately scorned his authority, he knelt down and prayed that if the boy persisted in following his own will, he might never return from the mountains unless as a corpse.   The imprecation, which was certainly as harsh as it was impious and senseless, might have startled many a mind from a purpose that was, to say the least of it, at variance with religion and the respect due to a father. It had no effect, however, upon the son, who is said to have replied, that whether he ever returned or not, he was determined on going ; and go accordingly he did.   He was not, however, alone, for it appears that three or four of the neighbouring young men accompanied him.   Whether their sport was good or otherwise, is not to the purpose, neither am I able to say ; but the story goes that towards the latter part of the day they started a larger and darker hare than any they had ever seen, and that she kept dodging on before them bit by bit, leading them to suppose that every succeeding cast of the cock-stick would bring her down. It was observed afterwards that she also led them into the recesses of the mountains, and that although they tried to turn her course homewards, they could not succeed in doing so. As evening advanced, the companions of M'Kenna began to feel the folly of pursuing her farther, and to perceive the danger of losing their way in the mountains should night or a snow-storm come upon them. They therefore proposed to give over the chase and return home ; but M'Kenna would not hear of it. "If you wish to go home, you may," said he ; "as for me, I'll never leave the hills till I have her with me." They begged and entreated of him to desist and return, but all to no purpose : he appeared to be what the Scotch call *fey*—that is, to act as if he were moved by some impulse that leads to death, and from the influence of which a man cannot withdraw himself. At length, on finding him invincibly obstinate, they left him pursuing the hare directly into the heart of the mountains, and returned to their respective homes.

In the meantime one of the most terrible snow-storms ever remembered in that part of the country came on, and the consequence was, that the self-willed young man, who had equally trampled on the sanctities of religion and parental authority, was given over for lost. As soon as the tempest became still, the neighbours assembled in a body and proceeded to look for him. The snow, however, had fallen so heavily that not a single mark of a footstep could be seen. Nothing but one wide waste of white undulating hills met the eye wherever it turned, and of M'Kenna no trace whatever was visible or could be found. His father, now remembering the unnatural character of his imprecation, was nearly distracted ; for although the body had not yet been found, still by every one who witnessed the sudden rage of the storm and who knew the mountains, escape or survival was felt to be impossible. Every day for about a week large parties were out among the hill-ranges seeking him, but to no purpose. At length there came a thaw, and his body was found on a snow-wreath, lying in a supine posture within a circle which he had drawn around him with his cock-stick. His prayer-book lay opened upon his mouth, and his hat was pulled down so as to cover it and his face. It is unnecessary to say that the rumour of his death, and of the circumstances under which he left home, created a most extraordinary sensation in the country—a sensation that was the greater in proportion to the uncertainty occasioned by his not having been found either alive or dead. Some affirmed that he had crossed the mountains, and was seen in Monaghan; others, that he had been seen in Clones, in Emyvale, in Five-mile-town; but despite of all these agreeable reports, the melancholy truth was at length made clear by the appearance of the body as just stated.

Now, it so happened that the house nearest the spot where he lay was inhabited by a man named Daly, I think —but of the name I am not certain—who was a herd or care-taker to Dr. Porter, then Bishop of Clogher. The situation of this house was the most lonely and desolate-looking that could be imagined. It was at least two miles distant from any human habitation, being surrounded by one wide and dreary waste of dark moor. By this house lay the route of those who had found the corpse, and I believe the door of it was borrowed for the purpose of conveying it home. Be this as it may, the family witnessed the melancholy procession as it passed slowly through the mountains, and when the place and circumstances are all considered, we may admit that to ignorant and superstitious people, whose minds, even upon ordinary occasions, were strongly affected by such matters, it was a sight calculated to leave behind it a deep, if not a terrible impression. Time soon proved that it did so.

An incident is said to have occurred at the funeral in fine keeping with the wild spirit of the whole melancholy event.

When the procession had advanced to a place called Mullaghtinny, a large dark-coloured hare, which was instantly recognised, by those who had been out with him on the hills, as the identical one that led him to his fate, is said to have crossed the roads about twenty yards or so before the coffin. The story goes, that a man struck it on the side with a stone, and that the blow, which would have killed any ordinary hare, not only did it no injury, but occasioned a sound to proceed from the body resembling the hollow one emitted by an empty barrel when struck.

In the meantime the interment took place, and the sensation began, like every other, to die away in the natural progress of time, when, behold, a report ran abroad like wild-fire that, to use the language of the people, " Frank M'Kenna was *appearing!* "

One night, about a fortnight after his funeral, the daughter of Daly, the herd, a girl about fourteen, while lying in bed saw what appeared to be the likeness of M'Kenna, who had been lost. She screamed out, and covering her head with the bed-clothes, told her father and mother that Frank M'Kenna was in the house. This alarming intelligence naturally produced great terror; still, Daly, who, notwithstanding his belief in such matters, possessed a good deal of moral courage, was cool enough to rise and examine the house, which consisted of only one apartment. This gave the daughter some courage, who, on finding that her father could not see him, ventured to look out, and she *then* could see nothing of him herself. She very soon fell asleep, and her father attributed what she saw to fear, or some accidental combination of shadows proceeding from the furniture, for it was a clear moonlight night. The light of the following day dispelled a great deal of their apprehensions, and comparatively little was thought of it until evening again advanced, when the fears of the daughter began to return. They appeared to be prophetic, for she said when night came that she knew he would appear again; and accordingly at the same hour he did so. This was repeated for several successive nights, until the girl, from the very hardihood of terror, began to become so far familiarised to the spectre as to venture to address it.

"In the name of God!" she asked, "what is troubling you, or why do you appear to me instead of to some of your own family or relations?"

The ghost's answer alone might settle the question involved in the authenticity of its appearance, being, as it was, an account of one of the most ludicrous missions that ever a spirit was despatched upon.

"I'm not allowed," said he, "to spake to any of my friends, for I parted wid them in anger; but I'm come to tell you that they are quarrelin' about my breeches—a new pair that I got made for Christmas day; an' as I was comin' up to thrace in the mountains, I thought the ould one 'ud do betther, an' of coorse I didn't put the new pair an me. My raison for appearin'," he added, "is, that you may tell my friends that none of them is to wear them—they must be given in charity."

This serious and solemn intimation from the ghost was duly communicated to the family, and it was found that the circumstances were exactly as it had represented them. This, of course, was considered as sufficient proof of the truth of its mission. Their conversations now became not only frequent, but quite friendly and familiar. The girl became a favourite with the spectre, and the spectre, on the other hand, soon lost all his terrors in her eyes. He told her that whilst his friends were bearing home his body, the handspikes or poles on which they carried him had cut his back, and *occasioned him great pain!* The cutting of the back also was known to be true, and strengthened, of course, the truth and authenticity of their dialogues. The whole neighbourhood was now in a commotion with this story of the apparition, and persons incited by curiosity began to visit the girl in order to satisfy themselves of the truth of what they had heard. Everything, however, was corroborated, and the child herself, without any symptoms of anxiety or terror, artlessly related her conversations with the spirit.   Hitherto their interviews had been all nocturnal, but now that the ghost found his footing made good, he put a hardy face on, and ventured to appear by daylight. The girl also fell into states of syncope, and while the fits lasted, long conversations with him upon the subject of God, the blessed Virgin, and Heaven, took place between them.   He was certainly an excellent moralist, and gave the best advice.   Swearing, drunkenness, theft, and every evil propensity of our nature, were declaimed against with a degree of spectral eloquence quite surprising.   Common fame had now a topic dear to her heart, and never was a ghost made more of by his best friends than she made of him.   The whole country was in a tumult, and I well remember the crowds which flocked to the lonely little cabin in the mountains, now the scene of matters so interesting and important.   Not a single day passed in which I should think from ten to twenty, thirty, or fifty persons, were not present at these singular interviews. Nothing else was talked of, thought of, and, as I can well testify, dreamt of.   I would myself have gone to Daly's were it not for a confounded misgiving I had, that perhaps the ghost might take such a fancy of appearing to *me*, as he had taken to cultivate an intimacy with the girl ; and it so happens, that when I see the face of an individual nailed down in the coffin—chilling and gloomy operation !—I experience no particular wish to look upon it again.

The spot where the body of M'Kenna was found is now marked by a little heap of stones, which has been collected since the melancholy event of his death.   Every person who passes it throws a stone upon the heap ; but why this old custom is practised, or what it means, I do not know, unless it be simply to mark the spot as a visible means of preserving the memory of the occurrence.

Daly's house, the scene of the supposed apparition, is now a shapeless ruin, which could scarcely be seen were it not for the green spot that once was a garden, and which now shines at a distance like an emerald, but with no agreeable or pleasing associations.   It is a spot which no solitary schoolboy will ever visit, nor indeed would the unflinching believer in the popular nonsense of ghosts wish to pass it without a companion. It is, under any circumstances, a gloomy and barren place; but when looked upon in connection with what we have just recited, it is lonely, desolate, and awful.

WITCHES, FAIRY DOCTORS.

WITCHES and fairy doctors receive their power from opposite dynasties; the witch from evil spirits and her own malignant will; the fairy doctor from the fairies, and a something—a temperament—that is born with him or her. The first is always feared and hated. The second is gone to for advice, and is never worse than mischievous. The most celebrated fairy doctors are sometimes people the fairies loved and carried away, and kept with them for seven years; not that those the fairies' love are always carried off—they may merely grow silent and strange, and take to lonely wanderings in the "gentle" places. Such will, in after-times, be great poets or musicians, or fairy doctors; they must not be confused with those who have a *Lianhaun shee* [*leannán-sidhe*], for the *Lianhaun shee* lives upon the vitals of its chosen, and they waste and die. She is of the dreadful solitary fairies. To her have belonged the greatest of the Irish poets, from Oisin down to the last century.

Those we speak of have for their friends the trooping fairies—the gay and sociable populace of raths and caves. Great is their knowledge of herbs and spices. These doctors, when the butter will not come on the milk, or the milk will not come from the cow, will be sent for to find out if the cause be in the course of common nature or if there has been witchcraft. Perhaps some old hag in the shape of a hare has been milking the cattle. Perhaps some user of "the dead hand" has drawn away the butter to her own churn. Whatever it be, there is the counter-charm. They will give advice, too, in cases of suspected changelings, and prescribe for the "fairy blast" (when the fairy strikes any one a tumour rises, or they become paralysed. This is called a "fairy blast" or a "fairy stroke").

The fairies are, of course, visible to them, and many a new-built house have they bid the owner pull down because it lay on the fairies' road.   Lady Wilde thus describes one who lived in Innis Sark :—" He never touched beer, spirits, or meat in all his life, but has lived entirely on bread, fruit, and vegetables. A man who knew him thus describes him—'Winter and summer his dress is the same—merely a flannel shirt and coat.   He will pay his share at a feast, but neither eats nor drinks of the food and drink set before him.   He speaks no English, and never could be made to learn the English tongue, though he says it might be used with great effect to curse one's enemy. He holds a burial-ground sacred, and would not carry away so much as a leaf of ivy from a grave.   And he maintains that the people are right to keep to their ancient usages, such as never to dig a grave on a Monday, and to carry the coffin three times round the grave, following the course of the sun, for then the dead rest in peace.   Like the people, also, he holds suicides as accursed ; for they believe that all its dead turn over on their faces if a suicide is laid amongst them.

" 'Though well off, he never, even in his youth, thought of taking a wife ; nor was he ever known to love a woman.   He stands quite apart from life, and by this means holds his power over the mysteries.   No money will tempt him to impart his know ledge to another, for if he did he would be struck dead—so he believes.   He would not touch a hazel stick, but carries an ash wand, which he holds in his hand when he prays, laid across his knees ; and the whole of his life is devoted to works of grace and charity, and though now an old man, he has never had a day's sickness.   No one has ever seen him in a rage, nor heard an angry word from his lips but once, and then being under great irritation, he recited the Lord's Prayer backwards as an imprecation on his enemy.   Before his death he will reveal the mystery of his power, but not till the hand of death is on him for certain.'   When he does reveal it, we may be sure it will be to one person only—his successor.   There are several such doctors in County Sligo, really well up in herbal medicine by all accounts, and my friends find them in their own counties.

All these things go on merrily.   The spirit of the age laughs in
vain, and is itself only a ripple to pass, or already passing,
away."

The spells of the witch are altogether different ; they smell of
the grave.   One of the most powerful is the charm of the dead
hand.   With a hand cut from a corpse they, muttering words
of power, will stir a well and skim from its surface a neighbour's
butter.

A candle held between the fingers of the dead hand can
never be blown out.   This is useful to robbers, but they appeal
for the suffrage of the lovers likewise, for they can make love-
potions by drying and grinding into powder the liver of a black
cat.   Mixed with tea, and poured from a black teapot, it is
infallible.   There are many stories of its success in quite recent
years, but, unhappily, the spell must be continually renewed, or
all the love may turn into hate.   But the central notion of
witchcraft everywhere is the power to change into some fictitious
form, usually in Ireland a hare or a cat.   Long ago a wolf was
the favourite.   Before Giraldus Cambrensis came to Ireland,
a monk wandering in a forest at night came upon two wolves,
one of whom was dying.   The other entreated him to give the
dying wolf the last sacrament.   He said the mass, and paused
when he came to the viaticum.   The other, on seeing this, tore
the skin from the breast of the dying wolf, laying bare the form
of an old woman.   Thereon the monk gave the sacrament.
Years afterwards he confessed the matter, and when Giraldus
visited the country, was being tried by the synod of the bishops.
To give the sacrament to an animal was a great sin.   Was it a
human being or an animal ?   On the advice of Giraldus they
sent the monk, with papers describing the matter, to the Pope
for his decision.   The result is not stated.

Giraldus himself was of opinion that the wolf-form was an
illusion, for, as he argued, only God can change the form.   His
opinion coincides with tradition, Irish and otherwise.

It is the notion of many who have written about these things
that magic is mainly the making of such illusions.   Patrick
Kennedy tells a story of a girl who, having in her hand a sod of

AN OLD HAG WITCH.

A FAIRY MUSICIAN.

grass containing, unknown to herself, a four-leaved shamrock, watched a conjurer at a fair. Now, the four-leaved shamrock guards its owner from all *pishogues* (spells), and when the others were staring at a cock carrying along the roof of a shed a huge beam in its bill, she asked them what they found to wonder at in a cock with a straw. The conjurer begged from her the sod of grass, to give to his horse, he said. Immediately she cried out in terror that the beam would fall and kill somebody.

This, then, is to be remembered—the form of an enchanted thing is a fiction and a caprice.

BEWITCHED BUTTER (DONEGAL).

MISS LETITIA MACLINTOCK.

NOT far from Rathmullen lived, last spring, a family called Hanlon ; and in a farm-house, some fields distant, people named Dogherty. Both families had good cows, but the Hanlons were fortunate in possessing a Kerry cow that gave more milk and yellower butter that the others.

Grace Dogherty, a young girl, who was more admired than loved in the neighbourhood, took much interest in the Kerry cow, and appeared one night at Mrs. Hanlon's door with the modest request—

"Will you let me milk your Moiley cow ? "

"An' why wad you wish to milk wee Moiley, Grace, dear ? " inquired Mrs. Hanlon.

"Oh, just becase you're sae throng at the present time."

"Thank you kindly, Grace, but I'm no too throng to do my ain work. I'll no trouble you to milk."

The girl turned away with a discontented air ; but the next evening, and the next, found her at the cow-house door with the same request.

At length Mrs. Hanlon, not knowing well how to persist in her refusal, yielded, and permitted Grace to milk the Kerry cow.

She soon had reason to regret her want of firmness. Moiley gave no more milk to her owner.

When this melancholy state of things lasted for three days, the Hanlons applied to a certain Mark McCarrion, who lived near Binion.

"That cow has been milked by someone with an evil eye," said he. "Will she give you a wee drop, do you think? The full of a pint measure wad do."

"Oh, ay, Mark, dear; I'll get that much milk frae her, any way."

"Weel, Mrs. Hanlon, lock the door, an' get nine new pins that was never used in clothes, an' put them into a saucepan wi' the pint o' milk. Set them on the fire, an' let them come to the boil."

The nine pins soon began to simmer in Moiley's* milk.

Rapid steps were heard approaching the door, agitated knocks followed, and Grace Dogherty's high-toned voice was raised in eager entreaty.

"Let me in, Mrs. Hanlon!" she cried. "Tak off that cruel pot! Tak out them pins, for they're pricking holes in my heart, an' I'll never offer to touch milk of yours again."

[There is hardly a village in Ireland where the milk is not thus believed to have been stolen times upon times. There are many counter-charms. Sometimes the coulter of a plough will be heated red-hot, and the witch will rush in, crying out that she is burning. A new horse-shoe or donkey-shoe, heated and put under the churn, with three straws, if possible, stolen at midnight from over the witches' door, is quite infallible.—ED.]

* In Connaught called a "mweeal" cow—*i.e.*, a cow without horns. Irish *maol*, literally, blunt. When the new hammerless breech-loaders came into use two or three years ago, Mr. Douglas Hyde, a Connaught gentleman, spoke of them as the "mweeal" guns, because they had no cocks.

A QUEEN'S COUNTY WITCH *

IT was about eighty years ago, in the month of May, that a Roman Catholic clergyman, near Rathdowney, in the Queen's County, was awakened at midnight to attend a dying man in a distant part of the parish. The priest obeyed without a murmur, and having performed his duty to the expiring sinner, saw him depart this world before he left the cabin. As it was yet dark, the man who had called on the priest offered to accompany him home, but he refused, and set forward on his journey alone. The grey dawn began to appear over the hills. The good priest was highly enraptured with the beauty of the scene, and rode on, now gazing intently at every surrounding object, and again cutting with his whip at the bats and big beautiful night-flies which flitted ever and anon from hedge to hedge across his lonely way. Thus engaged, he journeyed on slowly, until the nearer approach of sunrise began to render objects completely discernible, when he dismounted from his horse, and slipping his arm out of the rein, and drawing forth his "Breviary" from his pocket, he commenced reading his "morning office" as he walked leisurely along.

He had not proceeded very far, when he observed his horse, a very spirited animal, endeavouring to stop on the road, and gazing intently into a field on one side of the way where there were three or four cows grazing. However, he did not pay any particular attention to this circumstance, but went on a little farther, when the horse suddenly plunged with great violence, and endeavoured to break away by force. The priest with great difficulty succeeded in restraining him, and, looking at him more closely, observed him shaking from head to foot, and sweating profusely. He now stood calmly, and refused to move from where he was, nor could threats or entreaty induce him to proceed. The father was greatly astonished, but recollecting to have often heard of horses labouring under affright being induced to go by

blindfolding them, he took out his handkerchief and tied it
across his eyes. He then mounted, and, striking him gently,
he went forward without reluctance, but still sweating and
trembling violently. They had not gone far, when they
arrived opposite a narrow path or bridle-way, flanked at either
side by a tall, thick hedge, which led from the high road to
the field where the cows were grazing. The priest happened
by chance to look into the lane, and saw a spectacle which
made the blood curdle in his veins. It was the legs of a
man from the hips downwards, without head or body, trot-
ting up the avenue at a smart pace. The good father was
very much alarmed, but, being a man of strong nerve,
he resolved, come what might, to stand, and be further
acquainted with this singular spectre. He accordingly stood,
and so did the headless apparition, as if afraid to approach
him. The priest, observing this, pulled back a little from
the entrance of the avenue, and the phantom again resumed
its progress. It soon arrived on the road, and the priest now
had sufficient opportunity to view it minutely. It wore yellow
buckskin breeches, tightly fastened at the knees with green
ribbon ; it had neither shoes nor stockings on, and its legs
were covered with long, red hairs, and all full of wet, blood,
and clay, apparently contracted in its progress through the
thorny hedges. The priest, although very much alarmed,
felt eager to examine the phantom, and for this purpose
summoned all his philosophy to enable him to speak to it.
The ghost was now a little ahead, pursuing its march at its
usual brisk trot, and the priest urged on his horse speedily
until he came up with it, and thus addressed it—

" Hilloa, friend ! who art thou, or whither art thou going
so early ? "

The hideous spectre made no reply, but uttered a fierce
and superhuman growl, or "Umph."

" A fine morning for ghosts to wander abroad," again said
the priest.

Another " Umph " was the reply

" Why don't you speak ? "

" Umph."

"You don't seem disposed to be very loquacious this morning."

"Umph," again.

The good man began to feel irritated at the obstinate silence of his unearthly visitor, and said, with some warmth—

"In the name of all that's sacred, I command you to answer me, Who art thou, or where art thou travelling?"

Another "Umph," more loud and more angry than before, was the only reply.

"Perhaps," said the father," "a taste of whipcord might render you a little more communicative;" and so saying, he struck the apparition a heavy blow with his whip on the breech.

The phantom uttered a wild and unearthly yell, and fell forward on the road, and what was the priest's astonishment when he perceived the whole place running over with milk. He was struck dumb with amazement; the prostrate phantom still continued to eject vast quantities of milk from every part; the priest's head swam, his eyes got dizzy; a stupor came all over him for some minutes, and on his recovering, the frightful spectre had vanished, and in its stead he found stretched on the road, and half drowned in milk, the form of Sarah Kennedy, an old woman of the neighbourhood, who had been long notorious in that district for her witchcraft and superstitious practices, and it was now discovered that she had, by infernal aid, assumed that monstrous shape, and was employed that morning in sucking the cows of the village. Had a volcano burst forth at his feet, he could not be more astonished; he gazed awhile in silent amazement—the old woman groaning, and writhing convulsively.

"Sarah," said he, at length, "I have long admonished you to repent of your evil ways, but you were deaf to my entreaties; and now, wretched woman, you are surprised in the midst of your crimes."

"Oh, father, father," shouted the unfortunate woman, "can you do nothing to save me? I am lost; hell is open for me, and legions of devils surround me this moment, waiting to carry my soul to perdition."

The priest had not power to reply; the old wretch's pains increased; her body swelled to an immense size; her eyes flashed as if on fire, her face was black as night, her entire form writhed in a thousand different contortions; her outcries were appalling, her face sunk, her eyes closed, and in a few minutes she expired in the most exquisite tortures.

The priest departed homewards, and called at the next cabin to give notice of the strange circumstances. The remains of Sarah Kennedy were removed to her cabin, situate at the edge of a small wood at a little distance. She had long been a resident in that neighbourhood, but still she was a stranger, and came there no one knew from whence. She had no relation in that country but one daughter, now advanced in years, who resided with her. She kept one cow, but sold more butter, it was said, than any farmer in the parish, and it was generally suspected that she acquired it by devilish agency, as she never made a secret of being intimately acquainted with sorcery and fairyism. She professed the Roman Catholic religion, but never complied with the practices enjoined by that church, and her remains were denied Christian sepulture, and were buried in a sand-pit near her own cabin.

On the evening of her burial, the villagers assembled and burned her cabin to the earth. Her daughter made her escape, and never after returned.

THE WITCH HARE.

MR. AND MRS. S. C. HALL.

I WAS out thracking hares meeself, and I seen a fine puss of a thing hopping, hopping in the moonlight, and whacking her ears about, now up, now down, and winking her great eyes, and—" Here goes," says I, and the thing was so close to me that she turned round and looked at me, and then bounced back, as well as to say, do your worst! So I had the least grain in life of *blessed powder* left, and I put it in the gun—and bang at her! My jewel, the scritch she gave would frighten a rigment, and a mist, like, came betwixt me and her, and I seen her no more; but when the mist wint off I saw blood on the spot where she had been, and I followed its track, and at last it led me—whist, whisper—right up to Katey MacShane's door; and when I was at the thrashold, I heerd a murnin' within, a great murnin', and a groanin', and I opened the door, and there she was herself, sittin' quite content in the shape of a woman, and the black cat that was sittin' by her rose up its back and spit at me; but I went on never heedin', and asked the ould —— how she was and what ailed her.

"Nothing," sis she.

"What's that on the floor?" sis I.

"Oh," she says, "I was cuttin' a billet of wood," she says, "wid the reaping hook," she says, "an' I've wounded meself in the leg," she says, "and that's drops of my precious blood," she says.

BEWITCHED BUTTER (QUEEN'S COUNTY).*

ABOUT the commencement of the last century there lived in the vicinity of the once famous village of Aghavoe† a wealthy farmer, named Bryan Costigan. This man kept an extensive dairy and a great many milch cows, and every

---

* *Dublin University Magazine*, 1839.

† *Aghavoe*—"the field of kine"—a beautiful and romantic village near Borris-in-Ossory, in the Queen's County. It was once a place of considerable importance, and for centuries the episcopal seat of the diocese of Ossory, but for ages back it has gone to decay, and is now remarkable for nothing but the magnificent ruins of a priory of the Dominicans, erected here at an early period by St. Canice, the patron saint of Ossory.

year made considerable sums by the sale of milk and butter.
The luxuriance of the pasture lands in this neighbourhood
has always been proverbial; and, consequently, Bryan's
cows were the finest and most productive in the country,
and his milk and butter the richest and sweetest, and
brought the highest price at every market at which he offered
these articles for sale.

Things continued to go on thus prosperously with Bryan
Costigan, when, one season, all at once, he found his cattle
declining in appearance, and his dairy almost entirely profit-
less. Bryan, at first, attributed this change to the weather,
or some such cause, but soon found or fancied reasons to
assign it to a far different source. The cows, without any
visible disorder, daily declined, and were scarcely able to
crawl about on their pasture: many of them, instead of milk,
gave nothing but blood; and the scanty quantity of milk
which some of them continued to supply was so bitter that
even the pigs would not drink it; whilst the butter which it
produced was of such a bad quality, and stunk so horribly,
that the very dogs would not eat it. Bryan applied for
remedies to all the quacks and "fairy-women" in the
country—but in vain. Many of the impostors declared that
the mysterious malady in his cattle went beyond *their* skill;
whilst others, although they found no difficulty in tracing it
to superhuman agency, declared that they had no control in
the matter, as the charm under the influence of which his
property was made away with, was too powerful to be dissolved by anything less than the special interposition of
Divine Providence. The poor farmer became almost distracted; he saw ruin staring him in the face; yet what was
he to do? Sell his cattle and purchase others! No; that
was out of the question, as they looked so miserable and
emaciated, that no one would even take them as a present,
whilst it was also impossible to sell to a butcher, as the flesh
of one which he killed for his own family was as black as a
coal, and stunk like any putrid carrion.

The unfortunate man was thus completely bewildered.
He knew not what to do; he became moody and stupid;

his sleep forsook him by night, and all day he wandered
about the fields, amongst his "fairy-stricken" cattle like a
maniac.

Affairs continued in this plight, when one very sultry
evening in the latter days of July, Bryan Costigan's wife was
sitting at her own door, spinning at her wheel, in a very
gloomy and agitated state of mind.   Happening to look
down the narrow green lane which led from the high road
to her cabin, she espied a little old woman barefoot, and
enveloped in an old scarlet cloak, approaching slowly, with
the aid of a crutch which she carried in one hand, and a
cane or walking-stick in the other.   The farmer's wife felt
glad at seeing the odd-looking stranger; she smiled, and
yet she knew not why, as she neared the house.   A vague
and indefinable feeling of pleasure crowded on her imagination; and, as the old woman gained the threshold, she bade
her "welcome" with a warmth which plainly told that her
lips gave utterance but to the genuine feelings of her heart.

"God bless this good house and all belonging to it," said
the stranger as she entered.

"God save you kindly, and you are welcome, whoever
you are," replied Mrs. Costigan.

"Hem, I thought so," said the old woman with a signi-
ficant grin.   "I thought so, or I wouldn't trouble you."

The farmer's wife ran, and placed a chair near the fire for
the stranger; but she refused, and sat on the ground near
where Mrs. C. had been spinning.   Mrs. Costigan had now
time to survey the old hag's person minutely.   She appeared
of great age; her countenance was extremely ugly and
repulsive; her skin was rough and deeply embrowned as if
from long exposure to the effects of some tropical climate;
her forehead was low, narrow, and indented with a thousand
wrinkles; her long grey hair fell in matted elf-locks from
beneath a white linen skull-cap; her eyes were bleared,
blood-shotten, and obliquely set in their sockets, and her
voice was croaking, tremulous, and, at times, partially
inarticulate.   As she squatted on the floor, she looked round
the house with an inquisitive gaze; she peered pryingly

from corner to corner, with an earnestness of look, as if she had the faculty, like the Argonaut of old, to see through the very depths of the earth, whilst Mrs. C. kept watching her motions with mingled feelings of curiosity, awe, and pleasure.

"Mrs.," said the old woman, at length breaking silence, "I am dry with the heat of the day; can you give me a drink?"

"Alas!" replied the farmer's wife, "I have no drink to offer you except water, else you would have no occasion to ask me for it."

"Are you not the owner of the cattle I see yonder?" said the old hag, with a tone of voice and manner of gesticulation which plainly indicated her foreknowledge of the fact.

Mrs. Costigan replied in the affirmative, and briefly related to her every circumstance connected with the affair, whilst the old woman still remained silent, but shook her grey head repeatedly; and still continued gazing round the house with an air of importance and self-sufficiency.

When Mrs. C. had ended, the old hag remained a while as if in a deep reverie : at length she said—

"Have you any of the milk in the house?"

"I have," replied the other.

"Show me some of it."

She filled a jug from a vessel and handed it to the old sybil, who smelled it, then tasted it, and spat out what she had taken on the floor.

"Where is your husband?" she asked.

"Out in the fields," was the reply.

"I must see him."

A messenger was despatched for Bryan, who shortly after made his appearance.

"Neighbour," said the stranger, "your wife informs me that your cattle are going against you this season."

"She informs you right," said Bryan.

"And why have you not sought a cure?"

"A cure!" re-echoed the man; "why, woman, I have sought cures until I was heart-broken, and all in vain ; they get worse every day."

"What will you give me if I cure them for you?"

"Anything in our power," replied Bryan and his wife, both speaking joyfully, and with a breath.

"All I will ask from you is a silver sixpence, and that you will do everything which I will bid you," said she.

The farmer and his wife seemed astonished at the moderation of her demand. They offered her a large sum of money.

"No," said she, "I don't want your money; I am no cheat, and I would not even take sixpence, but that I can do nothing till I handle some of your silver."

The sixpence was immediately given her, and the most implicit obedience promised to her injunctions by both Bryan and his wife, who already began to regard the old beldame as their tutelary angel.

The hag pulled off a black silk ribbon or fillet which encircled her head inside her cap, and gave it to Bryan, saying—

"Go, now, and the first cow you touch with this ribbon, turn her into the yard, but be sure don't touch the second, nor speak a word until you return; be also careful not to let the ribbon touch the ground, for, if you do, all is over."

Bryan took the talismanic ribbon, and soon returned, driving a red cow before him.

The old hag went out, and, approaching the cow, commenced pulling hairs out of her tail, at the same time singing some verses in the Irish language in a low, wild, and unconnected strain. The cow appeared restive and uneasy, but the old witch still continued her mysterious chant until she had the ninth hair extracted. She then ordered the cow to be drove back to her pasture, and again entered the house.

"Go, now," said she to the woman, "and bring me some milk from every cow in your possession."

She went, and soon returned with a large pail filled with a frightful-looking mixture of milk, blood, and corrupt matter. The old woman got it into the churn, and made preparations for churning.

"Now," she said, "you both must churn, make fast the

door and windows, and let there be no light but from the fire ; do not open your lips until I desire you, and by observing my directions, I make no doubt but, ere the sun goes down, we will find out the infernal villain who is robbing you."

Bryan secured the doors and windows, and commenced churning. The old sorceress sat down by a blazing fire which had been specially lighted for the occasion, and commenced singing the same wild song which she had sung at the pulling of the cow-hairs, and after a little time she cast one of the nine hairs into the fire, still singing her mysterious strain, and watching, with intense interest, the witching process.

A loud cry, as if from a female in distress, was now heard approaching the house ; the old witch discontinued her incantations, and listened attentively. The crying voice approached the door.

" Open the door quickly," shouted the charmer.

Bryan unbarred the door, and all three rushed out in the yard, when they heard the same cry down the *boreheen*, but could see nothing.

" It is all over," shouted the old witch ; "something has gone amiss, and our charm for the present is ineffectual."

They now turned back quite crest-fallen, when, as they were entering the door, the sybil cast her eyes downwards, and perceiving a piece of horse-shoe nailed on the threshold,* she vociferated—

" Here I have it ; no wonder our charm was abortive. The person that was crying abroad is the villain who has your cattle bewitched ; I brought her to the house, but she was not able to come to the door on account of that horse-shoe. Remove it instantly, and we will try our luck again."

Bryan removed the horse-shoe from the doorway, and by

---

* It was once a common practice in Ireland to nail a piece of horse-shoe on the threshold of the door, as a preservative against the influence of the fairies, who, it is thought, dare not enter any house thus guarded. This custom, however, is much on the wane, but still it is prevalent in some of the more uncivilised districts of the country.

the hag's directions placed it on the floor under the churn, having previously reddened it in the fire.

They again resumed their manual operations. Bryan and his wife began to churn, and the witch again to sing her strange verses, and casting her cow-hairs into the fire until she had them all nearly exhausted. Her countenance now began to exhibit evident traces of vexation and disappointment. She got quite pale, her teeth gnashed, her hand trembled, and as she cast the ninth and last hair into the fire, her person exhibited more the appearance of a female demon than of a human being.

Once more the cry was heard, and an aged red-haired woman* was seen approaching the house quickly.

"Ho, ho!" roared the sorceress, "I knew it would be so; my charm has succeeded; my expectations are realised, and here she comes, the villain who has destroyed you."

"What are we to do now?" asked Bryan.

"Say nothing to her," said the hag; "give her whatever she demands, and leave the rest to me."

The woman advanced screeching vehemently, and Bryan went out to meet her. She was a neighbour, and she said that one of her best cows was drowning in a pool of water—that there was no one at home but herself, and she implored Bryan to go rescue the cow from destruction.

Bryan accompanied her without hesitation; and having rescued the cow from her perilous situation, was back again in a quarter of an hour.

It was now sunset, and Mrs. Costigan set about preparing supper.

During supper they reverted to the singular transactions of the day. The old witch uttered many a fiendish laugh at the success of her incantations, and inquired who was the woman whom they had so curiously discovered.

Bryan satisfied her in every particular. She was the wife of a neighbouring farmer; her name was Rachel Higgins; and she had been long suspected to be on familiar terms with the spirit of darkness. She had five or six cows;

* Red-haired people are thought to possess magic power.

but it was observed by her sapient neighbours that she sold more butter every year than other farmers' wives who had twenty. Bryan had, from the commencement of the decline in his cattle, suspected her for being the aggressor, but as he had no proof, he held his peace.

"Well," said the old beldame, with a grim smile, "it is not enough that we have merely discovered the robber; all is in vain, if we do not take steps to punish her for the past, as well as to prevent her inroads for the future."

"And how will that be done?" said Bryan.

"I will tell you; as soon as the hour of twelve o'clock arrives to-night, do you go to the pasture, and take a couple of swift-running dogs with you; conceal yourself in some place convenient to the cattle; watch them carefully; and if you see anything, whether man or beast, approach the cows, set on the dogs, and if possible make them draw the blood of the intruder; then ALL will be accomplished. If nothing approaches before sunrise, you may return, and we will try something else."

Convenient there lived the cow-herd of a neighbouring squire. He was a hardy, courageous young man, and always kept a pair of very ferocious bull-dogs. To him Bryan applied for assistance, and he cheerfully agreed to accompany him, and, moreover, proposed to fetch a couple of his master's best greyhounds, as his own dogs, although extremely fierce and bloodthirsty, could not be relied on for swiftness. He promised Bryan to be with him before twelve o'clock, and they parted.

Bryan did not seek sleep that night; he sat up anxiously awaiting the midnight hour. It arrived at last, and his friend, the herdsman, true to his promise, came at the time appointed. After some further admonitions from the *Collough*, they departed. Having arrived at the field, they consulted as to the best position they could chose for concealment. At last they pitched on a small brake of fern, situated at the extremity of the field, adjacent to the boundary ditch, which was thickly studded with large, old white-thorn bushes. Here they crouched themselves, and made the dogs, four in number, lie down beside them, eagerly expecting the appearance of their as yet unknown and mysterious visitor.

Here Bryan and his comrade continued a considerable time in nervous anxiety, still nothing approached, and it became manifest that morning was at hand; they were beginning to grow impatient, and were talking of returning home, when on a sudden they heard a rushing sound behind them, as if proceeding from something endeavouring to force a passage through the thick hedge in their rear. They looked in that direction, and judge of their astonishment, when they perceived a large hare in the act of springing from the ditch, and leaping on the ground quite near them. They were now convinced that this was the object which they had so impatiently expected, and they were resolved to watch her motions narrowly.

After arriving to the ground, she remained motionless for a few moments, looking around her sharply. She then began to skip and jump in a playful manner; now advancing at a smart pace towards the cows, and again retreating precipitately, but still drawing nearer and nearer at each sally. At length she advanced up to the next cow, and sucked her for a moment; then on to the next, and so respectively to every cow on the field—the cows all the time lowing loudly, and appearing extremely frightened and agitated. Bryan, from the moment the hare commenced sucking the first, was with difficulty restrained from attacking her; but his more sagacious companion suggested to him, that it was better to wait until she would have done, as she would then be much heavier, and more unable to effect her escape than at present. And so the issue proved; for being now done sucking them all, her belly appeared enormously distended, and she made her exit slowly and apparently with difficulty. She advanced towards the hedge where she had entered, and as she arrived just at the clump of ferns where her foes were couched, they started up with a fierce yell, and hallooed the dogs upon her path.

The hare started off at a brisk pace, squirting up the

milk she had sucked from her mouth and nostrils, and the dogs making after her rapidly. Rachel Higgins's cabin appeared, through the grey of the morning twilight, at a little distance; and it was evident that puss seemed bent on gaining it, although she made a considerable circuit through the fields in the rear. Bryan and his comrade, however, had their thoughts, and made towards the cabin by the shortest route, and had just arrived as the hare came up, panting and almost exhausted, and the dogs at her very scut. She ran round the house, evidently confused and disappointed at the presence of the men, but at length made for the door. In the bottom of the door was a small, semicircular aperture, resembling those cut in fowl house doors for the ingress and egress of poultry. To gain this hole, puss now made a last and desperate effort, and had succeeded in forcing her head and shoulders through it, when the foremost of the dogs made a spring and seized her violently by the haunch. She uttered a loud and piercing scream, and struggled desperately to free herself from his gripe, and at last succeeded, but not until she left a piece of her rump in his teeth. The men now burst open the door; a bright turf fire blazed on the hearth, and the whole floor was streaming with blood. No hare, however, could be found, and the men were more than ever convinced that it was old Rachel, who had, by the assistance of some demon, assumed the form of the hare, and they now determined to have her if she were over the earth. They entered the bed-room, and heard some smothered groaning, as if proceeding from some one in extreme agony. They went to the corner of the room from whence the moans proceeded, and there, beneath a bundle of freshly-cut rushes, found the form of Rachel Higgins, writhing in the most excruciating agony, and almost smothered in a pool of blood. The men were astounded; they addressed the wretched old woman, but she either could not, or would not answer them. Her wound still bled copiously; her tortures appeared to increase, and it was evident that she was dying. The aroused family thronged around her with cries and lamentations;

she did not seem to heed them, she got worse and worse, and her piercing yells fell awfully on the ears of the bystanders.   At length she expired, and her corpse exhibited a most appalling spectacle, even before the spirit had well departed.

Bryan and his friend returned home.   The old hag had been previously aware of the fate of Rachel Higgins, but it was not known by what means she acquired her super-natural knowledge.   She was delighted at the issue of her mysterious operations.   Bryan pressed her much to accept of some remuneration for her services, but she utterly rejected such proposals.   She remained a few days at his house, and at length took her leave and departed, no one knew whither.

Old Rachel's remains were interred that night in the neighbouring churchyard.   Her fate soon became generally known, and her family, ashamed to remain in their native village, disposed of their property, and quitted the country for ever.   The story, however, is still fresh in the memory of the surrounding villagers; and often, it is said, amid the grey haze of a summer twilight, may the ghost of Rachel Higgins, in the form of a hare, be seen scudding over her favourite and well-remembered haunts.

THE HORNED WOMEN.*

LADY WILDE.

A RICH woman sat up late one night carding and preparing wool, while all the family and servants were asleep. Suddenly a knock was given at the door, and a voice called—"Open! open!"

"Who is there?" said the woman of the house.

"I am the Witch of the one Horn," was answered.

The mistress, supposing that one of her neighbours had called and required assistance, opened the door, and a

* *Ancient Legends of Ireland.*

woman entered, having in her hand a pair of wool carders, and bearing a horn on her forehead, as if growing there. She sat down by the fire in silence, and began to card the wool with violent haste. Suddenly she paused, and said aloud : " Where are the women ? they delay too long."

Then a second knock came to the door, and a voice called as before, " Open ! open ! "

The mistress felt herself constrained to rise and open to the call, and immediately a second witch entered, having two horns on her forehead, and in her hand a wheel for spinning wool.

" Give me place," she said, " I am the Witch of the two Horns," and she began to spin as quick as lightning.

And so the knocks went on, and the call was heard, and the witches entered, until at last twelve women sat round the fire—the first with one horn, the last with twelve horns.

And they carded the thread, and turned their spinning-wheels, and wound and wove.

All singing together an ancient rhyme, but no word did they speak to the mistress of the house. Strange to hear, and frightful to look upon, were these twelve women, with their horns and their wheels ; and the mistress felt near to death, and she tried to rise that she might call for help, but she could not move, nor could she utter a word or a cry, for the spell of the witches was upon her.

Then one of them called to her in Irish, and said—

" Rise, woman, and make us a cake." Then the mistress searched for a vessel to bring water from the well that she might mix the meal and make the cake, but she could find none.

And they said to her, " Take a sieve and bring water in it."

And she took the sieve and went to the well ; but the water poured from it, and she could fetch none for the cake, and she sat down by the well and wept.

Then a voice came by her and said, " Take yellow clay and moss, and bind them together, and plaster the sieve so that it will hold."

THE HORNED WOMEN.

A WITCH CASTING A SPELL.

This she did, and the sieve held the water for the cake; and the voice said again—

"Return, and when thou comest to the north angle of the house, cry aloud three times and say, 'The mountain of the Fenian women and the sky over it is all on fire.'"

And she did so.

When the witches inside heard the call, a great and terrible cry broke from their lips, and they rushed forth with wild lamentations and shrieks, and fled away to Slievenamon,* where was their chief abode. But the Spirit of the Well bade the mistress of the house to enter and prepare her home against the enchantments of the witches if they returned again.

And first, to break their spells, she sprinkled the water in which she had washed her child's feet (the feet-water) outside the door on the threshold; secondly, she took the cake which the witches had made in her absence of meal mixed with the blood drawn from the sleeping family, and she broke the cake in bits, and placed a bit in the mouth of each sleeper, and they were restored; and she took the cloth they had woven and placed it half in and half out of the chest with the padlock; and lastly, she secured the door with a great crossbeam fastened in the jambs, so that they could not enter, and having done these things she waited.

Not long were the witches in coming back, and they raged and called for vengeance.

"Open! open!" they screamed, "open, feet-water!"

"I cannot," said the feet-water, "I am scattered on the ground, and my path is down to the Lough."

"Open, open, wood and trees and beam!" they cried to the door.

I cannot," said the door, "for the beam is fixed in the jambs and I have no power to move."

"Open, open, cake that we have made and mingled with blood!" they cried again.

"I cannot," said the cake, "for I am broken and bruised, and my blood is on the lips of the sleeping children."

---

* *Sliábh-na-mban—i.e.*, mountains of the women.

Then the witches rushed through the air with great cries, and fled back to Slievenamon, uttering strange curses on the Spirit of the Well, who had wished their ruin ; but the woman and the house were left in peace, and a mantle dropped by one of the witches in her flight was kept hung up by the mistress as a sign of the night's awful contest ; and this mantle was in possession of the same family from generation to generation for five hundred years after.

THE WITCHES' EXCURSION.*

PATRICK KENNEDY.

SHEMUS RUA† (Red James) awakened from his sleep one night by noises in his kitchen.   Stealing to the door, he saw half-a-dozen old women sitting round the fire, jesting and laughing, his old housekeeper, Madge, quite frisky and gay, helping her sister crones to cheering glasses of punch.   He began to admire the impudence and imprudence of Madge, displayed in the invitation and the riot, but recollected on the instant her officiousness in urging him to take a comfortable posset, which she had brought to his bedside just before he fell asleep.   Had he drunk it, he would have been just now deaf to the witches' glee.   He heard and saw them drink his health in such a mocking style as nearly to tempt him to charge them, besom in hand, but he restrained himself.

The jug being emptied, one of them cried out, " Is it time to be gone ? " and at the same moment, putting on a red cap, she added—

    " By yarrow and rue,
    And my red cap too,
      Hie over to England."

Making use of a twig which she held in her hand as a steed, she gracefully soared up the chimney, and was rapidly

---

* *Fictions of the Irish Celts.*

† Irish, *Séumus Ruadh*.   The Celtic vocal organs are unable to pronounce the letter j, hence they make Shon or Shawn of John, or Shamus of James, etc.

followed by the rest. But when it came to the house-keeper, Shemus interposed. "By your leave, ma'am," said he, snatching twig and cap. "Ah, you desateful ould crocodile! If I find you here on my return, there'll be wigs on the green—

> 'By yarrow and rue,
> And my red cap too,
> Hie over to England.'"

The words were not out of his mouth when he was soaring above the ridge pole, and swiftly ploughing the air. He was careful to speak no word (being somewhat conversant with witch-lore), as the result would be a tumble, and the immediate return of the expedition.

In a very short time they had crossed the Wicklow hills, the Irish Sea, and the Welsh mountains, and were charging, at whirlwind speed, the hall door of a castle. Shemus, only for the company in which he found himself, would have cried out for pardon, expecting to be *mummy* against the hard oak door in a moment; but, all bewildered, he found himself passing through the keyhole, along a passage, down a flight of steps, and through a cellar-door key-hole before he could form any clear idea of his situation.

Waking to the full consciousness of his position, he found himself sitting on a stillion, plenty of lights glimmering round, and he and his companions, with full tumblers of frothing wine in hand, hob-nobbing and drinking healths as jovially and recklessly as if the liquor was honestly come by, and they were sitting in *Shemus's* own kitchen. The red birredh* had assimilated *Shemus's* nature for the time being to that of his unholy companions. The heady liquors soon got into their brains, and a period of unconsciousness succeeded the ecstasy, the head-ache, the turning round of the barrels, and the "scattered sight" of poor Shemus. He woke up under the impression of being roughly seized, and shaken, and dragged upstairs, and subjected to a disagreeable examination by the lord of the castle, in his state parlour. There was much derision among the whole company, gentle

* Ir., *Birreud—i.e.*, a cap.

and simple, on hearing Shemus's explanation, and, as the thing occurred in the dark ages, the unlucky Leinster man was sentenced to be hung as soon as the gallows could be prepared for the occasion.

The poor Hibernian was in the cart proceeding on his last journey, with a label on his back, and another on his breast, announcing him as the remorseless villain who for the last month had been draining the casks in my lord's vault every night. He was surprised to hear himself addressed by his name, and in his native tongue, by an old woman in the crowd. "Ach, Shemus, alanna! is it going to die you are in a strange place without your *cappeen d'yarrag?*"* These words infused hope and courage into the poor victim's heart. He turned to the lord and humbly asked leave to die in his red cap, which he supposed had dropped from his head in the vault. A servant was sent for the head-piece, and Shemus felt lively hope warming his heart while placing it on his head. On the platform he was graciously allowed to address the spectators, which he proceeded to do in the usual formula composed for the benefit of flying stationers —"Good people all, a warning take by me;" but when he had finished the line, " My parents reared me tenderly," he unexpectedly added—"By yarrow and rue," etc., and the disappointed spectators saw him shoot up obliquely through the air in the style of a sky-rocket that had missed its aim. It is said that the lord took the circumstance much to heart, and never afterwards hung a man for twenty-four hours after his offence.

THE CONFESSIONS OF TOM BOURKE.

T. CROFTON CROKER.

TOM BOURKE lives in a low, long farm-house, resembling in outward appearance a large barn, placed at the bottom of the hill, just where the new road strikes off from the old one, leading from the town of Kilworth to that of Lismore. He

---

* Irish, *caipín dearg—i.e.*, red cap.

is of a class of persons who are a sort of black swans in Ireland : he is a wealthy farmer. Tom's father had, in the good old times, when a hundred pounds were no inconsiderable treasure, either to lend or spend, accommodated his landlord with that sum, at interest ; and obtained as a return for his civility a long lease, about half-a-dozen times more valuable than the loan which procured it. The old man died worth several hundred pounds, the greater part of which, with his farm, he bequeathed to his son Tom. But besides all this, Tom received from his father, upon his death-bed, another gift, far more valuable than worldly riches, greatly as he prized and is still known to prize them. He was invested with the privilege, enjoyed by few of the sons of men, of communicating with those mysterious beings called "the good people."

Tom Bourke is a little, stout, healthy, active man, about fifty-five years of age. His hair is perfectly white, short and bushy behind, but rising in front erect and thick above his forehead, like a new clothes-brush. His eyes are of that kind which I have often observed with persons of a quick, but limited intellect—they are small, grey, and lively. The large and projecting eyebrows under, or rather within, which they twinkle, give them an expression of shrewdness and intelligence, if not of cunning. And this is very much the character of the man. If you want to make a bargain with Tom Bourke you must act as if you were a general besieging a town, and make your advances a long time before you can hope to obtain possession ; if you march up boldly, and tell him at once your object, you are for the most part sure to have the gates closed in your teeth. Tom does not wish to part with what you wish to obtain ; or another person has been speaking to him for the whole of the last week. Or, it may be, your proposal seems to meet the most favourable reception. "Very well, sir ;" "That's true, sir ;" "I'm very thankful to your honour," and other expressions of kindness and confidence greet you in reply to every sentence ; and you part from him wondering how he can have obtained the character which he universally bears, of being a man whom no one can make anything of in a bargain. But when you next meet him the flattering illusion is dissolved : you find you are a great deal further from your object than you were when you thought you had almost succeeded ; his eye and his tongue express a total forgetfulness of what the mind within never lost sight of for an instant; and you have to begin operations afresh, with the disadvantage of having put your adversary completely upon his guard.

Yet, although Tom Bourke is, whether from supernatural revealings, or (as many will think more probable) from the tell-truth experience, so distrustful of mankind, and so close in his dealings with them, he is no misanthrope. No man loves better the pleasures of the genial board. The love of money, indeed, which is with him (and who will blame him ?) a very ruling propensity, and the gratification which it has received from habits of industry, sustained throughout a pretty long and successful life, have taught him the value of sobriety, during those seasons, at least, when a man's business requires him to keep possession of his senses. He has, therefore, a general rule, never to get drunk but on Sundays. But in order that it should be a general one to all intents and purposes, he takes a method which, according to better logicians than he is, always proves the rule. He has many exceptions ; among these, of course, are the evenings of all the fair and market-days that happen in his neighbourhood ; so also all the days in which funerals, marriages, and christenings take place among his friends within many miles of him. As to this last class of exceptions, it may appear at first very singular, that he is much more punctual in his attendance at the funerals than at the baptisms or weddings of his friends. This may be construed as an instance of disinterested affection for departed worth, very uncommon in this selfish world. But I am afraid that the motives which lead Tom Bourke to pay more court to the dead than the living are precisely those which lead to the opposite conduct in the generality of mankind—a hope of future benefit and a fear of future evil. For the good people, who are a race as powerful as they are capricious, have their favourites among those who inhabit this world; often show their affection by easing the objects of it from the load of this burdensome life; and frequently reward or punish the living according to the degree of reverence paid to the obsequies and the memory of the elected dead.

Some may attribute to the same cause the apparently humane and charitable actions which Tom, and indeed the other members of his family, are known frequently to perform. A beggar has seldom left their farm-yard with an empty wallet, or without obtaining a night's lodging, if required, with a sufficiency of potatoes and milk to satisfy even an Irish beggar's appetite; in appeasing which, account must usually be taken of the auxiliary jaws of a hungry dog, and of two or three still more hungry children, who line themselves well within, to atone for their nakedness without. If one of the neighbouring poor be seized with a fever, Tom will often supply the sick wretch with some untenanted hut upon one of his two large farms (for he has added one to his patrimony), or will send his labourers to construct a shed at a hedge-side, and supply straw for a bed while the disorder continues. His wife, remarkable for the largeness of her dairy, and the goodness of everything it contains, will furnish milk for whey; and their good offices are frequently extended to the family of the patient, who are, perhaps, reduced to the extremity of wretchedness, by even the temporary suspension of a father's or a husband's labour.

If much of this arises from the hopes and fears to which I above alluded, I believe much of it flows from a mingled sense of compassion and of duty, which is sometimes seen to break from an Irish peasant's heart, even where it happens to be enveloped in a habitual covering of avarice and fraud; and which I once heard speak in terms not to be misunderstood: "When we get a deal, 'tis only fair we should give back a little of it."

It is not easy to prevail on Tom to speak of those good

people, with whom he is said to hold frequent and intimate communications. To the faithful, who believe in their power, and their occasional delegation of it to him, he seldom refuses, if properly asked, to exercise his high prerogative when any unfortunate being is *struck* in his neighbourhood. Still he will not be won unsued : he is at first difficult of persuasion, and must be overcome by a little gentle violence. On these occasions he is un-usually solemn and mysterious, and if one word of reward be mentioned he at once abandons the unhappy patient, such a proposition being a direct insult to his supernatural superiors. It is true that, as the labourer is worthy of his hire, most persons gifted as he is do not scruple to receive a token of gratitude from the patients or their friends *after* their recovery. It is recorded that a very handsome gratuity was once given to a female practitioner in this occult science, who deserves to be mentioned, not only because she was a neighbour and a rival of Tom's, but from the singularity of a mother deriving her name from her son. Her son's name was Owen, and she was always called *Owen sa vauher* (Owen's mother). This person was, on the occasion to which I have alluded, *persuaded* to give her assistance to a young girl who had lost the use of her right leg ; *Owen sa vauher* found the cure a difficult one. A journey of about eighteen miles was essential for the pur-pose, probably to visit one of the good people who resided at that distance ; and this journey could only be performed by *Owen sa vauher* travelling upon the back of a white hen. The visit, however, was accomplished ; and at a particular hour, according to the prediction of this extraordinary woman, when the hen and her rider were to reach their journey's end, the patient was seized with an irresistible desire to dance, which she gratified with the most perfect freedom of the diseased leg, much to the joy of her anxious family. The gratuity in this case was, as it surely ought to have been, unusually large, from the difficulty of procuring a hen willing to go so long a journey with such a rider.

To do Tom Bourke justice, he is on these occasions, as

I have heard from many competent authorities, perfectly disinterested. Not many months since he recovered a young woman (the sister of a tradesman living near him), who had been struck speechless after returning from a funeral, and had continued so for several days. He steadfastly refused receiving any compensation, saying that even if he had not as much as would buy him his supper, he could take nothing in this case, because the girl had offended at the funeral of one of the *good people* belonging to his own family, and though he would do her a kindness, he could take none from her.

About the time this last remarkable affair took place, my friend Mr. Martin, who is a neighbour of Tom's, had some business to transact with him, which it was exceedingly difficult to bring to a conclusion. At last Mr. Martin, having tried all quiet means, had recourse to a legal process, which brought Tom to reason, and the matter was arranged to their mutual satisfaction, and with perfect good-humour between the parties. The accommodation took place after dinner at Mr. Martin's house, and he invited Tom to walk into the parlour and take a glass of punch, made of some excellent *poteen*, which was on the table : he had long wished to draw out his highly-endowed neighbour on the subject of his supernatural powers, and as Mrs. Martin, who was in the room, was rather a favourite of Tom's, this seemed a good opportunity.

" Well, Tom," said Mr. Martin, " that was a curious business of Molly Dwyer's, who recovered her speech so suddenly the other day."

" You may say that, sir," replied Tom Bourke ; " but I had to travel far for it : no matter for that now. Your health, ma'am," said he, turning to Mrs. Martin.

" Thank you, Tom. But I am told you had some trouble once in that way in your own family," said Mrs. Martin.

" So I had, ma'am ; trouble enough : but you were only a child at that time."

" Come, Tom," said the hospitable Mr. Martin, interrupting him, "take another tumbler;" and he then added, "I wish you would tell us something of the manner in which so many of your children died. I am told they dropped off, one after another, by the same disorder, and that your eldest son was cured in a most extraordinary way, when the physicians had given him over."

"'Tis true for you, sir," returned Tom; "your father, the doctor (God be good to him, I won't belie him in his grave), told me, when my fourth boy was a week sick, that himself and Dr. Barry did all that man could do for him; but they could not keep him from going after the rest. No more they could, if the people that took away the rest wished to take him too. But they left him; and sorry to the heart I am I did not know before why they were taking my boys from me; if I did, I would not be left trusting to two of 'em now."

"And how did you find it out, Tom?" inquired Mr. Martin.

"Why, then, I'll tell you, sir," said Bourke. "When your father said what I told you, I did not know very well what to do. I walked down the little *bohereen** you know, sir, that goes to the river-side near Dick Heafy's ground; for 'twas a lonesome place, and I wanted to think of myself. I was heavy, sir, and my heart got weak in me, when I thought I was to lose my little boy; and I did not well know how to face his mother with the news, for she doated down upon him. Besides, she never got the better of all she cried at his brother's *berrin†* the week before. As I was going down the *bohereen* I met an old *bocough*, that used to come about the place once or twice a-year, and used always to sleep in our barn while he staid in the neighbourhood. So he asked me how I was. 'Bad enough, Shamous,'‡ says I. 'I'm sorry for your trouble,' says he; 'but you're a foolish man, Mr. Bourke. Your son would be well enough if you would only do what you ought with him.' 'What more can I do with him, Shamous?'

* *Bohereen*, or *bogheen*, *i.e.*, a green lane.
† *Berrin*, burying.   ‡ *Shamous*, James.

says I ; 'the doctors give him over.'   'The doctors know no more what ails him than they do what ails a cow when she stops her milk,' says Shamous ; ' but go to such a one,' telling me his name, ' and try what he'll say to you.'"

"And who was that, Tom ?" asked Mr. Martin.

"I could not tell you that, sir," said Bourke, with a mysterious look ; " howsomever, you often saw him, and he does not live far from this.   But I had a trial of him before ; and if I went to him at first, maybe I'd have now some of them that's gone, and so Shamous often told me.   Well, sir, I went to this man, and he came with me to the house.   By course, I did everything as he bid me.   According to his order, I took the little boy out of the dwelling-house immediately, sick as he was, and made a bed for him and myself in the cow-house.   Well, sir, I lay down by his side in the bed, between two of the cows, and he fell asleep.   He got into a perspiration, saving your presence, as if he was drawn through the river, and breathed hard, with a great *impression* on his chest, and was very bad—very bad entirely through the night.   I thought about twelve o'clock he was going at last, and I was just getting up to go call the man I told you of ; but there was no occasion.   My friends were getting the better of them that wanted to take him away from me.   There was nobody in the cow-house but the child and myself.   There was only one halfpenny candle lighting it, and that was stuck in the wall at the far end of the house.   I had just enough of light where we were lying to see a person walking or standing near us : and there was no more noise than if it was a churchyard, except the cows chewing the fodder in the stalls.

Just as I was thinking of getting up, as I told you—I won't belie my father, sir, he was a good father to me—I saw him standing at the bedside, holding out his right hand to me, and leaning his other on the stick he used to carry when he was alive, and looking pleasant and smiling at me, all as if he was telling me not to be afeard, for I would not lose the child.   ' Is that you, father ? ' says I.   He said nothing. ' If that's **you**,' says I again, ' for the love of them that gone,

let me catch your hand.' And so he did, sir; and his hand
was as soft as a child's. He stayed about as long as you'd
be going from this to the gate below at the end of the
avenue, and then went away. In less than a week the child
was as well as if nothing ever ailed him; and there isn't
to-night a healthier boy of nineteen, from this blessed house
to the town of Ballyporeen, across the Kilworth mountains."

"But I think, Tom," said Mr. Martin, "it appears as if
you are more indebted to your father than to the man
recommended to you by Shamous; or do you suppose it
was he who made favour with your enemies among the good
people, and that then your father——"

"I beg your pardon, sir," said Bourke, interrupting him;
"but don't call them my enemies. 'Twould not be wishing
to me for a good deal to sit by when they are called so.
No offence to you, sir. Here's wishing you a good health
and long life."

"I assure you," returned Mr. Martin, "I meant no
offence, Tom; but was it not as I say?"

"I can't tell you that, sir," said Bourke; "I'm bound
down, sir. Howsoever, you may be sure the man I spoke
of and my father, and those they know, settled it between
them."

There was a pause, of which Mrs. Martin took advantage
to inquire of Tom whether something remarkable had not
happened about a goat and a pair of pigeons, at the time of
his son's illness—circumstances often mysteriously hinted at
by Tom.

"See that, now," said he, turning to Mr. Martin, "how
well she remembers it! True for you, ma'am. The goat I
gave the mistress, your mother, when the doctors ordered
her goats' whey?"

Mrs. Martin nodded assent, and Tom Bourke continued,
"Why, then, I'll tell you how that was. The goat was as
well as e'er goat ever was, for a month after she was sent to
Killaan, to your father's. The morning after the night I
just told you of, before the child woke, his mother was
standing at the gap leading out of the barn-yard into the

road, and she saw two pigeons flying from the town of Kilworth off the church down towards her. Well, they never stopped, you see, till they came to the house on the hill at the other side of the river, facing our farm. They pitched upon the chimney of that house, and after looking about them for a minute or two, they flew straight across the river, and stopped on the ridge of the cow-house where the child and I were lying. Do you think they came there for nothing, sir?"

"Certainly not, Tom," returned Mr. Martin.

"Well, the woman came in to me, frightened, and told me. She began to cry. 'Whisht, you fool?' says I; "'tis all for the better.' 'Twas true for me. What do you think, ma'am; the goat that I gave your mother, that was seen feeding at sunrise that morning by Jack Cronin, as merry as a bee, dropped down dead without anybody knowing why, before Jack's face; and at that very moment he saw two pigeons fly from the top of the house out of the town, towards the Lismore road. 'Twas at the same time my woman saw them, as I just told you."

"'Twas very strange, indeed, Tom," said Mr. Martin; "I wish you could give us some explanation of it."

"I wish I could, sir," was Tom Bourke's answer; "but I'm bound down. I can't tell but what I'm allowed to tell, any more than a sentry is let walk more than his rounds."

"I think you said something of having had some former knowledge of the man that assisted in the cure of your son," said Mr. Martin.

"So I had, sir,' returned Bourke. "I had a trial of that man. But that's neither here nor there. I can't tell you anything about that, sir. But would you like to know how he got his skill?"

"Oh! very much, indeed," said Mr. Martin.

"But you can tell us his Christian name, that we may know him better through the story," added Mrs. Martin.

Tom Bourke paused for a minute to consider this proposition.

"Well, I believe that I may tell you that, anyhow; his

name is Patrick. He was always a smart, 'cute* boy, and
would be a great clerk if he stuck to it. The first time I
knew him, sir, was at my mother's wake. I was in great
trouble, for I did not know where to bury her. Her people
and my father's people—I mean their friends, sir, among
the *good people*—had the greatest battle that was known for
many a year, at Dunmanwaycross, to see to whose churchyard she'd be taken. They fought for three nights, one
after another, without being able to settle it. The neighbours wondered how long I was before I buried my mother;
but I had my reasons, though I could not tell them at that
time. Well, sir, to make my story short, Patrick came on
the fourth morning and told me he settled the business, and
that day we buried her in Kilcrumper churchyard, with my
father's people."

"He was a valuable friend, Tom," said Mrs. Martin, with
difficulty suppressing a smile. "But you were about to tell
how he became so skilful."

"So I will and welcome," replied Bourke. "Your health,
ma'am. I'm drinking too much of this punch, sir; but
to tell the truth, I never tasted the like of it; it goes down
one's throat like sweet oil. But what was I going to say?
Yes—well—Patrick, many a long year ago, was coming
home from a *berrin* late in the evening, and walking by the
side of a river, opposite the big inch,† near Ballyhefaan
ford. He had taken a drop, to be sure; but he was only a
little merry, as you may say, and knew very well what he
was doing. The moon was shining, for it was in the month
of August, and the river was as smooth and as bright as a
looking-glass. He heard nothing for a long time but the
fall of the water at the mill weir about a mile down the river,
and now and then the crying of the lambs on the other side
of the river. All at once there was a noise of a great
number of people laughing as if they'd break their hearts,
and of a piper playing among them. It came from the inch
at the other side of the ford, and he saw, through the mist

---

* *'Cute,* acute.   † *Inch,* low meadow ground near a river.

that hung over the river, a whole crowd of people dancing on the inch. Patrick was as fond of a dance, as he was of a glass, and that's saying enough for him ; so he whipped off his shoes and stockings, and away with him across the ford. After putting on his shoes and stockings at the other side of the river he walked over to the crowd, and mixed with them for some time without being minded. He thought, sir, that he'd show them better dancing than any of themselves, for he was proud of his feet, sir, and a good right he had, for there was not a boy in the same parish could foot a double or treble with him. But pwah ! his dancing was no more to theirs than mine would be to the mistress' there. They did not seem as if they had a bone in their bodies, and they kept it up as if nothing could tire them. Patrick was 'shamed within himself, for he thought he had not his fellow in all the country round ; and was going away, when a little old man, that was looking at the company bitterly, as if he did not like what was going on, came up to him. ' Patrick,' says he. Patrick started, for he did not think anybody there knew him. ' Patrick,' says he, ' you're discouraged, and no wonder for you. But you have a friend near you. I'm your friend, and your father's friend, and I think worse* of your little finger than I do of all that are here, though they think no one is as good as themselves. Go into the ring and call for a lilt. Don't be afeard. I tell you the best of them did not do it as well as you shall, if you will do as I bid you.' Patrick felt something within him as if he ought not to gainsay the old man. He went into the ring, and called the piper to play up the best double he had. And sure enough, all that the others were able for was nothing to him ! He bounded like an eel, now here and now there, as light as a feather, although the people could hear the music answered by his steps, that beat time to every turn of it, like the left foot of the piper. He first danced a hornpipe on the ground. Then they got a table, and he danced a treble on it that drew down shouts from the whole company. At last he called for a trencher ;

* *Worse*, more.

and when they saw him, all as if he was spinning on it like a top, they did not know what to make of him. Some praised him for the best dancer that ever entered a ring; others hated him because he was better than themselves; although they had good right to think themselves better than him or any other man that ever went the long journey."

" And what was the cause of his great success?" inquired Mr. Martin.

" He could not help it, sir," replied Tom Bourke. " They that could make him do more than that made him do it. Howsomever, when he had done, they wanted him to dance again, but he was tired, and they could not persuade him. At last he got angry, and swore a big oath, saving your presence, that he would not dance a step more; and the word was hardly out of his mouth when he found himself all alone, with nothing but a white cow grazing by his side."

" Did he ever discover why he was gifted with these extraordinary powers in the dance, Tom?" said Mr. Martin.

" I'll tell you that too, sir," answered Bourke, "when I come to it. When he went home, sir, he was taken with a shivering, and went to bed; and the next day they found he had got the fever, or something like it, for he raved like as if he was mad. But they couldn't make out what it was he was saying, though he talked constant. The doctors gave him over. But it's little they knew what ailed him. When he was, as you may say, about ten days sick, and everybody thought he was going, one of the neighbours came in to him with a man, a friend of his, from Ballinlacken, that was keeping with him some time before. I can't tell you his name either, only it was Darby. The minute Darby saw Patrick he took a little bottle, with the juice of herbs in it, out of his pocket, and gave Patrick a drink of it. He did the same every day for three weeks, and then Patrick was able to walk about, as stout and as hearty as ever he was in his life. But he was a long time before he came to himself; and he used to walk the whole day sometimes by the ditch-side, talking to himself, like as if there was someone along with him. And so there was, surely, or he wouldn't be the man he is to-day."

"I suppose it was from some such companion he learned his skill," said Mr. Martin.

"You have it all now, sir," replied Bourke. "Darby told him his friends were satisfied with what he did the night of the dance; and though they couldn't hinder the fever, they'd bring him over it, and teach him more than many knew beside him. And so they did. For you see, all the people he met on the inch that night were friends of a different faction; only the old man that spoke to him, he was a friend of Patrick's family, and it went again his heart, you see, that the others were so light and active, and he was bitter in himself to hear 'em boasting how they'd dance with any set in the whole country round. So he gave Patrick the gift that night, and afterwards gave him the skill that makes him the wonder of all that know him. And to be sure it was only learning he was at that time when he was wandering in his mind after the fever."

"I have heard many strange stories about that inch near Ballyhefaan ford," said Mr. Martin. "'Tis a great place for the good people, isn't it, Tom?"

"You may say that, sir," returned Bourke. "I could tell you a great deal about it. Many a time I sat for as good as two hours by moonlight, at th' other side of the river, looking at 'em playing goal as if they'd break their hearts over it; with their coats and waistcoats off, and white handkerchiefs on the heads of one party, and red ones on th' other, just as you'd see on a Sunday in Mr. Simming's big field. I saw 'em one night play till the moon set, without one party being able to take the ball from th' other. I'm sure they were going to fight, only 'twas near morning. I'm told your grandfather, ma'am, used to see 'em there too," said Bourke, turning to Mrs. Martin.

"So I have been told, Tom," replied Mrs. Martin. "But don't they say that the churchyard of Kilcrumper is just as favourite a place with the good people as Ballyhefaan inch?"

"Why, then, maybe you never heard, ma'am, what happened to Davy Roche in that same churchyard," said Bourke; and turning to Mr. Martin, added, "'Twas a long time before he went into your service, sir. He was walking home, of an evening, from the fair of Kilcumber, a little merry, to be sure, after the day, and he came up with a berrin. So he walked along with it, and thought it very queer that he did not know a mother's soul in the crowd but one man, and he was sure that man was dead many years afore. Howsomever, he went on with the berrin till they came to Kilcrumper churchyard; and, faith, he went in and stayed with the rest, to see the corpse buried. As soon as the grave was covered, what should they do but gather about a piper that *come* along with 'em, and fall to dancing as if it was a wedding. Davy longed to be among 'em (for he hadn't a bad foot of his own, that time, whatever he may now); but he was loth to begin, because they all seemed strange to him, only the man I told you that he thought was dead. Well, at last this man saw what Davy wanted, and came up to him. 'Davy,' says he, 'take out a partner, and show what you can do, but take care and don't offer to kiss her.' 'That I won't,' says Davy, 'although her lips were made of honey.' And with that he made his bow to the *purtiest* girl in the ring, and he and she began to dance. 'Twas a jig they danced, and they did it to th' admiration, do you see, of all that were there. 'Twas all very well till the jig was over; but just as they had done, Davy, for he had a drop in, and was warm with the dancing, forgot himself, and kissed his partner, according to custom. The smack was no sooner off of his lips, you see, than he was left alone in the churchyard, without a creature near him, and all he could see was the tall tombstones. Davy said they seemed as if they were dancing too, but I suppose that was only the wonder that happened him, and he being a little in drink. Howsomever, he found it was a great many hours later than he thought it; 'twas near morning when he came home ; but they couldn't get a word out of him till the next day, when he woke out of a dead sleep about twelve o'clock."

When Tom had finished the account of Davy Roche and the berrin, it became quite evident that spirits, of some sort, were working too strong within him to admit of his telling many more tales of the good people. Tom seemed conscious of this. He muttered for a few minutes broken sentences concerning churchyards, river-sides, leprechauns, and *dina magh*,* which were quite unintelligible, perhaps, to himself, certainly to Mr. Martin and his lady. At length he made a slight motion of the head upwards, as if he would say, "I can talk no more;" stretched his arm on the table, upon which he placed the empty tumbler slowly, and with the most knowing and cautious air ; and rising from his chair, walked, or rather rolled, to the parlour door. Here he turned round to face his host and hostess ; but after various ineffectual attempts to bid them good-night, the words, as they rose, being always choked by a violent hiccup, while the door, which he held by the handle, swung to and fro, carrying his unyielding body along with it, he was obliged to depart in silence. The cow-boy, sent by Tom's wife, who knew well what sort of allurement detained him when he remained out after a certain hour, was in attendance to conduct his master home. I have no doubt that he returned without meeting any material injury, as I know that within the last month he was, to use his own words, "as stout and hearty a man as any of his age in the county Cork."

THE PUDDING BEWITCHED.

WILLIAM CARLETON.

"MOLL ROE RAFFERTY was the son—daughter I mane—of ould Jack Rafferty, who was remarkable for a habit he had

* *Daoine maithe, i.e.,* the good people.

of always wearing his head undher his hat; but indeed the same family was a quare one, as everybody knew that was acquainted wid them. It was said of them—but whether it was thrue or not I won't undhertake to say, for 'fraid I'd tell a lie—that whenever they didn't wear shoes or boots they always went barefooted; but I heard aftherwards that this was disputed, so rather than say anything to injure their character, I'll let that pass. Now, ould Jack Rafferty had two sons, Paddy and Molly—hut! what are you all laughing at?—I mane a son and daughter, and it was generally believed among the neighbours that they were brother and sisther, which you know might be thrue or it might not: but that's a thing that, wid the help o' goodness, we have nothing to say to. Troth there was many ugly things put out on them that I don't wish to repate, such as that neither Jack nor his son Paddy ever walked a perch widout puttin' one foot afore the other like a salmon; an' I know it was whispered about, that whinever Moll Roe slep', she had an out-of-the-way custom of keepin' her eyes shut. If she did, however, for that matther the loss was her own; for sure we all know that when one comes to shut their eyes they can't see as far before them as another.

"Moll Roe was a fine young bouncin' girl, large and lavish, wid a purty head o' hair on her like scarlet, that bein' one of the raisons why she was called *Roe*, or red; her arms an' cheeks were much the colour of the hair, an' her saddle nose was the purtiest thing of its kind that ever was on a face. Her fists—for, thank goodness, she was well sarved wid them too—had a strong simularity to two thumpin' turnips, reddened by the sun; an' to keep all right and tight, she had a temper as fiery as her head—for, indeed, it was well known that all the Rafferties were *warm*-hearted. Howandiver, it appears that God gives nothing in vain, and of coorse the same fists, big and red as they were, if all that is said about them is thrue, were not so much given to her for ornament as use. At laist, takin' them in connection wid her lively temper, we have it upon good authority, that there was no danger of their getting blue-moulded for want of practice. She had a twist, too, in one of her eyes that was very becomin' in its way, and made her poor husband, when she got him, take it into his head that she could see round a corner. She found him out in many quare things, widout doubt; but whether it was owin' to that or not, I wouldn't undertake to say *for fraid I'd tell a lie.*

"Well, begad, anyhow it was Moll Roe that was the *dilsy*.* It happened that there was a nate vagabone in the neighbourhood, just as much overburdened wid beauty as herself, and he was named Gusty Gillespie. Gusty, the Lord guard us, was what they call a black-mouth Prosbytarian, and wouldn't keep Christmas-day, the blagard, except what they call 'ould style.' Gusty was rather good-lookin' when seen in the dark, as well as Moll herself; and, indeed, it was purty well known that—accordin' as the talk went—it was in nightly meetings that they had an opportunity of becomin' detached to one another. The quensequence was, that in due time both families began to talk very seriously as to what was to be done. Moll's brother, Pawdien O'Rafferty, gave Gusty the best of two choices. What they were it's not worth spakin' about; but at any rate *one* of them was a poser, an' as Gusty knew his man, he soon came to his senses. Accordianly everything was deranged for their marriage, and it was appointed that they should be spliced by the Rev. Samuel M'Shuttle, the Prosbytarian parson, on the following Sunday.

"Now this was the first marriage that had happened for a long time in the neighbourhood betune a black-mouth an' a Catholic, an' of coorse there was strong objections on both sides aginst it; an' begad, only for one thing, it would never 'a tuck place at all. At any rate, faix, there was one of the bride's uncles, ould Harry Connolly, a fairy-man, who could cure all complaints wid a secret he had, and as he didn't wish to see his niece married upon sich a fellow, he fought bittherly against the match. All Moll's friends, however, stood up for the marriage barrin' him, an' of coorse the

---

* Perhaps from Irish *dilse—i.e.,* love.

Sunday was appointed, as I said, that they were to be dove-tailed together.

"Well, the day arrived, and Moll, as became her, went to mass, and Gusty to meeting, afther which they were to join one another in Jack Rafferty's, where the priest, Father M'Sorley, was to slip up afther mass to take his dinner wid them, and to keep Misther M'Shuttle, who was to marry them, company. Nobody remained at home but ould Jack Rafferty an' his wife, who stopped to dress the dinner, for, to tell the truth, it was to be a great let-out entirely. Maybe, if all was known, too, that Father M'Sorley was to give them a cast of his office over an' above the ministher, in regard that Moll's friends were not altogether satisfied at the kind of marriage which M'Shuttle could give them. The sorrow may care about that—splice here—splice there— all I can say is, that when Mrs. Rafferty was goin' to tie up a big bag pudden, in walks Harry Connolly, the fairy-man, in a rage, and shouts out,—'Blood and blunderbushes, what are yez here for?'

"'Arrah why, Harry? Why, avick?'

"'Why, the sun's in the suds and the moon in the high Horicks; there's a clipstick comin' an, an' there you're both as unconsarned as if it was about to rain mether. Go out and cross yourselves three times in the name o' the four Mandromarvins, for as prophecy says:—Fill the pot, Eddy, supernaculum—a blazing star's a rare spectaculum. Go out both of you and look at the sun, I say, an' ye'll see the condition he's in—off!'

"Begad, sure enough, Jack gave a bounce to the door, and his wife leaped like a two-year-ould, till they were both got on a stile beside the house to see what was wrong in the sky.

"'Arrah, what is it, Jack,' said she; 'can you see anything?'

"'No,' says he, 'sorra the full o' my eye of anything I can spy, barrin' the sun himself, that's not visible in regard of the clouds. God guard us! I doubt there's something to happen.'

"'If there wasn't, Jack, what 'ud put Harry, that knows so much, in the state he's in?'

"'I doubt it's this marriage,' said Jack: 'betune ourselves, it's not over an' above religious for Moll to marry a black-mouth, an' only for——; but it can't be helped now, though you see not a taste o' the sun is willin' to show his face upon it.'

"'As to that,' says the wife, winkin' wid both her eyes, 'if Gusty's satisfied wid Moll, it's enough. I know who'll carry the whip hand, anyhow; but in the manetime let us ax Harry 'ithin what ails the sun.'

"Well, they accordianly went in an' put the question to him:

"'Harry, what's wrong, ahagur? What is it now, for if anybody alive knows, 'tis yourself?'

"'Ah!' said Harry, screwin' his mouth wid a kind of a dhry smile, 'the sun has a hard twist o' the cholic; but never mind that, I tell you you'll have a merrier weddin' than you think, that's all;' and havin' said this, he put on his hat and left the house.

"Now, Harry's answer relieved them very much, and so, afther calling to him to be back for the dinner, Jack sat down to take a shough o' the pipe, and the wife lost no time in tying up the pudden and puttin' it in the pot to be boiled.

"In this way things went on well enough for a while, Jack smokin' away, an' the wife cookin' and dhressin' at the rate of a hunt. At last, Jack, while sittin', as I said, contentedly at the fire, thought he could persave an odd dancin' kind of motion in the pot that puzzled him a good deal.

"'Katty,' said he, 'what the dickens is in this pot on the fire?'

"'Nerra thing but the big pudden. Why do you ax?' says she.

"'Why,' said he, 'if ever a pot tuck it into its head to dance a jig, and this did. Thundher and sparbles, look at it!'

"Begad, it was thrue enough; there was the pot bobbin' up an' down and from side to side, jiggin' it away as merry as a grig; an' it was quite aisy to see that it wasn't the pot itself, but what was inside of it, that brought about the hornpipe.

"'Be the hole o' my coat,' shouted Jack, 'there's something alive in it, or it would never cut sich capers!'

"'Be gorra, there is, Jack; something sthrange entirely has got into it. Wirra, man alive, what's to be done?'

"Jist as she spoke, the pot seemed to cut the buckle in prime style, and afther a spring that 'ud shame a dancin'-masther, off flew the lid, and out bounced the pudden itself, hoppin', as nimble as a pea on a drum-head, about the floor. Jack blessed himself, and Katty crossed herself. Jack shouted, and Katty screamed. 'In the name of goodness, keep your distance; no one here injured you!'

"The pudden, however, made a set at him, and Jack lepped first on a chair and then on the kitchen table to avoid it. It then danced towards Kitty, who was now repatin' her prayers at the top of her voice, while the cunnin' thief of a pudden was hoppin' and jiggin' it round her, as if it was amused at her distress.

"'If I could get the pitchfork,' said Jack, 'I'd dale wid it —by goxty I'd thry its mettle.'

"'No, no,' shouted Katty, thinkin' there was a fairy in it; 'let us spake it fair. Who knows what harm it might do? Aisy now,' said she to the pudden, 'aisy, dear; don't harm honest people that never meant to offend you. It wasn't us —no, in troth, it was ould Harry Connolly that bewitched you; pursue *him* if you wish, but spare a woman like me; for, whisper, dear, I'm not in a condition to be frightened— troth I'm not.'

"The pudden, bedad, seemed to take her at her word, and danced away from her towards Jack, who, like the wife, believin' there was a fairy in it, an' that spakin' it fair was the best plan, thought he would give it a soft word as well as her.

"'Plase your honour,' said Jack, 'she only spaiks the truth; an', upon my voracity, we both feels much oblaiged to your honour for your quietness. Faith, it's quite clear that if you weren't a gentlemanly pudden all out, you'd act otherwise. Ould Harry, the rogue, is your mark; he's jist gone down the road there, and if you go fast you'll overtake him. Be me song, your dancin' masther did his duty, anyhow. Thank your honour! God speed you, an' may you never meet wid a parson or alderman in your thravels!'

"Jist as Jack spoke the pudden appeared to take the hint, for it quietly hopped out, and as the house was directly on the road-side, turned down towards the bridge, the very way that ould Harry went. It was very natural, of coorse, that Jack and Katty should go out to see how it intended to thravel; and, as the day was Sunday, it was but natural, too, that a greater number of people than usual were passin' the road. This was a fact; and when Jack and his wife were seen followin' the pudden, the whole neighbourhood was soon up and afther it.

"'Jack Rafferty, what is it? Katty, ahagur, will you tell us what it manes?'

"'Why,' replied Katty, 'it's my big pudden that's bewitched, an' it's now hot foot pursuin'——;' here she stopped, not wishin' to mention her brother's name—'*some one* or other that surely put *pishrogues* an it.'*

"This was enough; Jack, now seein' that he had assistance, found his courage comin' back to him; so says he to Katty, 'Go home,' says he, 'an' lose no time in makin' another pudden as good, an' here's Paddy Scanlan's wife, Bridget, says she'll let you boil it on her fire, as you'll want our own to dress the rest o' the dinner: and Paddy himself will lend me a pitchfork, for purshuin to the morsel of that same pudden will escape till I let the wind out of it, now that I've the neighbours to back an' support me,' says Jack.

"This was agreed to, and Katty went back to prepare a fresh pudden, while Jack an' half the townland pursued the other wid spades, graips, pitchforks, scythes, flails, and all possible description of instruments. On the pudden went, however, at the rate of about six Irish miles an hour, an' sich a chase never was seen. Catholics, Prodestants, an'

* Put it under fairy influence.

Prosbytarians, were all afther it, armed, as I said, an' bad end to the thing but its own activity could save it.   Here it made a hop, and there a prod was made at it ; but off it went, an' some one, as eager to get a slice at it on the other side, got the prod instead of the pudden.   Big Frank Farrell, the miller of Ballyboulteen, got a prod backwards that brought a hullabaloo out of him you might hear at the other end of the parish.   One got a slice of a scythe, another a whack of a flail, a third a rap of a spade that made him look nine ways at wanst.

"'Where is it goin'?' asked one.   'My life for you, it's on it's way to Meeting.   Three cheers for it if it turns to Carntaul.'   'Prod the sowl out of it, if it's a Prodestan',' shouted the others ; 'if it turns to the left, slice it into pancakes.   We'll have no Prodestan' puddens here.'

" Begad, by this time the people were on the point of beginnin' to have a regular fight about it, when, very fortunately, it took a short turn down a little by-lane that led towards the Methodist praichin-house, an' in an instant all parties were in an uproar against it as a Methodist pudden.   'It's a Wesleyan,' shouted several voices ; 'an' by this an' by that, into a Methodist chapel it won't put a foot to-day, or we'll lose a fall.   Let the wind out of it.   Come, boys, where's your pitchforks?'

"The divle purshuin to the one of them, however, ever could touch the pudden, an' jist when they thought they had it up against the gavel of the Methodist chapel, begad it gave them the slip, and hops over to the left, clane into the river, and sails away before all their eyes as light as an egg-shell.

" Now, it so happened that a little below this place, the demesne-wall of Colonel Bragshaw was built up to the very edge of the river on each side of its banks ; and so findin' there was a stop put to their pursuit of it, they went home again, every man, woman, and child of them, puzzled to think what the pudden was at all, what it meant, or where it was goin' !   Had Jack Rafferty an' his wife been willin' to let out the opinion they held about Harry Connolly bewitchin' it, there is no doubt of it but poor Harry might

be badly trated by the crowd, when their blood was up.
They had sense enough, howandiver, to keep that to
themselves, for Harry bein' an' ould bachelor, was a kind
friend to the Raffertys. So, of coorse, there was all kinds
of talk about it—some guessin' this, and some guessin' that
—one party sayin' the pudden was of there side, another
party denyin' it, an' insistin' it belonged to them, an' so on.

"In the manetime, Katty Rafferty, for 'fraid the dinner
might come short, went home and made another pudden
much about the same size as the one that had escaped, and
bringin' it over to their next neighbour, Paddy Scanlan's, it
was put into a pot and placed on the fire to boil, hopin' that
it might be done in time, espishilly as they were to have the
ministher, who loved a warm slice of a good pudden as well
as e'er a gintleman in Europe.

"Anyhow, the day passed; Moll and Gusty were made
man an' wife, an' no two could be more lovin'. Their
friends that had been asked to the weddin' were saunterin'
about in pleasant little groups till dinner-time, chattin' an'
laughin'; but, above all things, sthrivin' to account for the
figaries of the pudden; for, to tell the truth, its adventures
had now gone through the whole parish.

"Well, at any rate, dinner-time was dhrawin' near, and
Paddy Scanlan was sittin' comfortably wid his wife at the
fire, the pudden boilen before their eyes, when in walks
Harry Connolly, in a flutter, shoutin'—'Blood an' blunderbushes, what are yez here for?'

"'Arra, why, Harry—why, avick?' said Mrs. Scanlan.

"'Why,' said Harry, 'the sun's in the suds an' the moon
in the high Horicks! Here's a clipstick comin' an, an'
there you sit as unconsarned as if it was about to rain
mether! Go out both of you, an' look at the sun, I say,
and ye'll see the condition he's in—off!'

"'Ay, but, Harry, what's that rowled up in the tail of
your cothamore* (big coat)?'

"'Out wid yez,' said Harry, 'an' pray aginst the clipstick
—the sky's fallin'!'

* Irish, *cóta mór*.

" Begad, it was hard to say whether Paddy or the wife got out first, they were so much alarmed by Harry's wild thin face an' piercin' eyes ; so out they went to see what was wondherful in the sky, an' kep' lookin' an' lookin' in every direction, but not a thing was to be seen, barrin' the sun shinin' down wid great good-humour, an' not a single cloud in the sky.

"Paddy an' the wife now came in laughin', to scould Harry, who, no doubt, was a great wag in his way when he wished. 'Musha, bad scran to you, Harry——.' They had time to say no more, howandiver, for, as they were goin' into the door, they met him comin' out of it wid a reek of smoke out of his tail like a lime-kiln.

"'Harry,' shouted Bridget, 'my sowl to glory, but the tail of your cothamore's a-fire—you'll be burned. Don't you see the smoke that's out of it ? '

"'Cross yourselves three times,' said Harry, widout stoppin', or even lookin' behind him, 'for, as the prophecy says—Fill the pot, Eddy——' They could hear no more, for Harry appeared to feel like a man that carried something a great deal hotter than he wished, as anyone might see by the liveliness of his motions, and the quare faces he was forced to make as he went along.

"'What the dickens is he carryin' in the skirts of his big coat ? ' asked Paddy.

"'My sowl to happiness, but maybe he has stole the pudden,' said Bridget, 'for it's known that many a sthrange thing he does.'

"They immediately examined the pot, but found that the pudden was there as safe as tuppence, an' this puzzled them the more, to think what it was he could be carryin' about wid him in the manner he did. But little they knew what he had done while they were sky-gazin !

"Well, anyhow, the day passed and the dinner was ready, an' no doubt but a fine gatherin' there was to partake of it. The Prosbytarian ministher met the Methodist praicher—a divilish stretcher of an appetite he had, in throth—on their way to Jack Rafferty's, an' as he knew he

could take the liberty, why he insisted on his dinin' wid him ;
for, afther all, begad, in thim times the clargy of all
descriptions lived upon the best footin' among one another,
not all as one as now—but no matther. Well, they had
nearly finished their dinner, when Jack Rafferty himself
axed Katty for the pudden ; but, jist as he spoke, in it
came as big as a mess-pot.

"'Gintlemen,' said he, 'I hope none of you will refuse
tastin' a bit of Katty's pudden ; I don't mane the dancin'
one that tuck to its thravels to-day, but a good solid fellow
that she med since.'

"'To be sure we won't,' replied the priest ; 'so, Jack,
put a thrifle on them three plates at your right hand, and
send them over here to the clargy, an' maybe,' he said,
laughin'—for he was a droll good-humoured man—'maybe,
Jack, we won't set you a proper example.'

"'Wid a heart an' a half, yer reverence an' gintlemen ;
in throth, it's not a bad example ever any of you set us at
the likes, or ever will set us, I'll go bail. An' sure I only
wish it was betther fare I had for you ; but we're humble
people, gintlemen, and so you can't expect to meet here
what you would in higher places.'

"'Deither a male of herbs,' said the Methodist praicher,
'where pace is——.' He had time to go no farther, however ; for much to his amazement, the priest and the
ministher started up from the table jist as he was goin' to
swallow the first spoonful of the pudden, and before you
could say Jack Robinson, started away at a lively jig down
the floor.

" At this moment a neighbour's son came runnin' in, an'
tould them that the parson was comin' to see the new-
married couple, an' wish them all happiness ; an' the words
were scarcely out of his mouth when he made his appearance. What to think he knew not, when he saw the
ministher footing it away at the rate of a weddin'. He had
very little time, however, to think ; for, before he could sit
down, up starts the Methodist praicher, and clappin' his
two fists in his sides, chimes in in great style along wid him.

"'Jack Rafferty,' says he—and, by the way, Jack was his tenant—'what the dickens does all this mane?' says he; 'I'm amazed!'

"'The not a particle o' me can tell you,' says Jack; 'but will your reverence jist taste a morsel o' pudden, merely that the young couple may boast that you ait at their weddin'; for sure if *you* wouldn't, *who* would?'

"'Well,' says he, 'to gratify them I will; so just a morsel. But, Jack, this bates Bannagher,' says he again, puttin' the spoonful o' pudden into his mouth; 'has there been dhrink here?'

"'Oh, the divle a *spudh*,' says Jack, 'for although there's plinty in the house, faith, it appears the gintlemen wouldn't wait for it. Unless they tuck it elsewhere, I can make nothin' of this.'

"He had scarcely spoken, when the parson, who was an active man, cut a caper a yard high, an' before you could bless yourself, the three clargy were hard at work dancin', as if for a wager. Begad, it would be unpossible for me to tell you the state the whole meetin' was in when they seen this. Some were hoarse wid laughin'; some turned up their eyes wid wondher; many thought them mad, an' others thought they had turned up their little fingers a thrifle too often.

"'Be goxty, it's a burnin' shame,' said one, 'to see three black-mouth clargy in sich a state at this early hour!' 'Thundher an' ounze, what's over them at all?' says others; 'why, one would think they're bewitched. Holy Moses, look at the caper the Methodis cuts! An' as for the Recther, who would think he could handle his feet at such a rate! Be this an' be that, he cuts the buckle, and does the threblin' step aiquil to Paddy Horaghan, the dancin'-masther himself? An' see! Bad cess to the morsel of the parson that's not hard at *Peace upon a trancher*, an' it of a Sunday too! Whirroo, gintlemen, the fun's in yez afther all—whish! more power to yez!'

"The sorra's own fun they had, an' no wondher; but judge of what they felt, when all at once they saw ould Jack

Rafferty himself bouncin' in among them, and footing it away like the best o' them. Bedad, no play could come up to it, an' nothin' could be heard but laughin', shouts of encouragement, and clappin' of hands like mad. Now the minute Jack Rafferty left the chair where he had been carvin' the pudden, ould Harry Connolly comes over and claps himself down in his place, in ordher to send it round, of coorse ; an' he was scarcely sated, when who should make his appeaiance but Barney Hartigan, the piper. Barney, by the way, had been sent for early in the day, but bein' from home when the message for him went, he couldn't come any sooner.

" ' Begorra,' said Barney, 'you're airly at the work, gintlemen ! but what does this mane ? But, divle may care, yez shan't want the music while there's a blast in the pipes, anyhow !' So sayin' he gave them *Jig Polthogue*, an' after that *Kiss my Lady*, in his best style.

" In the manetime the fun went on thick an' threefold, for it must be remimbered that Harry, the ould knave, was at the pudden ; an' maybe he didn't sarve it about in double quick time too. The first he helped was the bride, and, before you could say chopstick, she was at it hard an' fast before the Methodist praicher, who gave a jolly spring before her that threw them into convulsions. Harry liked this, and made up his mind soon to find partners for the rest ; so he accordianly sent the pudden about like lightnin' ; an' to make a long story short, barrin' the piper an' himself, there wasn't a pair o' heels in the house but was as busy at the dancin' as if their lives depinded on it.

" ' Barney,' says Harry, ' just taste a morsel o' this pudden ; divle the such a bully of a pudden ever you ett ; here, your sowl ! thry a snig of it—it's beautiful.'

" ' To be sure I will,' says Barney. ' I'm not the boy to refuse a good thing ; but, Harry, be quick, for you know my hands is engaged, an' it would be a thousand pities not to keep them in music, an' they so well inclined. Thank you, Harry ; begad that is a famous pudden ; but blood an' turnips, what's this for ? '

"The word was scarcely out of his mouth when he bounced up, pipes an' all, an' dashed into the middle of the party. 'Hurroo, your sowls, let us make a night of it! The Ballyboulteen boys for ever! Go it, your reverence— turn your partner—heel an' toe, ministher. Good! Well done again—Whish! Hurroo! Here's for Ballyboulteen, an' the sky over it!'

"Bad luck to the sich a set ever was seen together in this world, or will again, I suppose. The worst, however, wasn't come yet, for jist as they were in the very heat an' fury of the dance, what do you think comes hoppin' in among them but another pudden, as nimble an' merry as the first! That was enough; they all had heard of—the ministhers among the rest—an' most o' them had seen the other pudden, and knew that there must be a fairy in it, sure enough. Well, as I said, in it comes to the thick o' them; but the very appearance of it was enough. Off the three clargy danced, and off the whole weddiners danced afther them, every one makin' the best of their way home; but not a sowl of them able to break out of the step, if they were to be hanged for it. Throth it wouldn't lave a laugh in you to see the parson dancin' down the road on his way home, and the ministher and Methodist praicher cuttin' the buckle as they went along in the opposite direction. To make short work of it, they all danced home at last, wid scarce a puff of wind in them; the bride and bridegroom danced away to bed; an' now, boys, come an' let us dance the *Horo Lheig* in the barn 'idout. But you see, boys, before we go, an' in ordher that I may make everything plain, I had as good tell you that Harry, in crossing the bridge of Bally-boulteen, a couple of miles below Squire Bragshaw's demense-wall, saw the pudden floatin' down the river—the truth is he was waitin' for it; but be this as it may, he took it out, for the wather had made it as clane as a new pin, and tuckin' it up in the tail of his big coat, contrived, as you all guess, I suppose, to change it while Paddy Scanlan an' the wife were examinin' the sky; an' for the other, he contrived to bewitch it in the same manner, by gettin' a fairy to go

into it, for, indeed, it was purty well known that the same
Harry was hand an' glove wid the *good people*.   Others will
tell you that it was half a pound of quicksilver he put into
it ; but that doesn't stand to raison.   At any rate, boys,
I have tould you the adventures of the Mad Pudden
of Ballyboulteen ; but I don't wish to tell you many other
things about it that happened—*for fraid I'd tell a lie.*"*

* Some will insist that a fairy-man or fairy-woman has the power to
bewitch a pudding by putting a fairy into it ; whilst others maintain
that a competent portion of quicksilver will make it dance over half the
parish.

T'YEER-NA-N-OGE.

———◆———

[THERE is a country called Tír-na-n-Og, which means the Country of the Young, for age and death have not found it; neither tears nor loud laughter have gone near it. The shadiest boskage covers it perpetually. One man has gone there and returned. The bard, Oisen, who wandered away on a white horse, moving on the surface of the foam with his fairy Niamh, lived there three hundred years, and then returned looking for his comrades. The moment his foot touched the earth his three hundred years fell on him, and he was bowed double, and his beard swept the ground. He described his sojourn in the Land of Youth to Patrick before he died. Since then many have seen it in many places; some in the depths of lakes, and have heard rising therefrom a vague sound of bells; more have seen it far off on the horizon, as they peered out from the western cliffs. Not three years ago a fisherman imagined that he saw it. It never appears unless to announce some national trouble.

There are many kindred beliefs. A Dutch pilot, settled in Dublin, told M. De La Boullage Le Cong, who travelled in Ireland in 1614, that round the poles were many islands; some hard to be approached because of the witches who inhabit them and destroy by storms those who seek to land. He had once, off the coast of Greenland, in sixty-one degrees of latitude, seen and approached such an island only to see it vanish. Sailing in an opposite direction, they met with the same island, and sailing near, were almost destroyed by a furious tempest.

According to many stories, Tír-na-n-Og is the favourite dwelling of the fairies. Some say it is triple—the island of the living, the island of victories, and an underwater land.]

THE LEGEND OF O'DONOGHUE.*

T. CROFTON CROKER.

IN an age so distant that the precise period is unknown, a chieftain named O'Donoghue ruled over the country which surrounds the romantic Lough Lean, now called the lake of Killarney. Wisdom, beneficence, and justice distinguished his reign, and the prosperity and happiness of his subjects were their natural results. He is said to have been as renowned for his warlike exploits as for his pacific virtues ; and as a proof that his domestic administration was not the less rigorous because it was mild, a rocky island is pointed out to strangers, called " O'Donoghue's Prison," in which this prince once confined his own son for some act of disorder and disobedience.

His end—for it cannot correctly be called his death—was singular and mysterious. At one of those splendid feasts for which his court was celebrated, surrounded by the most distinguished of his subjects, he was engaged in a prophetic relation of the events which were to happen in ages yet to come. His auditors listened, now wrapt in wonder, now fired with indignation, burning with shame, or melted into sorrow, as he faithfully detailed the heroism, the injuries, the crimes, and the miseries of their descendants. In the midst of his predictions he rose slowly from his seat, advanced with a solemn, measured, and majestic tread to the shore of the lake, and walked forward composedly upon its unyielding surface. When he had nearly reached the centre he paused for a moment, then, turning slowly round, looked toward his friends, and waving his arms to them with the cheerful air of one taking a short farewell, disappeared from their view.

The memory of the good O'Donoghue has been cherished by successive generations with affectionate reverence ; and

* *Fairy Legends of the South of Ireland.*

it is believed that at sunrise, on every May-day morning, the anniversary of his departure, he revisits his ancient domains : a favoured few only are in general permitted to see him, and this distinction is always an omen of good fortune to the beholders ; when it is granted to many it is a sure token of an abundant harvest,—a blessing, the want of which during this prince's reign was never felt by his people.

Some years have elapsed since the last appearance of O'Donoghue. The April of that year had been remarkably wild and stormy ; but on May-morning the fury of the elements had altogether subsided. The air was hushed and still ; and the sky, which was reflected in the serene lake, resembled a beautiful but deceitful countenance, whose smiles, after the most tempestuous emotions, tempt the stranger to believe that it belongs to a soul which no passion has ever ruffled.

The first beams of the rising sun were just gilding the lofty summit of Glenaa, when the waters near the eastern shore of the lake became suddenly and violently agitated, though all the rest of its surface lay smooth and still as a tomb of polished marble, the next morning a foaming wave darted forward, and, like a proud high-crested war-horse, exulting in his strength, rushed across the lake toward Toomies mountain. Behind this wave appeared a stately warrior fully armed, mounted upon a milk-white steed ; his snowy plume waved gracefully from a helmet of polished steel, and at his back fluttered a light blue scarf. The horse, apparently exulting in his noble burden, sprung after the wave along the water, which bore him up like firm earth, while showers of spray that glittered brightly in the morning sun were dashed up at every bound.

The warrior was O'Donoghue ; he was followed by numberless youths and maidens, who moved lightly and unconstrained over the watery plain, as the moonlight fairies glide through the fields of air ; they were linked together by garlands of delicious spring flowers, and they timed their movements to strains of enchanting melody. When O'Donoghue had nearly reached the western side of the lake, he suddenly turned his steed, and directed his course along the wood-fringed shore of Glenaa, preceded by the huge wave that curled and foamed up as high as the horse's neck, whose fiery nostrils snorted above it. The long train of attendants followed with playful deviations the track of their leader, and moved on with unabated fleetness to their celestial music, till gradually, as they entered the narrow strait between Glenaa and Dinis, they became involved in the mists which still partially floated over the lakes, and faded from the view of the wondering beholders: but the sound of their music still fell upon the ear, and echo, catching up the harmonious strains, fondly repeated and prolonged them in soft and softer tones, till the last faint repetition died away, and the hearers awoke as from a dream of bliss.

RENT-DAY.

"Oh, ullagone ! ullagone ! this is a wide world, but what will we do in it, or where will we go ? " muttered Bill Doody, as he sat on a rock by the Lake of Killarney. " What will we do ? To-morrow's rent-day, and Tim the Driver swears if we don't pay our rent, he'll cant every *ha'perth* we have ; and then, sure enough, there's Judy and myself, and the poor *grawls*,* will be turned out to starve on the high-road, for the never a halfpenny of rent have I !—Oh hone, that ever I should live to see this day ! "

Thus did Bill Doody bemoan his hard fate, pouring his sorrows to the reckless waves of the most beautiful of lakes, which seemed to mock his misery as they rejoiced beneath the cloudless sky of a May morning. That lake, glittering in sunshine, sprinkled with fairy isles of rock and verdure, and bounded by giant hills of ever-varying hues, might, with its magic beauty, charm all sadness but despair ; for alas,

---

* Children.

> " How ill the scene that offers rest
>   And heart that cannot rest agree ! "

Yet Bill Doody was not so desolate as he supposed ; there was one listening to him he little thought of, and help was at hand from a quarter he could not have expected.

"What's the matter with you, my poor man?" said a tall, portly-looking gentleman, at the same time stepping out of a furze-brake.   Now Bill was seated on a rock that commanded the view of a large field.   Nothing in the field could be concealed from him, except this furze-brake, which grew in a hollow near the margin of the lake.   He was, therefore, not a little surprised at the gentleman's sudden appearance, and began to question whether the personage before him belonged to this world or not.   He, however, soon mustered courage sufficient to tell him how his crops had failed, how some bad member had charmed away his butter, and how Tim the Driver threatened to turn him out of the farm if he didn't pay up every penny of the rent by twelve o'clock next day.

" A sad story, indeed," said the stranger ; " but surely, if you represented the case to your landlord's agent, he won't have the heart to turn you out."

" Heart, your honour ; where would an agent get a heart ! " exclaimed Bill.   " I see your honour does not know him ; besides, he has an eye on the farm this long time for a fosterer of his own ; so I expect no mercy at all at all, only to be turned out."

" Take this, my poor fellow, take this," said the stranger, pouring a purse full of gold into Bill's old hat, which in his grief he had flung on the ground.   " Pay the fellow your rent, but I'll take care it shall do him no good.   I remember the time when things went otherwise in this country, when I would have hung up such a fellow in the twinkling of an eye ! "

These words were lost upon Bill, who was insensible to everything but the sight of the gold, and before he could unfix his gaze, and lift up his head to pour out his hundred thousand blessings, the stranger was gone.   The bewildered peasant looked around in search of his benefactor, and at last he thought he saw him riding on a white horse a long way off on the lake.

"O'Donoghue, O'Donoghue!" shouted Bill; "the good, the blessed O'Donoghue!" and he ran capering like a madman to show Judy the gold, and to rejoice her heart with the prospect of wealth and happiness.

The next day Bill proceeded to the agent's; not sneakingly, with his hat in his hand, his eyes fixed on the ground, and his knees bending under him; but bold and upright, like a man conscious of his independence.

"Why don't you take off your hat, fellow? don't you know you are speaking to a magistrate?" said the agent.

"I know I'm not speaking to the king, sir," said Bill; "and I never takes off my hat but to them I can respect and love. The Eye that sees all knows I've no right either to respect or love an agent!"

"You scoundrel!" retorted the man in office, biting his lips with rage at such an unusual and unexpected opposition, "I'll teach you how to be insolent again; I have the power, remember."

"To the cost of the country, I know you have," said Bill, who still remained with his head as firmly covered as if he was the Lord Kingsale himself.

"But, come," said the magistrate; "have you got the money for me? this is rent-day. If there's one penny of it wanting, or the running gale that's due, prepare to turn out before night, for you shall not remain another hour in possession.

"There is your rent," said Bill, with an unmoved expression of tone and countenance; "you'd better count it, and give me a receipt in full for the running gale and all."

The agent gave a look of amazement at the gold; for it was gold—real guineas! and not bits of dirty ragged small notes, that are only fit to light one's pipe with. However willing the agent may have been to ruin, as he thought, the unfortunate tenant, he took up the gold, and handed the receipt to Bill, who strutted off with it as proud as a cat of her whiskers.

The agent going to his desk shortly after, was confounded at beholding a heap of gingerbread cakes instead of the money he had deposited there. He raved and swore, but all to no purpose; the gold had become gingerbread cakes, just marked like the guineas, with the king's head; and Bill had the receipt in his pocket; so he saw there was no use in saying anything about the affair, as he would only get laughed at for his pains.

From that hour Bill Doody grew rich; all his undertakings prospered; and he often blesses the day that he met with O'Donoghue, the great prince that lives down under the lake of Killarney.

LOUGHLEAGH (LAKE OF HEALING).*

"Do you see that bit of a lake," said my companion, turning his eyes towards the acclivity that overhung Loughleagh. "Troth, and as little as you think of it, and as ugly as it looks with its weeds and its flags, it is the most famous one in all Ireland. Young and ould, rich and poor, far and near, have come to that lake to get cured of all kinds of scurvy and sores. The Lord keep us our limbs whole and sound, for it's a sorrowful thing not to have the use o' them. 'Twas but last week we had a great grand Frenchman here; and, though he came upon crutches, faith he went home sound as a bell; and well he paid Billy Reily for curing him."

"And, pray, how did Billy Reily cure him?"

"Oh, well enough. He took his long pole, dipped it down to the bottom of the lake, and brought up on the top of it as much plaster as would do for a thousand sores!"

"What kind of plaster?"

* Dublin and London Magazine, 1825.

" What kind of plaster? why, black plaster to be sure;
for isn't the bottom of the lake filled with a kind of black
mud which cures all the world ? "

" Then it ought to be a famous lake indeed."

"Famous, and so it is," replied my companion, " but it
isn't for its cures neather that it is famous ; for, sure,
doesn't all the world know there is a fine beautiful city at
the bottom of it, where the good people live just like
Christians.   Troth, it is the truth I tell you; for *Shemus-
a-sneidh* saw it all when he followed his dun cow that was
stolen."

" Who stole her ? "

" I'll tell you all about it :—Shemus was a poor gossoon,
who lived on the brow of the hill, in a cabin with his ould
mother.   They lived by hook and by crook, one way and
another, in the best way they could.   They had a bit of
ground that gave 'em the preaty, and a little dun cow that
gave 'em the drop o' milk ; and, considering how times go,
they weren't badly off, for Shemus was a handy gossoon to
boot ; and, while minden the cow, cut heath and made
brooms, which his mother sould on a market-day, and
brought home the bit o' tobaccy, the grain of salt, and other
nic-nackenes, which a poor body can't well do widout.
Once upon a time, however, Shemus went farther than
usual up the mountain, looken for long heath, for town's-
people don't like to stoop, and so like long handles to their
brooms.   The little dun cow was a'most as cunning as a
Christian sinner, and followed Shemus like a lap-dog everywhere he'd go, so that she required little or no herden.   On
this day she found nice picken on a round spot as green as
a leek ; and, as poor Shemus was weary, as a body would
be on a fine summer's day, he lay down on the grass to rest
himself, just as we're resten ourselves on the cairn here.
Begad, he hadn't long lain there, sure enough, when, what
should he see but whole loads of ganconers* dancing about

* Ir. *gean-canach—i.e.*, love-talker, a kind of fairy appearing in
lonesome valleys, a dudeen (tobacco-pipe) in his mouth, making love
to milk-maids, etc.

the place. Some o' them were hurlen, some kicking a football, and others leaping a kick-step-and-a-lep. They were so soople and so active that Shemus was highly delighted with the sport, and a little tanned-skinned chap in a red cap pleased him better than any o' them, bekase he used to tumble the other fellows like mushrooms. At one time he had kept the ball up for as good as half-an-hour, when Shemus cried out, 'Well done, my hurler!' The word wasn't well out of his mouth when whap went the ball on his eye, and flash went the fire. Poor Shemus thought he was blind, and roared out, 'Mille murdher!'* but the only thing he heard was a loud laugh. 'Cross o' Christ about us,' says he to himself, 'what is this for?' and afther rubbing his eyes they came to a little, and he could see the sun and the sky, and, by-and-by, he could see everything but his cow and the mischievous ganconers. They were gone to their rath or mote; but where was the little dun cow? He looked, and he looked, and he might have looked from that day to this, bekase she wasn't to be found, and good reason why—the ganconers took her away with 'em.

"Shemus-a-sneidh, however, didn't think so, but ran home to his mother.

"'Where is the cow, Shemus?' axed the ould woman.

"'Och, musha, bad luck to her,' said Shemus, 'I donna where she is!'

"'Is that an answer, you big blaggard, for the likes o' you to give your poor ould mother?' said she.

"'Och, musha,' said Shemus, 'don't kick up saich a bollhous about nothing. The ould cow is safe enough, I'll be bail, some place or other, though I could find her if I put my eyes upon kippeens,† and, speaking of eyes, faith, I had very good luck o' my side, or I had naver a one to look after her.'

"'Why, what happened your eyes, agrah?' axed the ould woman.

"'Oh! didn't the ganconers—the Lord save us from all

* A thousand murders.　　† Ir. cipin—i.e., a stick, a twig.

hurt and harm !—drive their hurlen ball into them both ! and sure I was stone blind for an hour.'

" 'And may be,' said the mother, 'the good people took our cow ? '

" 'No, nor the devil a one of them,' said Shemus, 'for, by the powers, that same cow is as knowen as a lawyer, and wouldn't be such a fool as to go with the ganconers while she could get such grass as I found for her to-day.'

In this way, continued my informant, they talked about the cow all that night, and next mornen both o' them set off to look for her. After searching every place, high and low, what should Shemus see sticking out of a bog-hole but something very like the horns of his little beast !

" Oh, mother, mother," said he, " I've found her ! "

" Where, alanna ? " axed the ould woman.

" In the bog-hole, mother," answered Shemus.

At this the poor ould creathure set up such a *pullallue* that she brought the seven parishes about her ; and the neighbours soon pulled the cow out of the bog-hole. You'd swear it was the same, and yet it wasn't, as you shall hear by-and-by.

Shemus and his mother brought the dead beast home with them ; and, after skinnen her, hung the meat up in the chimney. The loss of the drop o' milk was a sorrowful thing, and though they had a good deal of meat, that couldn't last always ; besides, the whole parish *faughed* upon them for eating the flesh of a beast that died without bleeden. But the pretty thing was, they couldn't eat the meat after all, for when it was boiled it was as tough as carrion, and as black as a turf. You might as well think of sinking your teeth in an oak plank as into a piece of it, and then you'd want to sit a great piece from the wall for fear of knocking your head against it when pulling it through your teeth. At last and at long run they were forced to throw it to the dogs, but the dogs wouldn't smell to it, and so it was thrown into the ditch, where it rotted. This misfortune cost poor Shemus many a salt tear, for he was now obliged to work twice as hard as before, and be out cutten heath on the mountain late and early. One day he was passing by this cairn with a load of brooms on his back, when what should he see but the little dun cow and two red-headed fellows herding her.

" That's my mother's cow," said Shemus-a-sneidh.

" No, it is not," said one of the chaps.

" But I say it is," said Shemus, throwing the brooms on the ground, and seizing the cow by the horns. At that the red fellows drove her as fast as they could to this steep place, and with one leap she bounced over, with Shemus stuck fast to her horns. They made only one splash in the lough, when the waters closed over 'em, and they sunk to the bottom. Just as Shemus-a-sneidh thought that all was over with him, he found himself before a most elegant palace built with jewels, and all manner of fine stones. Though his eyes were dazzled with the splendour of the place, faith he had gomsh* enough not to let go his holt, but in spite of all they could do, he held his little cow by the horns. He was axed into the palace, but wouldn't go.

The hubbub at last grew so great that the door flew open, and out walked a hundred ladies and gentlemen, as fine as any in the land.

" What does this boy want?" axed one o' them, who seemed to be the masther.

" I want my mother's cow," said Shemus.

" That's not your mother's cow," said the gentleman.

" Bethershin!"† cried Shemus-a-sneid; " don't I know her as well as I know my right hand?"

" Where did you lose her?" axed the gentleman. And so Shemus up and tould him all about it : how he was on the mountain—how he saw the good people hurlen—how the ball was knocked in his eye, and his cow was lost.

" I believe you are right," said the gentleman, pulling out his purse, " and here is the price of twenty cows for you."

" No, no," said Shemus, " you'll not catch ould birds wid chaff. I'll have my cow and nothen else."

* Otherwise " gumshun—" *i.e.*, sense, cuteness.
† Ir. *B'éidir sin—i.e.*, " that is possible."

"You're a funny fellow," said the gentleman; "stop here and live in a palace."

"I'd rather live with my mother."

"Foolish boy!" said the gentleman; "stop here and live in a palace."

"I'd rather live in my mother's cabin."

"Here you can walk through gardens loaded with fruit and flowers."

"I'd rather," said Shemus, "be cutting heath on the mountain."

"Here you can eat and drink of the best."

"Since I've got my cow, I can have milk once more with the praties."

"Oh!" cried the ladies, gathering round him, "sure you wouldn't take away the cow that gives us milk for our tea?"

"Oh!" said Shemus, "my mother wants milk as bad as anyone, and she must have it; so there is no use in your palaver—I must have my cow."

At this they all gathered about him and offered him bushels of gould, but he wouldn't have anything but his cow. Seeing him as obstinate as a mule, they began to thump and beat him; but still he held fast by the horns, till at length a great blast of wind blew him out of the place, and in a moment he found himself and the cow standing on the side of the lake, the water of which looked as if it hadn't been disturbed since Adam was a boy—and that's a long time since.

Well, Shemus-a-sneidh drove home his cow, and right glad his mother was to see her; but the moment she said "God bless the beast," she sunk down like the *breesha** of a turf rick. That was the end of Shemus-a-sneidh's dun cow.

"And, sure," continued my companion, standing up, "it is now time for me to look after my brown cow, and God send the ganconers haven't taken her!"

Of this I assured him there could be no fear; and so we parted.

* Ir. *briseadh—i.e.*, breaking.

HY-BRASAIL—THE ISLE OF THE BLEST.

BY GERALD GRIFFIN.

On the ocean that hollows the rocks where ye dwell,
A shadowy land has appeared, as they tell ;
Men thought it a region of sunshine and rest,
And they called it *Hy-Brasail*, the isle of the blest.
From year unto year on the ocean's blue rim,
The beautiful spectre showed lovely and dim ;
The golden clouds curtained the deep where it lay,
And it looked like an Eden, away, far away !

A peasant who heard of the wonderful tale,
In the breeze of the Orient loosened his sail ;
From Ara, the holy, he turned to the west,
For though Ara was holy, *Hy-Brasail* was blest.
He heard not the voices that called from the shore—
He heard not the rising wind's menacing roar ;
Home, kindred, and safety, he left on that day,
And he sped to *Hy-Brasail*, away, far away !

Morn rose on the deep, and that shadowy isle,
O'er the faint rim of distance, reflected its smile ;
Noon burned on the wave, and that shadowy shore
Seemed lovelily distant, and faint as before ;
Lone evening came down on the wanderer's track,
And to Ara again he looked timidly back ;
Oh ! far on the verge of the ocean it lay,
Yet the isle of the blest was away, far away !

Rash dreamer, return !   O, ye winds of the main,
Bear him back to his own peaceful Ara again.
Rash fool ! for a vision of fanciful bliss,
To barter thy calm life of labour and peace.
The warning of reason was spoken in vain ;
He never revisited Ara again !
Night fell on the deep, amidst tempest and spray,
And he died on the waters, away, far away !

THE PHANTOM ISLE.

GIRALDUS CAMBRENSIS.*

AMONG the other islands is one newly formed, which they call the Phantom Isle, which had its origin in this manner. One calm day a large mass of earth rose to the surface of the sea, where no land had ever been seen before, to the great amazement of islanders who observed it. Some of them said that it was a whale, or other immense sea-monster; others, remarking that it continued motionless, said, "No; it is land." In order, therefore, to reduce their doubts to certainty, some picked young men of the island determined to approach nearer the spot in a boat. When, however, they came so near to it that they thought they should go on shore, the island sank in the water and entirely vanished from sight. The next day it re-appeared, and again mocked the same youths with the like delusion. At length, on their rowing towards it on the third day, they followed the advice of an older man, and let fly an arrow, barbed with red-hot steel, against the island; and then landing, found it stationary and habitable.

This adds one to the many proofs that fire is the greatest of enemies to every sort of phantom; in so much that those who have seen apparitions, fall into a swoon as soon as they are sensible of the brightness of fire. For fire, both from its position and nature, is the noblest of the elements, being a witness of the secrets of the heavens.

The sky is fiery; the planets are fiery; the bush burnt with fire, but was not consumed; the Holy Ghost sat upon the apostles in tongues of fire.

* "Giraldus Cambrensis" was born in 1146, and wrote a celebrated account of Ireland.

SAINTS, PRIESTS.

EVERYWHERE in Ireland are the holy wells. People as they pray by them make little piles of stones, that will be counted at the last day and the prayers reckoned up. Sometimes they tell stories. These following are their stories. They deal with the old times, whereof King Alfred of Northumberland wrote—

"I found in Innisfail the fair,
In Ireland, while in exile there,
Women of worth, both grave and gay men,
Many clericks and many laymen.

Gold and silver I found, and money,
Plenty of wheat, and plenty of honey;
I found God's people rich in pity,
Found many a feast, and many a city."

There are no martyrs in the stories. That ancient chronicler Giraldus taunted the Archbishop of Cashel because no one in Ireland had received the crown of martyrdom. "Our people may be barbarous," the prelate answered, "but they have never lifted their hands against God's saints; but now that a people have come amongst us who know how to make them (it was just after the English invasion), we shall have martyrs plentifully."

The bodies of saints are fastidious things. At a place called Four-mile-Water, in Wexford, there is an old graveyard full of saints. Once it was on the other side of the river, but they buried a rogue there, and the whole graveyard moved across in the night, leaving the rogue-corpse in solitude. It would have been easier to move merely the rogue-corpse, but they were saints, and had to do things in style.

THE PRIEST'S SOUL.*

LADY WILDE.

In former days there were great schools in Ireland, where every sort of learning was taught to the people, and even the poorest had more knowledge at that time than many a gentleman has now. But as to the priests, their learning was above all, so that the fame of Ireland went over the whole world, and many kings from foreign lands used to send their sons all the way to Ireland to be brought up in the Irish schools.

Now, at this time there was a little boy learning at one of them who was a wonder to everyone for his cleverness. His parents were only labouring people, and of course poor ; but young as he was, and as poor as he was, no king's or lord's son could come up to him in learning. Even the masters were put to shame ; for when they were trying to teach him he would tell them something they never heard of before, and show them their ignorance. One of his great triumphs was in argument ; and he would go on till he proved to you that black was white, and then when you gave in, for no one could beat him in talk, he would turn round and show you that white was black, or maybe that there was no colour at all in the world. When he grew up his poor father and mother were so proud of him that they resolved to make him a priest, which they did at last, though they nearly starved themselves to get the money. Well, such another learned man was not in Ireland, and he was as great in argument as ever, so that no one could stand before him. Even the bishops tried to talk to him, but he showed them at once they knew nothing at all.

Now, there were no schoolmasters in those times, but it was the priests taught the people ; and as this man was the cleverest in Ireland, all the foreign kings sent their sons to him, as long as he had house-room to give them. So he

* *Ancient Legends of Ireland.*

grew very proud, and began to forget how low he had been, and worst of all, even to forget God, who had made him what he was. And the pride of arguing got hold of him, so that from one thing to another he went on to prove that there was no Purgatory, and then no Hell, and then no Heaven, and then no God; and at last that men had no souls, but were no more than a dog or a cow, and when they died there was an end of them. "Whoever saw a soul?" he would say. "If you can show me one, I will believe." No one could make any answer to this; and at last they all came to believe that as there was no other world, everyone might do what they liked in this; the priest setting the example, for he took a beautiful young girl to wife. But as no priest or bishop in the whole land could be got to marry them, he was obliged to read the service over for himself. It was a great scandal, yet no one dared to say a word, for all the king's sons were on his side, and would have slaughtered anyone who tried to prevent his wicked goings-on. Poor boys; they all believed in him, and thought every word he said was the truth. In this way his notions began to spread about, and the whole world was going to the bad, when one night an angel came down from Heaven, and told the priest he had but twenty-four hours to live. He began to tremble, and asked for a little more time.

But the angel was stiff, and told him that could not be. "What do you want time for, you sinner?" he asked.

"Oh, sir, have pity on my poor soul!" urged the priest.

"Oh, no! You have a soul, then," said the angel. "Pray, how did you find that out?"

"It has been fluttering in me ever since you appeared," answered the priest. "What a fool I was not to think of it before."

"A fool, indeed," said the angel. "What good was all your learning, when it could not tell you that you had a soul?"

"Ah, my lord," said the priest, "If I am to die, tell me how soon I may be in Heaven?"

"Never," replied the angel. "You denied there was a Heaven."

"Then, my lord, may I go to Purgatory?"

"You denied Purgatory also; you must go straight to Hell," said the angel.

"But, my lord, I denied Hell also," answered the priest, "so you can't send me there either."

The angel was a little puzzled.

"Well," said he, "I'll tell you what I can do for you. You may either live now on earth for a hundred years, enjoying every pleasure, and then be cast into Hell for ever; or you may die in twenty-four hours in the most horrible torments, and pass through Purgatory, there to remain till the Day of Judgment, if only you can find some one person that believes, and through his belief mercy will be vouchsafed to you, and your soul will be saved."

The priest did not take five minutes to make up his mind.

"I will have death in the twenty-four hours," he said, "so that my soul may be saved at last."

On this the angel gave him directions as to what he was to do, and left him.

Then immediately the priest entered the large room where all the scholars and the kings' sons were seated, and called out to them—

"Now, tell me the truth, and let none fear to contradict me; tell me what is your belief—have men souls?"

"Master," they answered, "once we believed that men had souls; but thanks to your teaching, we believe so no longer. There is no Hell, and no Heaven, and no God. This is our belief, for it is thus you taught us."

Then the priest grew pale with fear, and cried out— "Listen! I taught you a lie. There is a God, and man has an immortal soul. I believe now all I denied before."

But the shouts of laughter that rose up drowned the priest's voice, for they thought he was only trying them for argument.

"Prove it, master," they cried. "Prove it. Who has ever seen God? Who has ever seen the soul?"

And the room was stirred with their laughter.

The priest stood up to answer them, but no word could he utter. All his eloquence, all his powers of argument had gone from him; and he could do nothing but wring his hands and cry out, "There is a God! there is a God! Lord have mercy on my soul!"

And they all began to mock him! and repeat his own words that he had taught them—

"Show him to us; show us your God." And he fled from them, groaning with agony, for he saw that none believed; and how, then, could his soul be saved?

But he thought next of his wife. "She will believe," he said to himself; "women never give up God."

And he went to her; but she told him that she believed only what he taught her, and that a good wife should believe in her husband first and before and above all things in Heaven or earth.

Then despair came on him, and he rushed from the house, and began to ask every one he met if they believed. But the same answer came from one and all—"We believe only what you have taught us," for his doctrine had spread far and wide through the country.

Then he grew half mad with fear, for the hours were passing, and he flung himself down on the ground in a lonesome spot, and wept and groaned in terror, for the time was coming fast when he must die.

Just then a little child came by. "God save you kindly," said the child to him.

The priest started up.

"Do you believe in God?" he asked.

"I have come from a far country to learn about him," said the child. "Will your honour direct me to the best school they have in these parts?"

"The best school and the best teacher is close by," said the priest, and he named himself.

"Oh, not to that man," answered the child, "for I am told he denies God, and Heaven, and Hell, and even that man has a soul, because he cannot see it; but I would soon put him down."

The priest looked at him earnestly. "How?" he inquired.

"Why," said the child, "I would ask him if he believed he had life to show me his life."

"But he could not do that, my child," said the priest. "Life cannot be seen; we have it, but it is invisible."

"Then if we have life, though we cannot see it, we may also have a soul, though it is invisible," answered the child.

When the priest heard him speak these words, he fell down on his knees before him, weeping for joy, for now he knew his soul was safe; he had met one at last that believed. And he told the child his whole story—all his wickedness, and pride, and blasphemy against the great God; and how the angel had come to him, and told him of the only way in which he could be saved, through the faith and prayers of someone that believed.

"Now, then," he said to the child, "take this penknife and strike it into my breast, and go on stabbing the flesh until you see the paleness of death on my face. Then watch—for a living thing will soar up from my body as I die, and you will then know that my soul has ascended to the presence of God. And when you see this thing, make haste and run to my school, and call on all my scholars to come and see that the soul of their master has left the body, and that all he taught them was a lie, for that there is a God who punishes sin, and a Heaven, and a Hell, and that man has an immortal soul destined for eternal happiness or misery."

"I will pray," said the child, "to have courage to do this work."

And he kneeled down and prayed. Then when he rose up he took the penknife and struck it into the priest's heart, and struck and struck again till all the flesh was lacerated; but still the priest lived, though the agony was horrible, for he could not die until the twenty-four hours had expired.

At last the agony seemed to cease, and the stillness of

death settled on his face. Then the child, who was watching, saw a beautiful living creature, with four snow-white wings, mount from the dead man's body into the air and go fluttering round his head.

So he ran to bring the scholars; and when they saw it, they all knew it was the soul of their master; and they watched with wonder and awe until it passed from sight into the clouds.

And this was the first butterfly that was ever seen in Ireland; and now all men know that the butterflies are the souls of the dead, waiting for the moment when they may enter Purgatory, and so pass through torture to purification and peace.

But the schools of Ireland were quite deserted after that time, for people said, What is the use of going so far to learn, when the wisest man in all Ireland did not know if he had a soul till he was near losing it, and was only saved at last through the simple belief of a little child.

THE PRIEST OF COLOONY.

W. B. YEATS.

Good Father John O'Hart
    In penal days rode out
To a *shoneen* in his freelands,
    With his snipe marsh and his trout.

In trust took he John's lands,
    —*Sleiveens* were all his race—
And he gave them as dowers to his daughters,
    And they married beyond their place.

But Father John went up,
    And Father John went down;
And he wore small holes in his shoes,
    And he wore large holes in his gown.

Shoneen—*i.e.*, upstart.   *Sleiveen*—*i.e.*, mean fellow.

All loved him, only the *shoneen*,
    Whom the devils have by the hair,
From their wives and their cats and their children,
    To the birds in the white of the air.

The birds, for he opened their cages,
    As he went up and down ;
And he said with a smile, "Have peace, now,"
    And went his way with a frown.

But if when anyone died,
    Came keener hoarser than rooks,
He bade them give over their keening,
    For he was a man of books.

And these were the works of John,
    When weeping score by score,
People came into Coloony,
    For he'd died at ninety-four.

There was no human keening ;
    The birds from Knocknarea,
And the world round Knocknashee,
    Came keening in that day,—

Keening from Innismurry,
    Nor stayed for bit or sup ;
This way were all reproved
    Who dig old customs up.

[Coloony is a few miles south of the town of Sligo. Father
O'Hart lived there in the last century, and was greatly beloved.
These lines accurately record the tradition. No one who has
held the stolen land has prospered. It has changed owners
many times.]

THE STORY OF THE LITTLE BIRD.*

T. CROFTON CROKER.

MANY years ago there was a very religious and holy man, one of the monks of a convent, and he was one day kneeling at his prayers in the garden of his monastery, when he heard a little bird singing in one of the rose-trees of the garden, and there never was anything that he had heard in the world so sweet as the song of that little bird.

And the holy man rose up from his knees where he was kneeling at his prayers to listen to its song; for he thought he never in all his life heard anything so heavenly.

And the little bird, after singing for some time longer on the rose-tree, flew away to a grove at some distance from the monastery, and the holy man followed it to listen to its singing, for he felt as if he would never be tired of listening to the sweet song it was singing out of its throat.

And the little bird after that went away to another distant tree, and sung there for a while, and then to another tree, and so on in the same manner, but ever further and further away from the monastery, and the holy man still following it farther, and farther, and farther, still listening delighted to its enchanting song.

But at last he was obliged to give up, as it was growing late in the day, and he returned to the convent; and as he approached it in the evening, the sun was setting in the west with all the most heavenly colours that were ever seen in the world, and when he came into the convent, it was nightfall.

And he was quite surprised at everything he saw, for they were all strange faces about him in the monastery that he had never seen before, and the very place itself, and everything about it, seemed to be strangely altered; and, altogether, it seemed entirely different from what it was when he had left in the morning; and the garden was not

* *Amulet*, 1827. T. C. Croker wrote this, he says, word for word as he heard it from an old woman at a holy well.

like the garden where he had been kneeling at his devotion when he first heard the singing of the little bird.

And while he was wondering at all he saw, one of the monks of the convent came up to him, and the holy man questioned him, "Brother, what is the cause of all these strange changes that have taken place here since the morning?"

And the monk that he spoke to seemed to wonder greatly at his question, and asked him what he meant by the change since morning? for, sure, there was no change; that all was just as before. And then he said, "Brother, why do you ask these strange questions, and what is your name? for you wear the habit of our order, though we have never seen you before."

So upon this the holy man told his name, and said that he had been at mass in the chapel in the morning before he had wandered away from the garden listening to the song of a little bird that was singing among the rose-trees, near where he was kneeling at his prayers.

And the brother, while he was speaking, gazed at him very earnestly, and then told him that there was in the convent a tradition of a brother of his name, who had left it two hundred years before, but that what was become of him was never known.

And while he was speaking, the holy man said, "My hour of death is come; blessed be the name of the Lord for all his mercies to me, through the merits of his only-begotten Son."

And he kneeled down that very moment, and said, "Brother, take my confession, for my soul is departing."

And he made his confession, and received his absolution, and was anointed, and before midnight he died.

The little bird, you see, was an angel, one of the cherubims or seraphims; and that was the way the Almighty was pleased in His mercy to take to Himself the soul of that holy man.

CONVERSION OF KING LAOGHAIRE'S DAUGHTERS.

ONCE when Patrick and his clericks were sitting beside a well in the Rath of Croghan, with books open on their knees, they saw coming towards them the two young daughters of the King of Connaught. 'Twas early morning, and they were going to the well to bathe.

The young girls said to Patrick, " Whence are ye, and whence come ye ? " and Patrick answered, " It were better for you to confess to the true God than to inquire concerning our race."

" Who is God ? " said the young girls, "and where is God, and of what nature is God, and where is His dwelling-place ? Has your God sons and daughters, gold and silver ? Is he everlasting ? Is he beautiful ? Did Mary foster her son ? Are His daughters dear and beauteous to men of the world ? Is He in heaven, or on earth, in the sea, in rivers, in mountainous places, in valleys ? "

Patrick answered them, and made known who God was, and they believed and were baptised, and a white garment put upon their heads ; and Patrick asked them would they live on, or would they die and behold the face of Christ ? They chose death, and died immediately, and were buried near the well Clebach.

KING O'TOOLE AND HIS GOOSE.

S. LOVER.

" By Gor, I thought all the world, far and near, heerd o' King O'Toole—well, well, but the darkness of mankind is ontellible ! Well, sir, you must know, as you didn't hear it afore, that there was a king, called King O'Toole, who was a fine ould king in the ould ancient times, long ago; and it was him that owned the churches in the early days.   The king, you see, was the right sort; he was the rale boy, and loved sport as he loved his life, and huntin' in partic'lar; and from the risin' o' the sun, up he got, and away he wint over the mountains beyant afther the deer; and the fine times them wor.

"Well, it was all mighty good, as long as the king had his health; but, you see, in coorse of time the king grew ould, by raison he was stiff in his limbs, and when he got sthriken in years, his heart failed him, and he was lost intirely for want o' divarshin, bekase he couldn't go a huntin' no longer; and, by dad, the poor king was obleeged at last for to get a goose to divart him.   Oh, you may laugh, if you like, but it's truth I'm tellin' you; and the way the goose divarted him was this-a-way: You see, the goose used for to swim acrass the lake, and go divin' for throut, and cotch fish on a Friday for the king, and flew every other day round about the lake, divartin' the poor king.   All went on mighty well, antil, by dad, the goose got sthriken in years like her master, and couldn't divart him no longer, and then it was that the poor king was lost complate. The king was walkin' one mornin' by the edge of the lake, lamentin' his cruel fate, and thinkin' o' drownin' himself, that could get no divarshun in life, when all of a suddint, turnin' round the corner beyant, who should he meet but a mighty dacent young man comin' up to him.

"'God save you,' says the king to the young man.

"'God save you kindly, King O'Toole,' says the young man.   'Thrue for you,' says the king.   'I am King O'Toole,' says he, 'prince and plennypennytinchery o' these parts,' says he; 'but how kem ye to know that?' says he.   'Oh, never mind,' says St. Kavin.

"You see it was Saint Kavin, sure enough—the saint himself in disguise, and nobody else.   'Oh, never mind,' says he, 'I know more than that.   May I make bowld to ax how is your goose, King O'Toole?' says he. 'Blur-an-agers, how kem ye to know about my goose?' says the king. 'Oh, no matther; I was given to understand it,' says Saint Kavin. After some more talk the king says, 'What are you?' 'I'm an honest man,' says Saint Kavin. 'Well, honest man,' says the king, 'and how is it you make your money so aisy?' 'By makin' ould things as good as new,' says Saint Kavin. 'Is it a tinker you are?' says the king. 'No,' says the saint; 'I'm no tinker by thrade, King O'Toole; I've a betther thrade than a tinker,' says he— 'what would you say,' says he, 'if I made your ould goose as good as new?'

"My dear, at the word o' making his goose as good as new, you'd think the poor ould king's eyes was ready to jump out iv his head. With that the king whistled, and down kem the poor goose, all as one as a hound, waddlin' up to the poor cripple, her masther, and as like him as two pays. The minute the saint clapt his eyes on the goose, 'I'll do the job for you,' says he, 'King O'Toole.' 'By *Jaminee!*' says King O'Toole, 'if you do, bud I'll say you're the cleverest fellow in the sivin parishes.' 'Oh, by dad,' says St. Kavin, 'you must say more nor that—my horn's not so soft all out,' says he, 'as to repair your ould goose for nothin'; what'll you gi' me if I do the job for you?—that's the chat,' says St. Kavin. 'I'll give you whatever you ax,' says the king; 'isn't that fair?' 'Divil a fairer,' says the saint; 'that's the way to do business. Now,' says he, 'this is the bargain I'll make with you, King O'Toole: will you gi' me all the ground the goose flies over, the first offer, afther I make her as good as new?' 'I will,' says the king. 'You won't go back o' your word?' says St. Kavin. 'Honor bright!' says King O'Toole, howldin' out his fist. 'Honor bright!' says St. Kavin, back agin, 'it's a bargain. Come here!' says he to the poor ould goose—'come here, you unfort'nate ould cripple, and it's I that'll make you the sportin' bird.' With that, my dear, he took up the goose by the two wings—'Criss o' my crass an you,' says he, markin' her to grace with the blessed sign at the same minute—and throwin' her up in the air, 'whew,' says he, jist givin' her a blast to help her; and with that, my jewel, she tuk to her heels, flyin' like one o' the aigles themselves, and cuttin' as many capers as a swallow before a shower of rain.

"Well, my dear, it was a beautiful sight to see the king standin' with his mouth open, lookin' at his poor ould goose flyin' as light as a lark, and betther nor ever she was : and when she lit at his fut, patted her an the head, and, '*Ma vourneen*,' says he, 'but you are the *darlint* o' the world.' 'And what do you say to me,' says Saint Kavin, 'for makin' her the like?' 'By gor,' says the king, 'I say nothin' bates the art o' man, barrin' the bees.' 'And do you say no more nor that?' says Saint Kavin. 'And that I'm behoulden to you,' says the king. 'But will you gi'e me all the ground the goose flew over?' says Saint Kavin. 'I will,' says King O'Toole, 'and you're welkim to it,' says he, 'though it's the last acre I have to give.' 'But you'll keep your word thrue?' says the saint. 'As thrue as the sun,' says the king. 'It's well for you, King O'Toole, that you said that word,' says he; 'for if you didn't say that word, *the devil receave the bit o' your goose id ever fly agin.*' Whin the king was as good as his word, Saint Kavin was *plazed* with him, and thin it was that he made himself known to the king. 'And,' says he, 'King O'Toole, you're a decent man, for I only kem here to *thry you.* You don't know me," says he, "bekase I'm disguised.' 'Musha! thin,' says the king, 'who are you? 'I'm Saint Kavin,' said the saint, blessin' himself. 'Oh, queen iv heaven!' says the king, makin' the sign 'o the crass betune his eyes, and fallin' down on his knees before the saint; 'is it the great Saint Kavin,' says he, 'that I've been discoorsin' all this time without knowin' it,' says he, 'all as one as if he was a lump iv a *gossoon?*—and so you're a saint?' says the king. 'I am,' says Saint Kavin. 'By gor, I thought I was only talking to a dacent boy,' says the king. 'Well, you know the differ now,' says the saint. 'I'm Saint Kavin,' says he, 'the greatest of all the saints.' And so the king had his goose as good as new, to divart him as long as he lived : and the saint supported him afther he kem into his property, as I tould

you, until the day iv his death—and that was soon afther;
for the poor goose thought he was ketchin' a throut one
Friday; but, my jewel, it was a mistake he made—and
instead of a throut, it was a thievin' horse-eel; and by gor,
instead iv the goose killin' a throut for the king's supper,—
by dad, the eel killed the king's goose—and small blame to
him; but he didn't ate her, bekase he darn't ate what
Saint Kavin laid his blessed hands on."

THE DEVIL.

THE DEMON CAT.*

LADY WILDE.

THERE was a woman in Connemara, the wife of a fisherman; as he had always good luck, she had plenty of fish at all times stored away in the house ready for market. But, to her great annoyance, she found that a great cat used to come in at night and devour all the best and finest fish. So she kept a big stick by her, and determined to watch.

One day, as she and a woman were spinning together, the house suddenly became quite dark; and the door was burst open as if by the blast of the tempest, when in walked a huge black cat, who went straight up to the fire, then turned round and growled at them.

"Why, surely this is the devil," said a young girl, who was by, sorting fish.

"I'll teach you how to call me names," said the cat; and, jumping at her, he scratched her arm till the blood came. "There, now," he said, "you will be more civil another time when a gentleman comes to see you." And with that he walked over to the door and shut it close, to prevent any of them going out, for the poor young girl, while crying loudly from fright and pain, had made a desperate rush to get away.

Just then a man was going by, and hearing the cries, he pushed open the door and tried to get in; but the cat stood

* *Ancient Legends of Ireland.*

229

on the threshold, and would let no one pass. On this the man attacked him with his stick, and gave him a sound blow; the cat, however, was more than a match in the fight, for it flew at him and tore his face and hands so badly that the man at last took to his heels and ran away as fast as he could.

"Now, it's time for my dinner," said the cat, going up to examine the fish that was laid out on the tables. "I hope the fish is good to-day. Now, don't disturb me, nor make a fuss; I can help myself." With that he jumped up, and began to devour all the best fish, while he growled at the woman.

"Away, out of this, you wicked beast," she cried, giving it a blow with the tongs that would have broken its back, only it was a devil; "out of this; no fish shall you have to-day."

But the cat only grinned at her, and went on tearing and spoiling and devouring the fish, evidently not a bit the worse for the blow. On this, both the women attacked it with sticks, and struck hard blows enough to kill it, on which the cat glared at them, and spit fire; then, making a leap, it tore their heads and arms till the blood came, and the frightened women rushed shrieking from the house.

But presently the mistress returned, carrying with her a bottle of holy water; and, looking in, she saw the cat still devouring the fish, and not minding. So she crept over quietly and threw holy water on it without a word. No sooner was this done than a dense black smoke filled the place, through which nothing was seen but the two red eyes of the cat, burning like coals of fire. Then the smoke gradually cleared away, and she saw the body of the creature burning slowly till it became shrivelled and black like a cinder, and finally disappeared. And from that time the fish remained untouched and safe from harm, for the power of the evil one was broken, and the demon cat was seen no more.

A WOMAN COUNTERING A DEVIL'S POWERS.

THE DEVIL AND HIS HOUNDS.

THE LONG SPOON.*

PATRICK KENNEDY.

THE devil and the hearth-money collector for Bantry set out one summer morning to decide a bet they made the night before over a jug of punch. They wanted to see which would have the best load at sunset, and neither was to pick up anything that wasn't offered with the good-will of the giver. They passed by a house, and they heard the poor ban-a-t'yee† cry out to her lazy daughter, "Oh, musha, —— take you for a lazy sthronsuch‡ of a girl! do you intend to get up to-day?" "Oh, oh," says the taxman, "there's a job for you, Nick." "Ovock," says the other, "it wasn't from her heart she said it; we must pass on." The next cabin they were passing, the woman was on the bawn-ditch§ crying out to her husband that was mending one of his brogues inside: "Oh, tattheration to you, Nick! you never rung them pigs, and there they are in the potato drills rootin' away; the —— run to Lusk with them." "Another windfall for you," says the man of the ink-horn, but the old thief only shook his horns and wagged his tail. So they went on, and ever so many prizes were offered to the black fellow without him taking one. Here it was a gorsoon playing *marvels* when he should be using his clappers in the corn-field; and then it was a lazy drone of a servant asleep with his face to the sod when he ought to be weeding. No one thought of offering the hearth-money man even a drink of butter-milk, and at last the sun was within half a foot of the edge of Cooliagh. They were just then passing Monamolin, and a poor woman that was straining her supper in a skeeoge outside her cabin-door, seeing the two standing at the bawn gate, bawled out, "Oh, here's the hearth-money man—run away wid him." "Got a bite at

---

* *Legendary Fictions of the Irish Celts.*
† Woman of the house.
‡ Ir. *strŏinse—i.e.*, a lazy thing.
§ Ir. *bádhun—i.e.*, enclosure, or wall round a house. From *ba*, cows, and *dún*, a fortress. Properly, cattle-fortress.

last," says Nick. "Oh, no, no! it wasn't from her heart," says the collector. "Indeed, an' it was from the very foundation-stones it came. No help for misfortunes; in with you," says he, opening the mouth of his big black bag; and whether the devil was ever after seen taking the same walk or not, nobody ever laid eyes on his fellow-traveller again.

THE COUNTESS KATHLEEN O'SHEA.*

A VERY long time ago, there suddenly appeared in old Ireland two unknown merchants of whom nobody had ever heard, and who nevertheless spoke the language of the country with the greatest perfection. Their locks were black, and bound round with gold, and their garments were of rare magnificence.

Both seemed of like age; they appeared to be men of fifty, for their foreheads were wrinkled and their beards tinged with grey.

In the hostelry where the pompous traders alighted it was sought to penetrate their designs; but in vain—they led a silent and retired life. And whilst they stopped there, they did nothing but count over and over again out of their money-bags pieces of gold, whose yellow brightness could be seen through the windows of their lodging.

"Gentlemen," said the landlady one day, "how is it that you are so rich, and that, being able to succour the public misery, you do no good works?"

"Fair hostess," replied one of them, "we didn't like to present alms to the honest poor, in dread we might be deceived by make-believe paupers. Let want knock at our door, we shall open it."

The following day, when the rumour spread that two rich strangers had come, ready to lavish their gold, a crowd besieged their dwelling; but the figures of those who came

* This was quoted in a London-Irish newspaper. I am unable to find out the original source.

out were widely different. Some carried pride in their mien ; others were shame-faced.

The two chapmen traded in souls for the demon. The souls of the aged was worth twenty pieces of gold, not a penny more ; for Satan had had time to make his valuation. The soul of a matron was valued at fifty, when she was handsome, and a hundred when she was ugly. The soul of a young maiden fetched an extravagant sum ; the freshest and purest flowers are the dearest.

At that time there lived in the city an angel of beauty, the Countess Kathleen O'Shea. She was the idol of the people and the providence of the indigent. As soon as she learned that these miscreants profited to the public misery to steal away hearts from God, she called to her butler.

" Patrick," said she to him, " how many pieces of gold in my coffers ? "

" A hundred thousand."

" How many jewels ? "

" The money's worth of the gold."

" How much property in castles, forests, and lands ? "

" Double the rest."

" Very well, Patrick ; sell all that is not gold ; and bring me the account. I only wish to keep this mansion and the demesne that surrounds it."

Two days afterwards the orders of the pious Kathleen were executed, and the treasure was distributed to the poor in proportion to their wants. This, says the tradition, did not suit the purposes of the Evil Spirit, who found no more souls to purchase. Aided by an infamous servant, they penetrated into the retreat of the noble dame, and purloined from her the rest of her treasure. In vain she struggled with all her strength to save the contents of her coffers ; the diabolical thieves were the stronger. If Kathleen had been able to make the sign of the Cross, adds the legend, she would have put them to flight, but her hands were captive. The larceny was effected.

Then the poor called for aid to the plundered Kathleen,

alas, to no good : she was able to succour their misery no longer ; she had to abandon them to the temptation.

Meanwhile, but eight days had to pass before the grain and provender would arrive in abundance from the western lands.   Eight such days were an age.   Eight days required an immense sum to relieve the exigencies of the dearth, and the poor should either perish in the agonies of hunger, or, denying the holy maxims of the Gospel, vend, for base lucre, their souls, the richest gift from the bounteous hand of the Almighty.   And Kathleen hadn't anything, for she had given up her mansion to the unhappy.   She passed twelve hours in tears and mourning, rending her sun-tinted hair, and bruising her breast, of the whiteness of the lily ; afterwards she stood up, resolute, animated by a vivid sentiment of despair.

She went to the traders in souls.

" What do you want ? " they said.

" You buy souls ? "

" Yes, a few still, in spite of you.   Isn't that so, saint, with the eyes of sapphire ? "

" To-day I am come to offer you a bargain," replied she.

" What ? "

" I have a soul to sell, but it is costly."

" What does that signify if it is precious ?   The soul, like the diamond, is appraised by its transparency."

" It is mine."

The two emissaries of Satan started.   Their claws were clutched under their gloves of leather ; their grey eyes sparkled ; the soul, pure, spotless, virginal of Kathleen—it was a priceless acquisition !

" Beauteous lady, how much do you ask ? "

" A hundred and fifty thousand pieces of gold."

" It's at your service," replied the traders, and they tendered Kathleen a parchment sealed with black, which she signed with a shudder.

The sum was counted out to her.

As soon as she got home she said to the butler, " Here, distribute this : with this money that I give you the poor can tide over the eight days that remain, and not one of of their souls will be delivered to the demon."

Afterwards she shut herself up in her room, and gave orders that none should disturb her.

Three days passed; she called nobody, she did not come out.

When the door was opened, they found her cold and stiff; she was dead of grief.

But the sale of this soul, so adorable in its charity, was declared null by the Lord; for she had saved her fellow-citizens from eternal death.

After the eight days had passed, numerous vessels brought into famished Ireland immense provisions in grain. Hunger was no longer possible. As to the traders, they disappeared from their hotel without anyone knowing what became of them. But the fishermen of the Blackwater pretend that they are enchained in a subterranean prison by order of Lucifer, until they shall be able to render up the soul of Kathleen, which escaped from them.

THE THREE WISHES.

W. CARLETON.

IN ancient times there lived a man called Billy Dawson, and he was known to be a great rogue. They say he was descended from the family of the Dawsons, which was the reason, I suppose, of his carrying their name upon him.

Billy, in his youthful days, was the best hand at doing nothing in all Europe; devil a mortal could come next or near him at idleness; and, in consequence of his great practice that way, you may be sure that if any man could make a fortune by it he would have done it.

Billy was the only son of his father, barring two daughters; but they have nothing to do with the story I'm telling you.   Indeed it was kind father and grandfather for Billy to be handy at the knavery as well as at the idleness ; for it was well known that not one of their blood ever did an honest act, except with a roguish intention.   In short, they were altogether a *dacent* connection, and a credit to the name.   As for Billy, all the villainy of the family, both plain and ornamental, came down to him by way of legacy ; for it so happened that the father, in spite of all his cleverness, had nothing but his roguery to *lave* him.

Billy, to do him justice, improved the fortune he got : every day advanced him farther into dishonesty and poverty, until, at the long run, he was acknowledged on all hands to be the completest swindler and the poorest vagabond in the whole parish.

Billy's father, in his young days, had often been forced to acknowledge the inconvenience of not having a trade, in consequence of some nice point in law, called the "Vagrant Act," that sometimes troubled him.   On this account he made up his mind to give Bill an occupation, and he accordingly bound him to a blacksmith ; but whether Bill was to *live* or *die* by *forgery* was a puzzle to his father,— though the neighbours said that *both* was most likely.   At all events, he was put apprentice to a smith for seven years, and a hard card his master had to play in managing him. He took the proper method, however, for Bill was so lazy and roguish that it would vex a saint to keep him in order.

" Bill," says his master to him one day that he had been sunning himself about the ditches, instead of minding his business, " Bill, my boy, I'm vexed to the heart to see you in such a bad state of health.   You're very ill with that complaint called an *All-overness ;* however," says he, " I think I can cure you.   Nothing will bring you about but three or four sound doses every day of a medicine called ' the oil o' the hazel.'   Take the first dose now," says he ; and he immediately banged him with a hazel cudgel until Bill's bones ached for a week afterwards.

" If you were my son," said his master, " I tell you that, as long as I could get a piece of advice growing convenient in the hedges, I'd have you a different youth from what you are. If working was a sin, Bill, not an innocenter boy ever broke bread than you would be. Good people's scarce, you think; but however that may be, I throw it out as a hint, that you must take you're medicine till you're cured, whenever you happen to get unwell in the same way."

From this out he kept Bill's nose to the grinding-stone; and whenever his complaint returned, he never failed to give him a hearty dose for his improvement.

In the course of time, however, Bill was his own man and his own master; but it would puzzle a saint to know whether the master or the man was the more precious youth in the eyes of the world.

He immediately married a wife, and devil a doubt of it, but if *he* kept *her* in whiskey and sugar, *she* kept *him* in hot water. Bill drank and she drank; Bill fought and she fought; Bill was idle and she was idle; Bill whacked her and she whacked Bill. If Bill gave her one black eye, she gave him another; *just to keep herself in countenance*. Never was there a blessed pair so well met; and a beautiful sight it was to see them both at breakfast-time, blinking at each other across the potato-basket, Bill with his right eye black, and she with her left.

In short, they were the talk of the whole town : and to see Bill of a morning staggering home drunk, his shirt sleeves rolled up on his smutted arms, his breast open, and an old tattered leather apron, with one corner tucked up under his belt, singing one minute, and fighting with his wife the next;—she, reeling beside him, with a discoloured eye, as aforesaid, a dirty ragged cap on one side of her head, a pair of Bill's old slippers on her feet, a squalling child on her arm—now cuffing and dragging Bill, and again kissing and hugging him! Yes, it was a pleasant picture to see this loving pair in such a state !

This might do for a while, but it could not last. They were idle, drunken, and ill-conducted; and it was not to be supposed that they would get a farthing candle on their words. They were, of course, *dhruv* to great straits ; and faith, they soon found that their fighting, and drinking, and idleness made them the laughing-sport of the neighbours; but neither brought food to their *childhre*, put a coat upon their backs, nor satisfied their landlord when he came to look for his own.   Still, the never a one of Bill but was a funny fellow with strangers, though, as we said, the greatest rogue unhanged.

One day he was standing against his own anvil, completely in a brown study—being brought to his wit's end how to make out a breakfast for the family.   The wife was scolding and cursing in the house, and the naked creatures of childhre squalling about her knees for food.   Bill was fairly at an amplush, and knew not where or how to turn himself, when a poor withered old beggar came into the forge, tottering on his staff.   A long white beard fell from his chin, and he looked as thin and hungry that you might blow him, one would think, over the house.   Bill at this moment had been brought to his senses by distress, and his heart had a touch of pity towards the old man ; for, on looking at him a second time, he clearly saw starvation and sorrow in his face.

"God save you, honest man!" said Bill.

The old man gave a sigh, and raising himself with great pain, on his staff, he looked at Bill in a very beseeching way.

"Musha, God save you kindly!" says he ; "maybe you could give a poor, hungry, helpless ould man a mouthful of something to ait?   You see yourself I'm not able to work ; if I was, I'd scorn to be beholding to anyone."

"Faith, honest man," said Bill, "if you knew who you're speaking to, you'd as soon ask a monkey for a churn-staff as me for either mate or money.   There's not a blackguard in the three kingdoms so fairly on the *shaughran* as I am for both the one and the other.   The wife within is sending the curses thick and heavy on me, and the childhre's playing the cat's melody to keep her in comfort.   Take my word for it, poor man, if I had either mate or money I'd help you, for I know particularly well what it is to want them at the present spaking; an empty sack won't stand, neighbour."

So far Bill told him truth. The good thought was in his heart, because he found himself on a footing with the beggar; and nothing brings down pride, or softens the heart, like feeling what it is to want.

"Why, you are in a worse state than I am," said the old man; "you have a family to provide for, and I have only myself to support."

"You may kiss the book on that, my old worthy," replied Bill; "but come, what I can do for you I will; plant yourself up here beside the fire, and I'll give it a blast or two of my bellows that will warm the old blood in your body. It's a cold, miserable, snowy day, and a good heat will be of service."

"Thank you kindly," said the old man; "I *am* cold, and a warming at your fire will do me good, sure enough. Oh, it *is* a bitter, bitter day; God bless it!"

He then sat down, and Bill blew a rousing blast that soon made the stranger edge back from the heat. In a short time he felt quite comfortable, and when the numbness was taken out of his joints, he buttoned himself up and prepared to depart.

"Now," says he to Bill, "you hadn't the food to give me, but *what you could you did*. Ask any three wishes you choose, and be they what they may, take my word for it, they shall be granted."

Now, the truth is, that Bill, though he believed himself a great man in point of 'cuteness, wanted, after all, a full quarter of being square; for there is always a great difference between a wise man and a knave. Bill was so much of a rogue that he could not, for the blood of him, ask an honest wish, but stood scratching his head in a puzzle.

"Three wishes!" said he. "Why, let me see—did you say *three*?"

"Ay," replied the stranger, "three wishes—that was what I said."

"Well," said Bill, "here goes,—aha!—let me alone, my

old worthy!—faith I'll overreach the parish, if what you say is true. I'll cheat them in dozens, rich and poor, old and young : let me alone, man,—I have it here ; " and he tapped his forehead with great glee. "Faith, you're the sort to meet of a frosty morning, when a man wants his breakfast ; and I'm sorry that I have neither money nor credit to get a bottle of whiskey, that we might take our *morning* together."

"Well, but let us hear the wishes," said the old man ; "my time is short, and I cannot stay much longer."

"Do you see this sledge-hammer ? " said Bill , "I wish, in the first place, that whoever takes it up in their hands may never be able to lay it down till I give them lave ; and that whoever begins to sledge with it may never stop sledging till it's my pleasure to release him."

"Secondly—I have an arm-chair, and I wish that whoever sits down in it may never rise out of it till they have my consent."

"And, thirdly—that whatever money I put into my purse, nobody may have power to take it out of it but myself!"

"You devil's rip ! " says the old man in a passion, shaking his staff across Bill's nose, "why did you not ask something that would sarve you both here and hereafter ? Sure it's as common as the market-cross, that there's not a vagabone in his Majesty's dominions stands more in need of both."

"Oh ! by the elevens," said Bill, "I forgot that altogether ! Maybe you'd be civil enough to let me change one of them ? The sorra purtier wish ever was made than I'll make, if you'll give me another chance."

"Get out, you reprobate," said the old fellow, still in a passion. "Your day of grace is past. Little you knew who was speaking to you all this time. I'm St. Moroky, you blackguard, and I gave you an opportunity of doing something for yourself and your family ; but you neglected it, and now your fate is cast, you dirty, bog-trotting profligate. Sure, it's well known what you are ! Aren't

you a by-word in everybody's mouth, you and your scold
of a wife? By this and by that, if ever you happen to
come across me again, I'll send you to where you won't
freeze, you villain!"

He then gave Bill a rap of his cudgel over the head, and
laid him at his length beside the bellows, kicked a broken
coal-scuttle out of his way, and left the forge in a fury.

When Billy recovered himself from the effects of the
blow, and began to think on what had happened, he
could have quartered himself with vexation for not asking
great wealth as one of the wishes at least; but now the die
was cast on him, and he could only make the most of the
three he pitched upon.

He now bethought him how he might turn them to the
best account, and here his cunning came to his aid. He
began by sending for his wealthiest neighbours on pretence
of business; and when he got them under his roof, he
offered them the arm-chair to sit down in. He now had
them safe, nor could all the art of man relieve them
except worthy Bill was willing. Bill's plan was to make the
best bargain he could before he released his prisoners; and
let him alone for knowing how to make their purses bleed.
There wasn't a wealthy man in the country he did not
fleece. The parson of the parish bled heavily; so did the
lawyer; and a rich attorney, who had retired from practice,
swore that the Court of Chancery itself was paradise
compared to Bill's chair.

This was all very good for a time. The fame of his chair,
however, soon spread; so did that of his sledge. In a short
time neither man, woman, nor child would darken his
door; all avoided him and his fixtures as they would a
spring-gun or man-trap. Bill, so long as he fleeced his
neighbours, never wrought a hand's turn; so that when his
money was out, he found himself as badly off as ever. In
addition to all this, his character was fifty times worse than
before; for it was the general belief that he had dealings
with the old boy. Nothing now could exceed his misery,
distress, and ill-temper. The wife and he and their children

all fought among one another. Everybody hated them, cursed them, and avoided them. The people thought they were acquainted with more than Christian people ought to know. This, of course, came to Bill's ears, and it vexed him very much.

One day he was walking about the fields, thinking of how he could raise the wind once more; the day was dark, and he found himself, before he stopped, in the bottom of a lonely glen covered by great bushes that grew on each side. "Well," thought he, when every other means of raising money failed him, "it's reported that I'm in league with the old boy, and as it's a folly to have the name of the connection without the profit, I'm ready to make a bargain with him any day;—so," said he, raising his voice, "Nick, you sinner, if you be convanient and willing, why stand out here; show your best leg—here's your man."

The words were hardly out of his mouth when a dark, sober-looking old gentleman, not unlike a lawyer, walked up to him. Bill looked at the foot and saw the hoof.— "Morrow, Nick," says Bill.

"Morrow, Bill," says Nick. "Well, Bill, what's the news?"

"Devil a much myself hears of late," says Bill; "is there anything *fresh* below?"

"I can't exactly say, Bill; I spend little of my time down now; the Tories are in office, and my hands are consequently too full of business here to pay much attention to anything else."

"A fine place this, sir," says Bill, "to take a constitutional walk in; when I want an appetite I often come this way myself—hem! *High* feeding is very bad without exercise."

"High feeding! Come, come, Bill, you know you didn't taste a morsel these four-and-twenty hours."

"You know that's a bounce, Nick. I eat a breakfast this morning that would put a stone of flesh on you, if you only smelt at it."

"No matter; this is not to the purpose. What's that

you were muttering to yourself awhile ago? If you want to come to the brunt, here I'm for you."

"Nick," said Bill, "you're complate; you want nothing barring a pair of Brian O'Lynn's breeches."

Bill, in fact, was bent on making his companion open the bargain, because he had often heard that, in that case, with proper care on his own part, he might defeat him in the long run. The other, however, was his match.

"What was the nature of Brian's garment," inquired Nick. "Why, you know the song," said Bill—

> "'Brian O'Lynn had no breeches to wear,
> So he got a sheep's skin for to make him a pair;
> With the fleshy side out and the woolly side in,
> They'll be pleasant and *cool*, says Brian O'Lynn.'

"A *cool* pare would sarve you, Nick."

"You're mighty waggish to-day, Misther Dawson."

"And good right I have," said Bill; "I'm a man snug and well to do in the world; have lots of money, plenty of good eating and drinking, and what more need a man wish for?"

"True," said the other; "in the meantime it's rather odd that so respectable a man should not have six inches of unbroken cloth in his apparel. You are as naked a tatter-demalion as I ever laid my eyes on; in full dress for a party of scare-crows, William."

"That's my own fancy, Nick; I don't work at my trade like a gentleman. This is my forge dress, you know."

"Well, but what did you summon me here for?" said the other; "you may as well speak out, I tell you; for, my good friend, unless *you* do, *I* shan't. Smell that."

"I smell more than that," said Bill; "and by the way, I'll thank you to give me the windy side of you—curse all sulphur, I say. There, that's what I call an improvement in my condition. But as you *are* so stiff," says Bill, "why, the short and long of it is—that—hem—you see I'm—tut —sure you know I have a thriving trade of my own, and that if I like I needn't be at a loss ; but in the meantime I'm rather in a kind of a so—so—don't you *take ?*"

And Bill winked knowingly, hoping to trick him into the first proposal.

"You must speak above-board, my friend," says the other. " I'm a man of few words, blunt and honest. If you have anything to say, be plain. Don't think I can be losing my time with such a pitiful rascal as you are."

"Well," says Bill, " I want money, then, and am ready to come into terms. What have you to say to that, Nick ? "

"Let me see—lét me look at you," says his companion, turning him about. " Now, Bill, in the first place, are you not as finished a scare-crow as ever stood upon two legs ? "

"I play second fiddle to you there again," says Bill.

"There you stand, with the blackguards' coat of arms quartered under your eye, and——"

"Don't make little of *black*guards," said Bill, " nor spake disparagingly of *your own* crest."

"Why, what would you bring, you brazen rascal, if you were fairly put up at auction ? "

"Faith, I'd bring more bidders than you would," said Bill, " if you were to go off at auction to-morrow. I tell you they should bid *downwards* to come to your value, Nicholas. We have no coin *small* enough to purchase you."

"Well, no matter," said Nick. " If you are willing to be mine at the expiration of seven years, I will give you more money than ever the rascally breed of you was worth."

"Done ! " said Bill ; "but no disparagement to my family, in the meantime ; so down with the hard cash, and don't be a *neger*."

The money was accordingly paid down ! but as nobody was present, except the giver and receiver, the amount of what Bill got was never known.

"Won't you give me a luck-penny ? " said the old gentleman.

"Tut," said Billy, "so prosperous an old fellow as you cannot want it ; however, bad luck to you, with all my heart! and it's rubbing grease to a fat pig to say so. Be off now, or I'll commit suicide on you. Your absence is a cordial to most people, you infernal old profligate. You have injured my morals even for the short time you have been with me; for I don't find myself so virtuous as I was."

" Is that your gratitude, Billy?"

" Is it gratitude *you* speak of, man? I wonder you don't blush when you name it. However, when you come again, if you bring a third eye in your head you will see what I mane, Nicholas, ahagur."

The old gentleman, as Bill spoke, hopped across the ditch, on his way to *Downing*-street, where of late 'tis thought he possesses much influence.

Bill now began by degrees to show off; but still wrought a little at his trade to blindfold the neighbours. In a very short time, however, he became a great man. So long indeed as he was a *poor* rascal, no decent person would speak to him; even the proud serving-men at the "Big House" would turn up their noses at him. And he well deserved to be made little of by others, because he was mean enough to make little of himself. But when it was seen and known that he had oceans of money, it was wonderful to think, although he was *now* a greater black-guard than ever, how those who despised him before began to come round him and court his company. Bill, however, had neither sense nor spirit to make those sunshiny friends know their distance; not he—instead of that he was proud to be seen in decent company, and so long as the money lasted, it was, "hail fellow, well met," between himself and every fair-faced *spunger* who had a horse under him, a decent coat to his back, and a good appetite to eat his dinners. With riches and all, Bill was the same man still; but, somehow or other, there is a great difference between a rich profligate and a poor one, and Bill found it so to his cost in *both* cases.

Before half the seven years was passed, Bill had his carriage, and his equipages; was hand and glove with my Lord This, and my Lord That; kept hounds and hunters;

was the first sportsman at the Curragh; patronised every boxing ruffian he could pick up; and betted night and day on cards, dice, and horses. Bill, in short, *should* be a blood, and except he did all this, he could not presume to mingle with the fashionable bloods of his time.

It's an old proverb, however, that "what is got over the devil's back is sure to go off under it;" and in Bill's case this proved true. In short, the old boy himself could not supply him with money so fast as he made it fly; it was "come easy, go easy," with Bill, and so sign was on it, before he came within two years of his time he found his purse empty.

And now came the value of his summer friends to be known. When it was discovered that the cash was no longer flush with him—that stud, and carriage, and hounds were going to the hammer—whish! off they went, friends, relations, pot-companions, dinner-eaters, black-legs, and all, like a flock of crows that had smelt gunpowder. Down Bill soon went, week after week, and day after day, until at last he was obliged to put on the leather apron, and take to the hammer again; and not only that, for as no experience could make him wise, he once more began his tap-room brawls, his quarrels with Judy, and took to his "high feeding" at the dry potatoes and salt. Now, too, came the cutting tongues of all who knew him, like razors upon him. Those that he scorned because they were poor and himself rich, now paid him back his own with interest; and those that he measured himself with, because they were rich, and who only countenanced him in consequence of his wealth, gave him the hardest word in their cheeks. The devil mend him! He deserved it all, and more if he had got it.

Bill, however, who was a hardened sinner, never fretted himself down an ounce of flesh by what was said to him, or of him. Not he; he cursed, and fought, and swore, and schemed away as usual, taking in every one he could; and surely none could match him at villainy of all sorts, and sizes.

At last the seven years became expired, and Bill was one morning sitting in his forge, sober and hungry, the wife cursing him, and the childhre squalling, as before; he was thinking how he might defraud some honest neighbour out of a breakfast to stop their mouths and his own too, when who walks in to him but old Nick, to demand his bargain.

"Morrow, Bill!" says he with a sneer.

"The devil welcome you!" says Bill; "but you have a fresh memory."

"A bargain's a bargain between two *honest* men, any day," says Satan; "when I speak of *honest* men, I mean *yourself* and *me*, Bill;" and he put his tongue in his cheek to make game of the unfortunate rogue he had come for.

"Nick, my worthy fellow," said Bill, "have bowels; you wouldn't do a shabby thing; you wouldn't disgrace your own character by putting more weight upon a falling man. You know what it is to get a *come down* yourself, my worthy; so just keep your toe in your pump, and walk off with yourself somewhere else. A *cool* walk will sarve you better than my company, Nicholas."

"Bill, it's no use in shirking," said his friend; "your swindling tricks may enable you to cheat others, but you won't cheat *me*, I guess. You want nothing to make you perfect in your way but to travel; and travel you shall under my guidance, Billy. No, no—*I'm* not to be swindled, my good fellow. I have rather a—a—better opinion of myself, Mr. D., than to think that you could outwit one Nicholas Clutie, Esq.—ahem!"

"You may sneer, you sinner," replied Bill; "but I tell you that I have outwitted men who could buy and sell you to your face. Despair, you villain, when I tell you that *no attorney* could stand before me."

Satan's countenance got blank when he heard this; he wriggled and fidgeted about, and appeared to be not quite comfortable.

"In that case, then," says he, "the sooner I *deceive* you the better; so turn out for the *Low Countries*."

"Is it come to that in earnest?" said Bill, "and are you going to act the rascal at the long run?"

"'Pon honour, Bill."

"Have patience, then, you sinner, till I finish this horse-shoe—it's the last of a set I'm finishing for one of your friend the attorney's horses. And here, Nick, I hate idle-ness, you know it's the mother of mischief; take this sledge-hammer, and give a dozen strokes or so, till I get it out of hands, and then here's with you, since it must be so."

He then gave the bellows a puff that blew half a peck of dust in Club-foot's face, whipped out the red-hot iron, and set Satan sledging away for bare life.

"Faith," says Bill to him, when the shoe was finished, "it's a thousand pities ever the sledge should be out of your hand; the great *Parra Gow* was a child to you at sledging, you're such an able tyke. Now just exercise yourself till I bid the wife and childhre good-bye, and then I'm off."

Out went Bill, of course, without the slightest notion of coming back; no more than Nick had that he could not give up the sledging, and indeed neither could he, but was forced to work away as if he was sledging for a wager. This was just what Bill wanted. He was now compelled to sledge on until it was Bill's pleasure to release him; and so we leave him very industriously employed, while we look after the worthy who outwitted him.

In the meantime, Bill broke cover, and took to the country at large; wrought a little journey-work wherever he could get it, and in this way went from one place to another, till, in the course of a month, he walked back very coolly into his own forge, to see how things went on in his absence. There he found Satan in a rage, the perspiration pouring from him in torrents, hammering with might and main upon the naked anvil. Bill calmly leaned his back against the wall, placed his hat upon the side of his head, put his hands into his breeches pockets, and began to whistle *Shaun Gow's* hornpipe. At length he says, in a very quiet and good-humoured way—

"Morrow, Nick!"

"Oh!" says Nick, still hammering away—"Oh! you double-distilled villain (hech!), may the most refined, ornamental (hech!), double-rectified, super-extra, and original (hech !) collection of curses that ever was gathered (hech !) into a single nosegay of ill-fortune (hech !), shine in the button-hole of your conscience (hech !) while your name is Bill Dawson ! I denounce you (hech !) as a double-milled villain, a finished, hot-pressed knave (hech !), in comparison of whom all the other knaves I ever knew (hech !), attorneys included, are honest men. I brand you (hech !) as the pearl of cheats, a tip-top take-in (hech !). I denounce you, I say again, for the villainous treatment (hech !) I have received at your hands in this most untoward (hech !) and unfortunate transaction between us ; for (hech !) unfortunate, in every sense, is he that has anything to do with (hech !) such a prime and finished impostor."

"You're very warm, Nicky," says Bill ; "what puts you into a passion, you old sinner ? Sure if it's your own will and pleasure to take exercise at my anvil, *I'm* not to be abused for it. Upon my credit, Nicky, you ought to blush for using such blackguard language, so unbecoming your grave character. You cannot say that it was I set you a hammering at the empty anvil, you profligate. However, as you are so industrious, I simply say it would be a thousand pities to take you from it. Nick, I love industry in my heart, and I always encourage it ; so work away, it's not often you spend your time so creditably. I'm afraid if you weren't at that you'd be worse employed."

" Bill, have bowels," said the operative ; "you wouldn't go to lay more weight on a falling man, you know ; you wouldn't disgrace your character by such a piece of iniquity as keeping an inoffensive gentleman, advanced in years, at such an unbecoming and rascally job as this. Generosity's your top virtue, Bill ; not but that you have many other excellent ones, as well as that, among which, as you say yourself, I reckon industry ; but still it is in generosity you *shine*. Come, Bill, honour bright, and release me."

"Name the terms, you profligate."

" You're above terms, William ; a generous fellow like you never thinks of terms."

" Good-bye, old gentleman ! " said Bill, very coolly ; " I'll drop in to see you once a month."

" No, no, Bill, you infern—a—a— you excellent, worthy, delightful fellow, not so fast ; not so fast. Come, name your terms, you sland——my dear Bill, name your terms."

" Seven years more."

" I agree ; but——"

" And the same supply of cash as before, down on the nail here."

" Very good ; very good. You're rather simple, Bill ; rather soft, I must confess. Well, no matter. I shall yet turn the tab—a—hem ! You are an exceedingly simple fellow, Bill ; still there will come a day, my *dear* Bill—there will come——"

" Do you grumble, you vagrant ? Another word, and I double the terms."

" Mum, William—mum ; *tace* is Latin for a candle."

" Seven years more of grace, and the same measure of the needful that I got before. Ay or no ? "

" Of grace, Bill ! Ay ! ay ! ay ! There's the cash. I accept the terms. Oh blood ! the rascal—of grace ! ! Bill ! "

" Well, now drop the hammer, and vanish," says Billy ; " but what would you think to take this sledge, while you stay, and give me a——eh ! why in such a hurry ? " he added, seeing that Satan withdrew in double-quick time.

" Hollo ! Nicholas ! " he shouted, " come back ; you forgot something ! " and when the old gentleman looked behind him, Billy shook the hammer at him, on which he vanished altogether.

Billy now got into his old courses ; and what shows the kind of people the world is made of, he also took up with his old company. When they saw that he had the money once more, and was sowing it about him in all directions, they immediately began to find excuses for his former extravagance.

" Say what you will," said one, " Bill Dawson's a spirited fellow, and bleeds like a prince."

"He's a hospitable man in his own house, or out of it, as ever lived," said another.

"His only fault is," observed a third, "that he is, if anything, too generous, and doesn't know the value of money; his fault's on the right side, however."

"He has the spunk in him," said a fourth; "keeps a capital table, prime wines, and a standing welcome for his friends."

"Why," said a fifth, "if he doesn't enjoy his money while he lives, he won't when he's dead; so more power to him, and a wider throat to his purse."

Indeed, the very persons who were cramming themselves at his expense despised him at heart. They knew very well, however, how to take him on the weak side. Praise his generosity, and he would do anything; call him a man of spirit, and you might fleece him to his face. Sometimes he would toss a purse of guineas to this knave, another to that flatterer, a third to a bully, and a fourth to some broken-down rake—and all to convince them that *he* was a sterling friend—a man of mettle and liberality. But never was he known to help a virtuous and struggling family—to assist the widow or the fatherless, or to do any other act that was *truly* useful. It is to be supposed the reason of this was, that as he spent it, as most of the world do, in the service of the devil, by whose aid he got it, he was prevented from turning it to a good account. Between you and me, dear reader, there are more persons acting after Bill's fashion in the same world than you dream about.

When his money was out again, his friends played him the same rascally game once more. No sooner did his poverty become plain, than the knaves began to be troubled with small fits of modesty, such as an unwillingness to come to his place when there was no longer anything to be got there. A kind of virgin bashfulness prevented them from speaking to him when they saw him getting out on the wrong side of his clothes. Many of them would turn away from him in the prettiest and most delicate manner when they thought he wanted to borrow money from them—all for fear of putting him to the blush by asking it. Others again, when they saw him coming towards their houses about dinner hour, would become so confused, from mere gratitude, as to think themselves in another place ; and their servants, seized, as it were, with the same feeling, would tell Bill that their masters were " not at home."

At length, after travelling the same villainous round as before, Bill was compelled to betake himself, as the last remedy, to the forge ; in other words, he found that there is, after all, nothing in this world that a man can rely on so firmly and surely as his own industry. Bill, however, wanted the organ of common sense ; for his experience— and it was sharp enough to leave an impression—ran off him like water off a duck.

He took to his employment sorely against his grain ; but he had now no choice. He must either work or starve, and starvation is like a great doctor—nobody tries it till every other remedy fails them. Bill had been twice rich ; twice a gentleman among blackguards, but always a blackguard among gentlemen ; for no wealth or acquaintance with decent society could rub the rust of his native vulgarity off him. He was now a common blinking sot in his forge ; a drunken bully in the tap-room, cursing and brow-beating every one as well as his wife ; boasting of how much money he had spent in his day ; swaggering about the high doings he carried on ; telling stories about himself and Lord This at the Curragh ; the dinners he gave—how much they cost him, and attempting to extort credit upon the strength of his former wealth. He was too ignorant, however, to know that he was publishing his own disgrace, and that it was a mean-spirited thing to be proud of what ought to make him blush through a deal board nine inches thick.

He was one morning industriously engaged in a quarrel with his wife, who, with a three-legged stool in her hand, appeared to mistake his head for his own anvil ; he, in the meantime, paid his addresses to her with his leather apron, when who steps in to jog his memory about the little agree-ment that was between them, but old Nick. The wife, it seems, in spite of all her exertions to the contrary, was getting the worst of it; and Sir Nicholas, willing to appear a gentleman of great gallantry, thought he could not do less than take up the lady's quarrel, particularly as Bill had laid her in a sleeping posture. Now Satan thought this too bad; and as he felt himself under many obligations to the sex, he determined to defend one of them on the present occasion; so as Judy rose, he turned upon the husband, and floored him by a clever facer.

"You unmanly villain," said he, "is this the way you treat your wife? 'Pon honour, Bill, I'll chastise you on the spot. I could not stand by, a spectator of such ungentlemanly conduct without giving up all claim to gallant——" Whack! the word was divided in his mouth by the blow of a churn-staff from Judy, who no sooner saw Bill struck, than she nailed Satan, who "fell" once more.

"What, you villain! that's for striking my husband like a murderer behind his back," said Judy, and she suited the action to the word, "that's for interfering between man and wife. Would you murder the poor man before my face? eh? If *he* bates me, you shabby dog you, who has a better right? I'm sure it's nothing out of your pocket. Must you have your finger in every pie?"

This was anything but *idle* talk; for at every word she gave him a remembrance, hot and heavy. Nicholas backed, danced, and hopped; she advanced, still drubbing him with great perseverance, till at length he fell into the redoubtable arm-chair, which stood exactly behind him. Bill, who had been putting in two blows for Judy's one, seeing that his enemy was safe, now got between the devil and his wife, *a situation that few will be disposed to envy him.*

"Tenderness, Judy," said the husband, "I hate cruelty. Go put the tongs in the fire, and make them red hot. Nicholas, you have a nose," said he.

Satan began to rise, but was rather surprised to find that he could not budge.

"Nicholas," says Bill, "how is your pulse? you don't look well; that is to say, you look worse than usual."

The other attempted to rise, but found it a mistake.

"I'll thank you to come along," said Bill. "I have a fancy to travel under your guidance, and we'll take the *Low Countries* in our way, won't we? Get to your legs, you sinner; you know a bargain's a bargain between two *honest men*, Nicholas; meaning *yourself* and *me*. Judy, are the tongs hot?"

Satan's face was worth looking at, as he turned his eyes from the husband to the wife, and then fastened them on the tongs, now nearly at a furnace heat in the fire, conscious at the same time that he could not move out of the chair.

"Billy," said he, "you won't forget that I rewarded your generosity the last time I saw you, in the way of business." "Faith, Nicholas, it fails me to remember any generosity I ever showed you. Don't be womanish. I simply want to see what kind of stuff your nose is made of, and whether it will stretch like a rogue's conscience. If it does, we will flatter it up the *chimly* with red-hot tongs, and when this old hat is fixed on the top of it, let us alone for a weather-cock." "Have a *fellow-feeling*, Mr. Dawson; you know *we* ought not to dispute. Drop the matter, and I give you the next seven years." "We know all that," says Billy, opening the red-hot tongs very coolly. "Mr. Dawson," said Satan, "if you cannot remember my friendship to yourself, don't forget how often I stood your father's friend, your grandfather's friend, and the friend of all your relations up to the tenth generation. I intended, also, to stand by your children after you, so long as the name of Dawson, and a respectable one it is, might last." "Don't be blushing, Nick," says Bill, "you are too modest; that was ever your failing; hould up your head, there's money bid for you. I'll give you such a nose, my good friend, that you will have to keep an outrider before you, to carry the end of it on his shoulder." "Mr. Dawson, I pledge my honour to raise your children in the world as high as they can go; no matter whether they desire it or not." "That's very kind of you," says the other, "and I'll do as much for your nose."

He gripped it as he spoke, and the old boy immediately sung out; Bill pulled, and the nose went with him like a piece of warm wax. He then transferred the tongs to Judy, got a ladder, resumed the tongs, ascended the chimney, and tugged stoutly at the nose until he got it five feet above the roof. He then fixed the hat upon the top of it, and came down.

"There's a weather-cock," said Billy; "I defy Ireland to show such a beauty. Faith, Nick, it would make the purtiest steeple for a church, in all Europe, and the old hat fits it to a shaving."

In this state, with his nose twisted up the chimney, Satan sat for some time, experiencing the novelty of what might be termed a peculiar sensation. At last the worthy husband and wife began to relent.

"I think," said Bill, "that we have made the most of the nose, as well as the joke; I believe, Judy, it's long enough." "What is?" says Judy.

"Why, the joke," said the husband.

"Faith, and I think so is the nose," said Judy."

"What do you say yourself, Satan?" said Bill.

"Nothing at all, William," said the other; "but that—ha! ha!—it's a good joke—an excellent joke, and a goodly nose, too, as it *stands*. You were always a gentlemanly man, Bill, and did things with a grace; still, if I might give an opinion on such a trifle——"

"It's no trifle at all," says Bill, "if you spake of the nose." "Very well, it is not," says the other; "still, I am decidedly of opinion, that if you could shorten both the joke and the nose without further violence, you would lay me under very heavy obligations, which I shall be ready to acknowledge and *repay* as I ought." "Come," said Bill, "shell out once more, and be off for seven years. As much as you came down with the last time, and vanish."

The words were scarcely spoken, when the money was at his feet, and Satan invisible. Nothing could surpass the mirth of Bill and his wife at the result of this adventure. They laughed till they fell down on the floor.

It is useless to go over the same ground again.   Bill was still incorrigible.   The money went as the devil's money always goes.   Bill caroused and squandered, but could never turn a penny of it to a good purpose.   In this way, year after year went, till the seventh was closed, and Bill's hour come. He was now, and had been for some time past, as miserable a knave as ever.   Not a shilling had he, nor a shilling's worth, with the exception of his forge, his cabin, and a few articles of crazy furniture.   In this state he was standing in his forge as before, straining his ingenuity how to make out a breakfast, when Satan came to look after him.   The old gentleman was sorely puzzled how to get at him.   He kept skulking and sneaking about the forge for some time, till he saw that Bill hadn't a cross to bless himself with.   He immediately changed himself into a guinea, and lay in an open place where he knew Bill would see him.   "If," said he, "I once get into his possession, I can manage him."   The honest smith took the bait, for it was well gilded; he clutched the guinea, put it into his purse, and closed it up.   "Ho! ho!" shouted the devil out of the purse, "you're caught, Bill; I've secured you at last, you knave you.   Why don't you despair, you villain, when you think of what's before you?"   "Why, you unlucky ould dog," said Bill, "is it there you are?   Will you always drive your head into every loop-hole that's set for you? Faith, Nick achora, I never had you bagged till now."

Satan then began to tug and struggle with a view of getting out of the purse, but in vain.

"Mr. Dawson," said he, "we understand each other. I'll give the seven years additional, and the cash on the nail."   "Be aisey, Nicholas.   You know the weight of the hammer, that's enough.   It's not a whipping with feathers you're going to get, anyhow.   Just be aisey."   "Mr. Dawson, I grant I'm not your match.   Release me, and I double the cash.   I was merely trying your temper when I took the shape of a guinea."

"Faith and I'll try your's before I lave it, I've a notion." He immediately commenced with the sledge, and Satan sang out with a considerable want of firmness. "Am I heavy enough!" said Bill.

"Lighter, lighter, William, if you love me. I haven't been well latterly, Mr. Dawson—I have been delicate—my health, in short, is in a very precarious state, Mr. Dawson." "I can believe *that*," said Bill, "and it will be more so before I have done with you. Am I doing it right?" "Bill," said Nick, "is this gentlemanly treatment in your own respectable shop? Do you think, if you dropped into my little place, that I'd act this rascally part towards you? Have you no compunction?" "I know," replied Bill, sledging away with vehemence, "that you're notorious for giving your friends a *warm* welcome. Divil an ould youth more so; but you must be daling in bad coin, must you? However, good or bad, you're in for a sweat now, you sinner. Am I doin' it purty?"

"Lovely, William—but, if possible, a little more delicate."

"Oh, how delicate you are! Maybe a cup o' tay would sarve you, or a little small gruel to compose your stomach."

"Mr. Dawson," said the gentleman in the purse, "hold your hand and let us understand one another. I have a proposal to make." "Hear the sinner anyhow," said the wife. "Name your own sum," said Satan, "only set me free." "No, the sorra may take the toe you'll budge till you let Bill off," said the wife; "hould him hard, Bill, barrin' he sets *you* clear of your engagement. "There it is, my posy," said Bill; "that's the condition. If you don't give *me up*, here's at you once more—and you must double the cash you gave the last time, too. So, if you're of that opinion, say *ay*—leave the cash and be off."

The money again appeared in a glittering heap before Bill, upon which he exclaimed—"The *ay* has it, you dog. Take to pour pumps now, and fair weather after you, you vagrant; but Nicholas—Nick—here, here——" The other looked back, and saw Bill, with a broad grin upon him, shaking the purse at him—"Nicholas come back," said he. "I'm short a guinea." Nick shook his fist, and disappeared.

It would be useless to stop now, merely to inform our

readers that Bill was beyond improvement. In short, he once more took to his old habits, and lived on exactly in the same manner as before. He had two sons—one as great a blackguard as himself, and who was also named after him ; the other was a well-conducted, virtuous young man, called James, who left his father, and having relied upon his own industry and honest perseverance in life, arrived afterwards to great wealth, and built the town called Castle Dawson ; which is so called from its founder until this day.

Bill, at length, in spite of all his wealth, was obliged, as he himself said, "to travel,"—in other words, he fell asleep one day, and forgot to awaken ; or, in still plainer terms, he died.

Now, it is usual, when a man dies, to close the history of his life and adventures at once ; but with our hero this cannot be the case. The moment Bill departed, he very naturally bent his steps towards the residence of St. Moroky, as being, in his opinion, likely to lead him towards the snuggest berth he could readily make out. On arriving, he gave a very humble kind of a knock, and St. Moroky appeared.

"God save your Reverence !" said Bill, very submissively.

"Be off ; there's no admittance here for so poor a youth as you are," said St. Moroky.

He was now so cold and fatigued that he cared little where he went, provided only, as he said himself, "he could rest his bones, and get an air of the fire." Accordingly, after arriving at a large black gate, he knocked, as before, and was told he would get *instant* admittance the moment he gave his name.

"Billy Dawson," he replied.

"Off, instantly," said the porter to his companions, "and let his Majesty know that the rascal he dreads so much is here at the gate."

Such a racket and tumult were never heard as the very mention of Billy Dawson created.

In the meantime, his old acquaintance came running towards the gate with such haste and consternation, that his tail was several times nearly tripping up his heels.

"Don't admit that rascal," he shouted; "bar the gate—make every chain, and lock and bolt, fast—I won't be safe —and I won't stay here, nor none of us need stay here, if he gets in—my bones are sore yet after him.   No, no—begone you villain—you'll get no entrance here—I know you too well."

Bill could not help giving a broad, malicious grin at Satan, and, putting his nose through the bars, he exclaimed —"Ha! you ould dog, I have you afraid of me at last, have I?"

He had scarcely uttered the words, when his foe, who stood inside, instantly tweaked him by the nose, and Bill felt as if he had been gripped by the same red-hot tongs with which he himself had formerly tweaked the nose of Nicholas.

Bill then departed, but soon found that in consequence of the inflammable materials which strong drink had thrown into his nose, that organ immediately took fire, and, indeed, to tell the truth, kept burning night and day, winter and summer, without ever once going out, from that hour to this.

Such was the sad fate of Billy Dawson, who has been walking without stop or stay, from place to place, ever since; and in consequence of the flame on his nose, and his beard being tangled like a wisp of hay, he has been christened by the country folk Will-o'-the-Wisp, while, as it were, to show the mischief of his disposition, the circulating knave, knowing that he must seek the coldest bogs and quagmires in order to cool his nose, seizes upon that opportunity of misleading the unthinking and tipsy night travellers from their way, just that he may have the satisfaction of still taking in as many as possible.

GIANTS.

◆

WHEN the pagan gods of Ireland—the *Tuath-De-Danān*—robbed of worship and offerings, grew smaller and smaller in the popular imagination, until they turned into the fairies, the pagan heroes grew bigger and bigger, until they turned into the giants.

THE GIANT'S STAIRS.*

T. CROFTON CROKER.

ON the road between Passage and Cork there is an old mansion called Ronayne's Court. It may be easily known from the stack of chimneys and the gable-ends, which are to be seen, look at it which way you will. Here it was that Maurice Ronayne and his wife Margaret Gould kept house, as may be learned to this day from the great old chimney-piece, on which is carved their arms. They were a mighty worthy couple, and had but one son, who was called Philip, after no less a person than the King of Spain.

Immediately on his smelling the cold air of this world the child sneezed, which was naturally taken to be a good sign of his having a clear head; and the subsequent rapidity of his learning was truly amazing, for on the very first day a primer was put into his hands he tore out the A, B, C page and destroyed it, as a thing quite beneath his notice. No wonder, then, that both father and mother were proud of their heir, who gave such indisputable proofs of genius, or, as they called it in that part of the world, "*genus.*"

One morning, however, Master Phil, who was then just

* *Fairy Legends of the South of Ireland.*

A GIANT.

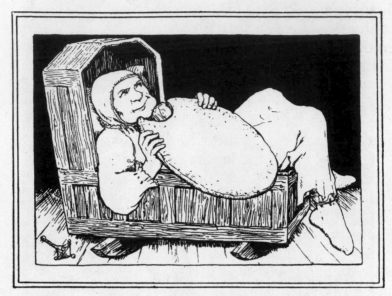

"A LEGEND OF KNOCKMANY."

seven years old, was missing, and no one could tell what had become of him : servants were sent in all directions to seek him, on horseback and on foot, but they returned without any tidings of the boy, whose disappearance altogether was most unaccountable. A large reward was offered, but it produced them no intelligence, and years rolled away without Mr. and Mrs. Ronayne having obtained any satisfactory account of the fate of their lost child.

There lived at this time, near Carrigaline, one Robert Kelly, a blacksmith by trade. He was what is termed a handy man, and his abilities were held in much estimation by the lads and the lasses of the neighbourhood ; for, independent of shoeing horses, which he did to great perfection, and making plough-irons, he interpreted dreams for the young women, sung "Arthur O'Bradley" at their weddings, and was so good-natured a fellow at a christening, that he was gossip to half the country round.

Now it happened that Robin had a dream himself, and young Philip Ronayne appeared to him in it, at the dead hour of the night. Robin thought he saw the boy mounted upon a beautiful white horse, and that he told him how he was made a page to the giant Mahon MacMahon, who had carried him off, and who held his court in the hard heart of the rock. "The seven years—my time of service—are clean out, Robin," said he, "and if you release me this night I will be the making of you for ever after."

"And how will I know," said Robin—cunning enough, even in his sleep—"but this is all a dream ?"

"Take that," said the boy, "for a token"—and at the word the white horse struck out with one of his hind legs, and gave poor Robin such a kick in the forehead that, thinking he was a dead man, he roared as loud as he could after his brains, and woke up, calling a thousand murders. He found himself in bed, but he had the mark of the blow, the regular print of a horse-shoe, upon his forehead as red as blood ; and Robin Kelly, who never before found himself puzzled at the dream of any other person, did not know what to think of his own.

Robin was well acquainted with the Giant's Stairs—as, indeed, who is not that knows the harbour? They consist of great masses of rock, which, piled one above another, rise like a flight of steps from very deep water, against the bold cliff of Carrigmahon. Nor are they badly suited for stairs to those who have legs of sufficient length to stride over a moderate-sized house, or to enable them to clear the space of a mile in a hop, step, and jump. Both these feats the giant MacMahon was said to have performed in the days of Finnian glory; and the common tradition of the country placed his dwelling within the cliff up whose side the stairs led.

Such was the impression which the dream made on Robin, that he determined to put its truth to the test. It occurred to him, however, before setting out on this adventure, that a plough-iron may be no bad companion, as, from experience, he knew it was an excellent knock-down argument, having on more occasions than one settled a little disagreement very quietly: so, putting one on his shoulder, off he marched, in the cool of the evening, through Glaun a Thowk (the Hawk's Glen) to Monkstown. Here an old gossip of his (Tom Clancey by name) lived, who, on hearing Robin's dream, promised him the use of his skiff, and, moreover, offered to assist in rowing it to the Giant's Stairs.

After a supper, which was of the best, they embarked. It was a beautiful still night, and the little boat glided swiftly along. The regular dip of the oars, the distant song of the sailor, and sometimes the voice of a belated traveller at the ferry of Carrigaloe, alone broke the quietness of the land and sea and sky. The tide was in their favour, and in a few minutes Robin and his gossip rested on their oars under the dark shadow of the Giant's Stairs. Robin looked anxiously for the entrance to the Giant's palace, which, it was said, may be found by any one seeking it at midnight; but no such entrance could he see. His impatience had hurried him there before that time, and after waiting a con-siderable space in a state of suspense not to be described,

Robin, with pure vexation, could not help exclaiming to his companion, " 'Tis a pair of fools we are, Tom Clancey, for coming here at all on the strength of a dream."

" And whose doing is it," said Tom, " but your own ? "

At the moment he spoke they perceived a faint glimmering of light to proceed from the cliff, which gradually increased until a porch big enough for a king's palace unfolded itself almost on a level with the water. They pulled the skiff directly towards the opening, and Robin Kelly, seizing his plough-iron, boldly entered with a strong hand and a stout heart. Wild and strange was that entrance, the whole of which appeared formed of grim and grotesque faces, blending so strangely each with the other that it was impossible to define any : the chin of one formed the nose of another ; what appeared to be a fixed and stern eye, if dwelt upon, changed to a gaping mouth ; and the lines of the lofty forehead grew into a majestic and flowing beard. The more Robin allowed himself to contemplate the forms around him, the more terrific they became ; and the stoney expression of this crowd of faces assumed a savage ferocity as his imagination converted feature after feature into a different shape and character. Losing the twilight in which these indefinite forms were visible, he advanced through a dark and devious passage, whilst a deep and rumbling noise sounded as if the rock was about to close upon him, and swallow him up alive for ever. Now, indeed, poor Robin felt afraid.

" Robin, Robin," said he, " if you were a fool for coming here, what in the name of fortune are you now ? " But, as before, he had scarcely spoken, when he saw a small light twinkling through the darkness of the distance, like a star in the midnight sky. To retreat was out of the question ; for so many turnings and windings were in the passage, that he considered he had but little chance of making his way back. He, therefore, proceeded towards the bit of light, and came at last into a spacious chamber, from the roof of which hung the solitary lamp that had guided him. Emerging from such profound gloom, the single lamp afforded Robin

abundant light to discover several gigantic figures seated
round a massive stone table, as if in serious deliberation,
but no word disturbed the breathless silence which prevailed. At the head of this table sat Mahon MacMahon
himself, whose majestic beard had taken root, and in the
course of ages grown into the stone slab. He was the first
who perceived Robin; and instantly starting up, drew his
long beard from out the hugh piece of rock in such haste
and with so sudden a jerk that it was shattered into a
thousand pieces.

"What seek you?" he demanded in a voice of thunder.

"I come," answered Robin, with as much boldness as he
could put on, for his heart was almost fainting within him;
"I come," said he, "to claim Philip Ronayne, whose time
of service is out this night."

"And who sent you here?" said the giant.

"'Twas of my own accord I came," said Robin.

"Then you must single him out from among my pages,"
said the giant; "and if you fix on the wrong one, your life
is the forfeit. Follow me." He led Robin into a hall of
vast extent, and filled with lights; along either side of which
were rows of beautiful children, all apparently seven years
old, and none beyond that age, dressed in green, and every
one exactly dressed alike.

"Here," said Mahon, "you are free to take Philip
Ronayne, if you will; but, remember, I give but one
choice."

Robin was sadly perplexed; for there were hundreds
upon hundreds of children; and he had no very clear recollection of the boy he sought. But he walked along the
hall, by the side of Mahon, as if nothing was the matter,
although his great iron dress clanked fearfully at every step,
sounding louder than Robin's own sledge battering on his
anvil.

They had nearly reached the end without speaking, when
Robin, seeing that the only means he had was to make
friends with the giant, determined to try what effect a few
soft words might have.

"'Tis a fine wholesome appearance the poor children carry," remarked Robin, "although they have been here so long shut out from the fresh air and the blessed light of heaven. 'Tis tenderly your honour must have reared them!"

"Ay," said the giant, "that is true for you; so give me your hand; for you are, I believe, a very honest fellow for a blacksmith."

Robin at the first look did not much like the huge size of the hand, and, therefore, presented his plough-iron, which the giant seizing, twisted in his grasp round and round again as if it had been a potato stalk. On seeing this all the children set up a shout of laughter. In the midst of their mirth Robin thought he heard his name called; and all ear and eye, he put his hand on the boy who he fancied had spoken, crying out at the same time, "Let me live or die for it, but this is young Phil Ronayne."

"It is Philip Ronayne—happy Philip Ronayne," said his young companions; and in an instant the hall became dark. Crashing noises were heard, and all was in strange confusion; but Robin held fast his prize, and found himself lying in the grey dawn of the morning at the head of the Giant's Stairs with the boy clasped in his arms.

Robin had plenty of gossips to spread the story of his wonderful adventure: Passage, Monkstown, Carrigaline— the whole barony of Kerricurrihy rung with it.

"Are you quite sure, Robin, it is young Phil Ronayne you have brought back with you?" was the regular question; for although the boy had been seven years away, his appearance now was just the same as on the day he was missed. He had neither grown taller nor older in look, and he spoke of things which had happened before he was carried off as one awakened from sleep, or as if they had occurred yesterday.

"Am I sure? Well, that's a queer question," was Robin's reply; "seeing the boy has the blue eye of the mother, with the foxy hair of the father; to say nothing of the *purty* wart on the right side of his little nose."

However Robin Kelly may have been questioned, the worthy couple of Ronayne's Court doubted not that he was the deliverer of their child from the power of the giant Mac-Mahon; and the reward they bestowed on him equalled their gratitude.

Philip Ronayne lived to be an old man; and he was remarkable to the day of his death for his skill in working brass and iron, which it was believed he had learned during his seven years' apprenticeship to the giant Mahon Mac-Mahon.

A LEGEND OF KNOCKMANY.

WILLIAM CARLETON.

WHAT Irish man, woman, or child has not heard of our renowned Hibernian Hercules, the great and glorious Fin M'Coul? Not one, from Cape Clear to the Giant's Causeway, nor from that back again to Cape Clear. And, by-the-way, speaking of the Giant's Causeway brings me at once to the beginning of my story. Well, it so happened that Fin and his gigantic relatives were all working at the Causeway, in order to make a bridge, or what was still better, a good stout pad-road, across to Scotland; when Fin, who was very fond of his wife Oonagh, took it into his head that he would go home and see how the poor woman got on in his absence. To be sure, Fin was a true Irishman, and so the sorrow thing in life brought him back, only to see that she was snug and comfortable, and, above all things, that she got her rest well at night; for he knew that the poor woman, when he was with her, used to be subject to nightly qualms and configurations, that kept him very anxious, decent man, striving to keep her up to the good spirits and health that she had when they were first married.

So, accordingly, he pulled up a fir-tree, and, after lopping off the roots and branches, made a walking-stick of it, and set out on his way to Oonagh.

Oonagh, or rather Fin, lived at this time on the very tip-top of Knockmany Hill, which faces a cousin of its own called Cullamore, that rises up, half-hill, half-mountain, on the opposite side—east-east by south, as the sailors say, when they wish to puzzle a landsman.

Now, the truth is, for it must come out, that honest Fin's affection for his wife, though cordial enough in itself, was by no manner of means the real cause of his journey home. There was at that time another giant, named Cucullin—some say he was Irish, and some say he was Scotch—but whether Scotch or Irish, sorrow doubt of it but he was a *targer*. No other giant of the day could stand before him; and such was his strength, that, when well vexed, he could give a stamp that shook the country about him. The fame and name of him went far and near; and nothing in the shape of a man, it was said, had any chance with him in a fight. Whether the story is true or not, I cannot say, but the report went that, by one blow of his fists he flattened a thunderbolt, and kept it in his pocket, in the shape of a pancake, to show to all his enemies, when they were about to fight him. Undoubtedly he had given every giant in Ireland a considerable beating, barring Fin M'Coul himself; and he swore, by the solemn contents of Moll Kelly's Primer, that he would never rest, night or day, winter or summer, till he would serve Fin with the same sauce, if he could catch him. Fin, however, who no doubt was the cock of the walk on his own dunghill, had a strong disinclination to meet a giant who could make a young earthquake, or flatten a thunderbolt when he was angry; so he accordingly kept dodging about from place to place, not much to his credit as a Trojan, to be sure, whenever he happened to get the hard word that Cucullin was on the scent of him. This, then, was the marrow of the whole movement, although he put it on his anxiety to see Oonagh; and I am not saying but there was some truth in that too.

However, the short and long of it was, with reverence be it spoken, that he heard Cucullin was coming to the Causeway to have a trial of strength with him; and he was naturally enough seized, in consequence, with a very warm and sudden sit of affection for his wife, poor woman, who was delicate in her health, and leading, besides, a very lonely, uncomfortable life of it (he assured them) in his absence. He accordingly pulled up the fir-tree, as I said before, and having *snedded* it into a walking-stick, set out on his affectionate travels to see his darling Oonagh on the top of Knockmany, by the way.

In truth, to state the suspicions of the country at the time, the people wondered very much why it was that Fin selected such a windy spot for his dwelling-house, and they even went so far as to tell him as much.

"What can you mane, Mr. M'Coul," said they, "by pitching your tent upon the top of Knockmany, where you never are without a breeze, day or night, winter or summer, and where you're often forced to take your nightcap* without either going to bed or turning up your little finger; ay, an' where, besides this, there's the sorrow's own want of water?"

"Why," said Fin, "ever since I was the height of a round tower, I was known to be fond of having a good prospect of my own; and where the dickens, neighbours, could I find a better spot for a good prospect than the top of Knockmany? As for water, I am sinking a pump,† and, plase goodness, as soon as the Causeway's made, I intend to finish it."

Now, this was more of Fin's philosophy; for the real state of the case was, that he pitched upon the top of Knockmany in order that he might be able to see Cucullin coming towards the house, and, of course, that he himself might go to look after his distant transactions in other parts of the

---

* A common name for the cloud or rack that hangs, as a forerunner of wet weather, about the peak of a mountain.

† There is upon the top of this hill an opening that bears a very strong resemblance to the crater of an extinct volcano.

country, rather than—but no matter—we do not wish to be too hard on Fin. All we have to say is, that if he wanted a spot from which to keep a sharp look-out—and, between ourselves, he did want it grievously—barring Slieve Croob, or Slieve Donard, or its own cousin, Cullamore, he could not find a neater or more convenient situation for it in the sweet and sagacious province of Ulster.

"God save all here!" said Fin, good-humouredly, on putting his honest face into his own door.

"Musha, Fin, avick, an' you're welcome home to your own Oonagh, you darlin' bully." Here followed a smack that is said to have made the waters of the lake at the bottom of the hill curl, as it were, with kindness and sympathy.

"Faith," said Fin, "beautiful; an' how are you, Oonagh —and how did you sport your figure during my absence, my bilberry?"

"Never a merrier—as bouncing a grass widow as ever there was in sweet 'Tyrone among the bushes.'"

Fin gave a short, good-humoured cough, and laughed most heartily, to show her how much he was delighted that she made herself happy in his absence.

"An' what brought you home so soon, Fin?" said she.

"Why, avourneen," said Fin, putting in his answer in the proper way, "never the thing but the purest of love and affection for yourself. Sure you know that's truth, anyhow, Oonagh."

Fin spent two or three happy days with Oonagh, and felt himself very comfortable, considering the dread he had of Cucullin. This, however, grew upon him so much that his wife could not but perceive something lay on his mind which he kept altogether to himself. Let a woman alone, in the meantime, for ferreting or wheedling a secret out of her good man, when she wishes. Fin was a proof of this.

"It's this Cucullin," said he, "that's troubling me. When the fellow gets angry, and begins to stamp, he'll shake you a whole townland; and it's well known that he can stop a thunderbolt, for he always carries one about him in the shape of a pancake, to show to anyone that might misdoubt it."

As he spoke, he clapped his thumb in his mouth, which he always did when he wanted to prophesy, or to know anything that happened in his absence; and the wife, who knew what he did it for, said, very sweetly,

"Fin, darling, I hope you don't bite your thumb at me, dear?"

"No," said Fin; "but I bite my thumb, acushla," said he.

"Yes, jewel; but take care and don't draw blood," said she. "Ah, Fin! don't, my bully—don't."

"He's coming," said Fin; "I see him below Dungannon."

"Thank goodness, dear! an' who is it, avick? Glory be to God!"

"That baste, Cucullin," replied Fin; "and how to manage I don't know. If I run away, I am disgraced; and I know that sooner or later I must meet him, for my thumb tells me so."

"When will he be here?" said she.

"To-morrow, about two o'clock," replied Fin, with a groan.

"Well, my bully, don't be cast down," said Oonagh; "depend on me, and maybe I'll bring you better out of this scrape than ever you could bring yourself, by your rule o' thumb."

This quieted Fin's heart very much, for he knew that Oonagh was hand and glove with the fairies; and, indeed, to tell the truth, she was supposed to be a fairy herself. If she was, however, she must have been a kind-hearted one, for, by all accounts, she never did anything but good in the neighbourhood.

Now it so happened that Oonagh had a sister named Granua, living opposite them, on the very top of Cullamore, which I have mentioned already, and this Granua was quite

as powerful as herself.   The beautiful valley that lies
between them is not more than about three or four miles
broad, so that of a summer's evening, Granua and Oonagh
were able to hold many an agreeable conversation across it,
from the one hill-top to the other.   Upon this occasion
Oonagh resolved to consult her sister as to what was best to
be done in the difficulty that surrounded them.

"Granua," said she, "are you at home?"

"No," said the other; "I'm picking bilberries in Althad-
hawan" (*Anglicé*, the Devil's Glen).

"Well," said Oonagh, "get up to the top of Cullamore,
look about you, and then tell us what you see."

"Very well," replied Granua; after a few minutes, "I am
there now."

"What do you see?" asked the other.

"Goodness be about us!" exclaimed Granua, "I see
the biggest giant that ever was known coming up from
Dungannon."

"Ay," said Oonagh, "there's our difficulty.   That giant
is the great Cucullin; and he's now commin' up to leather
Fin.   What's to be done?"

"I'll call to him," she replied, "to come up to Cullamore
and refresh himself, and maybe that will give you and Fin
time to think of some plan to get yourselves out of the
scrape.   But," she proceeded, "I'm short of butter, having
in the house only half-a-dozen firkins, and as I'm to have a
few giants and giantesses to spend the evenin' with me, I'd
feel thankful, Oonagh, if you'd throw me up fifteen or
sixteen tubs, or the largest miscaun you have got, and you'll
oblige me very much."

"I'll do that with a heart and a-half," replied Oonagh;
"and, indeed, Granua, I feel myself under great obligations
to you for your kindness in keeping him off of us till we see
what can be done; for what would become of us all if
anything happened Fin, poor man."

She accordingly got the largest miscaun of butter she had
—which might be about the weight of a couple a dozen
mill-stones, so that you may easily judge of its size—and

calling up to her sister, "Granua," said she, "are you ready? I'm going to throw you up a miscaun, so be prepared to catch it."

"I will," said the other; "a good throw now, and take care it does not fall short."

Oonagh threw it; but, in consequence of her anxiety about Fin and Cucullin, she forgot to say the charm that was to send it up, so that, instead of reaching Cullamore, as she expected, it fell about half-way between the two hills, at the edge of the Broad Bog near Augher.

"My curse upon you!" she exclaimed; "you've disgraced me. I now change you into a grey stone. Lie there as a testimony of what has happened; and may evil betide the first living man that will ever attempt to remove or injure you!"

And, sure enough, there it lies to this day, with the mark of the four fingers and thumb imprinted in it, exactly as it came out of her hand.

"Never mind," said Granua, "I must only do the best I can with Cucullin. If all fail, I'll give him a cast of heather broth to keep the wind out of his stomach, or a panada of oak-bark to draw it in a bit; but, above all things, think of some plan to get Fin out of the scrape he's in, otherwise he's a lost man. You know you used to be sharp and ready-witted; and my own opinion, Oonagh, is, that it will go hard with you, or you'll outdo Cucullin yet."

She then made a high smoke on the top of the hill, after which she put her finger in her mouth, and gave three whistles, and by that Cucullin knew he was invited to Culla-more—for this was the way that the Irish long ago gave a sign to all strangers and travellers, to let them know they were welcome to come and take share of whatever was going.

In the meantime, Fin was very melancholy, and did not know what to do, or how to act at all. Cucullin was an ugly customer, no doubt, to meet with; and, moreover, the idea of the confounded "cake" aforesaid flattened the very heart within him. What chance could he have, strong and brave though he was, with a man who could, when put in a passion, walk the country into earthquakes and knock thunderbolts into pancakes? The thing was impossible; and Fin knew not on what hand to turn him. Right or left—backward or forward—where to go he could form no guess whatsoever.

"Oonagh," said he, "can you do nothing for me? Where's all your invention? Am I to be skivered like a rabbit before your eyes, and to have my name disgraced forever in the sight of all my tribe, and me the best man among them? How am I to fight this man-mountain—this huge cross between an earthquake and a thunderbolt? —with a pancake in his pocket that was once——"

"Be easy, Fin," replied Oonagh; "troth, I'm ashamed of you. Keep your toe in your pump, will you? Talking of pancakes, maybe we'll give him as good as any he brings with him—thunderbolt or otherwise. If I don't treat him to as smart feeding as he's got this many a day, never trust Oonagh again. Leave him to me, and do just as I bid you."

This relieved Fin very much; for, after all, he had great confidence in his wife, knowing, as he did, that she had got him out of many a quandary before. The present, however, was the greatest of all; but still he began to get courage, and was able to eat his victuals as usual. Oonagh then drew the nine woollen threads of different colours, which she always did to find out the best way of succeeding in anything of importance she went about. She then platted them into three plats with three colours in each, putting one on her right arm, one round her heart, and the third round her right ankle, for then she knew that nothing could fail with her that she undertook.

Having everything now prepared, she sent round to the neighbours and borrowed one-and-twenty iron griddles, which she took and kneaded into the hearts of one-and-twenty cakes of bread, and these she baked on the fire in the usual way, setting them aside in the cupboard according as they were done. She then put down a large pot of

new milk, which she made into curds and whey, and gave
Fin due instructions how to use the curds when Cucullin
should come. Having done all this, she sat down quite
contented, waiting for his arrival on the next day about two
o'clock, that being the hour at which he was expected—for
Fin knew as much by the sucking of his thumb. Now, this
was a curious property that Fin's thumb had ; but, notwithstanding all the wisdom and logic he used, to suck out of it,
it could never have stood to him here were it not for the
wit of his wife. In this very thing, moreover, he was very
much resembled by his great foe, Cucullin ; for it was well
known that the huge strength he possessed all lay in the
middle finger of his right hand, and that, if he happened by
any mischance to lose it, he was no more, notwithstanding
his bulk, than a common man.

At length, the next day, he was seen coming across the
valley, and Oonagh knew that it was time to commence
operations. She immediately made the cradle, and desired
Fin to lie down in it, and cover himself up with the
clothes.

"You must pass for you own child," said she ; "so just
lie there snug, and say nothing, but be guided by me."
This, to be sure, was wormwood to Fin—I mean going
into the cradle in such a cowardly manner—but he knew
Oonagh well ; and finding that he had nothing else for it,
with a very rueful face he gathered himself into it, and lay
snug, as she had desired him.

About two o'clock, as he had been expected, Cucullin
came in. "God save all here !" said he ; "is this where
the great Fin M'Coul lives ? "

"Indeed it is, honest man," replied Oonagh ; "God save
you kindly—won't you be sitting ? "

"Thank you, ma'am," says he, sitting down ; "you're
Mrs. M'Coul, I suppose ? "

"I am," said she ; "and I have no reason, I hope, to be
ashamed of my husband."

"No," said the other, "he has the name of being the
strongest and bravest man in Ireland ; but for all that,

there's a man not far from you that's very desirous of taking a shake with him. Is he at home?"

"Why, then, no," she replied; "and if ever a man left his house in a fury, he did. It appears that some one told him of a big basthoon of a giant called Cucullin being down at the Causeway to look for him, and so he set out there to try if he could catch him. Troth, I hope, for the poor giant's sake, he won't meet with him, for if he does, Fin will make paste of him at once."

"Well," said the other, "I am Cucullin, and I have been seeking him these twelve months, but he always kept clear of me; and I will never rest night or day till I lay my hands on him."

At this Oonagh set up a loud laugh, of great contempt, by-the-way, and looked at him as if he was only a mere handful of a man.

"Did you ever see Fin?" said she, changing her manner all at once.

"How could I?" said he; "he always took care to keep his distance."

"I thought so," she replied; "I judged as much; and if you take my advice, you poor-looking creature, you'll pray night and day that you may never see him, for I tell you it will be a black day for you when you do. But, in the meantime, you perceive that the wind's on the door, and as Fin himself is from home, maybe you'd be civil enough to turn the house, for it's always what Fin does when he's here."

This was a startler even to Cucullin; but he got up, however, and after pulling the middle finger of his right hand until it cracked three times, he went outside, and getting his arms about the house, completely turned it as she had wished. When Fin saw this, he felt a certain description of moisture, which shall be nameless, oozing out through every pore of his skin; but Oonagh, depending upon her woman's wit, felt not a whit daunted.

"Arrah, then," said she, "as you are so civil, maybe you'd do another obliging turn for us, as Fin's not here to do it himself. You see, after this long stretch of dry weather we've had, we feel very badly off for want of water. Now, Fin says there's a fine spring-well somewhere under the rocks behind the hill here below, and it was his intention to pull them asunder; but having heard of you, he left the place in such a fury, that he never thought of it. Now, if you try to find it, troth I'd feel it a kindness."

She then brought Cucullin down to see the place, which was then all one solid rock; and, after looking at it for some time, he cracked his right middle finger nine times, and, stooping down, tore a cleft about four hundred feet deep, and a quarter of a mile in length, which has since been christened by the name of Lumford's Glen. This feat nearly threw Oonagh herself off her guard; but what won't a woman's sagacity and presence of mind accomplish?

"You'll now come in," said he, "and eat a bit of such humble fare as we can give you. Fin, even although he and you are enemies, would scorn not to treat you kindly in his own house; and, indeed, if I didn't do it even in his absence, he would not be pleased with me."

She accordingly brought him in, and placing half-a-dozen of the cakes we spoke of before him, together with a can or two of butter, a side of boiled bacon, and a stack of cabbage, she desired him to help himself—for this, be it known, was long before the invention of potatoes. Cucullin, who, by the way, was a glutton as well as a hero, put one of the cakes in his mouth to take a huge whack out of it, when both Fin and Oonagh were stunned with a noise that resembled something between a growl and a yell. "Blood and fury!" he shouted; "how is this? Here are two of my teeth out! What kind of bread is this you gave me?"

"What's the matter?" said Oonagh coolly.

"Matter!" shouted the other again; "why, here are the two best teeth in my head gone."

"Why," said she, "that's Fin's bread—the only bread he ever eats when at home; but, indeed, I forgot to tell you that nobody can eat it but himself, and that child in the cradle there. I thought, however, that, as you were reported to be rather a stout little fellow of your size, you might be able to manage it, and I did not wish to affront a man that thinks himself able to fight Fin. Here's another cake—maybe it's not so hard as that."

Cucullin at the moment was not only hungry, but ravenous, so he accordingly made a fresh set at the second cake, and immediately another yell was heard twice as loud as the first. "Thunder and giblets!" he roared, "take your bread out of this, or I will not have a tooth in my head; there's another pair of them gone!"

"Well, honest man," replied Oonagh, "if you're not able to eat the bread, say so quietly, and don't be wakening the child in the cradle there. There, now, he's awake upon me."

Fin now gave a skirl that startled the giant, as coming from such a youngster as he was represented to be. "Mother," said he, "I'm hungry—get me something to eat." Oonagh went over, and putting into his hand a cake *that had no griddle in it*, Fin, whose appetite in the meantime was sharpened by what he saw going forward, soon made it disappear. Cucullin was thunderstruck, and secretly thanked his stars that he had the good fortune to miss meeting Fin, for, as he said to himself, I'd have no chance with a man who could eat such bread as that, which even his son that's but in his cradle can munch before my eyes.

"I'd like to take a glimpse at the lad in the cradle," said he to Oonagh; "for I can tell you that the infant who can manage that nutriment is no joke to look at, or to feed of a scarce summer."

"With all the veins of my heart," replied Oonagh; "get up, acushla, and show this decent little man something that won't be unworthy of your father, Fin M'Coul."

Fin, who was dressed for the occasion as much like a boy as possible, got up, and bringing Cucullin out, "Are you strong?" said he.

"Thunder an' ounds!" exclaimed the other, "what a voice in so small a chap!"

"Are you strong?" said Fin again; "are you able to

squeeze water out of that white stone?" he asked, putting one into Cucullin's hand. The latter squeezed and squeezed the stone, but to no purpose; he might pull the rocks of Lumford's Glen asunder, and flatten a thunderbolt, but to squeeze water out of a white stone was beyond his strength. Fin eyed him with great contempt, as he kept straining and squeezing and squeezing and straining, till he got black in the face with the efforts.

"Ah, you're a poor creature!" said Fin.   "You a giant! Give me the stone here, and when I'll show what Fin's little son can do; you may then judge of what my daddy himself is."

Fin then took the stone, and slyly exchanging it for the curds, he squeezed the latter until the whey, as clear as water, oozed out in a little shower from his hand.

"I'll now go in," said he "to my cradle; for I scorn to lose my time with any one that's not able to eat my daddy's bread, or squeeze water out of a stone. Bedad, you had better be off out of this before he comes back; for if he catches you, it's in flummery he'd have you in two minutes."

Cucullin, seeing what he had seen, was of the same opinion himself; his knees knocked together with the terror of Fin's return, and he accordingly hastened in to bid Oonagh farewell, and to assure her, that from that day out, he never wished to hear of, much less to see, her husband. "I admit fairly that I'm not a match for him," said he, "strong as I am; tell him I will avoid him as I would the plague, and that I will make myself scarce in this part of the country while I live."

Fin, in the meantime, had gone into the cradle, where he lay very quietly, his heart at his mouth with delight that Cucullin was about to take his departure, without discovering the tricks that had been played off on him.

"It's well for you," said Oonagh, "that he doesn't happen to be here, for it's nothing but hawk's meat he'd make of you."

"I know that," says Cucullin; "divil a thing else he'd make of me; but before I go, will you let me feel what kind

of teeth they are that can eat griddle-bread like *that?*"—
and he pointed to it as he spoke.

"With all pleasure in life," said she; "only, as they're
far back in his head, you must put your finger a good way
in."

Cucullin was surprised to find such a powerful set of
grinders in one so young; but he was still much more so
on finding, when he took his hand from Fin's mouth, that
he had left the very finger upon which his whole strength
depended, behind him. He gave one loud groan, and fell
down at once with terror and weakness. This was all Fin
wanted, who now knew that his most powerful and bitterest
enemy was completely at his mercy. He instantly started
out of the cradle, and in a few minutes the great Cucullin,
that was for such a length of time the terror of him and all
his followers, lay a corpse before him. Thus did Fin,
through the wit and invention of Oonagh, his wife, succeed
in overcoming his enemy by stratagem, which he never
could have done by force: and thus also is it proved that
the women, if they bring us *into* many an unpleasant scrape,
can sometimes succeed in getting us *out* of others that are
as bad.

KINGS, QUEENS, PRINCESSES, EARLS, ROBBERS.

THE TWELVE WILD GEESE.*

PATRICK KENNEDY.

THERE was once a King and Queen that lived very happily together, and they had twelve sons and not a single daughter. We are always wishing for what we haven't, and don't care for what we have, and so it was with the Queen. One day in winter, when the bawn was covered with snow, she was looking out of the parlour window, and saw there a calf that was just killed by the butcher, and a raven standing near it. "Oh," says she, "if I had only a daughter with her skin as white as that snow, her cheeks as red as that blood, and her hair as black as that raven, I'd give away every one of my twelve sons for her." The moment she said the word, she got a great fright, and a shiver went through her, and in an instant after, a severe-looking old woman stood before her. "That was a wicked wish you made," said she, "and to punish you it will be granted. You will have such a daughter as you desire, but the very day of her birth you will lose your other children." She vanished the moment she said the words.

And that very way it turned out. When she expected her delivery, she had her children all in a large room of the

* *The Fireside Stories of Ireland* (Gill & Son, Dublin).

palace, with guards all round it, but the very hour her daughter came into the world, the guards inside and outside heard a great whirling and whistling, and the twelve princes were seen flying one after another out through the open window, and away like so many arrows over the woods. Well, the king was in great grief for the loss of his sons, and he would be very enraged with his wife if he only knew that she was so much to blame for it.

Everyone called the little princess Snow-white-and-Rose-red on account of her beautiful complexion. She was the most loving and lovable child that could be seen anywhere. When she was twelve years old she began to be very sad and lonely, and to torment her mother, asking her about her brothers that she thought were dead, for none up to that time ever told her the exact thing that happened them. The secret was weighing very heavy on the Queen's conscience, and as the little girl persevered in her questions, at last she told her. "Well, mother," said she, "it was on my account my poor brothers were changed into wild geese, and are now suffering all sorts of hardship; before the world is a day older, I'll be off to seek them, and try to restore them to their own shapes."

The King and Queen had her well watched, but all was no use. Next night she was getting through the woods that surrounded the palace, and she went on and on that night, and till the evening of next day. She had a few cakes with her, and she got nuts, and *mugoreens* (fruit of the sweet briar), and some sweet crabs, as she went along. At last she came to a nice wooden house just at sunset. There was a fine garden round it, full of the handsomest flowers, and a gate in the hedge. She went in, and saw a table laid out with twelve plates, and twelve knives and forks, and twelve spoons, and there were cakes, and cold wild fowl, and fruit along with the plates, and there was a good fire, and in another long room there were twelve beds. Well, while she was looking about her she heard the gate opening, and footsteps along the walk, and in came twelve young men, and there was great grief and surprise on all their faces when they laid eyes on her. "Oh, what misfortune sent you here?" said the eldest. "For the sake of a girl we were obliged to leave our father's court, and be in the shape of wild geese all day. That's twelve years ago, and we took a solemn oath that we would kill the first young girl that came into our hands. It's a pity to put such an innocent and handsome girl as you are out of the world, but we must keep our oath." "But," said she, "I'm your only sister, that never knew anything about this till yesterday; and I stole away from our father's and mother's palace last night to find you out and relieve you if I can." Every one of them clasped his hands, and looked down on the floor, and you could hear a pin fall till the eldest cried out, "A curse light on our oath! what shall we do?" "I'll tell you that," said an old woman that appeared at the instant among them. "Break your wicked oath, which no one should keep. If you attempted to lay an uncivil finger on her I'd change you into twelve *booliaun buis* (stalks of ragweed), but I wish well to you as well as to her. She is appointed to be your deliverer in this way. She must spin and knit twelve shirts for you out of bog-down, to be gathered by her own hands on the moor just outside of the wood. It will take her five years to do it, and if she once speaks, or laughs, or cries the whole time, you will have to remain wild geese by day till you're called out of the world. So take care of your sister; it is worth your while." The fairy then vanished, and it was only a strife with the brothers to see who would be first to kiss and hug their sister.

So for three long years the poor young princess was occupied pulling bog-down, spinning it, and knitting it into shirts, and at the end of the three years she had eight made. During all that time, she never spoke a word, nor laughed, nor cried : the last was the hardest to refrain from. One fine day she was sitting in the garden spinning, when in sprung a fine greyhound and bounded up to her, and laid his paws on her shoulder, and licked her forehead and her hair. The next minute a beautiful young prince rode up to the little garden gate, took off his hat, and asked for leave to come in. She gave him a little nod, and in he walked. He made ever so many apologies for intruding, and asked her ever so many questions, but not a word could he get out of her. He loved her so much from the first moment, that he could not leave her till he told her he was king of a country just bordering on the forest, and he begged her to come home with him, and be his wife. She couldn't help loving him as much as he did her, and though she shook her head very often, and was very sorry to leave her brothers, at last she nodded her head, and put her hand in his. She knew well enough that the good fairy and her brothers would be able to find her out. Before she went she brought out a basket holding all her bog-down, and another holding the eight shirts. The attendants took charge of these, and the prince placed her before him on his horse. The only thing that disturbed him while riding along was the displeasure his stepmother would feel at what he had done. However, he was full master at home, and as soon as he arrived he sent for the bishop, got his bride nicely dressed, and the marriage was celebrated, the bride answering by signs. He knew by her manners she was of high birth, and no two could be fonder of each other.

The wicked stepmother did all she could to make mischief, saying she was sure she was only a woodman's daughter; but nothing could disturb the young king's opinion of his wife. In good time the young queen was delivered of a beautiful boy, and the king was so glad he hardly knew what to do for joy. All the grandeur of the christening and the happiness of the parents tormented the bad woman more than I can tell you, and she determined to put a stop to all their comfort. She got a sleeping posset given to the young mother, and while she was thinking and thinking how she could best make away with the child, she saw a wicked-looking wolf in the garden, looking up at her, and licking his chops. She lost no time, but snatched the child from the arms of the sleeping woman, and pitched it out. The beast caught it in his mouth, and was over the garden fence in a minute. The wicked woman then pricked her own fingers, and dabbled the blood round the mouth of the sleeping mother.

Well, the young king was just then coming into the big bawn from hunting, and as soon as he entered the house, she beckoned to him, shed a few crocodile tears, began to cry and wring her hands, and hurried him along the passage to the bedchamber.

Oh, wasn't the poor king frightened when he saw the queen's mouth bloody, and missed his child? It would take two hours to tell you the devilment of the old queen, the confusion and fright, and grief of the young king and queen, the bad opinion he began to feel of his wife, and the struggle she had to keep down her bitter sorrow, and not give way to it by speaking or lamenting. The young king would not allow any one to be called, and ordered his step-mother to give out that the child fell from the mother's arms at the window, and that a wild beast ran off with it. The wicked woman pretended to do so, but she told underhand to everybody she spoke to what the king and herself saw in the bed-chamber.

The young queen was the most unhappy woman in the three kingdoms for a long time, between sorrow for her child, and her husband's bad opinion; still she neither spoke nor cried, and she gathered bog-down and went on with the shirts. Often the twelve wild geese would be seen lighting on the trees in the park or on the smooth sod, and looking in at her windows. So she worked on to get the shirts finished, but another year was at an end, and she had the twelfth shirt finished except one arm, when she was obliged to take to her bed, and a beautiful girl was born.

Now the king was on his guard, and he would not let the mother and child be left alone for a minute; but the wicked woman bribed some of the attendants, set others asleep, gave the sleepy posset to the queen, and had a person watching to snatch the child away, and kill it. But what should she see but the same wolf in the garden looking up, and licking his chops again? Out went the child, and away with it flew the wolf, and she smeared the sleeping mother's mouth and face with blood, and then roared, and bawled, and cried out to the king and to everybody she met, and the room was filled, and everyone was sure the young queen had just devoured her own babe.

The poor mother thought now her life would leave her. She was in such a state she could neither think nor pray, but she sat like a stone, and worked away at the arm of the twelfth shirt.

The king was for taking her to the house in the wood where he found her, but the stepmother, and the lords of the court, and the judges would not hear of it, and she was condemned to be burned in the big bawn at three o'clock the same day. When the hour drew near, the king went to the farthest part of his palace, and there was no more unhappy man in his kingdom at that hour.

When the executioners came and led her off, she took the pile of shirts in her arms. There was still a few stitches wanted, and while they were tying her to the stakes she still worked on. At the last stitch she seemed overcome and dropped a tear on her work, but the moment after she sprang up, and shouted out, "I am innocent; call my husband!" The executioners stayed their hands, except one wicked-disposed creature, who set fire to the faggot next him, and while all were struck in amaze, there was a rushing of wings, and in a moment the twelve wild geese were standing around the pile. Before you could count twelve, she flung a shirt over each bird, and there in the twinkling of an eye were twelve of the finest young men that could be collected out of a thousand. While some were untying their sister, the eldest, taking a strong stake in his hand, struck the busy executioner such a blow that he never needed another.

While they were comforting the young queen, and the king was hurrying to the spot, a fine-looking woman appeared among them holding the babe on one arm and the little prince by the hand. There was nothing but crying for joy, and laughing for joy, and hugging and kissing, and when any one had time to thank the good fairy, who in the shape of a wolf, carried the child away, she was not to be found. Never was such happiness enjoyed in any palace that ever was built, and if the wicked queen and her helpers were not torn by wild horses, they richly deserved it.

THE LAZY BEAUTY AND HER AUNTS.

THERE was once a poor widow woman, who had a daughter that was as handsome as the day, and as lazy as a pig, saving your presence. The poor mother was the most industrious person in the townland, and was a particularly good hand at the spinning-wheel. It was the wish of her heart that her daughter should be as handy as herself ; but she'd get up late, eat her breakfast before she'd finish her prayers, and then go about dawdling, and anything she handled seemed to be burning her fingers. She drawled her words as if it was a great trouble to her to speak, or as if her tongue was as lazy as her body. Many a heart-scald her poor mother got with her, and still she was only improving like dead fowl in August.

Well, one morning that things were as bad as they could be, and the poor woman was giving tongue at the rate of a mill-clapper, who should be riding by but the king's son. "Oh dear, oh dear, good woman!" said he, "you must have a very bad child to make you scold so terribly. Sure it can't be this handsome girl that vexed you!" "Oh, please your Majesty, not at all," says the old dissembler. "I was only checking her for working herself too much. Would your majesty believe it? She spins three pounds of flax in a day, weaves it into linen the next, and makes it all into shirts the day after." "My gracious," says the prince, "she's the very lady that will just fill my mother's eye, and herself's the greatest spinner in the kingdom. Will you put on your daughter's bonnet and cloak, if you please, ma'am, and set her behind me? Why, my mother will be so delighted with her, that perhaps she'll make her her daughter-in-law in a week, that is, if the young woman herself is agreeable."

Well, between the confusion, and the joy, and the fear of being found out, the women didn't know what to do ; and before they could make up their minds, young Anty (Anastasia) was set behind the prince, and away he and his attendants went, and a good heavy purse was left behind with the mother. She *pullillued* a long time after all was gone, in dread of something bad happening to the poor girl.

The prince couldn't judge of the girl's breeding or wit from the few answers he pulled out of her. The queen was struck in a heap when she saw a young country girl sitting behind her son, but when she saw her handsome face, and heard all she could do, she didn't think she could make too much of her. The prince took an opportunity of whispering her that if she didn't object to be his wife she must strive to please his mother. Well, the evening went by, and the prince and Anty were getting fonder and fonder of one another, but the thought of the spinning used to send the cold to her heart every moment. When bed-time came, the old queen went along with her to a beautiful bedroom, and when she was bidding her good-night, she pointed to a heap of fine flax, and said, " You may begin as soon as you like to-morrow morning, and I'll expect to see these three pounds in nice thread the morning after." Little did the poor girl sleep that night. She kept crying and lamenting that she didn't mind her mother's advice better. When she was left alone next morning, she began with a heavy heart ; and though she had a nice mahogany wheel and the finest flax you ever saw, the thread was breaking every moment. One while it was as fine as a cobweb, and the next as coarse as a little boy's whipcord. At last she pushed her chair back, let her hands fall in her lap, and burst out a-crying.

A small, old woman with surprising big feet appeared before her at the same moment, and said, " What ails you, you handsome colleen ? "   " An' haven't I all that flax to spin before to-morrow morning, and I'll never be able to have even five yards of fine thread of it put together."   " An' would you think bad to ask poor *Colliagh Cushmōr* (Old woman Big-foot) to your wedding with the young prince ? If you promise me that, all your three pounds will be made into the finest of thread while you're taking your sleep to-night."   " Indeed, you must be there and welcome, and I'll honour you all the days of your life."   " Very well ; stay in your room till tea-time, and tell the queen she may come in for her thread as early as she likes to-morrow morning." It was all as she said ; and the thread was finer and evener than the gut you see with fly-fishers.   " My brave girl you were ! " says the queen.   " I'll get my own mahogany loom brought into you, but you needn't do anything more to-day. Work and rest, work and rest, is my motto.   To-morrow you'll weave all this thread, and who knows what may happen ? "

The poor girl was more frightened this time than the last, and she was so afraid to lose the prince.   She didn't even know how to put the warp in the gears, nor how to use the shuttle, and she was sitting in the greatest grief, when a little woman, who was mighty well-shouldered about the hips, all at once appeared to her, told her her name was *Colliach Cromanmōr*, and made the same bargain with her as Colliach Cushmōr.   Great was the queen's pleasure when she found early in the morning a web as fine and white as the finest paper you ever saw.   " The darling you were ! " says she.   " Take your ease with the ladies and gentlemen to-day, and if your have all this made into nice shirts to-morrow you may present one of them to my son, and be married to him out of hand."

Oh, wouldn't you pity poor Anty the next day, she was now so near the prince, and, maybe, would be soon so far from him.   But she waited as patiently as she could with scissors, needle, and thread in hand, till a minute after noon.

Then she was rejoiced to see the third old woman appear. She had a big red nose, and informed Anty that people called her *Shron Mor Rua* on that account. She was up to her as good as the others, for a dozen fine shirts were lying on the table when the queen paid her an early visit.

Now there was nothing talked of but the wedding, and I needn't tell you it was grand. The poor mother was there along with the rest, and at the dinner the old queen could talk of nothing but the lovely shirts, and how happy herself and the bride would be after the honeymoon, spinning, and weaving, and sewing shirts and shifts without end. The bridegroom didn't like the discourse, and the bride liked it less, and he was going to say something, when the footman came up to the head of the table and said to the bride, "Your ladyship's aunt, Colliach Cushmōr, bade me ask might she come in." The bride blushed and wished she was seven miles under the floor, but well became the prince. "Tell Mrs. Cushmōr," said he, "that any relation of my bride's will be always heartily welcome wherever she and I are." In came the woman with the big foot, and got a seat near the prince. The old queen didn't like it much, and after a few words she asked rather spitefully, "Dear ma'am, what's the reason your foot is so big?" "*Musha*, faith, your majesty, I was standing almost all my life at the spinning-wheel, and that's the reason." "I declare to you, my darling," said the prince, "I'll never allow you to spend one hour at the same spinning-wheel." The same footman said again, "Your ladyship's aunt, Colliach Cromanmōr, wishes to come in, if the genteels and yourself have no objection." Very *sharoose* (displeased) was Princess Anty, but the prince sent her welcome, and she took her seat, and drank healths apiece to the company. "May I ask, ma'am?" says the old queen, "why you're so wide half-way between the head and the feet?" "That, your majesty, is owing to sitting all my life at the loom." "By my sceptre," says the prince, "my wife shall never sit there an hour." The footman again came up. "Your ladyship's aunt, Colliach Shron Mor Rua, is asking leave to come into the banquet." More blushing on the bride's face, but the bridegroom spoke out cordially, " Tell Mrs. Shron Mor Rua she's doing us an honour." In came the old woman, and great respect she got near the top of the table, but the people down low put up their tumblers and glasses to their noses to hide the grins. " Ma'am," says the old queen, " will you tell us, if you please, why your nose is so big and red ? " " Throth, your majesty, my head was bent down over the stitching all my life, and all the blood in my body ran into my nose." " My darling," said the prince to Anty, "if ever I see a needle in your hand, I'll run a hundred miles from you."

" And in troth, girls and boys, though it's a diverting story, I don't think the moral is good ; and if any of you *thuckeens* go about imitating Anty in her laziness, you'll find it won't thrive with you as it did with her. She was beautiful beyond compare, which none of you are, and she had three powerful fairies to help her besides. There's no fairies now, and no prince or lord to ride by, and catch you idling or working ; and maybe, after all, the prince and herself were not so very happy when the cares of the world or old age came on them."

Thus was the tale ended by poor old *Shebale* (Sybilla), Father Murphy's housekeeper, in Coolbawn, Barony of Bantry, about half a century since.

THE HAUGHTY PRINCESS.*

BY PATRICK KENNEDY.

THERE was once a very worthy king, whose daughter was the greatest beauty that could be seen far or near, but she was as proud as Lucifer, and no king or prince would she agree to marry. Her father was tired out at last, aud invited

* *Fireside Tales of Ireland.*

every king, and prince, and duke, and earl that he knew or didn't know to come to his court to give her one trial more. They all came, and next day after breakfast they stood in a row in the lawn, and the princess walked along in the front of them to make her choice. One was fat, and says she, "I won't have you, Beer-barrel!" One was tall and thin, and to him she said, "I won't have you, Ramrod!" To a white-faced man she said, "I won't have you, Pale Death;" and to a red-cheeked man she said, "I won't have you, Cockscomb!" She stopped a little before the last of all, for he was a fine man in face and form. She wanted to find some defect in him, but he had nothing remarkable but a ring of brown curling hair under his chin. She admired him a little, and then carried it off with, "I won't have you, Whiskers!"

So all went away, and the king was so vexed, he said to her, "Now to punish your *impedence*, I'll give you to the first beggarman or singing *sthronshuch* that calls;" and, as sure as the hearth-money, a fellow all over rags, and hair that came to his shoulders, and a bushy red beard all over his face, came next morning, and began to sing before the parlour window.

When the song was over, the hall-door was opened, the singer asked in, the priest brought, and the princess married to Beardy. She roared and she bawled, but her father didn't mind her. "There," says he to the bridegroom, " is five guineas for you. Take your wife out of my sight, and never let me lay eyes on you or her again."

Off he led her, and dismal enough she was. The only thing that gave her relief was the tones of her husband's voice and his genteel manners. "Whose wood is this?" said she, as they were going through one. "It belongs to the king you called Whiskers yesterday." He gave her the same answer about meadows and corn-fields, and at last a fine city. "Ah, what a fool I was!" said she to herself. "He was a fine man, and I might have him for a husband." At last they were coming up to a poor cabin. "Why are you bringing me here?" says the poor lady. "This was my house," said he, "and now it's yours." She began to cry, but she was tired and hungry, and she went in with him.

Ovoch! there was neither a table laid out, nor a fire burning, and she was obliged to help her husband to light it, and boil their dinner, and clean up the place after; and next day he made her put on a stuff gown and a cotton handkerchief. When she had her house readied up, and no business to keep her employed, he brought home *sallies* [willows], peeled them, and showed her how to make baskets. But the hard twigs bruised her delicate fingers, and she began to cry. Well, then he asked her to mend their clothes, but the needle drew blood from her fingers, and she cried again. He couldn't bear to see her tears, so he bought a creel of earthenware, and sent her to the market to sell them. This was the hardest trial of all, but she looked so handsome and sorrowful, and had such a nice air about her, that all her pans, and jugs, and plates, and dishes were gone before noon, and the only mark of her old pride she showed was a slap she gave a buckeen across the face when he *axed* her to go in an' take share of a quart.

Well, her husband was so glad, he sent her with another creel the next day; but faith! her luck was after deserting her. A drunken huntsman came up riding, and his beast got in among her ware, and made *brishe* of every mother's son of 'em. She went home cryin', and her husband wasn't at all pleased. "I see," said he, "you're not fit for business. Come along, I'll get you a kitchen-maid's place in the palace. I know the cook."

So the poor thing was obliged to stifle her pride once more. She was kept very busy, and the footman and the butler would be very impudent about looking for a kiss, but she let a screech out of her the first attempt was made, and the cook gave the fellow such a lambasting with the besom that he made no second offer. She went home to her husband every night, and she carried broken victuals wrapped in papers in her side pockets.

A week after she got service there was great bustle in

the kitchen. The king was going to be married, but no one knew who the bride was to be. Well, in the evening the cook filled the princess's pockets with cold meat and puddings, and, says she, "Before you go, let us have a look at the great doings in the big parlour." So they came near the door to get a peep, and who should come out but the king himself, as handsome as you please, and no other but King Whiskers himself. "Your handsome helper must pay for her peeping," said he to the cook, "and dance a jig with me." Whether she would or no, he held her hand and brought her into the parlour. The fiddlers struck up, and away went *him* with *her*. But they hadn't danced two steps when the meat and the *puddens* flew out of her pockets. Every one roared out, and she flew to the door, crying piteously. But she was soon caught by the king, and taken into the back parlour. "Don't you know me, my darling?" said he. "I'm both King Whiskers, your husband the ballad-singer, and the drunken huntsman. Your father knew me well enough when he gave you to me, and all was to drive your pride out of you." Well, she didn't know how she was with fright, and shame, and joy. Love was uppermost anyhow, for she laid her head on her husband's breast and cried like a child. The maids-of-honour soon had her away and dressed her as fine as hands and pins could do it ; and there were her mother and father, too ; and while the company were wondering what end of the handsome girl and the king, he and his queen, *who* they didn't know in her fine clothes, and the other king and queen, came in, and such rejoicings and fine doings as there was, none of us will ever see, any way.

THE ENCHANTMENT OF GEAROIDH IARLA.

BY PATRICK KENNEDY.*

IN old times in Ireland there was a great man of the Fitzgeralds. The name on him was Gerald, but the Irish, that always had a great liking for the family, called him *Gearoidh Iarla* (Earl Gerald). He had a great castle or rath at *Mullymast* (Mullaghmast); and whenever the English Government were striving to put some wrong on the country, he was always the man that stood up for it. Along with being a great leader in a fight, and very skilful at all weapons, he was deep in the *black art*, and could change himself into whatever shape he pleased. His lady knew that he had this power, and often asked him to let her into some of his secrets, but he never would gratify her.

She wanted particularly to see him in some strange shape, but he put her off and off on one pretence or other. But she wouldn't be a woman if she hadn't perseverance; and so at last he let her know that if she took the least fright while he'd be out of his natural form, he would never recover it till many generations of men would be under the mould. "Oh! she wouldn't be a fit wife for Gearoidh Iarla if she could be easily frightened. Let him but gratify her in this whim, and he'd see what a hero she was!" So one beautiful summer evening, as they were sitting in their grand drawing-room, he turned his face away from her and muttered some words, and while you'd wink he was clever and clean out of sight, and a lovely *goldfinch* was flying about the room.

The lady, as courageous as she thought herself, was a little startled, but she held her own pretty well, especially when he came and perched on her shoulder, and shook his wings, and put his little beak to her lips, and whistled the delightfulest tune you ever heard. Well, he flew in circles round the room, and played *hide and go seek* with his lady,

* *Legendary Fiction of the Irish Celts.*— (Macmillan.)

and flew out into the garden, and flew back again, and lay down in her lap as if he was asleep, and jumped up again.

Well, when the thing had lasted long enough to satisfy both, he took one flight more into the open air; but by my word he was soon on his return. He flew right into his lady's bosom, and the next moment a fierce hawk was after him. The wife gave one loud scream, though there was no need, for the wild bird came in like an arrow, and struck against a table with such force that the life was dashed out of him. She turned her eyes from his quivering body to where she saw the goldfinch an instant before, but neither goldfinch nor Earl Gerald did she ever lay eyes on again.

Once every seven years the Earl rides round the Curragh of Kildare on a steed, whose silver shoes were half an inch thick the time he disappeared; and when these shoes are worn as thin as a cat's ear, he will be restored to the society of living men, fight a great battle with the English, and reign king of Ireland for two-score years.*

Himself and his warriors are now sleeping in a long cavern under the Rath of Mullaghmast. There is a table running along through the middle of the cave. The Earl is sitting at the head, and his troopers down along in complete armour both sides of the table, and their heads resting on it. Their horses, saddled and bridled, are standing behind their masters in their stalls at each side; and when the day comes, the miller's son that's to be born with six fingers on each hand, will blow his trumpet, and the horses will stamp and whinny, and the knights awake and mount their steeds, and go forth to battle.

Some night that happens once in every seven years, while the Earl is riding round the Curragh, the entrance may be seen by any one chancing to pass by. About a hundred years ago, a horse-dealer that was late abroad and a little drunk, saw the lighted cavern, and went in. The lights, and the stillness, and the sight of the men in armour, cowed him a good deal, and he became sober. His hands began

* The last time *Gearoidh Iarla* appeared the horse-shoes were as thin as a sixpence.

to tremble, and he let a bridle fall on the pavement. The sound of the bit echoed through the long cave, and one of the warriors that was next him lifted his head a little, and said, in a deep hoarse voice, "Is it time yet?" He had the wit to say, "Not yet, but soon will," and the heavy helmet sunk down on the table. The horse-dealer made the best of his way out, and I never heard of any other one having got the same opportunity.

MUNACHAR AND MANACHAR.

TRANSLATED LITERALLY FROM THE IRISH BY DOUGLAS HYDE.

THERE once lived a Munachar and a Manachar, a long time ago, and it is a long time since it was, and if they were alive then they would not be alive now. They went out together to pick raspberries, and as many as Munachar used to pick Manachar used to eat. Munachar said he must go look for a rod to make a gad (a withy band) to hang Manachar, who ate his raspberries every one; and he came to the rod. "God save you," said the rod. "God and Mary save you." "How far are you going?" "Going looking for a rod, a rod to make a gad, a gad to hang Manachar, who ate my raspberries every one."

"You will not get me," said the rod, "until you get an axe to cut me." He came to the axe. "God save you," said the axe. "God and Mary save you." "How far are you going?" "Going looking for an axe, an axe to cut a rod, a rod to make a gad, a gad to hang Manachar, who ate my raspberries every one."

"You will not get me," said the axe, "until you get a flag to edge me." He came to the flag. "God save you," says the flag." "God and Mary save you." "How far are you going?" "Going looking for an axe, axe to cut a rod, a rod to make a gad, a gad to hang Manachar, who ate my raspberries every one."

"You will not get me," says the flag, "till you get water to wet me." He came to the water. "God save you," says the water. "God and Mary save you." "How far are you going?" "Going looking for water, water to wet flag to edge axe, axe to cut a rod, a rod to make a gad, a gad to hang Manachar, who ate my raspberries every one."

"You will not get me," said the water, "until you get a deer who will swim me." He came to the deer. "God save you," says the deer. "God and Mary save you." "How far are you going?" "Going looking for a deer, deer to swim water, water to wet flag, flag to edge axe, axe to cut a rod, a rod to make a gad, a gad to hang Manachar, who ate my raspberries every one."

"You will not get me," said the deer, "until you get a hound who will hunt me." He came to the hound. "God save you," says the hound. "God and Mary save you." "How far are you going?" "Going looking for a hound, hound to hunt deer, deer to swim water, water to wet flag, flag to edge axe, axe to cut a rod, a rod to make a gad, a gad to hang Manachar, who ate my raspberries every one."

"You will not get me," said the hound, "until you get a bit of butter to put in my claw." He came to the butter. "God save you," says the butter. "God and Mary save you." "How far are you going?" "Going looking for butter, butter to go in claw of hound, hound to hunt deer, deer to swim water, water to wet flag, flag to edge axe, axe to cut a rod, a rod to make a gad, a gad to hang Manachar, who ate my raspberries every one."

"You will not get me," said the butter, "until you get a cat who shall scrape me." He came to the cat. "God save you," said the cat. "God and Mary save you." "How far are you going?" "Going looking for a cat, cat to scrape butter, butter to go in claw of hound, hound to hunt deer, deer to swim water, water to wet flag, flag to edge axe, axe to cut a rod, a rod to make a gad, gad to hang Manachar, who ate my raspberries every one."

"You will not get me," said the cat, "until you will get milk which you will give me." He came to the cow. "God save you," said the cow. "God and Mary save you." "How far are you going?" "Going looking for a cow, cow to give me milk, milk I will give to the cat, cat to scrape butter, butter to go in claw of hound, hound to hunt deer, deer to swim water, water to wet flag, flag to edge axe, axe to cut a rod, a rod to make a gad, a gad to hang Manachar, who ate my raspberries every one."

"You will not get any milk from me," said the cow, "until you bring me a whisp of straw from those threshers yonder." He came to the threshers. "God save you," said the threshers. "God and Mary save ye." "How far are you going?" "Going looking for a whisp of straw from ye to give to the cow, the cow to give me milk, milk I will give to the cat, cat to scrape butter, butter to go in claw of hound, hound to hunt deer, deer to swim water, water to wet flag, flag to edge axe, axe to cut a rod, a rod to make a gad, a gad to hang Manachar, who ate my raspberries every one."

"You will not get any whisp of straw from us," said the threshers, "until you bring us the makings of a cake from the miller over yonder." He came to the miller. "God save you." "God and Mary save you." "How far are you going?" "Going looking for the makings of a cake, which I will give to the threshers, the threshers to give me a whisp of straw, the whisp of straw I will give to the cow, the cow to give me milk, milk I will give to the cat, cat to scrape butter, butter to go in claw of hound, hound to hunt deer, deer to swim water, water to wet flag, flag to edge axe, axe to cut a rod, a rod to make a gad, a gad to hang Manachar, who ate my raspberries every one."

"You will not get any makings of a cake from me," said the miller, "till you bring me the full of that sieve of water from the river over there."

He took the sieve in his hand and went over to the river, but as often as ever he would stoop and fill it with water, the moment he raised it the water would run out of

"MUNACHAR AND MANACHAR."

DONALD O'NEARY WITH HUDDEN AND DUDDEN.

it again, and sure, if he had been there from that day till this, he never could have filled it. A crow went flying by him, over his head. "Daub! daub!" said the crow. "My soul to God, then," said Munachar, "but it's the good advice you have," and he took the red clay and the daub that was by the brink, and he rubbed it to the bottom of the sieve, until all the holes were filled, and then the sieve held the water, and he brought the water to the miller, and the miller gave him the makings of a cake, and he gave the makings of the cake to the threshers, and the threshers gave him a whisp of straw, and he gave the whisp of straw to the cow, and the cow gave him milk, the milk he gave to the cat, the cat scraped the butter, the butter went into the claw of the hound, the hound hunted the deer, the deer swam the water, the water wet the flag, the flag sharpened the axe, the axe cut the rod, and the rod made a gad, and when he had it ready—I'll go bail that Manachar was far enough away from him.

There is some tale like this in almost every language. It resembles that given in that splendid work of industry and patriotism, Campbell's *Tales of the West Highlands* under the name of *Moonachug and Meenachug*. "The English House that Jack built," says Campbell, "has eleven steps, the Scotch Old Woman with the Silver Penny has twelve, the Novsk Cock and Hen A-nutting has twelve, ten of which are double. The German story in Grimm has five or six, all single ideas." This, however, is longer than any of them. It sometimes varies a little in the telling, and the actors' names are sometimes *Suracha* and *Muracha*, and the crow is sometimes a gull, who, instead of *daub! daub!* says *cuir cré rua lesh!*

DONALD AND HIS NEIGHBOURS.

From Hibernian Tales.*

HUDDEN and Dudden and Donald O'Nery were near neighbours in the barony of Balinconlig, and ploughed with three bullocks; but the two former, envying the present

* A chap book mentioned by Thackeray in his *Irish Sketch Book.*

prosperity of the latter, determined to kill his bullock, to prevent his farm being properly cultivated and laboured, that going back in the world he might be induced to sell his lands, which they meant to get possession of. Poor Donald finding his bullock killed, immediately skinned it, and throwing the skin over his shoulder, with the fleshy side out, set off to the next town with it, to dispose of it to the best of his advantage. Going along the road a magpie flew on the top of the hide, and began picking it, chattering all the time. The bird had been taught to speak, and imitate the human voice, and Donald, thinking he understood some words it was saying, put round his hand and caught hold of it. Having got possession of it, he put it under his great-coat, and so went on to town. Having sold the hide, he went into an inn to take a dram, and following the landlady into the cellar, he gave the bird a squeeze which made it chatter some broken accents that surprised her very much. "What is that I hear?" said she to Donald. "I think it is talk, and yet I do not understand." "Indeed," said Donald, "it is a bird I have that tells me everything, and I always carry it with me to know when there is any danger. Faith," says he, "it says you have far better liquor than you are giving me." "That is strange," said she, going to another cask of better quality, and asking him if he would sell the bird. "I will," said Donald, "if I get enough for it." "I will fill your hat with silver if you leave it with me." Donald was glad to hear the news, and taking the silver, set off, rejoicing at his good luck. He had not been long at home until he met with Hudden and Dudden. "Mr.," said he, "you thought you had done me a bad turn, but you could not have done me a better; for look here, what I have got for the hide," showing them a hatful of silver; "you never saw such a demand for hides in your life as there is at present." Hudden and Dudden that very night killed their bullocks, and set out the next morning to sell their hides. On coming to the place they went through all the merchants, but could only get a trifle for them; at last they had to take what they could get, and came home in a great rage, and vowing revenge on poor Donald. He had a pretty good guess how matters would turn out, and he being under the kitchen window, he was afraid they would rob him, or perhaps kill him when asleep, and on that account when he was going to bed he left his old mother in his place, and lay down in her bed, which was in the other side of the house, and they taking the old woman for Donald, choked her in her bed, but he making some noise, they had to retreat, and leave the money behind them, which grieved them very much. However, by daybreak, Donald got his mother on his back, and carried her to town. Stopping at a well, he fixed his mother with her staff, as if she was stooping for a drink, and then went into a public-house convenient and called for a dram. "I wish," said he to a woman that stood near him, "you would tell my mother to come in; she is at yon well trying to get a drink, and she is hard of hearing; if she does not observe you, give her a little shake and tell her that I want her." The woman called her several times, but she seemed to take no notice; at length she went to her and shook her by the arm, but when she let her go again, she tumbled on her head into the well, and, as the woman thought, was drowned. She, in her great surprise and fear at the accident, told Donald what had happened. "O mercy," said he, "what is this?" He ran and pulled her out of the well, weeping and lamenting all the time, and acting in such a manner that you would imagine that he had lost his senses. The woman, on the other hand, was far worse than Donald, for his grief was only feigned, but she imagined herself to be the cause of the old woman's death. The inhabitants of the town hearing what had happened, agreed to make Donald up a good sum of money for his loss, as the accident happened in their place, and Donald brought a greater sum home with him than he got for the magpie. They buried Donald's mother, and as soon as he saw Hudden he showed them the last purse of money he had got. "You thought to kill me last night," said he, "but it was good for me it happened on my mother, for I got all that purse for her to make gunpowder."

That very night Hudden and Dudden killed their mothers, and the next morning set off with them to town. On coming to the town with their burthen on their backs, they went up and down crying, "Who will buy old wives for gunpowder," so that everyone laughed at them, and the boys at last clotted them out of the place. They then saw the cheat, and vowed revenge on Donald, buried the old women, and set off in pursuit of him. Coming to his house, they found him sitting at his breakfast, and seizing him, put him in a sack, and went to drown him in a river at some distance. As they were going along the highway they raised a hare, which they saw had but three feet, and throwing off the sack, ran after her, thinking by her appearance she would be easily taken. In their absence there came a drover that way, and hearing Donald singing in the sack, wondered greatly what could be the matter. "What is the reason," said he, "that you are singing, and you confined?" "O, I am going to heaven," said Donald, "and in a short time I expect to be free from trouble." "O dear," said the drover, "what will I give you if you let me to your place?" "Indeed, I do not know," said he, "it would take a good sum." "I have not much money," said the drover, "but I have twenty head of fine cattle, which I will give you to exchange places with me." "Well," says Donald, "I do not care if I should loose the sack, and I will come out." In a moment the drover liberated him, and went into the sack himself, and Donald drove home the fine heifers, and left them in his pasture.

Hudden and Dudden having caught the hare, returned, and getting the sack on one of their backs, carried Donald, as they thought, to the river and threw him in, where he immediately sank. They then marched home, intending to take immediate possession of Donald's property, but how great was their surprise when they found him safe at home before them, with such a fine herd of cattle, whereas they knew he had none before. "Donald," said they, "what is all this? We thought you were drowned, and yet you are here before us." "Ah!" said he, "if I had but help along with me when you threw me in, it would have been the best job ever I met with, for of all the sight of cattle and gold that ever was seen is there, and no one to own them, but I was not able to manage more than what you see, and I could show you the spot where you might get hundreds." They both swore they would he his friend, and Donald accordingly led them to a very deep part of the river, and lifted up a stone. "Now," said he, "watch this," throwing it into the stream; "there is the very place, and go in, one of you first, and if you want help, you have nothing to do but call." Hudden jumping in, and sinking to the bottom, rose up again, and making a bubbling noise, as those do that are drowning, attempted to speak, but could not. "What is that he is saying now?" says Dudden. "Faith," says Donald, "he is calling for help; don't you hear him? Stand about," said he, running back, "till I leap in. I know how to do it better than any of you." Dudden, to have the advantage of him, jumped in off the bank, and was drowned along with Hudden, and this was the end of Hudden and Dudden.

THE JACKDAW.

TOM MOOR was a linen draper in Sackville Street. His father, when he died, left him an affluent fortune, and a shop of excellent trade.

As he was standing at his door one day a countryman came up to him with a nest of jackdaws, and accosting him, says, "Master, will you buy a nest of daws?" "No, I don't want any." "Master," replied the man, "I will sell them all cheap; you shall have the whole nest for nine-pence." "I don't want them," answered Tom Moor, "so go about your business."

As the man was walking away one of the daws popped out his head, and cried "Mawk, mawk." "Damn it," says

Tom Moor, "that bird knows my name; halloo, country-man, what will you take for the bird?" "Why, you shall have him for threepence." Tom Moor bought him, had a cage made, and hung him up in the shop.

The journeymen took much notice of the bird, and would frequently tap at the bottom of the cage, and say, "Who are you? Who are you? Tom Moor of Sackville Street."

In a short time the jackdaw learned these words, and if he wanted victuals or water, would strike his bill against the cage, turn up the white of his eyes, cock his head, and cry, "Who are you? who are you? Tom Moor of Sackville Street."

Tom Moor was fond of gaming, and often lost large sums of money; finding his business neglected in his absence, he had a small hazard table set up in one corner of his dining-room, and invited a party of his friends to play at it.

The jackdaw had by this time become familiar; his cage was left open, and he hopped into every part of the house; sometimes he got into the dining-room, where the gentlemen were at play, and one of them being a constant winner, the others would say, "Damn it, how he nicks them." The bird learned these words also, and adding them to the former, would call, "Who are you? who are you? Tom Moor of Sackville Street. Damn it, how he nicks them."

Tom Moor, from repeated losses and neglect of business, failed in trade, and became a prisoner in the Fleet; he took his bird with him, and lived on the master's side, supported by friends, in a decent manner. They would sometimes ask what brought you here? when he used to lift up his hands and answer, "Bad company, by G—." The bird learned this likewise, and at the end of the former words, would say, "What brought you here? Bad company, by G—."

Some of Tom Moor's friends died, others went abroad, and by degrees he was totally deserted, and removed to the common side of the prison, where the jail distemper soon attacked him; and in the last stage of life, lying on a straw bed; the poor bird had been for two days without food or water, came to his feet, and striking his bill on the floor, calls out, "Who are you? Tom Moor of Sackville Street; damn it, how he nicks them, damn it, how he nicks them. What brought you here? bad company, by G—, bad company, by G—."

Tom Moor, who had attended to the bird, was struck with his words, and reflecting on himself, cried out, "Good God, to what a situation am I reduced! my father, when he died, left me a good fortune and an established trade. I have spent my fortune, ruined my business, and am now dying in a loathsome jail; and to complete all, keeping that poor thing confined without support. I will endeavour to do one piece of justice before I die, by setting him at liberty."

He made a struggle to crawl from his straw bed, opened the casement, and out flew the bird. A flight of jackdaws from the Temple were going over the jail, and Tom Moor's bird mixed among them. The gardener was then laying the plats of the Temple gardens, and as often as he placed them in the day the jackdaws pulled them up by night. They got a gun and attempted to shoot some of them; but, being cunning birds, they always placed one as a watch in the stump of a hollow tree; who, as soon as the gun was levelled cried "Mawk," and away they flew.

The gardeners were advised to get a net, and the first night it was spread they caught fifteen; Tom Moor's bird was amongst them. One of the men took the net into a garret of an uninhabited house, fastens the doors and windows, and turns the birds loose. "Now," said he, "you black rascals, I will be revenged of you." Taking hold of the first at hand, he twists her neck, and throwing him down, cries, "There goes one." Tom Moor's bird, who had hopped up to a beam at one corner of the room unobserved, as the man lays hold of the second, calls out, "Damn it, how he nicks them." The man alarmed, cries, "Sure I heard a voice, but the house is uninhabited, and the door is fast; it could only be imagination." On laying hold of the third, and twisting his neck, Tom's bird again says, "Damn it, how he nicks them." The man dropped the bird in his hand, and turning to where the voice came from, seeing the other with his mouth open, cries out, "Who are you?" to which the bird answered, "Tom Moor of Sackville Street, Tom Moor of Sackville Street." "The devil you are; and what brought you here." Tom Moor's bird, lifting up his pinions, answered, "Bad company, by G—, bad company, by G—." The fellow, frightened almost out of his wits, opened the door, ran down stairs, and out of the house, followed by all the birds, who by this means regained their liberty.

THE STORY OF CONN-EDA; OR, THE GOLDEN APPLES OF LOUGH ERNE.*

Translated from the original Irish of the Story-teller, ABRAHAM McCOY, *by* NICHOLAS O'KEARNEY.

IT was long before the time the western districts of *Innis Fodhla†* had any settled name, but were indiscriminately called after the person who took possession of them, and whose name they retained only as long as his sway lasted, that a powerful king reigned over this part of the sacred island. He was a puissant warrior, and no individual was found able to compete with him either on land or sea, or question his right to his conquest. The great king of the west held uncontrolled sway from the island of Rathlin to the mouth of the Shannon by sea, and far as the glittering length by land. The ancient king of the west, whose name was Conn, was good as well as great, and passionately loved by his people. His queen was a *Breaton* (British) princess, and was equally beloved and esteemed, because she was the great counterpart of the king in every respect; for whatever

* Printed first in the *Cambrian Journal*, 1855; reprinted and re-edited in the *Folk-Lore Record*, vol. ii.
† *Innis Fodhla*—Island of Destiny, an old name for Ireland.

good qualification was wanting in the one, the other was certain to indemnify the omission. It was plainly manifest that heaven approved of the career in life of the virtuous couple; for during their reign the earth produced exuberant crops, the trees fruit ninefold commensurate with their usual bearing, the rivers, lakes, and surrounding sea teemed with abundance of choice fish, while herds and flocks were unusually prolific, and kine and sheep yielded such abundance of rich milk that they shed it in torrents upon the pastures; and furrows and cavities were always filled with the pure lacteal produce of the dairy. All these were blessings heaped by heaven upon the western districts of *Innis Fodhla*, over which the benignant and just Conn swayed his sceptre, in approbation of the course of goverment he had marked out for his own guidance. It is needless to state that the people who owned the authority of this great and good sovereign were the happiest on the face of the wide expanse of earth. It was during his reign, and that of his son and successor, that Ireland acquired the title of the "happy isle of the west" among foreign nations. Con Mór and his good Queen Eda reigned in great glory during many years; they were blessed with an only son, whom they named Conn-eda, after both his parents, because the Druids foretold at his birth that he would inherit the good qualities of both. According as the young prince grew in years, his amiable and benignant qualities of mind, as well as his great strength of body and manly bearing, became more manifest. He was the idol of his parents, and the boast of his people; he was beloved and respected to that degree that neither prince, lord, nor plebeian swore an oath by the sun, moon, stars, or elements, except by the head of Conn-eda. This career of glory, however, was doomed to meet a powerful but temporary impediment, for the good Queen Eda took a sudden and severe illness, of which she died in a few days, thus plunging her spouse, her son, and all her people into a depth of grief and sorrow from which it was found difficult to relieve them.

The good king and his subjects mourned the loss of

Queen Eda for a year and a day, and at the expiration of that time Conn Mór reluctantly yielded to the advice of his Druids and counsellors, and took to wife the daughter of his Arch-Druid. The new queen appeared to walk in the footsteps of the good Eda for several years, and gave great satisfaction to her subjects. But, in course of time, having had several children, and perceiving that Conn-eda was the favourite son of the king and the darling of the people, she clearly foresaw that he would become successor to the throne after the demise of his father, and that her son would certainly be excluded. This excited the hatred and inflamed the jealousy of the Druid's daughter against her step-son to such an extent, that she resolved in her own mind to leave nothing in her power undone to secure his death, or even exile from the kingdom. She began by circulating evil reports of the prince; but, as he was above suspicion, the king only laughed at the weakness of the queen; and the great princes and chieftains, supported by the people in general, gave an unqualified contradiction; while the prince himself bore all his trials with the utmost patience, and always repaid her bad and malicious acts towards him with good and benevolent ones. The enmity of the queen towards Conn-eda knew no bounds when she saw that the false reports she circulated could not injure him. As a last resource, to carry out her wicked projects, she determined to consult her *Cailleach-chearc* (hen-wife), who was a reputed enchantress.

Pursuant to her resolution, by the early dawn of morning she hied to the cabin of the *Cailleach-chearc*, and divulged to her the cause of her trouble. "I cannot render you any help," said the *Cailleach*, "until you name the *duais*" (reward). "What *duais* do you require?" asked the queen, impatiently. "My *duais*," replied the enchantress, "is to fill the cavity of my arm with wool, and the hole I shall bore with my distaff with red wheat." "Your *duais* is granted, and shall be immediately given you," said the queen. The enchantress thereupon stood in the door of her hut, and bending her arm into a circle with her side, directed the royal attendants to thrust the wool into her house through her arm, and she never permitted them to cease until all the available space within was filled with wool. She then got on the roof of her brother's house, and, having made a hole through it with her distaff, caused red wheat to be spilled through it, until that was filled up to the roof with red wheat, so that there was no room for another grain within. "Now," said the queen, "since you have received your *duais*, tell me how I can accomplish my purpose." "Take this chess-board and chess, and invite the prince to play with you ; you shall win the first game. The condition you shall make is, that whoever wins a game shall be at liberty to impose whatever *geasa* (conditions) the winner pleases on the loser. When you win, you must bid the prince, under the penalty either to go into *ionarbadh* (exile), or procure for you, within the space of a year and a day, the three golden apples that grew in the garden, the *each dubh* (black steed), and *coileen con na mbuadh* (hound of supernatural powers), called Samer, which are in the possession of the king of the Firbolg race, who resides in Lough Erne.* Those two things are so precious, and so well guarded, that he can never attain them by his own power ; and, if he would rashly attempt to seek them, he should lose his life."

The queen was greatly pleased at the advice, and lost no time in inviting Conn-eda to play a game at chess, under the conditions she had been instructed to arrange by the enchantress. The queen won the game, as the enchantress foretold, but so great was her anxiety to have the prince completely in her power, that she was tempted to challenge him to play a second game, which Conn-eda, to her astonishment, and no less mortification, easily won. "Now," said the prince, "since you won the first game, it is your duty to impose your *geis* first." "My *geis*," said the queen, "which I impose upon you, is to procure me the three golden apples

---

* The Firbolgs believed their elysium to be under water. The peasantry still believe many lakes to be peopled.—See section on *T'yeer-na-n-Oge.*

that grow in the garden, the *each dubh* (black steed), and
cuileen con na mbuadh (hound of supernatural powers), which
are in the keeping of the king of the Firbolgs, in Lough
Erne, within the space of a year and a day ; or, in case you
fail, to go into *ionarbadh* (exile), and never return, except
you surrender yourself to lose your head and *comhead
beatha* (preservation of life). " Well, then," said the prince,
" the *geis* which I bind you by, is to sit upon the pinnacle
of yonder tower until my return, and to take neither food
nor nourishment of any description, except what red-wheat
you can pick up with the point of your bodkin ; but if I do
not return, you are at perfect liberty to come down at the
expiration of the year and a day."

In consequence of the severe *geis* imposed upon him,
Conn-eda was very much troubled in mind ; and, well
knowing he had a long journey to make before he would
reach his destination, immediately prepared to set out on
his way, not, however, before he had the satisfaction of
witnessing the ascent of the queen to the place where she
was obliged to remain exposed to the scorching sun of the
summer and the blasting storms of winter, for the space of
one year and a day, at least. Conn-eda being ignorant of
what steps he should take to procure the *each dubh* and
cuileen con na mbuadh, though he was well aware that
human energy would prove unavailing, thought proper to
consult the great Druid, Fionn Dadhna, of Sleabh Badhna,
who was a friend of his before he ventured to proceed to
Lough Erne. When he arrived at the bruighean of the
Druid, he was received with cordial friendship, and the
failte (welcome), as usual, was poured out before him, and
when he was seated, warm water was fetched, and his feet
bathed, so that the fatigue he felt after his journey was greatly
relieved. The Druid, after he had partaken of refreshments,
consisting of the newest of food and oldest of liquors, asked
him the reason for paying the visit, and more particularly
the cause of his sorrow ; for the prince appeared exceedingly depressed in spirit. Conn-eda told his friend
the whole history of the transaction with his stepmother

from the beginning to end. "Can you not assist me?" asked the Prince, with downcast countenance. "I cannot, indeed, assist you at present," replied the Druid; "but I will retire to my *grianan* (green place) at sun-rising on the morrow, and learn by virtue of my Druidism what can be done to assist you." The Druid, accordingly, as the sun rose on the following morning, retired to his *grianan*, and consulted the god he adored, through the power of his *draoidheacht.** When he returned, he called Conn-eda aside on the plain, and addressed him thus: "My dear son, I find you have been under a severe—an almost impossible—*geis* intended for your destruction; no person on earth could have advised the queen to impose it except the Cailleach of Lough Corrib, who is the greatest Druidess now in Ireland, and sister to the Firbolg, King of Lough Erne. It is not in my power, nor in that of the Deity I adore, to interfere in your behalf; but go directly to Sliabh Mis, and consult *Eánchinn-duine* (the bird of the human head), and if there be any possibility of relieving you, that bird can do it, for there is not a bird in the western world so celebrated as that bird, because it knows all things that are past, all things that are present and exist, and all things that shall hereafter exist. It is difficult to find access to his place of concealment, and more difficult still to obtain an answer from him; but I will endeavour to regulate that matter for you; and that is all I can do for you at present."

The Arch-Druid then instructed him thus:—"Take," said he, "yonder little shaggy steed, and mount him immediately, for in three days the bird will make himself visible, and the little shaggy steed will conduct you to his place of abode. But lest the bird should refuse to reply to your queries, take this precious stone (*leag lorgmhar*), and present it to him, and then little danger and doubt exist but that he will give you a ready answer." The prince returned heartfelt thanks to the Druid, and, having saddled and mounted the little shaggy horse without much delay, received the precious stone from the Druid, and, after having taken his leave of him, set out on his journey. He

---

* *Draoidheacht, i.e.,* the Druidic worship; magic, sorcery, divination.

suffered the reins to fall loose upon the neck of the horse according as he had been instructed, so that the animal took whatever road he chose.

It would be tedious to relate the numerous adventures he had with the little shaggy horse, which had the extraordinary gift of speech, and was a *draoidheacht* horse during his journey.

The Prince having reached the hiding-place of the strange bird at the appointed time, and having presented him with the *leag lorgmhar*, according to Fionn Badhna's instructions, and proposed his questions relative to the manner he could best arrange for the fulfilment of his *geis*, the bird took up in his mouth the jewel from the stone on which it was placed, and flew to an inaccessible rock at some distance, and, when there perched, he thus addressed the prince, " Conn-eda, son of the King of Cruachan," said he, in a loud, croaking human voice, " remove the stone just under your right foot, and take the ball of iron and *corna* (cup) you shall find under it; then mount your horse, cast the ball before you, and having so done, your horse will tell you all the other things necessary to be done." The bird, having said this, immediately flew out of sight.

Conn-eda took great care to do everything according to the instructions of the bird. He found the iron ball and *corna* in the place which had been pointed out. He took them up, mounted his horse, and cast the ball before him. The ball rolled on at a regular gait, while the little shaggy horse followed on the way it led until they reached the margin of Lough Erne. Here the ball rolled in the water and became invisible. " Alight now," said the *draoidheacht* pony, " and put your hand into mine ear; take from thence the small bottle of *ice* (all-heal) and the little wicker basket which you will find there, and remount with speed, for just now your great dangers and difficulties commence." Conn-eda, ever faithful to the kind advice of his *draoidheacht* pony, did what he had been advised. Having taken the basket and bottle of *ice* from the animal's ear, he remounted and proceeded on his journey, while the water of the lake appeared only like an atmosphere above his head. When he entered the lake the ball again appeared, and rolled along until it came to the margin, across which was a causeway, guarded by three frightful serpents; the hissings of the monsters was heard at a great distance, while, on a nearer approach, their yawning mouths and formidable fangs were quite sufficient to terrify the stoutest heart. "Now," said the horse, "open the basket and cast a piece of the meat you find in it into the mouth of each serpent; when you have done this, secure yourself in your seat in the best manner you can, so that we may make all due arrangements to pass those *draoidheacht peists*. If you cast the pieces of meat into the mouth of each *peist* unerringly, we shall pass them safely, otherwise we are lost." Conn-eda flung the pieces of meat into the jaws of the serpents with unerring aim. "Bare a benison and victory," said the *draoidheacht* steed, "for you are a youth that will win and prosper." And, on saying these words, he sprang aloft, and cleared in his leap the river and ford, guarded by the serpents, seven measures beyond the margin. "Are you still mounted, prince Conn-eda?" said the steed. "It has taken only half my exertion to remain so," replied Conn-eda. "I find," said the pony, "that you are a young prince that deserves to succeed; one danger is now over, but two others remain." They proceeded onwards after the ball until they came in view of a great mountain flaming with fire. "Hold yourself in readiness for another dangerous leap," said the horse. The trembling prince had no answer to make, but seated himself as securely as the magnitude of the danger before him would permit. The horse in the next instant sprang from the earth, and flew like an arrow over the burning mountain. "Are you still alive, Conn-eda, son of Conn-mór?" inquired the faithful horse. "I'm just alive, and no more, for I'm greatly scorched," answered the prince. "Since you are yet alive, I feel assured that you are a young man destined to meet supernatural success and benisons," said the Druidic steed. "Our greatest dangers are over," added he, "and there is hope that we shall overcome the next and last danger." After they had proceeded a short distance, his faithful steed, addressing Conn-eda, said, " Alight, now, and apply a portion of the little bottle of *ice* to your wounds." The prince immediately followed the advice of his monitor, and, as soon as he rubbed the *ice* (all-heal) to his wounds, he became as whole and fresh as ever he had been before. After having done this, Conn-eda remounted, and following the track of the ball, soon came in sight of a great city surrounded by high walls. The only gate that was visible was not defended by armed men, but by two great towers that emitted flames that could be seen at a great distance. " Alight on this plain," said the steed, " and take a small knife from my other ear ; and with this knife you shall kill and flay me. When you have done this, envelop yourself in my hide, and you can pass the gate unscathed and unmolested. When you get inside you can come out at pleasure ; because when once you enter there is no danger, and you can pass and repass whenever you wish ; and let me tell you that all I have to ask of you in return is that you, when once inside the gates, will immediately return and drive away the birds of prey that may be fluttering round to feed on my carcass ; and more, that you will pour any drop of that powerful *ice*, if such still remain in the bottle, upon my flesh, to preserve it from corruption. When you do this in memory of me, if it be not too troublesome, dig a pit, and cast my remains into it."

" Well," said Conn-eda, " my noblest steed, because you have been so faithful to me hitherto, and because you still would have rendered me further service, I consider such a proposal insulting to my feelings as a man, and totally in variance with the spirit which can feel the value of gratitude, not to speak of my feelings as a prince. But as a prince I am able to say, Come what may—come death itself in its most hideous forms and terrors—I never will sacrifice private friendship to personal interest. Hence, I am, I swear by my arms of valour, prepared to meet the worst— even death itself—sooner than violate the principles of humanity, honour, and friendship ! What a sacrifice do you propose!" "Pshaw, man! heed not that; do what I advise you, and prosper." "Never! never!" exclaimed the prince. "Well, then, son of the great western monarch," said the horse, with a tone of sorrow, "if you do not follow my advice on this occasion, I tell you that both you and I shall perish, and shall never meet again; but, if you act as I have instructed you, matters shall assume a happier and more pleasing aspect than you may imagine. I have not misled you heretofore, and, if I have not, what need have you to doubt the most important portion of my counsel? Do exactly as I have directed you, else you will cause a worse fate than death to befall me. And, moreover, I can tell you that, if you persist in your resolution, I have done with you for ever."

When the prince found that his noble steed could not be persuaded from his purpose, he took the knife out of his ear with reluctance, and with a faltering and trembling hand essayed experimentally to point the weapon at his throat. Conn-eda's eyes were bathed in tears; but no sooner had he pointed the Druidic *scian* to the throat of his good steed, than the dagger, as if impelled by some Druidic power, stuck in his neck, and in an instant the work of death was done, and the noble animal fell dead at his feet. When the prince saw his noble steed fall dead by his hand, he cast himself on the ground, and cried aloud until his consciousness was gone. When he recovered, he perceived that the steed was quite dead; and, as he thought there was no hope of resuscitating him, he considered it the most prudent course he could adopt to act according to the advice he had given him. After many misgivings of mind and abundant showers of tears, he essayed the task of flaying him, which was only that of a few minutes. When he found he had the hide separated from the body, he, in the derangement of the moment, enveloped himself in it, and proceeding towards the magnificent city in rather a demented state of mind, entered it without any molestation or opposition. It was a surprisingly populous city, and an extremely wealthy place; but its beauty, magnificence, and wealth had no charms for Conn-eda, because the thoughts of the loss he sustained in his dear steed were paramount to those of all other earthly considerations.

He had scarcely proceeded more than fifty paces from the gate, when the last request of his beloved *draoidheacht* steed forced itself upon his mind, and compelled him to return to perform the last solemn injunctions upon him. When he came to the spot upon which the remains of his beloved *draoidheacht* steed lay, an appalling sight presented itself ; ravens and other carnivorous birds of prey were tearing and devouring the flesh of his dear steed. It was but short work to put them to flight ; and having uncorked his little jar of *ice*, he deemed it a labour of love to embalm the now mangled remains with the precious ointment. The potent *ice* had scarcely touched the inanimate flesh, when, to the surprise of Conn-eda, it commenced to undergo some strange change, and in a few minutes, to his unspeakable astonishment and joy, it assumed the form of one of the handsomest and noblest young men imaginable, and in the twinkling of an eye the prince was locked in his embrace, smothering him with kisses, and drowning him with tears of joy. When one recovered from his ecstasy of joy, the other from his surprise, the strange youth thus addressed the prince : "Most noble and puissant prince, you are the best sight I ever saw with my eyes, and I am the most fortunate being in existence for having met you ! Behold in my person, changed to the natural shape, your little shaggy *draoidheacht* steed ! I am brother of the king of the city ; and it was the wicked Druid, Fion Badhna, who kept me so long in bondage ; but he was forced to give me up when you came to *consult* him, for my *geis* was then broken ; yet I could not recover my pristine shape and appearance unless you had acted as you have kindly done. It was my own sister that urged the queen, your step-mother, to send you in quest of the steed and powerful puppy hound, which my brother has now in keeping. My sister, rest assured, had no thought of doing you the least injury, but much good, as you will find hereafter; because, if she were maliciously inclined towards you, she could have accomplished her end without any trouble. In short, she only wanted to free you from all future danger and disaster, and recover me from my relentless enemies through your instrumentality. Come with me, my friend and deliverer, and the steed and the puppy-hound of extraordinary powers, and the golden apples, shall be yours, and a cordial welcome shall greet you in my brother's abode; for you will deserve all this and much more."

The exciting joy felt on the occasion was mutual, and they lost no time in idle congratulations, but proceeded on to the royal residence of the King of Lough Erne. Here they were both received with demonstrations of joy by the king and his chieftains; and, when the purpose of Conn-eda's visit became known to the king, he gave a free consent to bestow on Conn-eda the black steed, the *coileen con-na-mbuadh*, called Samer, and the three apples of health that were growing in his garden, under the special condition, however, that he would consent to remain as his guest until he could set out on his journey in proper time, to fulfil his *geis*. Conn-eda, at the earnest solicitation of his friends, consented, and remained in the royal residence of the Firbolg, King of Lough Erne, in the enjoyment of the most delicious and fascinating pleasures during that period.

When the time of his departure came, the three golden apples were plucked from the crystal tree in the midst of the pleasure-garden, and deposited in his bosom; the puppy-hound, Samer, was leashed, and the leash put into his hand; and the black steed, richly harnessed, was got in readiness for him to mount. The king himself helped him on horseback, and both he and his brother assured him that he might not fear burning mountains or hissing serpents, because none would impede him, as his steed was always a passport to and from his subaqueous kingdom. And both he and his brother extorted a promise from Conn-eda, that he would visit them once every year at least.

Conn-eda took leave of his dear friend, and the king his brother. The parting was a tender one, soured by regret on both sides. He proceeded on his way without meeting anything to obstruct him, and in due time came in sight of the *dún* of his father, where the queen had been placed on the pinnacle of the tower, in full hope that, as it was the last day of her imprisonment there, the prince would not make his appearance, and thereby forfeit all pretensions and right to the crown of his father for ever. But her hopes were doomed to meet a disappointment, for when it had been announced to her by her couriers, who had been posted to watch the arrival of the prince, that he approached, she was incredulous; but when she saw him mounted on a foaming black steed, richly harnessed, and leading a strange kind of animal by a silver chain, she at once knew he was returning in triumph, and that her schemes laid for his destruction were frustrated. In the excess of grief at her disappointment, she cast herself from the top of the tower, and was instantly dashed to pieces. Conn-eda met a welcome reception from his father, who mourned him as lost to him for ever, during his absence; and, when the base conduct of the queen became known, the king and his chieftains ordered her remains to be consumed to ashes for her perfidy and wickedness.

Conn-eda planted the three golden apples in his garden, and instantly a great tree, bearing similar fruit, sprang up. This tree caused all the district to produce an exuberance of crops and fruits, so that it became as fertile and plentiful as the dominions of the Firbolgs, in consequence of the extraordinary powers possessed by the golden fruit. The hound Samer and the steed were of the utmost utility to him; and his reign was long and prosperous, and celebrated among the old people for the great abundance of corn, fruit, milk, fowl, and fish that prevailed during this happy reign. It was after the name Conn-eda the province of Connaucht, or *Conneda*, or *Connacht*, was so called.

NOTES.

GODS OF THE EARTH.—Par. 2, page 2.

Occultists, from Paracelsus to Elephas Levi, divide the nature spirits into gnomes, sylphs, salamanders, undines; or earth, air, fire, and water spirits. Their emperors, according to Elephas, are named Cob, Paralda, Djin, Hicks respectively. The gnomes are covetous, and of the melancholic temperament. Their usual height is but two spans, though they can elongate themselves into giants. The sylphs are capricious, and of the bilious temperament. They are in size and strength much greater than men, as becomes the people of the winds. The salamanders are wrathful, and in temperament sanguine. In appearance they are long, lean, and dry. The undines are soft, cold, fickle, and phlegmatic. In appearance they are like man. The salamanders and sylphs have no fixed dwellings.

It has been held by many that somewhere out of the void there is a perpetual dribble of souls ; that these souls pass through many shapes before they incarnate as men—hence the nature spirits. They are invisible—except at rare moments and times ; they inhabit the interior elements, while we live upon the outer and the gross. Some float perpetually through space, and the motion of the planets drives them hither and thither in currents. Hence some Rosicrucians have thought astrology may foretell many things ; for a tide of them flowing around the earth arouses there, emotions and changes, according to its nature.

Besides those of human appearance are many animal and bird-like shapes. It has been noticed that from these latter entirely come the familiars seen by Indian braves when they go fasting in the forest, seeking the instruction of the spirits. Though all at times are friendly to men—to some men—"They have," says Paracelsus, "an aversion to self-conceited and opinionated persons, such as dogmatists, scientists, drunkards, and gluttons, and against vulgar and quarrelsome people of all kinds ; but they love natural men, who are simple-minded and childlike, innocent and sincere, and the less there is of vanity and hypocrisy in a man, the easier will it be to approach them ; but otherwise they are as shy as wild animals."

Sir Samuel Ferguson.—Pages 13 and 38.

Many in Ireland consider Sir Samuel Ferguson their greatest poet. The English reader will most likely never have heard his name, for Anglo-Irish critics, who have found English audience, being more Anglo than Irish, have been content to follow English opinion instead of leading it, in all matters concerning Ireland.

Cusheen Loo.—Page 33.

Forts, otherwise raths or royalties, are circular ditches enclosing a little field, where, in most cases, if you dig down you come to stone chambers, their bee-hive roofs and walls made of unmortared stone. In these little fields the ancient Celts fortified themselves and their cattle, in winter retreating into the stone chambers, where also they were buried. The people call them Dane's forts, from a misunderstanding of the word Danān (Tuath-de-Danān). The fairies have taken up their abode therein, guarding them from all disturbance. Whoever roots them up soon finds his cattle falling sick, or his family or himself. Near the raths are sometimes found flint arrow-heads; these are called "fairy darts," and are supposed to have been flung by the fairies, when angry, at men or cattle.

Legend of Knockgrafton.—page 40.

Moat does not mean a place with water, but a tumulus or barrow. The words *La Luan Da Mort agus Da Dardeen* are Gaelic for " Monday, Tuesday, and Wednesday too." Da Hena is Thursday. Story-tellers, in telling this tale, says Croker, sing these words to the following music—according to Croker, music of very ancient kind :—

Mr. Douglas Hyde has heard the story in Connaught, with the song of the fairy given as "Peean Peean daw feean, Peean go leh agus leffin" [*pighin, pighin, dà phighin, pighin go ieith agus leith phighin*], which in English means, "a penny, a penny, twopence, a penny and a half, and a halfpenny."

STOLEN CHILD.—Page 59.

The places mentioned are round about Sligo. Further Rosses is a very noted fairy locality. There is here a little point of rocks where, if anyone falls asleep, there is danger of their waking silly, the fairies having carried off their souls.

SOLITARY FAIRIES.—Page 80.

The trooping fairies wear green jackets, the solitary ones red. On the red jacket of the Lepracaun, according to McAnally, are seven rows of buttons—seven buttons in each row. On the western coast, he says, the red jacket is covered by a frieze one, and in Ulster the creature wears a cocked hat, and when he is up to anything unusually mischievous, leaps on to a wall and spins, balancing himself on the point of the hat with his heels in the air. McAnally tells how once a peasant saw a battle between the green jacket fairies and the red. When the green jackets began to win, so delighted was he to see the green above the red, he gave a great shout. In a moment all vanished and he was flung into the ditch.

BANSHEE'S CRY.—Page 108.

Mr. and Mrs. S. C. Hall give the following notation of the cry :—

OMENS.—Page 108.

We have other omens beside the Banshee and the Dullahan and the Coach-a-Bower. I know one family where death is announced by the cracking of a whip. Some families are attended by phantoms of ravens or other birds. When McManus, of '48 celebrity, was sitting by his dying brother, a bird of vulture-like appearance came through the window and lighted on the breast of the dying man. The two watched in terror, not daring to drive it off. It crouched there, bright-eyed, till the soul left the body. It was considered a most evil omen. Lefanu worked this into a tale. I have good authority for tracing its origin to McManus and his brother.

A WITCH TRIAL.—Page 146.

The last trial for witchcraft in Ireland—there were never very many—is thus given in MacSkimin's *History of Carrickfergus* :—" 1711, March 31st, Janet Mean, of Braid-island ; Janet Latimer, Irish-quarter, Carrickfergus ; Janet Millar, Scotch-quarter, Carrickfergus ; Margaret Mitchel, Kilroot ; Catharine M'Calmond, Janet Liston, *alias* Seller, Elizabeth Seller, and Janet Carson, the four last from Island Magee, were tried here, in the County of Antrim Court, for witchcraft."

Their alleged crime was tormenting a young woman, called Mary Dunbar, about eighteen years of age, at the house of James Hattridge, Island Magee, and at other places to which she was removed. The circumstances sworn on the trial were as follows :—

" The afflicted person being, in the month of February, 1711, in the house of James Hattridge, Island Magee (which had been for some time believed to be haunted by evil spirits), found an apron on the parlour floor, that had been missing some time, tied with *five strange knots*, which she loosened.

" On the following day she was suddenly seized with a violent pain in her thigh, and afterwards fell into fits and ravings ; and, on recovering, said she was tormented by several women, whose dress and personal appearance she minutely described. Shortly after, she was again seized with the like fits, and on recovering she accused five other women of tormenting her, describing them also. The accused persons being brought from different parts of the country, she appeared to suffer extreme fear and additional torture as they approached the house.

" It was also deposed that strange noises, as of whistling, scratching, etc., were heard in the house, and that a sulphureous smell was observed in the rooms ; that stones, turf, and the like were thrown about the house, and the coverlets, etc., frequently taken off the beds and made up in the shape of a corpse ; and that a bolster once walked out of a room into the kitchen with a night-gown about it ! It likewise appeared in evidence that in some of her fits three strong men were scarcely able to hold her in the bed ; that at times she vomited feathers, cotton yarn, pins, and buttons ; and that on one occasion she slid off the bed and was laid on the floor, as if supported and drawn by an invincible power. The afflicted person was unable to give any evidence on the trial, being during that time dumb, but had no violent fit during its continuance."

In defence of the accused, it appeared that they were mostly sober, industrious people, who attended public worship, could repeat the Lord's Prayer, and had been known to pray both in public and private ; and that some of them had lately received communion.

Judge Upton charged the jury, and observed on the regular attendance of accused at public worship ; remarking that he thought it improbable that real witches could so far retain the form of religion as to frequent the religious worship of God, both publicly and privately, which had been proved in favour of the accused. He concluded by giving his opinion "that the jury could not bring them in guilty upon the sole testimony of the afflicted person's visionary images." He was followed by Judge Macarthy, who differed from him in opinion, "and thought the jury might, from the evidence, bring them in guilty," which they accordingly did.

This trial lasted from six o'clock in the morning till two in the afternoon ; and the prisoners were sentenced to be imprisoned twelve months, and to stand four times in the pillory of Carrickfergus.

Tradition says that the people were much exasperated against these unfortunate persons, who were severely pelted in the pillory with boiled cabbage stalks and the like, by which one of them had an eye beaten out.

T'YEER-NA-N-OGE.—Page 200.

" *Tir-na-n-óg,*" Mr. Douglas Hyde writes, "'The Country of the Young,' is the place where the Irish peasant will tell you *geabhaedh tu an sonas aer pighin,* ' you will get happiness for a penny,' so cheap and common it will be. It is sometimes, but not often, called *Tir-na-hóige ;* the ' Land of Youth.' Crofton Croker writes it, *Thierna-na-noge,* which is an unfortunate mistake of his, *Thiorna* meaning a lord, not a country. This unlucky blunder is, like many others of the same sort where Irish words are concerned, in danger of becoming stereotyped, as the name of Iona has been, from mere clerical carelessness."

THE GONCONER OR GANCANAGH [GEAN-CANACH].—Page 207.

O'Kearney, a Louthman, deeply versed in Irish lore, writes of the *gean-cānach* (love-talker) that he is "another diminutive being of the same tribe as the Lepracaun, but, unlike him, he personated love and idleness, and always appeared with a dudeen in his jaw in lonesome valleys, and it was his custom to make love to shepherdesses and milk-maids. It was considered very unlucky to meet him, and whoever was known to have ruined his fortune by devotion to the fair sex was said to have met a *gean-cānach.* The dudeen, or ancient Irish tobacco pipe, found in our raths, etc., is still popularly called a *gean-canach's* pipe."

The word is not to be found in dictionaries, nor does this spirit appear to be well known, if known at all, in Connacht. The word is pronounced *gánconâgh*.

In the MS. marked R.I.A. $\frac{23}{E.\ 13}$ in the Roy' Ir. Ac., there is a long poem describing such a fairy hurling-match as the one in the story, only the fairies described as the *shiagh*, or host, wore plaids and bonnets, like Highlanders. After the hurling the fairies have a hunt, in which the poet takes part, and they swept with great rapidity through half Ireland. The poem ends with the line —

"'*S gur shiubhail me na cúig cúig cúige's gan fúm acht buachallán buidhe;*"

"and I had travelled the five provinces with nothing under me but a yellow bohalawn (rag-weed)."—[*Note by Mr. Douglas Hyde.*]

Father John O'Hart.—Page 220.

Father O'Rorke is the priest of the parishes of Ballysadare and Kilvarnet, and it is from his learnedly and faithfully and sympathetically written history of these parishes that I have taken the story of Father John, who had been priest of these parishes, dying in the year 1739. Coloony is a village in Kilvarnet.

Some sayings of Father John's have come down. Once when he was sorrowing greatly for the death of his brother, the people said to him, "Why do you sorrow so for your brother when you forbid us to keen?" "Nature," he answered, "forces me, but ye force nature." His memory and influence survives, in the fact that to the present day there has been no keening in Coloony.

He was a friend of the celebrated poet and musician, Carolan.

Shoneen and Sleiveen.—Page 220.

Shoneen is the diminutive of *shone* [Ir. *Seón*]. There are two Irish names for John—one is *Shone*, the other is *Shawn* [Ir. *Seághan*]. Shone is the "grandest" of the two, and is applied to the gentry. Hence *Shoneen* means "a little gentry John," and is applied to upstarts and "big" farmers, who ape the rank of gentleman.

Sleiveen, not to be found in the dictionaries, is a comical Irish word (at least in Connaught) for a rogue. It probably comes from *sliabh*, a mountain, meaning primarily a mountaineer, and in a secondary sense, on the principle that mountaineers are worse than anybody else, a rogue. I am indebted to Mr. Douglas Hyde for these details, as for many others.

DEMON CAT.—Page 229.

In Ireland one hears much of Demon Cats. The father of one of the present editors of the *Fortnightly* had such a cat, say county Dublin peasantry. One day the priest dined with him, and objecting to see a cat feed before Christians, said something over it that made it go up the chimney in a flame of fire. " I will have the law on you for doing such a thing to my cat," said the father of the editor. "Would you like to see your cat?" said the priest. "I would," said he, and the priest brought it up, covered with chains, through the hearth-rug, straight out of hell. The Irish devil does not object to these undignified shapes. The Irish devil is not a dignified person. He has no whiff of sulphureous majesty about him. A centaur of the ragamuffin, jeering and shaking his tatters, at once the butt and terror of the saints !

A LEGEND OF KNOCKMANY.—Page 266.

Carleton says—"Of the grey stone mentioned in this legend, there is a very striking and melancholy anecdote to be told. Some twelve or thirteen years ago, a gentleman in the vicinity of the site of it was building a house, and, in defiance of the legend and curse connected with it, he resolved to break it up and use it. It was with some difficulty, however, that he could succeed in getting his labourers to have anything to do with its mutilation. Two men, however, undertook to blast it, but, some-how, the process of ignition being mismanaged, it exploded prema-turely, and one of them was killed. This coincidence was held as a fulfilment of the curse mentioned in the legend. I have heard that it remains in that mutilated state to the present day, no other person being found who had the hardihood to touch it. This stone, before it was disfigured, exactly resembled that which the country people term a miscaun of butter, which is precisely the shape of a complete prism, a circumstance, no doubt, which, in the fertile imagination of the old Senachies, gave rise to the superstition annexed to it."

SOME AUTHORITIES ON IRISH FOLK-LORE.

Croker's *Legends of the South of Ireland*. Lady Wilde's *Ancient Legends of Ireland*. Sir William Wilde's *Irish Popular Superstitions*. McAnally's *Irish Wonders*. *Irish Folk-Lore*, by Lageniensis. Lover's *Legends and Stories of the Irish Peasantry*. Patrick Kennedy's *Legend-ary Fictions of the Irish Celts*, *Banks of the Boro*, *Legends of Mount Leinster*, and *Banks of the Duffrey ;* Carlton's *Traits and Stories of the Irish Peasantry ;* and the chap-books, *Royal Fairy Tales*, *Hibernian Tales*, and *Tales of the Fairies*. Besides these there are many books on general subjects, containing stray folk-lore, such as Mr. and Mrs.

S. C. Hall's *Ireland ;* Lady Chatterton's *Rambles in the South of Ireland ;* Gerald Griffin's *Tales of a Jury-room ;* and the *Leadbeater Papers.* For banshee stories see Barrington's *Recollections* and Miss Lefanu's *Memoirs of my Grandmother.* In O'Donovan's introduction to the *Four Masters* are several tales. The principal magazine articles are in the *Dublin and London Magazine* for 1825-1828 (Sir William Wilde calls this the best collection of Irish folk-lore in existence) ; and in the *Dublin University Magazine* for 1839 and 1878, those in '78 being by Miss Maclintock. The *Folk-Lore Journal* and the *Folk-Lore Record* contain much Irish folk-lore, as also do the *Ossianic Society's* publications and the proceedings of the *Kilkenny Archæological Society.* Old Irish magazines, such as the *Penny Journal, Newry Magazine,* and *Duffy's Sixpenny Magazine* and *Hibernian Magazine,* have much scattered through them. Among the peasantry are immense quantities of ungathered legends and beliefs.

CUCHULAIN OF MUIRTHEMNE

THE STORY OF THE MEN OF THE RED BRANCH OF ULSTER

Arranged and Put into English by
Lady Isabella Augusta Gregory

"Deirim an móiɼ do beir mo muinntir," aɼ Cu-
culain, "go mbéið tɼáct aguɼ iompáð fóɼ aɼ mo
ᵹníomaɼtaið-ɼe ameaɼᵹ na n-áɼð-ᵹníom do ɼinne na
ᵹaiɼᵹiðiᵹ iɼ tɼéine."

"I SWEAR BY THE OATH OF MY PEOPLE," SAID CUCHULAIN, "I
WILL MAKE MY DOINGS BE SPOKEN OF AMONG THE GREAT DOINGS
OF HEROES IN THEIR STRENGTH."

CONTENTS

DEDICATION OF THE IRISH EDITION

TO THE PEOPLE OF KILTARTAN

My Dear Friends,

When I began to gather these stories together, it is of you I was thinking, that you would llke to have them and to be reading them. For although you have not to go far to get stories of Finn and Goll and Oisin from any old person in the place, there is very little of the history of Cuchulain and his friends left in the memory of the people, but only that they were brave men and good fighters, and that Deirdre was beautiful.

When I went looking for the stories in the old writings, I found that the Irish in them is too hard for any person to read that has not made a long study of it. Some scholars have worked well at them, Irishmen and Germans and Frenchmen, but they have printed them in the old cramped Irish, with translations into German or French or English, and these are not easy for you to get, or to understand, and the stories themselves are confused, every one giving a different account from the others in some small thing, the way there is not much pleasure in reading them. It is what

I have tried to do, to take the best of the stories, or whatever parts of each will fit best to one another, and in that way to give a fair account of Cuchulain's life and death. I left out a good deal I thought you would not care about for one reason or another, but I put in nothing of my own that could be helped, only a sentence or so now and again to link the different parts together. I have told the whole story in plain and simple words, in the same way my old nurse Mary Sheridan used to be telling stories from the Irish long ago, and I a child at Roxborough.

And indeed if there was more respect for Irish things among the learned men that live in the college at Dublin, where so many of these old writings are stored, this work would not have been left to a woman of the house, that has to be minding the place, and listening to complaints, and dividing her share of food.

My friend and your friend the *Craoibhin Aoibhin* has put Irish of to-day on some of these stories that I have set in order, for I am sure you will like to have the history of the heroes of Ireland told in the language of Ireland. And I am very glad to have something that is worth offering you, for you have been very kind to me ever since I came over to you from Kilchriest, two-and-twenty years ago.

AUGUSTA GREGORY.

March 1902.

PREFACE

I

I THINK this book is the best that has come out of Ireland in my time. Perhaps I should say that it is the best book that has ever come out of Ireland; for the stories which it tells are a chief part of Ireland's gift to the imagination of the world—and it tells them perfectly for the first time. Translators from the Irish have hitherto retold one story or the other from some one version, and not often with any fine understanding of English, of those changes of rhythm for instance that are changes of the sense. They have translated the best and fullest manuscripts they knew, as accurately as they could, and that is all we have the right to expect from the first translators of a difficult and old literature. But few of the stories really begin to exist as great works of imagination until somebody has taken the best bits out of many manuscripts. Sometimes, as in Lady Gregory's version of Deirdre, a dozen manuscripts have to give their best before the beads are ready for the necklace. It has been as necessary also to leave out as to add, for generations of copyists, who had often but little sympathy with the stories they copied, have mixed versions together in a clumsy fashion, often repeating one incident several times, and every century has ornamented what was once a simple story with its own often extravagant ornament. One does not perhaps exaggerate when one says that no story has come down to us in the form it had when the story-teller told it in the winter evenings. Lady Gregory has done her work of compression and selection at once so firmly and so reverently that I cannot believe that anybody, except now and then for a scientific purpose, will need another text than this, or than the version of it the Gaelic League is about to publish in Modern Irish. When she has added her translations from other cycles, she will have given Ireland its Mabinogion, its Morte D'Arthur, its Nibelungenlied. She has already put a great mass of stories, in which the ancient heart of Ireland still lives, into a shape at once harmonious and characteristic; and without writing more than a very few sentences of her own to link together incidents or thoughts taken from different manuscripts, without adding more indeed than the story-teller must often have added to amend the hesitation of a moment. Perhaps more than all she had discovered a fitting dialect to tell them in. Some years ago I wrote some stories of mediæval Irish life, and as I wrote I was sometimes made wretched by the thought that I knew of no kind of English that fitted them as the language of Morris' prose stories—the most beautiful language I had ever read—fitted his journeys to woods and wells beyond the world. I knew of no language to write about Ireland in but raw modern English; but now Lady Gregory has discovered a speech as beautiful as that of Morris, and a living speech into the bargain.

As she moved about among her people she learned to love the beautiful speech of those who think in Irish, and to understand that it is as true a dialect of English as the dialect that Burns wrote in. It is some hundreds of years old, and age gives a language authority. One finds in it the vocabulary of the translators of the Bible, joined to an idiom which makes it tender, compassionate, and complaisant, like the Irish language itself. It is certainly well suited to clothe a literature which never ceased to be folk-lore even when it was recited in the Courts of Kings.

II

Lady Gregory could with less trouble have made a book that would have better pleased the hasty reader. She could have plucked away details, smoothed out characteristics till she had left nothing but the bare stories; but a book of that kind would never have called up the past, or stirred the imagination of a painter or a poet, and would be as little thought of in a few years as if it had been a popular novel.

The abundance of what may seem at first irrelevant invention in a story like the death of Conaire, is essential if we are to recall a time when people were in love with a story, and gave themselves up to imagination as if to a lover. One may think there are too many lyrical outbursts, or too many enigmatical symbols here and there in some other story, but delight will always overtake one in the end. One comes to accept without reserve an art that is half epical, half lyrical,

like that of the historical parts of the Bible, the art of a
time when perhaps men passed more readily than they
do now from one mood to another, and found it harder
than we do to keep to the mood in which one tots up
figures or banters a friend.

III

The Church when it was most powerful created an
imaginative unity, for it taught learned and unlearned
to climb, as it were, to the great moral realities through
hierarchies of Cherubim and Seraphim, through clouds
of Saints and Angels who had all their precise duties
and privileges. The story-tellers of Ireland, perhaps of
every primitive country, created a like unity, only it was
to the great æsthetic realities that they taught people to
climb. They created for learned and unlearned alike,
a communion of heroes, a cloud of stalwart witnesses;
but because they were as much excited as a monk over
his prayers, they did not think sufficiently about the
shape of the poem and the story. One has to get a
little weary or a little distrustful of one's subject,
perhaps, before one can lie awake thinking how one
will make the most of it. They were more anxious
to describe energetic characters, and to invent beautiful
stories, than to express themselves with perfect dramatic
logic or in perfectly-ordered words. They shared
their characters and their stories, their very images,
with one another, and handed them down from generation to generation; for nobody, even when he had

added some new trait, or some new incident, thought of claiming for himself what so obviously lived its own merry or mournful life. The wood-carver who first put a sword into St Michael's hand would have as soon claimed as his own a thought which was perhaps put into his mind by St Michael himself. The Irish poets had also, it may be, what seemed a supernatural sanction, for a chief poet had to understand not only innumerable kinds of poetry, but how to keep himself for nine days in a trance. They certainly believed in the historical reality of even their wildest imaginations. And so soon as Christianity made their hearers desire a chronology that would run side by side with that of the Bible, they delighted in arranging their Kings and Queens, the shadows of forgotten mythologies, in long lines that ascended to Adam and his Garden. Those who listened to them must have felt as if the living were like rabbits digging their burrows under walls that had been built by Gods and Giants, or like swallows building their nests in the stone mouths of immense images, carved by nobody knows who. It is no wonder that one sometimes hears about men who saw in a vision ivy-leaves that were greater than shields, and blackbirds whose thighs were like the thighs of oxen. The fruit of all those stories, unless indeed the finest activities of the mind are but a pastime, is the quick intelligence, the abundant imagination, the courtly manners of the Irish country people.

IV

William Morris came to Dublin when I was a boy, and I had some talk with him about these old stories. He had intended to lecture upon them, but "the ladies and gentlemen"—he put a communistic fervour of hatred into the phrase—knew nothing about them. He spoke of the Irish account of the battle of Clontarf, and of the Norse account, and said, that one saw the Norse and Irish tempers in the two accounts. The Norseman was interested in the way things are done, but the Irishman turned aside, evidently well pleased to be out of so dull a business, to describe beautiful supernatural events. He was thinking, I suppose, of the young man who came from Aoibhell of the Grey Rock, giving up immortal love and youth, that he might fight and die by Murrugh's side. He said that the Norseman had the dramatic temper, and the Irishman had the lyrical. I think I should have said epical and romantic rather than dramatic and lyrical, but his words, which have so much greater authority than mine, mark the distinction very well, and not only between Irish and Norse, but between Irish and other un-Celtic literatures. The Irish story-teller could not interest himself with an unbroken interest in the way men like himself burned a house, or won wives no more wonderful than themselves. His mind constantly escaped out of daily circumstance, as a bough that has been held down by a weak hand suddenly straightens itself out. His imagination was always running off to Tir-nan-oge, to the Land of

Promise, which is as near to the country-people of to-day, as it was to Cuchulain and his companions. His belief in its nearness, cherished in its turn the lyrical temper, which is always athirst for an emotion, a beauty which cannot be found in its perfection upon earth, or only for a moment. His imagination, which had not been able to believe in Cuchulain's greatness, until it had brought the Great Queen, the red eye-browed goddess to woo him upon the battlefield, could not be satisfied with a friendship less romantic and lyrical than that of Cuchulain and Ferdiad, who kissed one another after the day's fighting, or with a love less romantic and lyrical than that of Baile and Aillinn, who died at the report of one another's deaths, and married in Tir-nan-oge. His art, too, is often at its greatest when it is most extravagant, for he only feels himself among solid things, among things with fixed laws and satisfying purposes, when he has reshaped the world according to his heart's desire. He understands as well as Blake that the ruins of time build mansions in eternity, and he never allows anything, that we can see and handle, to remain long unchanged. The characters must remain the same, but the strength of Fergus may change so greatly, that he, who a moment before was merely a strong man among many, becomes the master of Three Blows that would destroy an army, did they not cut off the heads of three little hills instead, and his sword, which a fool had been able to steal out of its sheath, has of a sudden the likeness of a rainbow. A wandering lyric moon must knead and kindle perpetually that moving world of cloaks made out of the fleeces of Manannan; of armed men who change themselves into sea-birds; of goddesses who become crows; of trees that bare fruit and flower at the same time. The great emotions of love, terror, and friendship must alone remain untroubled by the moon in that world, which is still the world of the Irish country-people, who do not open their eyes very wide at the most miraculous change, at the most sudden enchantment. Its events, and things, and people are wild, and are like unbroken horses, that are so much more beautiful than horses that have learned to run between shafts. One thinks of actual life, when one reads those Norse stories, which were already in decadence, so necessary were the proportions of actual life to their efforts, when a dying man remembered his heroism enough to look down at his wound and say, "Those broad spears are coming into fashion"; but the Irish stories make one understand why the Greeks call myths the activities of the dæmons. The great virtues, the great joys, the great privations come in the myths, and, as it were, take mankind between their naked arms, and without putting off their divinity. Poets have taken their themes more often from stories that are all, or half, mythological. than from history or stories that give one the sensation of history, under-standing, as I think, that the imagination which remembers the proportions of life is but a long wooing, and that it has to forget them before it becomes the torch and the marriage-bed.

V

One finds, as one expects, in the work of men who were not troubled about any probabilities or necessities but those of emotion itself, an immense variety of incident and character and of ways of expressing emotion. Cuchulain fights man after man during the quest of the Brown Bull, and not one of those fights is like another, and not one is lacking in emotion or strangeness ; and when one thinks imagination can do no more, the story of the Two Bulls, emblematic of all contests, suddenly lifts romance into prophecy. The characters too have a distinctness one does not find among the people of the Mabinogion, perhaps not even among the people of the Morte D'Arthur. One knows one will be long forgetting Cuchulain, whose life is vehement and full of pleasure, as though he always remembered that it was to be soon over ; or the dreamy Fergus who betrays the sons of Usnach for a feast, without ceasing to be noble ; or Conall who is fierce and friendly and trustworthy, but has not the sap of divinity that makes Cuchulain mysterious to men, and beloved of women. Women indeed, with their lamentations for lovers and husbands and sons, and for fallen rooftrees and lost wealth, give the stories their most beautiful sentences ; and, after Cuchulain, one thinks most of certain great queens—of angry, amorous Maeve, with her long pale face ; of Findabair, her daughter, who dies of shame and of pity ; of Deirdre who might be some mild modern housewife but for her prophetic wisdom. If one does not set Deirdre's lamentations among the

greatest lyric poems of the world, I think one may be
certain that the wine-press of the poets has been trodden
for one in vain; and yet I think it may be proud Emer,
Cuchulain's fitting wife, who will linger longest in the
memory. What a pure flame burns in her always,
whether she is the newly-married wife fighting for pre-
cedence, fierce as some beautiful bird, or the confident
housewife, who would awaken her husband from his
magic sleep with mocking words; or the great queen
who would get him out of the tightening net of his
doom, by sending him into the Valley of the Deaf, with
Niamh, his mistress, because he will be more obedient to
her; or the woman whom sorrow has sent with Helen and
seult and Brunnhilda, and Deirdre, to share their
immortality in the rosary of the poets.

"'And oh! my love!' she said, 'we were often in
one another's company, and it was happy for us; for if
the world had been searched from the rising of the sun to
sunset, the like would never have been found in one
place, of the Black Sainglain and the Grey of Macha,
and Laeg the chariot-driver, and myself and Cuchulain.'

"And after that Emer bade Conall to make a wide,
very deep grave for Cuchulain; and she laid herself
down beside her gentle comrade, and she put her mouth
to his mouth, and she said: 'Love of my life, my friend,
my sweetheart, my one choice of the men of the earth,
many is the women, wed or unwed, envied me until
to-day; and now I will not stay living after you.'"

VI

We Irish should keep these personages much in our hearts, for they lived in the places where we ride and go marketing, and sometimes they have met one another on the hills that cast their shadows upon our doors at evening.   If we will but tell these stories to our children the Land will begin again to be a Holy Land, as it was before men gave their hearts to Greece and Rome and Judea.   When I was a child I had only to climb the hill behind the house to see long, blue, ragged hills flowing along the southern horizon.   What beauty was lost to me, what depth of emotion is still perhaps lacking in me, because nobody told me, not even the merchant captains who knew everything, that Cruachan of the Enchantments lay behind those long, blue, ragged hills!

W. B. YEATS.

March 1902.

CUCHULAIN OF MUIRTHEMNE

I

BIRTH OF CUCHULAIN

IN the time long ago, Conchubar, son of Ness, was King of Ulster, and he held his court in the palace of Emain Macha. And this is the way he came to be king. He was but a young lad, and his father was not living, and Fergus, son of Rogh, who was at that time King of Ulster, asked his mother Ness in marriage.

Now Ness, that was at one time the quietest and kindest of the women of Ireland, had got to be unkind and treacherous because of an unkindness that had been done to her, and she planned to get the kingdom away from Fergus for her own son. So she said to Fergus: "Let Conchubar hold the kingdom for a year, so that his children after him may be called the children of a king; and that is the marriage portion I will ask of you."

"You may do that," the men of Ulster said to him; "for even though Conchubar gets the name of being king, it is yourself that will be our king all the time." So Fergus agreed to it, and he took Ness as his wife, and her son Conchubar was made king in his place.

But all through the year, Ness was working to keep the kingdom for him, and she gave great presents to the chief men of Ulster to get them on her side. And though Conchubar was but a young lad at that time, he was wise in his judgments, and brave in battle, and good in shape and in form, and they liked him well. And at the end of the year, when Fergus asked to have the kingship back again, they consulted together ; and it is what they agreed, that Conchubar was to keep it. And they said : " It is little Fergus thinks about us, when he was so ready to give up his rule over us for a year ; and let Conchubar keep the kingship," they said, " and let Fergus keep the wife he has got."

Now it happened one day that Conchubar was making a feast at Emain Macha for the marriage of his sister Dechtire with Sualtim son of Roig. And at the feast Dechtire was thirsty, and they gave her a cup of wine, and as she was drinking it, a mayfly flew into the cup, and she drank it down with the wine. And presently she went into her sunny parlour, and her fifty maidens along with her, and she fell into a deep sleep. And in her sleep, Lugh of the Long Hand appeared to her, and he said : " It is I myself was the mayfly that came to you in the cup, and it is with me you must come away now, and your fifty maidens along with you." And he put on them the appearance of a flock of birds, and they went with him southward till they came to Brugh na Boinne, the dwelling-place of the Sidhe. And no one at Emain Macha could get tale or tidings of them, or know where they had gone, or what had happened them.

It was about a year after that time, there was another feast in Emain, and Conchubar and his chief men were sitting at the feast. And suddenly they saw from the window a great flock of birds, that lit on the ground and began to eat up everything before them, so that not so much as a blade of grass was left.

The men of Ulster were vexed when they saw the birds destroying all before them, and they yoked nine of their chariots to follow after them. Conchubar was in his own chariot, and there were following with him Fergus son of Rogh, and Laegaire Buadach, the Battle-Winner, and Celthair son of Uithecar, and many others, and Bricriu of the bitter tongue was along with them.

They followed after the birds across the whole country southward, across Slieve Fuad, by Ath Lethan, by Ath Garach and Magh Gossa, between Fir Rois and Fir Ardae; and the birds before them always. They were the most beautiful that had ever been seen; nine flocks of them there were, linked together two and two with a chain of silver, and at the head of every flock there were two birds of different colours, linked together with a chain of gold; and there were three birds that flew by themselves, and they all went before the chariots, to the far end of the country, until the fall of night, and then there was no more seen of them.

And when the dark night was coming on, Conchubar said to his people: "It is best for us to unyoke the chariots now, and to look for some place where we can spend the night."

Then Fergus went forward to look for some place, and what he came to was a very small poor-looking house. A man and a woman were in it, and when they saw him they said: "Bring your companions here along with you, and they will be welcome." Fergus went back to his companions and told them what he had seen. But Bricriu said: "Where is the use of going into a house like that, with neither room nor provisions nor coverings in it; it is not worth our while to be going there."

Then Bricriu went on himself to the place where the house was. But when he came to it, what he saw was a grand, new, well-lighted house; and at the door there was a young man wearing armour, very tall and handsome and shining. And he said: "Come into the house, Bricriu; why are you looking about you?" And there was a young woman beside him, fine and noble, and with curled hair, and she said: "Surely there is a welcome before you from me." "Why does she welcome me?" said Bricriu. "It is on account of her that I myself welcome you," said the young man. "And is there no one missing from you at Emain?" he said. "There is surely," said Bricriu. "We are missing fifty young girls for the length of a year." "Would you know them again if you saw them?" said the young man. "If I would not know them," said Bricriu, "it is because a year might make a change in them, so that I would not be sure." "Try and know them again," said the man, "for the fifty young girls are in this house, and this woman beside me is their mistress, Dechtire. It was they themselves, changed into birds, that went to Emain Macha to bring you here." Then Dechtire gave Bricriu a purple cloak with gold fringes; and he went back to find his companions. But while he was going he thought to himself: "Conchubar would give great treasure to find these fifty young girls again, and his sister along with them. I will not tell him I have found them. I will only say I have found a house with beautiful women in it, and no more than that."

When Conchubar saw Bricriu, he asked news of him. "What news do you bring back with you, Bricriu?" he said. "I came to a fine well-lighted house," said Bricriu; "I saw a queen, noble, kind, with royal looks, with curled hair; I saw a troop of women, beautiful, well-dressed; I saw the man of the house, tall and open-handed and shining." "Let us go there for the night," said Conchubar. So they brought their chariots and their horses and their arms; and they were hardly in the house when every sort of food and of drink, some they knew and

some they did not know, was put before them, so that
they never spent a better night. And when they had
eaten and drunk and began to be satisfied, Conchubar
said to the young man: "Where is the mistress of the
house that she does not come to bid us welcome?"
"You cannot see her to-night," said he, "for she is in the
pains of childbirth."

So they rested there that night, and in the morning
Conchubar was the first to rise up; but he saw no more
of the man of the house, and what he heard was the cry
of a child. And he went to the room it came from,
and there he saw Dechtire, and her maidens about her,
and a young child beside her. And she bade Conchubar
welcome, and she told him all that had happened her,
and that she had called him there to bring herself and
the child back to Emain Macha. And Conchubar said:
"It is well you have done by me, Dechtire; you gave
shelter to me and to my chariots; you kept the cold from
my horses; you gave food to me and my people, and
now you have given us this good gift. And let our
sister, Finchoem, bring up the child," he said. "No, it
is not for her to bring him up, it is for me," said Sencha
son of Ailell, chief judge and chief poet of Ulster. "For
I am skilled; I am good in disputes; I am not forgetful;
I speak before any one at all in the presence of the king;
I watch over what he says; I give judgment in the
quarrels of kings; I am judge of the men of Ulster; no one
has a right to dispute my claim, but only Conchubar."

"If the child is given to me to bring up," said Blai,
the distributer, "he will not suffer from want of care
or from forgetfulness. It is my messages that do the
will of Conchubar; I call up the fighting men from
all Ireland; I am well able to provide for them for a
week, or even for ten days; I settle their business and
their disputes; I support their honour; I get satisfaction for their insults."

"You think too much of yourself," said Fergus. "It is I that will bring up the child; I am strong; I have knowledge; I am the king's messenger; no one can stand up against me in honour or riches; I am hardened to war and battles; I am a good craftsman; I am worthy to bring up a child. I am the protector of all the unhappy; the strong are afraid of me; I am the helper of the weak."

"If you will listen to me at last, now you are quiet," said Amergin, "I am able to bring up a child like a king. The people praise my honour, my bravery, my courage, my wisdom; they praise my good luck, my age, my speaking, my name, my courage, and my race. Though I am a fighter, I am a poet; I am worthy of the king's favour; I overcome all the men who fight from their chariots; I owe thanks to no one except Conchubar; I obey no one but the king."

Then Sencha said: "Let Finchoem keep the child until we come to Emain, and Morann, the judge, will settle the question when we are there"

So the men of Ulster set out for Emain, Finchoem having the child with her. And when they came there Morann gave his judgment. "It is for Conchubar," he said, "to help the child to a good name, for he is next of kin to him; let Sencha teach him words and speaking; let Fergus hold him on his knees; let Amergin be his tutor." And he said: "This child will be praised by all, by chariot drivers and fighters, by kings and by wise men; he shall be loved by many men; he will avenge all your wrongs; he will defend your fords; he will fight all your battles."

And so it was settled. And the child was left until he should come to sensible years, with his mother Dechtire and with her husband Sualtim. And they brought him up upon the plain of Muirthemne, and the name he was known by was Setanta, son of Sualtim.

II

BOY DEEDS OF CUCHULAIN

IT chanced one day, when Setanta was about seven years old, that he heard some of the people of his mother's house talking about King Conchubar's court at Emain Macha, and of the sons of kings and nobles that lived there, and that spent a great part of their time at games and at hurling. "Let me go and play with them there," he said to his mother. "It is too soon for you to do that," she said, "but wait till such time as you are able to travel so far, and till I can put you in charge of some one going to the court, that will put you under Conchubar's protection." "It would be too long for me to wait for that," he said, "but I will go there by myself if you will tell me the road." "It is too far for you," said Dechtire, "for it is beyond Slieve Fuad, Emain Macha is." "Is it east or west of Slieve Fuad?" he asked. And when she had answered him that, he set out there and then, and nothing with him but his hurling stick, and his silver ball, and his little dart and spear; and to shorten the road for himself he would give a blow to the ball and drive it from him, and then he would throw his hurling stick after it, and the dart after that again, and then he would make a run and catch them all in his hand before one of them would have reached the ground.

So he went on until he came to the lawn at Emain

Macha, and there he saw three fifties of king's sons hurling and learning feats of war. He went in among them, and when the ball came near him he got it between his feet, and drove it along in spite of them till he had sent it beyond the goal. There was great surprise and anger on them when they saw what he had done, and Follaman, King Conchubar's son, that was chief among them, cried out to them to come together and drive out this stranger and make an end of him. "For he has no right," he said, "to come into our game without asking leave, and without putting his life under our protection. And you may be sure," he said, "that he is the son of some common fighting man, and it is not for him to come into our game at all." With that they all made an attack on him, and began to throw their hurling sticks at him, and their balls and darts, but he escaped them all, and then he rushed at them, and began to throw some of them to the ground. Fergus came out just then from the palace, and when he saw what a good defence the little lad was making, he brought him in to where Conchubar was playing chess, and told him all that had happened. "This is no gentle game you have been playing," he said. "It is on themselves the fault is," said the boy; "I came as a stranger, and I did not get a stranger's welcome." "You did not know then," said Conchubar, "that no one can play among the boy troop of Emain unless he gets their leave and their protection." "I did not know that, or I would have asked it of them," he said. "What is your name and your family?" said Conchubar. My name is Setanta, son of Sualtim and of Dechtire," he said. When Conchubar knew that he was his sister's son, he gave him a great welcome, and he bade the boy troop to let him go safe among them. "We will do that," they said. But when they went out to play, Setanta began to break through them, and to overthrow them, so that they could not stand against him. "What are you wanting of them now?" said Conchubar. "I swear by the gods my people swear by," said the boy, "I will not lighten my hand off them till they have come under my protection the same way I have come under theirs." Then they all agreed to give in to this; and Setanta stayed in the king's house at Emain Macha, and all the chief men of Ulster had a hand in bringing him up.

There was a great smith in Ulster of the name of Culain, who made a feast at that time for Conchubar and for his people. When Conchubar was setting out to the feast, he passed by the lawn where the boy troop were at their games, and he watched them awhile, and he saw how the son of Dechtire was winning the goal from them all. "That little lad will serve Ulster yet," said Conchubar; "and call him to me now," he said, "and let him come with me to the smith's feast." "I cannot go with you now," said Setanta, when they had called to him, "for these boys have not had enough of play yet." "It would be too long for me to wait for you," said the king. "There is no need for you to wait; I will follow the track of the chariots," said Setanta.

So Conchubar went on to the smith's house, and there was a welcome before him, and fresh rushes were laid down, and there were poems and songs and recitals of laws, and the feast was brought in, and they began to be merry. And then Culain said to the king: "Will there be any one else of your people coming after you to-night?" "There will not," said Conchubar, for he forgot that he had told the little lad to follow him. "But why do you ask me that?" he said. "I have a great fierce hound," said the smith, "and when I take the chain off him, he lets no one come into the one district with himself, and he will obey no one but myself, and he has in him the strength of a hundred." "Loose him out," said Conchubar, "until he keeps a watch on the place." So Culain loosed him out, and the dog made a course round the whole district, and then he came back to the place where he was used to lie and to watch the house, and every one was in dread of him, he was so fierce and so cruel and so savage.

Now, as to the boys at Emain, when they were done playing, every one went to his father's house, or to who-ever was in charge of him. But Setanta set out on the track of the chariots, shortening the way for himself as he was used to do with his hurling stick and his ball. When he came to the lawn before the smith's house, the hound heard him coming, and began such a fierce yelling that he might have been heard through all Ulster, and he sprang at him as if he had a mind not to stop and tear him up at all, but to swallow him at the one mouthful. The little fellow had no weapon but his stick and his ball, but when he saw the hound coming at him, he struck the ball with such force that it went down his throat, and through his body. Then he seized him by the hind legs and dashed him against a rock until there was no life left in him.

When the men feasting within heard the outcry of the hound, Conchubar started up and said: "It is no good luck brought us on this journey, for that is surely my sister's son that was coming after me, and that has got his death by the hound." On that all the men rushed out, not waiting to go through the door, but over walls and barriers as they could. But Fergus was the first to get to where the boy was, and he took him up and lifted him on his shoulder, and brought him in safe and sound to Conchubar, and there was great joy on them all.

But Culain the smith went out with them, and when he saw his great hound lying dead and broken there was great grief in his heart, and he came in and said to Setanta: "There is no good welcome for you here." "What have you against the little lad?" said Conchubar.

SETANTA FOLLOWED CONCHUBAR'S CHARIOTS.

SETANTA AND THE SLAIN HOUND OF CULAIN.

"It was no good luck that brought him here, or that made me prepare this feast for yourself, King," he said; "for from this out, my hound being gone, my substance will be wasted, and my way of living will be gone astray. And, little boy," he said, "that was a good member of my family you took from me, for he was the protector of my goods and my flocks and my herds and of all that I had." "Do not be vexed on account of that," said the boy, "and I myself will make up to you for what I have done." "How will you do that?" said Conchubar. "This is how I will do it: if there is a whelp of the same breed to be had in Ireland, I will rear him and train him until he is as good a hound as the one killed; and until that time, Culain," he said, "I myself will be your watch-dog, to guard your goods and your cattle and your house." "You have made a fair offer," said Conchubar. "I could have given no better award myself," said Cathbad the Druid. "And from this out," he said, "your name will be Cuchulain, the Hound of Culain." "I am better pleased with my own name of Setanta, son of Sualtim," said the boy. "Do not say that," said Cathbad, "for all the men in the whole world will some day have the name of Cuchulain in their mouths." "If that is so, I am content to keep it," said the boy. And this is how he came by the name Cuchulain.

It was a good while after that, Cathbad the Druid was one day teaching the pupils in his house to the north-east of Emain. There were eight boys along with him that day, and one of them asked him: "Do your signs tell of any special thing this day is good or bad for?" "If any young man should take arms to-day," said Cathbad, "his name will be greater than any other name in Ireland. But his span of life will be short," he said.

Cuchulain was outside at play, but he heard what Cathbad said, and there and then he put off his playing suit, and he went straight to Conchubar's sleeping-room and said: "All good be with you, King!" "What is it you are wanting?" said Conchubar. "What I want is to take arms to-day." "Who put that into your head?" "Cathbad the Druid," said Cuchulain. "If that is so, I will not deny you," said Conchubar. Then he gave him his choice of arms, and the boy tried his strength on them, and there were none that pleased him or that were strong enough for him but Conchubar's own. So he gave him his own two spears, and his sword and his shield.

Just then Cathbad the Druid came in, and there was wonder on him, and he said: "Is it taking arms this young boy is?" "He is indeed," said the king. "It is sorry I would be to see his mother's son take arms on this day," said Cathbad. "Was it not yourself bade him do it?" said the king. "I did not surely," he said. "Then you have lied to me, boy," said Conchubar. "I told no lie, King," said Cuchulain, "for it was he indeed put it in my mind when he was teaching the others, for when one of them asked him if there was any special virtue in this day, he said that whoever would for the first time take arms to-day, his name would be greater than any other in Ireland, and he did not say any harm would come on him, but that his life would be short." "And what I said is true," said Cathbad, "there will be fame on you and a great name, but your lifetime will not be long." "It is little I would care," said Cuchulain, "if my life were to last one day and one night only, so long as my name and the story of what I had done would live after me." Then Cathbad said: "Well, get into a chariot now, and let us see if it was the truth I spoke."

Then Cuchulain got into a chariot and tried its strength, and broke it to pieces, and he broke in the same way the seventeen chariots that Conchubar kept for the boy troop at Emain, and he said: "These chariots

are no use, Conchubar, they are not worthy of me."
"Where is Ibar, son of Riangabra?" said Conchubar.
"Here I am," he answered. "Make ready my own
chariot, and yoke my own horses to it for this boy to
try," said Conchubar. So he tried the king's chariot
and shook it and strained it, and it bore him. "This is
the chariot that suits me," he said. "Now, little one,"
said Ibar, "let us take out the horses and turn them
out to graze." "It is too early for that, Ibar; let us
drive on to where the boy troop are, that they may
wish me good luck on the day of my taking arms." So
they drove on, and all the lads shouted when they saw
him—"Have you taken arms?" "I have indeed," said
Cuchulain. "That you may do well in wounding and
in first killing and in spoil-winning," they said; "but
it is a pity for us, you to have left playing."

"Let the horses go graze now," said Ibar. "It is too
soon yet," said Cuchulain, "and tell me where does that
great road that goes by Emain lead to?" "It leads to
Ath-an-Foraire, the watchers' ford in Slieve Fuad," said
Ibar. "Why is it called the watchers' ford?" "It is
easy to tell that; it is because some choice champion of
the men of Ulster keeps watch there every day to do
battle for the province with any stranger that might
come to the boundary with a challenge." "Do you
know who is in it to-day?" said Cuchulain. "I know
well it is Conall Cearnach, the Victorious, the chief
champion of the young men of Ulster and of all
Ireland." "We will go on then to the ford," said
Cuchulain. So they went on across the plain, and at the
water's edge they found Conall, and he said: "And are
those arms you have taken to-day, little boy?" "They
are indeed," Ibar said for him. "May they bring him
triumph and victory and shedding of first blood," said
Conall. "But I think, little Hound," he said, "that you
are too ready to take them; for you are not fit as yet

to do a champion's work." "What is it you are doing here, Conall?" said the boy. "I am keeping watch and guard for the province." "Rise out of it, Conall," he said, "and for this one day let me keep the watch." "Do not ask that, little one," said Conall; "for you are not able yet to stand against trained fighting men." "Then I will go down to the shallows of Lough Echtra and see if I can redden my arms on either friend or enemy." "Then I will go with you myself," said Conall, "to take care of you and to protect you, that no harm may happen you." "Do not," said Cuchulain. "I will indeed," said Conall, "for if I let you go into a strange country alone, all Ulster would avenge it on me."

So Conall's horses were yoked to his chariot, and he set out to follow Cuchulain, for he had waited for no leave, but had set out by himself. When Cuchulain saw Conall coming up with him he thought to himself, "If I get a chance of doing some great thing, Conall will never let me do it." So he picked up a stone, the size of his fist, from the ground, and made a good cast at the yoke of Conall's chariot, so that he broke it, and the chariot came down, and Conall himself was thrown to the ground sideways. "What did you do that for?" he said. "It was to see could I throw straight, and if there was the making of a good champion in me." "Bad luck on your throwing and on yourself," said Conall. "And any one that likes may strike your head off now, for I will go with you no farther." "That is just what I wanted," said Cuchulain. And with that, Conall went back to his place at the ford.

As for the lad, he went on towards Lough Echtra in the south. Then Ibar said: "If you will listen to me, little one, I would like that we would go back now to Emain; for at this time the carving of the food is beginning there, and it is all very well for you that have your place kept for you between Conchubar's knees.

But as to myself," he said, "it is among the chariot-drivers and the jesters and the messengers I am, and I must find a place and fight for myself where I can." "What is that mountain before us?" said Cuchulain. "That is Slieve Mourne, and that is Finncairn, the white cairn, on its top." "Let us go to it," said Cuchulain. "We would be too long going there," said Ibar. "You are a lazy fellow," said Cuchulain; "and this my first adventure, and the first journey you have made with me." "And that it may be my last," said Ibar, "if ever I get back to Emain again." They went on then to the cairn. "Good Ibar," said the boy, "show me now all that we can see of Ulster, for I do not know my way about the country yet." So Ibar showed him from the cairn all there was to see of Ulster, the hills and the plains and the duns on every side. "What is that sloping square plain before us to the south?" "That is Magh Breagh, the fine meadow." "Show me the duns and strong places of that plain." So Ibar showed him Teamhair and Tailte, Cleathra and Cnobhach and the Brugh of Angus on the Boyne, and the dun of Nechtan Sceine's sons. "Are those the sons of Nechtan that say in their boasting they have killed as many Ulstermen as there are living in Ulster to-day?" "They are the same," said Ibar. "On with us then to that dun," said Cuchulain. "No good will come to you through saying that," said Ibar; "and whoever may go there I will not go," he said. "Alive or dead, you must go there for all that," said Cuchulain. "Then if so, it is alive I will go there," said Ibar, "and it is dead I will be before I leave it."

They went on then to the dun of Nechtan's sons, and when they came to the green lawn, Cuchulain got out of the chariot, and there was a pillar-stone on the lawn, and an iron collar about it, and there was Ogham writing on it that said no man that came there, and he carrying arms, should leave the place without giving a challenge to some one of the people of the dun. When Cuchulain had read the Ogham, he put his arms around the stone and threw it into the water that was there at hand. "I don't see it is any better there than where it was before," said Ibar; "and it is likely this time you will get what you are looking for, and that is a quick death." "Good Ibar," said the boy, "spread out the coverings of the chariot now for me, until I sleep for a while." "It is no good thing you are going to do," said Ibar, "to be going to sleep in an enemy's country." He put out the coverings then, and Cuchulain lay down and fell asleep.

It was just at that time, Foill, son of Nechtan Sceine, came out, and when he saw the chariot, he called out to Ibar, "Let you not unyoke those horses." "I was not going to unyoke them," said Ibar; "the reins are in my hands yet." "What horses are they?" "They are Conchubar's two speckled horses." "So I thought when I saw them," said Foill. "And who is it has brought them across our boundaries?" "A young little lad," said Ibar, "that has taken arms to-day for luck, and it is to show himself off he has come across Magh Breagh." "May he never have good luck," said Foill, "and if he were a fighting man, it is not alive but dead he would go back to Emain to-day." "Indeed he is not able to fight, or it could not be expected of him," said Ibar, "and he but a child that should be in his father's house." At that the boy lifted his head from the ground, and it is red his face was, and his whole body, at hearing so great an insult put on him, and he said: "I am indeed well able to fight." But Foill said: "I am more inclined to think you are not." "You will soon know what to think," said the boy, "and let us go down now to the ford. But go first and get your armour," he said, "for I would not like to kill an un-

armed man." There was anger on Foill then, and he
went running to get his arms. "You must have a care
now," said Ibar, "for that is Foill, son of Nechtan, and
neither point of spear or edge of sword can harm him."
"That suits me very well," said the boy. With that
out came Foill again, and Cuchulain stood up to him,
and took his iron ball in his hand, and hurled it at his
head, and it went through the forehead and out at the
back of his head, and his brains along with it, so that
the air could pass through the hole it made. And
then Cuchulain struck off his head.

Then Tuachel, the second son of Nechtan, came out
on the lawn. "It is likely you are making a great
boast of what you are after doing," he said. "I see
nothing to boast of in that," said Cuchulain, "a single
man to have fallen by me." "You will not have long to
boast of it," said Tuachel, "for I myself am going to
make an end of you on the moment." "Then go back
and bring your arms," said Cuchulain, "for it is only a
coward would come out without arms." He went back
into the house then, and Ibar said: "You must have a
care now, for that is Tuachel, son of Nechtan, and if he
is not killed by the first stroke, or the first cast, or the
first thrust, he cannot be killed at all, for there is no way
of getting at him after that." "You need not be telling
me that, Ibar," said Cuchulain, "for it is Conchubar's
great spear, the Venomous, I will take in my hand, and
that is the last thrust that will be made at him, for after
that, there is no physician will heal his wounds for ever."

Then Tuachel came out on the lawn, and Cuchulain
took hold of the great spear, and made a cast at him,
that went through his shield and broke three of his ribs,
and made a hole through his heart. And then he struck
his head off, before the body reached the ground.

Then Fainnle, the youngest of the three sons of
Nechtan, came out. "Those were foolish fellows," he

said, "to come at you the way they did. But come out now, after me," he said, "into the water where your feet will not touch the bottom," and with that he made a plunge into the water. "Mind yourself well now," said Ibar, "for that is Fainnle, the Swallow, and it is why that name was put on him, he travels across water with the swiftness of a swallow, and there is not one of the swimmers of the whole world can come near him." "It is not to me you should be saying that," said Cuchulain, "for you know the river Callan that runs through Emain, and it is what I used to do," he said, "when the boy troop would break off from their games and plunge into the river to swim, I used to take a boy of them on each shoulder and a boy on each hand, and I would bring them through the river without so much as to wet my back." With that he made a leap into the water, where it was very deep, and himself and Fainnle wrestled together, and then he got a grip of him, and gave him a blow of Conchubar's sword, and struck his head off, and he let his body go away down the stream.

Then he and Ibar went into the house and destroyed what was in it, and they set fire to it, and left it burning, and turned back towards Slieve Fuad, and they brought the heads of the three sons of Nechtan along with them.

Presently they saw a herd of wild deer before them. "What sort of cattle are those?" said the boy. "They are not cattle, but the wild deer of the dark places of Slieve Fuad." "Make the horses go faster," said Cuchulain, "until we can see them better." But with all their galloping the horses could not come up with the wild deer. Then Cuchulain got down from the chariot and raced and ran after them until two stags lay moaning and panting from the hardness of their run through the wet bog, and he bound them to the back of the chariot with the thongs of it. Then they went on till they came to the plain of Emain, and there they saw a flock of white swans that were whiter than the swans of Conchubar's lake, and Cuchulain asked where they came from. "They are wild swans," said Ibar, "that are come from the rocks and the islands of the great sea to feed on the low levels of the country." "Would it be best to take them alive or to kill them?" "It would be best to take them alive," said Ibar, "for many a one kills them, and many a one makes casts at them, but you would hardly find any one at all would bring them in alive." With that, Cuchulain put a little stone in his sling and made a cast, and brought down eight birds of them, and then he put a bigger stone in, and with it he brought down sixteen more. "Get out now, Ibar," he said, "and bring me the birds here." "I will not," said Ibar, "for it would not be easy to stop the horses the way they are going now, and if I leap out, the iron wheels of the chariot will cut through me, or the horns of the stags will make a hole in me." "You are no good of a warrior, Ibar; but give me the reins and I will quiet the horses and the stags." So then Ibar went and brought in the swans, and tied them, and they alive, to the chariot and to the harness. And it is like that they went on till they came to Emain.

It was Levarcham, daughter of Aedh, the conversation woman and messenger to the king, that was there at that time, and was sometimes away in the hills, was the first to see them coming. "There is a chariot-fighter coming, Conchubar," she said, "and he is coming in anger. He has the bleeding heads of his enemies with him in the chariot, and wild stags are bound to it, and white birds are bearing him company. By the oath of my people!" she said, "if he comes on us with his anger still upon him, the best of the men of Ulster will fall by his hand." "I know that chariot-fighter," said Conchubar. "It is the young lad, the son of Dechtire, that went over the boundaries this very day. He has surely reddened his hand, and if his anger cannot be cooled, the young men of Emain will be in danger from him," he said.

Then they all consulted together, and it is what they agreed, to send out three fifties of the women of Emain red-naked to meet him. When the boy saw the women coming, there was shame on him, and he leaned down his head into the cushions of the chariot, and hid his face from them. And the wildness went out of him, and his feasting clothes were brought, and water for washing; and there was a great welcome before him.

This is the story of the boy deeds of Cuchulain, as it was told by Fergus to Ailell and to Maeve at the time of the war for the Brown Bull of Cuailgne.

III

THE COURTING OF EMER

WHEN Cuchulain was growing out of his boyhood at Emain Macha, all the women of Ulster loved him for his skill in feats, for the lightness of his leap, for the weight of his wisdom, for the sweetness of his speech, for the beauty of his face, for the loveliness of his looks, for all his gifts. He had the gift of caution in fighting, until such time as his anger would come on him, and the hero light would shine about his head ; the gift of feats, the gift of chess-playing, the gift of draught-playing, the gift of counting, the gift of divining, the gift of right judgment, the gift of beauty. And all the faults they could find in him were three, that he was too young and smooth-faced, so that young men who did not know him would be laughing at him, that he was too daring, and that he was too beautiful.

The men of Ulster took counsel together then about Cuchulain, for their women and their maidens loved him greatly, and it is what they settled among themselves, that they would seek out a young girl that would be a fitting wife for him, the way that their own wives and their daughters would not be making so much of him. And besides that they were afraid he might die young, and leave no heir after him.

So Conchubar sent out nine men into each of the provinces of Ireland to look for a wife for Cuchulain, to see if in any dun or in any chief place, they could find the daughter of a king or of an owner of land or a house-holder, who would be pleasing to him, that he might ask her in marriage.

All the messengers came back at the end of a year, but not one of them had found a young girl that would please Cuchulain. And then he himself went out to court a young girl he knew in Luglochta Loga, the Garden of Lugh, Emer, the daughter of Forgall Manach, the Wily.

He set out in his chariot, that all the chariots of Ulster could not follow by reason of its swiftness, and of the chariot chief who sat in it. And he found the young girl on her playing field, with her companions about her, daughters of the landowners that lived near Forgall's dun, and they learning needlework and fine embroidery from Emer. And of all the young girls of Ireland, she was the one Cuchulain thought worth courting ; for she had the six gifts—the gift of beauty, the gift of voice, the gift of sweet speech, the gift of needlework, the gift of wisdom, the gift of chastity. And Cuchulain had said that no woman should marry him but one that was his equal in age, in appearance, and in race, in skill and handiness ; and one who was the best worker with her needle of the young girls of Ireland, for that would be the only one would be a fitting wife for him. And that is why it was Emer he went to ask above all others.

And it was in his rich clothes he went out that day, his crimson five-folded tunic, and his brooch of inlaid gold, and his white hooded shirt, that was embroidered with red gold. And as the young girls were sitting together on their bench on the lawn, they heard coming towards them the clatter of hoofs, the creaking of a chariot, the cracking of straps, the grating of wheels, the rushing of horses, the clanking of arms. "Let one of you see," said Emer, "what is it that is coming towards us." And

Fiall, daughter of Forgall, went out and met him, and he came with her to the place where Emer and her companions were, and he wished a blessing to them. Then Emer lifted up her lovely face and saw Cuchulain, and she said, "May the gods make smooth the path before you." "And you," he said, "may you be safe from every harm." "Where are you come from?" she asked him. And he answered her in riddles, that her companions might not understand him, and he said, "From Intide Emna." "Where did you sleep?" "We slept," he said, "in the house of the man that tends the cattle of the plain of Tethra." "What was your food there?" "The ruin of a chariot was cooked for us," he said. "Which way did you come?" "Between the two mountains of the wood." "Which way did you take after that?" "That is not hard to tell," he said. "From the Cover of the Sea, over the Great Secret of the Tuatha De Danaan, and the Foam of the horses of Emain, over the Morrigu's Garden, and the Great Sow's back; over the Valley of the Great Dam, between the God and his Druid; over the Marrow of the Woman, between the Boar and his Dam; over the Washing-place of the horses of Dea; between the King of Ana and his servant, to Mandchuile of the Four Corners of the World; over Great Crime and the Remnants of the Great Feast; between the Vat and the Little Vat, to the Gardens of Lugh, to the daughters of Tethra, the nephew of the King of the Fomor." "And what account have you to give of yourself?" said Emer. "I am the nephew of the man that disappears in another in the wood of Badb," said Cuchulain.

"And now, maiden," he said, "what account have you to give of yourself?" "That is not hard to tell," said Emer, "for what should a maiden be but Teamhair upon the hills, a watcher that sees no one, an eel hiding in the water, a rush out of reach. The daughter of a king should be a flame of hospitality, a road that cannot be entered. And I have champions that follow me," she said, "to keep me from whoever would bring me away against their will, and against the will and the knowledge of Forgall, the dark king."

"Who are the champions that follow you, maiden?" said Cuchulain.

"It is not hard to tell you that," said Emer. "Two of the name of Lui; two Luaths; Luath and Lath Goible, sons of Tethra; Triath and Trescath; Brion and Bolor; Bas, son of Omnach; the eight Condla, and Cond, son of Forgall. Every man of them has the strength of a hundred and the feats of nine. And it would be hard for me," she said, "to tell of all the many powers Forgall has himself. He is stronger than any labouring man, more learned than any Druid, more quick of mind than any poet. You will have more than your games to do when you fight against Forgall, for many have told of his power and of the strength of his doings."

"Why do you not count me as a strong man as good as those others?" said Cuchulain. "Why would I not indeed, if your doings had been spoken of like theirs?" she said. "I swear by the oath of my people," said Cuchulain, "I will make my doings be spoken of among the great doings of heroes in their strength." "What is your strength, then?" said Emer. "That is easily told; when my strength in fighting is weakest I defend twenty; a third part of my strength is enough for thirty; in my full strength I fight alone against forty; and a hundred are safe under my protection. For dread of me, fighting men avoid fords and battles; armies and armed men go backward from the fear of my face."

"That is a good account for a young boy," said Emer, "but you have not reached yet to the strength of chariot chiefs." "But, indeed," said Cuchulain, "it is well I have been reared by Conchubar, my dear foster-father. It is not as a countryman strives to bring up his children, between the flags and the kneading trough, between the fire and the wall, on the floor of the one room, that Conchubar has brought me up; but it is among chariot chiefs and heroes, among jesters and Druids, among poets and learned men, among landowners and farmers of Ulster I have been reared, so that I have all their manners and their gifts."

"Who are these men, then, that have brought you up to do the things you are boasting of?" said Emer.

"That is easily told," he said. "Fair-speaking Sencha taught me wisdom and right judgment; Blai, lord of lands, my kinsman, took me to his house, so that I have entertained the men of Conchubar's province; Fergus brought me up to fights and to battles, so that I am able to use my strength. I stood by the knee of Amergin the poet, he was my tutor, so that I can stand up to any man, I can make praises for the doings of a king. Finchoem helped to rear me, so that Conall Cearnach is my foster-brother. Cathbad of the Gentle Face taught me, for the sake of Dechtire, so that I understand the arts of the Druids, and I have learned all the goodness of knowledge. All the men of Ulster have had a hand in bringing me up, chariot-drivers and chiefs of chariots, kings and chief poets, so that I am the darling of the whole army, so that I fight for the honour of all alike. And as to yourself, Emer," he said, "what way have you been reared in the Garden of Lugh?"

"It is easy to tell you that," said Emer. "I was brought up," she said, "in ancient virtues, in lawful behaviour, in the keeping of chastity, in stateliness of form, in the rank of a queen, in all noble ways among the women of Ireland." "These are good virtues indeed," said Cuchulain. "And why, then, would it not be right for us two to become one? For up to this time," he said, "I have never found a young girl able to hold talk with me the way you have done." "Have you no wife already?" said Emer. "I have not, indeed." "I may not marry before my sister is married," she said then, "for she is older than myself." "Truly, it is not with your sister, but with yourself, I have fallen in love," said Cuchulain.

While they were talking like this, Cuchulain saw the breasts of the maiden over the bosom of her dress, and he said: "Fair is this plain, the plain of the noble yoke." And Emer said, "No one comes to this plain who does not overcome as many as a hundred on each ford, from the ford at Ailbine to Banchuig Arcait."

"Fair is the plain, the plain of the noble yoke," said Cuchulain. "No one comes to this plain," said she, "who does not go out in safety from Samhain to Oilmell, and from Oilmell to Beltaine, and again from Beltaine to Bron Trogain."

"Everything you have commanded, so it will be done by me," said Cuchulain.

"And the offer you have made me, it is accepted, it is taken, it is granted," said Emer.

With that Cuchulain left the place, and they talked no more with one another on that day.

When he was driving across the plain of Bregia, Laeg, his chariot-driver, asked him, "What, now, was the meaning of the words you and the maiden Emer were speaking together?" "Do you not know," said Cuchulain, "that I came to court Emer? And it is for this reason we put a cloak on our words, that the young girls with her might not understand what I had come for. For if Forgall knew it, he would not consent to it, but to you, Laeg," he said, "I will tell the meaning of our talk.

"'Where did you come from,' said she. 'From Intide Emna,' said I, and I meant by that, from Emain Macha. For it took its name from Macha, daughter of Aed the Red, one of the three kings of Ireland. When he died

Macha asked for the kingship, but the sons of Dithorba said they would not give kingship to a woman. So she fought against them and routed them, and they went as exiles to the wild places of Connaught. And after a while she went in search of them, and she took them by treachery, and brought them all in one chain to Ulster. The men of Ulster wanted to kill them, but she said, ' No, for that would be a disgrace on my good government. But let them be my servants,' she said, 'and let them dig a rath for me, that shall be the chief seat of Ulster for ever.' Then she marked out the rath for them with the gold pin on her neck, and its name came from that; a brooch in the neck of Macha.

"The man, in whose house we slept, is Ronca, the fisherman of Conchubar. 'A man that tends cattle,' I said. For he catches fish on his line under the sea, and the fish are the cattle of the sea, and the sea is the plain of Tethra, a king of the kings of the Fomor.

"'Our food was the ruin of a chariot,' I said. For a foal was cooked for us on the hearth, and it is the horse that holds up the chariot.

"'Between the two mountains of the wood,' I said. These are the two mountains between which we came, Slieve Fuad to the west, and Slieve Cuilinn to the east of us, and we were in Oircil between them, the wood that is between the two.

"' The road,' I said, ' from the Cover of the Sea.' That is from the plain of Muirthemne. And it is from this it got its name; there was at one time a magic sea on it, with a sea turtle in it that was used to suck men down, until the Dagda came with his club of anger and sang these words, so that it ebbed away on the moment :—

'Silence on your hollow head ;
Silence on your dark body ;
Silence on your dark brow.'

"'Over the Great Secret of the men of Dea,' I said. That

is a wonderful secret and a wonderful whisper, because it was there that the gathering to the battle of Magh Tuireadh was first whispered of by the Tuatha De Danaan.

"'Over the horses of Emain,' I said. When Ema Nemed, son of Nama, reigned over the Gael, he had his two horses reared for him in Sidhe Ercman of the Tuatha De Danaan, and when those horses were let loose from the Sidhe, a bright stream burst out after them, and the foam spread over the land for a great length of time, and was there to the end of a year, so that the water was called Uanib, that is, foam on the water, and it is Uanib to-day.

"'The Back of the Great Sow,' I said. That is Drimne Breg, the Ridge of Bregin. For the shape of a sow appeared to the sons of Milid on every hill and on every height in Ireland, when they came over the sea, and wanted to land by force, after a spell had been cast on it by the Tuatha De Danaan.

"'The Valley of the Great Dam,' I said, 'between the God and his Druid.' That is, between Angus Og of the Sidhe of the Brugh and his Druid, to the west of the Brugh, and between them was the one woman, the wife of the Smith. That is the way I went, between the hill of the Sidhe of the Brugh where Angus is, and the Sidhe of Bresal, the Druid.

"'Over the Marrow of the Woman,' I said. That is the Boinne, and it gets its name from Boann, the wife of Nechtan, son of Labraid. She went down to the hidden well at the bottom of the dun with the three cup-bearers of Nechtan, Flex and Lex and Luam. No one came back from that well without blemish unless the three cup-bearers went with him. But the queen went out of pride and overbearing to the well, and it is what she said, that nothing would spoil her shape or put a blemish on her. She passed left-hand-wise round the well, to mock at its powers. Then three waves broke over her and bruised her two knees and her right hand and one of her eyes, and she ran out of the dun to escape until she came to the sea, and wherever she ran, the water followed after her. Segain was its name on the dun ; the River Segsa from the dun to the Pool of Mochua ; the hand of the wife of Nechtan and the knee of the wife of Nechtan after that ; the Boinne in Meath ; Arcait it is called from the Finda to the Troma ; the Marrow of the Woman from the Troma to the sea.

" ' The Boar,' I said, ' and his Dam.' That is, between Cleitech and Fessi. For Cleitech is the name for a boar, but it is also the name for a king, the leader of great hosts, and Fessi is the name for the great sow of a farmer's house.

" ' The King of Ana,' I said, ' and his servant.' That is Cerna, through which we passed, and that is its name since Enna Aignech put Cerna, king of Ana, to death on that hill, and he put his steward to death in the east of that place.

" ' The Washing of the Horses of Dea,' I said. That is Ange, for in it the men of Dea washed their horses when they came from the battle of Magh Tuireadh. And it was called Ange, because the Tuatha De Danaan washed their horses in it.

" ' The Four-cornered Mandchuile,' I said. That is Muincille. It is there Mann, the farmer, was, and there he made spells in his great four-cornered chambers underground, to keep off the plague from the cattle of Ireland in the time of Bresel Brec, king of Leinster.

" ' Great Crime,' I said. That is Ailbine. There was a king here in Ireland, Ruad, son of Rigdond of Munster. He had an appointment of meeting with foreigners, and he set out for the meeting round the south of Alban with three ships, and thirty men were in each ship. But the ships were stopped, and were held from below in the middle of the sea, and throwing jewels and precious things into the sea did not get them off. Then lots were cast among them who should go into the sea and find out what was holding them. The lot fell on the king himself, Ruad, son of Rigdond, and he leaped into the sea, and it closed over him. He lit upon a large plain, where nine beautiful women met him, and they confessed that it was they themselves had stopped the ships, the way that he might come to them. And he stopped with them nine days, and they gave him nine vessels of gold; and through the length of that time his men were not able to go on, through the power of the women. When he was going away, a woman of them said she would bear him a son, and that he must come back to them and bring away his son, when he would be coming from the east.

"Then he joined his men, and they went on their voyage, and they stopped away seven years, and then they came back by a different way, and they did not go near the same spot. They landed in the bay, and the sea-women came up to them there, and the men heard them playing music in their brazen ship. And then the women came to the shore, and they put the boy out of the ship on the land where the men were. And the harbour was stony and rocky, and the boy slipped and fell on one of the rocks, so that he died there. And the women saw it, and they cried all together, 'Olbine, Olbine,' that is 'Great Crime.' And it is from that it is called Ailbine.

"'The Remnants of the Great Feast,' I said. That is Tailne. It was there the great feast was given to Lugh, son of Ethlenn, to comfort him after the battle of Magh Tuireadh, for that was his wedding feast of kingship.

"'In the Garden of Lugh, to the daughters of Tethra's nephew,' I said; for Forgall Manach is sister's son of Tethra, king of the Fomor.

"As to the account of myself I gave her, there are

two rivers in the land of Ross; Conchubar is the name
of one of them, and it mixes with the other; and I am
the nephew of Conchubar; and as to the plague that
comes on dogs, it is wild fierceness, and truly I am a
strong fighter of that plague, for I am wild and fierce in
battles and in fights. And the Wood of Badb, that is
the land of Ross, the Wood of the Morrigu, the Battle
Crow, the Goddess of Battle.

"And when she said that no man should come to the
plain of her breasts until he had killed three times nine
men with one blow, and yet had saved one man from
each nine, it is what she meant, that three brothers of
her own will be guarding her, Ibur and Seibur and Catt,
and a company of nine with each of them. And it is
what I must do, I must strike a blow on each nine, from
which eight will die, but no stroke will reach any of her
brothers among them; and I must carry her and her
foster-sister, with their share of gold and silver, out of
the dun of Forgall.

"'Go out from Samhain to Oimell,' she said. That
is, that I shall fight without harm to myself from
Samhain, the end of summer, to Oimell, the beginning
of spring; and from the beginning of spring to Beltaine,
and from that to Bron Trogain. For Oi, in the
language of poetry, is a name for sheep, and Oimell is
the time when the sheep come out and are milked, and
Suain is a gentle sound, and it is at Samhain that gentle
voices sound; and Beltaine is a favouring fire; for it is
at that time the Druids used to make fires with spells
and to drive the cattle between them against the plagues
every year. And Bron Trogain, that is the beginning
of autumn, for it is then the earth is in labour, that is, the
earth under fruit, Bron Trogain, the trouble of the earth."

Then Cuchulain went on his way, and he slept that
night in Emain Macha.

When Forgall came back to his dun, and his lords of land with him, their daughters were telling them of the young man that had come in a splendid chariot, and how himself and Emer had been talking together, and they could not understand their talk with one another. The lords of land told this to Forgall, and it is what he said, "You may be sure it is the mad boy from Emain Macha has been here, and he and the girl have fallen in love with one another. But they will gain nothing by that," he said; "for it is I will hinder them."

With that Forgall went out to Emain, with the appearance of a foreigner on him, and he gave out that he was sent by the king of the Gall, to speak with Conchubar, and to bring him a present of golden treasures, and wine of the Gall, and many other things. And he brought some of his men with him, and there was a great welcome before them.

And on the third day, Cuchulain and Conall and other chariot chiefs of Ulster were praised before him, and he said it was right for them to be praised, and that they did wonderful feats, and Cuchulain above them all. But he said that if Cuchulain would go to Scathach, the woman-warrior that lived in the east of Alban, his skill would be more wonderful still, for he could not have perfect knowledge of the feats of a warrior without that.

But his reason for saying this was that he thought if Cuchulain set out, he would never come back again, through the dangers he would put around him on the journey, and through the wildness and the fierceness of the people about Scathach.

So then Forgall went home, and Cuchulain rose up in the morning, and made ready to set out for Alban, and Laegaire Buadach, the Battle Winner, and Conall Cearnach said they would go with him. But first Cuchulain went across the plain of Bregia to visit Emer, and to talk with her before going in the ship. And she told him how it was Forgall had gone to Emain, and had advised him to go and learn warriors' feats, the way they two might not meet again. Then each of them promised to be true to the other till they would meet again, unless death should come between them, and they said farewell to one another, and Cuchulain turned towards Alban.

When they came there, they stopped for a while at the forge of Donall, the smith, and then they set out to go to the east of Alban. But before they had gone far, a vision came before their eyes of Emain Macha, and Laegaire and Conall were not able to pass by it, and they turned back. It was Forgall raised that vision, to draw them away from Cuchulain, that he might be in the more danger, being alone. Then Cuchulain went on by himself on a strange road, and he was sad and tired and down-hearted for the loss of his comrades, but he held to his word that he would not go back to Emain without finding Scathach, even if he should die in the attempt.

But now he was astray and ignorant, and not knowing which way to take, and he saw a terrible great beast like a lion coming towards him, and it watching him, but it did not try to harm him. Whatever way he went, the beast went before him, and then it stopped and turned its side to him. So he made a leap and was on its back, and he did not guide it, but went whatever way it chose. They travelled like that through four days, till they came to the end of the bounds of men, and to an island where lads were rowing in a small loch ; and the lads began to laugh when they saw a beast of that sort, and a man riding it. And then Cuchulain leaped off, and the beast left him, and he bade it farewell.

He passed on till he came to a large house in a deep

valley, and a comely young girl in it, and she spoke to
him, and bade him welcome. "A welcome before you,
Cuchulain," she said. He asked her how did she know
him, and she said, "I was a foster-child of Wulfkin, the
Saxon, the time you came there to learn sweet speech
from him." And she gave him meat and drink, and he
went away from her. Then he met with a young man,
and he gave him the same welcome, and he said his
name was Eochu, and they talked together, and
Cuchulain asked him what was the way to Scathach's
dun. The young man told him the way, across the
Plain of Ill-Luck, that lay before him, and he said that
on the near side of the plain the feet of men would stick
fast, and on the far side every blade of grass would rise
and hold them fast on its points. And he gave him a
wheel, and bade him to follow its track across the one
half of the plain. And he gave him an apple along
with that, and bade him to throw it, and to follow the
way it went, till he would reach the end of the plain.
And he told him many other things that would happen
him, and how he would win a great name at the last.
And then each of them wished a blessing to the other,
and Cuchulain did as he bade him, and so he got across
the plain and went on his journey. And then, as the
young man had told him, he came to a valley, and it
full of monsters, sent there by Forgall to destroy him,
and only one narrow path through it, but he went
through it safely. And after that his road led through
a terrible, wild mountain. Then he came to the place
where Scathach's scholars were, and among them he
saw Ferdiad, son of Daman, and Naoise, Ainnle, and
Ardan, the three sons of Usnach, and when they knew
that he was from Ireland they welcomed him with
kisses, and asked for news of their own country. He
asked them where was Scathach. "In that island
beyond," they said. "What way must I take to reach

her ? " he asked. " By the bridge of the cliff," they said, " and no man can cross it till he has proved himself a champion, and many a king's son has got his death there."

And this is the way the bridge was : the two ends of it were low, and the middle was high, and whenever any one would leap on it, the first time it would narrow till it was as narrow as the hair of a man's head, and the second time it would shorten till it was as short as an inch, and the third time it would get slippery till it was as slippery as an eel of the river, and the fourth time it would rise up on high against you till it was as tall as the mast of a ship.

All the warriors and people on the lawn came down to see Cuchulain making his attempt to cross the bridge, and he tried three times to do it, and he could not, and the others were laughing at him, that he should think he could cross it, and he so young. Then his anger came on him, and the hero light shone round his head, and it was not the appearance of a man that was on him, but the appearance of a god ; and he leaped upon the end of the bridge and made the hero's salmon leap, so that he landed on the middle of it, and he reached the other end of the bridge before it could raise itself fully up, and threw himself from it, and was on the ground of the island where Scathach's sunny house was, and it having seven great doors, and seven great windows between every two doors, and three times fifty couches between every two windows, and three times fifty young girls, with scarlet cloaks and beautiful blue clothing on them, waiting on Scathach.

And Scathach's daughter, Uacthach, was sitting by a window, and when she saw the young man, and he a stranger, and comeliest of the men of Ireland, making his attempt to cross the bridge, she loved him, and her face and her colour began to change continually, so that now she would be as white as a little flower, and then again she would grow crimson red. And in her needlework that she was doing, she would put the gold thread where the silver thread should be, and the silver thread in the place where the gold thread should be. And when Scathach saw that, she said : " I think this young man has pleased you." And Uacthach said : " There would be great grief on me indeed, were he not to return alive to his own people, in whatever part of the world they may be, for I know there is surely some one to whom it would be great anguish to know the way he is now."

Then, when Cuchulain had crossed the bridge, he went up to the house, and struck the door with the shaft of his spear, so that it went through it. And when Scathach was told that, she said, " Truly this must be some one who has finished his training in some other place." Then Uacthach opened the door for him, and he asked for Scathach, and Uacthach told him where she was, and what he had best do when he found her. So he went out to the place where she was teaching her two sons, Cuar and Cett, under the great yew-tree ; and he took his sword and put its point between her breasts, and he threatened her with a dreadful death if she would not take him as her pupil, and if she would not teach him all her own skill in arms. So she promised him she would do that.

Now it was while Cuchulain was with Scathach that a great king in Munster, Lugaid, son of Ros, went northward with twelve chariot chiefs to look for a wife among the daughters of the men of Mac Rossa, but they had all been promised before.

And when Forgall Manach heard this, he went to Emain, and he told Lugaid that the best of the maidens of Ireland, both as to form and behaviour and handiwork, was in his house unwed. Lugaid said he was well pleased to hear that, and Forgall promised him his daughter Emer in marriage. And to the twelve chariot chiefs that were with him, he promised twelve daughters of twelve lords of land in Bregia, and Lugaid went back with him to his dun for the wedding.

But whem Emer was brought to Lugaid to sit by his side, she laid one of her hands on each side of his face, and she said on the truth of her good name and of her life, that it was Cuchulain she loved, although her father was against him, and that no one that was an honourable man should force her to be his wife.

Then Lugaid did not dare take her, for he was in dread of Cuchulain, and so he returned home again.

As to Cuchulain, after he had been a good time with Scathach, a war began between herself and Aoife, queen of the tribes that were round about. The armies were going out to fight, but Cuchulain was not with them, for Scathach had given him a sleeping-drink that would keep him safe and quiet till the fight would be over, for she was afraid some harm would come to him if he met Aoife, for she was the greatest woman-warrior in the world, and she understood enchantments and witchcraft. But after one hour, Cuchulain started up out of his sleep, for the sleeping-drink that would have held any other man for a day and a night, held him for only that length of time. And he followed after the army, and he met with the two sons of Scathach, and they three went against the three sons of Ilsuanach, three of the best warriors of Aoife, and it was by Cuchulain they were killed, one after the other.

On the morning of the morrow the fight was begun again, and the two sons of Scathach were going up the path of feats to fight against three others of the best champions of Aoife, Cire, Bire, and Blaicne, sons of Ess Enchenn. When Scathach saw them going up she gave a sigh, for she was afraid for her two sons, but just then Cuchulain came up with them, and he leaped before them on to the path of feats, and met the three champions, and all three fell by him.

When Aoife saw that her best champions were after being killed, she challenged Scathach to fight against herself, but Cuchulain went out in her place. And before he went, he asked Scathach, "What things does Aoife think most of in all the world?" "Her two horses and her chariot and her chariot-driver," said Scathach.

So then Cuchulain and Aoife attacked one another and began a fierce fight, and she broke Cuchulain's spear in pieces, and his sword she broke off at the hilt. Then Cuchulain called out, "Look, the chariot and the horses and the driver of Aoife are fallen down into the valley and are lost!" At that Aoife looked about her, and Cuchulain took a sudden hold of her, and lifted her on his shoulders, and brought her down to where the army was, and laid her on the ground, and held his sword to her breast, and she begged for her life, and he gave it to her. And after that she made peace with Scathach, and bound herself by sureties not to go against her again. And she gave her love to Cuchulain; and out of that love great sorrow came afterwards.

And as Cuchulain was going home by the narrow path, he met an old hag, and she blind of the left eye. She asked him to leave room for her to pass by, but he said there was no room on that path, unless he would throw himself down the great sea-cliff that was on the one side of it. But she asked him again to leave the road to her, and he would not refuse, and he dropped down the cliff, with only his one hand keeping a hold of the path. Then she came up, and as she passed him, she gave a hit of her foot at his hand, the way he would leave his hold and drop into the sea. But at that, he gave a leap up again on the path, and struck off the hag's head. For she was Ess Enchenn, the mother of the last three warriors that had fallen by him, and it was to destroy him she had come out to meet him, for she knew that under his rules of championship, he would make way for her when she asked it.

After that, he stayed for another while with Scathach, until he had learned all the arts of war and all the feats of a champion; and then a message came to him to come back to his own country, and he bade her farewell. And Scathach told him what would happen him in the time to come, for she had the Druid gift; and she told him there were great dangers before him, and that he would have to fight against great armies, and he alone; and that he would scatter his enemies, so that his name would come again to Alban; but that his life would not be long, for he would die in his full strength.

Then Cuchulain went on board his ship to set out for Ireland, and in the same ship with him were Lugaid and Luan, the two sons of Loch, and Ferbaeth and Larin and Ferdiad, and Durst, son of Derb.

On the night of Samhain they came to the island of Rechrainn, and Cuchulain left his ship and came to the strand. And there he heard a sound of crying, and he saw a beautiful young girl, and she sitting there alone. He asked her who was she, and what ailed her, and she said she was Devorgill, daughter of the king of Rechrainn, and that every year he was forced to pay a heavy tax to the Fomor, and this year, when he could not pay it, they made him leave her there near the sea, till they would come and bring her away in place of it.

"Where do these men come from?" said Cuchulain. "From that far country over there," she said, "and let you not stop here or they will see you when they come." But Cuchulain would not leave her, and presently three fierce men of the Fomor landed in the bay, and made straight for the spot where the girl was.   But before they had time to lay a hand on her, Cuchulain leaped on them and he killed the three of them, one after the other. The last man wounded him in the arm, and the girl tore a strip from her dress, and gave it to him to bind round the wound.   And then she ran to her father's house and told him all that had happened.   After that Cuchulain came to the king's house, like any other guest, and his companions with him, and Conall Cearnach and Laegaire Buadach were there before them, where they had been sent from Emain Macha to collect tribute.   For at that time a tribute was paid to Ulster from the islands of the Gall.

And they were all talking about the escape Devorgill had, and some were boasting that it was they themselves had saved her, for she could not be sure who it was had come to her, because of the dusk of the evening.   Then there was water brought for them all to wash before they would go to the feast; and when it came to Cuchulain's turn to bare his arms, she knew by the strip of her dress that was bound about it, that it was he had saved her. " I will give the girl to you as your wife," said the king, " and I myself will pay her wedding portion."   " Not so," said Cuchulain, " for I must make no delay in going back to Ireland."

So then he made his way back to Emain Macha, and he told his whole story and all that had happened him. And as soon as he had rested from the journey, he set out to look for Emer at her father's house.   But Forgall and his sons had heard he was come home again, and they had made the place so strong, and they kept so good a watch round it, that for the whole length of a year he could not get so much as a sight of her.

It was one day at that time he went down to the shore of Lough Cuan with Laeg, his chariot-driver, and

with Lugaid. And when they were there, they saw two
birds coming over the sea. Cuchulain put a stone in his
sling, and made a cast at the birds, and hit one of them.
And when they came to where the birds were, they
found in their place two women, and one of them the
most beautiful in the world, and they were Devorgill,
daughter of the king of Rechrainn, that had come from
her own country to find Cuchulain, and her serving-maid
along with her ; and it was Devorgill that Cuchulain had
hit with the stone. "It is a bad thing you have done,
Cuchulain," she said, "for it was to find you I came,
and now you have wounded me." Then Cuchulain put
his mouth to the wound and sucked out the stone and
the blood along with it. And he said, "You cannot be
my wife, for I have drunk your blood. But I will give
you to my comrade," he said, "to Lugaid of the Red
Stripes." And so it was done, and Lugaid gave her
his love all through her life, and when she died he died
of the grief that was on him after her.

After that, Cuchulain got his scythe chariot made
ready, and he set out again for Forgall's dun. And
when he got there, he leaped with his hero leap over the
three walls, so that he was inside the court, and there he
made three attacks, so that eight men fell from each
attack, but one escaped in every troop of nine ; that is the
three brothers of Emer, Seibur and Ibur and Catt. And
Forgall made a leap from the wall of the court to escape
Cuchulain, and he fell in the leap and got his death from
the fall.

And then Cuchulain went out again, and brought
Emer with him and her foster-sister, and their two
loads of gold and silver.

And then they heard cries all around them, and
Scenmend, Forgall's sister, came following them with
her men, and came up with them at the ford ; and
Cuchulain killed her in the fight, and it is from that

it is called the Ford of Scenmend. And her men came
up with them again at the next ford, and he killed a
hundred of them there. "It is a great thing you have
done," said Emer. "You have killed a hundred
strong armed men ; and Glondath, the Ford of Deeds,
is the name that shall be on it for ever." Then they
came to Raeban, the white field, and he gave three great
angry blows to his enemies there, so that streams of
blood went over it on every side. "This white hill is a
hill of red sods to-day, through your work, Cuchulain,"
said Emer. And from that time it has been called the
Ford of the Sods.

Then they were overtaken again at another ford on
the Boinne, and Emer quitted the chariot, and
Cuchulain followed his enemies along the banks, so that
the sods were flying from the feet of the horses across
the ford northward ; and then he turned and followed
them northward, so that the sods flew over the ford
southward. And from that it is called Ath na Imfuait,
the Ford of the Two Clods. And at each of these fords
Cuchulain killed a hundred, and so he kept his word to
Emer, and he came safely out of it all, and they came
to Emain Macha, toward the fall of night.

And then Cuchulain was given the headship of the
young men of Ulster, of the warriors, the poets, the
trumpeters, the musicians, the three pipers, the three
jesters to say sharp words ; the three distributers of
fame. It is of them the poet spoke, and set out their
names, and it is what he said :—"The young men of
Ireland, when they were in the Red Branch, it is they
were the fairest of all hosts." And of Cuchulain he said,
"He is as hard as steel and as bright, Cuchulain, the
victorious son of Dechtire."

And then Cuchulain took Emer for his wife, after that
long courting, and all the hardships he had gone through.
And he brought her into the House of the Red Branch,

and Conchubar and all the chief men of Ulster gave her a great welcome.

It was at Emain Macha, that was sometimes called Macha of the Spears, Conchubar, the High King, had the Eachrais Uladh, the Assembly House of Ulster, and it was there he had his chief palace.

A fine palace it was, having three houses in it, the Royal House, and the Speckled House, and the House of the Red Branch.

In the Royal House there were three times fifty rooms, and the walls were made of red yew, with copper rivets. And Conchubar's own room was on the ground, and the walls of it faced with bronze, and silver up above, with gold birds on it, and their heads set with shining carbuncles; and there were nine partitions from the fire to the wall, and thirty feet the height of each partition. And there was a silver rod before Conchubar with three golden apples on it, and when he shook the rod or struck it, all in the house would be silent.

It was in the House of the Red Branch were kept the heads and the weapons of beaten enemies, and in the Speckled House were kept the swords and the shields and the spears of the heroes of Ulster. And it was called the Speckled House because of the brightness and the colours of the hilts of the swords, and the bright spears, green or grey, with rings and bands of silver and gold about them, and the gold and silver that were on the rims and the bosses of the shields, and the brightness of the drinking-cups and the horns.

It was the custom with the men of the Red Branch, if one of them heard a word of insult, to get satisfaction for it on the moment. He would get up in the feasting hall itself, and make his attack; and it was to prevent that, the arms were kept together in one place. Conchubar's shield, the Ochain, that is the Moaning One, was hanging there; whenever Conchubar would be in danger, it would moan, and all the shields of Ulster would moan in answer to it. And Conall Cearnach's Lam-tapaid, the Quick Hand, was in it. And Fergus's Leochain, and Dubthach's Uathach, and Laegaire's Nithach; and Sencha's Sciath-arglan and Celthair's Comla Catha, the Gate of Battle, and a great many others along with these.

And Cuchulain's shield was there, and the way he got it was this.

There was a law made by the men of the Red Branch that the carved device on every shield should be different from every other. And the name of the man that used to make the shields was Mac Enge. Cuchulain went to him after coming back from Scathach, and bade him make him a shield, and put some new device on it. " I cannot do that," said Mac Enge, " for all I can do I have done already on the shields of the men of Ulster." There was anger on Cuchulain then, and he threatened Mac Enge with death, was he, or was he not, under Conchubar's protection.

Mac Enge was greatly put out at what had happened, and he was thinking what was best for him to do, when he saw a man coming towards him. " There is some trouble on you," he said. " There is, indeed," said the shield-maker, " for I am in danger of death unless I make a shield for Cuchulain." " Clear out your workshop," said the strange man, "and spread ashes a foot deep on the floor."

And when this was done, Mac Enge saw the man coming over the outer wall to him again, and a fork in his hand, and it having two prongs. And he put one of the prongs in the ashes, and with the other he made the pattern that was to be cut on Cuchulain's shield. And so Cuchulain got it, and the name it had was Dubhan, the Black One.

And as to Cuchulain's sword that was hanging along

with the shield, its name was the Cruaidin Cailid-cheann; that is, the Hard, Hard Headed. And it had a hilt of gold with ornaments of silver, and if the point of the sword would be bent back to its hilt, it would come as straight as a rod back again. It would cut a hair on the water, or it would cut a hair off the head without touching the skin, or it would cut a man in two, and the one half of him would not miss the other for some time after.

And as to Cuchulain's spear, the Gae Bulg, whether it was or was not kept in the Speckled House, this is the way he came by it. There were two monsters fighting in the sea one time, the Curruid and the Coinchenn their names were, and at the last the Coinchenn made for the strand to escape; but the other followed him and killed him there.

Then Bolg, son of Buan, a champion of the eastern part of the world, found the bones of the Coinchenn on the strand, and he made a spear with them. And he gave it to a great fighting man, the son of Jubar, and it went from one to another till it came to the woman - champion, Aoife. And Aoife gave it to Cuchulain, and he brought it to Ireland. And it was with it he killed his own son, and his friend Ferdiad afterwards.

There were three hundred and sixty-five men belonging to Conchubar's household; and one among them served the supper every night, and when the year came round, he would take his turn again. And it is not a small thing that supper was: beef and pork and beer for every man. But the three days before and the three days after Samhain, the chief men of Ulster used to come together, and to eat together in Conchubar's palace, and Conchubar himself took charge of the supper at that feast; for every man that did not come on Samhain night, his wits would go from him, and it was as well to make his grave and to put his memorial stone over him the next day.

And there were a great many poets and learned men used to come to Conchubar's court, for they were made welcome there when they were driven out of other places. Cathbad, the Druid, was among them, and his son, bright-faced Geanann, and Sencha, and Ferceirtne, that was very learned, and Morann, that could not give a wrong judgment, for if he did, the collar round his neck would tighten; and many others.

Adhna was the chief poet there at one time, and after he died Athairne was made chief poet of Ulster in his place. But Neidhe, Adhna's son, came back from Alban, expecting to be made chief poet. And it was the waves of the sea, breaking on the strand where he was, that told him of his father's death. And when he got to Emain, he went into the palace and sat down in the chief poet's chair, that he found empty, and put the chief poet's cloak about him, that was lying there, and that was ornamented with beautiful birds' feathers. And then Athairne came in and found him there, and they began an argument with one another in the language of poetry, and Conchubar and all the chief men of Ulster came in to listen to them, and some of the other poets joined in the argument.

And Neidhe proved himself to be the best, but if he did, as soon as it was given in his favour, he came down from the chair, and took off the cloak and put it about Athairne, and said that, his father being dead, he would take him for his master.

So Athairne was chief poet, but no one had any great liking for him, for he was too fond of riches, and was no way hospitable or open-handed. It was he went to Midhir, and brought away secretly his three cranes of churlishness and denial, the way none of the men of Ireland would get a good reception if they would come to ask anything at his house. "Do not come, do not come," the first crane would say. "Get away, get away," the second would say. "Go past the house, past the house," the third would say to any one that came near it.

It was after that argument between Athairne and Neidhe, king Conchubar made a change in the laws. For it had been a law that no one that was not a poet could be a judge. But the language of the poets was hard to understand, and the king was vexed when he could understand but a small part of their argument. So he said that from that time out, any fitting man might be made judge, was he or was he not a poet. And all the people agreed to that, and the new law turned out very well in the end.

And the twelve chief heroes of Conchubar's Red Branch were these: Fergus, son of Rogh; Conall Cearnach, the Victorious; Laegaire Buadach, the Battle-Winner; Cuchulain, son of Sualtim; Eoghan, son of Durthact, chief of Fernmaige; Celthair, son of Uthecar; Dubthach Doel Uladh, the Beetle of Ulster; Muinremar, son of Geirgind; Cethern, son of Findtain; and Naoise, Ainnle, and Ardan, the three sons of Usnach.

BRICRIU'S FEAST, AND THE WAR OF WORDS OF THE WOMEN OF ULSTER

BRICRIU of the Bitter Tongue made a great feast one time for Conchubar, son of Ness, and for all the chief men of Ulster. He was the length of a year getting the feast ready, and he built a great house to hold it in at Dun-Rudraige. He built it in the likeness of the House of the Red Branch in Emain, but it was entirely beyond all the buildings of that time in shape and in substance, in plan and in ornament, in pillars and in facings, in doors and in carvings, so that it was spoken of in all parts. It was on the plan of the drinking-hall at Emain it was made inside, and it having nine divisions from hearth to wall, and every division faced with bronze that was overlaid with gold, thirty feet high. In the front part of the hall there was a royal seat made for Conchubar, high above all the other seats of the house. It was set with carbuncles and other precious stones of all colours, that shone like gold and silver, so that they made the night the same as the day ; and round about it were the twelve seats of the twelve heroes of Ulster.

Good as the material was, the work done on it was as good. It took six horses to bring home every beam, and the strength of six men to fix every pole, and thirty of the best skilled men in Ireland were ordering it and directing it.

Then Bricriu made a sunny parlour for himself, on a level with Conchubar's seat and the seats of the heroes of valour, and it had every sort of ornament, and windows of glass were put on every side of it, the way he could see the hall from his seat, for he knew the men of Ulster would not let him stop inside.

When he had finished building the hall and the sunny parlour, and had furnished them with quilts and coverings, beds and pillows, and with a full supply of meat and drink, so that nothing was wanting, he set out for Emain Macha to see Conchubar and the chief men of Ulster.

It happened that day they were all gathered together at Emain Macha, and they made him welcome, and they put him to sit beside Conchubar, and he said to Conchubar and to them all, "Come with me to a feast I have made ready." "I am willing to go," said Conchubar, "if the men of Ulster are willing."

But Fergus, son of Rogh, and the others, said: "We will not go, for if we do, our dead will be more than our living, after Bricriu has set us to quarrel with one another." "It will be worse for you if you do not come," said Bricriu. "What will you do if they do not go with you?" said Conchubar. "I will stir up strife," said Bricriu, "between the kings and the leaders, and the heroes of valour, and the swordsmen, till every one makes an end of the other, if they will not come with me to use my feast." "We will not go for the sake of pleasing you," said Conchubar. "I will stir up anger between father and son, so that they will be the death of one another," said Bricriu; "if I fail in doing that, I will make a quarrel between mother and daughter; if that fails, I will put the two breasts of every woman of Ulster striking one against the other, and destroying one another." "It is better for us to go," said Fergus. "Let us consult with the chief men of Ulster," said Sencha, son of Ailell. "Some harm will come of it," said Conchubar, "if we do not consult together against this man."

On that, all the chief men met together in council, and it is what Sencha advised: "It is best for you to get securities from Bricriu, as you have to go along with him; and put eight swordsmen around him, to make him leave the house as soon as he has laid out the feast for you." So Ferbenn Ferbeson, son of Conchubar, brought the answer to Bricriu. "I am satisfied to do that," said Bricriu. With that the men of Ulster set out from Emain, host, troop, and company under king, chief, and leader, and it was a good march they all made together to Dun-Rudraige.

Then Bricriu set himself to think how with the securities that were given for him, he could best manage to set the men of Ulster one against the other. After he had been thinking a while, he went over to Laegaire Buadach, son of Connad, son of Iliath. "All good be with you, Laegaire, Winner of Battles, you mighty mallet of Bregia, you hot hammer of Meath, you flame-red thunderbolt, what hinders you from getting the championship of Ireland for ever?" "If I want it I can get it," said Laegaire. "You will be head of all the champions of Ireland," said Bricriu, "if you do as I advise." "I will do that, indeed," said Laegaire.

"Well," said Bricriu, "if you can get the Champion's Portion at the feast in my house, the championship of Ireland will be yours for ever. And the Champion's Portion of my house is worth fighting for," he said, "for it is not the portion of a fool's house. There goes with it a vat of good wine, with room enough in it to hold three of the brave men of Ulster; with that a seven-year-old boar, that has been fed since it was born on no other thing but fresh milk, and fine meal in spring-time, curds and sweet milk in summer, the kernel of nuts and wheat in harvest, beef and broth in the winter; with that a seven-year-old bullock that never had in its mouth, since it was a sucking calf, either heather or twig tops, but only sweet milk and herbs, meadow hay and corn; along with that, five-score wheaten cakes made with honey. That is the Champion's Portion of my house. And since you are yourself the best hero among the men of Ulster," he said, "it is but right to give it to you; and that is my wish, you to get it. And at the end of the day, when the feast is spread out, let your chariot-driver rise up, and it is to him the Champion's Portion will be given." "There will be dead men if that is not done," said Laegaire. Then Bricriu laughed, for he liked to hear that.

When he had done stirring up Laegaire Buadach, he went on till he met with Conall Cearnach. "May good be with you, Conall," he said. "It is you are the hero of fights and of battles; it is many victories you have won up to this over the heroes of Ulster. By the time the men of Ulster cross the boundary of a strange country, it is three days and three nights in advance of them you are, over many a ford and river; it is you who protect their rear coming back again, so that no enemy can get past you or through you, or over you. What would hinder you from being given the Champion's Portion of Emain to hold for ever?" Great as was his treachery with Laegaire, he showed twice as much in what he said to Conall Cearnach.

When he had satisfied himself that Conall was stirred up to a quarrel, he went on to Cuchulain. "May all good be with you, Cuchulain, conqueror of Bregia, bright banner of the Lifé, darling of Emain, beloved by wives and by maidens, Cuchulain is no nickname for you to-day, for you are the champion of the men of Ulster; it is you keep off their great quarrels and disputes; it is you get justice for every man of them; it is you have what all the men of Ulster are wanting in; all the men of Ulster acknowledge that your bravery, your valour, and your deeds are beyond their own. Why, then, would you leave the Champion's Portion for some other one of the men of Ulster, when not one of them would be able to keep it from you?"

"By the god of my people," said Cuchulain, " whoever comes to try and keep it from me will lose his head." With that Bricriu left them and followed after the army, as if he had done nothing to stir up a quarrel at all.

After that they came to the feasting-houses and went in, and every one took his place, king, prince, landowner, swordsman, and young fighting man. One half of the house was set apart for Conchubar and his following, and the other half was kept for the wives of the heroes of Ulster.

And there were attending on Conchubar in the front part of the house Fergus, son of Rogh; Celthair, son of Uthecar; Eoghan, son of Durthact; the two sons of the king, Fiacha and Fiachaig; Fergus, son of Leti; Cuscraid, the Stutterer of Macha; Sencha, son of Ailell; the three sons of Fiachach, that is Rus and Dare and Imchad; Muinremar, son of Geirgind; Errge Echbel; Amergin, son of Ecit; Mend, son of Salchah; Dubthach Doel Uladh, the Beetle of Ulster; Feradach Find Fectnach; Fedelmid, son of Ilair Cheting; Furbaide Ferbend; Rochad, son of Fathemon; Laegaire Buadach; Conall Cearnach; Cuchulain; Conrad, son of Mornai; Erc, son of Fedelmid; Iollan, son of Fergus; Fintan, son of Nial; Cethern, son of Fintan; Factna, son of Sencad; Conla the False; Ailell the Honey-Tongued; the chief men of Ulster, with the young men and the song-makers.

While the feast was being spread out, the musicians and players made music for them. As soon as Bricriu had spread the feast with its well-tasting, savoury meats, he was ordered by his sureties to leave the hall on the moment; and they rose up with their drawn swords in their hands to put him out. So he and his followers went out, and when he was on the threshold of the house he turned and called out: "The Champion's Portion of my house is not the portion of a fool's house; let it be given to whoever you think the best hero of Ulster." And with that he left them.

Then the distributers rose up to divide the food, and the chariot-driver of Laegaire Buadach, Sedlang, son of Riangabra, rose up and said to them, "Let you give the Champion's Portion to Laegaire, for he has the best right to it of all the young heroes of Ulster."

Then Id, son of Riangabra, chariot-driver to Conall Cearnach, rose up, and bade them to give it to his master. But Laeg, son of Riangabra, said, "It is to Cuchulain it must be brought; and it is no disgrace for all the men of Ulster to give it to him, for it is he is the bravest of you all." "That is not true," said Conall, and Laegaire said the same.

With that they got up upon the floor, and put on their shields and took hold of their swords, and they attacked and struck at one another till the one half of the hall was as if on fire with the clashing of swords and spears, and the other half was as white as chalk with the whiteness of the shields. There was fear on the whole gathering; all the men were put from their places, and there was great anger on Conchubar himself and on Fergus, son of Rogh, to see the injustice and the hardship of two men fighting against one, Conall and Laegaire both together attacking Cuchulain; but there was no one among the men of Ulster dared part them till Sencha spoke to Conchubar. "It is time for you to part these men," he said.

With that, Conchubar and Fergus came between them, and the fighters let their hands drop to their sides. "Will you do as I advise?" said Sencha

"We will do it," they said. "Then my advice is," said Sencha, "for this night to divide the Champion's Portion among the whole gathering, and after that to let it be settled according to the judgment of Ailell, king of Connaught, for it will be better for the men of Ulster, this business to be settled in Cruachan."

So with that they sat down to the feast again, and gathered round the fire and drank and made merry.

All this time Bricriu and his wife were in their upper room, and from there he had seen how things were going on in the great hall. And he began to search his mind how he could best stir up the women to quarrel with one another as he had stirred up the men. When he had done searching his mind, it just chanced as he could have wished, that Fedelm of the Fresh Heart came from the hall with fifty women after her, laughing and merry. Bricriu went to meet her. "All good be with you to-night, wife of Laegaire Buadach. Fedelm of the Fresh Heart is no nickname for you, with respect to your appearance and your wisdom and your family. Conchubar, king of Ulster, is of your kindred; Laegaire Buadach is your husband. I would not think well of it that any of the women of Ulster should go before you into the hall, for it is at your heel that all the other women of Ulster should walk. If you go first into the hall to-night, you will be queen over them all for ever and ever."

Fedelm went on after that, the length of three ridges from the hall.

After that there came out Lendabair, the Favourite, daughter of Eoghan, son of Durthact, wife of Conall Cearnach.

Bricriu came over to her, and he said, "Good be with you, Lendabair; and that is no nickname, for you are the favourite and the darling of the men of the whole world, because of the brightness of your beauty. As far as your husband is beyond the whole world in bravery and in comeliness, so far are you before the women of Ulster." Great as his deceit was in what he said to Fedelm, it was twice as great in what he said to Lendabair.

Then Emer came out and fifty women after her. "Health be with you, Emer, daughter of Forgall Manach, wife of the best man in Ireland! Emer of the Beautiful Hair is no nickname for you; the kings and princes of Ireland are quarrelling with one another about you. So far as the sun outshines the stars of heaven, so far do you outshine the women of the whole world in form, and shape, and birth, in youth, and beauty, and nicety, in good name, and wisdom, and speech." However great his deceit was towards the other women, it was twice as much towards Emer.

The three women went on then till they met at one spot, three ridges from the house, but none of them knew that Bricriu had been speaking to the other. They set out then to go back to the house. Their walk was even and quiet and easy on the first ridge; hardly did one of them put her foot before the other. But on the next ridge their steps were closer and quicker; and when they came to the ridge next the house, it was hardly one of them could keep up with the other, so that they took up their skirts nearly to their knees, each one trying to get first into the hall, because of what Bricriu had said to them, that whoever would be first to enter the house, would be queen of the whole province. And such was the noise they made in their race, that it was like the noise of forty chariots coming. The whole palace shook, and all the men started up for their arms, striking against one another.

"Stop," said Sencha, "it is not enemies that are coming, it is Bricriu has set the women quarrelling

By the god of my people!" he said, "unless the hall is shut against them, those that are dead among us will be more than those that are living." With that the doorkeepers shut the doors. But Emer was quicker than the other women, and outran them, and put her back against the door, and called to the doorkeepers before the other women came up, so that the men rose up, each of them to open the door before his own wife, so that she might be the first to come within.

"It is a bad night this will be," said Conchubar; and he struck the silver rod he had in his hand against the bronze post of the hall, and they all sat down. "Quiet yourselves," said Sencha; "it is not a war of arms we are going to have here, it is a war of words." Each woman then put herself under the protection of her husband outside, and then there followed the war of words of the women of Ulster.

Fedelm of the Fresh Heart was the first to speak, and it is what she said:

"The mother who bore me was free, noble, equal to my father in rank and in race; the blood that is in me is royal; I was brought up like one of royal blood. I am counted beautiful in form and in shape and in appearance; I was brought up to good behaviour, to courage, to mannerly ways. Look at Laegaire, my husband, and what his red hand does for Ulster. It was by himself alone its boundaries were kept from the enemies that were as strong as all Ulster put together; he is a defence and a protection against wounds; he is beyond all the heroes; his victories are greater than their victories. Why should not I, Fedelm, the beautiful, the lovely, the joyful, be the first to step into the drinking-hall to-night?"

Then Lendabair spoke, and it is what she said;

"I myself have beauty too, and good sense and good

carriage; it is I should walk into the hall with free, even steps before all the women of Ulster.

" For my husband is pleasant Conall of the great shield, the Victorious; he is proud, going with brave steps up to the spears of the fight; he is proud coming back to me after it, with the heads of his enemies in his hands.

" He brings his hard sword into the battle for Ulster; he defends every ford or he destroys it to keep out the enemy; he is a hero will have a stone raised over him.

" The son of noble Amergin, who can speak against his courage or his deeds? It is Conall who leads the heroes.

" All eyes look on the glory of Lendabair; why would she not go first into the hall of the king?"

Then Emer spoke, and it is what she said:

" There is no woman comes up to me in appearance, in shape, in wisdom; there is no one comes up to me for goodness of form, or brightness of eye, or good sense, or kindness, or good behaviour.

" No one has the joy of loving or the strength of loving that I have; all Ulster desires me; surely I am a nut of the heart. If I were a light woman, there would not be a husband left to any of you to-morrow.

" And my husband is Cuchulain. It is he is not a hound that is weak; there is blood on his spear, there is blood on his sword, his white body is black with blood, his soft skin is furrowed with sword cuts, there are many wounds on his thigh.

" But the flame of his eyes is turned westward; he is the strong protector; his chariot is red, its cushions are red; he fights from over the ears of horses, from over the breath of men; he leaps in the air like a salmon when he makes his hero leap; he does strange feats, the dark feat, the blind feat, the feat of nine; he breaks down armies in the hard fight; he saves the life of proud armies; he finds joy in the terror of the ignorant.

"Your fine heroes of Ulster are not worth a stalk of grass compared with my husband, Cuchulain, letting on to have a woman's sickness on them; he is like the clear red blood, they are like the scum .and the leavings, worth no more than a stalk of grass.

"Your fine women of Ulster, they are shaped like cows and led like cows, when they are put beside the wife of Cuchulain."

"When the men in the hall heard what the women said, Laegaire and Conall made a rush at the wall, and broke a plank out of it at their own height, to let their own wives in. But Cuchulain raised up that part of the house that was opposite to his place, so that the stars and the sky could be seen through the wall. By that opening Emer came in with the fifty women that waited on her, and with them the women that waited on the other two. None of the other women could be compared at all with Emer, and no one at all could be compared with her husband. And then Cuchulain let the wall he had lifted fall suddenly again, so that seven feet of it went into the ground, and the whole house shook, and Bricriu's upper room was laid flat in such a way that Bricriu himself and his wife were thrown into the dirt among the dogs. "My grief," cried Bricriu, "enemies are come in!" And he got up quickly and took a turn round, and he saw that the hall was now crooked and leaning entirely to one side. He clapped his hands together and went inside, but he was so covered with dirt that none of the Ulster people could know him, it was only by his way of speaking they made out who he was.

Then he said, from the middle of the floor, "It is a pity I ever made a feast for you, men of Ulster.

My house is more to me than everything else I have. I put *geasa*, that is, bonds, on you, not to drink or to eat or to sleep till you leave my house the same way as you found it." At that, all the men of Ulster went out and tried to pull the house straight, but they did not raise it by so much as a hand's breadth.

"What are we to do?" they said. "There is nothing for you to do," said Sencha, "but to ask the man that pulled it crooked to set it straight again."

Upon that they bid Cuchulain to put the wall up straight again, and Bricriu said, "O king of the heroes of Ireland, unless you can set it up straight, there is no man in the world can do it." And all the men of Ulster begged and prayed of Cuchulain to settle the matter. And that they might not have to go without food or drink, Cuchulain rose up and tried to lift the house with a tug, and he failed. Anger came on him then, and the hero light shone about him, and he put out all his strength, and strained himself till a man's foot could find place between each of his ribs, and he lifted the house up till it was as straight as it was before. After that they enjoyed the feast, with the chief men on the one side round about Conchubar, High King of Ulster, and their wives on the other side—Fedelm of the Nine Shapes (nine shapes she could take on, and each shape more beautiful than the other), and Findchoem, daughter of Cathbad, wife of Amergin of the Iron Jaw, and Devorgill, wife of Lugaid of the Red Stripes, besides Emer, and Fedelm of the Fresh Heart, and Lendabair; and it would be too long to count and to tell of all the other noble women besides.

There was soon a buzzing of words in the hall again, with the women praising their men, as if to stir up another quarrel between them. Then Sencha, son of

Ailell, got up and shook his bell branch, and they all stopped to listen to him, and then to quiet the women he said :

"Have done with this word-fighting, lest you drive the men of Ulster to grow white-faced in the anger and the pride of battle with one another.

"It is through the fault of women the shields of men are broken, heroes go out to fight and struggle with one another in their anger.

"It is the folly of women brings men to do these things, to bruise what they cannot bind up again, to strike down what they cannot raise up again. Wives of heroes, keep yourself from this."

But Emer answered him, and it is what she said :

"It is right for me to speak, Sencha, and I the wife of the comely, pleasant hero, who is beyond all others in beauty, in wisdom, in speaking, since the learning that was easy to him is done with.

"No one can do his feats, the over-breath feat, the apple feat, the ghost feat, the screw feat, the cat feat, the red-whirling feat, the barbed-spear feat, the quick stroke, the fire of the mouth, the hero's cry, the wheel feat, the sword-edge feat; no one can throw himself against hard-spiked places the way he does.

"There is no one is his equal in youth, in form, in brightness, in birth, in mind, in voice, in bravery, in boldness, in fire, in skill; no one is his equal in hunting, in running, in strength, in victories, in greatness. There is no man to be found who can be put beside Cuchulain."

"If it is truth you are speaking, Emer," said Conall Cearnach, "let this lad of feats stand up, that we may see them."

"I will not," said Cuchulain. "I am tired and broken to-day, I will do no more till after I have had food and sleep." It was true what he said, for it was on that morning he had met with the Grey of Macha by the side of the grey lake at Slieve Fuad. When it came out of the lake, Cuchulain slipped his hands round the neck of the horse, and the two of them struggled and wrestled with one another, and in that way they went all round Ireland, till late in the day he brought the horse home to Emain. It was in the same way he got the Black Sainglain from the black lake of Sainglen.

And Cuchulain said: " To-day myself and the Grey of Macha have gone through the great plains of Ireland, Bregia of Meath, the seashore marsh of Muirthemne Macha, through Moy Medba, Currech Cleitech Cerna, Lia of Linn Locharn, Fer Femen Fergna, Curros Domnand, Ros Roigne, and Eo. And now I would sooner eat and sleep than do any other thing. But I swear by the gods my people swear by," he said, " I would be ready to fight with any man of you if I had but my fill of food and of sleep." " Well," said Bricriu, " this has gone on long enough. Let food and drink be brought, and let the women's war be put a stop to till the feast is done."

They did so, and it was a pleasant time they had till the end of three days and three nights.

V

THE CHAMPIONSHIP OF ULSTER

AFTER they were gone back to Emain after Bricriu's feast, a quarrel began between Conall and Laegaire and Cuchulain about the Champion's Portion, and Conchubar and the chief men of Ulster came between them to settle it. And Conchubar bade them to go to Cruachan in Connaught, to have the matter judged by Ailell and by Maeve. "And if that fails you," he said, "what you have to do is to go to Curoi, son of Daire, at Slieve Mis, in Munster. And it is a true judgment he will give, for he is just and fair-minded, his house is open to guests, his hand is good in battle, in leading he is a king. He will give you a right judgment, but it is only a brave man will ask it from him, for he is wise in all sorts of enchantments, and can do things that no other man can do."

"We will go first to Cruachan," said Cuchulain. "I agree to that," said Laegaire. "Let us go then," said Conall Cearnach. "Let horses be brought, and your chariot yoked, Conall," said Cuchulain; "and go on the first." "I would not like that," said Conall. "That is no wonder," said Cuchulain, "for every one knows the awkwardness of your horses, and the unsteadiness of your chariot; it is so heavy that each of the wheels raises the sod on each side wherever it goes, the way that for the length of a year it is easy for the men of Ulster to know the track it has left after it."

"Do you hear that, Laegaire?" said Conall. "It is for you to go first." "Do not begin to mock at me," said Laegaire, "for I am good at crossing fords, and I am ready to go up and face a storm of spears before any man. But do not put me beside chariot kings till I practise going through hard and narrow places, and racing against single chariots, till the champion of a single chariot will be afraid to pass me."

With that Laegaire had his chariot yoked, and leaped into it. He drove over Magh da Gabal, the Plain of the Two Forks, over Bernaid na Foraire, the Gap of the Watch, over the Ford of Carpat Fergus, over the Ford of the Morrigu, to Caerthund Cluana da Dam, the Rowan Meadow of the Two Oxen, in the Fews of Firbuide; by the four ways, past Dundealgan, across Magh Slicech, the Peeled Plain, westward by Bregia. And it was not long till Conall Cearnach followed after him, and many of the chief men of Ulster with them.

But Cuchulain stayed behind the others, amusing the women of Ulster with his feats. He did nine feats with apples, nine with spears, and nine with knives, without ever letting one touch the other. And he took three times fifty needles from the women, and threw them up, one after the other, so that each needle went into the eye of the other, and in that way they were all joined together. Then he gave every woman her needle back into her own hand.

But Laeg, son of Riangabra, went to look for him, and reproached him, and said: "You pitiful squinter, your courage has gone from you! The Champion's Portion is lost to you, the men of Ulster have got to Cruachan before this." "I never thought of it, my Laeg," said Cuchulain; "but yoke the chariot for me now." So Laeg yoked it, and they set out on their journey. By that time the men of Ulster were come to Magh Breagh, the Fine Meadow; but Cuchulain, after he was roused up by Laeg, travelled so fast, and the Grey of Macha and the Black Sainglain went racing in such a way with his chariot across the whole province of Conchubar, across Slieve Fuad and the plain of Bregia, that he came up with the others before they came to Cruachan.

The noise the whole troop made was so great, going at such speed as they did, that a great shaking came on Cruachan, and the arms fell from the racks to the ground, and the whole of the dun began to shake, so that every man was trembling like a rush in a stream. On that Maeve said: "Since the day I first came to Cruachan I never before heard thunder, there being no clouds in the sky." Then Findabair of the Fair Eyebrows, daughter of Ailell and of Maeve, went up, for she had a bird's sight, to her sunny parlour over the great door of the fort, to tell them what was coming. "Dear mother," she said, "I see a chariot coming over the plain." "Tell me what is its appearance," said Maeve, "and the colour of its horses, and the appearance of the man that sits in it." "I see well," said Findabair, "the two horses that are in the chariot. Two fiery dappled greys, of the one colour, shape, and goodness, having the one speed, keeping the one pace; their ears pricked, their heads high, their nostrils broad, foreheads broad, manes and tails curled, thin-sided, wide-chested, galloping together. The chariot is made of fine wood with wicker-work newly polished, the yoke curved, with silver ornaments on it; it has two black wheels, soft looped yellow reins. I see in the chariot a big stout man, with reddish yellow hair, with long forked beard. He has a soft purple coat about him, and it striped with bright gold. His bronze shield is edged with gold; there is a five-pronged javelin at his wrist, a cover of strange birds' feathers over his head."

"I know well who that man is," said Maeve, and it is what she said: "A companion of kings, an old bestower of victories, a storm of war, a flame of judgment a long knife of victory that will cut us to pieces, mighty Laegaire of the Red Hand. His sword cuts through men as a knife cuts through a leek; his stroke is the back stroke of the wave to the land. And I swear by the gods my people swear by," she said, "if it is in anger and for fighting Laegaire Buadach is coming at us, that as leeks are cut close to the ground with a sharp knife, the same way we will be cut down, as many of us as are in Cruachan, unless we smooth down his anger by giving in to everything he asks."

"Good mother," said Findabair, "I see another chariot as good as the first coming over the plain." "Tell me what is its appearance," said Maeve.

"I see," she said, "yoked to the chariot, on the one side a red horse, taking strong, high strides across fords and splashes, over banks and gaps, over plains and hollows, with the quickness of birds that the quick eye loses in following. On the other side a bay horse of great strength; it is at full speed he races over the plain, between stones and hard places; he finds no hindrance in the land of oaks, hurrying on his way. A chariot of fine wood with wicker-work, on two wheels of bright bronze; its pole bright with silver, its frame very high and creaking, having a curved, firm yoke, with looped yellow reins.

"In the chariot a fair man, with wavy, hanging hair; his face white and red, his vest clean and white, his cloak blue and crimson, his shield brown with yellow bosses, its edge worked with bronze. In his hand a bright spear; a cover of the feathers of strange birds over the wicker frame of his chariot."

"I know who that man is," said Maeve, and she said then: "The growling of a lion; a flame that can cut like a sharpened stone; he heaps head on head, battle on battle. As a trout is cut upon red sandstone, so would the son of Finchoem cut us if he came on us in anger.

"For, by the oath of my people," she said, "as a speckled fish is beaten upon a shining red stone with iron rods, so would we be broken by Conall Cearnach, if he came against us."

"I see another chariot coming over the plain," said Findabair. "Tell me what its appearance is," said Maeve. "I see two horses of the one size and beauty, the one fierceness and speed, with ears pricked, heads high, spirited and powerful, with fine nostrils, wide foreheads, mane and tail curled, leaping together. The one grey, handsome, with broad thighs, eager, leaping, thundering, and trampling. As he goes, his fierce hoofs throw up sods of earth like a flock of swift birds after him. As he gallops on his way, he breathes out a blast of hot breath, a fire comes from his curbed jaws. The other, dark, small-headed, well-shaped, broad-hoofed, thin-sided, high-couraged, broad-backed, sure-footed, spirited; he takes long strides in the race; he leaps over streams, he throws off heaviness, he crosses the plains of the middle valley. They come together with fast, joyful steps, moving over the plain like a swift mountain mist, or like the speed of a hill hind, or like a hare on level ground, or like the rushing of a loud wind in winter.

"The chariot is of fine wood with wicker-work, having two iron wheels, a bright silver pole with bronze ornaments, a frame very high and creaking strengthened with iron, a curved yoke overlaid with gold, two soft looped yellow reins.

"I see in the chariot a dark, sad man, comeliest of the men of Ireland. A pleated crimson tunic about him, fastened at the breast with a brooch of inlaid gold; a long-sleeved linen cloak on him with a white hood embroidered with flame-red gold. His eyebrows as black as the blackness of a spit, seven lights in his eyes, seven colours about his head, love and fire in his look. Across his knees there lies a gold-hilted sword, there is a blood-red spear ready to his hand, a sharp-tempered blade with a shaft of wood. Over his shoulders a crimson shield with a rim of silver, overlaid with shapes of beasts in gold.

"There is before him in the chariot a driver, a very thin, tall, freckled man; very bright red hair, kept back from his face with a golden thread, a cup of gold at each side of his head. A short cloak about him with sleeves opening at the two elbows; in his hand a goad of red gold to guide his horses."

"That is truly a drop before a downpour," said Maeve. "I know well who that man is." And it is what she said: "Like the sound of an angry sea, like a great moving wave, with the madness of a wild beast that is vexed, he leaps through his enemies in the crash of battle, they hear their death in his shout. He heaps deed upon deed, head upon head; his is a name to be put in songs. As fresh malt is ground in the mill, so shall we be ground by Cuchulain.

"For I swear by the oath of my people," she said, "that as a mill of ten spokes grinds very hard malt, so he, with only himself, would grind us to dust and to gravel, if we had the whole province with us, unless his anger and his heat go down.

"And what way are the rest of the men of Ulster coming?" she said. And Findabair answered her, and it is what she said: "Hand to hand, arm to arm, side to side, shoulder to shoulder, wheel to wheel, axle to axle, that is the way they are coming. Their horses are coming on us like thunder on the roof, like heavy waves stirred by the storm; the trampling of their feet makes the earth shake under them."

And Maeve said, "Let our women be ready before them with vats of cold water; let the beds be made ready, bring the best of food, the best of ale. Open the courtyard, have a welcome before them, and surely they will not harm us."

Then Maeve went out by the high door of the dun into the courtyard, and three times fifty young girls attending her, with three vats of cold water to cool the heat of the three heroes in front of the rest. And she gave them their choice, would each man have a house for himself, or would they have one house for the three? "A house for each to himself," said Cuchulain. And when the rest of the men of Ulster came, Ailell and Maeve with their whole household went out and bade them welcome. "We are well pleased with the welcome," said Sencha for them.

After that, they all came into the fort and into the palace. They went round from one door to the other, and there was room for them all, and the musicians were playing music while everything was being made ready. And Conchubar, and Fergus, son of Rogh, were in Ailell's division, with nine others along with them, and there was a great feast made ready then, and they stopped there the length of three days and three nights.

At the end of that time Ailell asked Conchubar what was the business that had brought them there. And Sencha told him the whole story, about the quarrel of the women as to who should walk first, and the quarrel of their husbands for the Champion's Portion. "And they were not satisfied to be judged by any one but yourself," he said. Ailell did not seem to be well pleased at that. "Indeed, it was no friend of mine that left this judgment on me," he said. "There is no better judge than yourself," said Sencha. "Well," said Ailell, "you must give me time to think upon it." "Do not make too much delay," said Sencha, "for we cannot spare our heroes long from us." "Three days and three nights will be enough for me," said Ailell. "That much will not break friendship," said Sencha.

With that the men of Ulster went home to Emain, leaving Laegaire and Conall and Cuchulain to be judged by Ailell, and they left their blessing with Ailell and with Maeve, and their curse with Bricriu, because it was he had first started the quarrel.

That night the three heroes were given as good a feast as before, but they were put to eat it in a room by themselves. When night came on, three enchanted monsters, with the shape of cats, were let out from the cave that was in the hill of the Sidhe at Cruachan, to attack them. When Conall and Laegaire saw them, they got up into the rafters, leaving their food after them, and there they stayed till morning. Cuchulain did not leave his place, but when one of the monsters came to attack him, he gave a blow of his sword at its head; but the sword slipped off as if from a stone. Then the monster stayed quiet, and Cuchulain sat there through the night watching it. With the break of day the cats were gone, and Ailell came in and saw what way the three heroes were. "Are you not satisfied to give the Championship to Cuchulain, after this?" he said. "We are not," said Conall and Laegaire; "it is not against beasts we are used to fight, but against men."

Then Maeve said to them, "Go and spend the night with my foster-father, Ercol, and his wife Garmna." So they went, but first they were given their choice of food for their horses. Conall and Laegaire chose oats two years old for theirs, but Cuchulain chose barley grain for his. Then they set out, racing all the way, and Cuchulain winning the race.

Ercol and Garmna bade them welcome, and they knew it was to try them they had been sent there, so they sent them out that night, one after the other, to fight with the witches of the valley.

Laegaire went first, but he could not stand against them, and he came back, and left his arms and his clothes with them.

Then Conall went, and he was driven back, and left his spear with them, but he brought his sword that was his best weapon away with him.

Then Cuchulain went down into the valley and the witches screamed at him and attacked him, and he and they fought together till his spear was in splinters, his shield broken and his clothes torn off him. The witches were beating him and getting the better of him, but Laeg saw it, and he called out. "O Cuchulain," he said, "you poor coward, you squinting clown! Your courage is gone from you, witches to be beating you!" Then great anger came on Cuchulain, and he turned on the witches and cut and gashed them till the valley was filled with their blood, and he brought away their cloaks of battle with him, and went back to the house where his comrades were. And Garmna and her daughter Buan made much of him and bade him welcome.

They slept there that night, and the next day Ercol challenged them to come one by one, each man with his horse, to fight against himself and his horse. Laegaire was the first to go against him, and his horse was killed by Ercol's horse, and he himself was overcome by Ercol, so that he took to flight, and did not stop till he got back to Cruachan, and he brought the story there that both his companions had been killed by Ercol. Conall was the next to run away, after his horse being killed by Ercol's horse; and his servant Rathand was drowned in the river as he ran, and it takes its name after him, Snam Rathand, from that day.

But the Grey of Macha killed Ercol's horse, and Cuchulain put down Ercol and tied him behind his chariot and set out for Cruachan. And Buan, Garmna's daughter, ran out after the chariot for love of Cuchulain to follow him. And she knew the track of his chariot, for it was no roundabout track it used to take, but to be breaking through gaps or going over them; and in following it at last she gave a great leap and fell, and her forehead struck against a rock, and she died; and it is from this the place was given the name of Buan's Grave.

And when Conall and Cuchulain got back to Cruachan, they found the people of the dun keening them, for by the report Laegaire brought, they were sure they had been killed.

Then Ailell went to his inner room, and leaned his back against the wall, for he was not quiet in his mind, and he knew there was danger in whatever judgment he might give; and he had not eaten or slept for three days and three nights. Then Maeve said to him, "It is a coward you are, and if you do not settle this matter I will settle it myself." "It is hard for me to give judgment," said Ailell, "it is a misfortune for any one to have to do it." "It is easy enough," said Maeve, "for Laegaire and Conall Cearnach are as different as bronze and silver, and Conall Cearnach and Cuchulain are as different as silver and red gold."

After a while, when Maeve had searched her mind, Laegaire Buadach was called to her. "Welcome, Laegaire Buadach," she said, "it is right for you to have the Champion's Portion. We give you the headship of the heroes of Ireland from this out, and the Champion's Portion, and along with that this cup of bronze, having a bird in raised silver on the bottom. Take it with you as a token of the judgment, but let no one see it till you come to Conchubar and his Red Branch at the end of the day. When the Champion's Portion is set out, then bring out your cup in the presence of all the great men of Ulster, and not one of them will dispute it with you any more, for they will know by this token that the Championship has been given to you." With that, the cup was given to him with its full of rich wine, and he drank it off at a draught. "Now you have the Championship," said Maeve; "and I wish you may enjoy it a hundred years at the head of all Ulster."

So Laegaire left her, and Conall Cearnach was called up to the queen. "Welcome, Conall Cearnach," she said; "it is right for us to give you the Champion's Portion, and a silver cup along with it, having a bird on the bottom in raised gold." And she said the same to him as she had said to Laegaire before.

Then Conall went away, and a messenger was sent to bring Cuchulain. "Come up to speak with the king and queen," said the messenger.

Cuchulain was playing chess at the time with Laeg, his chariot-driver. "I am not a fool to be mocked at," he said, and he hurled one of the chessmen at the messenger, and hit him between the eyes, so that it is hardly he could get back to Ailell and Maeve.

"By my word," said Maeve, "this Cuchulain is hard to deal with." And then she came down herself to Cuchulain, and put her two arms round his neck. "Give your flattery to some other one," said Cuchulain.

But Maeve said, "Great son of Ulster, flame of the heroes of Ireland, there is no flattery in our mind when it is you we have to do with. For if all the heroes of Ireland should come here, it is to you we would give the Champion's Portion, for as to bravery and a great name, and as to youth and great deeds, it is well-known that you are far beyond all the men of Ireland."

Cuchulain rose up then, and went with Maeve into the palace, and Ailell gave him a great welcome. And he was given a gold cup full of wine, and it having on the bottom of it a bird in precious stones. "Now, you have the Championship," said Maeve, "and it is my wish you may enjoy it a hundred years at the head of all the heroes of Ulster." "And besides that," Ailell and Maeve said, "it is our judgment, that as much as you are beyond the heroes of Ulster, so far is your wife beyond their wives. And we think it right that she should walk before all the women of Ulster when they go together into the drinking-hall."

Then Cuchulain drank at one draught the full of the cup, and bade farewell to the king and the queen and the whole household. And he went till he came to Emain Macha at the end of the day. And there was no one among the men of Ulster would venture to ask news of any of the three until the time came to eat and to drink in the great hall.

When the feast was laid out, they all stopped their arguing and their talking, and gave themselves up to eating and to enjoyment. It was Sualtim, son of Roig, father of Cuchulain, was attending the feast that night, and Conchubar's great vat had been filled for it. The distributers began serving out the meat, but at first they kept back the Champion's Portion. Then Dubthach of the Chafer Tongue said, "Why is not the Champion's Portion given to one of these three heroes that are come back from Cruachan? They must surely have brought some token with them, that we may know which one is to have it."

Upon that, Laegaire Buadach rose up and held out the bronze cup with the silver bird on it. "The Champion's Portion is mine," he said, "and no one can dispute it with me."

"That is not so," said Conall Cearnach; "here is my token. Yours is a bronze cup but mine is a silver cup. You see by the difference in them it is to me the Champion's Portion belongs."

"It belongs to neither of you," said Cuchulain, and

he rose up and he said, " It was only to deceive you and to keep up the quarrel between us, the king and queen we went to gave you those. It is to me the Champion's Portion belongs, for you see my token, that it is far above the others."

With that he lifted high up the cup of red gold, with the bird on it of precious stones, and all the men in the feasting-hall saw it. " It is I myself that will get the Championship," he said, " if I get fair play." " It is yours indeed," said Conchubar, and Fergus, and all the chief men. " It is yours by the judgment of Ailell and Maeve." " I swear by the oath of my people," said Laegaire, " that the cup you have with you was not given to you, but bought. You gave riches and treasures for it to Ailell and Maeve, the way the Championship would not go to any other person; but by my hand of valour," he said, " that judgment shall not stand."

Then, with their swords drawn, they sprang at one another, but Conchubar went between them, and then they let down their hands and sheathed their swords. " It is best," said Sencha, " for you to go to Curoi for judgment." " We agree to that," said they.

So on the morning of the morrow, the three—Cuchulain, Conall, and Laegaire—set out for Curoi's dun. At the gate of the dun they unyoked their chariots, and they went into the courtyard, and Blanad, daughter of Mind, Curoi's wife, gave them a good welcome. Curoi was not at home that night, but knowing, by his enchantments, they would come, he had left instructions with his wife how to entertain them; and she did according to his wish, giving them water for washing, and drinks for refreshing, and beds of the best, so that they were well satisfied.

When bedtime came, Blanad told them they were each to take a night to watch the fort, till Curoi would come back. "And it is what he said, that you should take your turn according to age."

Now in whatever part of the world Curoi was, he made a spell every night over the dun, so that it went round like a mill, and no entrance could be found in it after the setting of the sun.

The first night Laegaire Buadach took the watch, for he was the oldest of the three. As he was keeping watch, towards the end of the night he saw a great shadow coming towards him from the sea westward. Very huge and ugly and terrible he thought it, and it took the shape of a giant and reached up to the sky, and the shining of the sea could be seen between its legs. It is how it came, its hands full of what had the appearance of stripped oaks, and each of them enough for a load for six horses ; and he hurled one of them at Laegaire, but it went past him. He did this two or three times, but the beam did not reach either the skin or the shield of Laegaire. Then Laegaire hurled a spear at him, and it did not hit him.

He stretched out his hand then to Laegaire, and the length of it reached across the three ridges that were between them while they were throwing at one another, and he gripped hold of him. Big and strong as Laegaire was, he fitted like a child of a year old into his hand. The giant turned him round between his two palms as a chessman is turned in a groove, and then he threw him half dead over the wall of the fort, into a heap of mud. There was no opening there, and the people inside the dun thought he had leaped over from outside, as a challenge to the others to do the same.

There they stayed until the end of the day, and at the fall of night Conall went out to take the watch, as he was older than Cuchulain. Everything happened as it did to Laegaire the first night. And when the third night came, Cuchulain went into the seat of the watch.

When midnight was come he heard a noise, and by the light of the cold moon he saw nine grey shapes coming towards him over the marsh. "Stop," said Cuchulain, "who is there? If they are friends, let them not stir; if they are enemies, let them come on." Then they raised a great shout at him, and Cuchulain rushed at them and attacked them, so that the nine fell dead to the ground, and he cut their heads off and made a heap of them, and sat down again to keep the watch. Another nine and then another shouted at him, but he made an end of the three nines, and made one heap of their heads and their arms.

While he was watching on through the night, tired and down-hearted, he heard a sound rising from the lake, like the sound of a very heavy sea. However tired he was, his mind would not let him keep quiet, without going to see what was the cause of that great noise he heard. Then he saw a great worm coming up from the lake, and it raised itself into the air over him and made for the dun, and opened its mouth, and it seemed to him that one of the houses would fit into its gullet.

Then Cuchulain with one leap reached its head and put his arm round its neck, and stretched his hand across its gullet, and tore the monster's heart out and threw it to the ground. Then the beast fell down, and Cuchulain hacked it with his sword, and made little bits of it, and brought the head along with him to the heap of skulls.

He was sitting there, towards the break of day, worn out and discouraged, and he saw the great shadow shaped like a giant coming to him westward from the sea. "This is a bad night," he said. "It will be worse for you yet," said Cuchulain. Then he threw one of the beams at Cuchulain, but it passed by him, and he did that two or three times, but it did not reach either his shield or his skin. Then he stretched out his hand to grip Cuchulain as he did the others, but Cuchulain

leaped his salmon leap at the head of the monster, with
his drawn sword, and brought him down. "Life for
life, Cuchulain," he said, and with that he vanished and
was no more seen.

Then Cuchulain wondered to himself how his fellows
had made their leap over the fort, for the wall was big
and broad and high, and twice he tried it and failed.
Then anger came on him, and he went a good way back
and made a run, and with the dint of the anger that was
on him, and the courage of his heart and of his mind, he
hardly took the dew off the tips of the grass in the run,
and he made one leap over the wall, and lit in the
middle, at the door of the house. Then he went in
through the door and gave a sigh. And Blanad, wife of
Curoi, said, "That is not the sigh of a beaten man, but a
conqueror's sigh of triumph." For the daughter of the
King of the Isle of the Men of Falga knew well all
Cuchulain had gone through that night.

"The Champion's Portion must go now to Cuchulain,"
she said to the others; "for you see by this that you
are not equal to him." "We do not agree to that," said
they; "for we know it was one of his friends among
the Sidhe came to put us down and to put us out of the
Championship. We will not give up for that," they
said.

Then she gave them a message she had from Curoi,
that the three champions were to go back to Emain,
until he would bring his judgment there himself. So
they bade her farewell, and went back to the Red
Branch.

It was a good while after this, as the men of Ulster
were in Emain, tired after the gathering and the games,
Conchubar and Fergus, son of Rogh, with the chief men,
went from the field of sports outside, and sat down in
the house of the Red Branch; but Cuchulain was not

there that night, or Conall Cearnach, but all the rest of the chief heroes were in it.

As they were sitting there towards evening, and the day wearing to its close, they saw a big awkward fellow, very ugly, coming to them into the hall. It seemed to them as if none of the men of Ulster could reach to half his height. He was frightful to look at; next his skin he had an old cow's hide, and a grey cloak around him, and over him he had a great spreading branch the size of a winter shed under which thirty cattle could find shelter. Ravenous yellow eyes he had, and in his right hand an axe weighing fifty cauldrons of melted metal, its sharpness such that it would cut through hairs, if the wind would blow them against its edge.

He went over and leaned against the branched beam that was beside the fire.

"Who are you at all?" said Dubthach of the Chafer Tongue. "Is there no other place for you in the hall that you come up here? Is it to be candlestick to the house you want, or is it to set the house on fire you want?"

"Uath, the Stranger, is my name," said he; "and neither of those things is the thing I want. The thing I want is the thing I cannot find, and I after going through the world of Ireland and the whole world looking for it, and that is a man that will keep his word and will hold to his agreement with me."

"What agreement is that?" said Fergus. "Here is this axe," he said, "and the man into whose hands it is put is to cut off my head to-day, I to cut his head off to-morrow. And as you men of Ulster have a name beyond the men of all other countries for strength and skill, for courage, for greatness, for highmindedness, for behaviour, for truth and generosity, for worthiness, let you find one among you that will hold to his word

A GREAT WORM CAME FLYING TOWARDS HIM.

UATH ROSE UP AND GATHERED HIS HEAD AND HIS AXE.

and keep to his bargain. Conchubar I put aside because of his kingship, and Fergus, son of Rogh, for the same reason. But outside these two, come, whichever of you will venture, he to cut off my head to-night, I to cut off his head to-morrow night."

"It is not right for dishonour to be put on a whole province," said Fergus, "for the want of one man that will keep his word." "Sure there is no champion here after these two are left out," said Dubthach. "By my word, there will be one this moment," said Laegaire, and he leaped out on the floor of the hall. "Stoop down, clown, that I may cut off your head to-night, you to cut off mine to-morrow night." "By the oath of my people," said Dubthach, "it is no good prospect you have if the man killed to-night comes to kill you to-morrow."

Then Uath put spells on the edge of the axe and laid his neck down on a block, and Laegaire struck a blow across it with the axe, till it went into the block underneath, and the head fell on the floor and the house was filled with the blood. But presently Uath rose up and gathered his head and his axe to his breast and went out from the hall, his neck streaming with blood, so that there was terror on all the people in the house.

"I swear," said Dubthach, "if this stranger, being killed, comes back to-morrow night, he will not leave a man alive in Ulster."

Back he came the next night to have his agreement kept. But Laegaire's heart failed him, and he was nowhere to be found. But Conall Cearnach was in the hall, and he said he would make a new agreement with him. So all happened the same as the night before, but when Uath came the next day, it was the same with Conall as with Laegaire, his heart failed him when it came to the keeping of his bargain.

Cuchulain was there that night when Uath came in and began to reproach and to mock at them all. "As for you, men of Ulster," he said, "all your courage and your daring is gone from you; you covet a great name, but you are not able to earn it. Where is that poor squinting fellow that is called Cuchulain," he said, "till I see if his word is any better than the word of the others?" "I will keep my word without any agreement," said Cuchulain. "That is likely, you miserable fly, it is in great fear of death you are."

On that, Cuchulain made a leap towards him and gave him a blow with the axe, and hurled his head to the top rafter of the hall, so that the whole house shook.

On the morrow the men of Ulster were watching Cuchulain to see if he would break his word to the stranger, as the others had done. As Cuchulain sat there waiting for him, they saw that he was very down-hearted, and they made sure his life was at its end, and that they might as well begin keening him. And then Cuchulain said to Conchubar, and there was hanging of the head on him, "Do not go from this till my agreement is fulfilled, for death is coming to me, but I would sooner meet with death than break my word."

They were there till the close of day, and then they saw Uath coming. "Where is Cuchulain?" he said. "Here I am," he answered. "It is dull your speech is to-night," said the stranger; "it is in great fear of death you are. But however great your fear, you have not failed me."

Then Cuchulain went to him and laid his head on the block. "Stretch out your head better," said he. "You are keeping me in torment," said Cuchulain; "put an end to me quickly. For last night," he said, "by my oath, I made no delay with you." Then he stretched out his neck, and Uath raised his axe till it reached the rafters of the hall, and the creaking of the old hide that was about him, and the crashing of the axe through the rafters, was like the loud noise of a wood in a stormy night. But when the axe came down, it was with its blunt side, and it was the floor it struck, so that Cuchulain was not touched at all. And all the chief men of Ulster were standing around looking on, and they saw on the moment that it was no strange clown was in it, but Curoi, son of Daire, that had come to try the heroes through his enchantments.

"Rise up, Cuchulain," he said. "Of all the heroes of Ulster, whatever may be their daring, there is not one to compare with you in courage and in bravery and in truth. The Championship of the heroes of Ireland is yours from this out, and the Champion's Portion with it, and to your wife the first place among all the women of Ulster. And whoever tries to put himself before you after this," he said, "I swear by the oath my people swear by, his own life will be in danger."

With that he left them. And this was the end of the Women's War of Words, and of the quarrel among the heroes for the Championship of Ulster.

VI

THE HIGH KING OF IRELAND

THERE was a king over Ireland before this time whose name was Eochaid Feidlech, and it is he was grandfather to Conaire the Great.

He was going one time over the fair green of Bri Leith, and he saw at the side of a well a woman, with a bright comb of silver and gold, and she washing in a silver basin, having four golden birds on it, and little bright purple stones set in the rim of the basin. A beautiful purple cloak she had, and silver fringes to it, and a gold brooch; and she had on her a dress of green silk with a long hood embroidered in red gold, and wonderful clasps of gold and silver on her breasts and on her shoulders. The sunlight was falling on her, so that the gold and the green silk were shining out. Two plaits of hair she had, four locks in each plait, and a bead at the point of every lock, and the colour of her hair was like yellow flags in summer, or like red gold after it is rubbed.

There she was, letting down her hair to wash it, and her arms out through the sleeve-holes of her shift. Her soft hands were as white as the snow of a single night, and her eyes as blue as any blue flower, and her lips as red as the berries of the rowan-tree, and her body as white as the foam of a wave. The bright light of the moon was in her face, the highness of pride in her eyebrows, a dimple of delight in each of her cheeks, the light of wooing in her eyes, and when she walked she had a step that was steady and even, like the walk of a queen.

Of all the women of the world she was the best and the nicest and the most beautiful that had ever been seen, and it is what King Eochaid and his people thought, that she was from the hills of the Sidhe. It is of her it was said, " All are dear and all are shapely till they are put beside Etain."

Then Eochaid sent his people to bring her to him, and when she came, he said, " Who are you yourself, and where do you come from ? " " It is easy to say that," she said ; " I am Etain, daughter of Etar, king of the Riders of the Sidhe. And I have been in this place ever since I was born, twenty years ago, in a hill of the Sidhe, and kings and great men among them have been asking my love, but they got nothing from me, for since the time I could first speak I have loved yourself, and given you a child's love, because of the great talk I heard of your grandeur. And when I saw you now I knew you by all I had heard of you ; and so I have reached to you at last."

" It is no bad friend you have been looking for," said Eochaid, " but there will be a welcome before you, and I will leave every other woman for you, and it is with yourself I will live from this out, so long as you keep good behaviour."

Then he gave her the bride price, and she lived with him till he died. But one time she was brought away from him by Midhir, and Eochaid brought her back by force, and the Sidhe had no good will towards him after that, but brought a revenge on his house, and on his grandson, Conaire.

They had one daughter, that was called by the same name as her mother, Etain, and that was married to

Cormac, king of Ulster.   And, like her mother, she had but the one daughter, and there was vexation on Cormac when she had no son, and he bade two of his serving-men to bring the child away out of his sight, and to do away with her.   So they brought her to a pit, but when they were putting her in, she smiled a laughing smile at them, and they had not the heart to harm her.   So they brought her to a calf-shed belonging to the herds that minded the cattle of Eterscel, great-grandson of Iar, king of Teamhair ; and they cared her well there, and there was not a king's daughter in Ireland was nicer than herself.   And they made a little house of wicker-work for her, with no door, but only a window high up in it.

King Eterscel's people thought it was provisions the herds used to keep in that house.   But one day a man of them got up and looked in through the window, and what he saw was the nicest and the most beautiful young girl of the whole world.

When King Eterscel heard that, he sent his people to break into the house and to bring her away, and ask no leave of the cowherds.   For he had no child, and it is what his Druids had foretold, that it was a woman of unknown race would bear him a son ; and he was sure this was the woman that had been foretold for him.

But before the king's messengers reached the house in the morning, Etain saw a bird coming in at the window.   And when it came in, it left its birdskin on the floor, and what she saw was a man before her.   And he said, " The king is sending messengers to bring you to him, that he may have a son.   But it is to me you will bear a son, and no bird must ever be killed by him. And his name will be Conaire, son of Mess Buachall, that is, son of the cowherd's foster-child."

Then she was brought away to the king, and the herds

that had fostered her went with her, and they all got good treatment. And it is what she asked, when her son Conaire was born, that he might be brought up between three households, the household of her own fosterers, and of the two honey-worded Maines, and her own. And she said that if any of the men of Ireland had a mind to give help in his bringing up, they should give it to those three households

So it was like that the boy was reared, and there were five other boys reared along with him, Ferger, Fergel, Ferogain, Ferobain, and Lomna Druth the Fool, of the house of Dond Dessa, the champion of the army from Muclesi. And they all used the same food, and their clothing and their armour and the colour of their horses were the same.

And after a while King Eterscel died, and there was a bull feast made ready at Teamhair, as the custom was, to find out by it the best man for the kingship.

It is this way the bull feast was made. A white bull was killed, and one man would eat his fill of the meat and of the broth, and in his sleep after that meal, a charm of truth would be said over him by four Druids. And whoever he would see in his sleep would be king, and he would tell them his appearance; and if he told what was not true, his lips would perish. And what the dreamer saw in his sleep this time was a young man, and he naked, and having a stone in his sling, passing the road to Teamhair.

Now just at that time Conaire was out playing games near the Lifé River with his foster-brothers, and the cowherds that had reared him came and bid him go up to Teamhair to attend the bull feast that was going on there.

So he left his foster-brothers at their games, and turned his chariot and went on till he came to Ath Cliath. And there he saw great white speckled birds, the best in size and appearance he had ever seen, and he followed after them till his horses were tired, but he could not come up with them, for they always kept just out of his reach. Then he got down from his chariot and took his sling and followed them to the strand, and they went into the sea and were swimming on the waves, and he went after them to take hold of them. Then they left their birdskins, and it was men he saw before him, and they turning to face him with spears and swords.

But one of them took him under his protection and said, "I am Nemglan, king of your father's birds, and there was a command put on you never to make a cast at birds, for there is not one here but should be dear to you." "I never knew of that command till this day," said Conaire. Then Nemglan said, "What you have to do is to go to Teamhair to-night, to the bull feast, and it is through it you will be made king, for it is a man that will go naked, and having a sling and a stone in his hand, along one of the roads to Teamhair, towards the end of the night, that will be king.

"And your bird reign will be great," he said. "But there is *geasa*, that is a bond, on you not to do these things :

"Do not go righthandwise round Teamhair, and lefthandwise round Bregia; do not hunt the evil beasts of Cerna ; do not go out beyond Teamhair every ninth night; do not settle the quarrel of two of your own people ; let no robbery be done in your reign ; do not sleep in a house you can see the firelight shining from after sunset; do not let one woman or one man come into the house where you are after sunset ; do not let three Reds go before you to the House of Red."

Then Conaire set out for Teamhair, naked, and having a stone in his sling. And on every one of

the four roads to Teamhair there were three kings
waiting, and having clothing with them, for the king
that was foretold.   And when the three kings on
Conaire's road saw him coming, they met him, and
put royal clothes on him, and brought him in a
chariot to Teamhair.   But the people of Teamhair
said when they saw him : " Our bull feast and our
charm of truth were not worth much, when it is only
a young, beardless lad they have brought us ! "

" That is no matter," said Conaire, " for it is no dis
grace for you to have a young king, when my father
and my grandfather held the same place."   " That is
true," they all said then, and they gave him the kingship, and he said, " I will learn of wise men, that I
myself may be wise."

Now there was great plenty in Ireland through his
reign ; seven ships coming at the one time to Inver
Colptha, and corn and nuts up to the knees in every
harvest, and the trees bending from the weight of fruit,
and the Buais and the Boinne full of fish every summer,
and that much law and peace and good-will among the
people, that each one thought the other's voice as sweet
as the strings of harps.   And the wolves themselves were
held by hostages not to kill more than one calf in every pen.
There was no thunder or storm in his reign, and from
spring to harvest there was not as much wind as would
stir a cow's tail, and the cattle were without keepers
because of the greatness of peace.   And in his reign
there were the three crowns in Ireland, the crown of
flowers, the crown of acorns, and the crown of
wheatears.

But after a while there began to be discontent on the
sons of Donn Dessa, because they were hindered from
the robbery and killing there used to be in the old
time.   And to vex the king, and to see what would he
do, they stole three things, a pig and a bullock and a

cow, from the same man every year for three years. And every year the countryman would come to the king to make his complaint, and every year the king would say, " It is to the sons of Donn Dessa you should go, for it is they took the beasts." But whenever he would go and speak to them, they would go near to kill him, and he would not go back to the king for fear he might be vexed.

So the sons of Donn Dessa went on with their robbery, and three times fifty other young men joined with them, sons of the great men of Ireland.

But one time they went doing their bad work in Connaught, and they followed a swineherd that ran from them, and he called out for help, and the people gathered to him, and the robbers were taken and brought back to Teamhair.

King Conaire was asked to give judgment then, and it is what he said, " Let every father of a robber put his own son to death, but let my foster-brothers be spared." " Give us leave," said all the people, " and we will put them to death for you." " I will not consent to that, indeed," said Conaire. " Their life must be spared. But if they must do robbery," he said, " let them go across the sea, and do it on the men of Alban."

So the sons of Donn Dessa and their men were driven out of the country, and some of the Maines went with them, the sons of Ailell and Maeve, and three great fighting men of Leinster, that were called the Three Red Hounds of Cualu, and they brought a troop of wild restless men with them.

They set out then in their ships, and when they were out on the rough sea, they met with the ship of Ingcel, the One-Eyed, grandson of Cormac of Britain. They were going to make an attack on him, but Ingcel said, " It would be best for us to come to an agreement together, for you have been driven out of Ireland, and I myself have been driven out from Britain. Let us make this agreement," he said. "Let you come and spoil the people of my country, and then I will go back with you and spoil the people of your country."

So they agreed to that, and they cast lots as to where they would go first, and it is how the lot fell, that they should go first to Britain with Ingcel. And when they got there it chanced that the father and mother and the seven brothers of Ingcel had been sent for to the house of the king of the district, and Ingcel and his comrades made an attack on them, and killed them all in the one night.

Then they made for Alban, and there they did every sort of destruction and robbery. And at last they turned back again to Ireland, that Ingcel might spoil their people the same way as they had spoiled his.

Now just at that time peace was after being broken in Ireland by the two Carbres that were at war with one another in Tuathmumain of Munster, and no one was able to put an end to their quarrel till Conaire himself went there to make peace. And he did that, although by doing it he broke two of the bonds put on him by the Man of the Waves. And on his way back to Teamhair, when he was passing Usnach in Meath, he and his people thought they saw fighting from east to west, and from north to south, and armies of naked men, and the country of the Ua Neills like a cloud of fire around them.

"What is that?" said Conaire. "It is easy to know that," said his people. "The king's law has broken down, and the country is on fire." "What way had we best go?" said Conaire. "To the north-west," said his people.

So then they went righthandways round Teamhair, and lefthandways round Bregia, and that was another breaking of his bonds, and they met with beasts and hunted them, and he did not know till afterwards that they were the evil beasts of Cerna.

And it was the Sidhe had made that Druid mist of smoke about him, because he had begun to break his bonds.

Great fear came on Conaire then, and he did not know what way would be best to go, and they went on by the sea-coast, towards the south by the road of Cualu. And then Conaire said, "Where shall we go to spend the night?"

"I can say this truly," said Mac Cecht, one of his fighting men, he that kept three of the Fomor as hostages at the king's court, the way their people would not spoil corn or milk in Ireland through his reign; "it is oftener the men of Ireland have been quarrelling to have you in the house, than you have been straying about, looking for a lodging." "I have a friend not far from this," said Conaire, "if we but knew the way to his house." "What is his name?" said Mac Cecht. "Da Derga of Leinster, that keeps the great Inn," said Conaire. "He came to ask a gift of me, and it is not a refusal he met with. I gave him a hundred head of cattle, I gave him a hundred fat swine, I gave him a hundred cloaks of fine cloth, I gave him a hundred swords and spears, I gave him a hundred red-gilded brooches, I gave him ten vats of good brown ale, I gave him three times nine white hounds in silver chains, I gave him a hundred swift horses. I would give him the same if he would come again. He will make a return to me to-night, for it would be a strange thing, he to begrudge me anything when I come to his house."

"When I knew his house," said Mac Cecht, "the road we are in now led straight to it. Seven doorways there are in it, and seven sleeping-rooms between every two doorways." "We will go to the house with all our people," said Conaire. "If that is so," said Mac Cecht,

"I will go on first till I light a fire in the house before you."

They went on then towards Ath Cliath, and presently a man with hair cut short, with a dreadful appearance, with but one hand and one foot and one eye, overtook them. A forked pole of black iron he had in his hand, and on his back a black-bristled singed pig, and it squealing; and there was a woman coming after him, ugly and big-mouthed. "Welcome to you, my master, Conaire," he said. "It is long we have known of your coming." "Who gives that welcome?" said Conaire. "Fer Coille, the Man of the Wood," he said, "and his black pig with him, that you may not be fasting to-night, for you are the best king that ever came into the world." "Leave me for to-night," said Conaire, "and I will go to you any other night that pleases you." "We will not," said he; "but we will go to the place you will be in to-night, O fair little master, Conaire."

So he went on towards the Inn, and his wife behind him, and his black pig squealing on his back.

After that Conaire saw before him three horsemen going towards the Inn. Red cloaks they had, and red shields, and red spears in their hands, and they riding on red horses.

"What men are these before me?" said Conaire. "It is in my bonds not to let them go before me; three Reds to the House of Red, that is, of Derga. Who will follow them and bid them to come back and to follow after me?" "I will follow them," said Lefriflaith, Conaire's son.

So he struck his horse and went after them, but he could not come up with them. So he called to them to turn back, and not to go on before the king. And he did this three times, and the third time one of the three men turned his head and said, "There is great news before us, my son ; wetting of swords, destroying of life, shields with broken bosses, after the fall of night. Our horses are tired ; we are riding the horses of the Sidhe ; although we are alive we are dead." And with that they went from him, and he went back to his father.

"You did not keep back the men," said Conaire. "It was not my fault, indeed," said Lefriflaith. Then he told the answer they had given him, and Conaire and his people were not well pleased to hear that, and uneasiness came on them. "All my bonds are ended to-night," said Conaire, "and those three Reds before me are sent by the Sidhe."

Now while he and his people were in the road of Cualu going towards the Inn, Ingcel and the outlaws of Ireland were come in their ships to the coast of Bregia against Etair. And the sons of Donn Dessa said, "Strike the sails now, and let some light-footed messenger go on shore and see can we keep our bargain with Ingcel, and give him a spoil for the spoil he gave us." "Let some man go," said Ingcel, "that has the gift of hearing and of far sight and of judgment."

"I have the gift of hearing," said Maine Milscothach. "I have the gift of far sight and of judgment," said Maine Andoe. "It is as well for you to go, so," said the others.

So they landed and went on till they came to Beinn Etair, and they stopped there to try what they might see and hear. "Be quiet now," said Maine Milscothach, "and listen." "What do you hear?" said Maine Andoe. "I hear the coming of a king," he said, "and look now and tell me what you see." "I see," he said, "a great company of men, travelling over hills and rivers. Clothes of every colour they have, and grey spears over their chariots, and swords with

ivory hilts beside them, and silver shields; and I swear
by the oath my people swear by," he said, "the horses
they have with them are the horses of some good lord.
And it is my opinion that it is Conaire, son of Eterscel,
and a good share of the men of Ireland with him, that
is travelling the road."

With that they went back and told their comrades
what they had heard and seen. And when they
heard it they brought the boats to shore and landed
on the strand of Furbuithe. And it was just at the
same moment Mac Cecht was striking a spark to kindle
a fire at the Inn before the High King.

Then Conaire came to the lawn of the Inn, and he
went in, and his people, and they took their seats,
and the three Red Men sat down along with them, and
the Man of the Wood that was a swineherd of the Sidhe
with his squealing pig.

And Da Derga came to them with three times fifty
fighting men, every one of them having a long head
of hair and a short cloak and a great blackthorn stick
with bands of iron in his hand. "Welcome, my master,
Conaire," said Da Derga, "and if you were to bring
the whole of the men of Ireland with you, there would
be a welcome before them all."

After the fall of evening they saw a lone woman
coming to the door of the Inn; long hair she had, and
a grey woollen cloak, and her mouth was drawn to
one side of her head. She came and leaned up against
the doorpost, and she threw an evil eye on the king
and the young men about him. "Well, woman," said
Conaire, "if you have the Druid sight, what is it you
see for us?" "It is what I see for you," she said,
"that nothing of your skin or of your flesh will escape
from the place you are in, except what the birds will
bring away in their claws. And let me come into the
house now," she said. "There are bonds on me," said

Conaire, "not to let one woman come by herself into the house after the setting of the sun. And bring her out," he said, "a good share of food from my own table, but let her stop for the night in some other place."

"If the king's hospitality is gone from him," she said, "and if it is the way with him not to have room in his house for one lone woman to be fed and lodged, I will go and get food and lodging from some better man." "Let her in, in spite of my bonds," said Conaire, when he heard that. So they let her in, but none of them felt easy in their minds after what she had said.

Now all this time the outlaws were on their way to the Inn, and they stopped at Leccaibcend Slebe. And when they saw the great light that was shining from the Inn through the wheels of the chariots that were outside the doors, Ingcel said to Ferogain, "What is that great light beyond?" "It is what I think," said Ferogain, "that it is the fire of Conaire, the High King. And I would be glad he not to be there to-night, for it would be a pity if harm would come on him, or his life be shortened, for he is a branch in its blossom."

"It is good luck for me," said Ingcel, "it he is there. Spoil for spoil. It is no worse for you than it was for me when I gave up my father and mother and my seven brothers and the king of my country into your hands." "That is true, that is true," said all the others.

Then every man of them brought up a stone from the strand to make a cairn, as they were used to do before they would make an attack on any place, to know by it afterwards how many men they had lost. For every man that would come from the fight would take his stone from the cairn, and the stones of all that would be killed would be left there.

After that they held a council, and it is what they agreed, that one man should go and spy out what way

things were at the Inn. And it was Ingcel himself
went to do that, and he was a good while looking in
by the seven doors of the house, but at last some one
of the men inside caught sight of him, and he made
his way back to his comrades, where they were all
sitting down, and their leaders in the middle, waiting
to hear his news.

"Did you see the house, Ingcel?" said Ferogain. "I
did see it," said Ingcel; "and whether or not there is a
king in it, it is a royal house, and I will take it as my
share when the time comes." "You may do that," said
Conaire's foster-brothers. "But we will not go against
it before we know who is in it."

"The first I saw," said Ingcel, "was a large man, of
good race, with bright eyes, with hair like flax; his face
open, wide above and narrow below; with modest looks,
and having no beard. A five-barbed spear in his hand,
and a shield with five gold circles on it. Nine men he
had about him, all beautiful and all alike, so that you
would think they had the one father and mother. Who
were those men, Ferogain?" he said.

"It is easy to say that," said Ferogain. "That was
Cormac Conloingeas, son of Conchubar, the best fighter
behind a shield in all Ireland, but he is modest with all
that. And those were his nine comrades about him;
they have never put men to death because of their
poverty, or spared them because of their riches. He is
a good leader they have with them. I swear by the
gods my people swear by, it is no small slaughter they
will make before the Inn to-night."

"It is a pity for him that will make the attack," said
Lomna Druth, the Fool, "because of that man only,
Cormac Conloingeas. And if I had my way," he said,
"the attack would not be made, for the sake of that man
alone and his beauty and his goodness."

"You will not be able to hinder it, Lomna," said

Ingcel. "You are no good of a fighter; I know you well, there are clouds of weakness coming on you. No one, whether old man or story-teller, will be able to say I drew back from this fight before I had gone through with it."

"It is well enough for you, Ingcel," said Lomna; "you will escape after the fight, and you will bring away the head of a strange king with you, but as for myself," he said, "it is my head will be the first to be tossed to and fro to-night."

"What did you see after that?" said Ferogain.

"I saw a room with three soft young boys in it and they wearing cloaks of silk with gold brooches. Long yellow hair they had, as curly as a ram's head; a golden shield and a candle of a king's house over each of them, and every one in the house humours them. Who were those, Ferogain?" he said.

But Ferogain was crying tears down, so that the front of his cloak was wet, and it was a long time before he could bring out his voice. "O little ones," he said then, "I have good reason for crying. Those are the three sons of the king, Oball and Obline and Corpre Findmor."

"There is grief on us if that story is true," said the other sons of Donn Dessa; "for it is good those three are. They are as mannerly as young girls, and they have the hearts of brothers, and the courage of lions. Whoever has been with them and parts from them, it is little he sleeps or eats till the end of nine days, fretting after their company. It is a pity for him that will destroy them."

"I saw after that," said Ingcel, "a very fair man, having a golden bush of hair, the size of a reaping basket. A long, heavy three-edged sword in his hand, a red shield speckled with rivets of white bronze between plates of gold."

"That man is known to all the men of Ireland," said Ferogain. "It is Conall Cearnach, son of Amergin, and he is the man Conaire thinks most of in the world; and that shield in his hand is the Lam-tapaid. There are seven doorways in that inn, and when the attack is made, Conall Cearnach will be at every one of them. What did you see after that, Ingcel?" he said.

"I saw," he said, "a brown big man, with short brown hair and a red speckled cloak, and a black shield with clasps of gold; and with him two chief men, in their first greyness, and black swords at their sides. And one of them had in his hand a great spear, with fifty rivets through it, and he shook it over his head, and struck the haft against the palm of his hand three times, and then he plunged it into a great pot that stood before them, with some black thing in it, and when he was putting it in there were flames on the shaft. Who were those men, Ferogain?"

"That brown man is Muinremar, son of Geirgind, one of the champions of the Red Branch. And another is Sencha, the beautiful son of Ailell; and the man with the spear is Dubthach, the Beetle of Ulster, and the spear in his hand is Celthair's Luin, that was in the battle of Magh Tuireadh, and that was brought from the east by the three children of Tuireann, and when a battle is coming near, it flames up of itself, and it must be kept quenched in a vessel, or it will go through whoever has it in his hand."

"I saw after that," said Ingcel, "a room with nine men in it, fair-haired and beautiful, with speckled cloaks, and above them were nine bagpipes, and light was shining from the ornaments that were on them."

"Those are the nine pipers that came to Conaire out of the hill of the Sidhe at Bregia," said Ferogain, "because of the great stories about him. The best pipers they are in the whole world. And they are good fighters, but to fight with them is to fight with a shadow, for they kill but cannot be killed, because they are from the Sidhe."

"I saw after that," said Ingcel, "three very big men, with terrible looks. A dress of rough hair they had, and a club of iron with chains on it in every man's hand. There was sadness on them, and they standing alone, and every one in the house avoiding them. Who were those, Ferogain?"

Ferogain was silent for a while, and he said then, "I do not know of any such men in the world, unless they might be the three giants Cuchulain spared, the time he took them from the men of Falga, he would not let them be killed because of their strangeness; Conaire bought them from Cuchulain after that, so it is along with him they are."

"I saw nine men in the north side of the house," said Ingcel, "having very yellow manes of hair, and short linen dresses, and purple cloaks without brooches; broad spears, and red curved shields."

"I know those men," said Ferogain; "three royal princes of Britain that are with the king, Oswald and his two foster-brothers, Osbrit of the Long Hand and his two foster-brothers, Lindas and his two foster-brothers."

"Three red men I saw after that," said Ingcel; "red shields above them, red spears in their hands, their three red horses in their bridles in front of the Inn."

"Those are the three champions that did deceit and falsehood among the Sidhe," said Ferogain, "and it is the punishment was put on them by the king of the Sidhe, to be three times destroyed by the King of Teamhair; and Conaire is the last king through whom they will be destroyed; yet they will not be killed, nor will they kill any one. It is to work out their own destruction they are come."

"I saw after that," said Ingcel, "a big man, and his

hair white, and the shame of baldness on him, and gold earrings in his ears. Nine swords he had in his hand, and nine silver shields, and nine golden apples. He was throwing each of them upwards, and not one would fall on the ground, but each of them rising and falling past each other like bees on a sunny day. But as I looked at him, he let all fall to the ground, and the people about him cried out, and the king that was sitting there said to him, 'We have been together since I was a little boy, and your tricks never failed till to-night.'

"'My grief!' he said. 'Fair master, Conaire, I have good cause for it; an unfriendly eye looked at me; there is some bad thing in front of the Inn.'

"And when the king heard that, it is what he said: 'I had a dream in my sleep a while ago, of the howling of my dog Ossar, of wounded men, of a wind of terror, of keening that overcame laughter.'"

"That was Taulchinne, Conaire's juggler," said Ferogain. "And tell me now," he said, "what was the appearance of the king?"

"Of all the men I ever saw in the world," said Ingcel, "he is the best in shape, and the most beautiful; young he is, and wise and kinglike. The colour of his hair was like the shining of purified gold; the cloak about him was like the mist of a May morning, changing from colour to colour, every colour more beautiful than another; a wheel brooch of gold reaching from his chin to his waist; his golden-hilted sword within his reach."

"That was Conaire, the High King, indeed," said Ferogain; "and it is he is the greatest and the best and the comeliest of the kings of the whole world, and there is no fault in him, either as to wisdom or bravery or knowledge or words or worthiness. Tender he is, a sleepy, simple man, till he chances on some brave thing to do, but when his anger is awaked, the champions of Ireland and of Scotland will not win their battle so long as he is against them. And I swear by the oath my people swear by, unless drink should fail him, or the like, that man alone would hold the Inn till help would gather to him from the Wave of Cliodna in the south, to the Wave of Essruadh in the north."

"It is time for us to rise up," said Ingcel then, "and to get on to the house."

So with that the outlaws rose up and went on to the Inn, and the noise of their voices was heard about it.

"Be quiet now and listen," said Conaire. "What is that we hear?"

"Fighting men about the house," said Conall Cearnach. "There are fighting men to meet them here," said Conaire. "They will be wanted to-night," said Conall.

Then Lomna Druth, the Fool, broke in first to the house, and the doorkeepers struck off his head, and it was tossed three times in and out of the Inn, just as he himself had foretold.

Then they all attacked one another, and Conaire himself went out with his people and killed a great many of the outlaws outside. And three times the Inn was set on fire, and three times it was put out again. And Conaire got to his arms then, for he had not got them in the first attack, and he went out again and made a great slaughter, so that the outlaws were driven back. "I told you," said Ferogain, "that all the men of Ireland and of Alban could not take the house till Conaire's rage would be quenched." "It is short his time will be," said the Druids that were along with the outlaws. And what they put on him by their enchantments was a great thirst, so that he went back to the house and called for a drink. "A drink to me, Mac Cecht," he said. "That is not the order you are used to give me," said

Mac Cecht. "What I have to do is to keep you from the men that are attacking you all round the house; ask a drink of your steward and of your cup-bearers," he said.

Then Conaire called to his cup-bearers for a drink. "There is none," they said, "for every drop in the house was thrown on the fire to put it out." "Get me a drink, Mac Cecht," he said again then; "for if I am to die, it is all the same to me by what death I die."

Then Mac Cecht gave a choice to the champions of Ireland that were in the house, would they go out and look for a drink for Conaire, or would they stop in the house and defend him. And Conall Cearnach called out: "Leave the defence of the king to us, and go you and look for the drink, for it was of you it was asked." And he was vexed with Mac Cecht for putting the choice to them, and there was never a very friendly feeling between them afterwards.

Then Mac Cecht went to look for a drink, and he brought Conaire's great golden cup with him, and an iron spit, the cauldron spit, in his other hand.

He burst out on the outlaws, and attacked them with blows of the spit, so that many got their death; and then he took his shield and made a round with his sword above his head, and cut down all before him, and got through the whole band.

And it would be too long to tell, and it would tire the hearers, all that happened after that; the people of the Inn coming out and making attacks, and some of them getting their death, and the most part making their escape. And at last there were none left in the Inn with Conaire but Conall, and Sencha, and Dubthach.

Now from the rage that was on Conaire, and the greatness of the fight he had fought, a great drouth came on him again, and such a fever of thirst, and no drink to get, that he died of it in the end.

Then the other three, when they saw the High King was dead, went out and cut their way through their enemies, and got away with their lives, but if they did, they were wounded, and hurt, and broken.

And Conall Cearnach, after he got away, went on to his father's house, and but half his shield left in his hand, and a few bits left of his two spears. And he found Amergin, his father, out before his dun in Tailltin.

"Those are fierce wolves that have hunted you, my son," said he. "It was not wolves that wounded me, but a sharp fight with fighting-men," said Conall. "Have you news from Da Derga's Inn?" said Amergin. "Is your lord living?" "He is not living," said Conall. "I swear by the gods the great tribes of Ulster swear by, the man is a coward that came out alive, leaving his lord dead among his enemies," said Amergin. "My own wounds are not white, old hero," said Conall. And with that he showed him his right arm, that was full of wounds. "That arm fought there, my son," said Amergin. "That is true," said Conall. "There are many in front of the Inn now it gave drinks of death to last night."

Now, as to Mac Cecht, after he got away from the Inn, he went on to the well of Casair, that was near him in Crith Cualann, but he could not find so much as the full of the cup of water in it. Then he went on through the night, from lake to lake, and from river to river, but he could not find the full of the cup of water in any one of them. But at last he came to Uaran Garad on Magh Ai, and it could not hide itself from him, and he filled the cup, and went back again, and reached Da Derga's Inn before morning. And when he got there, he saw two men, and they striking off Conaire's head; and Mac Cecht struck off the head of one of them, and then the other man was going away with the king's head, and he took up a stone and threw it at him, that it broke his back.

Then Mac Cecht stooped down and poured the water into Conaire's mouth and his throat. And when the water was poured in, the head spoke and it said: "A good man Mac Cecht is, a good man, a good champion without and within. He gives drink, he saves a king, he does a deed; it is well he fought at the door, it is well he made an end of fighting men. It is good I would be, and I alive, to Mac Cecht of the great name."

And it was after that, Mac Cecht brought the body of the High King on his back to Teamhair, and buried him there as some say. And he himself went to his own country, into Connaught. And the place he stopped in was called, from his sharp grief, Magh Bron-gear.

And there was no High King chosen to rule over Ireland for a good many years after that.

VII

FATE OF THE SONS OF USNACH

NOW it was one Fedlimid, son of Doll, was harper to King Conchubar, and he had but one child, and this is the story of her birth.

Cathbad, the Druid, was at Fedlimid's house one day. "Have you got knowledge of the future?" said Fedlimid. "I have a little," said Cathbad. "What is it you are wanting to know?" "I was not asking to know anything," said Fedlimid, "but if you know of anything that may be going to happen me, it is as well for you to tell me."

Cathbad went out of the house for a while, and when he came back he said: "Had you ever any children?" "I never had," said Fedlimid, "and the wife I have had none, and we have no hope ever to have any; there is no one with us but only myself and my wife." "That puts wonder on me," said Cathbad, "for I see by Druid signs that it is on account of a daughter belonging to you, that more blood will be shed than ever was shed in Ireland since time and race began. And great heroes and bright candles of the Gael will lose their lives because of her." "Is that the foretelling you have made for me?" said Fedlimid, and there was anger on him, for he thought the Druid was mocking him; "if that is all you can say, you can keep it for yourself; it is little I think of your share

448

of knowledge." "For all that," said Cathbad, "I am certain of its truth, for I can see it all clearly in my own mind."

The Druid went away, but he was not long gone when Fedlimid's wife was found to be with child. And as her time went on, his vexation went on growing, that he had not asked more questions of Cathbad, at the time he was talking to him, and he was under a smouldering care by day and by night, for it is what he was thinking, that neither his own sense and understanding, or the share of friends he had, would be able to save him, or to make a back against the world, if this misfortune should come upon him, that would bring such great shedding of blood upon the earth; and it is the thought that came, that if this child should be born, what he had to do was to put her far away, where no eye would see her, and no ear hear word of her.

The time of the delivery of Fedlimid's wife came on, and it was a girl-child she gave birth to. Fedlimid did not allow any living person to come to the house or to see his wife, but himself alone.

But just after the child was born, Cathbad, the Druid, came in again, and there was shame on Fedlimid when he saw him, and when he remembered how he would not believe his words. But the Druid looked at the child and he said: "Let Deirdre be her name; harm will come through her.

"She will be fair, comely, bright-haired; heroes will fight for her, and kings go seeking for her."

And then he took the child in his arms, and it is what he said: "O Deirdre, on whose account many shall weep, on whose account many women shall be envious, there will be trouble on Ulster for your sake, O fair daughter of Fedlimid.

"Many will be jealous of your face, O flame of beauty; for your sake heroes shall go to exile. For your sake deeds of anger shall be done in Emain; there is harm in your face, for it will bring banishment and death on the sons of kings.

"In your fate, O beautiful child, are wounds, and ill-doings, and shedding of blood.

"You will have a little grave apart to yourself; you will be a tale of wonder for ever, Deirdre."

Cathbad went away then, and he sent Levarcham, daughter of Aedh, to the house; and Fedlimid asked her would she take the venture of bringing up the child, far away where no eye would see her, and no ear hear of her. Levarcham said she would do that, and that she would do her best to keep her the way he wished.

So Fedlimid got his men, and brought them away with him to a mountain, wide and waste, and there he bade them to make a little house, by the side of a round green hillock, and to make a garden of apple-trees behind it, with a wall about it. And he bade them put a roof of green sods over the house, the way a little company might live in it, without notice being taken of them.

Then he sent Levarcham and the child there, that no eye might see, and no ear hear of Deirdre. He put all in good order before them, and he gave them pro-visions, and he told Levarcham that food and all she wanted would be sent from year to year as long as she lived.

And so Deirdre and her foster-mother lived in the lonely place among the hills without the knowledge or the notice of any strange person, until Deirdre was fourteen years of age. And Deirdre grew straight and clean like a rush on the bog, and she was comely beyond comparison of all the women of the world, and her movements were like the swan on the wave, or the deer on the hill. She was the young girl of the greatest beauty and of the gentlest nature of all the women of Ireland.

Levarcham, that had charge of her, used to be giving Deirdre every knowledge and skill that she had herself. There was not a blade of grass growing from root, or a bird singing in the wood, or a star shining from heaven, but Deirdre had the name of it. But there was one thing she would not have her know, she would not let her have friendship with any living person of the rest of the world outside their own house.

But one dark night of winter, with black clouds overhead, a hunter came walking the hills, and it is what happened, he missed the track of the hunt, and lost his way and his comrades.

And a heaviness came upon him, and he lay down on the side of the green hillock by Deirdre's house. He was weak with hunger and going, and perished with cold, and a deep sleep came upon him. While he was lying there a dream came to the hunter, and he thought that he was near the warmth of a house of the Sidhe, and the Sidhe inside making music, and he called out in his dream, " If there is any one inside, let them bring me in, in the name of the Sun and the Moon." Deirdre heard the voice, and she said to Levarcham, " Mother, mother, what is that ? " But Levarcham said, " It is nothing that matters ; it is the birds of the air gone astray, and trying to find one another. But let them go back to the branches of the wood." Another troubled dream came on the hunter, and he cried out a second time. " What is that ? " asked Deirdre again. " It is nothing that matters," said Levarcham. " The birds of the air are looking for one another ; let them go past to the branches of the wood." Then a third dream came to the hunter, and he cried out a third time, if there was any one in the hill to let him in for the sake of the Elements, for he was perished with cold and overcome with hunger. " Oh !

what is that, Levarcham?" said Deirdre. "There is nothing there for you to see, my child, but only the birds of the air, and they lost to one another, but let them go past us to the branches of the wood. There is no place or shelter for them here to-night." "Oh, mother," said Deirdre, " the bird asked to come in for the sake of the Sun and the Moon, and it is what you yourself told me, that anything that is asked like that, it is right for us to give it. If you will not let in the bird that is perished with cold and overcome with hunger, I myself will let it in." So Deirdre rose up and drew the bolt from the leaf of the door, and let in the hunter. She put a seat in the place for sitting, food in the place for eating, and drink in the place for drinking, for the man who had come into the house. "Come now and eat food, for you are in want of it," said Deirdre. "Indeed it is I was in want of food and drink and warmth when I came into this house ; but by my word, I have forgotten that since I saw yourself," said the hunter. "How little you are able to curb your tongue," said Levarcham. "It is not a great thing for you to keep your tongue quiet when you get the shelter of a house and the warmth of a hearth on a dark winter night." "That is so," said the hunter, " I may do that much, to keep my mouth shut ; but I swear by the oath my people swear by, if some others of the people of the world saw this great beauty that is hidden away here, they would not leave her long with you." "What people are those?" said Deirdre. "I will tell you that," said the hunter; "they are Naoise, son of Usnach, and Ainnle and Ardan, his two brothers." "What is the appearance of these men, if we should ever see them?" said Deirdre. "This is the appearance that is on those three men," said the hunter : "the colour of the raven is on their hair, their skin is like the swan on the wave, their cheeks like the blood of the speckled red calf, and their swiftness and their leap are like the

DEIRDRE SAID, "MOTHER, MOTHER, WHAT IS THAT?"

DEIRDRE AND THE HUNTER.

salmon of the stream and like the deer of the grey mountain; and the head and shoulders of Naoise are above all the other men of Ireland." "However they may be," said Levarcham, "get you out from here, and take another road; and by my word, little is my thankfulness to yourself, or to her that let you in." "You need not send him out for telling me that," said Deirdre, "for as to those three men, I myself saw them last night in a dream, and they hunting upon a hill."

The hunter went away, but in a little time after he began to think to himself how Conchubar, High King of Ulster, was used to lie down at night and to rise up in the morning by himself, without a wife or any one to speak to; and that if he could see this great beauty it was likely he would bring her home to Emain, and that he himself would get the good-will of the king for telling him there was such a queen to be found on the face of the world.

So he went straight to King Conchubar at Emain Macha, and he sent word in to the king that he had news for him, if he would hear it. The king sent for him to come in. "What is the reason of your journey?" he said. "It is what I have to tell you, King," said the hunter, "that I have seen the greatest beauty that ever was born in Ireland, and I am come to tell you of it."

"Who is this great beauty, and in what place is she to be seen, when she was never seen before you saw her, if you did see her?" "I did see her, indeed," said the hunter, "but no other man can see her, unless he knows from me the place where she is living." "Will you bring me to the place where she is, and you will have a good reward?" said the king. "I will bring you there," said the hunter. "Let you stay with my household to-night," said Conchubar, "and I myself and my people will go with you early on the morning of to-morrow." "I will stay," said the hunter, and he stayed that night in the household of King Conchubar.

Then Conchubar sent to Fergus and to the other chief men of Ulster, and he told them of what he was about to do. Though it was early when the songs and the music of the birds began in the woods, it was earlier yet when Conchubar, king of Ulster, rose up with his little company of near friends, in the fresh spring morning of the fresh and pleasant month of May, and the dew was heavy on every bush and flower as they went out towards the green hill where Deirdre was living

But many a young man of them that had a light glad, leaping step when they set out, had but a tired, slow, failing step before the end, because of the length and the roughness of the way. "It is down there below," said the hunter, "in the house in that valley, the woman is living, but I myself will not go nearer it than this.

Conchubar and his troop went down then to the green hillock where Deirdre was, and they knocked at the door of the house. Levarcham called out that neither answer nor opening would be given to any one at all, and that she did not want disturbance put on herself or her house. "Open," said Conchubar, "in the name of the High King of Ulster." When Levarcham heard Conchubar's voice, she knew there was no use trying to keep Deirdre out of sight any longer, and she rose up in haste and let in the king, and as many of his people as could follow him.

When the king saw Deirdre before him, he thought in himself that he never saw in the course of the day, or in the dreams of the night, a creature so beautiful, and he gave her his full heart's weight of love there and then. It is what he did; he put Deirdre up on the shoulders of his men, and she herself and Levarcham were brought away to Emain Macha.

With the love that Conchubar had for Deirdre, he wanted to marry her with no delay, but when her leave was asked, she would not give it, for she was young yet, and she had no knowledge of the duties of a wife, or the ways of a king's house. And when Conchubar was pressing her hard, she asked him to give her a delay of a year and a day. He said he would give her that, though it was hard for him, if she would give him her certain promise to marry him at the year's end. She did that, and Conchubar got a woman teacher for her, and nice, fine, pleasant, modest maidens to be with her at her lying down and at her rising up, to be companions to her. And Deirdre grew wise in the works of a young girl, and in the understanding of a woman; and if any one at all looked at her face, whatever colour she was before that, she would blush crimson red. And it is what Conchubar thought, that he never saw with the eyes of his body a creature that pleased him so well.

One day Deirdre and her companions were out on a hill near Emain Macha, looking around them in the pleasant sunshine, and they saw three men walking together. Deirdre was looking at the men and wondering at them, and when they came near, she remembered the talk of the hunter, and the three men she saw in her dream, and she thought to herself that these were the three sons of Usnach, and that this was Naoise, that had his head and shoulders above all the men of Ireland. The three brothers went by without turning their eyes at all upon the young girls on the hillside, and they were singing as they went, and whoever heard the low singing of the sons of Usnach, it was enchantment and music to them, and every cow that was being milked and heard it, gave two-thirds more of milk. And it is what happened, that love for Naoise came into the heart of Deirdre, so that she could not but follow him. She gathered up her skirt and went after the three men that had gone past the foot of the hill, leaving her companions there after her.

But Ainnle and Ardan had heard talk of the young girl that was at Conchubar's Court, and it is what they thought, that if Naoise their brother would see her, it is for himself he would have her, for she was not yet married to the king. So when they saw Deirdre coming after them, they said to one another to hasten their steps, for they had a long road to travel, and the dusk of night coming on. They did so, and Deirdre saw it, and she cried out after them, "Naoise, son of Usnach, are you going to leave me?" "What cry was that came to my ears, that it is not well for me to answer, and not easy for me to refuse?" said Naoise. "It was nothing but the cry of Conchubar's wild ducks," said his brothers; "but let us quicken our steps and hasten our feet, for we have a long road to travel, and the dusk of the evening coming on." They did so, and they were widening the distance between themselves and her. Then Deirdre cried, "Naoise! Naoise! son of Usnach, are you going to leave me?" "What cry was it that came to my ears and struck my heart, that it is not well for me to answer, or easy for me to refuse?" said Naoise. "Nothing but the cry of Conchubar's wild geese," said his brothers; "but let us quicken our steps and hasten our feet, the darkness of night is coming on." They did so, and were widening the distance between themselves and her. Then Deirdre cried the third time, "Naoise! Naoise! Naoise! son of Usnach, are you going to leave me?" "What sharp, clear cry was that, the sweetest that ever came to my ears, and the sharpest that ever struck my heart, of all the cries I ever heard," said Naoise. "What is it but the scream of Conchubar's lake swans," said his brothers. "That was the third cry of some person beyond there," said Naoise, "and I swear by my hand of valour," he said, "I will go no further until I see where the cry comes from." So Naoise turned back and met Deirdre, and Deirdre and Naoise kissed one another three times, and she gave a kiss to each of his brothers. And with the confusion that was on her, a blaze of red fire came upon her, and her colour came and went as quickly as the aspen by the stream. And it is what Naoise thought to himself, that he never saw a woman so beautiful in his life; and he gave Deirdre, there and then, the love that he never gave to living thing, to vision, or to creature, but to herself alone.

Then he lifted her high on his shoulder, and he said to his brothers to hasten their steps; and they hastened them.

"Harm will come of this," said the young men. "Although there should harm come," said Naoise, "I am willing to be in disgrace while I live. We will go with her to another province, and there is not in Ireland a king who will not give us a welcome." So they called their people, and that night they set out with three times fifty men, and three times fifty women, and three times fifty greyhounds, and Deirdre in their midst.

They were a long time after that shifting from one place to another all around Ireland, from Essruadh in the south, to Beinn Etair in the east again, and it is often they were in danger of being destroyed by Conchubar's devices. And one time the Druids raised a wood before them, but Naoise and his brothers cut their way through it. But at last they got out of Ulster and sailed to the country of Alban, and settled in a lonely place; and when hunting on the mountains failed them, they fell upon the cattle of the men of Alban, so that these gathered together to make an end of them. But the sons of Usnach called to the king of Scotland, and he took them into his friendship, and they gave him their help when he went out into battles or to war.

But all this time they had never spoken to the king of Deirdre, and they kept her with themselves, not to let any one see her, for they were afraid they might get their death on account of her, she being so beautiful.

But it chanced very early one morning, the king's steward came to visit them, and he found his way into the house where Naoise and Deirdre were, and there he saw them asleep beside one another. He went back then to the king, and he said : "Up to this time there has never been found a woman that would be a fitting wife for you; but there is a woman on the shore of Loch Ness now, is well worthy of you, king of the East. And what you have to do is to make an end of Naoise, for it is of his wife I am speaking." "I will not do that," said the king; "but go to her," he said, "and bid her to come and see me secretly." The steward brought her that message, but Deirdre sent him away, and all that he had said to her, she told it to Naoise afterwards. Then when she would not come to him, the king sent the sons of Usnach into every hard fight, hoping they would get their death, but they won every battle, and came back safe again. And after a while they went to Loch Eitche, near the sea, and they were left to themselves there for a while in peace and quietness. And they settled and made a dwelling house for themselves by the side of Loch Ness, and they could kill the salmon of the stream from out their own door, and the deer of the grey hills from out their window. But when Naoise went to the court of the king, his clothes were splendid among the great men of the army of Scotland, a cloak of bright purple, rightly shaped, with a fringe of bright gold; a coat of satin with fifty hooks of silver; a brooch on which were a hundred polished gems; a gold-hilted sword in his hand, two blue-green spears of bright points, a dagger with the colour of yellow gold on it, and a hilt of silver. But the two children they had, Gaiar and Aebgreine, they gave into the care of Manannan, Son of the Sea. And he cared them well in Emhain of the Apple Trees, and he brought Bobaras the poet to give learning to Gaiar. And Aebgreine of the Sunny Face he gave in marriage afterwards to Rinn, son of Eochaidh Juil of the Land of Promise.

Now it happened after a time that a very great feast was made by Conchubar, in Emain Macha, for all the great among his nobles, so that the whole company were easy and pleasant together. The musicians stood up to play their songs and to give poems, and they gave out the branches of relationship and of kindred. These are the names of the poets that were in Emain at the time, Cathbad, the Druid, son of Conall, son of Rudraige; Geanann of the Bright Face, son of Cathbad; Ferceirtne, and Geanann Black-Knee, and many others, and Sencha, son of Ailell.

They were all drinking and making merry until Conchubar, the king, raised his voice and spoke aloud, and it is what he said: " I desire to know from you, did you ever see a better house than this house of Emain, or a hearth better than my hearth in any place you were ever in? " " We did not," they said. " If that is so," said Conchubar, " do you know of anything at all that is wanting to you? " " We know of nothing," said they. " That is not so with me," said Conchubar. " I know of a great want that is on you, the want of the three best candles of the Gael, the three noble sons of Usnach, that ought not to be away from us for the sake of any woman in the world, Naoise, Ainnle, and Ardan; for surely they are the sons of a king, and they would defend the High Kingship against the best men of Ireland." "If we had dared," said they, "it is long ago we would have said it, and more than that, the province of Ulster would be equal to any other province in Ireland, if there was no Ulsterman in it but those three alone, for it is lions they are in hardness and in bravery." "If that is so," said Conchubar, "let us send word by a messenger to Alban, and to the dwelling-place of the sons of Usnach, to ask them back again." "Who will go there with the message?" said they all. "I cannot know that," said Conchubar, "for there is *geasa*, that is bonds, on Naoise not to come back with any man only one of the three, Conall Cearnach, or Fergus, or Cuchulain, and I will know now," said he, "which one of those three loves me best." Then he called Conall to one side, and he asked him, "What would you do with me if I should send you for the sons of Usnach, and if they were destroyed through me—a thing I do not mean to do?" "As I am not going to undertake it," said Conall, "I will say that it is not one alone I would kill, but any Ulsterman I would lay hold of that had harmed them would get shortening of life from me and the sorrow of death." "I see well," said Conchubar, "you are no friend of mine," and he put Conall away from him. Then he called Cuchulain to him, and asked him the same as he did the other. "I give my word, as I am not going," said Cuchulain, "if you want that of me, and that you think to kill them when they come, it is not one person alone that would die for it, but every Ulsterman I could lay hold of would get shortening of life from me and the sorrow of death." "I see well," said Conchubar, "that you are no friend of mine." And he put Cuchulain from him. And then he called Fergus to him, and asked him the same question, and Fergus said, "Whatever may happen, I promise your blood will be safe from me, but besides yourself there is no Ulsterman that would try to harm them, and that I would lay hold of, but I would give him shortening of life and the sorrow of death." "I see well," said Conchubar, "it is yourself must go for them, and it is to-morrow you must set out, for it is with you they will come, and when you are coming back to us westward, I put you under bonds to go first to the fort of Borach, son of Cainte, and give me your word now that as soon as you get there, you will send on the sons of Usnach to Emain, whether it be day or night at the time." After that the two of them went in together, and Fergus told all the company how it was under his charge they were to be put.

Then Conchubar went to Borach and asked had he a feast ready prepared for him. "I have," said Borach, "but although I was able to make it ready, I was not able to bring it to Emain." "If that is so," said Conchubar, "give it to Fergus when he comes back to Ireland, for it is *geasa* on him not to refuse your feast." Borach promised he would do that, and so they wore away that night.

So Fergus set out in the morning, and he brought no guard nor helpers with him, but himself and his two sons, Fair-Haired Iollan, and Rough-Red Buinne, and Cuillean, the shield-bearer, and the shield itself. They went on till they got to the dwelling-place of the sons of Usnach, and to Loch Eitche in Alba. It is how the sons of Usnach lived; they had three houses, and the house where they made ready the food, it is not there they would eat it, and the house where they would eat it, it is not there they would sleep.

When Fergus came to the harbour he let a great shout out of him. And it is how Naoise and Deirdre were, they had a chessboard between them, and they playing on it. Naoise heard the shout, and he said,

"That is the shout of a man of Ireland." "It is not, but the cry of a man of Alban," said Deirdre. She knew at the first it was Fergus gave the shout, but she denied it. Then Fergus let another shout out of him. "That is an Irish shout," said Naoise again. "It is not, indeed," said Deirdre, "let us go on playing." Then Fergus gave the third shout, and the sons of Usnach knew this time it was the shout of Fergus, and Naoise said to Ardan to go out and meet him. Then Deirdre told him that she herself knew at the first shout that it was Fergus. "Why did you deny it, then, Queen?" said Naoise. "Because of a vision I saw last night," said Deirdre. "Three birds I saw coming to us from Emain Macha, and three drops of honey in their mouths, and they left them with us, and three drops of our blood they brought away with them." "What meaning do you put on that, Queen?" said Naoise. "It is," said Deirdre, "Fergus that is coming to us with a message of peace from Conchubar, for honey is not sweeter than a message of peace sent by a lying man." "Let that pass," said Naoise. "Is there anything in it but troubled sleep and the melancholy of woman? And it is a long time Fergus is in the harbour. Rise up, Ardan, to be before him, and bring him with you here." And Ardan went down to meet him, and gave a fond kiss to himself and to his two sons. And it is what he said: "My love to you, dear comrades." After that he asked news of Ireland, and they gave it to him, and then they came to where Naoise and Ainnle and Deirdre were, and they kissed Fergus and his two sons, and they asked news of Ireland from them. "It is the best news I have for you," said Fergus, "that Conchubar, king of Ulster, has sworn by the earth beneath him, by the high heaven above him, and by the sun that travels to the west, that he will have no rest by day nor sleep by night, if the sons of Usnach, his own foster-brothers, will not come back to the land of their home and the country of their birth ; and he has sent us to ask you there." "It is better for them to stop here," said Deirdre, "for they have a greater sway in Scotland than Conchubar himself has in Ireland." "One's own country is better than any other thing," said Fergus, "for no man can have any pleasure, however great his good luck and his way of living, if he does not see his own country every day." "That is true," said Naoise, "for Ireland is dearer to myself than Alban, though I would get more in Alban than in Ireland." "It will be safe for you to come with me," said Fergus. "It will be safe indeed," said Naoise, "and we will go with you to Ireland ; and though there were no trouble beneath the sun, but a man to be far from his own land, there is little delight in peace and a long sleep to a man that is an exile. It is a pity for the man that is an exile ; it is little his honour, it is great his grief, for it is he will have his share of wandering."

It was not with Deirdre's will Naoise said that, and she was greatly against going with Fergus. And she said : "I had a dream last night of the three sons of Usnach, and they bound and put in the grave by Conchubar of the Red Branch." But Naoise said : "Lay down your dream, Deirdre, on the heights of the hills, lay down your dream on the sailors of the sea, lay down your dream on the rough grey stones, for we will give peace and we will get it from the king of the world and from Conchubar." But Deirdre spoke again, and it is what she said : "There is the howling of dogs in my ears ; a vision of the night is before my eyes, I see Fergus away from us, I see Conchubar without mercy in his dun ; I see Naoise without strength in battle ; I see Ainnle without his loud-sounding shield ; I see Ardan without shield or breastplate, and the Hill of Atha without delight. I see Conchubar asking for blood; I see Fergus caught with hidden lies; I see Deirdre crying with tears, I see Deirdre crying with tears."

"A thing that is unpleasing to me, and that I would never give in to," said Fergus, "is to listen to the howling of dogs, and to the dreams of women; and since Conchubar, the High King, has sent a message of friendship, it would not be right for you to refuse it." "It would not be right, indeed," said Naoise, "and we will go with you to-morrow." And Fergus gave his word, and he said, "If all the men of Ireland were against you, it would not profit them, for neither shield nor sword or a helmet itself would be any help or protection to them against you, and I myself to be with you." "That is true," said Naoise, "and we will go with you to Ireland."

They spent the night there until morning, and then they went where the ships were, and they went on the sea, and a good many of their people with them, and Deirdre looked back on the land of Alban, and it is what she said: "My love to you, O land to the east, and it goes ill with me to leave you; for it is pleasant are your bays and your harbours and your wide flowery plains and your green-sided hills; and little need was there for us to leave you." And she made this complaint: "Dear to me is that land, that land to the east, Alban, with its wonders; I would not have come from it hither but that I came with Naoise.

"Dear to me, Dun Fiodhaigh and Dun Fionn; dear is the dun above them; dear to me Inis Droignach, dear to me Dun Suibhne.

"O Coill Cuan! Ochone! Coil Cuan! where Ainnle used to come. My grief! it was short I thought his stay there with Naoise in Western Alban. Glen Laoi, O Glen Laoi, where I used to sleep under soft coverings;

fish and venison and badger's flesh, thât was my portion in Glen Laoi.

"Glen Masan, my grief! Glen Masan! high its hart's-tongue, bright its stalks; we were rocked to pleasant sleep over the wooded harbour of Masan.

"Glen Archan, my grief! Glen Archan, the straight valley of the pleasant ridge; never was there a young man more light-hearted than my Naoise used to be in Glen Archan.

"Glen Eitche, my grief! Glen Eitche, it was there I built my first house; beautiful were the woods on our rising; the home of the sun is Glen Eitche.

"Glen-da-Rua, my grief! Glen-da-Rua, my love to every man that belongs to it; sweet is the voice of the cuckoo on the bending branch on the hill above Glen-da-Rua.

"Dear to me is Droighin over the fierce strand, dear are its waters over the clean sand; I would never have come out from it at all but that I came with my beloved!"

After she had made that complaint they came to Dun Borach, and Borach gave three fond kisses to Fergus and to the sons of Usnach along with him. It was then Borach said he had a feast laid out for Fergus, and that it was *geasa* for him to leave it until he would have eaten it. But Fergus reddened with anger from head to foot, and it is what he said: "It is a bad thing you have done, Borach, laying out a feast for me, and Conchubar to have made me give my word that as soon as I would come to Ireland, whether it would be by day or in the night-time, I would send on the sons of Usnach to Emain Macha." "I hold you under bonds," said Borach, "to stop and use the feast."

Then Fergus asked Naoise what should he do about the feast. "You must choose," said Deirdre, "whether you will forsake the children of Usnach or the feast, and it would be better for you to refuse the feast than to forsake the sons of Usnach." "I will not forsake them," said he, "for I will send my two sons, Fair-Haired Iollan and Rough-Red Buinne, with them, to Emain Macha." "On my word," said Naoise, "that is a great deal to do for us; for up to this no other person ever protected us but ourselves." And he went out of the place in great anger; and Ainnle, and Ardan, and Deirdre, and the two sons of Fergus followed him, and they left Fergus dark and sorrowful after them. But for all that, Fergus was full sure that if all the provinces of Ireland would go into one council, they would not consent to break the pledge he had given.

As for the sons of Usnach, they went on their way by every short road, and Deirdre said to them, "I will give you a good advice, Sons of Usnach, though you may not follow it." "What is that advice, Queen?" said Naoise. "It is," said she, "to go to Rechrainn, between Ireland and Scotland, and to wait there until Fergus has done with the feast; and that will be the keeping of his word to Fergus, and it will be the lengthening of your lives to you." "We will not follow that advice," said Naoise; and the children of Fergus said it was little trust she had in them, when she thought they would not protect her, though their hands might not be so strong as the hands of the sons of Usnach; and besides that, Fergus had given them his word. "Alas! it is sorrow came on us with the word of Fergus," said Deirdre, "and he to forsake us for a feast," and she made this complaint: "It is grief to me that ever I came from the east on the word of the unthinking son of Rogh. It is only lamentations I will make. Och! it is very sorrowful my heart is!

"My heart is heaped up with sorrow; it is to-night my great hurt is. My grief! my dear companions, the end of your days is come."

And it is what Naoise answered her : "Do not say that in your haste, Deirdre, more beautiful than the sun. Fergus would never have come for us eastward to bring us back to be destroyed."

And Deirdre said, "My grief! I think it too far for you, beautiful sons of Usnach, to have come from Alban of the rough grass; it is lasting will be its life-long sorrow."

After that they went forward to Finncairn of the watch-tower on sharp-peaked Slieve Fuad, and Deirdre stayed after them in the valley, and sleep fell on her there.

When Naoise saw that Deirdre was left after them, he turned back as she was rising out of her sleep, and he said, "What made you wait after us, Queen?" "Sleep that was on me," said Deirdre; "and I saw a vision in it." "What vision was that?" said Naoise. "It was," she said, "Fair-Haired Iollan that I saw without his head on him, and Rough-Red Buinne with his head on him; and it is without help of Rough-Red Buinne you were, and it is with the help of Fair-Haired Iollan you were." And she made this complaint:

"It is a sad vision has been shown to me, of my four tall, fair, bright companions; the head of each has been taken from him, and no help to be had one from another."

But when Naoise heard this he reproached her, and said, "O fair, beautiful woman, nothing does your mouth speak but evil. Do not let the sharpness and the great misfortune that come from it fall on your friends." And Deirdre answered him with kind, gentle words, and it is what she said: "It would be better to me to see harm come on any other person than upon any one of you three, with whom I have travelled over the seas and over the wide plains; but when I look on you, it is only Buinne I can see safe and whole, and

I know by that his life will be longest among you ; and indeed it is I that am sorrowful to-night."

After that they came forward to the high willows, and it was then Deirdre said, " I see a cloud in the air, and it is a cloud of blood ; and I would give you a good advice, sons of Usnach," she said. " What is that advice?" said Naoise. " To go to Dundealgan where Cuchulain is, until Fergus has done with the feast, and to be under the protection of Cuchulain, for fear of the treachery of Conchubar." " Since there is no fear on us, we will not follow that advice," said Naoise. And Deirdre complained, and it is what she said : " O Naoise, look at the cloud I see above us in the air ; I see a cloud over green Macha, cold and deep red like blood. I am startled by the cloud that I see here in the air ; a thin, dreadful cloud that is like a clot of blood. I give a right advice to the beautiful sons of Usnach not to go to Emain to-night, because of the danger that is over them.

" We will go to Dundealgan, where the Hound of the Smith is ; we will come to-morrow from the south along with the Hound, Cuchulain."

But Naoise said in his anger to Deirdre, " Since there is no fear on us, we will not follow your advice." And Deirdre turned to the grandsons of Rogh, and it is what she said : " It is seldom until now, Naoise, that yourself and myself were not of the one mind. And I say to you, Naoise, that you would not have gone against me like this, the day Manannan gave me the cup in the time of his great victory."

After that they went on to Emain Macha. " Sons of Usnach," said Deirdre, " I have a sign by which you will know if Conchubar is going to do treachery on you." " What sign is that?" said Naoise. " If you are let come into the house where Conchubar is, and the nobles of Ulster, then Conchubar is not going to do treachery on you. But if it is in the House of the Red Branch you are put, then he is going to do treachery on you."

After that they came to Emain Macha, and they took the handwood and struck the door, and the doorkeeper asked who was there. They told him that it was the sons of Usnach, and Deirdre, and the two sons of Fergus were there.

When Conchubar heard that, he called his stewards and serving men to him, and he asked them how was the House of the Red Branch for food and for drink. They said that if all the seven armies of Ulster would come there, they would find what would satisfy them. "If that is so," said Conchubar, "bring the sons of Usnach into it."

It was then Deirdre said, "It would have been better for you to follow my advice, and never to have come to Emain, and it would be right for you to leave it, even at this time." "We will not," said Fair-Haired Iollan, "for it is not fear or cowardliness was ever seen on us, but we will go to the house." So they went on to the House of the Red Branch, and the stewards and the serving-men with them, and well-tasting food was served to them, and pleasant drinks, till they were all glad and merry, except only Deirdre and the sons of Usnach; for they did not use much food or drink, because of the length and the greatness of their journey from Dun Borach to Emain Macha. Then Naoise said, "Give the chessboard to us till we go playing." So they gave them the chessboard and they began to play.

It was just at that time Conchubar was asking, "Who will I send that will bring me word of Deirdre, and that will tell me if she has the same appearance and the same shape she had before, for if she has, there is not a woman in the world has a more beautiful shape or appearance than she has, and I will bring her out with edge of blade and point of sword in spite of the sons of Usnach, good though they be. But if not, let Naoise have her for himself." " I myself will go there," said Levarcham, " and I will bring you word of that." And it is how it was, Deirdre was dearer to her than any other person in the world; for it was often she went through the world looking for Deirdre and bringing news to her and from her. So Levarcham went over to the House of the Red Branch, and near it she saw a great troop of armed men, and she spoke to them, but they made her no answer, and she knew by that it was none of the men of Ulster were in it, but men from some strange country that Conchubar's messengers had brought to Emain.

And then she went in where Naoise and Deirdre were, and it is how she found them, the polished chessboard between them, and they playing on it; and she gave them fond kisses, and she said: " You are not doing well to be playing; and it is to bring Conchubar word if Deirdre has the same shape and appearance she used to have that he sent me here now; and there is grief on me for the deed that will be done in Emain to-night, treachery that will be done, and the killing of kindred, and the three bright candles of the Gael to be quenched, and Emain will not be the better of it to the end of life and time," and she made this complaint sadly and wearily:

" My heart is heavy for the treachery that is being done in Emain this night; on account of this treachery, Emain will never be at peace from this out.

" The three that are most king-like to-day under the sun; the three best of all that live on the earth, it is grief to me to-night they to die for the sake of any woman. Naoise and Ainnle whose deeds are known, and Ardan, their brother; treachery is to be done on the young, bright-faced three; it is not I that am not sorrowful to-night."

When she had made this complaint, Levarcham said to the sons of Usnach and to the children of Fergus to shut close the doors and the windows of the house and to do bravery. "And oh, sons of Fergus," she said, "defend your charge and your care bravely till Fergus comes, and you will have praise and a blessing for it." And she cried with many tears, and she went back to where Conchubar was, and he asked news of Deirdre of her. And Levarcham said, "It is good news and bad news I have for you." "What news is that?" said Conchubar. "It is the good news," she said, "the three sons of Usnach to have come to you and to be over there, and they are the three that are bravest and mightiest in form and in looks and in countenance, of all in the world; and Ireland will be yours from this out, since the sons of Usnach are with you; and the news that is worst with me is, the woman that was best of the women of the world in form and in looks, going out of Emain, is without the form and without the appearance she used to have."

When Conchubar heard that, much of his jealousy went backward, and he was drinking and making merry for a while, until he thought on Deirdre again the second time, and on that he asked, "Who will I get to bring me word of Deirdre?" But he did not find any one would go there. And then he said to Gelban, the merry, pleasant son of the king of Lochlann: "Go over and bring me word if Deirdre has the same shape and the same appearance she used to have, for if she has, there is not on the ridge of the world or on the waves of the earth, a woman more beautiful than herself."

So Gelban went to the House of the Red Branch, and he found the doors and the windows of the fort shut, and fear came on him. And it is what he said: "It is not an easy road for any one that would get to the sons of Usnach, for I think there is very great anger on them." And after that he found a window that was left open by forgetfulness in the house, and he was looking in. Then Deirdre saw him through the window, and when she saw him looking at her, she went into a red blaze of blushes, and Naoise knew that some one was looking at her from the window, and she told him that she saw a young man looking in at them. It is how Naoise was at that time, with a man of the chessmen in his hand, and he made a fair throw over his shoulder at the young man, that put the eye out of his head. The young man went back to where Conchubar was. "You were merry and pleasant going out," said Conchubar, "but you are sad and cheerless coming back." And then Gelban told him the story from beginning to end. "I see well," said Conchubar, "the man that made that throw will be king of the world, unless he has his life shortened. And what appearance is there on Deirdre?" he said. "It is this," said Gelban, "although Naoise put out my eye, I would have wished to stay there looking at her with the other eye, but for the haste you put on me; for there is not in the world a woman is better of shape or of form than herself."

When Conchubar heard that, he was filled with jealousy and with envy, and he bade the men of his army that were with him, and that had been drinking at the feast, to go and attack the place were the sons of Usnach were. So they went forward to the House of the Red Branch, and they gave three great shouts around it, and they put fires and red flames to it. When the sons of Usnach heard the shouts, they asked who those men were that were about the house. "Conchubar and the men of Ulster," they all said together. "Is it the pledge of Fergus you would break?" said Fair-Haired Iollan. "On my word," said Conchubar, "there will be sorrow on the sons of Usnach, Deirdre to be with them." "That is true," said Deirdre, "Fergus had deceived you." "By my oath," said Rough-Red Buinne, "if he betrayed, we will not betray." It was then Buinne went out and killed three-fifths of the fighting men outside, and put great disturbance on the rest; and Conchubar asked who was there, and who was doing destruction on his men like that. "It is I, myself, Rough-Red Buinne, son of Fergus," said he. "I will give you a good gift if you will leave off," said Conchubar. "What gift is that?" said Rough-Red Buinne. "A hundred of land," said Conchubar. "What besides?" said Rough-Red Buinne. "My own friendship and my counsel," said Conchubar. "I will take that," said Rough-Red Buinne. It was a good mountain that was given him as a reward, but it turned barren in the same night, and no green grew on it again for ever, and it used to be called the Mountain of the Share of Buinne.

Deirdre heard what they were saying. "By my word," she said, "Rough-Red Buinne has forsaken you, and in my opinion, it is like the father the son is." "I give my word," says Fair-Haired Iollan, "that is not so with me; as long as this narrow, straight sword stays in my hand, I will not forsake the sons of Usnach."

After that, Fair-Haired Iollan went out, and made three courses around the house, and killed three-fifths of heroes outside, and he came in again where Naoise was, and he playing chess, and Ainnle with him. So Iollan went out the second time, and made three other courses round the fort, and he brought a lighted torch with him on the lawn, and he went destroying the hosts, so that they dared not come to attack the house. And he was a good son, Fair-Haired Iollan, for he never refused any person on the ridge of the world anything that he had, and he never took wages from any person but only Fergus.

It was then Conchubar said: "What place is my own son, Fiacra the Fair?" "I am here, High Prince," said Fiacra. "By my word," said Conchubar, "it is on the one night yourself and Iollan were born, and as it is the arms of his father he has with him, let you take my arms with you, that is, my shield, the Ochain, my two spears, and my great sword, the Gorm Glas, the Blue Green—and do bravery and great deeds with them."

Then Fiacra took Conchubar's arms, and he and Fair-Haired Iollan attacked one another, and they made a stout fight, one against the other. But however it was, Fair-Haired Iollan put down Fiacra, so that he made him lie under the shelter of his shield, till it roared for the greatness of the strait he was in; for it was the way with the Ochain, the shield of Conchubar, to roar when the person on whom it would be was in danger; and the three chief waves of Ireland, the Wave of Tuagh, the Wave of Cliodna, and the Wave of Rudraige, roared in answer to it.

It was at that time Conall Cearnach was at Dun Sobairce, and he heard the Wave of Tuagh. "True it is," said Conall, "Conchubar is in some danger, and it is not right for me to be here listening to him."

Conall rose up on that, and he put his arms and his armour on him, and came forward to where Conchubar was at Emain Macha, and he found the fight going on on the lawn, and Fiacra, the son of Conchubar, greatly pressed by Fair-Haired Iollan, and neither the king of Ulster nor any other person dared to go between them. But Conall went aside, behind Fair-Haired Iollan and thrust his sword through him. "Who is it has wounded me behind my back?" said Fair-Haired Iollan. "Whoever did it, by my hand of valour, he would have got a fair fight, face to face, from myself." "Who are you yourself?" said Conall. "I am Iollan, son of

Fergus, and are you yourself Conall?" "It is I," said Conall. "It is evil and it is heavy the work you have done," said Iollan, "and the sons of Usnach under my protection." "Is that true?" said Conall. "It is true, indeed," said Iollan. "By my hand of valour," said Conall, "Conchubar will not get his own son alive from me to avenge it," and he gave a stroke of the sword to Fiacra, so that he struck his head off, and he left them so. The clouds of death came upon Fair-Haired Iollan then, and he threw his arms towards the fortress, and called out to Naoise to do bravery, and after that he died.

It is then Conchubar himself came out and nineteen hundred men with him, and Conall said to him: "Go up now to the doorway of the fort, and see where your sister's children are lying on a bed of trouble." And when Conchubar saw them he said: "You are not sister's children to me; it is not the deed of sister's children you have done me, but you have done harm to me with treachery in the sight of all the men of Ireland." And it is what Ainnle said to him: "Although we took well-shaped, soft-handed Deirdre from you, yet we did a little kindness to you at another time, and this is the time to remember it. That day your ship was breaking up on the sea, and it full of gold and silver, we gave you up our own ship, and ourselves went swimming to the harbour." But Conchubar said: "If you did fifty good deeds to me, surely this would be my thanks; I would not give you peace, and you in distress, but every great want I could put on you."

And then Ardan said: "We did another little kindness to you, and this is the time to remember it; the day the speckled horse failed you on the green of Dundealgan, it was we gave you the grey horse that would bring you fast on your road."

But Conchubar said: "If you had done fifty good

deeds to me, surely this would be my thanks; I would not give you peace, and you in distress, but every great want I could put on you."

And then Naoise said: "We did you another good deed, and this is the time to remember it; we have put you under many benefits; it is strong our right is to your protection.

"The time when Murcael, son of Brian, fought the seven battles at Beinn Etair, we brought you, without fail, the heads of the sons of the king of the South-East."

But Conchubar said: "If you had done me fifty good deeds, surely this is my thanks; I would not give you peace in your distress, but every great want I could put upon you.

"Your death is not a death to me now, young sons of Usnach, since he that was innocent fell by you, the third best of the horsemen of Ireland."

Then Deirdre said: "Rise up, Naoise, take your sword, good son of a king, mind yourself well, for it is not long that life will be left in your fair body."

It is then all Conchubar's men came about the house, and they put fires and burning to it. Ardan went out then, and his men, and put out the fires and killed three hundred men. And Ainnle went out in the third part of the night, and he killed three hundred, and did slaughter and destruction on them.

And Naoise went out in the last quarter of the night, and drove away all the army from the house.

He came into the house after that, and it is then Deirdre rose up and said to him: "By my word, it is well you won your way; and do bravery and valour from this out, and it was bad advice you took when you ever trusted Conchubar."

As for the sons of Usnach, after that they made a good protection with their shields, and they put Deirdre in the middle and linked the shields around her, and they gave three leaps out over the walls of Emain, and they killed three hundred men in that sally.

When Conchubar saw that, he went to Cathbad, the Druid, and said to him : " Go, Cathbad, to the sons of Usnach, and work enchantment on them ; for unless they are hindered they will destroy the men of Ulster for ever if they go away in spite of them ; and I give the word of a true hero, they will get no harm from me, but let them only make agreement with me." When Cathbad heard that, he agreed, believing him, and he went to the end of his arts and his knowledge to hinder the sons of Usnach, and he worked enchantment on them, so that he put the likeness of a dark sea about them, with hindering waves. And when Naoise saw the waves rising he put up Deirdre on his shoulder, and it is how the sons of Usnach were, swimming on the ground as they were going out of Emain ; yet the men of Ulster did not dare to come near them until their swords had fallen from their hands. But after their swords fell from their hands, the sons of Usnach were taken. And when they were taken, Conchubar asked of the children of Durthacht to kill them. But the children of Durthacht said they would not do that. There was a young man with Conchubar whose name was Maine, and his surname Rough-Hand, son of the king of the fair Norwegians, and it is Naoise had killed his father and his two brothers ; Athrac and Triathrach were their names And he said he himself would kill the sons of Usnach. " If that is so," said Ardan, " kill me the first, for I am younger than my brothers, so that I will not see my brothers killed." " Let him not be killed but myself," said Ainnle. " Let that not be done," said Naoise, " for I have a sword that Manannan, son of Lir, gave me, and the stroke of it leaves nothing after it, track nor trace ; and strike the three of us together, and we will die at the one time." "That is well," said they all, "and let you lay down your heads," they said. They did that, and Maine gave a strong quick blow of the sword on the three necks together on the block, and struck the three heads off them with one stroke ; and the men of Ulster gave three loud sorrowful shouts, and cried aloud about them there.

As for Deirdre, she cried pitifully, wearily, and tore her fair hair, and she was talking on the sons of Usnach and on Alban, and it is what she said :

"A blessing eastward to Alban from me ; good is the sight of her bays and valleys, pleasant was it to sit on the slopes of her hills, where the sons of Usnach used to be hunting.

"One day, when the nobles of Scotland were drinking with the sons of Usnach, to whom they owed their affection, Naoise gave a kiss secretly to the daughter of the lord of Duntreon. He sent her a frightened deer, wild, and a fawn at its foot ; and he went to visit her coming home from the host of Inverness. When myself heard that, my head filled full of jealousy ; I put my boat on the waves, it was the same to me to live or to die. They followed me swimming, Ainnle and Ardan, that never said a lie ; they turned me back again, two that would give battle to a hundred ; Naoise gave me his true word, he swore three times with his arms as witness, he would never put vexation on me again, until he would go from me to the hosts of the dead.

"Och! if she knew to-night, Naoise to be under a covering of clay, it is she would cry her fill, and it is I would cry along with her."

After she had made this complaint, seeing they were all taken up with one another, Deirdre came forward on the lawn, and she was running round and round, up and down, from one to another, and Cuchulain met

NAOISE PUT DEIRDRE ON HIS SHOULDER AS THE WAVES ROSE.

DEIRDRE'S LAMENT.

her, and she told him the story from first to last, how
it had happened to the sons of Usnach. It is sorrowful Cuchulain was for that, for there was not in the
world a man was dearer to him than Naoise. And
he asked who killed him. "Maine Rough-Hand," said
Deirdre. Then Cuchulain went away, sad and sorrowful, to Dundealgan.

After that Deirdre lay down by the grave, and
they were digging earth from it, and she made this
lament after the sons of Usnach:

"Long is the day without the sons of Usnach; it
was never wearisome to be in their company; sons of
a king that entertained exiles; three lions of the Hill of
the Cave.

"Three darlings of the women of Britain; three
hawks of Slieve Cuilenn; sons of a king served by
valour, to whom warriors did obedience. The three
mighty bears; three lions of the fort of Conrach;
three sons of a king who thought well of their praise;
three nurslings of the men of Ulster.

"Three heroes not good at homage; their fall is a
cause of sorrow; three sons of the sister of a king;
three props of the army of Cuailgne.

"Three dragons of Dun Monad, the three valiant
men from the Red Branch; I myself will not be living
after them, the three that broke hard battles.

"Three that were brought up by Aoife, to whom
lands were under tribute; three pillars in the breach
of battle; three pupils that were with Scathach.

"Three pupils that were with Uathach; three
champions that were lasting in might; three shining sons of Usnach; it is weariness to be without
them.

"The High King of Ulster, my first betrothed, I
forsook for love of Naoise; short my life will be after
him; I will make keening at their burial.

"That I would live after Naoise let no one think on the earth; I will not go on living after Ainnle and after Ardan.

"After them I myself will not live; three that would leap through the midst of battle; since my beloved is gone from me I will cry my fill over his grave.

"O young man, digging the new grave, do not make the grave narrow; I will be along with them in the grave, making lamentation and ochones!

"Many the hardship I met with along with the three heroes; I suffered want of house, want of fire, it is myself that used not to be troubled.

"Their three shields and their spears made a bed for me often. O young man, put their three swords close over their grave.

"Their three hounds, their three hawks, will be from this time without huntsmen; three helpers of every battle; three pupils of Conall Cearnach.

"The three leashes of those three hounds have brought a sigh from my heart; it is I had the care of them, the sight of them is a cause of grief.

"I was never one day alone to the day of the making of this grave, though it is often that myself and yourselves were in loneliness.

"My sight is gone from me with looking at the grave of Naoise; it is short till my life will leave me, and those who would have keened me do not live.

"Since it is through me they were betrayed I will be tired out with sorrow; it is a pity I was not in the earth before the sons of Usnach were killed.

"Sorrowful was my journey with Fergus, betraying me to the Red Branch; we were deceived all together with his sweet, flowery words. I left the delights of Ulster for the three heroes that were bravest; my life will not be long, I myself am alone after them.

" I am Deirdre without gladness, and I at the end of my life; since it is grief to be without them, I myself will not be long after them."

After that complaint Deirdre loosed out her hair, and threw herself on the body of Naoise before it was put in the grave and gave three kisses to him, and when her mouth touched his blood, the colour of burning sods came into her cheeks, and she rose up like one that had lost her wits, and she went on through the night till she came to where the waves were breaking on the strand. And a fisherman was there and his wife, and they brought her into their cabin and sheltered her, and she neither smiled nor laughed, nor took food, drink, or sleep, nor raised her head from her knees, but crying always after the sons of Usnach.

But when she could not be found at Emain, Conchubar sent Levarcham to look for her, and to bring her back to his palace, that he might make her his wife. And Levarcham found her in the fisherman's cabin, and she bade her come back to Emain, where she would have protection and riches and all that she would ask. And she gave her this message she brought from Conchubar : " Come up to my house, O branch with the dark eye-lashes, and there need be no fear on your fair face, of hatred or of jealousy or of reproach." And Deirdre said : " I will not go up to his house, for it is not land or earth or food I am wanting, or gold or silver or horses, but leave to go to the grave where the sons of Usnach are lying, till I give the three honey kisses to their three white, beautiful bodies." And she made this complaint :

" Make keening for the heroes that were killed on their coming to Ireland ; stately they used to be, coming to the house, the three great sons of Usnach.

" The sons of Usnach fell in the fight like three branches that were growing straight and nice, and they destroyed in a heavy storm that left neither bud nor twig of them.

"Naoise, my gentle, well-learned comrade, make no delay in crying him with me; cry for Ardan that killed the wild boars, cry for Ainnle whose stength was great.

"It was Naoise that would kiss my lips, my first man and my first sweetheart; it was Ainnle would pour out my drink, and it was Ardan would lay my pillow.

"Though sweet to you is the mead that is drunk by the soft-living son of Ness, the food of the sons of Usnach was sweeter to me all through my lifetime.

"Whenever Naoise would go out to hunt through the woods or the wide plains, all the meat he would bring back was better to me than honey.

"Though sweet to you are the sounds of pipes and of trumpets, it is truly I say to the king, I have heard music that is sweeter.

"Delightful to Conchubar, the king, are pipes and trumpets; but the singing of the sons of Usnach was more delightful to me.

"It was Naoise had the deep sound of the waves in his voice; it was the song of Ardan that was good, and the voice of Ainnle towards their green dwelling-place.

"Their birth was beautiful and their blossoming, as they grew to the strength of manhood; sad is the end to-day, the sons of Usnach to be cut down.

"Dear were their pleasant words, dear their young, high strength; in their going through the plains of Ireland there was a welcome before the coming of their strength.

"Dear their grey eyes that were loved by women, many looked on them as they went; when they went freely searching through the woods, their steps were pleasant on the dark mountain.

"I do not sleep at any time, and the colour is gone from my face; there is no sound can give me delight since the sons of Usnach do not come.

"I do not sleep through the night; my senses are scattered away from me, I do not care for food or drink. I have no welcome to-day for the pleasant drink of nobles, or ease, or comfort, or delight, or a great house, or the palace of a king.

"Do not break the strings of my heart as you took hold of my young youth, Conchubar; though my darling is dead, my love is strong to live. What is country to me, or land, or lordship? What are swift horses? What are jewels and gold? Och! it is I will be lying to-night on the strand like the beautiful sons of Usnach."

So Levarcham went back to Conchubar to tell him what way Deirdre was, and that she would not come with her to Emain Macha.

And when she was gone, Deirdre went out on the strand, and she found a carpenter making an oar for a boat, and making a mast for it, clean and straight, to put up a sail to the wind. And when she saw him making it, she said: "It is a sharp knife you have, to cut the oar so clean and so straight, and if you will give it to me," she said, "I will give you a ring of the best gold in Ireland for it, the ring that belonged to Naoise, and that was with him through the battle and through the fight; he thought much of it in his lifetime; it is pure gold, through and through." So the carpenter took the ring in his hand, and the knife in the other hand, and he looked at them together, and he gave her the knife for the ring, and for her asking and her tears. Then Deirdre went close to the waves, and she said: "Since the other is not with me now, I will spend no more of my lifetime without him." And with that she drove the black knife into her side, but she drew it out again and threw it in the sea to her right hand, the way no one would be blamed for her death.

Then Conchubar came down to the strand and five hundred men along with him, to bring Deirdre away to Emain Macha, but all he found before him was her white body on the ground, and it without life. And it is what he said :

"A thousand deaths on the time I brought death on my sister's children ; now I am myself without Deirdre, and they themselves are without life.

"They were my sister's children, the three brothers I vexed with blows, Naoise, and Ainnle, and Ardan ; they have died along with Deirdre."

And they took her white, beautiful body, and laid it in a grave, and a flagstone was raised over her grave, and over the grave of the sons of Usnach, and their names were written in Ogham, and keening was made for their burial.

And as to Fergus, son of Rogh, he came on the day after the children of Usnach were killed, to Emain Macha. And when he found they had been killed and his pledge to them broken, he himself, and Cormac Conloingeas, Conchubar's own son, and Dubthach, the Beetle of Ulster, with their men, made an attack on Conchubar's house and men, and a great many were killed by them, and Emain Macha was burned and destroyed.

And after doing that, they went into Connaught, to Ailell and to Maeve at Cruachan, and they were made welcome there, and they took service with them and fought with them against Ulster because of the treachery that was done by Conchubar. And that is the way Fergus and the others came to be on the side of the men of Connaught in the war for the Brown Bull of Cuailgne.

And Cathbad laid a curse on Emain Macha, on account of that great wrong. And it is what he said, that none of the race of Conchubar should have the kingdom, to the end of life and time.

And that came true, for the most of Conchubar's sons died in his own lifetime, and when he was near his death, he bade the men of Ulster bring back Cormac Conloingeas out of Cruachan, and give him the kingdom.

So they sent messengers to Cormac, and he set out and his three troops of men with him, and he left his blessing with Ailell and with Maeve, and he promised them a good return for all the kind treatment they had given him. And they crossed the river at Athluain, and there they saw a red woman at the edge of the ford, and she washing her chariot and her harness. And after that they met a young girl coming towards them, and a light green cloak about her, and a brooch of precious stones at her breast. And Cormac asked her was she coming with them, and she said she was not, and it would be better for himself to turn back, for the ruin of his life was come.

And he stopped for the night at the House of the Two Smiths on the hill of Bruighean Mor, the great dwelling-place.

But a troop of the men of Connaught came about the house in the night, for they were on the way home after destroying and robbing a district of Ulster, and they thought to make an end of Cormac before he would get to Emain.

And it chanced there was a great harper, Craiftine, living close by, and his wife, Sceanb, daughter of Scethern, a Druid of Connaught, loved Cormac Conloingeas, and three times she had gone to meet him at Athluain, and she planted three trees there—Grief, and Dark, and Dumbness.

And there was great hatred and jealousy of Cormac on Craiftine, so when he knew the men of Connaught were going to make an attack on him, he went outside the house with his harp, and played a soft sleepy tune to him, the way he had not the strength to rouse himself up, and himself and the most of his people were killed. And Amergin, that had gone with the message to him, made his grave and his mound, and the place is called Cluain Duma, the Lawn of the Mound.

VIII

THE DREAM OF ANGUS OG

ANGUS, son of the Dagda, was asleep in his bed one night, and he saw what he thought was a young girl standing near him at the top of the bed, and she the most beautiful he had ever seen in Ireland. He put out his hand to take her hand, but she vanished on the moment, and in the morning when he awoke there were no trace or tidings of her.

He got no rest that day thinking of her, and that she had gone away before he could speak to her. And the next night he saw her again, and this time she brought a little harp in her hand, the sweetest he ever heard, and she played a song to him, so that he fell asleep and slept till morning. And the same thing happened every night for a year. She would come to his bedside and be playing on the harp to him, but she would be gone before he could speak with her. And at the end of the year she came no more, and Angus began to pine away with love of her and with fretting after her ; and he would take no food, but lay upon the bed, and no one knew what it was ailed him. And all the physicians of Ireland came together, but they could not put a name on his sickness or find any cure for him.

But at last Fergne, the physician of Conn, was brought to him, and as soon as he looked at him he knew it was not on his body the sickness was, but on his mind. And he sent every one away out of the room, and he said : " I think it is for the love of some woman that you are wasting away like this." "That is true, indeed," said Angus ; "and it is my sickness has betrayed me." And then he told him how the woman with the most beautiful appearance of any woman in Ireland, used to come and to be playing the harp to him through the night, and how she had vanished away.

Then Fergne went and spoke with Boann, Angus's mother, and he told her all that happened, and he bade her to send and search all through Ireland if she could find a young girl of the same appearance as the one Angus had seen in his sleep. And then he left him in his mother's care, and she had all Ireland searched for a year, but no young girl of that appearance could be found.

At the end of the year, Boann sent for Fergne to come again, and she said : "We have not got any help from our search up to this." And Fergne said : "Send for the Dagda, that he may come and speak to his son." So they sent for the Dagda, and when he came, he said : "What have I been called for?" "To give an advice to your son," said Fergne, "and to help him, for he is lying sick on account of a young girl that appeared to him in his sleep, and that cannot be found ; and it would be a pity for him to die." "What use will it be, I to speak to him?" said the Dagda, "for my knowledge is no higher than your own." "By my word," said Fergne, "you are the king of all the Sidhe of Ireland, and what you have to do is to go to Bodb, the king of the Sidhe of Munster, for he has a name for knowledge all through Ireland." So messengers were sent to Bodb, at his house in Sidhe Femain, and he bade them welcome. "A welcome before you, messenger of the Dagda," he said, "and what is the message you have brought?" "This is the message," they said, "Angus

Og, son of the Dagda, is wasting away these two years
with love of a woman he saw in his dreams, and we
have not been able to find her in any place. And this
is an order to you," they said, "from the Dagda, to
search out through Ireland a young girl of the same
form and appearance as the one he saw." "The search
will be made," said Bodb, "if it lasts me a year."

And at the end of a year he sent messengers to the
Dagda. "Is it a good message you have brought?"
said the Dagda. "It is, indeed," they said; "and this
is the message Bodb bade us give you, 'I have searched
all Ireland until I found the young girl with the same
form and appearance that you said, at Loch Beul
Draguin, at the Harp of Cliach.' And now," they said,
"he bids Angus to come with us, till he sees if it is the
same woman that appeared to him in his dream."

So Angus set out in his chariot to Sidhe Femain,
and Bodb bade him welcome, and made a great feast
for him, that lasted three days and three nights. And
at the end of that time he said: "Come out now
with me, and see if this is the same woman that came
to you."

So they set out together till they came to the sea,
and there they saw three times fifty young girls, and
the one they were looking for among them; and she
was far beyond them all. And there was a silver chain
between every two of them, but about her own neck
there was a necklace of shining gold. And Bodb said
"Do you see that woman you were looking for?" I
see her, indeed," said Angus. "But tell me who is she,
and what her name is." "Her name is Caer Ormaith,
daughter of Ethal Anbual, from Sidhe Uaman, in the
province of Connaught. But you cannot bring her
away with you this time," said Bodb.

Then Angus went to visit his father, the Dagda,
and his mother, Boann, at Brugh na Boinne; and Bodb

went with him, and they told how they had seen the
girl, and they had heard her own name, and her father's
name. "What had we best do now?" said the Dagda.
"The best thing for you to do," said Bodb, "is to go
to Ailell and Maeve, for it is in their district she lives,
and you had best ask their help."

So the Dagda set out until he came into the province
of Connaught, and sixty chariots with him; and Ailell
and Maeve made a great feast for him. And after
they had been feasting and drinking for the length
of a week, Ailell asked the reason of their journey.
And the Dagda said: "It is by reason of a young girl
in your district, for my son has sickness upon him on
account of her, and I am come to ask if you will give
her to him." "Who is she?" said Ailell. "She is Caer
Ormaith, daughter of Ethal Anbual." "We have no
power over her that we could give her to him," said
Ailell and Maeve. "The best thing for you to do,"
said the Dagda, "would be to call her father here to
you."

So Ailell sent his steward to Ethal Anbual, and he
said: "I am come to bid you to go and speak with
Ailell and with Maeve." "I will not go," he said; "I
will not give my daughter to the son of the Dagda."
So the steward went back and told this to Ailell. "He
will not come," he said, "and he knows the reason you
want him for."

Then there was anger an Ailell and on the Dagda,
and they went out, and their armed men with them,
and they destroyed the whole place of Ethal Anbual,
and he was brought before them. And Ailell said to
him: "Give your daughter now to the son of the
Dagda." "That is what I cannot do," he said, "for
there is a power over her that is greater than mine."
"What power is that?" said Ailell. "It is an enchantment," he said, "that is on her, she to be in the shape

of a bird for one year, and in her own shape the next year," "Which shape is on her at this time?" said Ailell. "I would not like to say that," said her father. "Your head from you if you will not tell it," said Ailell.

"Well," said he, "I will tell you this much; she will be in the shape of a swan next month at Loch Beul Draguin, and three fifties of beautiful birds will be along with her, and if you will go there, you will see her."

So then Ethal was set free, and he made friends again with Ailell and Maeve; and the Dagda went home and told Angus all that had happened, and he said: "Go next summer to Loch Beul Draguin, and call her to you there."

So when the time came, Angus Og went to the loch, and he saw the three times fifty white birds there, with their silver chains about their necks. And Angus stood in a man's shape at the edge of the loch, and he called to the girl: "Come and speak with me, O Caer!" "Who is calling me?" said Caer. "Angus calls you," he said, "and if you come, I swear by my word, I will not hinder you from going into the loch again." "I will come," she said. So she came to him, and he laid his two hands on her, and then, to hold to his word, he took the shape of a swan on himself, and they went into the loch together, and they went around it three times. And then they spread their wings and rose up from the loch, and went in that shape till they were at Brugh na Boinne. And as they were going, the music they made was so sweet that all the people that heard it fell asleep for three days and three nights.

And Caer stopped there with him ever afterwards, and from that time there was friendship between Angus Og and Ailell and Maeve. And it was on account of that friendship, Angus gave them his help at the time of the war for the Brown Bull of Cuailgne.

IX

CRUACHAN

NOW as to Cruachan, the home of Ailell and of Maeve, it is on the plain of Magh Ai it was, in the province of Connaught.

And this is the way the plain came by its name. In the time long ago, there was a king whose name was Conn, that had the Druid power, so that when the Sidhe themselves came against him, he was able to defend himself with enchantments as good as their own. And one time he went out against them, and broke up their houses, and carried away their cattle, and then, to hinder them from following after him, he covered the whole province with a deep snow.

The Sidhe went then to consult with Dalach, the king's brother, that had the Druid knowledge even better than himself; and it is what he told them to do, to kill three hundred white cows with red ears, and to spread out their livers on a certain plain. And when they had done this, he made spells on them, and the heat the livers gave out melted the snow over the whole plain and the whole province, and after that the plain was given the name of Magh Ai, the Plain of the Livers.

Ailell was son of Ross Ruadh, king of Leinster, and Maeve was daughter of Eochaid, king of Ireland, and her brothers were the Three Fair Twins that rose up against their father, and fought against him at Druim Criadh. And they were beaten in the fight, and went back over the Sionnan, and they were overtaken and their heads were cut off, and brought back to their father, and he fretted after them to the end of his life.

Seven sons Ailell and Maeve had, and the name of every one of them was Maine. There was Maine Mathremail, like his mother, and Maine Athremail, like his father, and Maine Mo Epert, the Talker, and Maine Milscothach, the Honey-Worded, and Maine Andoe the Quick, and Maine Mingor, the Gently Dutiful, and Maine Morgor, the Very Dutiful. Their own people they had, and their own place of living.

This now was the appearance of Cruachan, the Royal house of Ailell and of Maeve, that some called Cruachan of the poets; there were seven divisions in the house, with couches in them, from the hearth to the wall; a front of bronze to every division, and of red yew with carvings on it; and there were seven strips of bronze from the foundation to the roof of the house. The house was made of oak, and the roof was covered with oak shingles; sixteen windows with glass there were, and shutters of bronze on them, and a bar of bronze across every shutter. There was a raised place in the middle of the house for Ailell and Maeve, with silver fronts and strips of bronze around it, and four bronze pillars on it, and a silver rod beside it, the way Ailell and Maeve could strike the middle beam and check their people.

And outside the royal house was the dun, with the walls about it that were built by Brocc, son of Blar, and the great gate; and it is there the houses were for strangers to be lodged.

And besides this, there was at Cruachan the Hill of the Sidhe, or, as some called it, the Cave of Cruachan. It was there Midhir brought Etain one time, and it is there the people of the Sidhe lived; but it is seldom any living person had the power to see them.

It is out of that hill a flock of white birds came one time, and everything they touched in all Ireland withered up, until at last the men of Ulster killed them with their slings. And another time enchanted pigs came out of the hill, and in every place they trod, neither corn nor grass nor leaf would sprout before the end of seven years, and no sort of weapon would wound them. But if they were counted in any place, or if the people so much as tried to count them, they would not stop in that place, but they would go on to another. But however often the people of the country tried to count them, no two people could ever make out the one number, and one man would call out, " There are three pigs in it," and another, " No, but there are seven," and another that it was eleven were in it, or thirteen, and so the count would be lost. One time Maeve and Ailell themselves tried to count them on the plain, but while they were doing it, one of the pigs made a leap over Maeve's chariot, and she in it. Every one called out, " A pig has gone over you, Maeve!" "It has not," she said, and with that she caught hold of the pig by the shank, but if she did, its skin opened at the head, and it made its escape. And it is from that the place was called Magh-mucrimha, the Plain of Swine-counting.

Another time Fraech, son of Idath, of the men of Connaught, that was son of Boann's sister, Befind, from the Sidhe, came to Cruachan. He was the most beautiful of the men of Ireland or of Alban, but his life was not long. It was to ask Findabair for his wife he came, and before he set out his people said : " Send a message to your mother's people, the way they will send you clothing of the Sidhe." So he went to Boann, that was at Magh Breagh, and he brought away fifty blue cloaks with four black ears on each cloak, and a brooch of red gold with each, and pale white shirts with looped beasts of gold around them; and fifty silver shields with edges, and a candle of a king's house in the hand of each of the men, knobs of carbuncle under them, and their points of precious stones. They used to light up the night as if they were sun's rays.

And he had with him seven trumpeters with gold and silver trumpets, with many coloured clothing, with golden, silken, heads of hair, with coloured cloaks; and three harpers with the appearance of a king on each of them, every harper having the white skin of a deer about him and a cloak of white linen, and a harp-bag of the skins of water-dogs.

The watchman saw them from the dun when they had come into the Plain of Cruachan. "I see a great crowd," he said, "coming towards us. Since Ailell was king and Maeve was queen, there never came and there never will come a grander or more beautiful crowd than this one. It is like as if I had my head in a vat of wine, with the breeze that goes over them."

Then Fraech's people let out their hounds, and the hounds found seven deer and seven foxes and seven hares and seven wild boars, and hunted them to Rath Cruachan, and there they were killed on the lawn of the dun.

Then Ailell and Maeve gave them a welcome, and they were brought into the house, and while food was being made ready, Maeve sat down to play a game of chess with Fraech. It was a beautiful chess-board they had, all of white bronze, and the chessmen of gold and silver, and a candle of precious stones lighting them.

Then Ailell said: "Let your harpers play for us while the feast is being made ready." "Let them play, indeed," said Fraech.

So the harpers began to play, and it was much that the people of the house did not die with crying and with sadness. And the music they played was the Three Cries of Uaithne. It was Uaithne, the harp of the Dagda, that first played those cries the time Boann's sons were born. The first was a song of sorrow for the hardness of her pains, and the second was a song of smiling and joy for the birth of her sons, and the third was a sleeping song after the birth.

And with the music of the harpers, and with the light that shone from the precious stones in the house, they did not know the night was on them, till at last Maeve started up, and she said: "We have done a great deed to keep these young men without food." "It is more you think of chess-playing than of providing for them," said Ailell; "and now, let them stop from the music," he said, "till the food is given out."

Then the food was divided. It was Lothar used to be sitting on the floor of the house, dividing the food with his cleaver, and he not eating himself, and from the time he began dividing, food never failed under his hand.

After that, Fraech was brought into the conversation-house, and they asked him what was it he wanted.

"A visit to yourselves," he said, but he said nothing of Findabair. So they told him he was welcome, and he stopped with them for a while, and every day they went out hunting, and all the people of Connaught used to come and to be looking at them.

But all this time Fraech got no chance of speaking with Findabair, until one morning at daybreak, he went down to the river for washing, and Findabair and her young girls had gone there before him. And he took her hand, and he said: "Stay here and talk with me, for it is for your sake I am come, and would you go away with me secretly?" "I will not go secretly," she said, "for I am the daughter of a king and of a queen."

So she went from him then, but she left him a ring to remember her by. It was a ring her mother had given her.

Then Fraech went to the conversation-house to Ailell and to Maeve. "Will you give your daughter to me?" he said. "We will give her if you will give the marriage portion we ask," said Ailell, "and that is, sixty black-grey horses with golden bits, and twelve milch cows, and a white red-eared calf with each of them; and you to come with us with all your strength and all your musicians at whatever time we go to war in Ulster." "I swear by my shield and my sword, I would not give that for Maeve herself," he said; and he went away out of the house.

But Ailell had taken notice of Findabair's ring with Fraech, and he said to Maeve: "If he brings our daughter away with him, we will lose the help of many of the kings of Ireland. Let us go after him and make an end of him before he has time to harm us." "That would be a pity," said Maeve, "and it would be a reproach on us." "It will be no reproach on us, the way I will manage it," said he. And Maeve agreed to it, for there was vexation on her that it was Findabair that Fraech wanted, and not herself. So they went into the palace, and Ailell said: "Let us go and see the hounds hunting until mid-day." So they did so, and at mid-day they were tired, and they all went to bathe in the river. And Fraech was swimming in the river, and Ailell said to him: "Do not come back till you bring me a branch of the rowan-tree there beyond, with the beautiful berries." For he knew there was a prophecy that it was in a river Fraech would get his death.

So he went and broke a branch off the tree and brought it back over the water, and it is beautiful he looked over the black water, his body without fault, and his face so nice, and his eyes very grey, and the branch with the red berries between the throat and the white face. And then he threw the branch to them out of the water. "It is ripe and beautiful the berries are," said Ailell; "bring us more of them."

So he went off again to the tree, and the water-worm that guarded the tree caught a hold of him. "Let me have a sword," he called out, but there was not a man on the land would dare to give it to him, through fear of Ailell and of Maeve. But Findabair made a leap to go into the water with a gold knife she had in her hand, but Ailell threw a sharp-pointed spear from above, through her plaited hair, that held her; but she threw the knife to Fraech, and he cut off the head of the monster, and brought it with him to the land, but he himself had got a deep wound. Then Ailell and Maeve went back to the house. "It is a great deed we have done," said Maeve. "It is a pity, indeed, what we have done to the man," said Ailell. "And let a healing-bath be made for him now," he said, "of the marrow of pigs and of a heifer." Fraech was put in the bath then, and pleasant music was played by the trumpeters, and a bed was made for him.

Then a sorrowful crying was heard on Cruachan, and they saw three times fifty women with purple gowns, with green head-dresses, and pins of silver on their wrists, and a messenger went and asked them who was it they were crying for. "For Fraech, son of Idath," they said, "boy darling of the king of the Sidhe of Ireland."

Then Fraech heard their crying, and he said: "Lift me out of this, for that is the cry of my mother, and of the women of Boann." So they lifted him out, and the women came round him and brought him away into the Hill of Cruachan.

And the next day he came out, and he whole and

sound, and fifty women with him, and they with the appearance of women of the Sidhe. And at the door of the dun they left him, and they gave out their cry again, so that all the people that heard it could not but feel sorrowful. It is from this the musicians of Ireland learned the sorrowful cry of the women of the Sidhe.

And when he went into the house, the whole household rose up before him and bade him welcome, as if it was from another world he was come. And there was shame and repentance on Ailell and on Maeve for trying to harm him, and peace was made, and he went away to his own place.

And it was after that he came to help Ailell and Maeve, and that he got his death in a river as was foretold, at the beginning of the war for the Brown Bull of Cuailgne.

And one time the Hill was robbed by the men of Cruachan, and this is the way it happened.

One night at Samhain, Ailell and Maeve were in Cruachan with their whole household, and the food was being made ready.

Two prisoners had been hanged by them the day before, and Ailell said: "Whoever will put a gad round the foot of either of the two men on the gallows, will get a prize from me."

It was a very dark night, and bad things would always appear on that night of Samhain, and every man that went out to try came back very quickly into the house. "I will go if I will get a prize," said Nera, then. "I will give you this gold-hilted sword," said Ailell.

So Nera went out and he put a gad round the foot of one of the men that had been hanged. Then the man spoke to him. "It is good courage you have," he said, "and bring me with you where I can get a drink, for I was very thirsty when I was hanged." So Nera brought him where he would get a drink, and then he put him on the gallows again, and went back to Cruachan.

But what he saw was the whole of the palace as if on fire before him, and the heads of the people of it lying on the ground, and then he thought he saw an army going into the Hill of Cruachan, and he followed after the army. "There is a man on our track," the last man said. "The track is the heavier," said the next to him, and each said that word to the other from the last to the first. Then they went into the Hill of Cruachan. And they said to their king: "What shall be done to the man that is come in?" "Let him come here till I speak with him," said the king. So Nera came, and the king asked him who it was had brought him in. "I came in with your army," said Nera. "Go to that house beyond," said the king: "there is a woman there will make you welcome. Tell her it is I myself sent you to her. And come every day," he said, "to this house with a load of firing."

So Nera went where he was told, and the woman said: "A welcome before you, if it is the king sent you." So he stopped there, and took the woman for his wife. And every day for three days he brought a load of firing to the king's house, and on each day he saw a blind man, and a lame man on his back, coming out of the house before him. They would go on till they were at the brink of a well before the Hill. "Is it there?" the blind man would say. "It is, indeed," the lame man would say. "Let us go away," the lame man would say then.

And at the end of three days, as he thought, Nera asked the woman about this. "Why do the blind man and the lame man go every day to the well?" he said. "They go to know is the crown safe that is in the well. It is there the king's crown is kept." "Why do these two go?" said Nera. "It is easy to tell that," she said; "they are trusted by the king to visit the crown, and one of them was blinded by him, and the other was lamed. And another thing," she said, "go now and give a warning to your people to mind themselves next Samhain night, unless they will come to attack the hill, for it is only at Samhain," she said, "the army of the Sidhe can go out, for it is at that time all the hills of the Sidhe of Ireland are opened. But if they will come, I will promise them this, the crown of Briun to be carried off by Ailell and by Maeve."

"How can I give them that message," said Nera, 'when I saw the whole dun of Cruachan burned and destroyed, and all the people destroyed with it?" "You did not see that, indeed," she said. "It was the host of the Sidhe came and put that appearance before your eyes. And go back to them now," she said, "and you will find them sitting round the same great pot, and the meat has not yet been taken off the fire."

"How will it be believed that I have gone into the Hill?" said Nera. "Bring flowers of summer with you," said the woman. So he brought wild garlic with him, and primroses and golden fern.

So he went back to the palace, and he found his people round the same great pot, and he told them all that had happened him, and the sword was given to him, and he stopped with his people to the end of a year.

At the end of the year Ailell said to Nera: "We are going now against the Hill of the Sidhe, and let you go back," he said, "if you have anything to bring out of it." So he went back to see the woman, and she bade him welcome. "Go now," she said, "and bring in a load of firing to the king, for I went in myself every day for the last year with the load on my back, and I said there was sickness on you." So he did that.

Then the men of Connaught and the black host of the exiles of Ulster went into the Hill and robbed it and brought away the crown of Briun, son of Smetra, that was made by the smith of Angus, son of Umor, and that was kept in the well at Cruachan, to save it from the Morrigu. And Nera was left with his people in the hill, and he has not come out till now, and he will not come out till the end of life and time.

Now one time the Morrigu brought away a cow from the Hill of Cruachan to the Brown Bull of Cuailgne, and after she brought it back again its calf was born. And one day it went out of the Hill, and it bellowed three times. At that time Ailell and Fergus were playing draughts, for it was after Fergus had come as an exile from Ulster, because of the death of the sons of Usnach, and they heard the bellowing of the bull-calf in the plain. Then Fergus said : " I do not like the sound of the calf bellowing. There will be calves without cows," he said, " when the king goes on his march."

But now Ailell's bull, Finbanach, the White-Horned, met the calf in the plain of Cruachan, and they fought together, and the calf was beaten and it bellowed. " What did the calf bellow ? " Maeve asked her cow-herd Buaigle. " I know that, my master, Fergus," said Bricriu. " It is the song that you were singing a while ago." On that Fergus turned and struck with his fist at his head, so that the five men of the chessmen that were in his hand went into Bricriu's head, and it was a lasting hurt to him. " Tell me now, Buaigle, what did the calf bellow ? " said Maeve. " It said indeed," said Buaigle, " that if its father the Brown of Cuailgne would come to fight with the White-Horned, he would not be seen any more in Ai, he would be beaten through the whole plain of Ai on every side." And it is what Maeve said : " I swear by the gods my people swear by, I will not lie down on feathers, or drink red or white ale, till I see those two bulls fighting before my face."

X

THE WEDDING OF MAINE MORGOR

WHEN Maine Morgor, the Very Dutiful, the son of Ailell and of Maeve, set out for his wedding with Ferb, daughter of Gerg of Rath Ini, in Ulster, he brought three troops of young men with him, and fifty men in each troop, and this is the appearance that was on the first two troops. Shining white shirts they had, striped with purple down the sides; gold shields on their backs with borders of white silver, with figures engraved on them, and with edges of white bronze as sharp as knives. Great two-edged swords with silver hilts at their belts; chains of white silver round their necks. And there were neither helmets on their heads, or shoes on their feet.

And as to the third troop, the one Maine himself was in, there were fifty reddish-brown horses in it, and fifty white horses with red ears, with long manes and tails coloured purple, and bridles on them, with a ball of red gold on the one side, and a ball of white silver on the other side, and a gold or a silver bit to every one of them. A collar of gold with bells from it on the neck of every horse, and when the horses would be moving, the sound of these bells would be as sweet as the strings of a harp when the player strikes it with his hand. There was a chariot of white bronze ribbed with gold and silver to every two of the horses;

purple cushions sewed with gold bound to every chariot; fifty fair slender young men in these fifty chariots, and not one among them but was the son of a king and a queen, and was a hero and a brave man of Connaught, and they wearing purple cloaks about them, that had borders ornamented with gold and silver, and a clasp of pure red gold to every cloak ; fine silk coats fastened with hooks of gold close to their white bodies; fifty silver shields on their backs with gold rims studded with carbuncles and other precious stones of every colour; two candles of valour were the two shining spears on the hand of every man of them ; fifty rivets of bronze and of gold in every spear, and if any man of them had a debt of a bushel of silver or gold, one rivet from his spear would pay it. And there were precious stones on their spears that would flame in the night like the rays of the sun. At their belts they had long, gold-hilted swords with silver sheaths ; goads in their hands of white bronze with silver crooks. And as to the young men themselves, they were very handsome and stately, and large and shining ; curled yellow hair on them, hanging down on their shoulders ; proud, clear, blue eyes ; their cheeks like the flowers of the woods in May, or like the foxglove of the mountains. There were seven greyhounds following Maine's chariot in chains of silver, and apples of gold on every chain. There were seven trumpeters with gold and silver trumpets, wearing clothes of many colours, and having all of them light yellow hair. And three Druids went in front of them, and they having bands of silver on their heads, and speckled cloaks on them, and carrying shields of bronze with ornaments of red copper. And there were three harpers with them, that had the appearance of kings.

It is like that they gathered at the royal house of Cruachan, and they went three times round the lawn before the house. And they said farewell to Maeve and to Ailell, and then they set out for Rath Ini.

"It is a fine setting out you are having," said Bricriu ; "but maybe the coming back will not be so fine." "It is a journey that will be heard of in every place," said Maine. "I suppose," said Bricriu, "it is but a day visit you will make there, for you will hardly stop to feast through the night in a district that is under Conchubar." "I give my word," said Maine, "we will not turn back to Cruachan till we have feasted three days and three nights in Gerg's house." He did not waste any more time talking, but set out on the journey.

When the messengers they sent before them came to Gerg's house at Rath Ini, the people there began to make all ready before them, and they laid down green-leaved birch branches and fresh green rushes in the house. Then Ferb sent her foster-sister, Findchoem, daughter of Erg, and bade her go a part of the way with the messengers, and bring her back word what appearance was on Maine and on his companions. She was not long away, and as soon as she came back she went with her report to the sunny parlour where Ferb was, and it is what she said: "I never saw since Conchubar was in Emain, and I never will see till the end of life and time, a finer, or grander, or a more beautiful troop, than the troop that is coming now over the plain. It was the same as if I was in a sweet apple-garden, from the sweetness that came to me when the light wind passed over them and stirred their clothes."

With that, the men of Connaught came to the dun, and the people within pressed upon one another to look at them. And the gates were set open, and their chariots unyoked, and baths of pure water were made ready for them. And then they were brought into the hall of heroes in the middle of the house, and they were given every sort of food and of drink that is to be found on the whole ridge of the world.

But as they were using the feast and making merry, there came a sudden blast of wind that shook the whole place, so that the hall they were in trembled, and the shields fell from their hooks, and the spears from their places, and the tables fell like leaves in an oak wood. All the young men were astonished, and Gerg asked Maine's Druids what meaning they could put on that blast. And Ollgaeth, Maine's chief Druid, said: "I think it is no good sign for those who are come to-night to this wedding. A blast of wind," he said; "a sorrowful sound; it is the man that will conquer.

"A shield struck out of a white hand; the bodies of dead men laid under stones; a high stone over stiff bodies; the story is sorrowful!

"And if you will take my advice," he said, "you will quit this feast this very night."

But he got a sharp rebuke from Maine for saying that, and Gerg said: "There is no cause for any uneasiness, for the men of Ulster are not gathered at Emain at this time. And if they were itself," he said, "I and my two sons would be ready to go out and fight against Conchubar along with you."

They hung up their arms then again, and gave no more heed to what the Druid had said.

Now on the mornihg of this very day, when Conchubar was lying in his sleep at Emain, he saw in a dream a beautiful woman coming to his bedside, and she having the appearance of a queen. Yellow plaited hair she had, and folds of silk over her white skin, and a cloak of green silk from her shoulders, and two sandals of white bronze between her soft feet and the ground. "All good be with you, Conchubar," she said. "What is the reason of your coming?" said Conchubar. "It is not long from this time," she said,

"that Ulster will be attacked and will be robbed, and
the Brown Bull of Cuailgne will be driven away.   And
the son of the man that will do this thing," she said,
"Maine Morgor, son of Ailell and of Maeve, is coming
this very night to his wedding with Ferb, daughter of
Gerg of Rath Ini, and three times fifty young men with
him.   Rise up now," she said, "there are but three times
fifty men against you, and the victory will be with
you."

Then Conchubar sprang up, and sent for Cathbad, the
Druid, and told him his vision.   "It is likely enough,"
he said, "that it is meant to warn us against the men
of Connaught.   And you may be sure," he said, "that
if we stop here quietly, they will be doing their robbery.
And let me have the truth from you now, and tell me
what is best to do, for there is not the like of you
among the Druids."

And Cathbad said: "It is what your vision means,
that many men will get their death, and Maine of
Connaught, he that is above all disgrace, along with
them; and he and his companions will never go back
again to beautiful Cruachan.   But you yourself will come
back safe," he said, "with fame and victory."

Then Conchubar set out, and there went with him
Cathrach Catuchenn, a queen with a great name, that
had come to Emain from the country of Spain for love
of Cuchulain; and she went out now with Conchubar's
army.   And there went with him as well, the three
outlaws of the race of the Fomor, Siabarcha, son of
Suilremar, and Berngal Brec, and Buri of the Rough
Word.   And Facen, son of Dublongsech of the old
stock of Ulster came, and Fabric Fiacail from Great
Asia, and Forais Fingalach from the Isle of Man.
So Conchubar set out, and three times fifty men with
him, but he brought none of the men of Ulster with
him, but himself and his chariot-driver Brod, and

Imrinn the Druid, Cathbad's son. And none of them
brought a servant with him, except only Conchubar,
but their shields on their backs, and their bright green
spears in their hands, and their heavy swords in their
belts. And if they were not many in number, the pride
of their minds was great.

When they were come within sight of Rath Ini, they
saw a great heavy cloud over it, the one end of it black
and the middle red, and the other end green. And
Conchubar asked Imrinn the Druid, "What is this cloud
over the house a token of?" "I know well," said Imrinn,
"it is a sign there will be fighting to-night, and the sorrow
of death will be on the house like a cloud, and it is for a
young man the death darkness is made ready."

Then Conchubar went on towards the dun, and just
at that time the great vat that belonged to the house,
and that got afterwards the name of the Ol Guala, was
brought into the feasting hall, and it full of wine. But
whoever went to draw it let the silver vessel fall into
the vat, so that the wine flowed over the edges in three
waves. "My grief!" said Ollgaeth the Druid, "it is not
long before these vessels will be with strangers. He is
not a happy son born of a mother that is in this house
to-night."

Then Conchubar came to the door, and the strangers
that were with him gave their shout of attack around
the dun, as their custom was. At that Gerg rose up, and
his two sons with him, Conn Coscorach and Cobthach
Cnesgel, and they took hold of their arms. And Gerg
said to Maine : "Let this be fought out now between us
men of Ulster till you see which of us are the bravest.
And we are all answerable for you, and it is best for you
that we should fight together. But if we fall, then let
you hold the place if you can."

And then Gerg went out and his two sons along with
him and their people. And they held the place, and

fought Conchubar outside ; and for a long time they did not let any one go past them. And Gerg stood outside the door, and a hewing and cutting was aimed at him on every side, and five men of the Fomor fell by him, and Imrinn the Druid, along with them, and he cut his head off and brought it to the door with him.

Then Cathrach Catuchenn came between him and the door, and she made a sharp attack on him, and Gerg struck her head off, and brought it back with him into the house, for he had got a hard wound. And he threw the heads down before Maine, and he sat down on a bed, and gave a heavy sigh and asked for a drink. And then Conchubar and his people came up to the wall, and they were holding their shields over their heads with their left hands, and tearing down the wall with their right hands, till they were able to make their way through it.

Then Brod, Conchubar's chariot-driver, threw one of the spears he had in his hand into the house, and it went through Gerg's body, and through the body of Airisdech his servant that was behind him, so that the two of them fell together. And Conchubar attacked Gerg's people in the house, so that thirty of them fell, and he killed Conn, Gerg's son, by his own hand, and many of his own people got their death as well.

Then Nuagal, Gerg's wife, rose up, and she gave three great angry cries of grief, and she took the head of her husband into her bosom. " By my word," she said, " it is a fine servant's deed, Brod to have killed Gerg in his own house. But there are many," she said, " that will keen you, and as you have fallen on account of your daughter, many women shall have sorrow on account of you." And she made this complaint :

" It is a good fight Gerg made, that is lying here now, the fair-haired champion with the red sword ; he that was proud, open-handed, brave, wise, beautiful.

"Where is there a better hero than Gerg? Where is the man that has not anger on him. Where is the army that does not keen for your death?

"It is grief to me to see you on your bed of death, O beautiful fair-haired Gerg! It is a pity for me, you to be dead.

"Before you here in Rath Ini, and at Loch Ane and at Irard, and in the valleys of the south, there were many women that gave you their love.

"You were the friend of every army; every one gave you full obedience; your friendly word was dear to every one; surely it is you were the good adviser.

"It is great indeed your deeds were, it is stately your assemblies were; you were a king among great lords.

"Your house was great, it was well-known, the house within which harm came to you; it was there Brod killed you in the hall of kings.

"It was a great harm and a great curse Brod put on us, he to kill a king of Ireland before his time; he has killed him; he has killed all of us along with him."

Then Gerg's two sons said they would hold the place, and they were not without killing many in the fight. Then Maine could not hold in his strength any longer, and he went out to avenge his father-in-law. And his three times fifty companions rose up along with him, and it was not easy to stand against them. There was great pride in the mind, and great courage in the heart of every one of them, and there was great desire and longing on them to do high deeds.

And as to Maine, the king's son, he was stately, kind, mannerly, and although he was hardly out of his boyhood, he was braver in the fight than any other. He was gentle in the drinking-house, and he was hard in battle, and he was mindful of his enemies, and he was pitiful in wounding, and a spender of treasure, and a stone of anger, and a wave of justice; and he was the head in the gatherings of the three Connaughts, and their hand in spending, and their fitting king.

He thought it would be dishonour on him, ever to be overcome in equal fight by any men in the world, or the place to be taken that he was defending. And he went out and drove the Fomor away from the house, and it is not a hand of healing Maine had that time; and nine of the Fomor fell by his first attack. Then the outlaw of Great Asia, Fabric Fiacail, came up to the threshold, and began destroying the men before him, and no one stood against him till he came to the place where Maine was. And then they two set their shields one against the other, and they were fighting together till after midnight; and Fabric gave Maine three deep wounds, and when they were tired out with the fight, Maine struck off his head. Then Conchubar came, and thirty of Gerg's men were killed by him, and the two armies fell upon one another, and it is much that even the toes of their feet did not make an attack of their own. And the blood that was in the dun was as high as a man's knees, and in all the district round nothing could be heard but the striking of blows on shields, and the clinking of spears, and the clash of swords against one another, and the roar of beaten men.

And Maine, when he had overcome the Fomor, came where Facen, son of Dublongsech was, and they fought together a good while, and then Facen was killed. Then Maine and Cobthach were driven up into the house after their people were put down, and they held it bravely till morning, and no one was able to make a way in.

In this same night, the same woman that had brought news to Conchubar, went to where Maeve was lying in her sleep at Cruachan, and said to her: "If you had the Druid sight, Maeve," she said, "you would not be in your sleep now." "What has happened?" said Maeve. "Conchubar is at this very moment," said the strange woman, "getting the upper hand of Maine, and he is on the point of putting him to death. Rise up now, and gather your men together," she said, "and go out and avenge him."

With that Maeve wakened out of her sleep, and she called to Ailell and told him the vision, and told it to her people as well. "There is no truth in it," said Bricriu.

But when Fiannamail, the innkeeper's son at Cruachan, heard it, he waited for no one and made no delay, but set out for the place where Maine was, for Maine was his foster-brother. And Maeve chose out seven hundred armed men, the best that were to be found in Cruachan at that time. And then Donall Dearg came, that was the best fighter in the province, and that was another of Maine's foster-brothers. And he set out in the same way, before the others, and thirty fighting men with him, and the name of every one of them was Donall. And then Maeve set out after them on her journey.

But as to Maine, he held the house till the bright rising of the sun on the morrow, and it was not pleasant rest this night brought to either side. When they could see each other by the light of day, each remembered the other to his hurt, and Conchubar began to rouse up his people. "If it was the men of Ulster I had with me now," he said, "they would not be dragging on with this battle, the way the Fomor are doing." When the Fomor heard that sharp reproach, their courage rose up in them, and they pressed on hard in the fight, and never left off till they were through the door of the house. The house they came into had a great name for grandeur, but it was bad work that was done in it now. There were a hundred tables of white silver in it, and three hundred of brass, and three hundred of white bronze. And there were thirty vessels with pure silver from Spain on their rims, and two hundred cowhorns ornamented with gold or silver, and thirty silver cups, and thirty brass cups, and on the walls there were hangings of white linen with wonderful figures worked on them.

Then the two armies met one another in the middle of the house, and a great many were killed there. And Cobthach, Gerg's son, after he had killed many of the Fomor, came to where Berngal Brec was hewing the heads off the men of Connaught, and they fought together, and Berngal was worsted in the end.

And as to Maine, he killed Buri of the Rough Word, and after that he went mad and raging through the house, and thirty other men fell by him. But when Conchubar saw the madness that was on Maine, he turned to him, and Maine waited for him, and they fought a long while, and Maine threw his casting spear so strong and straight, that it went through Conchubar's body; and while Conchubar was striving to draw out that spear, Maine wounded him with the long spear that was in his hand. Then Brod came to help Conchubar, and Maine gave him three heavy wounds, so that he was able to fight no more. But then Conchubar attacked him with blows on every side, until he laid him dead before him.

And after he had killed Maine, he began to attack the crowd about him, so that they fell, foot to foot, and neck to neck, all through the house. And at the end, there was not one of Maine's people left living; and of the three times fifty men that came with Conchubar, there was not one left living but himself and Brod, and if they were itself, they did not come whole out of it.

Then Conchubar drove Cobthach, Gerg's son, out of the house; and while he was following him over the plain, Ferb came with her foster-sister to the place where Maine was lying, and she cried and lamented over him, and she said: "My grief! you are alone now, you that spent so many nights in company." And she made this complaint:—

"O young man, it is red your bed is! It is bad the signs were, and you coming into the house, a foretelling of tears to all your people.

"O son of Maeve! O branch of high honour! O son of Ailell who is not weak! It is a pity it is for my heart and my body, you to be lying there for ever!

"O young man, the best I ever saw; a rod of gold and you lying on the pillow; whenever you and an enemy met together, that was the last meeting there was between you.

"There is grief on me, you to be lying there, young man, son of Maeve; your face was ruddy, your hand was rough in battle; it is grief has been put into my heart that was waiting for you.

"It is seldom you were without arms up to this, until you were struck down, lying dead. The shining spear pierced you, the hard sword wounded you, till blood was dropping down on your cheeks.

"Och! What were you to me, and I not to have seen your death; my darling, my choice among men, he that was worth good treasure.

"He is my husband for all my days, great Maine, Ailell's son; I will die for the want of him, and he not able to come and care me.

"His purple cloak is grief to me, and himself lying there on the floor of the house, and his hand that was struck off after he fell, and his head in the hand of Conchubar;

"And his sword that was strong, heavy in striking, Conchubar has carried it far away; and his shield there where he fell, and he defending his people

"He himself a hero, and no lie in it; it is he divided

much riches ; it is not a little thing he did to die like that, and he defending his people.

"The fair young man of Connaught to be lying there cold, and the best of his troop along with him ; it is a pity for his people that died defending him ; it is a pity for me, his unmarried wife.

"There is nothing I can do for you, Maine ; it is on myself the hurt is come ; my heart is broken with it, and I looking at you, Maine."

Then Fiannamail, the innkeeper's son from Cruachan, came to the house, and Ferb saw him, and she said : "Here is Fiannamail come to visit us, but whatever companions he has left at home, he will find none before him here." "That is rough news you are giving me, Ferb," said Fiannamail ; "and indeed I am parted from my companions if it is they that are lying here," he said. "They are your companions indeed," said Ferb ; "they overcame others, and now they are overcome themselves."

And Fiannamail said : "And Maine, is he living ? my comrade, my dear friend, my prince at home !" And Ferb said : "It is bitter to me, you to ask this, for I know you did not think it was Maine's last bed you would find here."

And then she told Fiannamail all that had happened. And Fiannamail said ; "When this news of the thing the people of Ulster have done goes out, they will be attacked in the west and in the east as long as there is a man living in Connaught." But Ferb said : "There are not left of the army of Ulster but Conchubar himself and Brod his chariot-driver, and the both of them were wounded by Maine before Conchubar killed him at the last."

Then Fiannamail went out to follow after Conchubar, to get satisfaction for Maine's death. And he met with Niall of the Fair Head, Conchubar's son, and a hundred men with him, and they looking for Conchubar ; and for all they were so many, he fought a hot battle with them, till he fell dead.

And after he left Ferb, she was looking at the young men of Connaught, and she made this complaint:

"A pity it is, young men of Connaught, that there is not soft down in your pillows under you; you that took the defence and would not give it up. What troop was there better than yourselves, and now you are lying like a loosened thread.

"It is a heavy hand was laid on your eyes; you were given the sour drink of beaten men; your story is hard, it will be a cause of battles; it will be a foretelling of many tears.

"It is a pity there is no help for me to bring you, but only to be keening and crying over you; it would be better for me to go with you, and my ashes to be scattered abroad.

"You were the best of the armies of Ireland, young men of Connaught, and I keening you; many women will cry Och! Och! after your proud ways.

"It is proud you were coming into the house; it is not common men you had for your fathers. O beautiful young men of Connaught, it is a pity it is the way you are now!"

Then Donall Dearg came to the lawn before the dun. And Ferb's foster-sister saw him, and she said: "It is a pity he was not here and Maine living, for he would have given him good help." And when Ferb heard he was there, she went out to him and she said: "Well, Donall, hawk of valour, here is a thing for you to do, to avenge your foster-brother that has got his death." And it is what Donall said: "If Maine has fallen, the man has fallen that was above all hls companions, in courage, in wisdom, and in gentleness." And Ferb said: "It is not the work of a hero, you to be sighing and keening and crying Ochone! But since Maine will not come back for

that, it is better for you to go out against his enemies."
And Donall said: "I will go; I will destroy Conchubar,
I will destroy his two sons in revenge for Maine." And
Ferb said: "If it had been yourself, Donall Dearg, that
had got your death from the men of Ulster on account of
me, the story of the great vengeance Maine did for it
would be told in every place." Then Donall said:
"And as it is Maine Morgor himself has got his death,
I will never go home westward so long as there is a man
left living in Ulster.

So Donall went out, and he had not long to wait till
he saw a great troop coming towards him, and Feradach
of the Long Hand, Conchubar's son, with them. And
Donall and his men attacked them, but they were out-
numbered, and all his men fell. And he himself
wounded Feradach twice, but then his men came at him,
and Feradach struck his head off, and let out his shout
of victory, and his people shouted along with him.

And Ferb was gone into the house again, and she was
looking at Maine. "There is no good appearance on
you now, the way you are, Maine," she said; "and my
father got his death through you, and my father's son;
but even so, I will die with the fret of losing you." And
it is what she said: "There are many women and many
young girls will be lonely after you, you to be the only
one to fail them.

"It is beautiful you were up to this, proud and tall,
going out with your young hounds to the hunting; it
is spoiled your body is now, it is pale your hands are.

"It is bad the news is that will travel westward to
Findabair of the Fair Eyebrows; the story of her
brother that failed Ferb; it is not I that have not my
fill of sorrow."

Then Maeve and her men came up to where
Conchubar was, and his two sons that had joined him,
and they faced one another, and the fight began; and

Maeve broke through the army of Ulster to get satisfaction for her son and for her people, and she killed Conchubar's two sons. But Conchubar stood out and faced her in spite of his wounds, and in spite of being tired out; for his hurts were healed by the greatness of his anger after his two sons being kiiled.

Then Maeve was driven back and lost the battle; and the Druids brought her away as was their custom; and Conchubar followed after them till they had passed Magh Ini. And then he turned back to spoil Gerg's dun, and he carried away with him all he could find of treasures; and he took away the great brass vat that was in the house, and brought it to Emain. And when it was filled with beer, all the province of Ulster used to drink from it; and it got the name of the Champion's Drinking Vat.

And Ferb died with grief for Maine, and Nuagal died with grief for her husband and for her two sons. And a grave was made for them, and a stone put over it, and their names were written in Ogham; and Rath Ini got the name of Duma Ferb, Ferb's Mound, after that.

And this was the first blood shed in Ulster on the account of the Brown Bull of Cuailgne.

XI

THE WAR FOR THE BULL OF CUAILGNE

IT happened one time before Maeve and Ailell rose up
from their royal bed in Cruachan, they began to
talk with one another. "It is what I am thinking," said
Ailell, "it is a true saying, 'Good is the wife of a good
man.'" "A true saying, indeed," said Maeve, "but why
do you bring it to mind at this time?" "I bring it to
mind now because you are better to-day than the day I
married you." "I was good before I ever had to do
with you," said Maeve. "How well we never heard of
that and never knew it until now," said Ailell, "but
only that you stopped at home like any other woman,
while the enemies at your boundaries were slaughtering
and destroying and driving all before them, and you not
able to hinder them." "That is not the way it was at
all," said Maeve, "but of the six daughters of my father
Eochaid, King of Ireland, I was the best and the one
that was thought most of. As to dividing gifts and
giving counsel, I was the best of them, and as to battle
feats and arms and fighting, I was the best of them.
It was I had fifteen hundred soldiers sons of exiles, and
fifteen hundred sons of chief men. And I had these,"
she said, "for my own household; and along with that
my father gave me one of the provinces of Ireland, the
province of Cruachan; so that Maeve of Cruachan is the
name that was given to me.

"And as to being asked in marriage," she said, "messengers came to me from your own brother, Finn, son of Ross Ruadh, king of Leinster, and I gave him a refusal; and after that there came messengers from Cairbre Niafer, son of Rossa, king of Teamhair; and from Conchubar, son of Ness, king of Ulster; and after that again from Eochu Beag, son of Luchta, and I refused them all. For it is not a common marriage portion would have satisfied me, the same as is asked by the other women of Ireland," she said; "but it is what I asked as a marriage portion, a man without stinginess, without jealousy, without fear. For it would not be fitting for me to be with a man that would be close-handed, for my own hand is open in wage-paying and in free-giving; and it would be a reproach on my husband, I to be a better wage-payer than himself. And it would not be fitting for me to be with a man that would be cowardly, for I myself go into struggles and fights and battles and gain the victory; and it would be a reproach to my husband, his wife to be braver than himself. And it would not be fitting for me to be with a husband that would be jealous, for I was never without one man being with me in the shadow of another. Now I have got such a husband as I looked for in yourself, Ailell, for you are not close-handed or jealous or cowardly. And I gave you good wedding gifts," she said, "suits of clothing enough for twelve men; a chariot that was worth three times seven serving-maids; the width of your face in red gold, the round of your arm in a bracelet of white bronze. And the fine or the tribute you can ask of your enemies is no more than the fine or the tribute I have a right to ask, for you are nothing of yourself, but it is in the pay of a woman you are," she said. "That is not so," said Ailell, "for I am a king's son, and I have two brothers that are kings, Finn, king of Leinster, and Cairbre, king of Teamhair, and I would have been king in their places but that they are older than myself. And as to giving of wages and dividing of gifts," he said, "you are no better than myself; and if this province is under the rule of a woman, it is the only province in Ireland that is so; and it is not through your right I took the kingship of it, but through the right of my mother, Mata of Murrisk, daughter of Magach. And if I took the daughter of the chief king of Ireland for my wife, it was because I thought she was a fitting wife for me." "You know well," said Maeve, "the riches that belong to me are greater than the riches that belong to you." "That is a wonder to me," said Ailell, "for there is no one in Ireland has a better store of jewels and riches and treasure than myself, and you know well there is not."

"Let our goods and our riches be put beside one another, and let a value be put on them," said Maeve, "and you will know which of us owns most." "I am content to do that," said Ailell.

With that, orders were given to their people to bring out their goods and to count them, and to put a value on them. They did so, and the first things they brought out were their drinking vessels, their vats, their iron vessels, and all the things belonging to their households, and they were found to be equal. Then their rings were brought out, and their bracelets and chains and brooches, their clothing of crimson and blue and black and green and yellow and saffron and speckled silks, and these were found to be equal. Then their great flocks of sheep were driven from the green plains of the open country and were counted, and they were found to be equal; and if there was a ram among Maeve's flocks that was the equal of a serving-maid in value, Ailell had one that was as good. And their horses were brought in from the meadows, and their herds of swine out of the woods and the valleys, and they were equal one to another. And the last thing that was done was to bring in the herds of cattle from the forest and the wild places of the province, and when they were put beside one another they were found to be equal, but for one thing only. It happened a bull had been calved in Maeve's herd, and his name was Fionnbanach, the White-horned. But he would not stop in Maeve's herds, for he did not think it fitting to be under the rule of a woman, and he had gone into Ailell's herds and stopped there ; and now he was the best bull in the whole province of Connaught. And when Maeve saw him, and knew he was better than any bull of her own, there was great vexation on her, and it was as bad to her as if she did not own one head of cattle at all. So she called Mac Roth, the herald, to her, and bade him to find out where there was a bull as good as the White-horned to be got in any province of the provinces of Ireland.

"I myself know that well," said Mac Roth, "for there is a bull that is twice as good as himself at the house of Daire, son of Fachtna, in the district of Cuailgne, and that is Donn Cuailgne, the Brown Bull of Cuailgne." "Rise up, then," said Maeve, "and make no delay, but go to Daire from me, and ask the loan of that bull for a year, and I will return him at the end of the year, and fifty heifers along with him, as fee for the loan. And there is another thing for you to say, Mac Roth ; if the people of Daire's district and country think bad of him for sending away that wonderful jewel the Donn of Cuailgne, let Daire himself come along with him, and I will give him the equal of his own lands on the smooth plain of Ai, and a chariot that is worth three times seven serving-maids, and my own close friendship along with that."

So Mac Roth set out on his journey, and nine men along with him, and when they came to Daire's house there was a good welcome before them, as there should be, for Mac Roth was the chief herald of all Ireland.

Daire asked him then what was the reason of his journey, and Mac Roth told him the whole story of the quarrel between Maeve and Ailell and of the counting of their herds, and of the great rewards Maeve offered him if he would give her the loan for one year of the Brown Bull of Cuailgne. Daire was so well pleased when he heard this, that he wagged himself till the stitches of the feathers under him burst, and he said : "I will send him to Maeve into Connaught, whether the men of Ulster like it or do not like it." Mac Roth was well content with that ; and he and his men were attended to, and fresh rushes were spread, and a feast was put before them, with every sort of food and of drink, so that after a while they were not so clear in their wits as they were before.

Two of them began talking to one another then, and one said : "This is a good man in whose house we are." "He is good indeed," said the other. "Is there any man in Ulster better than himself?" said the first. "There is, surely," said the other, "for Conchubar the High King is a better man, and it is no shame for all the men of Ulster to gather to him." "It is a wonder," said the first, "Daire to have given up to us what it would have taken the strength of the four provinces of Ireland to bring away by force." "That I may see the mouth that spoke those words filled with blood," said another of the men ; "for if Daire had refused to give it willingly, the strength of Ailell and of Maeve, and the knowledge of Fergus, son of Rogh, would have brought it from him against his will."

Just as they were talking, the chief steward of Daire's house came in, and servants along with him bringing meat and drink ; and he heard what the men of Connaught said and great anger came on him, and he bade the servants put down the food for them, but he never told them to use it or not to use it, but he went to where Daire was and said : " Was it you, Daire, promised the Brown Bull of Cuailgne to these messengers ? " " It was myself indeed," said Daire. " Then what they have said is true ? " " What is that ? " said Daire. " They say that you knew if you did not give him willingly you would have had to give him against your will by the strength of Ailell and Maeve and by the guidance of Fergus, son of Rogh." " If they say that," said Daire, " I swear by the gods my people swear by, that they will not take him away till they take him by force."

On the morning of the morrow the messengers rose up and went into the house where Daire was. " Show us now," they said, " the place where the bull is." " I will not indeed," said Daire ; " but if it was a habit with me," he said, " to do treachery to messengers or to travellers or to men on their road, not one of you would go back alive to Cruachan." " What reason have you for this change ? " said Mac Roth. " I have a good reason for it, for you were saying last night that if I did not give the bull willingly, I would be forced to give it against my will by Ailell and by Maeve and by Fergus." " If that was said, it was the talk of common messengers, and they after eating and drinking," said Mac Roth, " and it is not fitting for you to take notice of a thing like that."

" It may be so " said Daire ; " but for all that," he said " I will not give the bull this time."

They went back then to Cruachan, and Maeve asked news of them, and Mac Roth told her the whole story, how Daire gave them the promise of the bull at first, and refused it afterwards. " What was the reason of that ? " she asked. And when it was told her she said : " This riddle is not hard to guess ; they did not intend to let us get the bull at all; but now we will take him from them by force," she said.

And this was the cause of the great war for the Brown Bull of Cuailgne.

Then Maeve sent messengers to the six Maines, her sons, to come to Cruachan, the brothers of Maine Morgor that got his death at Dun Gerg. And she sent messengers to the sons of Magach; and they came, with thirty hundred armed men, and to Cormac Conloingeas, son of King Conchubar, and to Fergus, son of Rogh; and they came, and thirty hundred armed men with them.

This is the appearance that was on the first troop. Black heads of hair they had, and green cloaks about them, held with silver brooches, and on their bodies shirts of gold thread, embroidered with red gold, and they had swords with white sheaths and hilts of silver.

As to the second troop, they had short-cut hair, and grey cloaks about them, and on their bodies pure white shirts; and they had swords with knobbed hilts of gold, and sheaths of silver. Every one asked: "Is that Cormac among them?" "It is not indeed," said Maeve.

As to the last troop, they had gold-yellow hair, falling loose like manes, and crimson cloaks, well ornamented, about them, and gold brooches with jewels at their breasts, and long silk shirts coming down to their ankles. And as they walked they lifted up their feet and put them down again all together. "Is that Cormac among them?" every one asked. "It is, surely," said Maeve.

So they made their camp there, and between the four fords of Ai, Athmaga, Athslisen, Athberena, and Athcoltna, there were red fires blazing through the night.

And they stopped a fortnight there at Cruachan, eating drinking, and resting themselves, that they might be the better able for the journey and the marching.

Then Maeve bade her chariot-driver to yoke her horses, that she might go and consult with her Druid and ask a prophecy from him, to foretell for her if the army she was bringing out would get the victory, and would come back safely. And she said to the Druid : "There are many that will part here to-day from their companions and their friends, from their country and their lands, from their father and their mother. And if it happens that the whole of them do not come back again safe and sound, it is on me the complaints and the curses will fall. And besides that," she said, "there is no one that goes out or that stops behind, that is dearer to us than we are to ourselves. So find out for us now whether we shall return, or not return." And the Druid said : "Whoever returns or does not return, you yourself will return."

Her chariot was turned then, and she went back again homeward. But presently she saw a thing she wondered at, a woman sitting on the shaft of the chariot, facing her, and this is how she was : a sword of white bronze in her hand, with seven rings of red gold on it and she seemed to be weaving a web with it ; a speckled green cloak about her, fastened at the breast with a brooch of red gold ; a ruddy, pleasant face she had, her eyes grey, and her mouth like red berries, and when she spoke her voice was sweeter than the strings of a curved harp, and her skin showed through her clothes like the snow of a single night. Long feet she had, very white, and the nails on them pink and even ; her hair gold-yellow, three locks of it wound about her head, and another that fell down loose below her knee.

Maeve looked at her, and she said : "What are you doing here, young girl ?" "It is looking into the future

QUEEN MAEVE CONSULTED WITH HER DRUID.

CUCHULAIN IN BATTLE.

for you I am," she said, "to see what will be your
chances and your fortunes, now you are gathering the
provinces of Ireland to the war for the Brown Bull of
Cuailgne." "And why would you be doing this for me?"
said Maeve. "There is good reason for it," she said,
"for I am a serving-maid of your own people." "Which
of my people do you belong to?" said Maeve. "I am
Fedelm of the Sidhe, of Rath Cruachan." "It is well,
Fedelm of the Sidhe; tell me what way you see our
hosts." "I see crimson on them, I see red." "Yet
Conchubar is lying in his weakness at Emain; my
messengers are come back from there, and we need not
be in dread of anything from Ulster," said Maeve. "But
look again, Fedelm of the Sidhe, and tell me the truth
of the matter." "I see crimson on them, I see red,"
said the girl. "Yet Eoghan, son of Durthacht, is in his
weakness at Rathairthir; my messengers are come back
from him; we need not be afraid of anything from Ulster.
Look again, Fedelm of the Sidhe; how do you see our
hosts?" "I see them all crimson, I see them all red."
"Celtchair, son of Uthecar, is lying in his weakness
within his fort; my messengers are come back from him.
Tell me again, Fedelm of the Sidhe, how do you see our
hosts?" "I see crimson on them, I see red." "There
may be no harm in what you see," said Maeve, "for
when all the men of Ireland are gathered together in one
place, there will surely be quarrels and fights among
them, about going first or last over fords and rivers, or
about the first wounding of some stag or boar, or such
like. Tell me truly now, Fedelm of the Sidhe, what
way do you see our hosts?" "I see crimson on them,
I see red. And I see," she said, "a low-sized man doing
many deeds of arms; there are many wounds on his
smooth skin; there is a light about his head, there is
victory on his forehead; he is young and beautiful, and
modest towards women; but he is like a dragon in the

battle. His appearance and his courage are like the appearance and the courage of Cuchulain of Muirthemne; and who that Hound from Muirthemne may be I do not know; but I know this much well, that all this host will be reddened by him. He is setting out for the battle; he will make your dead lie thickly, the memory of the blood shed by him will be lasting; women will be keening over the bodies brought low by the Hound of the Forge that I see before me."

This is the foretelling that was made for Maeve by Fedelm of the Sidhe, before the setting out of the hosts at Cruachan for Ulster.

Now, when Maeve told Fedelm of the Sidhe that there need be no fear of the men of Ulster coming out to attack the army, for they were lying in their weakness, she meant that they were under the curse and the enchantment that was put on them one time by a woman they had ill-treated. And the story of it is this :—

There was a man of the name of Crunden, son of Agnoman, that lived in a lonely part of Ulster, among the mountains, and he had a good way of living ; but his wife had died, and he had the care of all his children on him. One day he was sitting in the house, and he saw a woman come in at the door, tall and handsome, and with good clothes on her, and she did not say a word, but she sat down by the hearth and began to make up the fire. And then she went to where the meal was, and took it out and mixed it, and baked a cake. And when the evening was drawing on, she took a vessel and went out and milked the cows, but all the time she never spoke a word. Then she came back into the house, and took a turn to the right, and was the last to stop up and to cover over the fire.

She stayed on there, and Crunden, the man of the

house, married her, and she tended him and his sons, and everything he had prospered.

It happened, one day, there was to be a great gathering of the men of Ulster, for games and races and all sorts of amusements, and all that could go, both of men and women, used to go to that gathering. " I will go there to-day," said Crunden, " the same as every other man is going." " Do not," said his wife, " for if you so much as say my name there at the fair," she said, " I will be lost to you for ever." " Then indeed I will not speak of you at all," said Crunden. So he set out with the others to the fair, and there was every sort of amusement there, and all the people of the country were at it.

At the ninth hour, the royal chariot was brought on the ground, and the king's horses won the day. Then the bards and poets, and the Druids, and the servants of the king, and the whole gathering, began to praise the king and the queen and their horses, and they cried out: " There were never seen such horses as these ; there are no better runners in all Ireland." " My wife is a better runner than those two horses," said Crunden. When the king was told of that he said : " Take hold of the man, and keep him until his wife can be brought to try her chance and to run against the horses."

So they took hold of him, and kept him, and messengers were sent from the king to the woman. She bade the messengers welcome, and asked what brought them. " We are come by the king's order," they said, " to bring you to the fair, to see if you will run faster than the king's horses ; for your husband boasted that you would, and he is kept prisoner now until you will come and release him." " It is foolish my husband was to speak like that," she said ; " and as for myself, I am not fit to go, for I am soon going to give birth to a child." " That is a pity," said the messengers, " for if you do not come, your husband will be put to death." "If that is so, I must go, whatever happens," she said.

So with that she set out for the gathering, and when she got there all the people were crowding about her to see her. "It is not fitting to be looking at me, and I the way I am," she said; "and what have I been brought here for?" "To run against the two horses of the king," the people called out. "Ochone!" she said, "do not ask me, for I am close upon my hour." "Take out your swords and put the man to death," said the king. "Give me your help," she said to the people, "for every one of you has been born of a mother." And then she said to the king: "Give me even a delay until my child is born." "I will give no delay," said the king. "Then the shame that is on you will be greater than the shame that is on me," she said. "And because you have showed no pity and no respect to me," she said, "it is a heavier punishment will fall on you than has fallen upon me. And bring out the horses beside me now." Then they started, and the woman outran the horses and gained the race; and at the goal the pains of childbirth came on her, and she bore two children, a boy and a girl, and she gave a great cry in her pain.

And a weakness came suddenly on all that heard the cry, so that they had no more strength than the woman as she lay there. And it is what she said: "From this out, and till the ninth generation, the shame that you have put on me will fall on you; and at whatever time you most want your strength, at the time your enemies are closing on you, that is the time the weakness of a woman in childbirth will come upon all the men of the province of Ulster."

And so it happened; and of all the men of Ulster that were born after that day, there was no one escaped that curse and that enchantment but only Cuchulain.

When the men of Connaught set out from Cruachan for the north they stopped towards evening at Cuilsilinne, and there they made their encampment for the night. Ailell took his place in the middle of the camp, and on his right was Fergus, son of Rogh, and Cormac Conloingeas next to him again, and their people on the same side; and on Ailell's left there was a place made for Maeve and Findabair her daughter. But Maeve stopped behind until the whole of the army had come up, and then she went in her chariot to see if all was in order, and after that she came and took her seat at Ailell's right hand. "Which of the troops do you think the best?" said Ailell. "None of them are any good at all," said Maeve, "compared with the men of Leinster, the Gailiana." "What have they done beyond all the others that you praise them so much?" said Ailell. "There is reason for praising them," said Maeve; "for while the others were choosing a place for themselves, the Gailiana had their huts and their shelters made, and while the others were making their shelters, they had their share of food and drink cooked and set out, and while the others were making ready their food they had theirs eaten, and while the others were eating, they were laid down and sleeping. And as their servants have been better than the servants of the men of Ireland," she said, "so will their young men and their fighting men be better than the young men of Ireland on this march." "I am well pleased to hear that," said Ailell, "for it was with me they came, and they are of my own province." "Then you need not be so well pleased," said Maeve, "for they shall march no further with you, for I will not have them boasted of, before me or to me." "Let them stop in this camp, then," said Ailell. "They shall not do that either," said Maeve. "What must they do, then?" said Findabair, "if they are neither to go on nor to stop in the camp?" "They will get death and destruction from myself," said Maeve. " It is a pity you to say that," said Ailell, " and they only just after joining us." " If you think to harm them," said Fergus, "you will have to fight with me as well as with them ; for by the oath of my people," he said, " it is only over my body and the bodies of the men of Ulster that are with me, you can come at their death." " Do not speak that way, Fergus," said Maeve ; " for if you were to join with these strangers against me, I would have the six Maines and their men on my side, and the sons of Magach and their men, and my own troops along with them. And I think we would be well able for you," she said. " It is not right for you to say that," said Fergus, " for there are no men in Ireland better than the young men of Ulster that came to Connaught with me, and they have been a good help to you up to this. But I will tell you another thing to do," he said : " let the men of Leinster be divided through all the other troops of the men of Ireland, the way there will not be more than five of them together in any one place." " I will agree to that," said Maeve, " for I know there would be nothing but fighting and jealousy if they were left together the way they are now."

On the morning of the morrow, they made ready to set out again, but the chief men among them consulted together first, what way they could best keep the peace between so many troops and tribes and families ; and it is what they settled, to put every troop under its own leader, and to let it, great or small, take a road of its own. And besides that, they consulted who would be the best man to put over the whole army, to lead them and to show them the way. And they all said Fergus would be the best, for he had been king of Ulster seventeen years, until Conchubar put him out of the kingship, and he had stopped on in Ulster after that until the time Conchubar killed the sons of Usnach in spite of the guarantee he had given them.

So Fergus was made leader of the whole army; but as they went on, a great love for his own province and his home came on him, and instead of going on northwards he turned to the south.   And while he was delaying the army like that, he sent messsengers into Ulster to give warning and news of their coming.   But Maeve was keeping a watch on him, and when she saw what had happened, she went to him and said : "Why is it, Fergus, that we have turned again to the south?"   Then Fergus knew it was no use to try and deceive her, and they turned again, but they did not go far, but only to the place they had left in the morning, Cuilsilinne.

Then Fergus called to mind that they were coming near the borders of Ulster, and that it was likely it would not be long before they would meet with Cuchulain ; and he gave a warning to the army to mind themselves well, lest the Hound of Muirthemne should fall on them, angry and beautiful, and destroy them.

And then the men of Connaught set out again eastward, and when they came to Monecolthan, they saw before them eight-score deer, in the one herd, and the whole army surrounded them, and all the deer were killed ; but if they were, it was the Gailiana, scattered as they were, that killed all the deer but five, and those five were all that were killed by the rest of the men of Ireland.

It was on that same day Cuchulain and his father, Sualtim, came to the pillar-stone at Ardcullin, for they had got the warning Fergus had sent, and there they let their horses graze, and Sualtim's horses cropped the grass to the north of the pillar-stone to the earth, but Cuchulain's horses, at the south side, cropped it to the bare flags.

"It is in my mind, Sualtim," said Cuchulain, "that the army of Connaught is not far away from us now. Go now, then," he said, "and bring a warning to the men of Ulster, and tell them not to stop in the open plains, but to go into the woods and the valleys of the province, that the men of Ireland may not come upon them." "And you yourself, little son, what will you do?" said Sualtim. "I must go," said Cuchulain, "southward to Teamhair, for I promised to go there to-day, to see a young girl of the household of Fedelm of the Fair Shape, Laegaire's wife." "It is a pity for you to go for a thing like that," said Sualtim, "and you leaving Ulster under the feet of enemies and strangers." "I must go, indeed," said Cuchulain, "for if I break my word to a woman, it will be said from this out that a woman's word is better than a man's."

So Sualtim set out then, to give a warning to the men of Ulster, and Cuchulain went into the oak woods and cut down an oak sapling, and twisted it into a ring, and cut a message on it in Ogham. And then he forced the ring over the top of the pillar-stone, and down to the thick part of it. And then he went on to keep his appointment at Teamhair.

As to the men of Ireland, they went on till they came to Ardcullin, and the whole country of Ulster lay there before them. And then they saw the pillar-stone and the oak ring that was on it; and Ailell took it off, and gave it to Fergus, and bade him read the Ogham. And what he read on it was Cuchulain's name, and the warning on it that the men of Ulster should not pass the pillar-stone that night, for if they did, he would do a great revenge on them at the sunrise of the morrow.

"It would be a pity," said Maeve, "that the first blood to be shed after going into the province should be the blood of our own people: it would be best for us to draw blood first on the people of Ulster." "I agree to that," said Ailell, "for I am loth to go against this ring or the man that twisted it; but let us go into the wood and make our camp there for the night." So they went into the wood, and cut a way for the chariots with their swords as they went, and it is from that the place is called Sleact na Gearbat, the Cut Way of the Chariots, until this time. And a great snow fell that night, so that it made one plain of the five provinces of Ireland, and they could make no shelter or prepare food, and none of the men in the camp knew through the whole night was it friend or enemy was near him, until the clear light of the sun fell on the snow in the morning. And then they left that place, and went on into Ulster.

As to Cuchulain, he did not rise very early that morning, and when he did, there was food made ready for him, and a bath of pure water. Then he bade Laeg to make his chariot ready, and they set out; and after a while they came to the track of the army of Ireland where it had gone over the border into Ulster. "Well, Laeg," said Cuchulain, " I have not much luck out of my appointment that I kept last night; for it is expected of one that is watching the borders that the least he should do is to raise a cry or give a warning of the enemy that is coming, and I have missed doing this, so that the men of Ireland have slipped by without news or notice into Ulster." " I told you, Cuchulain," said Laeg, "that if you kept to your meeting last night, some vexation like this would fall on you." "Well, Laeg," said Cuchulain, "let you follow their track now, and count them, and see what number of the men of Ireland are come over the border." Laeg did this, and he came back and told their number, as he had counted them. "There is a mistake in your counting," said Cuchulain. "I will count them myself this time." Then he told their number. "It is with yourself the mistake is, Cuchulain," said Laeg. "It is not," he said, "but there are eighteen divisions have passed the border, but the eighteenth is broken up and distributed among the others, so that no sure reckoning can be made of it."

This, now, was one of the three best estimates ever made in Ireland, and the other two were made by Lugh of the Long Hand, and by Angus at Brugh na Boinne.

"But now, Laeg," he said, "turn the chariot towards the army, and hurry on the horses; for unless I can make an end of some of them to-day," he said, "I will not live through the night myself."

So they went on to the place that is called now Athgowla, northward from Knowth.

There they met with the two young men, the sons of Neara, that were sent out in front of Maeve's army, to see was there any hindrance before it, and Cuchulain struck off their heads and the heads of their chariot-drivers.

And he cut down a tree with his sword, and it having four branches, and he lopped them short, and cleared the tree ; and he stood up in his chariot, and with one cast he drove the tree into the ground that it stood deep and firm, and he set the four heads he had struck off on the four lopped branches of it. And then he turned back their horses in their chariots towards the army.

Now it is the way Maeve used to be going, she in a chariot by herself, and two chariots on each side of her, and behind her and before her, the way no sod from the feet of the horses of the army, or foam from their mouths, would touch her clothing. And when she saw the two chariots coming back, and the bodies in them without heads, she stopped to see what had happened. "What are these?" she said. "They are the chariots and the bodies of the two sons of Neara that went on before us," said her chariot-driver.

Then she held a council with her chief men, and it is what they agreed, that it must be some part of the army of Ulster was there before them at the ford they were drawing near, and that it was best to send out

Cormac Conloingeas and his men to see who was in it, for the men of Ulster would not be willing to harm the son of their High King.

So Cormac and his troop went on to the ford, but when he got there all he saw was a lopped tree and four heads on it, and the blood dripping down from them, and the track of one chariot only, going eastward out of the ford. Then the rest of the army came with the other chief men. "There is wonder on me," said Ailell; "our four men to have been made an end of so easily as this." "You may wonder as well," said Fergus, "at the way this pole was driven into the ground by one man, and it will be hard for you to find a man of your army will drag it out again." "Do it yourself, Fergus," said Maeve, "for you are of my army." So Fergus called for a chariot, and stood up in it, and gave such a strong pull at the pole, that the chariot broke under him. "Give me another chariot," he said. And when he had broken seventeen of the war-chariots of Connaught one after another, and had not so much as loosened the pole, Maeve said: "Leave off now, Fergus, from breaking my people's chariots; and if you yourself had not been with us on this march," she said, "we would have been up with the men of Ulster before now, and we would have taken men and cattle. And I know well why you did this; it was to give the men of Ulster time to get over their weakness and their pains, and to come out against us to defend their bull and their cattle." "Give me my own chariot, then," said Fergus. So they gave him his own chariot, and he got up in it and gave a great pull at the pole; and neither the frame nor the wheels of his chariot started or strained like the others, and he pulled up the pole and gave it into Ailell's hand, and Ailell looked at it and said: "There is dread on me, of the man that set that pole there; do you think, Fergus," he said, "was it Conchubar the High King that did it?" "It was not," said Fergus, "for if Conchubar had come here, his army would have come along with him, and all the men of Ulster, and he would not have been so near to you without offering you battle, and by this time whichever got the better would be boasting of it." "Do you think was it Cuscraid, Conchubar's son?" said Ailell; "or Eoghan, son of Durthacht, king of Fernmaighe; or Celthair, son of Uthecar?" "I do not," said Fergus, "but it is what I think, that it was my own foster-son and Conchubar's that was here, Cuchulain, son of Sualtim." "We heard you often talking at Cruachan about that young man, and what is his age at this time?" "His age is of no great matter," said Fergus, "for he did great deeds, when he was but a soft child." "He is young enough yet," said Maeve, "and I think it will not be hard to find some one of our own men that will get the better of this wild Hound, for he has but the one body to wound or to put to flight." "You will get no one," said Fergus, "among your fighting men and your young men and your champions that will be able to put down Cuchulain."

They stopped there then and made their camp, and rested that night, with food and with music.

And it was in that night Fergus gave Maeve and Ailell the whole story of the boy deeds of Cuchulain, and how he used to have a stone for a pillow, and no one dared wake him, lest he might chance to give them a blow of the stone in his anger. And he told of one night when he was asleep, and Conchubar was attacked and was beaten by Eoghan, son of Durthacht. And Cuchulain was awakened by the cries of the beaten men that were running away, and he went out in the darkness of the night to look for Conchubar; and where the battle had been, he saw a man with the half of a man's body on his back, and he called to

Cuchulain to help him, and threw the half-body to him, and Cuchulain threw it back again, and they fought, and he struck off the man's head. And then he found Conchubar lying in a grave, and he dug him out of that, and as they went home, they met Cuscraid that was wounded, and Cuchulain brought him home to Emain on his back. And another time he went into a wood and saw a terrible-looking man having a wild boar in one hand, and his weapon in the other hand, and he killed him, and brought home the boar. And another time when the men of Ulster were in their weakness, three times nine sea-robbers came to Emain, and the women ran shrieking to the palace when they saw them, and when the boys that were at play on the lawn knew what they were running from, they ran along with them. But Cuchulain went out and killed nine of the sea-robbers and wounded the rest of them, so that he drove them all back. And he told them many other stories of his doings beside these.

The next day, the army marched on eastward beyond the mountain. But there was a narrow place they had to pass through, and Cuchulain cut down a great oak tree, and laid it across the gap, and wrote an Ogham on it; and when the men of Ireland came up to it, it hindered them, and they could not move it, and they made their camp there that night. And early in the morning they sent the young man Fraech, son of Idath, to get the hindrance cleared away. But Fraech went on beyond it, till he came to a river, and there he found Cuchulain bathing. And they attacked one another in the water, and Fraech was beaten, and Cuchulain went away and left his body on the bank.

And when the men of Ireland found his body they began to keen him. And then they saw a great band of women of the Sidhe, with green dresses on them, coming for his body, and they gave out a great cry over him and brought him away to a hill of the Sidhe. And Findabair cried after him, and went to see the green bank where he was lying.

And they knew that Cuchulain was not far from them, for presently Maeve's little dog, Baiscne, got his death by a stone from a sling. There was anger on Maeve then, and she urged her men to follow after Cuchulain, so that they broke the poles of their chariots in their hurry.

The next day Cuchulain was going through the wood, and he heard the sound of blows on the trees.

"It is too bold the men of Ulster are, Laeg," he said, "to be cutting down trees like this, with the men of Ireland coming on them; and stop here," he said, "till I find out who is it that is in the wood."

He went on till he met with a young man of Connaught, that was chariot-driver to Orlam, son of Maeve and Ailell. "What is it you are doing there, young man?" he asked. "I am cutting holly poles," said the young man, "for we have broken our chariots hunting that notable deer, Cuchulain. And now, good friend," he said, "lend me a hand with these poles, lest that same notable Cuchulain should come upon me here." "Your choice, boy; shall I cut the holly poles, or shall I trim them for you?" "Let you do the trimming," said he. So Cuchulain took them and trimmed them straight and smooth, that a fly could not have kept his footing on them. The chariot-driver looked at the poles, and he said: "I am thinking this is not the work you have a right to be put to. And who are you at all?" he said. "I am that notable Cuchulain you were speaking of just now." "That is bad news for me," said the driver, "for surely I am a dead man." "There need be no fear on you," said Cuchulain, "for I do not fight against drivers or messengers or unarmed men. But where is your master?" he said. "He is out before you on the plain." "Go to him, then, and give him this warning, that I am here, and that if we meet, he will surely get his death from me." With that the young man went to look for his master, but quick as he went, Cuchulain was quicker, and as soon as he came up with Orlam he struck off his head, and held it up and shook it before the men of Ireland.

After that, the three sons of Garach came out and made an attack on him, but he overcame them, and struck off their heads, and he killed their chariot-drivers as well, that they had armed against him. And Lethan and his chariot-driver came against him, and he killed them in the same way.

At that time the harpers of Cainbile came to Maeve's camp, and played on their magic harps; but the men of Ireland thought it might be as spies they came, and they drove them out of the camp, and followed after them till they came to the great stone of Lecmore. But when they thought to overtake them there, the harpers took on themselves the shape of wild deer, and went away. And it was on the same day that Cuchulain, with two casts of a sling stone, killed the marten and the pet bird that were sitting on Maeve's two shoulders.

Then the men of Ireland came into Magh Breagh and Muirthemne, and carried off and destroyed all before them. And Fergus warned them that Cuchulain was not far off, and that he would do a great vengeance on them, since they had spoiled Muirthemne. And it was at that time Lugaid, son of Nois, that had gone into Connaught with Fergus, went secretly to Cuchulain and told him of all that was going on in the camp, and of the dread of him that was on all the men of Ireland, so that they did not dare to stir out alone, and that he himself was true to him yet.

And now that the army was coming so near to

Cuailgne, the War-goddess, the Battle Crow, the Morrigu, came and sat on a pillar-stone at Teamhair, and gave a warning to the Brown Bull of Cuailgne, and it is what she said : "Have a care, and keep a good watch, my poor bull, or the men of Ireland will come on you and will drive you away to their camp." And when the bull heard the warning, he brought fifty of his heifers with him, and went away to a valley of Slieve Cuilinn.

And the men of Ireland came on, bringing the herds of cattle they took on the way, where there was no one to defend them. And they stopped for the night at Conaille Muirthemne, and there Maeve bade one of her women go down to the stream for water. And the woman was wearing Maeve's golden covering on her head, and Cuchulain saw her, and he thought it was Maeve herself that was in it, and he made a cast of a stone that killed her, and the gold covering was broken in pieces.

And they were delayed there for a while, for the river was in flood, and when they tried to cross it, the chariots that went in were swept away to the sea ; and one of Maeve's best men, Uala, that she sent to try the depth of it, was swept away along with them. And while they were stopping there, Cuchulain killed Raen and Rae, that were come to tell the story of the war, and a hundred men along with them.

Then Maeve said : "Some man of you must go out and stand against Cuchulain to save the army." "It is not I that will go," said one of them. "It is not I," said all the others, "for Cuchulain is no easy man to stand against." And they were for going round by the head of the river, but Maeve made them cut a way through the mountain before them, that it might be left as a lasting disgrace to Ulster. So they did this, and it is called Berna Ulaid, the Gap of Ulster, to this day.

Now, when they were setting out to cross the moun-

tain, Maeve gave orders that the army was to be
divided in two parts, each with its own share of cattle,
and of all other things, and she said that she herself
and Fergus would go with the one part, by the Gap of
Ulster, and that Ailell should go with the other part,
by the road of Midluachair.

So Ailell set out, and his chariot-driver, Ferloga, with
him, and that was the same Ferloga that made a bargain
with Conchubar, the High King, one time; and this is
the way it happened. It was at the time Mac Datho of
Leinster had stirred up a fight between the men of
Ulster and the men of Connaught, about the dividing
of a pig at a feast he made, the same way Bricriu had
stirred up a fight about the Championship, and
Conchubar was following after the men of Connaught
over the plain of Fearbile; and all of a sudden Ferloga,
that had been left behind by Ailell, and that was
hiding himself, made a leap to the back of Conchubar's
chariot, and took a hold of his neck between his two
hands. "What will you give me to let you loose, king?"
he said. "What is it you are asking?" said Conchubar.
"Indeed it is no great gift I am asking," said Ferloga,
"but only you to bring me along with you to Emain
Macha, and the young women and the young girls of
Ulster to sing a song around me every evening, and
every one of them to say, 'Ferloga is my favourite.'"
Conchubar agreed to that, and Ferloga went with him
to Emain; but at the end of a year they sent him back,
and presents with him, to Ailell and to Maeve.

At that time, a suspicion came on Ailell, that there
was some understanding between Maeve and Fergus,
and he bade Ferloga to keep a watch on them. After a
while, Ferloga saw that Maeve and Fergus had stopped
in a wood behind the rest of the army, and he followed
after them quietly, the way they would not hear him,
and there he found Fergus's sword lying on the ground.

So he took the sword out of the sheath, and he cut a wooden sword and shaped it, and put it into the sheath in its place, and he brought Fergus's sword back to Ailell, and told him how he had found it, and Ailell bade him hide it in his chariot. When Fergus saw that his sword was gone and a wooden sword was put in its place, there was great confusion on him ; but Ailell said nothing of it when they met, but asked him to come and play a game of chess with him. And at the game they quarrelled, and Ailell said sharp words of blame to Fergus and to Maeve, and they answered him back, and Fergus bade him give him up his sword. But Ailell said he would never give it to him until the day of the great battle would come, between the men of Ireland and the men of Ulster.

Then Cuchulain came there and stood on a height and shook his spears and his sword before them, so that great dread came on them.

After that, Maeve sent Fiacha, son of Firaba, to talk with Cuchulain, and to try could he win him over. "What will you offer him ?" said Fiacha. "I will give him full payment for all that has been spoiled of his goods, and a good place for himself in Cruachan Ai, and my own protection and Ailell's, if he will give up Conchubar's service and come into ours. And indeed that would be better for him," she said, "than to stop under a little king like Conchubar."

So Fiacha went to speak with Cuchulain, and he gave him a good welcome. And Fiacha told him the message he had brought from Maeve, and the offer she had made if he would quit Conchubar's service. "I will not do that," said Cuchulain ; "I will not betray my mother's brother for the sake of any strange king. But I will consent to go myself to-morrow," he said, "to speak with Maeve and Ailell and with Fergus." So Fiacha bade him farewell, and went back to the army.

On the morning of the morrow Cuchulain went to Glen Ochain, and Maeve and Fergus came to meet him ; and Maeve looked at him and she said : " Is this the same Cuchulain you put such a great name on, Fergus ? I see that he has not yet grown out of his boyhood." Then she spoke with Cuchulain and made her offer again, and he refused it, and they left the place with great anger on them one against the other. And that night, and the two nights after it, the men of Ireland were afraid either to eat or to sleep or to make music ; for Cuchulain killed so many of their men before the clear light of every morning, that it was as if the whole army was melting away. " Some one must go and make him another offer," said Maeve, and this time she sent Mac Roth, the herald. " Where will I find him ? " said Mac Roth. " Ask Fergus for news of him," said Maeve. " It is likely," said Fergus, " he will be between Ochain and the sea, letting the sun shine and the wind blow upon him after so many nights spent without sleep."

It was there he found him sure enough, and Laeg keeping a watch a good way off. " There is an armed man coming towards us, Cuchulain," said Laeg. " What sort of a man is he ? " said Cuchulain. " A brown-haired, broad-faced, handsome young man ; a fine brown cloak on him ; a bright bronze spear-like brooch fastening his cloak ; a well-fitting shirt next his skin ; two strong shoes between his feet and the ground. There is a white hazel rod in one hand, and a sword with a sea-horse tooth for a hilt in the other." " Well, Laeg," said Cuchulain, " let him come, for these are the tokens of a herald."

Mac Roth came up to him then and asked : " Who are you serving under, young man ? " " We are serving under Conchubar, High King of Ulster." " Can you tell me where can I find Cuchulain, that has killed so many of the men of Ireland ? " " Whatever you would say to him, you may say it to me," said Cuchulain. Then Mac Roth told him all the new offers he had brought from

Maeve, and Cuchulain said: "I am Cuchulain that you are looking for, and I refuse all your offers." So Mac Roth went back to the camp. "Did you find Cuchulain?" said Maeve. "I found," he said, "an angry boy between Ochain and the sea, and I do not know if it was Cuchulain." "Did he take your offer?" said Maeve. "He did not," said Mac Roth. "It is Cuchulain he was talking to," said Fergus. "You must go to him again," said Maeve, "and make new offers." So Mac Roth went out again to make some terms with Cuchulain, but he refused all his offers. "And another thing," he said, "I would never consent to give in to a woman, or to be under a woman's rule." "Is there any bargain you would make?" said Mac Roth. "If there is," said Cuchulain, "you must find it out for yourselves, and there is one in the camp can tell you of it," he said; "and if he himself comes to me, I will speak with him, but if any other man comes to me again with offers, that will be the last day of his life."

So Mac Roth went back again and told all this to Maeve. "And I will not go near him again, myself," he said, "for all that any king in Ireland could give me." Then Maeve said to Fergus: "Have you any knowledge of the terms Cuchulain would take?" "I have not," said Fergus. But after she had questioned him a while, he said: "It is what he wants, that one man of the men of Ireland should meet him and fight alone with him every day. And while that fight is going on, he will put no hindrance on the rest of the army, but it may march on. But so soon as he has killed the man set against him, the army must stop, and make its camp until the morning of the morrow." "I will agree to that," said Maeve, "for it is better to lose one man every day than a hundred every night. And who will go and make this agreement with him?" "Fergus must go," they all said. "I will not go,"

said Fergus. "Why so?" said Ailell. "I will not go,"
he said, "unless you bind yourselves on your oath to
keep to your agreement with him." "We will do that,"
they said; and so Fergus bound them on their oath, and
his horses were yoked to his chariot.

Then a young lad, Etarcomal by name, of the people
of Maeve and of Ailell, made ready his own chariot.
"What side are you going, Etarcomal?" said Fergus.
"I am going with you," he said, "the way I will get a
sight of Cuchulain." "If you take my advice, you will
not make that journey," said Fergus. "Why so?"
"Because if your pride and his pride meet together, some
misfortune will surely happen." "I give my word not
to anger him in any way," said Etarcomal.

They went on then to where Cuchulain was, between
Ochain and the sea, and himself and Laeg were playing a game with their casting spears. "There is an
armed man coming to us," said Laeg. "What sort of
man is he?" said Cuchulain. "He is large and proud,
and he standing in a high chariot, and the waving
yellow hair about his head gives him the appearance
of the top of a tall tree that stands on a green lawn,"
said Laeg. "He has a crimson cloak about him with a
deep border of gold thread, and an inlaid gold brooch in
the cloak; a broad green spear in his hand; a shield
with a boss of red gold over him; a long sword in a
toothed sheath across his knees." "It is Fergus that is
in it," said Cuchulain. Then Fergus came where he was
and got out of his chariot, and Cuchulain gave him
a great welcome. "Do you welcome me indeed?"
said Fergus. "I do surely," said Cuchulain; "but if
it is to look for a feast from me you are come, when
a flock of birds passes over the plain a wild goose will
fall to your share, and when fish rise in the invers a
salmon will fall to your share; a handful of seaweed
and a handful of water-cress." "We know well your
hospitality is straitened in this war," said Fergus.

But I am come for the men of Ireland, to agree to your
conditions. And from this out they will send one of
their best men to fight with you alone every day." "I
agree to keep to my part of the bargain," said Cuchulain,
"and let us not stop talking here any more," he said,
"or the men of Ireland will be thinking you are doing
some treachery on them."

So Fergus went back to the camp, but Etarcomal
stopped for a while looking at Cuchulain. "What are you
looking at?" said Cuchulain. "I am looking at yourself," he said. "Then take your eyes off me, and go after
Fergus; and maybe you think yourself a better fighting
man than the one you are looking at," said Cuchulain.
"You look to me as good a fighter as I ever saw for one
of your age," said Etarcomal, "but you would not be
thought much of among trained fighters and grown
men." "It is well for you," said Cuchulain, "it is under
Fergus's protection you came, or I swear, by the gods
my people swear by, you would not go back safe and
sound to the camp." "You have no right to say that,"
said Etarcomal; "and what you want of the men of
Ireland, I will give it to you," he said, "for you ask for
one champion at a time to fight with, and I myself will
be the first to come to you to-morrow." "Come, then,"
said Cuchulain, "and however early you may come in
the morning, you will find me here before you."

So Etarcomal set out, and he began to tell his chariot-
driver all he had said, and how he had promised to go
out and fight with Cuchulain on the morrow. "Did you
make that promise?" said his driver. "I did," said
Etarcomal, "and I have given my word I will go; and I
do not know," he said, "would it be better for me to wait
till to-morrow, or to go back and fight with him to-day."
"You will not get the better of him to-morrow," said his
driver, "and it would be just as well for you to be beaten
to-night." "Turn the chariot and let us go back," said

Etarcomal, "for I swear by the oath of my people, I will not go back to the camp without bringing Cuchulain's head in my hand." So they turned back again towards the sea.

Then Laeg said : "That chariot that was here a while ago has turned back again to us, Cuchulain." "It is Etarcomal coming back to challenge me, and it is not I that will fall in this fight," said Cuchulain. "But bring me my arms," he said, "for it would not be right for me not to be ready to meet him." So he went to meet him, and took his sword out of the sheath, and said : "What are you come back for?" "I am come to fight with you." "I am loth to fight with you," said Cuchulain, "for it was under the protection of Fergus you came here."

And with that he gave a blow of his sword that cut the sod clean away from under the soles of Etarcomal's feet, so that he fell on his back. "Go back now," he said, "for you have had a warning." "I will not go back until I have fought with you." Then Cuchulain gave another stroke with the edge of his sword that cut the hair close off his head, but drew no blood. "You may go back now, at least," he said. "I will not go," said Etarcomal, "until I have made an end of you, or you have made an end of me." "Well," said Cuchulain, "if you are set upon that, it is I must make an end of you." With that he made a cross blow at him that cut him through and through, so that he fell dead.

Fergus, now, had seen nothing of all this, for it was his custom, when he was travelling, never to look back, but always to be looking before him ; and presently, Etarcomal's chariot-driver came up with him, and he said : "Where have you left your master?" "Cuchulain is after attacking and making an end of him on the plain," said the man. "It was not right of him to do that," said Fergus, "to any one that came under my protection. Turn my chariot about now," he said, "until I go back and talk with him." And when he came to where Cuchulain was, he said : " It was not right of you, my own foster-son, to kill one that came under my protection." " Ask his chariot-driver," said Cuchulain, "on which of us the blame should be laid." Then the chariot-driver told the whole story, and when Fergus heard it, he said : "There is no blame on you, Cuchulain." Then he bound the body of Etarcomal to his chariot, so that it was dragged after it along the road and through the camp to the door of Ailell and Maeve. "There is the young man you sent out," he said, "and this is the treatment Cuchulain will give to every other man that goes out against him." And Maeve came out of the door and spoke high, angry, loud words : " I had put great hopes in that young man," she said, "and I did not think it was under bad protection he was going, when he went under the protection of Fergus." And Fergus said : "What business had he going out at all, to meddle with Cuchulain ? And if I went there myself," he said, "it is well pleased I was to get back again safely."

The next day, the men of Ireland consulted together as to who should go against Cuchulain, and they agreed that it was best to send Natchrantal, that was a great fighting man.

So he set out, but he would bring no arms with him but three times nine holly rods, and they having hardened points.

Cuchulain was at that time following after a flock of wild birds, to bring some of them down for the evening's food, and he took no notice of Natchrantal, but went on following after the birds. But Natchrantal thought it was afraid of him he was, and he went back to the door of Maeve's tent and gave a loud shout, and he said : " That great Cuchulain there is so much talk about, is running away now after the challenge I gave him." " I would hardly believe that," said Maeve, "for he has stood against many good fighting men before now, and why would he not stand against you?" Fergus heard what was said, and it vexed him, any man to say Cuchulain had run before him; and he sent Fiacha, son of Firaba, to reproach him, for letting such a thing be said, and Cuchulain bade him welcome. "I am come from Fergus," said Fiacha, "and it is what he says, that it would have been more fitting for you to spill the blood of the man that was sent against you, than to run from him." "Who did I run from?" said Cuchulain. "Tell me who makes that boast." "It is Natchrantal," said Fiacha. "What would Fergus have me do?" said Cuchulain; "would he have me kill an unarmed man? For he brought nothing with him but wooden rods, and it is not my custom to wound chariot-drivers or messengers or unarmed men. But let him come out armed to meet me," he said, "on the morning of to-morrow."

So Fiacha went back to the camp, and the day seemed long to Natchrantal till he could meet Cuchulain. But when he went out in the morning and came to the plain he said to Cormac Conloingeas: "Where is Cuchulain?" "He is there before you," said he. "That is not the appearance that was on him yesterday," said Natchrantal; for Cuchulain's anger had come on him so that the appearance he had was changed, and he was leaning against a pillar-stone, and in the strength of his anger, as he was throwing his cloak about him, he broke off the pillar-stone, and he never noticed that it was wrapped between the cloak and himself; and Natchrantal threw his sword at him, and it broke to pieces against the pillar-stone, and then Cuchulain gave him a blow over the top of his shield that struck off his head.

While this fight was going on, Maeve, having a third part of the army with her, set out Northward to Dun-Sobairce, to look for the Brown Bull. And Cuchulain followed after her for a while ; but then he turned back to defend his own country. And he saw before him Buac, son of Bainblai, that was the man Maeve trusted better than any other, and twenty-four men along with him, and they driving the Brown Bull before them and fifteen of his heifers, that they had brought out of Glen-na-masc in Slieve Cuilinn. "Where are you bringing these cattle from ? " said Cuchulain. " Out of that mountain beyond." "What is your name ? " he said. "If I tell it, it is not either through love of you or through fear of you," he said. " I am Buac, son of Bainblai, from Ailell's country and Maeve's." " Take this from me, then," said Cuchulain, and with that he threw his spear at him so that it went through his body, and he fell dead. But while he was doing this, the rest of the men drove away the Bull with great haste to the camp of the men of Ireland ; and this was the greatest affront that was put on Cuchulain through the whole of the war for the Brown Bull of Cuailgne.

Then the men of Ireland began saying to one another that Cuchulain would not have the mastery over them but for the bronze spear he had, and that there must be enchantment on it, for none of them could stand against it. And they said to Maeve that she should send Rae, the satirist, to ask it of him, for he could not refuse a satirist ; so Rae went and asked it of him. "Give me your spear," he said. "I will not give you that indeed," said Cuchulain, " but I will give you other things." " I will not take any other thing," said Rae, "and I will put a bad name on you, if you refuse me the spear." "Take it, then," said Cuchulain, and with that he threw it with all his force at his head. "That is a weighty present," said the satirist, and he dropped dead.

Then Cur, son of Daltach, was sent out, for the men of Ireland thought he would be able ro rid them of

Cuchulain. But it was hard to persuade Cur, because he thought it was not worth his while to go and fight with a young beardless boy. And when he went out in the morning, Cuchulain was practising all his feats that he had learned, and Cur was for a while trying to get near enough to come at him with his weapons, but he could not ; and Cuchulain was so taken up with doing his feats that he never noticed him at all. Then Laeg saw him and said : " Have a care, Cuchulain ; there is an armed man making ready to attack you." Cuchulain was doing his apple feat at that time, keeping nine apples, and his shield, and his sword in the air, that none of them fell to the ground. And when he saw Cur, he threw the apple that was in his hand straight at his forehead, and it went through, and brought out a share of his brains the size of itself, at the other side.

And after that, other fighting men were sent out every day through a week, and he killed them all. And one day he said : " Go, Laeg, to the camp, to my friends, Lugaid and Ferbaeth and Ferdiad, and say you are come from me, and ask him which of the men of Ireland is to be sent against me to-morrow." So Laeg went, and when he came back he said : " It is your own comrade and fellow-pupil with Scathach, Ferbaeth, your blood-friend, is coming against you ; for he has only lately joined the army, and he has brought four-fifths of his men with him, and Maeve has promised him her daughter Findabair, and he has drunk from her cup, and been fed by her hand. And it is not to every one Maeve gives the ale that she gave out for Ferbaeth." " I am sorry to hear that," said Cuchulain, " for I think worse of a comrade of my own coming against me, than of any other man." And when Ferbaeth came out to fight against him in the morning, Cuchulain did his best to make him give up the fight, for the sake of their old friendship, but Ferbaeth would not listen. Cuchulain turned from him then in anger, and he struck the sole of his own foot with a spear, that it drew blood, and then he threw his spear at Ferbaeth, but he did not look to see did it hit him or not. But the spear went through his head and out of his mouth, and this is the way Ferbaeth came to his death.

Then Ailell made up a plan by which he thought to make Cuchulain give up the stand he was making against the army, and his plan was to offer Findabair to him if he would give his word to leave off attacking the men of Ireland, and he sent Lugaid to make the offer to him. Cuchulain was not very well pleased with the message, and he thought there might be some treachery in it, but he agreed that he would meet Ailell and Findabair, and speak with them. But when the time came, Ailell made his fool put on his clothes, and wear his gold circle on his head, and go with Findabair; and he bade him stop as far back as he could, the way Cuchulain would not know it was not the king that was in it; and then Findabair was to bind him over to their side, not to fight any more against the men of Ireland, and when that was done, she herself and the fool were to hurry back to the camp together. But when Cuchulain saw them, he knew the fool, and he sent a stone out of his sling and killed him. And because Findabair had taken a share in the treachery, he cut off her two plaits of hair and took them away. And after a while Ailell and Maeve came to see what had happened them, and there they found Findabair beside the dead body of the fool. And they brought her home and said nothing of it, but all the same the story was talked of in the camp.

Then Cuchulain sent Laeg into the camp again to ask news of Lugaid. And it is what Lugaid told him that the next to be sent against him was his own brother Larine, that Maeve had persuaded with wine, and with the promise of Findabair, to go against him. "And it is what they think," said Lugaid, "that if Cuchulain should kill my brother, I myself would have to go and get satisfaction for his death; and tell Cuchulain," he said, "not to make an end of Larine, but only to give him some punishment he will not forget." So when Larine came out, at the breaking of the day, Cuchulain struck the weapons out of his hands as one might strike toys out of the hands of a child, and he took him in his two hands and shook him, and left him there with the life still in him. But he was never the better of the shaking he got to the end of his life.

As Cuchulain lay in his sleep one night a great cry from the North came to him, so that he started up and fell from his bed to the ground like a sack. He went out of his tent, and there he saw Laeg yoking the horses to the chariot. "Why are you doing that?" he said. "Because of a great cry I heard from the plain to the north-west," said Laeg. "Let us go there then," said Cuchulain. So they went on till they met with a chariot, and a red horse yoked to it, and a woman sitting in it, with red eyebrows, and a red dress on her, and a long red cloak that fell on to the ground between the two wheels of the chariot, and on her back she had a grey spear. "What is your name, and what is it you are wanting?" said Cuchulain. "I am the daughter of King Buan," she said, "and what I am come for is to find you and to offer you my love, for I have heard of all the great deeds you have done." "It is a bad time you have chosen for coming," said Cuchulain, "for I am wasted and worn out with the hardship of the war, and I have no mind to be speaking with women." "You will have my help in everything you do," she said, "and it is protecting you I was up to this, and I will protect you from this out." "It is not trusting to a woman's protection I am in this work I have in my hands," said Cuchulain. "Then if you will not take my help." she said, "I will turn it against you; and at the time when you will be fighting with some man as good as yourself, I will come against you in all shapes, by water and by land, till you are beaten." There was anger on Cuchulain then, and he took his sword, and made a leap at the chariot. But on the moment, the chariot and the horse and the woman had disappeared, and all he saw was a black crow, and it sitting on a branch; and by that he knew it was the Morrigu had been talking with him.

After that, Loch, son of Mofebis, was sent for to Maeve, and she asked him would he go out to the next day's fight. "I will not go," he said, "for it would not be fitting for me to go out against a young boy, whose beard is not grown; but I have one to meet him," he said, "and that is my brother Long, son of Emonis, and you can make an agreement with him." So then Long was sent for, and Maeve promised him a great reward, suits of armour for twelve men, and a chariot, and Findabair for a wife, and the right of coming to every feast at Cruachan. Then Long went out to the fight, but Cuchulain killed him.

Then Maeve said to her women: "Go now to Cuchulain, and tell him to put some likeness of a beard on himself, and say to him there is no good warrior in the camp thinks it fitting to go out and fight him, he being young and beardless."

When Cuchulain heard what Maeve had said, he smeared his face, the way he would have the appearance of a beard, and then he came out on the hill and showed himself to the men of Ireland. When Loch, son of Mofebis, saw him, he said: "Is that a beard on Cuchulain?" "That is certainly what I see," said Maeve. "Then I will go out and meet him," said Loch. So they met beside the ford, where Long had got his death. "Come to the ford that is higher up," said Loch, for he would not fight at the ford where his brother died. So they fought at the upper ford, and while they were fighting, the Morrigu came against

Cuchulain with the appearance of a white, red-eared heifer, and fifty other heifers along with her, and a chain of white bronze between every two of them, and they made a rush into the ford. But Cuchulain made a cast at her, and wounded one of her eyes. Then she came down the stream in the shape of a black eel, and wound herself about Cuchulain's legs in the water; and while he was getting himself free of her, and bruising her against a green stone of the ford, Loch wounded his body. Then she took the appearance of a grey wolf, and took hold of his right arm, and while he was getting free of her, Loch wounded him again. Then great anger came on him, and he took the spear Aoife had given him, the Gae Bulg, and gave him a deadly wound. "I ask one thing for the sake of your great name, Cuchulain," he called out. "What thing is that?" "It is not to spare my life I am asking you," said Loch, "but let me rise up, the way I may fall on my face, and not backwards towards the men of Ireland, so that none of them can say it was in running away or in going backward I fell." "I will surely give that leave," said Cuchulain, "for the thing you ask is a right gift for a fighting man." And after that he went back to his own camping-place.

Now, on that day above any other, a very downhearted feeling came on Cuchulain, he to be fighting alone against the four provinces of Ireland. And he bade Laeg to go to Conchubar and to the men of Ulster, and to say to them that he, the son of Dechtire, was tired with fighting every day, and with the wounds he had got, and not one of his people or his friends coming to help him.

After that Maeve sent out six all together against him, three men and three women that understood enchantments; but he destroyed them all. And now that Maeve had broken her agreement with him, not to send more than one against him at a time, he did not spare her men any longer, but from where he was he used his sling so well that in the whole army there was neither dog, horse, or man, that dared turn his face towards Cuchulain.

It was one day at that time the Morrigu came to try and get healing of her wounds from him, for it was only by his own hand the wounds he gave could be healed. She took the appearance of an old woman on her, and she milking a cow with three teats. Cuchulain was passing by, and there was thirst on him, and he asked a drink, and she gave him the milk of one teat. " May this be to the good of the giver," he said, and with that her eye that was wounded was healed. Then she gave him milk from another teat, and he said the same words ; then she gave him the milk from the third teat. " The full blessing of the gods, and of the people of the plough, on you," he said. And with that, all the wounds of the Great Queen were healed.

Then the men of the four great provinces of Ireland made their camp, and put up walls at the place called the Great Breach, on the plain of Muirthemne ; but they sent the cattle they had with them southward. And Cuchulain took his place on a mound ; and in the evening Laeg made a fire for him there, and the flame flashed on the bright shining weapons of the men of Ireland. And when Cuchulain saw so many of them, and they so near him, great anger came on him, and he took his spears and his shield and his sword and shook them, and he gave out his loud hero cry, and it was such a great cry he gave that the Bocanachs and Bananachs and the witches of the valley answered it from all parts.

And when the men in the camp heard these great cries, they thought it was an attack that was being made upon them, and they ran against one another, and fought one another in their fright, so that a hundred of them were killed in that night.

Then Laeg saw a man coming through the camp from the north-east. "There is a man coming towards us, little Hound," he said. "What is the appearance on him?" said Cuchulain. "He is very tall and handsome and shining, and he has a green cloak about him, fastened with a silver brooch; a shirt of silk that is embroidered with red gold, falling to his knees; a black shield in his hand, with a border of white bronze, and a spear with five prongs. And it is a strange thing," he said, "that no one in the whole camp seems to see him or to take any heed of him." "That is so," said Cuchulain; "and the men of Ireland take no heed of him because they cannot see him; and I know well it is one of my friends among the Sidhe that is coming to give me help and relief; for they know it is hard for me to be standing alone against the four provinces of Ireland."

Then the man of the Sidhe, that was Lugh of the Long Hand, came and spoke with Cuchulain, and it is what he said, that he knew he was tired out and in want of sleep. "And sleep now, Cuchulain," he said, "by the grave in the Lerga, and I myself will keep watch over you till the end of three days and three nights. So Cuchulain fell asleep there and then by the grave that is in the Lerga, and no wonder in that, for he had been fighting since before the feast of Samhain without sleep, but all the while killing and attacking and destroying the men of Ireland—unless he might sleep a little while beside his spear in the middle of the day, his head on his hand, and his hand on his spear, and his spear on his knee. And while he was lying in his heavy sleep, the man of the Sidhe put Druid herbs on his wounds, so that they were all healed. So he slept for three days and three nights, and at the end of that time he rose up and passed his hand over his face, and he blushed red from head to foot with the strengthening of his courage that he felt in him, and he would have been ready to go there and then into any great gathering or feasting hall in all Ireland. "How long have I been in my sleep?" he asked the man. "Three days and three nights." "Then you have done me a bad turn indeed," he said, "for the men of Ireland have been left in quiet all that time." "They were not indeed," said the man. "Who was it stood up to them then?" said Cuchulain. "It was the boy troop came from the North, from Emain Macha," he said; "three times fifty sons of the chief men of Ulster, and they attacked the army three times, and they killed three times their own number, but they themselves were all killed in the end. And Follaman, son of Conchubar, was leading them, and he had made a boast that he would never go home again unless he could bring Ailell's head along with him, and the gold crown that was on it. But two foster-sons of Ailell, the two sons of Betchach, son of Baen, fell on him and wounded him, so that he got his death." "My grief, and oh! my grief that I was not there," said Cuchulain; "for if I had been in it, the boy troop would never have been destroyed, and Conchubar's son would not have come to his death." "Do not be fretting, little Hound," said the strange man; "there is no reproach on your name by it." "Stop here with me to-night," said Cuchulain, "and the two of us together will avenge the boy troop." "I will not indeed," said he; "but let you yourself play the game out now with the men of Ireland, for it is not they that have power over your life at this time."

With that he went away, and Cuchulain said to Laeg, "Yoke the scythed chariot for me now, if you have the things belonging to it." Then Laeg rose up and got ready the chariot, and he put on his light dress of deer-skins, that was spotted and striped and close-fitting, so that his arms were left free. And over that he put his raven-black cloak, and his shining helmet on his head; and on his forehead he put the narrow band of gold that chariot-drivers were used to wear. And then he threw over the horses the cloths that covered them all over, and that were studded with little blades, and spikes, and points, so that every time the chariot moved, it brought some sharp point against those that were near it, the way every point and every head of the chariot would cut its sure path; and he gathered the reins in his hand, and the goad, and the long whip.

And then Cuchulain put on his armour, and took his spears, and his sword, and his shield that had a rim so sharp it would cut a hair against the stream, and his cloak that was made of the precious fleeces of the land of the Sidhe, that had been brought to him by Manannan from the King of Sorcha. He went out then against the men of Ireland, and attacked them, and his anger came on him, so that it was not his own appearance he had on him, but the appearance of a god. And after that he turned back and left them, and there was no wound on himself, or on the horses, or on Laeg that day. And he made a round of the whole army, mowing men down on every side, in revenge for the boy troop of Emain.

But the next day he was standing on the hill, young, and comely, and shining, and the cloud of his anger had gone from him. Then the women and the young girls in the camp, and the poets and the singers, came out to look at him; but Maeve hid her face behind a shelter of shields, thinking he might make a cast at her with his sling. And there was wonder on these women to see him so quiet and so gentle to-day, and he such a terror to the whole army yesterday; and they bade the men lift them up on their shields to the height of their shoulders, the way they could have a good sight of him.

But Dubthach, the Beetle of Ulster, saw his own wife climbing up with the other women to look at Cuchulain, and great anger and jealousy came on him; and he said to the chief men of the army that it would be best for them to surround Cuchulain secretly on all sides, and then to let on to be fighting among themselves, so as to lead him down where he could not escape them. But when Fergus was told this, he gave a great kick of his foot to Dubthach, that sent him from where he was. And he spoke angry words against Dubthach, and he told him he would be well paid for the harm he had planned, whenever the men of Ulster would get up from their weakness, and come out to help Cuchulain.

And that night the army of Ireland made their camp at the great stone in the country of Ross; and then Maeve asked which of them would go out and fight with Cuchulain on the morrow. But every one of the men of Ireland said: "It is not I that will go." "It is not one of my family that should be sent to his death." Then Maeve asked Fergus to go out and fight him. "It is not right for you," said Fergus, "to ask me to go against a young boy, and he my own pupil and my foster-son." But Maeve pressed him so hard that he could not but take the work in hand; and early in the morning he went out to the ford of fighting where Cuchulain was. When Cuchulain saw him coming he said: "Truly, my master, it is not safe for you to come and fight, and you without a sword," for Ailell had not given him back his own sword yet. "It is no matter," he said, "for if I had a sword in my sheath, it is not on you I would use it. And now, Cuchulain," he said, "for the sake of all I did for you, and all Conchubar and the whole of Ulster did for you in your bringing-up, let you give way before me to-day, in the sight of the men of Ireland." "Indeed I am loth to give way before any man in this war," said Cuchulain. "You need not mind that," said Fergus, "for I will do the same for you when the great last battle of this war is fought; it is then I will turn and run before you, when you are covered with wounds and with blood. And if I run then," he said, "all the men of

Ireland will run along with me. So Cuchulain agreed to do that, because it would be for the profit of Ulster. And he bade Laeg make ready his chariot; and presently, as if he had been beaten by Fergus, he gave way to him in the sight of the men of Ireland. When they saw it, they called out: " He is running before you, Fergus." And Maeve called out: " Follow him, Fergus— make haste, the way he will not escape you." " I will not indeed," said Fergus, " I will follow him no farther; and if you think I did not make him run far enough," he said, " I did more than all the rest of the men that went against him up to this; and I will make no other attack on him," he said, "until all the men of Ireland have fought with him, one by one."

So that was the end of the fight between Fergus and Cuchulain.

There was a man of Connaught at that time whose name was Ferchu, and he had been at war with Ailell and Maeve from the time they got the kingdom, and he used to be robbing the country and destroying it, so that he was made an outlaw. And some of his men heard that the whole army of Connaught was being vexed and hindered by one man; and when they told it to Ferchu, he said: " It would be a good chance for us to go and attack that man, and to bring his head with us to Ailell and Maeve, for if we do that," he said, "they will forgive us all the harm we have done their country."

So he himself and his twelve men went forward to where Cuchulain was, and they attacked him all together. But Cuchulain was not long in making an end of them, and he struck off their heads, and put them on twelve stones; and he put Ferchu's head on a stone by itself.

Then the men of Ireland consulted together again who they would send out to fight on the next day; and it is what they all said, that it was Calatin and his twenty-seven sons and his sister's son, Glas, son of Delga, should go out. Now it is the way they were, every man of them had poison in himself and in his weapons; and there was not one of them ever made a cast of a spear or a stone that missed, and there was no one that would be wounded by them but he would die, either on the spot or within nine days. So great rewards were promised them, if they would go out against Cuchulain. And Fergus was there at the time the business was knotted. "And surely," every one said, "they are only one man, for they are all members of Calatin's body." After that, Fergus went into his tent, to his people, and he gave a deep groan of trouble, and he said : "My grief for the thing that is to be done to-morrow." "What thing is that?" said they all. "Cuchulain to be killed," he said. "Who would kill him?" said they. "Calatin and his sons," he said, "and if there is any one of you would go and watch the fight and bring me word what happens, I would give him a good reward, and my blessing." "I will go," said Fiacha, son of Firaba.

So in the morning Calatin, with his sons and his sister's son, rose up and went to where Cuchulain was, and Fiacha, son of Firaba, went along with them. And as soon as they came near him, they threw their twenty-nine spears at him all together, in one cast, and not one of them drew blood, for he caught them all on his shield. Then Cuchulain drew his sword from the sheath to hack off the spears and to lighten his shield ; but while he was doing that, they all ran at him as one man and put their twenty-nine right hands on his head, and forced his face down to the gravel and the sand of the ford. And he gave out his great hero cry, and the cry of a man in unequal fight, and there was not a man in the camp, and he not dead or asleep, but heard it.

Then Fiacha, son of Firaba, came up, and when he saw what had happened, the love of his own countryman came over him, and he pulled out his sword and hit the nine-and-twenty hands off Calatin and his sons, with one blow. Cuchulain raised up his head then, and gave a deep sigh of relief, and he saw who it was had come to his help. "That was done quiet and easy, my good comrade," he said. "You may think it is quiet and easy I was," said Fiacha, "but if what I did is heard of in the camp, the reward that will fall on me will not be quiet and easy. For if the men of the children of Rudraige should hear of the stroke I made for you, it is with sword and spear my reward will be paid." "I give you my word," said Cuchulain, "that now I have lifted my head and got my breath again, unless you tell tales on yourself, none of these men will tell tales on you."

With that he made an attack on Calatin and his sons, and he began to hack and to cut at them till there was nothing left of them but limbs and little pieces eastward and westward over the whole face of the ford. Only one man of them, Glas, son of Delga, got away and ran, but Cuchulain rushed after him and gave him a great blow. But he got as far as Ailell and Maeve's tent, and all he could say was, "Fiacha! Fiacha!" before he fell dead.

Fergus and Maeve said: "What debts are those he called out about?"—for Fiacha is the word for a debt in Irish. "I do not know indeed," said Fergus, "unless it might be that some one in the camp owed him a debt, and that it was on his mind." "That must have been so," said Ailell. "By my word," said Fergus, "however it was, all his debts are paid now."

And at the ford where Calatin and his sons got their death, there is a stone with the marks of their sword-hilts, and the butt-ends of their spears on it to this day.

Then it was settled by the men of Ireland that it was

Ferdiad, son of Daire, the great champion of the men
of Domnand, should go out and meet Cuchulain the
next day. For they had the same way of fighting, and
it was with the same teachers they had learned the
knowledge of arms, with Scathach and with Uathach
and with Aoife ; and neither of them had an advantage
over the other, except that Cuchulain had the feat of
the Gae Bulg. But Ferdiad had good armour to protect him against any man he would fight with.

So they sent messengers to bring Ferdiad, but he
refused and would not come, for he knew it was what
they wanted of him, to fight against his friend, his
companion and his fellow pupil, Cuchulain.

Then Maeve sent the Druids and the satirists to him,
that they might make three hurtful satires and three hill-
top satires on him, if he would not come with them, that
would raise three blisters on his face, Shame and Blemish
and Reproach, so that if he did not die on the moment,
he would be dead before the end of nine days.

Then Ferdiad came with them for the sake of his
good name, for he thought it better to fall by spears
than by satires. And when he came he was received
with honour and attendance, and he was served with
pleasant drinks, so that he grew merry, and his mind
was confused. And great rewards were offered him if
he would go out against Cuchulain ; clothes of all
colours for his men, and speckled satins, and silver
and gold, and the equal of his own lands of the level
plains of Magh Ai, without rent or disturbance, secure
to his son and to his grandson and to their children to
the end of life and time.

And it is what Maeve said : " It is a great reward I am
giving you, Ferdiad, and why would you not accept it ? "
And Ferdiad was making excuses. " I will not take
your reward without good pledges," he said, " for it is a
heavy fight is before me ; he that has the name of

Cuchulain is surely a good Hound." "I will give you a champion's pledge," said Maeve; "you will not be bound to come to our gatherings, you will get horses and bridles; I will call you my friend above all other men." "I will not go to this fight," said Ferdiad, "without some other securities, for this is a fight will be heard of till the end of life and time." "Take all you want," said Maeve. "There is no delay except with yourself. Bind us till you are satisfied by the right hand of kings and of princes; there is nothing I will refuse you." "I must have six securities and no less," said Ferdiad, "before I will go out and be destroyed by Cuchulain, and all the whole army looking on." "I will give you whatever securities you want," said Maeve, "however hard it may be to come at them; Domnall in his chariot; Niaman of the Slaughter, both of them protectors of bards; bind Morann if you want sure payment; bind Carpre Min of Manand, he that has a string of knowledge in his harp; bind our own two sons." "O Maeve, it is a bitter woman you are," said Ferdiad. "And it is not a gentle wife to a husband you are, but it is a fit queen you are for Cruachan of the Swords, with your high talk and your fierce strength. But in spite of all the words you are stirring me up with," he said, "if you would offer me the land and the sea, I would not take them, without the sun and the moon along with them." "You need not wait longer than to-day and to-morrow," said Maeve, "before you will get your fill of all sorts of the jewels of the earth. And here is my brooch with its hooked pin," she said; "and more than all that, Ferdiad, so soon as you have killed this Hound of feats, I will give you Findabair of the champions, queen of the west of Elga." Then every one was saying what great rewards those were. "But however great they are," said Ferdiad, "it is with Maeve herself they will stay and not with myself; and I will not take them to go into battle with my fellow and my near friend, that is Cuchulain." And it is what he said:

"A pity indeed a woman to have come between myself and himself! The half of my heart is Cuchulain's without fault, and I am the half of his own heart.

"By my shield! If Cuchulain were killed from Ath Cliath, it is I would thrust my sword through my heart, through my side, through my breast.

"By my sword! If Cuchulain were killed from Glen Bolg, I would kill no man after him till I had leaped over the edge of the well.

"By my hand! If the Hound were killed from Glen an Scail, I would make an end of Maeve and her army and of no one else of the men of Ireland.

"By my spear! If it were from Ath Cro the Hound was killed, it is I would be buried in his grave; the one grave would be for the two of us.

"Say to him, the Hound without blemish, that Scathach without fear made a prophecy I would be put down by him at a ford.

"Misfortune on Maeve, misfortune on Maeve, that put her face between us! Sending us one against the other, myself and strong Cuchulain."

Then Maeve said to her people, the way she would stir him up: "It is a true word Cuchulain spoke." "What word was that?" said Ferdiad. "He said it would be no great wonder if you would fall by him in the first trial of arms in this country." "He had no right to say that," said Ferdiad; "for it is not fear or want of skill he learned of me up to this time. And I swear by my arms if it is true he said this thing, that I will be the first to fight with him to-morrow before the men of Ireland." "May good be with you for saying that," said Maeve; "and this is better to me than to see you show fear or weakness, for every man cares for his own country, and why has he a right to do more for the profit of Ulster than you would do for the profit of Connaught?"

Ferdiad gave in to her then, and he bound her on the sureties of the aforesaid six for the fulfilment of her promises of the reward; and she bound him to fight with Cuchulain on the morrow.

Then Fergus got his horses harnessed and his chariot yoked, and he went out to where Cuchulain was, to tell him of all that had happened. "My welcome before you, my master Fergus," said Cuchulain. "I am glad of that welcome, my pupil," said Fergus. "But what I am come for is to tell you who it is that is coming to fight at the early hour of the morning of to-morrow." "I will listen to that," said Cuchulain. "Your own friend and companion, and fellow-pupil, the man that learned the use of arms with you, Ferdiad, son of Daire, the hero of the men of Domnand." "I give my word," said Cuchulain, "it is not my wish, my friend to come out against me." "And now," said Fergus, "you must be careful and ready more than any other time, for there was not the like of Ferdiad among any of the men who have fought you up to this." "I am here," said Cuchulain, "hindering and delaying the four great provinces of Ireland, from the beginning of the winter to the beginning of spring, and I have not drawn back one foot before any man in that time, and I think it likely I will not draw back before him." "Neither has Ferdiad any fear on him before you, now his anger is stirred up," said Fergus, "and besides that, he has good armour to protect him." "Be quiet now, Fergus, and do not let me hear any more of that story," said Cuchulain. "I was always well able to stand against him in any place, or on any ground." "It is not easy to get the better of him," said Fergus, "for he is fierce in fighting, and he has the strength of a hundred." "There will be a sharp fight when myself and Ferdiad come to the ford," said Cuchulain; "it will not be without being told in stories." "O Cuchulain of the red sword," said Fergus, "it would be better to me than a great reward, you to carry proud Ferdiad's purple cloak eastward." "I give my word and my oath," said Cuchulain, "it is I myself will get the victory over Ferdiad." Then Fergus went back to the encampment.

At the same time Ferdiad went to his tent and to his people, and told them how he was bound by Maeve to fight with Cuchulain on the morrow, and he told how he had bound Maeve by six sureties for the fulfilment of her promises, if Cuchulain should fall by him.

It is not happy in their minds the people of Ferdiad's tent were that night, but gloomy and heavy-hearted; for they were sure that wherever Cuchulain and Ferdiad would meet, it was there one of them would get his death, and they were sure that one would be their own master; for no one at all had been able to stand against Cuchulain since the beginning of the war.

Ferdiad slept through the early part of the night very heavily, and when the latter end of the night came, his sleep went from him, and his drunkenness had passed away, and the thought of the fight was pressing on him. And he bade his driver to harness the horses, and to yoke his chariot. But the driver tried to turn him from it. "It would be better for you to stop here than to go," he said, "for my liking of it is not more than my disliking."

"Be silent, boy," said Ferdiad, "for I will not be turned from this journey by any young lad; but I will go to the ford, a ford the ravens will be croaking over; I will fight with Cuchulain till I wound his strong body, till I crush the courage out of him the way that he will die."

"It would be better for you to stop here," said the driver, "for it is not gentle your threats are; your parting will be sorrowful; there is one to whom it will be a sickness; grief will come of that meeting with Cuchulain; it is long it will be remembered; it is a pity for him who goes that journey." "It is not right what you are saying," said Ferdiad; "it is not for a brave man to refuse—it is not in our race. I will delay no longer, courage is better than fear; let us set out now to the ford."

Then Ferdiad's horses were harnessed, and his chariot was yoked, and he went forward to the ford, and the day with its full light came upon him there. "Now, boy," he said, "spread out the skins and the cushions of my chariot under me here, until I get some sleep and rest, for I got no sleep at the end of the night, with the care of the fight upon me."

So his servant unharnessed the horses, and settled the skins and cushions of the chariot under him, and the heavy rest of sleep came upon him.

But as to Cuchulain, he did not rise up at all till the day had come with its full light, the way the men of Ireland would not say it was fear that was on him that made him rise. And when the day came: "It would be as well, Laeg," he said, "to yoke the chariot, for it is an early-rising man that is coming to meet us to-day."

"The horses are harnessed, and the chariot is yoked," said Laeg; "let you get into it, and there will be no hindrance to your courage."

With that the ready-handed, battle-winning son of Sualtim leaped into the chariot, and there shouted around him the Bocanachs and Bananachs, and witches of the valley. For the Tuatha de Danaan were used to set up their shouts around him, the way the fear and the wonder would be great before him in every fight he would go into.

And it was not long until Ferdiad's driver heard the noise coming near, the straining of the harness, the creaking of the chariot, the ringing of the armour and of the shield, the trampling of the horses, the joyful coming of Cuchulain to the ford.

The driver came and laid his hand on his master. "Good Ferdiad," he said, " rise up ; here they are coming. For I hear," he said, " the creaking of a chariot ; it has come over Breg Ross, over Braine ; it has come over the highway by the foot of Baile-in-Bile ; he is a mighty Hound that urges it ; he is a good driver that yokes it ; he is a free hawk that hurries his horses towards the south. It is not he that will be slow in the fight. It is a pity for him that is on the height waiting for the Hound of valour. It is a year ago I foretold there would come a Hound, the Hound of Emain, a Hound with all colours about him—the Hound of Ulster, the Hound of Battle ; I hear him—I have heard him coming."

"Good servant," said Ferdiad, "why is it you have been praising that man ever since you came out from the house ? It is likely you are not without wages for your great praise of him. Yet it has been foretold to me by Ailell and by Maeve, it is he that will fall by me. And it is a time to help me," he said ; "and let you be silent, and give up praising him, that your foretelling may not come true. It is not for you to give up on the brink of the fight ; surely I will soon have the reward."

And the driver said : " He is coming, not slowly, but quick as the wind, or as water from a high cliff, or like swift thunder." " Surely you have taken wages for these great praises you put upon him," said Ferdiad ; " it is not against him you are, but praising him, and putting a great name on him."

It was not long then until Ferdiad saw Cuchulain coming towards him in his chariot, and it is how his two horses were going, like a hawk sweeping from a cliff on a day of hard wind, or like a sweeping gust of the spring wind on a March day over a smooth plain, or like the swiftness of a wild stag when he is first started by the hounds in his first field ; as if they were on fiery flagstones, so that the earth was shaking and trembling with the quickness of their going.

So Cuchulain reached the ford, and Ferdiad came to the south side, and Cuchulain drew up on the north side, and Ferdiad bade Cuchulain welcome. " I am happy at your coming, Cuchulain," he said. " I would have been glad of that welcome up to this time," said Cuchulain, " but to-day I do not take it as the welcome of a friend. And, Ferdiad," he said, "it would be fitter for me to welcome you than for you to welcome me, for it is you have come to me in the country and province where I am, and it is not right for you to come to fight with me, but it is I should go to fight with you, for it is out before you are the women and the children, the young men and the horses, the flocks, the herds, and the cattle of the province of Ulster."

" Good Cuchulain," said Ferdiad, " what has brought you to fight with me at all ? For when we were with Scathach and with Uathach and with Aoife, you were my serving-boy, to tie up my spears and to make ready my bed." " That is true indeed," said Cuchulain ; " but it was as less in age than you I was used to do so ; but that is not the story that will be told of us after this day, for there is not a man in the whole world I would not fight to-day."

And it is then each of them spoke sharp, unfriendly words against the other ; and it is what Ferdiad said : " What has brought you, O Hound, to fight with a strong fighter ? It is red your blood will be, flowing over the harness of your horses ; it is a pity for your journey ; it is long it will be spoken of ; you will be in much want of healing if you ever get back to your own house," he said.

" I have fought with heroes, with chiefs of armies, with

troops, with hundreds before now," said Cuchulain, "and what I have to do to-day is to make an end of you, to bring you down in our first path of battle."

"You have met now with a man that will put reproach on you," said Ferdiad, "for it is I myself will do that. It is well the loss of the men of Ulster will be remembered," he said, "their champion to be put down, and they looking on."

"What way shall we meet one another?" said Cuchulain. "Is it in our chariots we had best fight, or is it with my sword and spear I am to overthrow you, if the time has come?" And Ferdiad said: "Before the setting of the sun to-night, you will be fighting as if with a mountain, and it is not white that battle will be. The men of Ulster will be shouting for you," he said, "till you grow overbold; but it is sorrowful they will be, when your ghost passes over them and through them." "You are fallen into the gap of danger, Ferdiad," said Cuchulain; "the end of your life has come, not by treachery, but by sharp weapons. You may think much of yourself till we meet one another, but you will never fight in a battle again, from this day to the end of time." "Leave off now from your boastings," said Ferdiad; "it is you are the greatest boaster in the world. I know well you are no fighter at all, you heart of a bird in a cage; you are but a giggling fellow, without courage, without strength." But Cuchulain said: "When we were together with Scathach, we used to be practising together, we used to go to every battle together, because of our bravery that was equal. You were my heart companion, you were my people, you were my family—I never found one was dearer; it is sorrowful your death would be to me."

"Where is the use of all this talk?" said Ferdiad; "your great name will be lost, your head will be on a stake before the crowing of the cock. Madness and grief are taking hold of you, Cuchulain," he said, "and it is bad treatment you will get from me, because it is on yourself the fault is."

"Good Ferdiad," Cuchulain said then, "it was not right for you to come out against me, through the stirring up and the meddling of Ailell and of Maeve; and none of those who came before you got victory or success, but they all fell by me, and you will fall along with them. And, O Ferdiad, strong fighter," he said, "do not come against me; the meeting will bring sorrow to many, and what is worse than sorrow to you. Have you not been bought with many presents? A purple belt, a suit of armour? But, Ferdiad," he said, "the woman for whom you are come to this fight, Findabair, daughter of Maeve, however comely she may be, will never be given to you; for she has been offered to many before you," he said, "and many like you have been wounded for her sake." And he said, and Ferdiad began to listen to him:

"Do not break your oath not to fight with me; do not break friendship. Do not break the word you gave me, do not come against me.

"The woman has been promised to fifty others; it was a heavy gift for them; it is by me they were sent to their grave; it was by me they got the end that was fitting for them.

"Though Ferbaeth was boastful, he who had a houseful of brave men, it is short the time was till I quieted his rage; I killed him by the one cast.

"The striking down of Srub Daire's courage was bitter to him; it is he held the secrets of a hundred women; he had a great name at one time; it is not silver thread but gold thread was in his clothes.

"If it were to me the woman was promised on whom the kings of the fair province smile, I would not bring the red blood on your body for it, south or north, east or west.

"And, good Ferdiad," he said, "this is why it is not right for you to come to this fight. When we were with Scathach, it is together we used to go to every battle, to every wild place, through every darkness and every hardship. We were heart companions; we were comrades in gatherings; we shared the one bed where we used to sleep sound sleep. We used to practise together, in many far countries; we used to go to hard fights; we used to go through every forest together."

"O Cuchulain of the wonderful feats," said Ferdiad, "although we learned knowledge together, and although I know the bonds friendship put upon us, it is I that will give you your first wounds; do not be remembering our companionship, for it will not protect you. And it is too long we are delaying like this," he said; "and what arms shall we use to-day, Cuchulain?"

"It is you have the choice of arms to-day," said Cuchulain, "for it is you were the first to reach the ford." "Do you remember at all," said Ferdiad, "the casting spears we used to practise with Scathach and with Uacthach and with Aoife?" "I remember them indeed," said Cuchulain. "If you remember, let us begin with them," said Ferdiad.

So they began with their casting weapons, and they took their protecting shields, and their round-handled spears, and their little quill spears, and their ivory-hilted knives, and their ivory-hafted spears, eight of each of them they had. And these were flying from them and to them like bees on the wing on a fine summer day; there was no cast that did not hit, and each one went on shooting at the other with those weapons from the twilight of the early morning to the full midday, until all their weapons were blunted against the faces and the bosses of the shields. And as good as the throwing was, the defence was so good that neither of them drew blood from the other through that time.

"Let us leave these weapons now, Cuchulain," said Ferdiad, "for it is not by the like of them our fight will be settled." "Let us leave them indeed if the time is come," said Cuchulain.

They stopped then, and threw their darts into the hands of their chariot-drivers. "What weapons shall we use now, Cuchulain?" said Ferdiad. "The choice of weapons is yours till night," said Cuchulain. "Let us, then," said Ferdiad, "take to our straight spears, with the flaxen strings in them." "Let us now indeed," said Cuchulain. And then they took two stout shields, and they took to their spears.

Each of them went on throwing at the other with the spears from the middle of mid-day until the fall of evening. And good as the defence was, yet the throwing was so good that each of them wounded the other in that time.

"Let us leave this now," said Ferdiad. "Let us leave it indeed if the time has come," said Cuchulain.

So they left off, and they threw their spears away from them into the hands of their chariot-drivers. Each of them came to the other then, and each put his hands round the neck of the other, and gave him three kisses. Their horses were in the one enclosure that night, and their chariot-drivers at the one fire; and their chariot-drivers spread beds of green rushes for them, with wounded men's pillows on them. The men that had knowledge of healing came then, and put herbs of healing to their wounds. And of every herb and plant that was put to Cuchulain's wounds, he would send an equal share from him westward over the ford to Ferdiad, the way the men of Ireland might not say if Ferdiad should fall by him, that it was by better means of cure he was able to overcome him.

And of every kind of food and of drink that was sent by the men of Ireland to Ferdiad, he would send a fair share over the ford northward to Cuchulain ; because the providers of Ferdiad were more than the providers of Cuchulain. All the men of Ireland were providers to Ferdiad for beating off Cuchulain from them, but only the Bregians were providers to Cuchulain. They used to come and to be talking with him at the dusk of every night.

They rested there that night, and they rose up early on the morrow, and came forward to the ford of battle.

"What weapons shall we use to-day, Ferdiad?" said Cuchulain. "It is you have the choice of weapons until night," said Ferdiad, "because I had my choice of them the last day." "Let us then," said Cuchulain, "take to our great broad spears to-day ; for we shall be nearer to the end of our battle by the thrusting to-day than we were by the throwing yesterday."

Each of them continued to cut, and to wound, and to redden the other, from the twilight of the early morning till the fall of the evening. If it were the custom for birds in their flight to pass through the bodies of men, they could have passed through their bodies on that day, and they could have carried pieces of flesh and blood through their stabs and cuts, into the clouds and the sky all around. And when the fall of evening came, their horses were tired, and their chariot-drivers were down-hearted, and they were tired themselves as well.

"Let us stop from this now, Ferdiad," said Cuchulain, "for our horses are tired, and our chariot-drivers are down-hearted ; and when they are tired, why would not we be tired as well? And we are not bound to go on for ever," he said, "as is the custom with the Fomor. Let us put the quarrel away for a while, now the noise of the fighting is over." "Let us leave off indeed if the time is come," said Ferdiad.

They threw their spears from them then into the

hands of their chariot-drivers, and each of them came towards the other. Each of them put his hand round the neck of the other and gave him three kisses. Their horses were in the one enclosure that night, and their chariot-drivers at the one fire.

Their chariot-drivers made beds of green rushes for them, with wounded men's pillows on them, and the men that had knowledge of healing came to examine them that night, but they could do nothing more for them, because of the deepness of their many wounds, but to use charms and spells on them, to staunch their blood. Every charm and every spell that was used on the wounds of Cuchulain, he sent a full share of them over the ford westward to Ferdiad. And of every sort of food and of drink that was sent to Ferdiad, he sent a share of them over the ford northward to Cuchulain.

They rested there that night, and they rose up early on the morrow, and they came forward to the ford of battle. Cuchulain saw a sort of a dark look on Ferdiad that day. "It is bad you are looking to-day, Ferdiad," he said ; " there is a darkness on your face, and a heaviness on your eyes, and your own appearance is gone from you." "It is not from fear or dread of you I am like this to-day," said Ferdiad ; "for there is not a champion in Ireland to-day I could not put down." And Cuchulain was fretted to see him that way, and it is what he said : "O Ferdiad, if it is you yourself, I am sure you are a miserable man, to have come at the bidding of a woman to fight against your own companion." But Ferdiad said : "O Cuchulain, giver of wounds, true hero, every man must come in the end to the sod where his last grave shall be."

"As to Findabair, daughter of Maeve," said Cuchulain, "whatever her beauty may be, it is not for love of you she was given to you, but only for the sake of your great strength." "O Hound of the gentle sway," said Ferdiad, "it is long ago my strength was tried ; but I never heard of any man braver in fight than yourself ; I never met so brave a man until to-day." "It is your own fault what has happened," said Cuchulain ; "you to have come at the bidding of a woman to try your sword against your fellow." "If I had gone back," said Ferdiad, "without doing battle with you, it is little my name and my word would be thought of by Ailell and by Maeve of Cruachan." "No one has ever put food to his lips," said Cuchulain, "and no one has ever been born in honour of a king or queen, for whose sake I would have harmed you." "O Cuchulain, winner of battles," said Ferdiad ; "it was not you but Maeve that betrayed me ; let you take the victory and the fame, for it is not on you the blame is."

And Cuchulain said : "My faithful heart is like a clot of blood ; my life is nearly gone from me ; I have no strength for high deeds, fighting with you, Ferdiad." "Much as you are complaining over me now," said Ferdiad, "what arms shall we use to-day ?" "It is you have the choice to-day," said Cuchulain, "because it was I had it yesterday." "Let us then," said Ferdiad, "take to our swords to-day, for we will be nearer the end of our battle by the hewing to-day, than we were by the thrusting yesterday." "Let us do so indeed," said Cuchulain.

And then they put two long wide shields on them, and they took to their swords, and each of them continued to hack at the other, from the dawn of the early morning till the time of the fall of evening. "Let us leave off from this now," said Cuchulain. So they left off.

They threw their swords from them into the hands of their chariot-drivers, and it was the parting, mournful, sorrowful, downhearted, of two men that night.

Their horses were not in the one enclosure that night,

their chariot-drivers were not at the one fire. They rested that night there.

And Ferdiad rose up early next morning, and went forward by himself to the ford. For he knew that day would decide the fight, and he knew one of them would fall on that day there, or they would both fall.

And then he put on his battle suit, before the coming of Cuchulain to him. He put on his shirt of striped silk, with its border of speckled gold, next his white skin. He put on his coat of brown leather, well sewed, over the outside. He put on his apron of purified iron, through dread of the Gae Bulg that day. He put his crested helmet of battle on his head, on which were forty gems, carbuncles, in each division, and it was studded with crystal and with shining rubies of the eastern world. He took his strong spear into his right hand, and his curved sword upon his left side, with its golden hilt, and its knobs of red gold, and his great large, bossed shield on his back.

And then he began to show off many changing, wonderful feats, that he had never learned with any other person, neither with nurse or with tutor, or with Scathach or with Uacthach, or with Aoife, but that were made up that day by himself against Cuchulain.

Then Cuchulain came to the ford, and when he saw all Ferdiad was doing: "I see, my friend Laeg," he said, "all those feats will be tried on me one after another; and because of that," he said, "if it is I that begin to give in to-day, it is for you to reproach me, and to speak hard words to me, the way that the strength of my anger may grow the more on me. But if I am getting the better of him, then you are to praise me, and make much of me, that my courage may be the greater." "I will do that indeed, my master Cuchulain," said Laeg.

And then Cuchulain put on his battle suit, and he said: "What arms shall we take to-day, Ferdiad?" "The choice is yours to-day," said Ferdiad. "Let us try the ford feat then," said Cuchulain. "Let us indeed," said Ferdiad. But though Ferdiad agreed to it, it is sorry he was to say those words, for he knew Cuchulain was used to put an end to every fighter that was against him in the feat of the ford.

It was great work, now, that was done on that day at the ford; the two champions of western Europe, the two gift-giving and wage-giving hands of the northwest of the world; the two pillars and the two keys of the courage of the Gael; to be brought from far off, to fight one against the other, through the stirring up and the meddling of Ailell and Maeve. Each of them began to throw his weapons at the other, from the dawn of early morning to the middle of mid-day. And when mid-day came, the anger of the men grew hotter, and each of them drew nearer to the other. And then it was that Cuchulain leaped on to the boss of Ferdiad's shield, to strike at his head over the rim of the shield. But Ferdiad gave the shield a blow of the left elbow, and threw Cuchulain from him like a bird on the brink of the ford. Cuchulain leaped up again to the boss of the shield, but Ferdiad gave it a stroke of his left knee, and threw Cuchulain from him like a little child.

Laeg saw that done. "My grief indeed," he said, "the fighter that is against you, Cuchulain, casts you away as a light woman would cast her child. He throws you as foam is thrown by the river; he grinds you as a mill would grind fresh malt; he cuts through you as the axe cuts through the oak; he binds you as the woodbine binds the tree; he darts on you as the hawk darts on little birds; and from this out, you have no call nor claim to courage or a brave name to the end of life and time, you little fairy fighter," said Laeg.

It is then Cuchulain leaped up with the quickness of the wind, and with the readiness of the swallow, and with the fierceness of the lion, towards the troubled clouds of the air the third time, until he lit on the boss on Ferdiad's shield, to strike at his head from above. And Ferdiad gave his shield a shake and cast Cuchulain from him, the same as if he had never been cast off before at all.

And it is then Cuchulain's anger came on him, and the flames of the hero light began to shine about his head, like a red-thorn bush in a gap, or like the sparks of a fire, and he lost the appearance of a man, and what was on him was the appearance of a god.

So close was the fight they made now, that their heads met above and their feet below, and their hands in the middle, over the rims and bosses of their shields. So close was the fight, that they broke and loosened their shields from the rim to the middle. So close was the fight, that they turned and bent and shattered their spears from the points to the hilts. So close was the fight, that the Bocanachs and Bananachs and the witches of the valley screamed from the rims of their shields and from the hilts of their swords, and from the handles of their spears. So close was the fight, that they drove the river out of its bed and out of its course, so that it might have been a place for a king or a queen to rest in, so that there was not a drop of water in it, unless it dropped into it by the trampling and the hewing the two champions made in the middle of the ford.

So great was the fight, that the horses of the men of Ireland broke away in fright and shyness, with fury and madness, breaking their chains and their yokes, their ropes and their traces; and the women and the young lads and the children and the crazy and the followers of the men of Ireland broke out of the camp to the south-west.

They were using the edge of their swords through that time; and it was then Ferdiad found a time when Cuchulain was off his guard, and he gave him a stroke of the sword, and hid it in his body, and the ford was reddened with Cuchulain's blood. and Ferdiad kept on making great strokes at him. And Cuchulain could not bear with this, and he called to Laeg for the Gae Bulg, and it was sent down the stream to him, and he caught it with his foot. And when Ferdiad heard the name of the Gae Bulg, he made a stroke of his shield down to protect his body. But Cuchulain made a straight cast of the spear, the Gae Bulg, off the middle of his hand, over the rim of the shield, and it passed through his armour and went out through his body, so that its sharp end could be seen.

Ferdiad gave a stroke of his shield up to protect the upper part of his body, though it was "the relief after danger," as the saying is. "That is enough," said Ferdiad; "I die by that. And I may say, indeed, you have left me sick after you, and it was not right that I should fall by your hand. O Hound of the beautiful feats, it was not right, you to kill me; the fault of my death is yours, it is on you my blood is. A foolish man does not escape when he goes into the gap of danger; my grief! I am going away, my end is come. My ribs will not hold my heart, my heart is all turned to blood. I have not done well in the battle; you have killed me, Cuchulain."

Cuchulain ran towards him after that, and put his two arms about him, and lifted him across the ford northwards, so that his body should be by the ford on the north, and not on the west of the ford with the men of Ireland.

He laid him down then, and a cloud and a weakness came on him as he stood over Ferdiad. Laeg saw that, and he saw that all the men of Ireland were rising up to come towards him. "Good Cuchulain," said Laeg, "rise up now, for the men of Ireland are coming towards us, and it is not one man they will put to fight against us now that Ferdiad has fallen by you." "What use is it to me to rise up now, and he after falling by me?" said Cuchulain. But Laeg said: "Rise up, O chained Hound of Emain ; it is glad and shouting you have a right to be now, since Ferdiad of the hosts has fallen by you." "What are joy and shouting to me now?" said Cuchulain ; "it is to madness and to grief I am driven after the thing I have done, and the body I wounded so hard." "It is not right for you to be lamenting him," said Laeg. "It is making rejoicings over him you should be. It was at you he aimed his spears." But Cuchulain said : "Even if he had cut one arm and one leg from me, it is my grief Ferdiad not to be riding his horses through the long days of his lifetime." And Laeg said : "It is better pleased the women of the Red Branch will be, he to have died and you to be living. They know it is not few but many you have sent away for ever ; for from the day you came out of Cuailgne to meet Maeve of the great name, it is a grief to her all you have killed of her people and of her fighting men. You have not taken quiet sleep since the spoiling of your country began ; though there were few along with you, many were the mornings you rose up early."

Then Cuchulain began to keen and to lament for Ferdiad there, and it is what he said : "Well, Ferdiad, it is a pity for you it was not one of the men that knew my courage you asked an advice of before you came to meet me in the fight that was too hard for you. It is a pity it was not Laeg, son of Riangabra, you asked how we stood one to another. It is a pity you did not ask a true advice of Fergus. It is a pity it was not pleasant comely Conall you asked which of us would put down the other.

"And these men know well," he said, "there will never be born one among the men of Connaught who will do deeds equal to yours, to the end of life and time. And they know that if they looked among the places, the gatherings, the swearings, the false promises of the fair-haired women of Connaught, or in the playing with targets and shields, the playing with shields and swords, the playing backgammon and chess, the playing with horses and chariots, there will not be found the hand of a man that will wound like Ferdiad's hand, or a man to bring the red-mouthed birds croaking over the speckled battle, nor one that will fight for Cruachan, that will be your equal to the end of life and time, O red-cheeked son of Daman." And then he rose up and stood over Ferdiad. "Well, Ferdiad," he said, "it is great wrong and treachery was played on you by the men of Ireland, to bring you out to fight with me. For it has not been easy to stand against me in the war for the Bull of Cuailgne." And he made this complaint :—

"O Ferdiad, you were betrayed to your death ; your last end was sorrowful ; you to die, I to be living ; our parting for ever is a grief for ever.

"When we were far away, with Scathach the victorious, we gave our word that to the end of time we would never go against one another.

"Dear to me was your beautiful ruddiness ; dear to me your comely form ; dear to me your clear grey eye ; dear to me your wisdom and your talk.

"There has not come to the battle, there has not been made angry in the fight, there has not held up shield on the field of spears, the like of you, O red son of Daman.

"Findabair, the daughter of Maeve, with all her great beauty, it was putting a gad on the sand, or on the sun, for you to think to get her, Ferdiad."

Then Cuchulain was still looking down on Ferdiad, "Well, my friend Laeg," he said, "strip Ferdiad now, and take his armour and his clothes off him, until I see the brooch for the sake of which he undertook the fight."

Laeg stripped Ferdiad then, and when Cuchulain saw the brooch, he began to lament and complain over him again, and it is what he said :

"My grief, O gold brooch ! O Ferdiad of the poets, O strong striker of many blows, it is brave your arm was.

"Your yellow hair, curled, well-loved; your soft, leaf-like belt about you until death.

"Dear was our fellowship, dear the brightness of your eyes; your shield with its rim of gold; your chessboard that was worth riches.

"It was not right, you to fall by my hand; it was not a friendly ending. My grief, O gold brooch, my grief!

"Well, my friend Laeg," he said then, "come now and take the Gae Bulg out of him, for I cannot afford to be without my spear." So Laeg took the Gae Bulg out of him, and when Cuchulain saw his reddened spear lying beside Ferdiad, he said: "O Ferdiad, it is a sorrowful story to me, that I should see you so red and so pale, I with my spear reddened, and you in a bed of blood.

"When we were over in the east with Scathach, there would not have been angry words between us, or destroying weapons.

"Scathach spoke fiery words to us, 'Go all of you to the battle that will be fought by Germain the terrible.'

"I said to Ferdiad and to Lugaid, the always generous, and to the son of Baetan the fair, 'Let us all go against Germain.'

"We all of us came to the battle-ground on the shore of the lake of Lind Formait; we brought four hundred out with us from the islands of the Athisech.

"As I and brave Ferdiad were together in the door of Germain's dun, I killed Rind, the son of Niul, I killed Ruad, son of Finnial.

"Ferdiad killed upon the shore Blath, son of Calba of the red swords. Lugaid killed Mugarne of the Torrian Sea, a surly, fierce man.

"We spoiled the dun of Germain the crafty; we brought him with us alive over the wide sea of speckled waters; we brought him to Scathach of the broad shield.

"She, our teacher, whose name was well known, bound us to friendship together, the way our anger would not turn against one another among the fair tribes of Elga.

"Sorrowful the morning when the strength was taken from the son of Daman. My grief! I loved the friend to whom I have given a drink of red blood.

"It is a sorrowful thing has happened to us the pupils of Scathach—I myself red and wounded; you yourself not driving your chariot.

"It is a sorrowful thing has happened to us the pupils of Scathach—I myself hard with blood; you yourself entirely dead.

"It is a sorrowful thing has happened to us the pupils of Scathach—yourself to have died, myself to be alive and strong; it is angry we were in the battle."

"Good Cuchulain," said Laeg, "let us leave this ford now; it is too long we are here." "Let us leave it now indeed, my friend Laeg," said Cuchulain. "But every other fight I ever made was as a game and a sport beside the fight with Ferdiad." And it is what he said:

"Each fight was a game, each one was a jest, until Ferdiad came to the ford; we got the same teaching, we got the same rewards; our teacher was kind to us both alike, setting us both above all the others.

"Each was as a game, each was as a jest, until Ferdiad came to the ford; we had the same ways, we used to do the same deeds; it was at the one time Scathach gave a shield to me, and a shield to Ferdiad.

"Each was a game, each was a jest, until Ferdiad came to the ford; dear to me was the pillar of gold that I broke down on the ford; he who, when he attacked the tribes, was braver than any other.

"Each was a game, each was a jest, until Ferdiad came to the ford, like a proud swelling wave, threatening to destroy all before him.

"Each was a game, each was a jest, until Ferdiad came to the ford; this thing will hang over me for ever. Yesterday he was larger than a mountain; to-day there is nothing of him but a shadow."

XII

THE AWAKENING OF ULSTER

THEN some of the men of Ulster came to comfort Cuchulain, and among them were Senoll Uathach and the two sons of Gege, Muredach and Cotreb. They brought him away to the five streams of Conaille Muirthemne, to wash his hurts in them. And the Sidhe threw all sorts of herbs and plants into the streams for his healing, so that they were all strewed over with green leaves.

Then when Ailell and Maeve heard there were men beginning to come from Ulster, they sent Mac Roth, the herald, to watch at Slieve Fuad, and to warn them if he could see any one coming. And after a while he came back, and Ailell asked news of him. " I saw," he said, " one chariot only, to the north of Slieve Fuad, and it coming straight on, and the man that was in it naked, and without armour or weapons, but only an iron spit in his hand, and he goading on the horses as if he would never get to the army alive." " Who do you think was that man, Fergus ? " said Ailell. " I think," said Fergus, " it was Cethern, son of Fintan, from the North, and he will soon be upon us." With that, Cethern came bursting into the camp, and he attacked everyone he met with his spit, and he himself got many wounds back again, so that he had to hold up the board of the chariot to his body to keep his bowels from falling out; and at last he made his escape, and came to the place where Cuchulain was lying. Then Cuchulain said to Laeg: "Rise up now, and go into the camp, and bring some of Ailell's physicians to cure Cethern; for I give my word, if they do not come before this time to-morrow, I will bring death and destruction on them." So Laeg went, and he brought back the physicians with him, and it was only the dread of Cuchulain that made them come. Then Cethern showed the first one of them his wounds, and it is what he said, that he could not be cured. Then Cethern gave him a blow that sent him out of the house. And the same thing happened with all the rest, fifteen there were of them altogether. Then he asked Cuchulain would he get him another physician, for those of the men of Ireland had done him no good. "Rise up, Laeg," said Cuchulain; "go to Slieve Fuad, to Fingan, the Druid physician of Conchubar, and bid him to come here and to heal Cethern." Now, Fingan was the greatest physician in all Ireland, and it was said of him that he could tell what a person's sickness was by looking at the smoke of the house he was in; and he knew by looking at a wound what sort the person was that gave it. Then he came, and Cethern showed him his wounds. "Look at this wound for me, good Fingan," he said. "There came at me two young men, with clear noble looks, with strange foreign clothes on them, and each of them threw a spear into me, and I threw my spear into each of them. "I know those two very well," said Cuchulain; "they are two choice men of Norway, and they were sent against you by Ailell and Maeve." "Look at this wound for me, Fingan," said Cethern. Fingan looked at it. "That is the work of two brothers," he said. "That is true indeed," said Cethern. "Two young men came at me, and they were like one another; but one had curling

brown hair, and the other had curling yellow hair.
Two green cloaks about them, with brooches of bright
silver; two soft shirts of yellow silk; bright swords in
their belts they had, and shields with bright silver
fastenings, and spears with veins of silver on their
handles." "I know those two very well," said Cuchulain;
"they are Maine Athremail and Maine Mathremail, two
sons of Ailell and Maeve."

"Look at this wound for me, good Fingan," said
Cethern. Fingan looked at the wound, and he said: "It
was a father and a son made that together." "That is
true," said Cethern; "there came at me two large men
with flaming eyes, and they having gold bands on their
heads, and the dress of kings, and gold swords at their
sides." "I know those two very well," said Cuchulain;
"it was Ailell and his son Maine Andoe that gave you
that wound." "Look at this wound, good Fingan," said
Cethern. Fingan looked at the wound. "That is the
work of a proud woman," he said. "That is true," said
Cethern; "there came at me a beautiful, pale, long-faced
woman, with long, flowing yellow hair on her, a crimson
cloak with a brooch of gold over her breast, and a
straight spear shining red in her hand. It was she gave
me that wound, and she got a little wound from me."
"I know that woman well," said Cuchulain. "She is
Maeve, daughter of the High King of Ireland, and Queen
of Connaught. She would have thought it a great
victory and a great triumph, you to have fallen by her
hand." "Good Fingan," said Cethern then, "tell me
now, what do you think of the way I am, and what can
you do for me?" "It is what I think," said Fingan,
"you will hardly see the calves that are following
your cows at this time grow to be yearlings; or if you
do itself," he said, "it will not be much use your life will
be to you." "That is what all the others said to me,"
said Cethern, "and it is not much profit or credit they got

by it, and it is not much you yourself will get"; and with that he made a kick at him, to drive him out of the house. But in spite of that treatment, Fingan gave him his choice of two things : the first to be a long time on his bed, so that he would see the men of Ulster coming in the end to avenge him ; or to be made well enough at the end of three days to go out himself and spend what he had of strength on his enemies.

"I will choose that," he said, "for I would not like to leave my enemies after me; and I would sooner get satisfaction from them myself." So then Fingan bade Cuchulain to make a healing bath that would ease Cethern. So Cuchulain went down to the camp, and he brought away with him all that he met of the cattle of the men of Ireland. Then their flesh was cut up with their bones and their skins to make a Druid bath, and Cethern was put in it for the length of three days and three nights. And at the end of that time he rose up and got into his chariot, to do vengeance on the men of Ireland. And his wife Ionda, daughter of Eochaid, came to him from the North, and brought him his sword that he had forgotten in his hurry at his first setting out.

But it happened that one of the physicians he had driven out with a blow had fallen down outside the tent, and lay there, not able to stir from that. But when Cethern was making ready to set out, he rose up and made his way back to the camp, and he said to the men of Ireland : "Cethern is after being cured by Fingan, the Druid, and he is coming at you now, and do you lay some trap for him." So it is what they did : they took Ailell's cloak and his shirt, and they put them about the pillar-stone, at the boundary of Ross, and his crown on top of it, and left them there. Cethern came rushing on them, and when he saw the pillar-stone, he thought it was Ailell was standing there, and he made at it, and gave a great blow of his sword, that it broke in pieces against the stone.

Then he saw what it was, and he said : "This is some trick they have played on me. And by the oath of my people," he said, "I will not stop my hand from killing, until such time as I have killed some man having a dress like this."

When Maine Andoe heard that, he put on his father's armour, and came out to meet him. And Cethern saw him, and made for him, and threw his shield at him, so that he was cut through and through the body by the rim of the shield.

And when the men of Ireland saw that, they pressed on Cethern from all sides and made an end of him. And his wife Ionda, daughter of Eochaid, came and cried over him there. And it is what she said :

"It is all one to me, it is all one, since there will be no hand of a man under my head for ever; since a grave has been made in the earth for Cethern from the Dun of the Two Hills.

"Cethern, son of Fintan, he that was like a king, was in no need of arms for his work; with nothing in his hand but a two-headed spit, his anger did not spare the men of Connaught.

"I will not take a mate for ever from the flocks of the living world; I will not wed with a man; my husband is sleeping with no woman.

"Dear the little hill, dear the dun where our fighting men were used to gather; dear the sweet fair water, dear was Inis Ruadh.

"Pitiful the grief, pitiful the grief the War for the Bull has brought on me; I will be keening him until my death, I Ionda, daughter of Eochaid !"

And then Fintan, Cethern's father, came with three times fifty men to get satisfaction for his son, and he made three attacks on the army, and killed a great many of Ailell's men; but Fintan lost a good many of his own men, and his son Crimthan was made prisoner. And the men of Ireland were afraid their army would be too much weakened by little fights of this sort before the great last battle that was foretold would come, and they made an agreement with Fintan to give him back his son, and to fall back themselves a day's march; and he gave his word not to vex them again until the time of the last battle. And they found, where the fight had been, one of Fintan's men and one of Ailell's men lying dead together, and they with their teeth fixed into one another. And it is from this the fight was given the name of Fintan's Tooth-fight.

Then Rochad, son of Fatheman, came to help Cuchulain, and three times fifty men with him. Now Findabair loved him, and when she heard he was coming, she told her secret, and she said to her mother: "That is my love and my choice out of all the men of Ireland." And when Maeve heard that, she made a plan to draw him off, and she said to Findabair: "If he is dear to you, go and spend the night with him, and bid him to go back with his men until the day of the great battle, and I give you my leave to be his wife." So Findabair went and did as Maeve bade her, and he went back to the North. But this was heard of in the camp, and the twelve kings of Munster that were in Maeve's army began speaking with one another; and it is what they all said, that Maeve had secretly promised Findabair as a wife to each one of them as a reward, if he would join in the war. "And the best thing we can do now," they said, "is to go and avenge ourselves on Maeve's men, and on Rochad, for the treachery that was done on us."

So they went out and made an attack on them, and Ailell and Maeve's men and Rochad made ready to defend themselves; but Fergus went out and tried to make them leave off, and to make peace between them, and before he could do that, seven hundred men had got their death.

And it was told to Findabair how these seven hundred men had got their death on account of her, and how Maeve had promised her in marriage to every one of the twelve kings of Munster. And when she heard that, her heart broke with the shame and the pity that came on her, and she fell dead there and then, and they buried her.

Now at that time Iliach, son of Cas, of the race of Rudraige, was living in the North with his son's son, Laegaire Buadach. And it was told him how the four provinces of Ireland were plundering and destroying the people of Ulster since the day before Samhain, and driving off their cattle and their goods, and all that they had. So he consulted with his people, and it is what he said, that he would go out himself and make an attack on the men of Ireland, and let loose his strength on them, and destroy what he could of them, and do what he could for Ulster. "For as to myself," he said, "if I come out of it, or do not come out of it, is all one to me." Then his two old spent horses, that had been let loose for life, were brought from where they were on the shore by the dun, and yoked to his old chariot, that had neither cushions nor skins in it. And he took his rough, dark, iron shield, with its hard rim of silver, over his shoulder, and his rough, grey, heavy sword at his left side. And he put in the chariot his two rusty, blunt spears, and his people gave him a store of stones and bits of rocks in a heap about him; and that is the way he went out against the army, and no armour on him at all.

When the men of Ireland saw him coming that way, they began mocking and laughing at him, but it is what Maeve said: "I would be glad indeed all the men of Ulster to come and meet us like that." Then Doche, son of Magach, chanced to meet him, and bade him welcome. "Who is it bids me welcome?" said Iliach.

" The comrade and friend of Laegaire Buadach," said he;
" Doche, son of Magach."   " I am glad of that welcome,"
said Iliach, "and for the sake of it, let you come to me
when I have spent my rage on the army, and when my
strength is going, and when my hand is tired, and let
you, and no other of the men of Ireland, make an end
of me.   And keep my sword," he said, "for your friend,
Laegaire Buadach."

Then he made an attack on the men of Ireland, and
when his spears were all broken in pieces, he began
hitting and throwing with the stones he had.   And when
they were out, he attacked the men that were near him
with the strength of his own hands, so that he made an
end of some of them.   And when all he could do was
done, he saw Doche, son of Magach, near him, and he
said : " Come to me now, Doche, and strike my head off,
and take charge of my sword for Laegaire Buadach."
And Doche did as he bade him, but he brought his
head to Ailell and to Maeve.

At this time Sualtim, son of Roig, was told that
Cuchulain had fought with Calatin and his sons, and
with Ferdiad, and of the hard fight he had made, and
the wounds he had got.   And it is what Sualtim said :
" Is it the sky bursting I hear, or is it the sea going
backward, or the earth breaking up, or is it the groaning
of my son in his weakness ? "   With that he set out to
visit him, and he found him covered with hurts and
wounds, and he began to cry over him.   But that did
not please Cuchulain, and he knew Sualtim would do
no good by stopping there, for he was not the man to
avenge him, for he was no great hero ; not that he was a
coward, but just like any other good fighting man.   And
Cuchulain said to him : " Well, Sualtim, stop your crying
over me, and rise up and go to Emain, and tell the men
of Ulster they must come themselves and follow on with
the war from this out, for I am not able to defend them

any more; for after all I went through, not one of them comes to help me or to comfort me.   And tell them," he said, "what way you found me, that I cannot bear to have my clothing next my skin, but it is with crooks of hazel I have to hold it off me, and it is grass that is laid over my wounds; for there is not the place of the point of a needle on me from head to foot but has some hurt on it, except my left hand that was holding my shield; and tell them to make no delay in coming," he said.

Then Sualtim set out on the Grey of Macha to give his message; and when he got close to Emain he called out: "Men are being killed, women brought away, cattle driven off in Ulster," but he got no word of answer. Then he went up to the very wall, and he cried again: "Men are being killed, women brought away, cattle brought away in Ulster"; but the second time he got no answer. Then he went on to the Stone of the Hostages at Emain, and he called out the same words the third time.   Then Cathbad, the Druid, asked: "Who are taken, and who is it is taking them?"   "It is Ailell and Maeve that are robbing you and destroying you," said Sualtim; "they are bringing away your women, your little boys, your cattle and your horses, and there is only Cuchulain to delay and to hinder the four great provinces of Ireland in the gaps and the passes of Muirthemne; the lad is wounded and no one is coming to his help." But Cathbad was vexed at being waked out of his sleep, and he said: "Any man that comes to scold at the king this way has a right to be put to death." But Conchubar, the king, said: "It is true what Sualtim is saying."   "It is true indeed," said all the men of Ulster.

Then anger came on Sualtim that he got no better answer than that, and he turned sharply, and the Grey of Macha reared up, the way the sharp edge of Sualtim's shield came against his own head, and cut it clean off.

Then the Grey turned again to Emain, and the shield dragged after him by its thongs, and Sualtim's head in the hollow of it, and the head said the same words as before: "Men are being killed, women brought away, cattle brought away in Ulster." Then Conchubar said: "The sky is over our heads, the earth is under our feet, the sea is round about us; and unless the sky with all its shower of stars comes down on earth, or the earth breaks open under our feet, or the blue sea goes over the whole face of the world, I swear that I will bring back every cow to its own shed, and every woman to her own dwelling-house."

Then he called to one of his messengers, Finnched, son of Troiglethan, that chanced to be there, and he bade him to go and to call out the men of Ulster. But with the sleep that was on him still, and the weakness, he bade him go and call those of his people that were dead, as well as those that were living. And one of the names he gave him to call to was Cuchulain, son of Sualtim.

It was easy work Finnched had to do now, for the men of Ulster were rising from out of their weakness, and they all made ready to come out with Conchubar, and some of them did not wait for Conchubar at all, but set out on the track of the army of Ireland.

Then Conchubar and his men set out from Emain, and the first day they went as far as Irard Cuillenn, and there they made a halt. "What are we stopping here for?" said Conchubar. "We are waiting for your own two sons," his men said, "Fiachna and Fiacha, that are gone to meet your grandson Erc, son of Fedelm, and of Cairbre, king of Teamhair, to bring him with us." "By my word," said Conchubar, "I will not make any more delay here, for fear the men of Ireland might hear I am risen from my weakness; for they do not know it up to this," he said, "or even if I am alive at all."

CUCHULAIN PUT HIS TWO ARMS ABOUT FERDIAD.

SUALTIM'S HEAD SAID THE SAME WORDS AS BEFORE.

So he himself and Celthair, and thirty hundred fierce chariot-fighters, went on, and it was not long before they came on eight times twenty strong men belonging to Ailell and to Maeve, and each of them bringing away a woman of the women of Ulster with him. And Conchubar and Celthair struck their heads off, and set the women free; and then they went back to Irard Cuillenn.

Now, as to the men of Ireland, they spent that night at Sleamhain of Meath. And in the night Cormac Conluin-geas started up out of his sleep, and he called out that there had a warning dream come to him, and that there was a terrible battle before them. And after a while Dubthach, the Beetle of Ulster, started up out of his sleep, and called out the same thing, that there had a warning dream come to him, and that it would not be long till there would be a great clashing of shields. And with these dreams and foretellings, great fear came on the men of Ireland, and it was an uneasy night they spent at Sleamhain that time.

And in the morning Ailell said: "We have been harrying Ulster and Cuailgne this long time, and we have taken the women and the cattle and the goods of the men of Ulster, and we have cut down hills behind us; and now," he said, "it is time for us to turn back to Magh Ai, and they can follow us and fight with us there if they have a mind to. But before that," he said, "I will send a messenger to look out across the great plain of Meath, to see if any of them are coming against us; and if they are," he said, "I will not go from this without giving battle to them, for he would not be a good king that would be good at running away."

So he sent out Mac Roth, the herald. And he had not long to wait before he heard a noise that was like the falling of the sky, or the breaking in of the sea over the land, or the falling of trees on one another in a great storm. And he saw the plain covered with wild creatures that had broken away out of the woods. Then he went back to Ailell and to Maeve, and told them his story, and they asked him what had he seen; and he said: "I thought I saw a grey mist far away across the plain, and then I saw something like falling snow, and then through the mist I saw something shining like sparks from a fire, or like the stars on a very frosty night." "What was it he saw, Fergus?" said Ailell. And Fergus said: "The mist he saw was the dust that went up from the march of the men of Ulster, and the flakes of snow were the foam flakes from the bits of their horses; and what he saw shining like sparks from the fire, or like stars on a frosty night, was the angry light of their eyes shining under their helmets."

"It is little I care for that," said Maeve; "we have good fighting men to meet them." "It is a pity for you to think that," said Fergus; "for there is neither in Alban nor in Ireland an army that can put down the men of Ulster when once their weakness is gone from them and their anger is kindled."

That night the men of Ireland made their camp in Clartha, and they put Mac Roth and another man to keep a good watch, the way the men of Ulster would not fall on them without warning. Now Conchubar and Celtchair, with their thirty hundred men, had followed them to Slieve Sleamhain, and when they found them gone from there they followed on to Clartha, for they thought to get the start of the rest of Ulster in reddening their hands upon the men of Ireland. So Mac Roth was not long waiting when he saw men and horses coming from the north-east, and he went back into the camp. "Well, Mac Roth," said Ailell, "have you seen any of the men of Ulster on our track?" "I saw men and horses coming," he said. "What is the number of them?" said Ailell. "Not less than thirty hundred chariots." "Those are the men of Ulster coming with Conchubar," said Ailell; "and what did you mean a while ago, Fergus, threatening us with the dust of a great army in the plain, when a little troop like that is all that can be brought against us?" "You are too quick in complaining of that," said Fergus, "and you will soon know what their number is."

"Let us make some good plan now," said Maeve, "for I am sure it is that hot, rude man, Conchubar, king of Ulster, that is coming to attack us. Let us make a pen before him," she said, "of all the army standing round on three sides, and thirty hundred men ready to shut the mouth of it on him when he comes in. For we must take these fellows alive and not kill them, for it would be unworthy of our name to do more than make prisoners of them, and they so few." Now this was one of the most laughable things that was said in the whole course of the war, Conchubar and his thirty hundred of the best men of Ulster to be taken alive. And when Conchubar's son, Cormac Conloingeas, heard this, there was great anger on him, and it is what he thought: "If I do not get satisfaction now at once from Maeve for this boast of hers, I will never get it again." So he rose up with his three thousand men to make an attack on her, and on Ailell; and they rose up as well, and their sons the Maines along with them, and the sons of Magach. But then the Gailiana, and the men of Munster, and of Teamhair, came between them, and made peace, and persuaded them to lay down their arms. But for all that, Maeve did make a pen of the army of Ireland to shut up Conchubar, and she had men ready to close it up when once he would be in. But it is what Conchubar did, he never so much as looked for an opening, but when he saw the army before him, he went straight through it, and he broke open a gap of two hundred on the right hand, and a gap of two hundred on the left, and went through them all, and cut them down in the very middle, so that eight hundred men of them were killed.

And then he went away from them, back to Slieve Sleamhain, to join the army of Ulster.

Then the men of Ulster began to gather upon the plain in their full strength, and when Ailell heard it, he said: "Let some one go up and watch them coming, and bring us a report of the appearance that is on them, and of the chief men that are leading them." "Let Mac Roth go," said Fergus.

So Mac Roth went out and took a post on the plain from the early light of the morning till the fall of evening, and through all that time the men of Ulster were coming, so that the ground was not naked under them, every division under its own chief man, and every troop under its own lord, and each one of them apart from the others, and they came on till they had covered the Hill of Sleamhain.

And when evening came, Mac Roth came back to Ailell and to Maeve, and they questioned him and said: "What sort were the men of Ulster as they came across the plain?" And Mac Roth said: "The first troop I saw coming had three thousand men in it, and as soon as they got to the hill, they took their armour off, and they began to dig and to make a seat of sods and of earth on the highest part of the hill, for their leader to sit on until the rest of the army would come.

"He had the appearance of a tall, proud man, used to giving orders; and he had yellow, curling hair on him, and a yellow forked beard, and a red, pleasant face, and blue eyes you would be afraid of. A five-folded crimson cloak he had on him, and a gold pin over his breast, and a white shirt with threads of gold woven into it next his body." "Who was that man, Fergus?" said Ailell. "He was Conchubar, son of Fachtna and of Ness, High King of Ulster." "There was a man stood beside him," said Mac Roth, "with scattered white hair, and a purple cloak, and a shield with bosses of red brass, and a long iron sword of foreign make. And he looked up to the sky, and threw his hand upwards, and with that the clouds seemed like as if they were rushing at one another, and fire came from them towards the men of Ireland." "That was Cathbad the Druid," said Fergus, "and he trying by his enchantments to know how the battle would go to-morrow."

"I saw another man with Conchubar," said Mac Roth, "and he having a smooth, dark face, and white eyes in his head; a long bronze rod in his hand, and a little bell beside him, and when he touched it with his rod, all the people near him began to laugh." "Who is that man?" said Ailell. "It is easy to know that," said Fergus; "that is Rocmid, the king's fool. There was never trouble or tiredness on any man of Ulster that he would not forget if he saw Rocmid." "There came another troop then," said Mac Roth, "and it is what I thought, that the leader they had was the handsomest and the most comely of all the men of Ireland, tall and well formed. Deep red-yellow hair he had, his face wide at the top and narrow below; thin, red lips, and grey eyes that were laughing. A red and white cloak on him, that the wind stirred as he walked, a white shield with gold fastenings at his shoulder, a long, dark green spear in his hand." "Who was that man, Fergus?" said Ailell. "That man is himself half an army, Rochad, son of Fatheman, from Rachlainn, in the North," said Fergus. Now this was the same Rochad that Findabair had loved. "There was another troop came then," said Mac Roth, "and a quiet, grey-haired man at the head of it. A dark-green, long-woolled cloak he had about him, and a white shirt, and a silver belt around his waist, and a bell branch at his shoulder. He sat before King Conchubar when he came to the hill,

and his whole company sat about him.   And the sound
of his voice when he spoke before the king, and when
he was advising him, was sweeter than a three-cornered
harp in the player's hand." "Who was that man,
Fergus?" said Ailell. "That was Sencha, the orator,
the best-spoken of all the men of the whole world, and
the peace-maker of the army of Ulster," said Fergus;
"and the whole of the men of the world, from the rising
to the setting of the sun, he would pacify with his three
fair words. But by my word, it is no cowardly or no
peaceful counsel that man will give his king to-day, but
counsel of courage, and of strength, and of battle."

"There came another troop," said Mac Roth, "and
a man at the head of them, and it would not be easy
to find a man with a better appearance, or with hair
more like gold than what he has. There was a sword
with an ivory hilt in his hand, and he throwing it up
and catching it in his hand again, as it was coming on
the heads of the people near him." "That is Aithirne,
the poet and satirist," said Fergus. It was said now of
that man that he was very covetous, and that he would
ask the one-eyed man for his one eye, and that the rivers
and the lakes went back before him when he made a
satire on them, and rose when he praised them. And one
time when the men of Ulster were fighting to protect
him against the men of Leinster, that he had stirred up,
and were shut up in Beinn Etair, he had plenty of cows
himself in the fort, but he would not give a drop of
milk to man or boy, or to a wounded man itself, but
left them without food and without drink, unless they
would eat the clay or drink the salt water of the sea.

"I saw another troop coming," said Mac Roth, "wild-
looking, and in the middle of it a young little lad, red
and freckled. He had a silk shirt on him with a border of
red gold, and a shield faced with gold, with a golden rim,
and a little bright gold sword at his side." "Who is

that, Fergus?" said Ailell. "I do not remember leaving any such boy as that when I left Ulster," said Fergus; "but it is likely it may be Erc, son of Cairbre, that has come without leave of his father to help his grandfather, Conchubar; and the men of Teamhair with him. And if what I think is true," he said, "you will find that troop to be a drowning sea, and it is by that troop and by that little boy the battle will be won against you."

Now that was the same Erc that fought afterwards in the last battle against Cuchulain at Muirthemne, and some said it was he that made an end of Cuchulain, but others said it was only the Grey of Macha he made an end of. And Conall Cearnach killed him afterwards in his red vengeance; and his sister Acaill came to Teamhair where he was buried, and cried for him through nine days, till her heart broke like a nut inside her, and she desired that her grave and her mound should be made in a place where the grave and the mound of Erc could be seen from it. And it was made in the place that used to be called the place of the poet Maine, but that is called now the place of Acaill.

"I saw another company," said Mac Roth, "having at its head a tall, large man, with high looks, with soft brown hair in thin smooth locks on his forehead; a deep grey cloak wrapped around him, having a silver brooch in it; a soft white shirt next his skin." "I know that man," said Fergus; "he is Eoghan, son of Durthact, king of Fernmaige, one of the twelve chief heroes of the Red Branch."

"I saw another company coming," said Mac Roth, "and a great many in it; and they red with the fire of their anger, strong and eager and destroying. At their head an angry man, dreadful to look at, long-nosed, large-eared, with coarse grey hair; a striped cloak on him, an iron skewer in place of a brooch, a coarse striped shirt next his skin, a great spear in his hand."

"I know that man," said Fergus; "Celthair, son of Uthecar; a head of battle in Ulster. And the spear in his hand is the great spear, the Luin, that was brought back from the East by the three sons of Tuireann."

"I saw the troop that came last," said Mac Roth, "and it without a leader. There were thirty hundred in it, of proud, clean, ruddy men; long fair hair they had, and shining eyes, and long shining cloaks with good brooches, blue shining spears, good coverings on their heads, and shirts of striped silk. But they seemed to have some great trouble on them, and to be very down-hearted." "What men are those, Fergus?" said Ailell. "I know them well," said Fergus. "It is well for those on whose side they are, and it is a pity for those they are against; for they are able by themselves," he said, "to fight the whole army of Ireland; for they are Cuchulain's men from Muirthemne."

Now all this time Cuchulain was lying on his bed, with the dint of his wounds. But when he knew by the noise on the plain that the men of Ulster were gathering for the battle, he used all his strength and tried to rise up; and he gave a great shout, that all his own troop heard it, and all the whole army. But his people that were about him laid him down on the bed again by force, and put ropes and fastenings over him, the way he could not move from it to open his wounds again. And as he was lying there, two mocking women came from Ailell's camp, and stood beside his bed, and let on to be crying and lamenting; and it is what they told him, that the men of Ulster were beaten, and that Conchubar was killed, and that Fergus was killed along with him. And in the night the Morrigu came like a lean, grey-haired hag, shrieking from the one army to the other, hopping over the points of their weapons, to stir up anger between them, and she called out that ravens would be picking men's necks on the morrow. And with all this outcry, Cuchulain could not sleep, and when the day began to break he said to Laeg: "Look out now, and bring me word of everything that happens on this day." So Laeg looked out, and he said: "I see a little herd of cattle breaking out from the west of Ailell's camp, and there are lads following after them and trying to bring them back; and I see more lads coming out from the army of Ulster to attack them." "That little herd on the plain is the beginning of a great battle," said Cuchulain, "for it is the Brown Bull of Cuailgne and his heifers are in it, and now the young men of the east and of the west will come out against one another. And go now, Laeg," he said, "for I cannot go out myself, and call to the men of Ulster, and stir them up to the battle." So Laeg went out and called to them in Cuchulain's name to get themselves ready and to come out to the battle.

When the men of Ulster heard that message from Cuchulain, they rose up, and rushed out without stopping to put on their clothing, but only taking their weapons in their hands; and such of them as had the door of their tents facing eastwards did not wait to go through it, but broke out to the west.

But Conchubar was not in such haste to bring his own men out, but he said to Sencha: "Keep them back till the right time will have come, when the sun will have lighted all the valleys and the hills."

Then Laeg went to look out again, and he saw the army of Ireland coming out to meet the men of Ulster, and there began a great fight between them, and it went on a good while without one side getting the better of the other. And when Cuchulain heard it he said: "My grief! I not to be able to go among them!"

Now as to Maeve, she was sending out her men, the three Conaires from Slieve Lis, the three red Luachras, the three nimble Suibhnes, the three sky-like Eochaids, the three bards from Lough Riach, the three Fachtnas from the woods of Navan, the three sad-faced Murroughs, the three boiling Laegaires, the three dove-like Conalls, the three sons of Driscoll that fought together, the three Fintans from beside the sea. And some say that besides these there were three young men of the Sidhe in shining armour, that mixed through the army to stir up courage, and that none of the men of the army could see among them, Delbhaeth, son of Eithlin, and Cermat Honey-mouth, and Angus Og, son of the Dagda.

But when Maeve saw the battle going on, and neither side getting the victory, she called to Fergus, and she said : " It is time for you, Fergus, to go out and avenge yourself on your enemy Conchubar ; and besides that," she said, " it is right for you to go and to fight for us now, after all the good treatment you got from us in Connaught." " I would go out willingly," said Fergus, " if I had my own sword again, the Caladcholg, the sword that Leite brought from the country of the Sidhe." Then Ailell said to his chariot - driver, Ferloga : " Go now and bring Fergus's sword that I bade you to hide away." So Ferloga brought the sword, and put it in Fergus's hand, and Fergus gave it a great welcome. " Come out now into the battle, Fergus," said Maeve, " and spare no one to-day, unless it might be some very dear friend."

Then Fergus and Maeve and Ailell went out into the battle, and three times they made the army of Ulster go back before them. And when Conchubar heard his people were being driven back, he called out to the household of the Red Branch : " Let you hold the place I am in now, till I go see who has turned back our men against us three times on the north side."

And the men of the Red Branch called back to him : " We will do that, and unless the sky should fall on us, or the earth give way under us, we will not give up one inch of ground before the men of Ireland till you come to us again, or till we get our death."

Then Conchubar went to see who it was that was driving back his army, and it was Fergus he found before him ; and Fergus struck three great blows on Conchubar's shield, the Ochain, so that the shield screamed out loud, and all the shields of the army of Ulster screamed with it, and the three great waves of Ireland answered it.

Then Fergus said : " Who is it is holding his shield against me ? " And Conchubar knew then who was before him, and he cried out : " It is the man, Fergus, that is greater and more comely and younger and better than yourself, the man whose father and mother were better than your own ; the man that put to death the three great candles of the valour of the Gael, the three prosperous sons of Usnach, in spite of your guarantee and your protection ; the man that banished you out of your own country ; the man that made your house a dwelling-place for deer and foxes ; the man that never left you so much as the breadth of your foot of land in Ulster ; the man that drove you to the entertainment of a woman ; and the man that will drive you back to-day in the presence of the men of Ireland, Conchubar, son of Fachtna Fathach, High King of Ulster, the High King of Ireland."

When Fergus heard that, he took his sword, the Caladcholg, in his two hands, and he was swinging it over his head, that it seemed to have the size and appearance of a rainbow, and he was about to give his three great strokes on the men of Ulster.

But Conchubar's son, Cormac Conloingeas, saw what he was doing, and he made a rush at Fergus, and put his arms about his knees, and he said : " Do not put out your great strength, my master Fergus, to destroy the whole army of Ulster." " Let me go," said Fergus, " for I will not live through the day unless I strike my three blows on the men of Ulster." But Cormac Conloingeas would not leave off from asking him, and then he said : " Tell Conchubar to go back to his own place in the battle, and I will spare the army." So Conchubar went back, and then Fergus struck his three blows on three little hills that were near him, and cut their tops off, and they are called "the three bare hills of Meath" to this day.

But when Cuchulain heard the scream of Conchubar's shield the time Fergus struck it, he called out to Laeg: "Who has dared to strike those three blows upon the Ochain, and I still living?" "It is Fergus, son of Rogh, struck them," said Laeg. "Where is the battle going on now?" said Cuchulain. "The armies are come as far as Gairech," said Laeg. "By my hand of valour," said Cuchulain, "they will not have reached to Ilgairech before I will be with them." With that he put out all his strength, and he broke the ropes that were about him, and threw them off, and he scattered the grass that was on his wounds into the high air. And the two mocking women were there yet, and he dashed them one against the other, and left them there on the ground. And he looked for his arms, but he could see none of them; but only his chariot, that was broken, was lying there. And he took hold of a shaft of it, and rushed, with all his wounds, straight into the battle, till he found Fergus, and he called to him to go back before him now, as he had promised he would do. But Fergus gave him no answer. Then Cuchulain said: "Go back, now, Fergus, or by the oath of my people," he said, "I will grind you to pieces as a mill grinds the malt." Then Fergus said: "Do not be giving out threats to me, for my army is well able for the army of Ulster." "You gave me your promise, Fergus," said Cuchulain, "to go back before me when we would meet in the great battle, and when I would be covered with wounds. You bound yourself to that the time I went back before you, and you without your sword."

Then Fergus, when he heard that, went back three steps, and then he turned, and his men with him, and gave way before Cuchulain. And all the men of Ireland turned when they saw that, and broke out of their ranks, and ran over the hill westward, and Cuchulain and the men of Ulster followed after them, making a great slaughter. And Cuchulain came up with Maeve, and she called out: "A gift to me, Cuchulain." "What is it you are asking of me?" he said. "Take what is left of my army under your protection, and let it pass over the great ford westward." So he agreed to do that, and what was left of the army of Ireland went over the great ford of the Sionnan at Athluain, and Maeve and Ailell and Fergus, and the Maines, and the sons of Magach stopped to the last, and drew their shields of protection behind the men of Ireland, till they had got back to Cruachan in Connaught, the place they set out from.

It was mid-day when Cuchulain came into the battle, and the sun was setting when the last of them went over the ford. And then Cuchulain took his sword that Laeg had brought him, for he had but a few splinters left of the shaft of the chariot he had used in the fight, and he made three blows at three rocks, and cut the tops off them, for an insult to Connaught for ever, the way if any one should speak of the three bare hills of Meath, the three bare rocks of Athluain would be there to give the answer.

And Fergus was watching the army of Ireland going back over the ford, and it is what he said: "This army is swept away to-day; it is wandering and going astray like a mare among her foals that goes astray in a strange place, not knowing what path to take. And it is following the lead of a woman," he said, "has brought it into this distress."

This then was the end of the battle of Gairech and Ilgairech, and the end of the war for the Brown Bull of Cuailgne.

XIII

THE TWO BULLS

THIS, now, is the story of the two bulls, the Brown of Cuailgne, and the White-horned of Cruachan Ai, and this is the way it was with them—for they were not right bulls, but there was enchantment on them. In the time long ago Bodb was king of the Sidhe of Munster, and it is in Femen, of Slieve-na-man he was, and Ochall Ochne was king of the Sidhe of Connaught, and it is in Cruachan he used to be. They used at one time to be fighting one against the other, but afterwards they made peace, and were good friends. Now Bodb had a swineherd, whose name was Friuch, and Ochall had a swineherd whose name was Rucht, and they were friendly with one another the same as their masters. And they had the knowledge of enchantments, and could turn themselves to every shape. And when there was a great plenty of mast in Munster, the swineherd from Connaught would bring his lean swine to the south, and in the same way, when mast was plentiful in Connaught, the swineherd would bring his swine northward, and would bring them home again fat.

But after a while some bad feeling rose up between the two, for the men of Connaught and the men of Munster began to set them one against the other. So one year when there was great mast in Munster, and Rucht brought his herd from Connaught, so soon as his comrade Friuch had bade him welcome, he said : " The

612

people are all saying your power is greater than mine."
"It is no less any way," said Ochall's herd. "We will
soon know that," said Friuch. "I will put an enchantment on your swine, and even though they eat their
share of mast, they will not be fat, like mine will be."
And so it happened, he put an enchantment on the
Connaught swine, and when Rucht went home with
them they could hardly walk at all, they were so thin
and so weak, and all the people were laughing at the
state they were in. "It was a bad day for you, you went
to the South," they said, "for your comrade has greater
power than what you have." "That is not so," said he.
"Wait till it is our turn to have mast, and I will play
the same trick on him."

So the next year he did as he had said, and the
Munster swine pined away, so that every one said their
power was the same. And when Bodb's swineherd
went back home to Munster with his lean swine, his
master put him out of the place. And Ochall put his
herd out of his place as well, because of the swine
coming back in so bad a state from Munster.

One day, two full years after that, the men of Munster
were gathered together near Femen, and they took
notice of two ravens that were making a great cawing.
"What a noise those birds have been making all through
the year!" they said. "They never stop scolding at one
another." Just then Findell, Ochall's steward from
Cruachan, came towards them on the hill, and they bade
him welcome. "What a noise those birds are making!"
he said; "any one would think them to be the same
two birds we had in Cruachan last year." With that,
they saw the two ravens change into the shape of men,
and they knew them to be the two swineherds, and
they bade them welcome. "It is not right you to
welcome us," said Bodb's swineherd, "for there will be
many dead bodies of friends, and much crying on

account of us two." What has happened you all
through this time?" they asked. "Nothing good," he said.
"Since we went from you we have been all the time in
the shape of birds, and you saw the way we were scolding at one another all through this year. And we were
quarrelling in the same way the whole of last year at
Cruachan, and the men of the North and of the South
have seen what our power is. And now," he said, "we
will go into the shape of water beasts, and be under the
water for the length of two years." And with that one
of them went into the Sionnan, and the other into the
Suir, and they were seen for a year in the Suir, and for
a year in the Sionnan, and they devouring one another.
And one day the men of Connaught had a great
gathering at Ednecha, on the Sionnan, and they saw these
two beasts in the river; each one of them looked to be
as big as the top of a hill, and they made such a furious
attack on one another that fiery swords seemed to be
coming from their jaws, and the people came round
them on every side. They came out of the Sionnan
then, and as soon as they touched the shore, they
changed again into the shape of the two swineherds.
Ochall bade them welcome. "Where have you been
wandering?" he asked them. "Indeed it is tired we
are with our wanderings," they said. "You saw what we
were doing before your eyes, and that is what we were
doing through these two years, under seas and waters.
And now we must take new shapes on us, till we try
one another's strength again." And with that they
went away.

It happened a good while after that there was a great
gathering of the men of Connaught at Loch Riach, for
Bodb was coming on a friendly visit to Ochall. And
Bodb brought a great troop with him, the most splendid
ever seen; speckled horses they had, and green cloaks
with silver brooches, and shoes with clasps of red bronze,

and every one of them had a collar of gold, with a stone worth a newly-calved cow set in it. When Ochall saw what grand clothes and horses they had, he called to his people secretly, and asked could they match Bodb's people in dress and in horses and arms, and they said they could not. Then Ochall said: "That is a pity, and our great name is lost." But just then a troop of men were seen coming from the North, and black horses with them, that you would think had been cast up by the sea, and bridle-bits of gold in their mouths. And the men had black-grey cloaks, and a gold brooch at the breast of each, and a white tunic with crimson stripes, and fifty coils of bright gold round every man. And every man of them had black hair, as smooth as if a cow had licked it. And they stopped a little way off, and then the men of Connaught stood up and gave up their place to them. There was a Druid from Britain there, and when he saw them make way he said: "From this out, to the end of life and time, the Connaught men will be under the yoke, attending on hounds and on sons of kings and queens for ever."

Then after they had been feasting for a while, Bodb asked could any Connaught man be found that would fight against his champion Rinn, that was with him, and that had a great name, but no one knew where he came from. And at first there could no one be found, but then a strange champion came out from among the men of Connaught, and he said, "I will go against him." "That is no welcome news," said Rinn. Then they fought against one another for three days and three nights, and before the end of that time the two armies began to join into the fight, and a troop came from Leinster and joined with Bodb, and another troop came from Meath and joined with Ochall. And four kings were killed there, and Ochall among them, and then Bodb went back to Slieve-na-man. But as to the two champions, they were seen no more, and it was known they were the two swineherds. After that they were for two years with the appearance of shadows, threatening one another, the way that many people died of fright after seeing them.

And after that, they were in the shape of eels, and one went into the river Cruind, in Cuailgne; and after a while a cow belonging to Daire, son of Fachna, drank it down. And the other went into the Spring of Uaran Garad, in Connaught; and one day Maeve went out to the spring, and a small bronze vessel in her hand, and she dipped it in the water, and the little eel went into it, and every colour was to be seen on him. And she was a long time looking at him, she thought the colours so beautiful. Then the water went away, and the eel was alone in the vessel. "It is a pity you cannot speak to me," said Maeve. "What is it you want to know?" said the eel. "I would like to know what way it is with you in that shape of a beast," she said; "and I would like to know what will happen me after I get the sway over Connaught." "Indeed it is a tormented beast I am," he said, "and it is in many shapes I have been. And as to yourself," he said, "handsome as you are, you should take a good man to be with you in your sway." "I have no wish," said Maeve, "to let a man of Connaught get the upper hand over me," and with that she went home again.

But she married Ailell after that, and as for the eel, he was swallowed down by one of Maeve's cows that came to drink at the spring.

And it was from that cow, and from the cow that belonged to Daire, son of Fachna, the two bulls were born, the White-horned and the Brown. They were the finest ever seen in Ireland, and gold and silver were put on their horns by the men of Ulster and Connaught. In Connaught no bull dared bellow before the White-horned, and in Ulster no bull dared bellow before the Brown.

As to the Brown, he that had been Friuch, the Munster swineherd, his lowing when he would be coming home every evening to his yard was good music to the people of the whole of Cuailgne. And wherever he was, neither Bocanachs nor Bananachs nor witches of the valley, could come into the one place with him. And it was on account of him the great war broke out.

Now, when Maeve saw at Ilgaireth that the battle was going against her, she sent eight of her own messengers to bring away the Brown Bull, and his heifers. "For whoever goes back or does not go back," she said, "the Brown Bull must go to Cruachan."

Now when the Brown Bull came into Connaught, and saw the beautiful trackless country before him, he let three great loud bellowings out of him. As soon as the White-horned heard that, he set out for the place those bellowings came from, with his head high in the air.

Then Maeve said that the men of her army must not go to their homes till they would see the fight between the two bulls.

And they all said some one must be put to watch the fight, and to give a fair report of it afterwards. And it is what they agreed, that Bricriu should be sent to watch it, because he had not taken any side in the war; for he had been through the whole length of it under care of physicians at Cruachan, with the dint of the wound he got the day he vexed Fergus, and that Fergus drove the chess-men into his head. " I will go willingly," said Bricriu. So he went out and took his place in a gap, where he could have a good view of the fight.

As soon as the bulls caught sight of one another they pawed the earth so furiously that they sent the sods flying, and their eyes were like balls of fire in

their heads; they locked their horns together, and they
ploughed up the ground under them and trampled it,
and they were trying to crush and to destroy one
another through the whole length of the day.

And once the White-horned went back a little way
and made a rush at the Brown, and got his horn into
his side, and he gave out a great bellow, and they
rushed both together through the gap where Bricriu
was, the way he was trodden into the earth under
their feet. And that is how Bricriu of the bitter
tongue, son of Cairbre, got his death.

Then when the night was coming on, Cormac
Conloingeas took hold of a spear-shaft, and he laid
three great strokes on the Brown Bull from head to
tail, and he said: " This is a great treasure to be boasting of, that cannot get the better of a calf of his own
age." When the Brown Bull heard that insult, great
fury came on him, and he turned on the White-horned
again. And all through the night the men of Ireland
were listening to the sound of their bellowing, and they
going here and there, all through the country.

On the morrow, they saw the Brown Bull coming
over Cruachan from the west, and he carrying what
was left of the White-horned on his horns. Then
Maeve's sons, the Maines, rose up to make an attack
on him on account of the Connaught bull he had destroyed. " Where are those men going:" said Fergus.
" They are going to kill the Brown Bull of Cuailgne."
" By the oath of my people," said Fergus, " if you do
not let the Brown Bull go back to his own country in
safety, all he has done to the White-horned is little to
what I will do now to you."

Then the Brown Bull bellowed three times, and set
out on his way. And when he came to the great ford
of the Sionnan he stopped to drink, and the two loins of
the White-horned fell from his horns into the water.

And that place is called Ath-luain, the ford of the loin, to this day. And its liver fell in the same way into a river of Meath, and it is called Ath-Truim, the ford of the liver, to this day.

Then he went on till he came to the top of Slieve Breagh, and when he looked from it he saw his own home, the hills of Cuailgne; and at the sight of his own country, a great spirit rose up in him, and madness and fury came on him, and he rushed on, killing everyone that came in his way.

And when he got to his own place, he turned his back to a hill and he gave out a loud bellowing of victory. And with that his heart broke in his body, and blood came bursting from his mouth, and he died.

XIV

THE ONLY JEALOUSY OF EMER

IT happened one time, near to the day of Samhain, the men of Ulster came together for games and for feasting upon the plain of Muirthemne.

And they were all of them there but Conall Cearnach and Lugaid of the Red Stripes. "Let the feast be begun," they said. "It shall not be begun," said Cuchulain, "till Conall and Lugaid are here."

Sencha, the poet, said then : "Let us play chess while we are waiting, and let poems be sung for us, and let games be played." And they agreed to that.

While they were doing these things, a flock of birds came down on the lake before them, and in all Ireland there were not birds to be seen that were more beautiful.

A great longing came on the women that were there to have the birds that were on the lake, and they began to quarrel with one another as to who should have them.

King Conchubar's wife said : "I must have a bird of these birds on each of my two shoulders." "We must all have the same," said the other women. "If any one is to get them, it is I that must first get them," said Eithne Inguba, who loved Cuchulain. "What shall we do ?" said the women. "It is I will tell you that," said Levarcham, "for I will go to Cuchulain from you to ask him to get them."

So she went to Cuchulain and said : "The women of

Ulster desire that you will get these birds for them."
Cuchulain put his hand upon his sword as if to strike
her, and he said: "Have the idle women of Ulster
nothing better to do than to send me catching birds to-
day?" "It is not for you," said Levarcham, "to be
angry with the women of Ulster; for there are many
of them are half blind to-day with looking at you, from
the greatness of their love for you."

Then Cuchulain told Laeg to yoke his chariot for him,
and he went in it to the lake, and he gave the birds a
side stroke of his sword, so that their feet and their
wings could not rise from the water.

They caught them all then, and divided them among
the women, so that there was not a woman among them
who did not get two birds, but Eithne Inguba only.
Cuchulain came last to her. "It is vexed you seem to
be," he said. "Is it because I have given the birds to
the other women?" "You have good reason for that,"
she said, "for there is not a woman of them but would
share her love and her friendship with you; while, as to
me, no person shares my love but you alone."

"Do not be vexed then," said Cuchulain; "for whatever birds may come to the plain of Muirthemne, or to
the Boinne, from this out, you shall have the two most
beautiful among them."

It was not long after that, two other birds came on
the lake, and they linked together with a chain of red
gold, and they were singing soft music that went near
to put sleep on the whole gathering.

Cuchulain went over towards the birds, but Laeg said
to him not to go, and Eithne said: "If you would take
our advice, you would not go near them, for there is
enchantment behind these birds; let some other birds be
got for me besides these."

"Do you think you can put me from what I have a
mind to do?" said Cuchulain. And he said to Laeg:

"Put a stone into that sling." Laeg took a stone and put it in a sling, and Cuchulain made a cast, but it missed. "My grief!" he said. Then he took another stone, and made another cast, and it passed by them. "I am good for nothing," he said, "for since I first took arms I never made a bad cast till this day." Then he threw his heavy spear, and it went through the flying wing of one of the birds, and the two of them dived down under the water.

Cuchulain went away then with vexation on him, and he lay down with his head against a rock, and sleep came on him. And he saw two women coming towards him, one of them having a green cloak about her, and the other a five-folded crimson cloak.

The woman with the green cloak went up to him, and smiled at him, and she gave him a stroke of a rod. The other went up to him then, and smiled at him, and gave him a stroke in the same way; and they went on doing this for a long time, each of them striking him in turn, till he was more dead than alive. And then they went away and left him there.

All the men of Ulster saw that something had happened, and they asked if they would awaken him. "Do not," said Conall; "do not move him before night."

After that Cuchulain stood up in his sleep, and the men of Ulster asked him who was it had used him like that, but he could not speak with them. But after a while he said: "Bring me and lay me on my bed, not to Dundealgan, but to the Speckled House at Emain." "Let him be brought to Dundealgan, where Emer his wife is," said Laeg. "Not so," said Cuchulain, "but bring me to the Speckled House." So he was brought there, and he stopped to the end of a year in that place without speaking to any person.

One day before the next feast of Samhain, at the end of the year, Conchubar and the men of Ulster were

SENCHA ANNOUNCED THAT THE SUN HAD LIGHTED THE VALLEY.

THE SMILING WOMEN IN GREEN AND CRIMSON STRUCK CUCHULAIN.

around him in the house; that is, Laegaire between him and the wall, and Conall Cearnach between him and the door, Lugaid of the Red Stripes beside his pillow, and Eithne Inguba at his feet.

As they were sitting like this, one who had the appearance of a man came into the house to them, and sat down on the side of the bed where Cuchulain was lying.

"What has brought you here?" said Conall. "I will tell you that," said he. "It is to speak with the man lying here on the bed I am come. And if the man lying here were in his health, he would be a protection to all the men of Ulster; but as he is, under great sickness and weakness, he is a better protection to them." And he stood up then, and it is what he said:

"If Cuchulain, son of Sualtim, would take my friendship to-day, all he has seen in his sleep would be his, with no help from his army.

"Liban, she who sits at the right hand of Labraid of the quick sword, has said that the coming of Cuchulain would bring great joy to the heart of Fand her sister.

"O Cuchulain, it is not long your sickness would be on you if they would come, the two daughters of Aedh Abrat. Here to the south, to the plain of Muirthemne, I will send Liban to cure your sickness, Cuchulain."

"Who are you yourself?" they said to him then.

"I am Angus," he said, and with that he went out; and they did not know where he came from, or where he went. And then Cuchulain sat up and spoke to them. "It is time indeed," said the men of Ulster, "for you to tell us all that has happened you." "I saw," he said, "a vision about this time last year": and then he told them all he had seen, and of the women that had come and had struck him with their rods. "And what is to be done now, my master, Conchubar?" he said. "This must be done," said Conchubar: "you must go back till you come to the same rock."

So then Cuchulain set out, and came to the same rock, and there he saw the same woman with the green cloak coming towards him. "That is well, Cuchulain," said she. "It is not well indeed; and tell me what did you want with me when you came last year?" said Cuchulain.

"It was not to harm you, indeed, we came," said the woman, "but to ask your love; and I am come now to speak to you," she said, "from Fand, daughter of Aedh Abrat; for Manannan, Son of the Sea, has left her, and her love has fallen on you; and my own name is Liban, wife of Labraid of the quick sword. And I have a message for you from him," she said, "that he will give all you can wish for, if you will give him one day's help against Senach of the crooked body, and against Eochaid Juil, and against Eoghan of Inver, that is Eoghan of the River's Mouth."

"My weakness is on me yet," said Cuchulain, "and I could not go out fighting against men to-day." "You will not be long so," said Liban; "you will be healed, and what is lost of your strength will be given back to you again; and you ought to do this much for Labraid," she said, "because he is the best of the heroes of the world."

"In what place is he?" said Cuchulain. "He is in Magh Mell, the Happy Plain," she said. "I will not go," said Cuchulain, "until I see Emer, my wife. And you are to go for me, Laeg," he said, "to where she is, and tell her it was the women of the Sidhe came to me from the hills and struck me; and tell her I am getting better now, and bid her come and visit me."

So Laeg went to Emer, and he told her what way Cuchulain was. And Emer said: "It is a bad servant you are, Laeg, you that are coming and going by the hills, and that cannot find a cure for your master; and it is a pity for the men of Ulster," she said, "that they do not find a certain cure for him. If it had been Conchubar that was in bonds, or Fergus that could not sleep, or Conall Cearnach that had wounds on him, it is Cuchulain that would give them relief." And it is what she said:

"My grief! son of Riangabra, you who go early and late among the hills, you are not early but late in bringing a cure for the beautiful son of Dechtire.

"It is a pity for the brave men of Ulster, with all the knowledgeable men and the learners among them, that they have not searched the whole face of the world for a cure for their friend Cuchulain.

"If it was Fergus had lost his sleep, and that any enchantment could cure him, it is the son of Dechtire would not sleep at home till he had found a Druid to do it.

"If it were Conall in the same way was suffering from wounds and from sores, it is the Hound would search the wide world till he would find one that would cure him.

"If it was Laegaire of many gifts was wounded in battle, Cuchulain would have searched through all Ireland to cure the grandson of Iliach.

"If it were on Celthair the revengeful sleep had fallen and long sickness, night and day would see the journeys of Setanta among the hills.

"If it had been Furbaigh, chief of fighters, that lay wasting in his bed, he would have searched the ridge of the world until he had found what would save him.

"The host of the hill of Truin has killed him; they have taken from him his great courage; the Hound of Muirthemne is no better than any other hound since the sleep of the hill of Bruagh came on him.

"My grief! sickness has laid hold of me for the Hound

of the smith of Conchubar; it will be sickness to my heart and my body, I to fail in bringing him a cure.

"My grief! It hurts my heart, sickness to be on the rider of the plain, so that he could not come here, to the gathering at the plain of Muirthemne.

"It is why he does not come from Emain, the appearance he had is gone from him; my voice is weak and dead because of the way he is. A month and a quarter and a year without sleep, that is the way I am, and without hearing any one speak pleasant words, son of Riangabra, O son of Riangabra."

After she had made this complaint, Emer went forward to Emain Macha to attend on Cuchulain, and she sat on the side of the bed where he was, and it is what she was saying:

"Rise up, champion of Ulster, awake from your sleep, in health and happiness. Look at the well-shaped king of Macha; he will not allow your long sleep. Look at his shoulder, smooth like crystal; look at his drinking-horns and battle spoils; look at his chariots that sweep the valleys; look at the movements of his chess-men.

"Think on his heroes in their strength; think on his high, fine women; think on his kings of brave doings; think on their high noble queens.

"Think on the beginning of clear winter; think on its wonders in their turn; think in yourself of what it brings forth—its cold, its length, its want of beauty. This stupor, it is not good wholesome sleep; it is idleness and the fear of battle; long sleep is the same as drunkenness; weakness is only second to death.

"Awake from the sleep of the Sidhe you have drunk; cast it off with all your great strength. You have had your fill of sweet flowery words; rise up, O hero of Ulster."

Cuchulain rose up then, and he drew his hand across his face, and he put his stupor and his heaviness off

him. Then Laeg said: "It is great idleness for a hero
to give in to the sleep of a sick-bed because women
from Magh Mell have appeared to you, who overcame
you, who bound you, who put you within the power
of idle women. Rise up out of death, you who are
wounded by women of the Sidhe, for your strength
has come, the strength of a hero among heroes; rise
up till you go to the place of fighting men, till you do
great deeds, where Labraid of the quick hand leads
his men. Rise up that you may be great, and leave
this idleness."

Then Cuchulain went again to the rock, and he saw
Liban coming towards him, and she asked him again
to go with her to her country. "What place is Labraid
in at this time?" said Cuchulain. "I will tell you that,"
said Liban, and it is what she said:

"Labraid is at this time upon a clear lake, where
companies of women come to. It is not tired you
would be coming to his country, if you would but visit
Labraid of the quick sword.

"A happy house ordered by a kind woman; a
hundred men in it that are masters of learning; the
beauty of redness is on the cheek of Labraid.

"He shakes a wolf's head before his thin red sword;
he bruises the armour of rushing hosts; he breaks the
shields of heroes.

"His appearance in the fight is the delight of the
eye; he does his brave deeds at all points; it is he is
worth more than any other man.

"The greatest of fighters, the one told of in stories,
has reached the country of Eochaid Juil; his hair is
like rings of gold upon him; his coming is like the
smell of wine.

"A man of many strange deeds, Labraid of the quick
hand at sword; he does not strike till he is forced; he
keeps his people in quietness.

"There are bridles and collars of red gold on his horses, and this is not all his riches; the house he lives in is supported by pillars of silver and of crystal."

"I will not go on a woman's asking," said Cuchulain. "Let Laeg come with me then," said Liban, "to see and to know everything." "Let him go then," said Cuchulain.

Then Laeg went along with the women, and they went past Magh Luada, the Racing Plain, and past the Bile Buada, the Tree of Victory, and past Oenach Emna, the gathering-place of Emain, and to Oenach Fidhga, the gathering-place of the woods; and it was there Aedh Abrat used to be with his daughters. And Liban caught Laeg by the shoulder: "You will not escape to-day, Laeg," she said, "unless you are protected by a woman." "That is not what we were much used to up to this," said Laeg, "to be under women protection." "My grief for ever, Cuchulain not to be in your place now!" said Liban. "I would be glad indeed he to be here," said Laeg.

They went away then towards the Island of Labraid, and when they came to the lake they saw a little copper ship upon the water before them. Then they went into the ship, and they came to the island, and there they went to the door of a house. And they saw a man coming towards them, and Liban said to him: "Where is Labraid of the quick sword?" And the man said: "Labraid is putting courage into the people, and he is gathering them for battle. There will be great slaughter made there, that will fill the plain of Fidgha."

Then they went up to the house, and Laeg thought he had seen it before, and yet it was strange. And in it were beds, crimson, green, white and gold; and the great candle there was a bright precious stone. And at the western door, where the sun goes down, there was a stud of horses with grey speckled manes, and others of red-brown. And at the eastern door were three tall trees of pure crimson, with lasting flowers, and birds singing from them for the young men of the king's rath. And there was a tree at the door of the court that there was not the like of for beauty, a silver tree, and when the sun was shining on it, it was like gold. And there were three times twenty other trees there, and the top of every one meeting the other, and three hundred could be fed from every tree with fruit that is different, that is always ripe. And there was a fountain in the great court, and three times fifty striped cloaks, and a shining gold pin in the ear of every cloak. And there was a vat of merry mead for dividing among the household; it is a lasting custom that it is always full, ever and always. And in the house were three times fifty women, and they all bade welcome to Laeg, and it is what they all said to him: "There is a welcome before you, Laeg, for the sake of the woman with whom you come, and for the sake of him from whom you come, and for your own sake."

"What will you do now, Laeg?" said Liban. "Will you go first and speak with Fand?" "I will, if I know the place she is in," said Laeg. "I will tell you that, for she is apart in a room by herself," said Liban. So they went to speak with her, and she bade Laeg welcome in the same way as the others. And the meaning of the name Fand is a tear that passes over the fire of the eye. It was for her purity she was called that, and for her beauty; for there was nothing in life with which she could be compared besides it.

And when she had bade Laeg welcome, she said: "For what reason did Cuchulain not come?" "He had no mind to come on a woman's asking," said Laeg. "And besides that," he said, "he did not know if it was from yourself the message came." "It was from myself indeed," she said, "and let him not be long in coming, for it is on this day the battle is to be fought."

While they were there together, they heard the sound of Labraid's chariot coming to the island. "It is troubled Labraid's mind is to-day," said Liban. "Let us go out before him." So they went out, and Liban bade him welcome, and it is what she said:

"Welcome, Labraid of the quick hand at sword, yourself an army, a destroyer of heroes; welcome, welcome, Labraid."

Labraid made no answer, and Liban spoke again:

"Welcome, Labraid of the quick hand at sword; his hand is open to all; his word is faithful; his justice is right; kind his sway; strong his right arm; gentle to his horses; welcome, welcome, Labraid!"

Still Labraid did not answer, and she spoke again, and it is what she said:

"Welcome, Labraid of the quick sword; lifter up of the weak; subduer of the strong; welcome, Labraid; welcome, Labraid!"

Then Labraid said: "Leave your praises, woman, for it is not pride or happiness or high thoughts of myself I have in my mind to-day. A battle is near, and the striking of swords in right and left hands; the one heart of Eochaid Juil is equal to many. It is not a time for pride."

"There is good news before you," said Liban then. "Laeg, the chariot-driver of Cuchulain, is here, and he has brought a message from him that he will go into the battle with you." Then Labraid bade him welcome as the women had done, and he said: "Go back home now, and tell Cuchulain to make no delay in coming, for it is to-day the battle is to be fought."

So Laeg went away then to Emain Macha, and told his story to Cuchulain, and to all the rest, and it is what he said:

"Labraid is a king of great armies. I saw his country, bright, free, where no lies are spoken, and no bad thing. I saw the masters of music within, giving delight to the daughters of Aedh. If I had not come away quickly, they would have taken my strength from me.

"I saw all this at the hill of the Sidhe. The women there are beautiful, their gifts are beyond counting; as to Fand, the daughter of Aedh Abrat, no one could reach her beauty but the queens of the kings.

"Eithne Inguba is a beautiful woman, but the woman I am speaking of now takes away the wits from whole armies.

"It is a pity, Cuchulain, you did not go a while ago, and every one asking you to do it, that you might see the way it is in the great house I have seen.

"If all Ireland were mine, and I king over the happy hills, I would give it, and that would be no small thing, to live for ever in the place I have been in."

"That is good," said Cuchulain. "It is good," said Laeg, "and it is right to go to reach it, and everything in that country is good."

Then Cuchulain rose up, and he passed his hand over his face, and he spoke pleasantly with Laeg, and he felt that the things the young man was telling him were a strengthening to his mind. And Laeg said : "It is time to come, for the battle is being fought to-day."

Cuchulain went along with him then to that country, and took his chariot with him till they reached the island. Labraid bade them welcome, and all the women ; and Fand bade Cuchulain her own welcome.

"What is to be done here now?" said Cuchulain.

"This is what we have to do," said Labraid ; "to go and take a turn round the army that is against us."

They went forward then till they reached the gathering-place of the armies, and till they cast an eye over

them, and it seemed as if there was no end to them.
"Go you away for a while," said Cuchulain to Labraid.
So Labraid went away then, and Cuchulain stayed before
the armies.   Then two black ravens croaked, and all the
armies laughed.   "It is likely," they said, "the ravens
are telling of the coming of the angry man from
Muirthemne."   And they hunted them away.

After that Eochaid Juil went to wash his hands at
the spring, and Cuchulain saw his bare shoulder through
the shirt, and he threw a spear at him, and it passed
through him ; and then he attacked the army alone, and
killed a great many.   Then he was attacked by Senach
Siabartha the Unearthly, and they fought very hard,
and Cuchulain overcame him in the end.   And Labraid
came then, and broke the armies before him, and he
called to Cuchulain to leave off from killing.   But Laeg
said : "I am in dread he will spend his rage on us, since
he has not had enough of fighting.   And let your people
go," he said, "and let them make ready three vats of
water to put out his heat.   The first vat he will go into
will boil over ; the second vat, no person could bear its
heat ; but the heat of the third vat will be fit to bear."

When the women saw Cuchulain coming back, it was
then Fand sang before him : "Stately is the man that
comes in his chariot ; young he is, and without a beard ;
his course is splendid across the plain at evening, at
Senach Fidhga, the gathering-place of the woods.

"It is not the music of the Sidhe would keep him in
a bed ; it is the red colour of blood that is upon him ; I
stand looking at the horses of his chariot ; their like is
not known, they are as fast as the winds of spring.

"It is Cuchulain that is coming, the young hero from
Muirthemne ; it is a pity for the man against whom he
is angered."

Then Liban asked him what he had done in the fight.
And Cuchulain said : "Fair, ruddy-faced men attacked

me on every side from the back of horses, the people of
Manannan, Son of the Sea, called there by Eochaid of
Inver; I gave them wound for wound. I threw my spear
at Eochaid Juil; it was not with the uncertain cast
of a man among mists I threw it. I heard his groan, and
its sound was friendly to me; if those who have spoken
have told the truth, it was that throw won the battle."

It was to the son, now, of this Eochaid Juil of the
Land of Promise, that Aebgreine, the daughter of
Naoise and Deirdre was given afterwards in marriage
by Manannan.

After that, Cuchulain stopped a month in that country
with Fand, and at the end of the month he bade her
farewell, and she said to him: "In whatever place you
tell me to go and meet you, I will go there." And the
place they settled to meet at was at Ibar Cinn Tracta,
the yew at the head of Baile's strand.

But when all this was told to Emer, there was great
anger on her, and she had knives made ready to kill the
woman with, and she came, and fifty young girls with
her, to the place where they had settled to meet.

Cuchulain and Laeg were playing chess there, and they
did not see the women coming. It was Fand saw them
first, and she said to Laeg: "Look, Laeg, at what I see."
"What is that?" said Laeg. Then he looked, and it is
what Fand said: "Look behind you, Laeg; there are
women listening to you, wise, with sharp, green knives in
their right hands, with gold at their well-shaped breasts;
they move as brave men do, going through a battle of
chariots. Well does Emer, daughter of Forgall, change
colour in her anger."

"No harm shall be done to you by her," said Cuchulain;
"and she shall not reach to you at all. Come into the
sunny seat of the chariot, opposite myself, for I will
defend you against all the many women of the four
points of Ulster; for though Forgall's daughter may

threaten," he said, "on the strength of her companions, to do some daring thing, it is surely not against me she will dare it."

Then Cuchulain said to Emer : " It is little I mind you, woman, in spite of my affection for you, more than any other man minds a woman. The spear in your shaking hand does not wound me, nor your weak, thin knife, nor your vain, gathered anger ; for it would be a pity my strength to be put down by a woman's strength."

" I ask then," said Emer, " what was it led you, Cuchulain, to dishonour me before all the women of the province, and before all the women of Ireland, and before all honourable people in the same way? For it was under your shelter I came, and on the strength of your faithfulness ; for although you threaten a great quarrel in your pride, it is certain, Cuchulain, you cannot put me away, even if you would try to do it."

" I ask you, Emer," said Cuchulain, " why I may not have my turn in the company of this woman ; for in the first place she is well-behaved, comely, well-mannered, worthy of a king, this woman from beyond the waves of the great sea ; with form and countenance and high descent ; with embroidery and handiness, with sense and quickness ; for there is not anything under the skies her husband could ask, but she would do it, even if she had not given her promise. And O Emer," he said, "you will never find any brave, comely man so good as myself."

" It is certain," said Emer, " that I will not refuse this woman if you follow her. But all the same, everything red is beautiful, everything new is fair, everything high is lovely, everything common is bitter, everything we are without is thought much of ; everything we know is thought little of, till all knowledge is known. And O Cuchulain," she said, " I was at one time in esteem with you and I would be so again, if it were pleasing to you."

JEALOUS EMER CAME UPON FAND AND CUCHULAIN AT THEIR TRYST.

CUCHULAIN WAS REBUKED BY EMER.

And grief came upon her, and overcame her. "By my word, now," said Cuchulain, "you are pleasing to me, and will be pleasing as long as I live."

"Let me be given up," said Fand. "It is better for me to be given up," said Emer. "Not so," said Fand, "it is I that will be given up in the end, and it is I that have been in danger of it all this time."

And great grief and trouble of mind came on Fand, because she was ashamed to be given up, and to have to go back to her home there and then; and the great love she had given Cuchulain troubled her; and so she was lamenting, and she made this complaint:

"It is I will go on the journey; I agree to it with great sorrow; though my father has so great a name, I would sooner stay with Cuchulain. It would be better for me to be here, to be under your rule without grief, than to go, though you may wonder at it, to the sunny house of Aedh Abrat.

"O Emer, the man is yours, and well may you wear him, for you are worthy; what my arm cannot reach, that at least I may wish well to.

"Many were the men asking for me, in the court and in country places; I never went to meet one of them, for it is myself was of right behaviour.

"A pity it is to give love to a man, and he to take no heed to it. It is better to be turned away, if you are not loved as you love.

"It was not right of you, Emer of the yellow hair, to take hold of Fand, to kill her in her misery."

Now all this was told to Manannan, that Fand, daughter of Aedh Abrat was fighting alone against the women of Ulster, and that Cuchulain was putting her away. Manannan came then from the east in search of her, and he was near them, and no one of them saw him but only Fand. And then great fear and trouble of mind came on her at seeing Manannan, and it is what she said:

"Look on the great son of the sea, from the plains of Eoghan of Inver; Manannan, lord of the fair hills of the world; there was a time when he was dear to me.

"He may even to-day be constant; my mind is no friend to jealousy. There is a road love leads us in.

"The time I and the friend of Lugh were in the sunny palace of Dun Inver, we thought, without a doubt, that we should never be parted from one another.

"When Manannan the great married me, I was a wife worthy of him; he gave me a bracelet of heavy gold, as the price of my beauty.

"I see, coming over the sea, no earthly person sees him, the crested horseman of the high-maned waves; he has no need of long ships.

"As for me myself, because there is foolishness in the minds of women, the man I loved exceedingly has left me here astray.

"Farewell to you, beautiful Cuchulain; I go away from you with a kind heart. Though I do not come back again, let me have your good will; all things are good in comparison with a parting.

"It is time for me to go away; there is one to whom it is not grief, but for all that, it is a great disgrace to me, O Laeg, son of Riangabra.

"It is with my own husband I will go, because he will do as I desire. Look now at my going, that it may not be said I went away secretly."

Then Fand went over to Manannan, and Manannan bade her welcome, and he said: "Well, woman, is it after Cuchulain you will be going from this time, or is it with me you will go?" "By my word now," said she, "there is one of you I would sooner follow than the other; but it is along with you I will go and I will not wait on Cuchulain, because he has left me. And another thing," she said, "you have not a queen that is fitting for you, and that is what Cuchulain has."

But when Cuchulain saw the woman going away from him with Manannan, he said to Laeg : " What is that ? " " It is Fand," said Laeg, " that is going to Manannan, Son of the Sea, because she was not pleasing to you."

It is then there was great anger on Cuchulain, and he went with great leaps southward to Luachair, the place of rushes ; and he stopped for a long while without drink, without food, among the mountains, and where he slept every night, was on the road of Midluachan.

And when Emer heard that, she went to visit Conchubar in Emain Macha, and she told him the way Cuchulain was.

Then Conchubar sent the poets and the skilled men and the Druids of Ulster to visit him, that they might lay hold of him, and bring him to Emain Macha along with them. But when they came to him, he would have killed them, but the Druids did enchantment on him, until they had laid hold of him, and until his wits began to come back to him. Then he asked them for a drink, and the Druids gave him a drink of forgetfulness. From the moment he drank that drink, he did not remember Fand, and all the things he had done. And they gave a drink of forgetfulness to Emer as well, that she might forget her jealousy, for the state she was in was no better than his own.

And after that, Manannan shook his cloak between Cuchulain and Fand, the way they should never meet one another again.

XV

ADVICE TO A PRINCE

THERE was a meeting of the three provinces of
Ireland held about this time in Teamhair, to try
could they find some person to give the High Kingship of
Ireland to; for they thought it a pity the Hill of the
Lordship of Ireland, that is Teamhair, to be without the
rule of a king on it, and the tribes to be without a
king's government to judge their houses. For the men
of Ireland had been without the government of a High
King over them since the death of Conaire at Da
Derga's Inn.

And the kings that met now at the court of Cairbre
Niafer were Ailell and Maeve of Connaught, and Curoi,
and Tigernach, son of Luchta, king of Tuathmumain,
and Finn, son of Ross, king of Leinster. But they
would not ask the men of Ulster to help them in
choosing a king, for they were all of them against the
men of Ulster.

There was a bull-feast made ready then, the same
way as the time Conaire was chosen, to find out who was
the best man to get the kingship.

After a while the dreamer screamed out in his sleep,
and told what he saw to the kings. And what he saw
this time, was a young strong man, with high looks, and
with two red stripes on his body, and he sitting over the
pillow of a man that was wasting away in Emain
Macha.

A message was sent then with this account to Emain Macha. The men of Ulster were gathered at that time about Cuchulain, that was on his sick-bed. The messenger told his story to Conchubar and to the chief men of Ulster.

"There is a young man of good race and good birth with us now that answers to that account," said Conchubar ; "that is Lugaid of the Red Stripes, son of Clothru, daughter of Eochaid Feidlech, the pupil of Cuchulain ; and he is sitting by his pillow within, caring him, for he is on his sick-bed."

And when it was told Cuchulain that messengers were come for Lugaid, to make him King in Teamhair, he rose up and began to advise him, and it is what he said :

"Do not be a frightened man in a battle ; do not be light-minded, hard to reach, or proud. Do not be ungentle, or hasty, or passionate ; do not be overcome with the drunkenness of great riches, like a flea that is drowned in the ale of a king's house. Do not scatter many feasts to strangers ; do not visit mean people that cannot receive you as a king. Do not let wrongful possession stand because it has lasted long , but let witnesses be searched to know who is the right owner of land. Let the tellers of history tell truth before you ; let the lands of brothers and their increase be set down in their lifetime ; if a family has increased in its branches, is it not from the one stem they are come ? Let them be called up, let the old claims be established by oaths ; let the heir be left in lawful possession of the place his fathers lived in ; let strangers be driven off it by force.

"Do not use too many words. Do not speak noisily ; do not mock, do not give insults, do not make little of old people. Do not think ill of any one ; do not ask what is hard to give. Let you have a law of lending, a law of oppression, a law of pledging. Be obedient to the advice of the wise; keep in mind the advice of the old. Be a follower of the rules of your fathers. Do not be cold-hearted to friends; be strong towards your enemies; do not give evil for evil in your battles. Do not be given to too much talking. Do not speak any harm of others. Do not waste, do not scatter, do not do away with what is your own. When you do wrong, take the blame of it; do not give up the truth for any man. Do not be trying to be first, the way you will not be jealous; do not be an idler, that you may not be weak; do not ask too much, that you may not be thought little of. Are you willing to follow this advice, my son?"

Then Lugaid answered Cuchulain, and it is what he said: "As long as all goes well, I will keep to your words, and every one will know that there is nothing wanting in me; all will be done that can be done."

Then Lugaid went away with the messengers to Teamhair, and he was made king, and he slept in Teamhair that night. And after that all the people that had gathered there went to their own homes.

XVI

THE SONS OF DOEL DERMAIT

ONE time Cuchulain was gone west to Carraige, in the province of Connaught, and Lugaid of the Red Stripes with him, and Laeg. And one day they saw a young girl standing on the burial-hill of Tetach. "What is it you are wanting?" said Lugaid. "I want Cuchulain, son of Sualtim," she said, "for I have set my love on him on account of his great deeds that I have heard of." "There he is, beyond," said Lugaid. Then she went over to him, and put her arms about his neck, and kissed him; and she told him she was Finnchoem, daughter of Eocho Rond, king of Hy Maine.

Then Cuchulain took her into his keeping, and they travelled northward through the night, towards Emain. And one time in the darkness of the night, towards Fid Manach, they saw three fires in a wood before them, and nine men at every fire; outlaws they were, that were robbing the country. And Cuchulain killed three of them at every fire.

And in the morning they saw a troop of men coming towards them on the plain, and Finnchoem's father, the king of Hy Maine, leading them, and he having on him a four-folded crimson cloak, with four borders of gold, and a shield with eight borders of white bronze, and a gold-hilted sword at his side. And he had light yellow hair falling down on each side to the flanks of his grey-black horse; and there was a gold chain of the

641

weight of seven ounces hanging from his hair, and it was from that he took his name, Eocho Rond, that is, Eocho of the gold chain. And as soon as he saw Cuchulain, he threw his spear at him. But Cuchulain caught the spear and threw it back again, and it struck the horse in the neck, so that he reared up and threw his master. And Cuchulain lifted Eocho in his arms, and carried him as far as Cruachan, that they were near at the time, to leave him with Ailell and with Maeve. And there was great shame on the king of Hy Maine at what had happened.

And when Cuchulain was leaving him he said: "May you never have rest in sitting, or in lying down, until you find out what it was brought away the three sons of Doel Dermait, the Beetle of Forgetfulness, out of their own country."

And Cuchulain went on to Emain. But when he sat down in his place, it seemed to him the walls of the house and the ground under him to be on fire. Then he said to his people: "I think what Eocho Rond threatened me with is coming on me, and I will get my death if I do not do as he bade me."

Then he went back to his own place, Dundealgan, and out westward to Baile's strand. And there he saw a boat coming, and the king of Alban's son in it, and his people, and they bringing presents for king Conchubar, of purple, and of golden drinking-cups. And when they saw the three men on the strand, Cuchulain and Lugaid and Laeg, they said to them: "It is likely if the king knew we were here, he would send us food and drink by you." "Is it a steward you would make of me?" said Cuchulain, and anger came on him, and he took the sword in his hand to strike them. "Give us our life, Cuchulain, for we did not know you," said the king's son.

"Do you know what was it drove the three sons of Doel Dermait from their own country?" said Cuchulain.

"I do not know that," said the king's son. "But I have a sea charm, and I will set it for you, and I will give it to you, and you will find the knowledge you are looking for."

Then Cuchulain gave him his little spear, and scratched an Ogham on it, and said to him : "Set out now, and go and take my seat at Emain Macha."

Then they took the things out of the boat, and Cuchulain got in, and Lugaid of the Red Stripes, and Laeg ; and they put up the sail, and went on for a day and a night until they came to an island. It was a fine, large, beautiful island, having a silver wall about it, and a paling of bronze.

Then Cuchulain landed, and he saw a house with pillars of white bronze, and three times fifty beds in the house, and a chessboard, and a draughtboard, and a harp hanging over every bed. And he saw a grey king and queen in the house, with purple cloaks on them, worked with dark-coloured gold, and three young girls of the one age, having a dress worked with gold thread on each of them.

And the king gave them a friendly welcome, and he said : "Cuchulain is welcome to us for Lugaid's sake, and Laeg is welcome for his father and his mother's sake."

Then Cuchulain asked him did he know what was it drove the three sons of Doel Dermait out of their own country. "You will soon know that," he said, "for their sister and their sister's husband are in that island there to the south."

Then three pieces of iron were put in the fire, and when they were red-hot, the three young girls took them out, and put them in three vats, and Cuchulain and Lugaid and Laeg bathed in the vats. And they were brought cups of mead. And then they heard a noise of arms and of trumpets, and they saw fifty armed men coming to the house, and every two of them bringing a pig and an ox, and every one a cup of mead of hazel nuts. And then every man of them came again, and a load of firing on his back; and then the oxen and the pigs were cooked, and a feast for hundreds was given to Cuchulain and his comrades.

And the next day they went on to the island where the daughter of Doel Dermait was, and the boat went on, steering itself, to the island. And Condla, son-in-law of Doel Dermait, was lying on the strand, and his head against a pillar at the east of the island, and his feet at the west of the island, and every time he breathed, he made a wave in the sea that turned the boat back. But then he called out to Cuchulain: "Come to land, for there is no fear of you on us; for however great your anger may be, it is not in the prophecy that it is by you this island will be destroyed." Then Cuchulain came to land, and Condla and his wife bade him welcome. And Cuchulain asked if they knew what it was had driven the three sons of Doel Dermait from their own country. "I know it," said the woman, "and I will show you where they are, for it is foretold that their healing is to come by you; and it is glad my true, warm heart would be, they to be healed." And then she said: "Go to where that wall is, and you will find Cairpre Cundail, and he will bring you to the valley where they are kept by Eocho Glas, the strong man."

So they went on to the wall, and they saw two women that were cutting rushes, and Cuchulain said to one of them: "What is the name of this country I have come to?" And the woman rose up, and it is what she said: "There are seven princes in this country, and every one of them has had seven victories; and there are seven women in this country, every one of them having a king under her feet. And every one of them has seven armies; and when a thief comes to this place, he does not go back again to tell the story of it."

Then Cuchulain struck her down with his hand, and the other woman went away to tell Cairpre Cundail what had happened.

Cairpre Cundail came out then, and he and Cuchulain fought through the day, and neither got the better of the other. But at night Cairpre said : "That is enough, Cuchulain." And they left off for the night. And next morning Cairpre brought Cuchulain to the valley where Eocho Glas was, that he himself was always at war with. And Eocho Glas called out : "Is any one there of your miserable fighters?" "There is some one here," said Cuchulain. At that Eocho said : "That is not a voice that pleases me, for it is the voice of the angry man from Muirthemne."

Then he came out, and they fought together in the valley, and then they fought beside the sea. And in the end Cuchulain took the Gae Bulg and put it through him, and he fell, and Cuchulain struck his head off.

Then the prisoners of Eocho Glas came running from the hills on every side, east and west, and bathed themselves in his blood, for he had been doing them every sort of hurt and harm, and they all got healing.

And the three sons of Doel Dermait came with them, and were healed along with them, and they told their whole story to Cuchulain. And then they set out for their own country.

And Cuchulain went back the same way as he came ; and he brought wonderful presents with him from Cairpre Cundail.

And when he got back to Ulster, he went on to Emain Macha, and his share of food and drink were waiting there for him yet. And he told his whole story to Conchubar and to the heroes of the Red Branch, and to Eocho Rond, king of Hy Maine ; and that is the way he made his peace with him.

XVII

BATTLE OF ROSNAREE

THERE was a time, now, after the war for the Bull of Cuailgne, when King Conchubar got someway down-hearted, and there was a heaviness on his mind.

And the men of Ulster thought it might be lonesome he was, and fretting after Deirdre yet, and they searched about through the whole province for a wife for him.

And at last they found a beautiful young girl of good race, whose name was Luain, and they brought her to Emain Macha, and a great wedding was made, and great feasting ; and the king grew to be quiet and happy in his mind. But among the men that came to the wedding were the two sons of the poet Aithirne, that had such a bad name for covetousness and for cruelty.

The two sons were poets as well, Cuingedach and Abhartach, and when they saw Luain, Conchubar's queen, and she so beautiful, the two of them fell in love with her there and then. And they stopped at Emain, and after a while each of them tried to gain her secret love. But there was great anger and displeasure on Luain at that, and she drove them from her.

They went home then to their father, Aithirne, and the three of them, to avenge themselves on Luain, made satires on her, that brought blotches out on her face. And when her face that was so beautiful was spoiled like that, she went back and hid herself in her father's house, and with the shame and the sorrow that were on her, she died there.

Then great anger and rage came on Conchubar, and he sent the men of Ulster to Aithirne's house, and they killed himself and his two sons, and they pulled his house down to the ground.

But the rest of the poets of Ulster were not well pleased that Conchubar should put such disrespect on one of themselves and do such a great vengeance on him, and they gathered together and gave Aithirne a great burial and keened him, and it was Amergin that made a lament over his grave.

And then Conchubar stopped in Emain Macha, and the cloud of trouble came on him again, and he used to be thinking of the war for the Bull of Cuailgne, and of all that Maeve's army did when he was in his weakness; and he did not sleep in the night, and there was no food that pleased him.

And then the men of Ulster bid Cathbad, the Druid, go to Conchubar, and rouse him out of his sickness.

So Cathbad went to him, and he cried tears down when he saw him, and he said: "Tell me, Conchubar, what wound it is or what sickness has weakened you and has made your face so pale?" "It is no wonder sickness to be on me," said Conchubar, "when I think of the way the four provinces of Ireland came and destroyed my forts and my duns and my walled towns and the houses of my people, and when I think how Maeve brought away cattle and gold and silver, and how she came as far as Dun Sescind and Dun Sobairce, and brought away Daire's bull out of my own province. And it is what vexes me, Maeve herself to have got away safe from the battle; and it is time for me to go and avenge that time on the men of Ireland," he said. "That is no right thing you are saying," said Cathbad, "for the men of Ulster did a good vengeance on the

men of Ireland the time they gained the battle of
Ilgaireth." "I do not count any battle to be a battle,"
said Conchubar, "unless a king or a queen has fallen in
it; and I swear by the oath of my people, Cathbad," he
said, "that kings and great men will be brought to their
death by me, or else I myself will go to my death."

"This is my advice to you," said Cathbad, "not to set
out till the winter is gone by; for at this time the winds
are rough, and the roads are heavy, and the rivers are full
and flooded, and every windy gap is cold. It is best to
wait for the summer," he said, "till the fords are shallow
and the roads are smooth, till the thick leaves on the
bushes will be shelters, till every sod of grass will be a
pillow, till our colts will be strong, till the nights will be
short for keeping watch against an enemy. It is best to
wait," he said, "till you can gather together the men of
Ulster, and till you can send messengers to your friends
among the Gall." "I am willing to do that," said
Conchubar, "but I give my word," he said, "let them
come, or let them not come, I will go myself to Teamhair
to get satisfaction from Cairbre Niafer, my own son-in-
law, that did not come to help me at the gathering at
Ilgaireth, and to Lugaid, son of Curoi, and to Eocha, son
of Luchta, and to Maeve, and to Ailell, till I throw
down the stones over the graves of their chief men, till I
destroy and lay waste their country, the same way as
the men of Ireland destroyed my province."

So then Conchubar sent out messengers to Conall
Cearnach, that was raising his tribute in the islands of
Leodus, and of Cadd, and of Orc, and to the countries
of the Gall, to Olaib, grandson of the king of Norway,
and to Baire of the Scigger islands, and to Siugraid Soga,
king of Sudiam; to the seven sons of Romra, and to the
son of the king of Alban, and to the king of the island of
Orc.

And the first to answer the messengers, and to set out

for Ulster was Conall Cearnach, for there was great anger on him when he heard of all that had happened in Ulster in the war for the Bull of Cuailgne, and he not in it. "And if I had been in it," he said, "the men of Connaught would not have taken spoil from Ulster, without an equal vengeance being measured to them again." And Olaib, grandson of the king of Norway, came with him, and Baire, of the Scigger islands, and their men with them in their ships; and they came through the green waves, and the seals and the sword fishes rising about them, towards Dundealgan, and the place where they landed was at the Strand of Baile, son of Buan.

This, now, is the story of Baile that was buried at that strand.

He was of the race of Rudraige, and although he had but little land belonging to him, he was the heir of Ulster, and every one that saw him loved him, both man and woman, because he was so sweet-spoken; and they called him Baile of the Honey-Mouth. And the one that loved him best was Aillinn, daughter of Lugaidh, the King of Leinster's son. And one time she herself and Baile settled to meet one another near Dundealgan, beside the sea. Baile was the first to set out, and he came from Emain Macha, over Slieve Fuad, over Muirthemne, to the strand where they were to meet; and he stopped there, and his chariots were unyoked, and his horses were let out to graze. And while he and his people were waiting there they saw a strange, wild-looking man, coming towards them from the South, as fast as a hawk that darts from a cliff or as the wind that blows from off the green sea. "Go and meet him," said Baile to his people, "and ask him news of where he is going and where he comes from, and what is the reason of his haste." So they asked news of him, and he said: "I am going back now to Tuagh Inbhir, from Slieve Suidhe Laighen, and this is all the news I have, that Aillinn daughter of Lugaidh, was on her way to meet Baile, son of Buan, that she loved. And the young men of Leinster overtook her, and kept her back from going to him, and she died of the heartbreak there and then. For it was foretold by Druids that were friendly to them that they would not come together in their lifetime, but that after their death they would meet, and be happy for ever after." And with that he left them, and was gone again like a blast of wind, and they were not able to hinder him.

And when Baile heard that news, his life went out from him, and he fell dead there on the strand.

And at that time the young girl Aillinn was in her sunny parlour to the south, for she had not set out yet. And the same strange man came in to her, and she asked him where he came from. " I come from the North," he said, " from Tuagh Inver, and I am going past this place to Slieve Suidhe Laighen. And all the news I have," he said, " is that I saw the men of Ulster gathered together on the strand near Dundealgan, and they raising a stone, and writing on it the name of·Baile, son of Buan, that died there when he was on his way to meet the woman he had given his love to ; for it was not meant for them ever to reach one another alive, or that one of them should see the other alive." And when he had said that he vanished away, and as to Aillinn, her life went from her, and she died the same way that Baile had died.

And an apple-tree grew out of her grave, and a yew-tree out of Baile's grave. And it was near that yew-tree Conall Cearnach landed, and Baire, and the grandson of the king of Norway. And Cuchulain had made ready a great feast for them, and for Conchubar that had come to meet them, at bright-faced Dundealgan.

And the Hound bade them a kind, loving welcome, and he said : " Welcome to those I know, and those I do not know, to the good and the bad, the young and the old among you." And they stopped there a week, and Conchubar was well pleased to see the whole strand full of his friends that were come in their ships. And then he bade farewell to Emer, daughter of Forgall, and he said to Cuchulain : " Go now to the three fifties of old fighting men, that are resting in their age, under Irgalach, son of Macclach, and say to them to come with me to this gathering and to this war, the way I will have their help and their advice." " Let them go to it if they have a mind," said Cuchulain ; " but it is not I that will go and ask it of them."

So then Conchubar himself went to the great house, where the old fighting men used to be living that had laid by their arms. And when he came in, they raised their heads from their places to look at the great king. And then they leaped up, and they said : " What has brought you to us to day, our chief and our lord ? " " Did you get no word," he said, " of the way the four provinces of Ireland came against us, and how they burned down our forts and our houses, and how they brought their makers of poems and of stories along with them, that their deeds might be told, and our disgrace might be the greater. And I am going out against them now," he said, " to get satisfaction from them ; and let you come with me, and I will have your advice." Then the hearts of the old men rose in them, and they caught their old horses and yoked their old chariots. And they went on with the king to the mouth of the Water of Luachann that night.

And the next day Conchubar set out with his own men and his friends from beyond the sea, to Slieve Breagh, that is near Rosnaree on the Boinne. And they made their camp at Cuanglas, the green harbour, and lighted their fires, and music and merry songs were made for them. But Cuchulain stopped behind in

Dundealgan to gather his own people, and to make provision for them on the march.

Now news had been brought to Cairbre Niafer at Teamhair, that Conchubar was gathering his men to get satisfaction for all that had been done to Ulster in the war for the Bull of Cuailgne, and that it was likely he himself would be the first he would come against.

For there was some bad feeling between Cairbre and the men of Ulster, since the time he drove the sons of Umor into Connaught, with the heavy rent he put on them, and that after Conall Cearnach and Cuchulain giving their own security for their good behaviour. They turned on their securities after that, and fought with them, and Conall Cool, the son of their chief, fell; and Cuchulain, and his father, and his friends, raised the heap of stones over him that is called Carn Chonaill, in the province of Connaught.

And Cairbre sent a message to Cruachan, to say to Ailell and to Maeve: "If it is towards us Conchubar and the men of Ulster are coming, let you come to our help; but if it is past us they go, into the fair-headed province of Connaught, we will go to your help." So when Conchubar came to Cuanglas, at Rosnaree, there was a good army gathered there to make a stand against him; the three troops of the children of Deagha, and a great troop of the Collamnachs, and of the men of Bregia, and of the Gailiana. And he rose up early in the morning, and he could see the moving of men and the shining of spears, and he heard the noise of a great army, and he said: "We will send some one of our men to bring us word about them."

And he sent out Feic, son of Follaman. And Feic went up to a hill beside the Boinne, and he began to look at the army and to count it, and it vexed him to see how many were in it. "If I go back now and tell this," he said, "the men of Ulster will come and will begin the battle, and there will be no better chance for me to get a great name and do great deeds than for any other man. And why would I not go and begin a fight now by myself?" And with that he crossed the river.

But the men that were in front caught sight of him, and the whole army began shouting around him, and he had not courage to go against them, but he turned to cross the river again. But he gave a false leap, just where the water was deepest, and a wave laughed over him, and he died.

It seemed a long time to Conchubar that he was away, and he said to the men of Ulster: "What is your advice to us about this battle?" "It is what we advise," they said, "to wait till our strong fighters and our chief men are come. And they had not long to wait before they saw troops coming, Cathbad with twelve hundred men, and Amergin with twelve hundred men, and Eoghan, king of Fernmaighe, and Laegaire Buadach, and the three sons of Conall Buide.

And then they saw another troop coming, and in the front of it a fierce, brown man. Rough, dark hair he had, and a big nose and hollow cheeks, and his talk was quick and hurried. A blue cloak about him, and a brooch of silver as white as a bird, a heavy sword, and a shield with iron rims. And this is who he was, Daire of Cuailgne, that was come to get satisfaction for his bull and for his herds on the men of Ireland. "What is delaying you here," he said to Conchubar. "I have good reason for delaying," said Conchubar, "for there is a great army under Cairbre Niafer before us at Rosnaree, and there are not enough of us to go against them. And it is not refusing a battle we are, but waiting till we get our full number." "By my word," said Daire, "if you do not go out against them, it is I will go against them by myself."

Then Conchubar put on his armour, and took his

many-coloured shield, and his sword, the Ochain. And all the men of Ulster gathered around him, and they raised their spears and their shields, and it was like a great river breaking from the side of a mountain, and breaking what it meets of stones and trees before it, that they went to meet the men of Leinster at Rosnaree on the Boinne.

And when Cairbre Niafer and his friends and his men saw them coming, they made ready for them, and came towards the river.

And the men of Ulster crossed the river, and the two armies met, and each of them took to hacking and destroying the other. And the Gailiana pressed heavily on the men of Ulster, and came in to the middle of them, and cut them down like trees are cut in a wood. And as for Conchubar he did not give back, where he was, and Celthair on his right hand, and Amergin the poet on his right hand again, and Eoghan, king of Fernmaighe, on his left, and Daire of Cuailgne near him. These few stood against the Gailiana, and fought against them, stout and proud. But as to the young men and those that were never in a fight before, they turned round and burst through the battle northwards.

It was just then Conall Cearnach was coming in his chariot, and when the young men of Ulster saw the face of Conall, they came to a stop, and Conall saw that they were beaten and running from the battle, and he called out sharp words to them, for there was anger on him, they to have left the fight, and with no sign of blood or of wounds upon them.

But they were ashamed then, and content to go back to the battle, when they had Conall's hand to help them; and each one of them tore a green branch off the oak trees that were near them, and held it up, and they went with him; for they knew there would be no running away in any place where Conall's face would be seen.

And it happened just at that time Conchubar, the High King, was taking three backward steps out of the battle northward, but when he saw the face of Conall coming towards him, he called to him to stop the army from falling back. " I give my word," said Conall, " I think it easier to fight the battle by myself than to stop the rout now."

And just then the three royal poets of the king of Teamhair came to give him their help, Eochaid the Learned, and Diarment of the Songs, and Forgel the Just, and they went into the fight against Conall. And Conall looked at them and he said : "I give my true word," he said, "if you were not poets and men of learning, you would have got your death by me before this ; and now that you are come fighting with your master," he said, "where is there any reason for sparing you ?" And with that he made a blow at them with a heavy stick that was in his hand, that struck the three heads off them.

Then Conall drew his sword out of its sheath, and he played the music of his sword on the armies of Leinster, and the sound of it was heard on every side ; and when the men near him heard it their faces whitened, and each one of them went back to his place in the battle. And at that time Cuchulain came into the battle, and the men of the Gailiana gave wild shouts at him, and anger came on him and he scattered them.

And strength came again into the hearts of the men of Ulster, and their anger rose, and the earth shook under their feet, and there was clashing of swords on both sides, and the shouting of young men, and the screams of old men, and the groaning of chariot-fighters, and the crying of ravens. And there were many lying in cold pools, the white soles of their feet close together, and the red lips turning grey, and the bright faces very pale, and darkness coming on their grey eyes, and confusion on their clear wits.

It is then Cuchulain met with Cairbre Niafer, and he went against him, and put his shield against his shield and there they were face to face. And Cairbre said words of insult to Cuchulain, and Cuchulain answered him back and said: "It is all I ask of you, to fight with me now alone." "I will do that," said Cairbre Niafer, "for I am a king in my way of living, and a champion in battles."

Then each attacked the other, and it was hard for them to hold their feet firm, or to strike with their hands, in the closeness of the fight. And Cairbre broke all his weapons, but nine of his men came and kept up the fight against Cuchulain till more weapons could be brought to him. And then Cuchulain's weapons were broken, and Cairbre and nine of his men came and held up their shields before him till Laeg could bring him his own right weapons, the Dubach, the grim one, his spear, and the Cruaidin, his sword. And then they took to hitting at one another again, and at last Cuchulain took his spear into his left hand, and struck at Cairbre with it, and he lowered his shield to protect his body. And then Cuchulain changed it to his right hand, and struck at him over the rim of his shield, and it went through his heart; and before his body could reach the ground, Cuchulain made a spring and struck his head off. And then he held up the head, and shook it before the two armies.

Then Sencha, son of Ailell, rose up and shook the branch of peace, and the men of Ulster stood still. As to the men of Leinster, when they saw their king was killed, they fell back; but Iriel of the Great Knees, the son of Conall Cearnach, followed after them, and did a great slaughter on the Gailiana and on the rest of the army till they reached to the Rye of Leinster.

And then the men of Ulster went back to their homes. And as to Conchubar, he went back to Emain, and it was not till a good while after that he got the wound in his head that Fintan sewed up with gold thread, to match the colour of his hair, and that brought him to his death in the end.

XVIII

THE ONLY SON OF AOIFE

THE time Cuchulain came back from Alban, after he had learned the use of arms under Scathach, he left Aoife, the queen he had overcome in battle, with child.

And when he was leaving her, he told her what name to give the child, and he gave her a gold ring, and bade her keep it safe till the child grew to be a lad, and till his thumb would fill it; and he bade her to give it to him then, and to send him to Ireland, and he would know he was his son by that token. She promised to do so, and with that Cuchulain went back to Ireland.

It was not long after the child was born, word came to Aoife that Cuchulain had taken Emer to be his wife in Ireland. When she heard that, great jealousy came on her, and great anger, and her love for Cuchulain was turned to hatred; and she remembered her three champions that he had killed, and how he had overcome herself, and she determined in her mind that when her son would come to have the strength of a man, she would get her revenge through him. She told Conlaoch her son nothing of this, but brought him up like any king's son; and when he was come to sensible years, she put him under the teaching of Scathach, to be taught the use of arms and the art of war. He turned out as apt a scholar as his father, and it was not long before he had learnt all Scathach had to teach.

Then Aoife gave him the arms of a champion, and bade him go to Ireland, but first she laid three commands on him: the first never to give way to any living person, but to die sooner than be made turn back; the second, not to refuse a challenge from the greatest champion alive, but to fight him at all risks, even if he was sure to lose his life; the third, not to tell his name on any account, though he might be threatened with death for hiding it. She put him under *geasa*, that is, under bonds, not to do these things.

Then the young man, Conlaoch, set out, and it was not long before his ship brought him to Ireland, and the place he landed at was Baile's Strand, near Dundealgan.

It chanced that at that time Conchubar, the High King, was holding his court there, for it was a convenient gathering-place for his chief men, and they were settling some business that belonged to the government of that district.

When word was brought to Conchubar that there was a ship come to the strand, and a young lad in it armed as if for fighting, and armed men with him, he sent one of the chief men of his household to ask his name, and on what business he was come.

The messenger's name was Cuinaire, and he went down to the strand, and when he saw the young man he said: "A welcome to you, young hero from the east, with the merry face. It is likely, seeing you come armed as if for fighting, you are gone astray on your journey; but as you are come to Ireland, tell me your name and what your deeds have been, and your victories in the eastern bounds of the world."

"As to my name," said Conlaoch, "it is of no great account; but whatever it is, I am under bonds not to tell it to the stoutest man living."

"It is best for you to tell it at the king's desire," said

Cuinaire, "before you get your death through refusing
it, as many a champion from Alban and from Britain
has done before now." "If that is the order you put on
us when we land here, it is I will break it," said
Conlaoch, "and no one will obey it any longer from
this out."

So Cunaire went back and told the king what the
young lad had said. Then Conchubar said to his
people : "Who will go out into the field, and drag the
name and the story out of this young man ?" "I will
go," said Conall, for his hand was never slow in fighting.
And he went out, and found the lad angry and destroying,
handling his arms, and they attacked one another with
a great noise of swords and shouts, and they were
gripped together, and fought for a while, and then Conall
was overcome, and the great name and the praise that
was on Conall, it was on the head of Conlaoch it was
now.

Word was sent then to where Cuchulain was, in
pleasant, bright-faced Dundealgan. And the messenger
told him the whole story, and he said : "Conall is lying
humbled, and it is slow the help is in coming ; it is a
welcome there would be before the Hound."

Cuchulain rose up then and went to where Conlaoch
was, and he still handling his arms. And Cuchulain
asked him his name and said : "It would be well for you,
young hero of unknown name, to loosen yourself from
this knot, and not to bring down my hand upon you, for
it will be hard for you to escape death." But Conlaoch
said : "If I put you down in the fight, the way I put
down your comrade, there will be a great name on me ;
but if I draw back now, there will be mockery on me,
and it will be said I was afraid of the fight. I will never
give in to any man to tell the name, or to give an
account of myself. But if I was not held with a command," he said, "there is no man in the world I would

sooner give it to than to yourself, since I saw your face. But do not think, brave champion of Ireland, that I will let you take away the fame I have won, for nothing."

With that they fought together, and it is seldom such a battle was seen, and all wondered that the young lad could stand so well against Cuchulain.

So they fought a long while, neither getting the better of the other, but at last Cuchulain was charged so hotly by the lad that he was forced to give way, and although he had fought so many good fights, and killed so many great champions, and understood the use of arms better than any man living, he was pressed very hard.

And he called for the Gae Bulg, and his anger came on him, and the flames of the hero-light began to shine about his head, and by that sign Conlaoch knew him to be Cuchulain, his father. And just at that time he was aiming his spear at him, and when he knew it was Cuchulain, he threw his spear crooked that it might pass beside him. But Cuchulain threw his spear, the Gae Bulg, at him with all his might, and it struck the lad in the side and went into his body, so that he fell to the ground.

And Cuchulain said: "Now, boy, tell your name and what you are, for it is short your life will be, for you will not live after that wound."

And Conlaoch showed the ring that was on his hand, and he said: "Come here where I am lying on the field, let my men from the east come round me. I am suffering for revenge. I am Conlaoch, son of the Hound, heir of dear Dundealgan; I was bound to this secret in Dun Scathach, the secret in which I have found my grief."

And Cuchulain said: "It is a pity your mother not to be here to see you brought down. She might have stretched out her hand to stop the spear that wounded you." And Conlaoch said: "My curse be on my mother, for it was she put me under bonds; it was she sent me here to try my strength against yours." And Cuchulain said: "My curse be on your mother, the woman that is full of treachery; it is through her harmful thoughts these tears have been brought on us." And Conlaoch said: "My name was never forced from my mouth till now; I never gave an account of myself to any man under the sun. But, O Cuchulain of the sharp sword, it was a pity you not to know me the time I threw the slanting spear behind you in the fight."

And then the sorrow of death came upon Conlaoch, and Cuchulain took his sword and put it through him, sooner than leave him in the pain and the punishment he was in.

And then great trouble and anguish came on Cuchulain, and he made this complaint:

"It is a pity it is, O son of Aoife, that ever you came into the province of Ulster, that you ever met with the Hound of Cuailgne.

"If I and my fair Conlaoch were doing feats of war on the one side, the men of Ireland from sea to sea would not be equal to us together. It is no wonder I to be under grief when I see the shield and the arms of Conlaoch. A pity it is there is no one at all, a pity there are not hundreds of men on whom I could get satisfaction for his death.

"If it was the king himself had hurt your fair body, it is I would have shortened his days.

"It is well for the House of the Red Branch, and for the heads of its fair army of heroes, it was not they that killed my only son.

"It is well for Laegaire of Victories it is not from him you got your heavy pain.

"It is well for the heroes of Conall they did not join in the killing of you; it is well that travelling across the plain of Macha they did not fall in with me after such a fight.

"It is well for the tall, well-shaped Forbuide; well for Dubthach, your Black Beetle of Ulster.

"It is well for you, Cormac Conloingeas, your share of arms gave no help, that it is not from your weapons he got his wound, the hard-skinned shield or the blade.

"It is a pity it was not one on the plains of Munster, or in Leinster of the sharp blades, or at Cruachan of the rough fighters, that struck down my comely Conlaoch.

"It is a pity it was not in the country of the Cruithne, of the fierce Fians, you fell in a heavy quarrel, or in the country of the Greeks, or in some other place of the world, you died, and I could avenge you.

"Or in Spain, or in Sorcha, or in the country of the Saxons of the free armies; there would not then be this death in my heart.

"It is very well for the men of Alban it was not they that destroyed your fame; and it is well for the men of the Gall.

"Och! It is bad that it happened; my grief! it is on me is the misfortune, O Conlaoch of the Red Spear, I myself to have spilled your blood.

"I to be under defeat, without strength. It is a pity Aoife never taught you to know the power of my strength in the fight.

"It is no wonder I to be blinded after such a fight and such a defeat.

"It is no wonder I to be tired out, and without the sons of Usnach beside me.

"Without a son, without a brother, with none to come after me; without Conlaoch, without a name to keep my strength.

"To be without Naoise, without Ainnle, without Ardan; is it not with me is my fill of trouble?

"I am the father that killed his son, the fine green branch ; there is no hand or shelter to help me.

"I am a raven that has no home ; I am a boat going from wave to wave ; I am a ship that has lost its rudder ; I am the apple left on the tree ; it is little I thought of falling from it ; grief and sorrow will be with me from this time."

Then Cuchulain stood up and faced all the men of Ulster. "There is trouble on Cuchulain," said Conchubar ; "he is after killing his own son, and if I and all my men were to go against him, by the end of the day he would destroy every man of us. Go now," he said to Cathbad, the Druid, "and bind him to go down to Baile's Strand, and to give three days fighting against the waves of the sea, rather than to kill us all."

So Cathbad put an enchantment on him, and bound him to go down. And when he came to the strand, there was a great white stone before him, and he took his sword in his right hand, and he said : "If I had the head of the woman that sent her son to his death, I would split it as I split this stone." And he made four quarters of the stone.

Then he fought with the waves three days and three nights, till he fell from hunger and weakness, so that some men said he got his death there. But it was not there he got his death, but on the plain of Muirthemne.

XIX

THE GREAT GATHERING AT MUIRTHEMNE

NOW after all the battles Cuchulain had fought, and all the men he had killed, it is no wonder he had a good share of enemies watching to get the upper hand of him. And besides Maeve, those that had their minds most set against him were Erc, son of Cairbre Niafer, that he had killed at Rosnaree, and Lugaid, son of Curoi, that he had killed at his own house in Munster, and the three daughters of Calatin.

This, now, was the way it happened that Curoi got his death by him. He met with Blanad one time, a good while after Curoi had given him the championship of Ulster, and it is what she told him that there was not a man on the face of the earth she loved more than himself. And she bade him come, near Samhain time, to Curoi's dun at Finglas, and his men with him, and to bring her away by force.

So when the time came, Cuchulain set out, and his men with him, and they came to a wood near the dun, that had a stream running through it, and he sent word to Blanad he was waiting there. And Blanad sent him back word to come and bring her away at whatever time he would see the stream in the wood turning white. And when what she thought to be a good time came, when all the men of the place were sent out looking for stones to build a great new dun, she milked the three white

cows with red ears Curoi had brought away by force
from her father, Midhir, into the cauldron he had
brought away with them, and she poured a great vessel
of new milk into the stream, where it ran by the dun.
And when Cuchulain saw the stream turning white, he
went up to the dun. But he found Curoi there before
him, and they fought, and Curoi was killed, the son of
Daire, lord of the southern sea, that had a great name
and great praise on him before Blanad was his wife.

Then Cuchulain brought Blanad away with him to
Ulster. But Curoi's poet, Feirceirtne, followed after
them to avenge his master's death. And when they
were come as far as the headland of Cian Beara, he
saw Blanad standing on the edge of a high rock, and
she alone. And he went up to her, and took her in his
arms, and threw her, and himself along with her, over
the rock, and they both got their death by the fall on
the moment.

And as to the children of Calatin, this is the way it
was with them. At the time Cuchulain made an end of
Calatin at the ford, and of all his sons with him, Calatin's
wife was with child. And when her time came, there
were three daughters born at the one birth, and they deformed, and each of them having but one eye.

Then Maeve came from Cruachan to visit them, and
she brought away the children with her, and took the
charge of them. And when they were come to sensible
years, she came to see them, and she said: "Do you know
who it was killed your father?" "We know well," they
said, "it was Cuchulain, son of Sualtim, killed him."
"That is so," said Maeve, "and let you make a journey
now," she said, "through the whole world, to get knowledge of spells and enchantments from them that have it,
the way you will be able to avenge your father when the
time comes."

When the three one-eyed daughters of Calatin heard

that, they went out into Alban, and to every other country, from the rising to the setting of the sun, and they were learning every sort of enchantment and of witchcraft. And at the end they came back to Cruachan.

And as to Maeve, she went up one morning to her sunny parlour, and from there she saw the three daughters of Calatin sitting outside on the lawn. So she took her cloak, that had beautiful embroidery on it, and put it about her, and she went out on the lawn and bade them welcome, and she sat down before them, and asked news of all they had done since they left Ireland. And they told her all they had learned. "Do you remember it all?" said Maeve. "We remember it well," they said, "and we can do many things, and we can make the appearance of terrible battles by secret words."

Maeve brought them then into the royal house, and they were attended on, and they were given every sort of food and of drink, and of good treatment.

And then Maeve sent word to Lugaid, and he came to Cruachan, and himself and Maeve began to talk together. "Do you remember," she said, "who it was killed Curoi your father?" "I remember it well," he said; "it was Cuchulain killed him." Then Erc came to her, and she asked him the same question about his father Cairbre Niafer, and he made the same answer. "What you say is true," Maeve said then, "and the children of Calatin are come back to me now, after going through the whole world, to fight against Cuchulain with their enchantments. And there is no king or chief man, or fighting man in the four provinces of Ireland, but lost his friend or his comrade, his father or his brother, by him in the war for the Bull of Cuailgne, or at some other time. And now," she said, "it is best for us to gather together a great army of the men of Ireland to make an attack on him, for the men of Ulster have their weakness coming on them, and it is likely they will not be able to help him."

With that, Lugaid went away southward to the king of Munster, to bid him come, and bring his men with him; and Erc went and called to the chief men of Leinster in the same way.

Then all the provinces gathered together to Cruachan, and they stopped there with feasting and merriment for three days and three nights. And at the end of that time they went out of Cruachan. But Maeve did not bring Fergus with them this time, for she was sure the men of Ireland would never be able to make an end of Cuchulain if Fergus was along with them.

And this is the way they went, beyond Magh Finn to Athluain, and they rested there that night.

And the next day they went on their road till they came to Glean-na-loin, and from that to Glean-mor, and from that to Tailtin, and they stopped the night there; and then they went on by the borders of Magh Breagh, and Midhe, and Treathfa, and Cuailgne.

It is then Conchubar, King of Ulster, got word that the borders of his province were being robbed and destroyed by the men of Munster and Leinster, and of Connaught.

"Where is Levarcham?" said Conchubar. "I am here," she said. "Go out for me now," said Conchubar, "and bring Cuchulain here to Emain; for it is against him this army we have news of is gathered. Bid him to make no delay, but to leave Dundealgan and Muirthemne and to come here to advise with myself, and with Cathbad and Amergin, and all the knowledgeable men. For if he can put off this battle till I myself, and Conall, and all the men of Ulster, will be ready to go out with him, we will give them a great defeat, the way they will not come into my province again. For there are many bear him ill-will," he said, "on account of all he killed. Finn, son of Ross, Fraoch, son of Idath, and Dearg, son of Conroi, and many of the best men of Ulster; and

Cairbre Niafer at the battle of Rosnaree ; and Curoi, son
of Daire, High King of Munster, and many of the men of
Munster besides him ; Fircearna, and Fiamain, and Niall,
and Laoc Leathbuine, and many more along with them."

Levarcham went quickly then with that message, and
it is where she found Cuchulain, between sea and land,
on Baile's Strand, and he trying to bring down sea-birds
with his sling ; but with all the birds that were flying
over him and past him, he could not bring one down,
but they all escaped him.

And there was heaviness on him, not to be able to hit
them, for he knew it had some bad meaning. And indeed he had never been very happy in his mind since the
death of the blossomed branch, Aoife's son, there on that
strand.   Then he saw Levarcham coming, and he bade
her welcome.   "I am glad of that welcome," said
Levarcham, "and it with news from Conchubar I am
come to you."   "What is your news ?" said Cuchulain.
"I have news indeed," she said.   And then she told him
all that Conchubar had said, from beginning to end.
"And it is what all are asking of you," she said : "chief
men and fighting men, poets and learned men, women
and young girls, to keep aside from the men of Ireland
that are coming here to Muirthemne, and not to go out
alone against that great army."   "I would sooner stop
here and defend my own place," said Cuchulain.   "It is
best for you to go to Emain," said Laeg.   So after a while
he gave in to them, and they went back to Dundealgan,
and Emer came out on the lawn to meet them, and they
gave her the same advice, to go to Emain Macha where
Conchubar and his chief men were gathered together.
Then Emer got her chariot, and she sent her servants
and the herds, and the cattle to Slieve Cuilenn in the
North, and herself and Cuchulain set out for Emain.
And that was the first time Dundealgan was emptied
since Cuchulain had the sway over it.

And when Cuchulain came to Emain Macha, they brought him to the bright, sunny house. And when the women of the place heard he was there, they came and spoke sweet words, and the poets and the harpers came, and the skilled men, and they all made music, and feasting, and pleasant talk round about Cuchulain, in the wide, white, sunny house of the Red Branch ; for what always quieted Cuchulain best was the singing of songs and rhymes before him. It is that way Scumac, the story-teller, quieted him one time he was vexed, and had a mind to set fire to Emain, because Conchubar had gone to a feast given by Conall, son of Gleo Glas, in Cuailgne, and had left no word for him to follow.

And Conchubar bade Cathbad, and the learned men, and the women, to keep a good watch on Cuchulain, and to mind him well. " For I leave the charge of him on you," he said, "to save him from the plans Maeve has made against him, and from the power of the children of Calatin. For if he should fall," he said, "it is certain the safety and the prosperity of Ulster will fall with him for ever." " That is true," said Cathbad, and all the others said the same.

" Well," said Geanann, Cathbad's son, " I will go now and see him." He went then to the place Cuchulain and Emer were, and the poets, and the women, and the learned men with them, and a feast laid out on the table, and all of them at drinking and pleasantness and games.

Now as to the men of Ireland, they came to the plain of Muirthemne, and they made their camp there, and they began to destroy and to take all they could find there, and in Macaire Conall ; and when they knew Cuchulain had left Dundealgan, it is then the three daughters of Calatin went with the lightness and the quickness of the wind to Emain Macha. And they sat down on the lawn outside the house where Cuchulain was, and they began to tear up the earth and the grass, and by means of their witchcraft they put the appearance of troops of men and of armies on stalks and coloured oak-leaves, and little fuzz-balls ; and the sounds of fighting and striking, and the shouting of a great army were heard on every side, as if there was an attack being made on the dun.

It was bright-faced Geanann, son of Cathbad, was keeping a watch on Cuchulain that day, and he saw him sit up and look out on the lawn, and redness and shame came on his face, when he saw, as he thought, two armies fighting one another, and he put out his hand as if to take his sword, but Geanann threw his two arms about him and hindered him, and told him there was nothing before him but witchcraft and enchantment, and the appearance of fighting made up by the children of Calatin to bring him out to his death. And Cathbad and all the learned men came then and told him the same thing. But after all that, it was hardly they were able to hold him back and to persuade him.

The next day Cathbad himself came to keep a watch on him with the rest, and after a while the noise of shouting began again, and for all they could do, Cuchulain went and looked out at the window. And the first thing he thought he saw was the army of Ireland standing there upon the plain. And then he thought he saw Gradh, son of Lir, standing there; and after that he thought he heard the harp of the son of Meardha playing the sweet music of the Sidhe, and he knew when he heard those sounds that his time was come, and that his courage and his strength would soon be made an end of. And then one of the daughters of Calatin took the appearance of a crow, and came flying over him and saying mocking words, and she bade him go out and save his own house and his lands from the enemies that were destroying them. And though Cuchulain knew well by this time it was witchcraft was being worked against him, he was as ready as before to rush out when he heard the sounds and the shouting of battle ; and there came trouble and confusion on his mind with the noise of striking and of fighting, and with the sweet sounds of the harp of the Sidhe. But Cathbad did his best with him, and it is what he told him, that if he would but stop quiet for another three days in Emain, the power of the enchantments would be broken, and Conall Cearnach would have come to his help, and he could go out again, and the whole world would be full of his name and of his lasting victories.

And the women of Emain and the musicians closed round him, and they sang sweet songs, and led away his mind from what he had heard, until the day drew to a close.

And on the morning of the morrow, Conchubar called for Cathbad and Bright-Faced Geanann, and the rest of the Druids. And Emer came along with them, and Celthair's daughter, Niamh, that Cuchulain loved, and the rest of the women of the House of the Red Branch. And Conchubar asked them in what way they could best keep a watch on Cuchulain through the day. " We do not know that," they said. " I will tell you what is best to do," said Conchubar then. " Bring him away with you to Glean-na-Bodhar, the Deaf Valley. For if all the men of Ireland were letting out shouts and cries of war around it, no one that would be in that valley would hear any sound at all. Bring Cuchulain there, then," he said, " and keep him there with you till their enchantments will be spent, and till Conall Cearnach will come to his help out of the island of Leodus." " King," said Niamh, " we were asking him and persuading him all through yesterday to go to that valley, but he would not go there, for all I myself or the rest of the women of Ireland could say. And let you yourself go to him now," she said, " with Cathbad, and Geanann, and the poets, and with Emer, and let you bring him into that valley, and let there be music and pleasantness made about him there, the way he will not hear the shouts and the mocking words of the children of Calatin." It is not I will go with him," said Emer, " but let Niamh go, and my blessing with her, for it will be hard for him to refuse her." So they agreed to that, and they went to where Cuchulain was, and Conchubar's harper, Cobhtach, went along with them, making sweet music. Then Cathbad went out to Cuchulain where he was lying on the bed, and he began to ask him and to persuade him. "Dear son," he said, "come with me to-day to use the feast I am making, and all the women and the poets will come with us. And there are bonds on you not to refuse my feast." " My grief for that," said Cuchulain. " This is no fit time for me to be feasting and making merry, and the four provinces of Ireland burning and destroying Ulster, and the men of Ulster in their weakness, and Conall away, and the men of Ireland putting insults on me and reproaches, and saying I have run away before them. And but for yourself and Conchubar," he said, " and for Geanann and Amergin, I would fall on them and scatter them, that their dead would be more than their living." Then all the women persuaded him, and Emer spoke to him, and it is what she said : "Little Hound, I never hindered you until this hour from any deed or any adventure you had a mind for. So now, for my sake, my choice sweetheart, my first love and first darling of the men of the world, go with Cathbad and with Geanann, with Niamh and with the poets, to share Cathbad's feast."

Then Niamh went over to him and gave him three fond, loving kisses ; and then they all rose up, and he rose along with them, heavy and sorrowful, and in that way he went in their company into Glean-na-Bodhar. And when they came into it, he said : " My grief ! I ever to have come here, and I never came to any place I liked less than this : for now the men of Ireland will be saying it was to escape them I came here." "You gave me your word," said Niamh, "you would not go out to meet the men of Ireland without leave from me." If I gave it," said Cuchulain, "it is right for me to hold to it."

Their chariots were unyoked then, and the Grey of Macha and the Black Sainglain were let loose to graze in the valley, and they all went to the house Cathbad had made ready. And there was a great feast laid out, and Cuchulain was put in the chief place, and to his right hand were Cathbad and Geanann and the poets, and on the left was Niamh, daughter of Celthair, with the women. And opposite them were the musicians and the reciters. And then they all took to feasting and drinking and to games, and they made a great show of mirth and pleasantness before Cuchulain.

But as to the three deformed, one-eyed children of Calatin, they came quickly and lightly, the way they had come on the other days, to the lawn at Emain, to the place where they had got sight of Cuchulain in the house. And when they did not see him there, they searched through the whole of Emain, but when they did not find him with Conchubar, or with the men of the Red Branch, there was great wonder on them. And then they began to think it was Cathbad was hiding him from them, and they rose up high in the air, on a blast of moaning wind they made by their enchantments, and on it they went over the whole province, searching out every wood and valley, every cave and secret path. But they found nothing, till at last they came over Glean-na-Bodhar, and there in the middle of the valley they saw the Grey of Macha and the Black Sainglain and Laeg, son of Riangabra, beside them.

They knew then that Cuchulain must be in the valley, and presently they heard the sounds of music and of laughter and of women's voices, where all the people in the feasting-house were trying their best to raise the cloud and the heaviness off Cuchulain's mind.

Then the children of Calatin came down into the valley, and the same way as before they took thistle-stalks and little fuzz-balls and withered leaves, and put on them the appearance of troops of armed men, so that there seemed to be no hill or no place outside the whole valley but was filled with battalions, coming hundred by hundred. And the air was all filled with sounds of battle and shouts, and of trumpets and dreadful laughter, and the cries of wounded men. And there seemed to be fires in the country about, and a noise of the crying of women. And great dread came on all that heard that outcry, both men and women, and dogs of every kind.

But when the women that were with Cuchulain heard those shouts, they shouted back again and raised their voices, but with all they could do, they did not keep the outcry from reaching to Cuchulain. "My grief!" he said, " I hear the shouts of the men of Ireland that are spoiling the whole of the province; my fame is at an end, my great name is gone from me, Ulster is put down for ever." " Let the noise pass by," said Cathbad; "it is only the noise made by the children of Calatin, that want to draw you out from where you are, to make an end of you. Stop here with us now, and put the trouble off your mind."

Cuchulain stayed quiet then, but the children of Calatin went on a long time filling the air with battle noises. But they tired of it at last, for they saw that Cathbad and the women were too much for them.

Then anger came on Badb, one of Calatin's daughters, and she said: "Go on now, making sounds of fighting in the air, and I myself will go into the valley; for even if I get my death by it, I will speak with Cuchulain."

With that, she went on in the madness of her anger

to the very house where the feast was going on, and there she took the appearance of a woman of Niamh's women, and she beckoned Niamh out to speak with her.

So Niamh came out, thinking she had news to give her, and a good many of the other women of Emain with her, and Badb bade them follow her. And she led them a long way down the valley, and then by her enchantments she raised a thick mist between them and the house, so that they could not find their way, but were astray in the valley, not knowing where they were.

Then she went back to the feasting-house, and she put on herself the appearance of Niamh, and she came in to where Cuchulain was and called out: "Rise up, Cuchulain; Dundealgan is burned, Muirthemne is destroyed, and Conaille Muirthemne. The whole province is trampled down by the men of Ireland. And it is on myself the blame will be laid," she said, "and all Ulster will say that I hindered you, and kept you back from going out to check the army, and to get satisfaction from the men of Ireland. And it is from Conchubar himself I will get my death on account of that," she said. For she knew Cuchulain had given Niamh his promise that without leave from her, he would not go out to face the men of Ireland.

"My grief!" said Cuchulain then, "it is hard to trust in women. For I thought," he said, "that you would not have given me that leave for the whole riches of the world. But since you yourself give me leave to go out and face the men of Ireland, I will do it." And with that he rose up to go out. And as he rose up, he threw his cloak about him, and his foot caught in the cloak, and the gold brooch that was in the cloak fell on his foot and pierced it. "Truly the brooch is a friend that gives me a warning," said Cuchulain.

He went out then, and he bade Laeg to yoke the horses and to make ready the chariot. And Cathbad, and Geanann, and the women followed him out, and took hold of him, but they were not able to stop him. For the cries of battle were still in the air, and he thought he saw a great army standing on the lawn at Emain, and the whole plain filled up and crowded with troops and bands of men, with horses and arms and armour, and he thought he heard great shouts, and that he saw all Conchubar's city burning, and all the hills round about Emain full of things brought away, and he thought he saw Emer's sunny house thrown down, and the House of the Red Branch in one blaze, and all Emain under fire and smoke. And Cathbad tried to quiet him. "Dear son," he said, "for this day only, follow my advice, and do not go out against the men of Ireland, and I will be able to save you from all the enchantments of the children of Calatin." But Cuchulain said: "Dear master, there is no reason for me to care for my life from this out, for my time is at an end, and Niamh has given me leave to go and face the men of Ireland." And then Niamh herself came up to him and said: "My grief! my little Hound, I would never have given you that leave for all the riches of the world; and it was not I that gave you leave, but Badb, the daughter of Calatin, that took my shape on her. And stay with me now," she said, "my friend, my darling." But Cuchulain would not believe her, and he bade Laeg yoke the chariot, and put his arms in order. Laeg went to do that, but indeed that time above all others he had no mind for the work. And when he shook the bridles towards the horses as he was used to do, they went away from him; and the Grey of Macha would not let him come near him at all. "Truly," said Laeg, "this is a warning of some bad thing. And indeed, my life," he said to the Grey, "it is seldom you would not come to meet the bridle and to meet myself, up to this day." Then he went to Cuchulain and said: "I swear by the gods my people swear by, that if all the men in the province of Ulster were round about the Grey of Macha, they would not be able to bring him as far as the chariot, and I never refused you up to this," he said, " and come out now and speak to the Grey yourself."

So Cuchulain went out, and the horse turned his left side three times to his master. Then he reproached the horse. "You were not used," he said, "to behave like that to me." Then the Grey of Macha came up to him and he let big, round tears of blood fall on Cuchulain's feet.

Then the chariot was yoked; and it was the Morrigu had unyoked it and had broken it the night before, for she did not like Cuchulain to go out and to get his death in the battle. And Cuchulain set out and came to Emain, and to the house where Emer was, and she came out and bade him come down from his chariot. " I will not," he said, " until I go first to Muirthemne, to attack the four great provinces of Ireland, and to avenge all the hurts and the insults they have put on me, and on Ulster, for I have seen their gatherings and their armies." " Those were made up by enchantments," said Emer. " I tell you, woman," he said, "and I swear by my word, I will never come back here until I have made an attack upon them in their camp."

Then he turned his chariot towards the south, by the road of Meadhon Luachair, and Levarcham cried out after him, and the three times fifty queens that were in Emain Macha, and that loved him, cried out upon him miserably, and struck their hands together, for they knew he would not come back to them again.

XX

DEATH OF CUCHULAIN

CUCHULAIN went on then to the house of his mother, Dechtire, to bid her farewell. And she came out on the lawn to meet him, for she knew well he was going out to face the men of Ireland, and she brought out wine in a vessel to him, as her custom was when he passed that way. But when he took the vessel in his hand, it was red blood that was in it. "My grief!" he said, "my mother Dechtire, it is no wonder others to forsake me, when you yourself offer me a drink of blood." Then she filled the vessel a second, and a third time, and each time when she gave it to him, there was nothing in it but blood.

Then anger came on Cuchulain, and he dashed the vessel against a rock, and broke it, and he said: "The fault is not in yourself, my mother Dechtire, but my luck is turned against me, and my life is near its end, and I will not come back alive this time from facing the men of Ireland." Then Dechtire tried hard to persuade him to go back and to wait till he would have the help of Conall. "I will not wait," he said, "for anything you can say; for I would not give up my great name and my courage for all the riches of the world. And from the day I first took arms till this day, I have never drawn back from a fight or a battle. And it is not now I will begin to draw back," he said, "for a great name outlasts life."

Then he went on his way, and Cathbad, that had followed him, went with him. And presently they came to a ford, and there they saw a young girl, thin and white-skinned and having yellow hair, washing and ever washing, and wringing out clothing that was stained crimson red, and she crying and keening all the time. "Little Hound," said Cathbad, "do you see what it is that young girl is doing? It is your red clothes she is washing, and crying as she washes, because she knows you are going to your death against Maeve's great army. And take the warning now and turn back again." "Dear master," said Cuchulain, "you have followed me far enough; for I will not turn back from my vengeance on the men of Ireland that are come to burn and to destroy my house and my country. And what is it to me, the woman of the Sidhe to be washing red clothing for me? It is not long till there will be clothing enough, and armour and arms, lying soaked in pools of blood, by my own sword and my spear. And if you are sorry and loth to let me go into the fight, I am glad and ready enough myself to go into it, though I know as well as you yourself I must fall in it. Do not be hindering me any more, then," he said, "for, if I stay or if I go, death will meet me all the same. But go now to Emain, to Conchubar and to Emer, and bring them life and health from me, for I will never go back to meet them again. It is my grief and my wound, I to part from them! And O Laeg!" he said, "we are going away under trouble and under darkness from Emer now, as it is often we came back to her with gladness out of strange places and far countries."

Then Cathbad left him, and he went on his way. And after a while he saw three hags, and they blind of the left eye, before him in the road, and they having a venomous hound they were cooking with charms on rods of the rowan tree. And he was going by them, for he knew it was not for his good they were there.

But one of the hags called to him : " Stop a while with us, Cuchulain." " I will not stop with you," said Cuchulain. " That is because we have nothing better than a dog to give you," said the hag. " If we had a grand, big cooking-hearth, you would stop and visit us ; but because it is only a little we have to offer you, you will not stop. But he that will not show respect for the small, though he is great, he will get no respect himself."

Then he went over to her, and she gave him the shoulder-blade of the hound out of her left hand, and he ate it out of his left hand. And he put it down on his left thigh, and the hand that took it was struck down, and the thigh he put it on was struck through and through, so that the strength that was in them before left them.

Then he went down the road of Meadhon-Luachair, by Slieve Fuad, and his enemy, Erc, son of Cairbre, saw him in the chariot, and his sword shining red in his hand, and the light of his courage plain upon him, and his hair spread out like threads of gold that change their colour on the edge of the anvil under the smith's hand, and the Crow of Battle in the air over his head.

" Cuchulain is coming at us," said Erc to the men of Ireland, " and let us be ready for him." So they made a fence of shields linked together, and Erc put a couple of the men that were strongest here and there, to let on to be fighting one another, that they might call Cuchulain to them ; and he put a Druid with every couple of them, and he bid the Druid to ask Cuchulain's spears of him, for it would be hard for him to refuse a Druid. For it was in the prophecy of the children of Calatin that a king would be killed by each one of those spears in that battle.

And he bid the men of Ireland to give out shouts, and Cuchulain came against them in his chariot, doing his three thunder feats, and he used his spear and his sword in such a way, that their heads, and their hands, and their feet, and their bones, were scattered through the plain of Muirthemne, like the sands on the shore, like the stars in the sky, like the dew in May, like snow-flakes and hailstones, like leaves of the trees, like buttercups in a meadow, like grass under the feet of cattle on a fine summer day. It is red that plain was with the slaughter Cuchulain made when he came crashing over it.

Then he saw one of the men that was put to quarrel with the other, and the Druid called to him to come and hinder them, and Cuchulain leaped towards them. "Your spear to me," cried the Druid. "I swear by the oath of my people," said Cuchulain, "you are not so much in want of it as I am in want of it myself. The men of Ireland are upon me," he said, "and I am upon them." "I will put a bad name on you if you refuse it to me," said the Druid. "There was never a bad name put on me yet, on account of any refusal of mine," said Cuchulain, and with that he threw the spear at him, and it went through his head, and it killed the men that were on the other side of him.

Then Cuchulain drove through the host, and Lugaid, son of Curoi, got the spear. "Who is it will fall by this spear, children of Calatin?" said Lugaid. "A king will fall by it," said they. Then Lugaid threw the spear at Cuchulain's chariot, and it went through and hit the driver, Laeg, son of Riangabra, and he fell back, and his bowels came out on the cushions of the chariot. "My grief!" said Laeg, "it is hard I am wounded." Then Cuchulain drew the spear out, and Laeg said his farewell to him, and Cuchulain said: "To-day I will be a fighter and a chariot-driver as well."

Then he saw the other two men that were put to quarrel with one another, and one of them called out it would be a great shame for him not to give him his help. Then Cuchulain leaped towards them. " Your spear to me, Cuchulain," said the Druid. " I swear by the oath my people swear by," said he, " you are not in such want of the spear as I am myself, for it is by my courage, and by my arms, that I have to drive out the four provinces of Ireland that are sweeping over Muirthemne to-day." " I will put a bad name upon you," said the Druid. " I am not bound to give more than one gift in the day, and I have paid what is due to my name already," said Cuchulain. Then the Druid said : " I will put a bad name on the province of Ulster, because of your refusal."

" Ulster was never dispraised yet for any refusal of mine," said Cuchulain, " or for anything I did unworthily. Though little of my life should be left to me, Ulster will not be reproached for me to-day." With that he threw his spear at him, and it went through his head, and through the heads of the nine men that were behind him, and Cuchulain went through the host as he did before.

Then Erc, son of Cairbre Niafer, took up his spear. " Who will fall by this ? " he asked the children of Calatin. " A king will fall by it," they said. " I heard you say the same thing of the spear that Lugaid threw a while ago," said Erc. " That is true," said they, " and the king of the chariot-drivers of Ireland fell by it, Cuchulain's driver Laeg, son of Riangabra."

With that, Erc threw the spear, and it went through the Grey of Macha. Cuchulain drew the spear out, and they said farewell to one another. And then the Grey went away from him, with half his harness hanging from his neck, and he went into Glas-linn, the grey pool in Slieve Fuad.

Then Cuchulain drove through the host, and he saw the third couple disputing together, and he went between them as he did before. And the Druid asked his spear of him, but he refused him. " I will put a bad name on you," said the Druid. " I have paid what is due to my name to-day," said he ; " my honour does not bind me to give more than one request in a day." " I will put a bad name upon Ulster because of your refusal." " I have paid what is due for the honour of Ulster," said Cuchulain. " Then I will put a bad name on your kindred," said the Druid. " The news that I have been given a bad name shall never go back to that place I am never to go back to myself ; for it is little of my life that is left to me," said Cuchulain. With that he threw the spear at him, and it went through him, and through the heads of the men that were along with him.

" You do your kindness unkindly, Cuchulain," said the Druid, as he fell. Then Cuchulain drove for the last time through the host, and Lugaid took the spear, and he said : " Who will fall by this spear, children of Calatin ? " " A king will fall by it," said they. " I heard you saying that a king would fall by the spear Erc threw a while ago." " That is true," they said, " and the Grey of Macha fell by it, that was the king of the horses of Ireland."

Then Lugaid threw the spear, and it went through and through Cuchulain's body, and he knew he had got his deadly wound ; and his bowels came out on the cushions of the chariot, and his only horse went away from him, the Black Sainglain, with half the harness hanging from his neck, and left his master, the king of the heroes of Ireland, to die upon the plain of Muirthemne.

Then Cuchulain said : " There is great desire on me to go to that lake beyond, and to get a drink from it."

" We will give you leave to do that," they said, " if you will come back to us after."

" I will bid you come for me if I am not able to come back myself," said Cuchulain.

Then he gathered up his bowels into his body, and he went down to the lake. He drank a drink, and he washed himself, and he turned back again to his death. and he called to his enemies to come and meet him.

There was a pillar-stone west of the lake, and his eye lit on it, and he went to the pillar-stone, and he tied himself to it with his breast-belt, the way he would not meet his death lying down, but would meet it standing up. Then his enemies came round about him, but they were in dread of going close to him, for they were not sure but he might be still alive.

" It is a great shame for you," said Erc, son of Cairbre, "not to strike the head off that man, in revenge for his striking the head off my father."

Then the Grey of Macha came back to defend Cuchulain as long as there was life in him, and the hero-light was shining above him. And the Grey of Macha made three attacks against them, and he killed fifty men with his teeth, and thirty with each of his hoofs. So there is a saying : " It is not sharper work than this was done by the Grey of Macha, the time of Cuchulain's death."

Then a bird came and settled on his shoulder. " It is not on that pillar birds were used to settle," said Erc.

Then Lugaid came and lifted up Cuchulain's hair from his shoulders, and struck his head off, and the men of Ireland gave three great heavy shouts, and the sword fell from Cuchulain's hand, and as it fell, it struck off Lugaid's right hand, so that it fell to the ground. Then they cut off Cuchulain's hand, in satisfaction for it, and then the light faded away from about Cuchulain's head, and left it as pale as the snow of a single night. Then all the men of Ireland said that as it was Maeve had gathered the army, it would be right for her to bring away the head to Cruachan. " I will not bring it with me; it is for Lugaid that struck it off to bring it with him," said Maeve. And then Lugaid and his men went away, and they brought away Cuchulain's head and his

right hand with them, and they went south, towards tne
Lifé river.

At that time the army of Ulster was gathering to
attack its enemies, and Conall was out before them,
and he met the Grey of Macha, and his share of blood
dripping from him. And then he knew that Cuchulain
was dead, and himself and the Grey of Macha went
looking for Cuchulain's body. And when they saw his
body at the pillar-stone, the Grey of Macha went and
laid his head in Cuchulain's breast: "That body is a
heavy care to the Grey of Macha," said Conall.

Then Conall went after the army, thinking in his own
mind what way he could get satisfaction for Cuchulain's
death. For it was a promise between himself and
Cuchulain that whichever of them would be killed the
first, the other would get satisfaction for his death.

"And if I am the first that is killed," said Cuchulain
at that time, "how long will it be before you get satisfaction for me?"

"Before the evening of the same day," said Conall, "I
will have got satisfaction for you. And if it is I that
will die before you," he said, "how long will it be before
you get satisfaction for me?"

"Your share of blood will not be cold on the ground,"
said Cuchulain, "when I will have got satisfaction for
you."

So Conall followed after Lugaid to the river Lifé.

Lugaid was going down to bathe in the water, but he
said to his chariot-driver: "Look out there over the
plain, for fear would any one come at us unknown."

The chariot-driver looked around him. "There is a
man coming on us," he said, "and it is in a great
hurry he is coming; and you would think he has all the
ravens in Ireland flying over his head, and there are
flakes of snow speckling the ground before him."

"It is not in friendship the man comes that is coming

like that," said Lugaid. "It is Conall Cearnach it is, with Dub-dearg, and the birds that you see after him, they are the sods the horse has scattered in the air from his hoofs, and the flakes of snow that are speckling the ground before him, they are the froth that he scatters from his mouth and from the bit of his bridle. Look again," said Lugaid, "and see what way is he coming." "It is to the ford he is coming, the same way the army passed over," said the chariot-driver. "Let him pass by us," said Lugaid, "for I have no mind to fight with him."

But when Conall came to the middle of the ford, he saw Lugaid and his chariot-driver, and he went over to them. "Welcome is the sight of a debtor's face," said Conall. "The man you owe a debt to is asking payment of you now, and I myself am that man," he said, "for the sake of my comrade, Cuchulain, that you killed. And I am standing here now, to get that debt paid."

They agreed then to fight it out on the plain of Magh Argetnas, and in the fight Conall wounded Lugaid with his spear. From that they went to a place called Ferta Lugdac. "I would like that you would give me fair play," said Lugaid. "What fair play?" said Conall Cearnach.

"That you and I should fight with one hand, said he, "for I have the use of but one hand."

"I will do that," said Conall. Then Conall's hand was bound to his side with a cord, and then they fought for a long time, and one did not get the better of the other. And when Conall was not gaining on him, his horse, Dub-dearg, that was near by, came up to Lugaid, and took a bite out of his side.

"Misfortune on me," said Lugaid, "it is not right or fair that is of you, Conall."

"It was for myself I promised to do what is right and fair," said Conall. "I made no promise for a beast, that is without training and without sense."

"It is well I know you will not leave me till you take my head, as I took Cuchulain's head from him," said Lugaid. "Take it, then, along with your own head. Put my kingdom with your kingdom, and my courage with your courage; for I would like that you would be the best champion in Ireland."

Then Conall made an end of him, and he went back, bringing Cuchulain's head along with him to the pillar-stone where his body was.

And by that time Emer had got word of all that had happened, and that her husband had got his death by the men of Ireland, and by the powers of the children of Calatin. And it was Levarcham brought her the story, for Conall Cearnach had met her on his way, and had bade her go and bring the news to Emain Macha; and there she found Emer, and she sitting in her upper room, looking over the plain for some word from the battle.

And all the women came out to meet Levarcham, and when they heard her story, they made an outcry of grief and sharp cries, with loud weeping and burning tears; and there were long dismal sounds going through Emain, and the whole country round was filled with crying. And Emer and her women went to the place where Cuchulain's body was, and they gathered round it there, and gave themselves to crying and keening.

And when Conall came back to the place, he laid the head with the body of Cuchulain, and he began to lament along with them, and it is what he said: "It is Cuchulain had prosperity on him, a root of valour from the time he was but a soft child; there never fell a better hero than the hero that fell by Lugaid of the Lands. And there are many are in want of you," he said, "and until all the chief men of Ireland have fallen by me, it is not fitting there should ever be peace.

"It is grief to me, he to have gone into the battle

without Conall being at his side; it was a pity for him to go there without my body beside his body. Och! it is he was my foster-son, and now the ravens are drinking his blood; there will not be either laughter or mirth, since the Hound has gone astray from us."

"Let us bury Cuchulain now," said Emer. "It is not right to do that," said Conall, "until I have avenged him on the men of Ireland. And it is a great shouting I hear about the plain of Muirthemne, and it is full the country is of crying after Cuchulain; and it is good at keeping the country and watching the boundaries the man was that is here before me, a cross-hacked body in a pool of blood. And it is well it pleased Lugaid, son of Curoi, to be at the killing of Cuchulain, for it was Cuchulain killed the chiefs and the children of Deaguid round Famain, son of Foraoi, and round Curoi, son of Daire himself. And this shouting has taken away my wits and my memory from me," he said, "and it is hard for me, Cuchulain not to answer these cries, and I to be without him now; for there is not a champion in Ireland that was not in dread of the sword in his hand. And it is broken in halves my heart is for my brother, and I will bring my revenge through Ireland now, and I will not leave a tribe without wounding, or true blood without spilling, and the whole world will be told of my rout to the end of life and time, until the men of Munster and Connaught and Leinster will be crying for the rising they made against him. And without the spells of the children of Calatin, the whole of them would not have been able to do him to death."

After that complaint, rage and madness came on Conall, and he went forward in his chariot to follow after the rest of the men of Ireland, the same way as he had followed after Lugaid.

And Emer took the head of Cuchulain in her hands, and she washed it clean, and put a silk cloth about it.

and she held it to her breast ; and she began to cry heavily over it, and it is what she said :

"Ochone !" said she, "it is good the beauty of this head was, though it is low this day, and it is many of the kings and princes of the world would be keening it if they knew the way it is now, and the poets and the Druids of Ireland and of Alban ; and many were the goods and the jewels and the rents and the tributes that you brought home to me from the countries of the world, with the courage and the strength of your hands !"

And she made this complaint :

"Och, head ! Ochone, O head ! you gave death to great heroes, to many hundreds ; my head will lie in the same grave, the one stone will be made for both of us

"Och, hand ! Ochone, hand that was once gentle. It is often it was put under my head ; it is dear that hand was to me !

"Dear mouth ! Ochone, kind mouth that was sweet-voiced telling stories ; since the time love first came on your face, you never refused either weak or strong !

"Dear the man, dear the man, that would kill the whole of a great host ; dear his cold bright hair, and dear his bright cheeks !

"Dear the king, dear the king, that never gave a refusal to any ; thirty days it is to-night since my body lay beside your body.

"Och, two spears ! Ochone, two spears ! Och, shield ! Och, deadly sword ! Let them be given to Conall of the battles ; there was never any wage given like that.

"I am glad, I am glad, Cuchulain of Muirthemne, I never brought red shame on your face, for any unfaithfulness against you.

"Happy are they, happy are they, who will never

hear the cuckoo again for ever, now that the Hound has died from us.

"I am carried away like a branch on the stream; I will not bind up my hair to-day. From this day I have nothing to say that is better than Ochone!"

And then she said: "It is long that it was showed to me in a vision of the night, that Cuchulain would fall by the men of Ireland, and it appeared to me Dundealgan to be falling to the ground, and his shield to be split from lip to border, and his sword and his spears broken in the middle, and I saw Conall doing deeds of death before me, and myself and yourself in the one death. And oh! my love," she said, "we were often in one another's company, and it was happy for us; for if the world had been searched from the rising of the sun to sunset, the like would never have been found in one place, of the Black Sainglain and the Grey of Macha, and Laeg the chariot-driver, and myself and Cuchulain. And it is breaking my heart is in my body, to be listening to the pity and the sorrowing of women and men, and the harsh crying of the young men of Ulster keening Cuchulain, and Ulster to be in its weakness, and without strength to revenge itself upon the men of Ireland."

And after she had made that complaint, she brought Cuchulain's body to Dundealgan; and they all cried and keened about him until such time as Conall Cearnach came back from making his red rout through the army of the men of Ireland.

For he was not satisfied to make a slaughter of the men of Munster and Connaught, without reddening his hand in the blood of the men of Leinster as well.

And when he had done that, he came to Dundealgan, and his men along with him, but they made no rejoicing when they went back that time. And he brought the heads of the men of Ireland along with him in a gad, and he laid them out on the green lawn, and the people of the house gave three great shouts when they saw the heads.

And Emer came out, and when she saw Conall Cearnach, she said: "My great esteem and my welcome before you, king of heroes, and may your many wounds not be your death; for you have avenged the treachery done on Ulster, and now what you have to do is to make our grave, and to lay us together in the grave, for I will not live after Cuchulain.

"And tell me, Conall," she said, "whose are those heads all around on the lawn, and which of the great men of Ireland did they belong to?"

And she was asking, and Conall was answering, and it is what she said:

"Tell me, Conall, whose are those heads, for surely you have reddened your arms with them. Tell me the names of the men whose heads are there upon the ground."

And Conall said: "Daughter of Forgall of the Horses, young Emer of the sweet words, it is in revenge for the Hound of Feats I brought these heads here from the south."

"Whose is the great black head, with the smooth cheek redder than a rose; it is at the far end, on the left side, the head that has not changed its colour?"

"It is the head of the king of Meath, Erc, son of Cairbre of Swift Horses; I brought his head with me from far off, in revenge for my own foster-son."

"Whose is that head there before me, with soft hair, with smooth eyebrows, its eyes like ice, its teeth like blossoms; that head is more beautiful in shape than the others?"

"A son of Maeve; a destroyer of harbours, yellow-haired Maine, man of horses; I left his body without a head; all his people fell by my hand."

"O great Conall, who did not fail us, whose head is this you hold in your hand? Since the Hound of Feats is not living, what do you bring in satisfaction for his head?"

"The head of the son of Fergus of the Horses, a destroyer in every battle-field, my sister's son of the narrow tower; I have struck his head from his body."

"Whose is that head to the west, with fair hair, the head that is spoiled with grief? I used to know his voice; I was for a while his friend."

"That is he that struck down the Hound, Lugaid, son of Curoi of the Rhymes. His body was laid out straight and fair, I struck his head off afterwards."

"Whose are those two heads farther out, great Conall of good judgment? For the sake of your friendship, do not hide the names of the men put down by your arms."

"The heads of Laigaire and Clar Cuilt, two men that fell by my wounds. It was they wounded faithful Cuchulain; I made my weapons red in their blood."

"Whose are those heads farther to the east, great Conall of bright deeds? The hair of the two is of the one colour; their cheeks are redder than a calf's blood."

"Brave Cullain and hardy Cunlaid, two that were used to overcome in their anger. There to the east, Emer, are their heads; I left their bodies in a red pool."

"Whose are those three heads with evil looks I see before me to the north? Their faces blue, their hair black; even hard Conall's eye turns from them."

"Three of the enemies of the Hound, daughters of Calatin, wise in enchantments; they are the three witches killed by me, their weapons in their hands."

'O great Conall, father of kings, whose is that head that would overcome in the battle? His bushy hair is gold-yellow; his head-dress is smooth and white like silver."

"It is the head of the son of Red-Haired Ross, son of Necht Min, that died by my strength. This, Emer, is his head; the high king of Leinster of Speckled Swords."

"O great Conall, change the story. How many of the men that harmed him fell by your hand that does not fail, in satisfaction for the head of Cuchulain?"

"It is what I say, ten and seven scores of hundreds is the number that fell, back to back, by the anger of my hard sword and of my people."

"O Conall, what way are they, the women of Ireland, after the Hound? Are they mourning the son of Sualtim? are they showing respect through their grief?"

"O Emer, what shall I do without my Cuchulain, my fine nurseling, going in and out from me, to-night?"

"O Conall, lift me to the grave. Raise my stone over the grave of the Hound; since it is through grief for him I go to death, lay my mouth to the mouth of Cuchulain.

"I am Emer of the Fair Form; there is no more vengeance for me to find; I have no love for any man. It is sorrowful my stay is after the Hound."

And after that Emer bade Conall to make a wide, very deep grave for Cuchulain; and she laid herself down beside her gentle comrade, and she put her mouth to his mouth, and she said: "Love of my life, my friend, my sweetheart, my one choice of the men of the earth, many is the woman, wed or unwed, envied me till to-day: and now I will not stay living after you."

And her life went out from her, and she herself and Cuchulain were laid in the one grave by Conall. And he raised the one stone over them, and he wrote their names in Ogham, and he himself and all the men of Ulster keened them.

But the three times fifty queens that loved Cuchulain saw him appear in his Druid chariot, going through Emain Macha; and they could hear him singing the music of the Sidhe.

THE END

THE DEATH OF CUCHULAIN.

NOTE BY W. B. YEATS ON THE CONVER-SATION OF CUCHULAIN AND EMER.
(Page 367).

THIS conversation, so full of strange mythological information, is an example of the poet speech of ancient Ireland. One comes upon this speech here and there in other stories and poems. One finds it in the poem attributed to Ailbhe, daughter of Cormac Mac Art, and quoted by O'Curry in " MS. Materials," of which one verse is an allusion to a story given in Lady Gregory's book:

> " The apple tree of high Aillinn,
> The yew of Baile of little land,
> Though they are put into lays,
> Rough people do not understand them."

One finds it too in the poems which Brian, Son of Tuireann, chanted when he did not wish to be wholly understood. "That is a good poem, but I do not understand a word of its meaning," said the kings before whom he chanted ; but his obscurity was more in a roundabout way of speaking than in mythological allusions. There is a description of a banquet, quoted by Professor Kuno Meyer, where hens' eggs are spoken of as " gravel of Glenn Ai," and leek, as " a tear of a fair woman," and some eatable sea-weed, dulse, perhaps, as a " net of the plains of Rein "—that is to say, of the sea—and so on. He quotes also a poem that calls the sallow, " the strength of bees," and the hawthorn " the barking of hounds," and the gooseberry bush " the sweetest of trees," and the yew, " the oldest of trees."

This poet speech somewhat resembles the Icelandic court poetry, as it is called, which certainly required alike for the writing and understanding of it a great traditional culture. Its descriptions of shields and tapestry, and its praises of Kings, that were first written, it seems, about the tenth century, depended for their effects on just this heaping up of mythological allusions, and the "Eddas" were written to be a granary for the makers of such poems. But by the fourteenth and fifteenth centuries they have come to be as irritating to the new Christian poets and writers who stood outside their tradition, as are the more esoteric kinds of modern verse to unlettered readers. They were called "obscure," and "speaking in riddles," and the like.

It has sometimes been thought that the Irish poet speech was indeed but a copy of this court poetry, but Professor York Powell contradicts this, and thinks it is not unlikely that the Irish poems influenced the Icelandic, and made them more mythological and obscure.

I am not scholar enough to judge the Scandinavian verse, but the Irish poet speech seems to me at worst an over-abundance of the esoterism which is an essential element in all admirable literature, and I think it a folly to make light of it, as a recent writer has done. Even now, verse no less full of symbol and myth seems to me as legitimate as, let us say, a religious picture full of symbolic detail, or the symbolic ornament of a Cathedral.

Nash's—

> "Brightness falls from the air,
> Queens have died young and fair,
> Dust hath closed Helen's eye"—

must seem as empty as a Scald's song, or the talk of Cuchulain and Emer, to one who has never heard of Helen, or even to one who did not fall in love with her when he was a young man. And if we were not accustomed to be stirred by Greek myth, even without remembering it very fully, "Berenice's ever burning hair' would not stir the blood, and especially if it were put into some foreign tongue, losing those resounding "b's" on the way.

The mythological events Cuchulain speaks of give mystery to the scenery of the tales, and when they are connected with the battle of Magh Tuireadh, the most tremendous of mythological battles, or anything else we know much about, they are full of poetic meaning or historical interest. The hills that had the shape of a sow's back at the coming of the Children of Miled, remind one of Borlase's conviction that the pig was the symbol of the mythological ancestry of the Firbolg, which the Children of Miled were to bring into subjection, and of his suggestion that the magical pigs that Maeve numbered were some Firbolg tribe that Maeve put down in war. And everywhere that esoteric speech brings the odour of the wild woods into our nostrils.

The earlier we get, the more copious does this traditional and symbolical element in literature become. Till Greece and Rome created a new culture, a sense of the importance of man, all that we understand by humanism, nobody wrote history, nobody described anything as we understand description. One called up the image of a thing by comparing it with something else, and partly because one was less interested in man, who did not seem to be important, than in divine revelations, in changes among the heavens and the gods, which can hardly be expressed at all, and only by myth, by symbol, by enigma. One was always losing oneself in the unknown, and rushing to the limits of the world. Imagination was all in all. Is not poetry, when all is said, but a little of this habit of mind caught as in the beryl stone of a Wizard?

NOTES

THE Irish text, from which the greater number of the stories in this book have been taken, has been published either in *Irische Texte* or the *Revue Celtique*, or by O'Curry in *Atlantis* and elsewhere, and I have worked from this text, comparing it with the translations that have been already made. In some cases, as in the greater part of "The War for the Bull of Cuailgne," a very small part of the Irish text has as yet been printed, and I have had to work by comparing and piecing together various translations.

I have had to put a connecting sentence of my own here and there, and I have condensed many passages, and I have sometimes tried to give the meaning of a formula that has lost its old meaning. Thus I have exchanged for the grotesque accounts of Cuchulain's distortion—which no doubt merely meant that in time of great strain or anger he had more than human strength—the more simple formula that his appearance changed to the appearance of a god. In the same way, I have left out Levarcham's distortion, which was the recognised way of saying she was a swift messenger.

As to the date of the stories, I cannot do better than quote from Mr Alfred Nutt's "Cuchulain, the Irish Achilles":—

"It suffices to say that we possess a MS. literature of which Cuchulain and his contemporaries are the subject, the extent of which may be roughly reckoned at 2000 8vo pages. The great bulk of this is contained in MSS. which are older than the twelfth century, or which demonstrably are copied from pre-twelfth-century MSS.; where post-twelfth-century versions alone remain, the story itself is nearly always known from earlier sources; in fact, there is hardly a single scene or incident in the whole cycle which has reached us only in MSS. of the thirteenth and following centuries. At the same time a not inconsiderable portion of the cycle comes before us altered in language, and to some extent in content, style of narrative, and characterisation, showing that the saga as a whole remained a living element of Irish culture and participated in the accidents of its evolution.

"The great bulk of this literature is, as I have said, certainly older than the twelfth century; but we can carry it back much farther, apart from any considerations based upon the subject-matter. Arguments of a nature purely philological, based upon the language of the texts, or critical, based upon the relations of the various MSS. to each other, not only allow, but compel us to date the *redaction* of the principal Cuchulain stories, substantially in the form under which they have survived, back to the seventh to ninth centuries. Whether or no they are older yet, is a question that cannot be answered without preliminary examination of the subject-matter. In the meantime it is something to know that the Cuchulain stories were put into permanent literary form at about the same date as Beowulf, some 100 to 250 years before the Scandinavian mythology crystallised into its present form, at least 200 years before the oldest Charlemagne romances, and probably 300 years before the earliest draft of the Nibelungenlied. Irish is the most ancient *vernacular* literature of modern Europe, a fact which of itself commends it to the attention of the student."

A critical account of this and the other Irish cycles is also given in Dr Douglas Hyde's " Literary History of Ireland."

The Tuatha de Danaan, or the Sidhe, so often mentioned, were the divine race, the people of the Gods of Dana, who conquered the Fomor, the powers of darkness and their helpers the Firbolgs, in the battle of Magh Tuireadh, and possessed Ireland until they were in their turn conquered by the children of the Gael, under the leadership of the Sons of Miled. Then they became invisible, and made their home in hills and raths.

The Morrigu was their goddess of battle, and Angus Og, Son of the Dagda, their god of youth and love, and Lugh, the Master of many Arts, their Hermes, their Apollo, and Manannan, Son of Lir, their Sea-God, or, as some say, the sea itself.

The spelling of Irish names for English readers is always a difficulty. I have not gone by any fixed rule, but have taken the spelling of names from various good authorities. As to pronunciation, the modern is generally used, but we know so little what the ancient pronunciation was, that we are left some freedom, and some words have taken a shape from English-speaking generations, that it is hard to change. Teamhair, for instance, has become Tara through a mistaken use of the genitive ; Muirthemne is called by Irish speakers " Mur-hev-na," but others call it Muir'them-mé, and I am inclined to prefer this for the charm of its sound, and I do not see any stronger reason against using it than against sounding as we do the "s" in Paris. After all, it has not yet been definitely settled whether Trafalgar is to be spoken in the Spanish or the English way; English poets have given it one or the other emphasis. This is the approximate pronunciation of some of the more difficult names :—

Aedh	Ae (rhyming to "day").
Aoife	Eefa.
Badb	Bibe (as "jibe").
Bodb	Bove.
Cliodna	Cleevna.
Cobhthach	Cowhach.
Conchubar	Conachoor.
Cuailgne	Cooley.
Cuchulain	Cuhoolin, or Cu-hullin.
Dun Sobairce	Dom Sĕvĕrka.
Emain	Avvin.
Eochaid	Yohee.
Eocho	Yūchŏ.
Eoghan	Owen.
Fernmaighe	Farney.
Glen na (m) Bodhar	Glen na Mower (as "bower").
Inbhir	Inver.
Lugh	Loo.
Magh Tuireadh	Moytirra.
Muirthemne	Mŭr-hĕv-na.
Niamh	Nee-av.
Rudraige	Rury.
Sidhe	Shee.
Slieve Suidhe Laighen	Slieve see lihon.
Suibnes	Sivness.
Teamhair	T'yower.
Tuathmumain	Too-moon.

I give below some names of places that can still be identified—

Ard Inver	Mouth of the Avoca, Co. Wicklow.
Argatros	On the Nore, Co. Kilkenny.
Ath Cliath	Dublin.
Ath Firdiadh	(Ferdiad's Ford) Ardee.
Ath Truim	Trim.
Beinn Edair	Howth.
Boinne River	The Boyne.
Bregia	Bray.

Bri Leith	. .	In Co. Longford.
Brug na Boinne	. .	On the Boyne.
Carraige	. .	Kerry.
Cerna	. .	{ Probably River Muilchean, Co. Limerick.
Clarthe	. .	Clara, near Mullingar.
Cleitech	. .	On the Boyne.
Conaille-Muirthemne	.	{ Between the Cooley Mountains and the Boyne.
Cruachan	. .	In Co. Roscommon.
Cuailgne	. .	Cooley, Co. Louth.
Cuilsilinne	.	South-west of Kells.
Drium Criadh	. .	Drumcree, Co. Westmeath.
Dundealgan	. .	Dundalk.
Dun Rudraige	. .	Dundrum, Co. Down.
Dun Scathach	. .	Isle of Skye.
Dun Sobairce	. .	Dunseverick, Co. Antrim.
Emain Macha	. .	{ Navan fort, near Armagh. A description and plan of Emain Macha are given by D'Arbois de Jubainville in *Revue Celtique*, vol. xvi.
Esro	. .	Ballyshannon.
Fearbile	. .	In Co. Westmeath.
Femen	. .	At Slieve na Man, Co. Tipperary.
Gairech and Ilgaireth	.	Two hills near Mullingar.
Hill of Brughean Mor	.	{ In Parish of Drumany, Co. Westmeath.
Hy Maine	. .	{ A part of Roscommon, bordering Sligo and Mayo.
Inver Colptha	. .	Estuary of the Boyne.
Loch Cuan	. .	Strangford Loch.
Loch Riach	. .	In Co. Galway.
Leodus, Cadd, and Ork	.	Lewis, Shetland, and Orkney.
Magh Ai	. .	In Co. Roscommon.
Magh Breagh	. .	In East Meath.
Magh Mucrime	. .	Near Athenry, Co. Galway.
Magh Slecht	. .	Near Ballymagauran, Co. Cavan.
Muirthemne	. .	{ The part of Co. Louth bordering the sea, between the Boyne and Dundalk.
Road of Midluachair	. .	{ The north-eastern road from Teamhair.
Sionnan	. .	The Shannon.
Sleamhain of Meath	.	Near Mullingar.
Slieve Breagh	. .	Co. Louth.
Slieve Cuilinn	. .	Co. Londonderry.
Slieve Fuad	. .	Co. Armagh.

Slieve Mis .	.	.	Co. Kerry.
Slieve Suidhe Laighen	.		Mount Leinster.
Scigger Isles	.	.	Faröe Isles.
Sudiam .	.	.	Sweden.
Tailltin .	.	.	Telltown.
Teamhair .	.	.	Tara, Co. Meath.
Tuathmumain	.	.	Thomond.
Uaran Garad	.	.	River Cruind.
Usnech .	.	.	{ The Hill of Usnogh in West Meath.
Wave of Assaroe .		.	At Ballyshannon.
Wave of Cliodna .		.	At Glandore, Co. Cork.
Wave of Inbhir	.	.	Mouth of the Bann.

The following is a list of the authorities I have been chiefly helped by in putting these stories together. But I cannot make it quite accurate, for I have sometimes transferred a mere phrase, sometimes a whole passage from one story to another, where it seemed to fit better. I have occasionally used Scottish Gaelic versions, as in the account of Deirdre's birth, and the manner of her death, and in a part of "The Only Son of Aoife." "O'Curry" stands for his two books, "The Manners and Customs of Ancient Ireland," and "MS. Materials for Ancient Irish History," and his contributions to *Atlantis*.

BIRTH OF CUCHULAIN.—O'Curry; De Jubainville, *Epopée Celtique*; Nutt, *Voyage of Bran*; Kuno Meyer, *Revue Celtique*; Duvau, *Revue Celtique*; Windisch, *Irische Texte*; Stokes, *Irische Texte*.

BOY DEEDS OF CUCHLAIN.—Same as "War for the Bull of Cuailgne."

COURTING OF EMER.—Kuno Meyer, *Revue Celtique*; Kuno Meyer, *Archæological Review*; Dr Douglas Hyde, *Literary History of Ireland*; De Jubainville, *Epopée Celtique*; O'Curry.

BRICRIU'S FEAST, and THE CHAMPIONSHIP OF ULSTER.—Text, with Henderson's translation, published by Irish Texts Society; De Jubainville, *Epopée Celtique*; O'Curry; Windisch, *Irische Texte*.

THE HIGH KING OF IRELAND.—Whitley Stokes, *Revue Celtique*; O'Curry; Zimmer, *Keltische Studien*.

FATE OF THE CHILDREN OF USNECH.—Text and Translations published by the Society for the Preservation of the Irish Language; Hyde, *Literary History of Ireland*; Hyde, *Zeitschrift Celt. Philologie*; O'Curry; Whitley Stokes, *Irische Texte*; Windisch, *Irische Texte*; Cameron, *Reliquae Celticae*; O'Flanagan, *Transactions of Gaelic*

Society; O'Flanagan, *Reliquae Celticae;* Carmichael, *Transactions of Gaelic Society; Ultonian Ballads;* De Jubainville, *Epopée Celtique;* Dottin, *Revue Celtique.*

THE DREAM OF ANGUS.—Müller, *Revue Celtique.*

RUACHAN.—Kuno Meyer, *Revue Celtique;* O'Beirne Crowe, *Proceedings of Royal Irish Academy;* O'Curry; Rhys, *Celtic Heathendom.*

WEDDING OF MAINE MORGOR.—Windisch, *Irische Texte.*

WAR FOR THE BULL OF CUAILGNE, and AWAKENING OF ULSTER.—MS. translations by O'Daly in Royal Irish Academy; MS. translation by O'Looney in Royal Irish Academy; O'Curry; Standish Hayes O'Grady's Synopsis in Miss Hull's *Cuchulain Saga;* Zimmer, Synopsis in *Zeitschrift für Vergleichende Sprachforschung.*

THE TWO BULLS.—Windisch, *Irische Texte;* Nutt, *Voyage of Bran;* O'Curry.

THE ONLY JEALOUSY OF EMER, and INSTRUCTION TO A PRINCE.— O'Curry, *Atlantis;* De Jubainville, *Epopée Celtique.*

THE SONS OF DOEL DERMAIT.—Windisch, *Irische Texte;* Rhys, *Hibbert Lectures.*

BATTLE OF ROSNAREE.—Text with Father Hogan's translation; Todd Lecture Series; O'Curry; Kuno Meyer, *Revue Celtique.*

ONLY SON OF AOIFE.—Keating's *History of Ireland;* Miss Brooke's *Reliques;* Curtain's *Folk Tales;* Some Gaelic Ballads.

GATHERING AT MUIRTHEMNE, and DEATH OF CUCHULAIN.—"Brislech Mor Magh Muirthemne," and "Deargruatar Conaill Cearnaig"— published in *Gaelic Journal,* 1901; S. Hayes O'Grady in Miss Hull's *Cuchulain Saga;* Whitley Stokes, *Revue Celtique;* an unpublished MS. in Dr Hyde's possession.

We must be grateful to all these scholars, workers, or compilers, those who have passed away, and those who are living. And I am personally grateful to my friend Douglas Hyde for patient answering of many questions; and to my friend and critic, W. B. Yeats, for his kindness and for his severity.

A. G.